THE
ENCYCLOPEDIA
OF
SHIPS

THE
ENCYCLOPEDIA
OF
SHIPS

THE HISTORY AND SPECIFICATIONS OF OVER 1200 SHIPS

General Editor: Chris Marshall

Blitz Editions

This edition published in 1995 by:
Blitz Editions
an imprint of Bookmart Limited
Registered Number 2372865
Trading as Bookmart Limited
Desford Road
Enderby
Leicester LE9 5AD

ISBN 1-85605-288-5

Material previously published in 1994 as part of the Italian encyclopedia set *Navi e Velieri*
(De Agostini).

Editorial and design: Brown Packaging Ltd
255-257 Liverpool Rd, London N1 1LX

Printed in Hong Kong by
Dai Nippon Printing Co. (H.K.) Ltd

Picture credits
Brown Packaging: 10
Mary Evans Picture Library: 5, 6
TRH Pictures: 7, 8, 9

Introduction

This book is a pictorial record of the most interesting, innovative and important ships that have sailed the oceans since the earliest times, from Greek triremes to nuclear-powered aircraft carriers. As such, it is not only a list of ships from every historical period, it is also a testament to man's conquest of the seas and the advances that have been made in maritime technology. But to fully understand and appreciate maritime vessels, it is necessary to know the laws and technologies that determine the shape and size of ships, and how they have changed throughout history.

Three interdependent factors traditionally decided the basic form and nature of a ship or boat: the level of local construction expertise, the materials available, and the means of propulsion to be employed in the finished craft.

The changes in the nature of ships came about thanks to progress in developing new materials and methods. Until the start of the industrial revolution, the state of the shipbuilder's art – or his technology – changed but slowly. Then, quite suddenly, the whole

world was transformed. As a result, there is a definite divide in maritime history, and though we may not be able to place the watershed between the 'ancient' and the 'modern' in any one particular year, we can be sure it lies sometime just this side of the widespread introduction of the all-iron hull, the screw propeller, the vertical compound steam engine and the water-tube boiler, i.e. towards the mid-point of the second half the nineteenth century. Looking back, it is clear that the technological progress made during the nineteenth century greatly benefited the ship, which was at that time the most complex single entity in existence.

Written language clearly post-dates the development of the ship, for the earliest texts in existence refer to craft which were many stages more advanced than the simple pegged- or stitched-together plank boats of pre-Iron Age man. By the time of the Pharaohs and the Phoenicians, we find ships and boats that were sophisticated and quite beautiful objects, their hulls carefully formed to a shape which cut cleanly through the water. These peoples knew

Above: A nineteenth-century reconstruction of a Greek trireme. The principal weapon of these vessels was the long ram at the bow. The ram was constructed so that the whole ship would absorb the impact of ramming another ship, not just the keel.

nothing at all about streamlining or theoretical hydrodynamics, but they certainly knew what fish and aquatic mammals looked like, and they sought to copy their attributes.

Not all ships in ancient times were so shapely, though, for seafarers had already begun to make the distinction between the hull form of merchant ships and that of men o'war. Even in the earliest times, cargo ships tended to be deep, beamy craft, well-adapted to the carriage of barrels, bales and the like, and designed with an eye towards capacity rather than speed. Warships, on the other hand, were built and operated with a different set of criteria in mind: they were designed as fast and manoeuvrable fighting platforms, as well as being convincing weapons in their own right, thanks to the armoured ram incorporated into their bows.

Warfare during the Bronze and Iron Ages was a much more personal affair than in later periods. Though mechanical projectile weapons, such as catapults, were in use in the Mediterranean during pre-Christian times, at sea and on land the basic naval tactic was to close with the enemy and either ram or grapple him, so that the ships' fighting crews could engage in hand-to-hand combat. Sheer weight of numbers often decided naval battles, and ships had very large crews as a result (note that oarsmen did not fight in battle).

Given the state of the art in sailing technology, as opposed to boat- and ship-building, the early salt-water mariner had little choice but to row if he wanted to go a different way to that in which the wind was blowing. For many hundreds of years, ships and boats alike had nothing but a single square sail, set on a boom carried more or less at right angles to the vessel's keel, and braced around with lines and a pole. There was little chance of the craft making good a course under sail that was more than about 40 degrees either side of the direction in which the wind was blowing. The steering oars or boards (the steer-board was always slung on the right-hand-side looking forwards, hence the term 'starboard') then employed to stabilise the vessel on her course or heading hardly helped, being heavy and

cumbersome, and with limited travel. It was only in the thirteenth century that ship-building technology improved to the point where the straight sternpost and central, tiller-actuated rudder became a practical possibility.

Long before that, the sailors of the eastern Mediterranean had adopted the fore-and-aft-rigged lateen sail the Gulf and Indian Ocean Arabs used, and with that came a dramatic improvement in sailing performance, especially in coastal waters. The prototype fore-and-aft rig did have its drawbacks: it was considerably less efficient than a square rig when the wind was abaft the beam, which can often be the case on long ocean passages (where the mariner may wish to abandon a direct route with headwinds in favour of a longer course which will take him into areas where winds are more favourable). As long as half a millennium ago the distinction in the powers of the two rigs was already widely accepted. On Christopher Columbus's first voyage of exploration in 1492, for example, he had his third ship, the caravel *Nina*, re-rigged from lateen to square on the mainmast before he got beyond the Canaries. In changeable conditions, however, such as in the Mediterranean, and in circumstances where manoeuvrability was of paramount importance (most pirate ships and slavers, even of a later age, were fore-and-aft-rigged schooners, for

Above: Mediterranean cogs transporting French crusaders to the Holy Land in the thirteenth century. These vessels were large and could transport both men and horses, making them ideal for moving armies. They were usually two- or three-masted.

example), there was really nothing to beat the fore-and-aft rig, and it is much easier to handle with a small crew. Even hundreds of years later, in the latter days of sail, when owners cut back on every cost, it was to multi-masted schooners, such as the fore-and-aft-rigged *Thomas Lawson*, that they looked to turn a profit.

The earliest square-rigged sailing ships had but one mast, normally stepped somewhat abaft of amidships. The first step in the development of these ships was to add another, forwards. The improvement in performance off the wind – that is, with the wind blowing from anything but full astern, in the case of a square-rigger – was immediate, and not just for the obvious reason that the sail area was increased. In addition, the airstream across the sails when they were braced around was channelled, and caused a small degree of bernoulli effect (the aerodynamic principle which makes aeroplanes fly, and on which the fore-and-aft rig relies to head up into the wind). The next step was to add a mizzenmast, too (which often bore a fore-and-aft lateen sail, so that the vessel could enjoy the benefits conferred by both rigs at once), and then, as the technology to mount spars and to rig them successfully evolved, to add further sails above the courses. Some ships sprouted a fourth mast, which was known as the bonaventure. This also mounted a lateen sail, but it proved to be a short-lived experiment, for a square topsail on the mizzen itself soon proved to be both handier and more effective at

These structures did nothing whatsoever to enhance the ships' performance – the reverse, in fact – and they began to disappear as the gun became an effective weapon, in the sixteenth century.

Apart from their means of propulsion, the sailing warships and the galleys differed in one vital and essential way: the galley had to be of the lightest possible construction if it was to

size to accommodate them in large numbers on two, even three, full-length decks – something the galley could never do. The biggest, heaviest pieces, which were carried as low to the waterline as possible in order to maintain a low centre of gravity, were considerably longer than earlier guns, and needed more room in which to be worked. This meant that ships were much broader abeam at the waterline than at the upper deck level. This development had a useful secondary characteristic: it made boarding rather more difficult, too, since the bulwarks of two such ships hard alongside each other were a considerable distance apart.

The high forecastle of the carracks and cogs of the thirteenth, fourteenth and fifteenth centuries, which did so much to degrade a sailing ship's progress, was drastically reduced in the latter half of the sixteenth century, to a single deck only. The aftercastle was lowered, too, usually to two superior decks: a half-deck and a quarter-deck. It was eventually reduced still further, especially in smaller vessels. The ships, known now as galleons, also became longer in relation to their beam, by as much as 30 per cent, and by the end of the sixteenth century a typical 'great ship' would have been more than 50 metres (164ft) long between perpendiculars and perhaps 12-13 metres (39-42ft) abeam, and displacing over 1500 tons.

In addition to their basic shape change, during the sixteenth and seventeenth centuries warships also took on more and more flamboyant decoration in the form of carving, gilding and painting, often to the point where the cost of the embellishment was as much as – and sometimes greatly exceeded – that of the basic ship herself. Not that earlier ships had been drab, far from it. Topsides were painted in bright colours, and sails were frequently painted, too, often with heraldic devices – and the most prestigious ships wore sails woven in intricate designs from the most precious of cloths for ceremonial occasions.

By the later years of the seventeenth century, both the European merchant ship and the man o'war had developed to a point where they were fully capable of making long ocean passages in comparative comfort and safety. Most of the world's significant landmasses had been 'discovered' by then. Much of the world's surface had been mapped, and trade, as usual, had followed the various flags avidly. The leading maritime nations – Britain, Holland, France and Spain – were soon faced with the problems of policing overseas colonies and trade routes, and this led to the introduction of a new type of warship: the frigate.

At first, frigates were comparatively modest in size: about half as long as the smallest ship of the line (that is, a ship capable of fighting in the line of battle, often at point blank-range). They were much lighter in construction, carrying perhaps a dozen guns a side on a single deck and with a crew of not much more than 100. Later on, in the eighteenth and nineteenth centuries, the largest frigates were to be very

Above: French, British and Spanish ships of the line exchange broadsides at the Battle of Trafalgar in 1805. The batteries of guns on the gundecks of these vessels could deliver fearful broadsides, as evidenced by the state of the French ship *Redoutable* on the left.

supplying extra driving force. Bowsprits (a spar projecting from the bow of a sailing ship) became universal, both as a way of staying the foremast, and, briefly, as the location for a short extra mast, mounted at the tip and flying a square sail from a single yard. The spritmast proved even less effective than the bonaventure, for it was almost impossible to stay it securely, and working the sail was never easy. It disappeared in its turn, and gave way eventually to the flying jib, which was a much more effective sail in every way.

The other big change in the appearance of the sailing ship of the early years of the second millennium was in the introduction of high 'castles' – fighting platforms with some degree of protection – at both bow and stern. This change, pioneered in the galleys of the Mediterranean, came about originally not for any reason peculiar to maritime technology or fighting tactics, but simply to give archers, spearmen and stone throwers a height advantage, and a position from which they could dominate the enemy's oarsmen, who of necessity were low down near the waterline. The tactics of sailing warships switched to projectile weapons for that part of the fight which preceded boarding and hand-to-hand combat. This in turn led to the fore- and aftercastles increasing in size and importance.

achieve the high speeds which gave it its tactical advantage. The development of gunpowder and the cannon, a weapon aimed at destroying a ship's hull from a distance rather than disabling its crew, made them very vulnerable. It was this improvement in weapon technology, as much as any changes in the effectiveness of sail as a medium of propulsion, which spelled the end of the oared warship, except in very particular circumstances where manoeuvrability counted for more than sheer weight of firepower. Small frigates of some northern European navies, for example, were equipped with oars up until the early nineteenth century, though they were seldom used.

After the Battle of Lepanto in 1571, where they made their last serious attempt to compete as warships, the galleys began to decline in importance, and the three-masted sailing ship began what was to be three full centuries of dominance on the oceans of the world. By that time, of course, the cannon had long taken over as the most important naval weapon, and warships had already grown to a considerable

the level of the courses, but later also on the topsail yards. There were more and better mechanical aids to working the ship, too: the tiller had given way to wheel steering via a system of ropes and chains; and the capstan, while still used for the heaviest jobs, such as weighing anchor and warping the ship, had been supplemented by the lighter windlass.

Over the course of the next two centuries the pace of change slowed, as the wooden sailing ship reached the limits of its materials and technology. There were still developments in shipbuilding techniques which allowed the construction of bigger hulls. Diagonal cross-bracing, for example, allowed ships to grow to almost 75 metres (246ft) in length, and the new arrangement of superior decks, inherited from the frigates, increased the amount of available space. However, the law of diminishing returns had already begun to exercise control. By the time of the Crimean War in the mid-1850s, wooden warships had reached their effective maximum size, mounting up to 120 guns on three or four decks and displacing up to 5000 tons. They had not only reached their limits of manageability, but they had even exhausted (in Europe, anyway) the hardwood forests which supplied the timber to build them (the Royal Navy, for example, had long turned to both India and North America for wood).

Merchant ships of the period were considerably smaller, and very much lighter in construction, though in general they adhered to the same basic rules of design and building as warships. Already, however, there were signs of innovation on the horizon: by the end of the second decade of the nineteenth century steam engines were regularly (if not yet commonly) to be found in small ships, on inland waterways at first, but soon on short sea passages, too. And iron had already made its appearance as a construction medium, first of all in the form of the barge, but shortly thereafter for self-propelled ships. It was time for change.

The transition from wooden sailing ships to iron and steel steamers took a surprisingly short time. Despite an excursion down a dead-end road – the paddlewheel – it was completed in under half a century. The change came fastest and was most complete, after almost unbelievable resistance in most quarters, in the world's navies. This was because the advantages of steam power first of all, then armour, were undeniable. In addition, what one navy had, all the others clearly had to have also if they were to stay competitive. Sailing ships of the line met in battle for the last time at Navarino in 1827, and within less than 40 years their place had been taken by screw-driven, steam-propelled ironclad armoured warships.

Steam-powered merchant ships were rather slower to catch on, except on certain specific routes – the North Atlantic route from Liverpool to New York, for example, and on short crossings like the English Channel – chiefly because the space their fuel bunkers occupied consumed too much of the available cargo

much bigger vessels – of up to 2500 tons displacement and mounting 50-60 guns on two decks – though their scantlings were still very much lighter than those of a battleship. The eighteenth century frigates broke with the traditional form of the sailing ships of the day in that they were effectively flush-decked from the stem right through to the stern, losing their quarter-deck. The old well deck (that is, the main deck) was enclosed and covered by what is properly called a spar deck joining the foredeck with the half-deck aft. It was surmounted by a small raised command platform at the poop (at the stern of the ship) – a forerunner of the much later bridge. This development eventually found its way into bigger vessels, too.

By the time of the introduction of the first frigates in the mid-seventeenth century, the sailing ships of the world had already reached a high stage of development compared with only

Above: The British Dreadnought class battleship *Neptune*. The original HMS *Dreadnought*, launched in 1906, was truly revolutionary, because it made all other battleships obsolete. She immediately became the model for all future battleship developments. Note the two centreline turrets on different levels.

100 years before. The lateen sail on the mizzen had been reduced to a much more manageable size, by the simple expedient of lopping off its fore- and topmost triangles, and replacing the unwieldy antenna on which it had been set by lacing it to the mast and a cut-down remnant of the original long pole, thus creating a simple gaff sail. The spritsail and the mast on which it had flown had disappeared, replaced with triangular flying jibs. Similar triangular fore- and aftsails had made their appearance on the main and mizzen stays. Studding sails were set on outboard extensions of the yards, first of all at

routes for the carriage of passengers and perishable cargo.

Like the early merchant steamships, the first generation of steam warships carried a full suit of sails in addition to their engines, and used the latter sparingly. Their screw propellers were more often than not designed to be lifted up into a well when not in use, so that they would not adversely affect sailing performance.

The Royal Navy's first steam-powered ship of the line, HMS *Ajax,* entered service in 1846, by which time the Navy List actually included well over 100 steam-powered vessels, most of them tugboats. Four years later the French launched the first warship to be *built* as a steamer, the *Napoleon,* and the British replied two years later with HMS *Agamemnon.* It was to be almost 20 years more before sail finally disappeared from the Royal Navy, though, with the launching of HMS *Devastation,* the first battleship designed to be driven by steam alone.

The other significant development of that period was the substitution of iron for wood as the structural material of the ship's hull and the introduction of armour plating. The French ship *La Gloire* was the first armoured ship (following the successful use of ironclad armoured batteries during the Crimean war), launched in 1859. The British followed with the very much superior *Warrior* in 1860. Within two years, steam-powered ironclads were in action against each other when the *Monitor* met the *Merrimack* in Hampton Roads during the American Civil War. It was proof that no wooden sailing battlefleet in the world could stand against even one single armoured steam battleship.

Though the merchant marine was, in general, less sure about the economic benefits of steam, by 1850 it had certainly proved itself technically. Brunel's *Great Western,* the first steamship to ply regularly across the Atlantic, had already been in service for 12 years by then, and his prototype screw-driven ship, the *Great Britain,* joined her seven years later. His *Great Eastern,* launched in 1858, displaced almost 19,000 tons and was 211 metres (692ft) long. She was more than three times the size of any ship ever seen, and able to carry up to 4000 passengers and 6000 tons of cargo half-way around the world without re-fuelling.

Ironically, the introduction of iron and steel as a shipbuilding material gave the sailing ships a new lease of life, albeit a short one. In the last half of the nineteenth century, the composite wood-on-iron tea clippers enjoyed a brief heyday. They, in turn, were succeeded by all-metal barques and barquentines with four, five and even six masts, which continued to serve well into the twentieth century, particularly in the nitrate fertiliser trade from Chile to North America and Europe.

The last third of the nineteenth century was to see a drastic reduction in the size of powerplants, together with huge increases in their efficiency, thanks to the development of new types of boiler and compound multi-cylinder engines operating at previously

capacity. It was not until significant refinements in steam engine technology reduced their fuel consumption dramatically that merchant steamships finally took over from sailing ships. In essence, even if a steamer *could* make three voyages to a sailing ship's one, it was still only worthwhile in economic terms on high-traffic

Above: The US battleship *Iowa*. This ship was one of a class of battleships that was commisioned in 1943-44. These ships were formidable vessels, and have only recently been mothballed by the US Navy. Though it was thoroughly modernised during its life, the *Iowa's* original nine 16in guns were retained, allowing it to fire ordnance up to a range of 73km (46 miles).

impossible temperatures and pressures. These engines found application in warships and merchantmen alike, bringing the necessary fuel economy to the latter and unheard-of speed to the former. Then, a young engineer named Charles Parsons startled the British Royal Navy with an unofficial demonstration of what was a truly revolutionary new powerplant – the steam turbine – at the Diamond Jubilee Naval Review at Spithead in 1897.

With new, much more powerful engines available to them, naval architects, both civilian and military, began to increase the size of their designs, the former to provide greater carrying capacity, the latter to mount bigger guns and heavier armour. There was some confusion in naval design offices during the 1870s and 1880s as to just how the new heavy weapons should be deployed. For example, there was considerable controversy concerning the relative merits of revolving turrets and fixed barbettes, and even the old broadside battery, now protected within an armoured citadel, made a brief comeback. However, the launching of the turbine-powered HMS *Dreadnought* in 1906 convinced the more conservative elements that there was no point in loading a battleship down with useless secondary batteries of smaller-calibre guns which could do nothing that the bigger guns could not do.

Though the gun was still the most important weapon aboard ship, the work of an Italianised Englishman, Robert Whitehead, in the development of a self-propelled underwater weapon called the torpedo began to attract serious attention during the 1880s, particularly since they could be launched from submarines, which were the subject of intensive development at that time. In America, Britain and France, pioneers of the new craft worked to complete an effective design. First in the field was probably the Irish-American renegade John

Above: The purpose-built sail-assisted cruise liner *Club Med 1* is a remarkable marriage of modern technology and traditional grace. She can operate under sail alone, with a computer monitoring her progress and automatically switching to engine power if required.

Holland, if only because his prototype was the first one to be accepted for naval service. In almost no time at all, it seemed, the submarine went from being an unworkable notion to being a potent naval weapon, as Germany was to show during World War I.

The submarine wasn't the only means of delivering torpedoes, and virtually all types of surface combatants were soon equipped with them. In addition, they also gave rise to another type of small craft: the torpedo boat. Fast, low to the water and agile, these boats offered a real threat to even the biggest capital ships. The best defence against them was small-calibre, quick-firing guns, and so a new type of boat thus armed made its appearance – the torpedo boat destroyer. The latter could be used for other tasks, too, such as protecting merchant ships from submarines. Destroyers soon became the most numerous class of vessels in any surface fleet. Meanwhile, various types of cruisers patrolled the shipping routes, operating independently of the battlefleets in far-flung corners of the globe.

World War I failed to produce a truly clear-cut naval victory, though the Battle of Jutland was decisive in itself, i.e. it did convince the German High Seas Fleet that it was no match for the Royal Navy.

By the time the second global conflict of the twentieth century came around, aircraft carriers had become the new capital ships of the day, the bombs and torpedoes their aircraft could deliver being clearly more potent than the shot and shells of even the biggest battleship. The days of the big-gun platform were numbered,

though once again the in-bred conservatism of many senior naval officers served to disguise the inevitability of it for a while.

The submarine changed very little in the period between the wars. However, technical developments, particularly in electric propulsion and remote sensing, gave the boats a new potential. After the war, nuclear power, which, requiring no oxygen for the purposes of combustion to produce steam and generate electricity, allowed the boats to stay submerged as long as their rations lasted. Nuclear power also increased the interval between re-fuelling stops, and did away with the need to carry huge supplies of oil. Nuclear power was readily applied to carriers, too, the space originally required for bunkerage now being devoted to aircraft fuel. Steam began to disappear from smaller classes of vessel at about the same time as nuclear power proliferated, to be replaced by either diesel engines or gas turbines, though the German Navy had switched over to internal combustion engines considerably earlier.

Away from military considerations, World Wars I and II saw an enormous rise in mercantile marine traffic, and in the number and type of ships required to carry it. Until the coming of steam there had been very little specialisation in ship design, but by 1900 oil tankers, refrigerated carriers and bulk carriers had all been built in considerable numbers to sail alongside general cargo vessels and passenger liners. In addition, the demands for transportation of men and materiel during the wars saw to it that a huge fleet of merchant ships was available at the end of both of them. After 1945 in particular, this influx of shipping coincided with a vast increase in manufacturing capacity, first of all in the West, then in Asia, which led to further developments in maritime operations, especially in the way cargo was handled. The only area of seaborne trade which really suffered was the carriage of passengers on long routes – the airliner took over during the 1960s – and the few liners left became cruise ships. That said, short-range passenger and car ferries are still increasing in numbers.

As for the warship, the heavily armed battleship declined in importance in the years after World War II. In general, the aircraft carrier and the submarine have come to dominate strategic thinking.

Though the most important recent developments in ship design and operation have been in sub-systems, there have been some changes to the basic lines of the ship itself, most of them detailed improvements to hull form and in the placing of superstructure. The appearance of the commercial hovercraft in the 1960s looked like a major step forward, but has since proved to have only very limited civilian or military applications, such as amphibious landings in the latter category.

The ships listed in the following pages are a visual history of the design and construction of vessels through the ages. Sit back and enjoy a trip through the maritime archives.

A1

Type: The first British submarine
Displacement: 194 tonnes (191 tons) on surface, 274.5 tonnes (270 tons) submerged
Dimensions: 30.5m (100ft) long, 3.4m (11ft 2in) diameter hull
Machinery: 160hp petrol motor for surface work, 126hp electric motor for underwater propulsion
Top speed: 9.5 knots (surface), 6 knots (submerged)
Armament: Two 460mm (18.1in) torpedo tubes
Launched: July 1902

The A class vessels were the first submarines designed in Britain, although they were originally based on the earlier US Holland type which had entered Royal Navy service in 1901. *A1* was basically a slightly lengthened *Holland*, but from *A2* onwards they were much larger. They were also the first submarines to be made with a proper conning tower to allow surface running in heavy seas. Originally fitted with a single bow-mounted torpedo tube, the class was equipped with a second one from *A5* onwards. These boats were powered by a combined petrol and electric system, although *A13* was later fitted with a diesel engine. Built by Vickers, this class helped the Royal Navy to develop and refine their submarine doctrine and operating skills. Thirteen boats were built between 1902 and 1905. Some were still in service during the 1914-18 war, albeit only in a training role.

Aboukir

Type: British armoured cruiser
Displacement: 12,240 tonnes (12,047 tons)
Dimensions: 144m x 21.2m x 7.6m (472ft 5in x 69ft 7in x 24ft 11in)
Machinery: Triple expansion, 21,000hp
Top speed: 21 knots
Main armament: Two 234mm (9.2in), 12 150mm (6in) guns
Armour: 150mm (6in) on sides and guns, 75mm (3in) on deck
Launched: May 1900

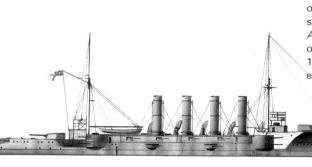

The first British cruiser since 1886 to be built with a belt of armour for better protection against the increasing size of guns in the late 19th and early 20th centuries. *Aboukir* was sunk by the German submarine *U-9* while on patrol in the southern North Sea on 22 September 1914, with her sister ships *Cressy* and *Hogue*, with enormous loss of life – 1,400 men died in total.

Admiral Graf Spee

Type: German pocket battleship
Displacement: 16,218 tonnes (15,963 tons)
Dimensions: 186m x 20.6m x 7.2m (610ft 3in x 67ft 7in x 23ft 7in)
Machinery: Diesels, 51,000hp
Top speed: 28 knots
Main armament: Six 279mm (11in), eight 150mm (6in) guns
Armour: 76mm (3in) belt, 140 to 76mm (5.5 to 3in) on turrets, 38mm (1.5in) on deck
Launched: April 1933

Limited by the 1919 Treaty of Versailles to a maximum displacement of 10,200 tonnes (10,039 tons), Germany produced the cleverly designed 'pocket' battleship. Great savings were achieved by using electric welding and light alloys in the hull. *Admiral Graf Spee*, with her two sister ships *Deutschland* and *Admiral Scheer*, were intended primarily as commerce-raiders. The ship was scuttled off Montevideo, Uruguay, after engaging three British cruisers in the Battle of the River Plate in December 1939.

Affondatore

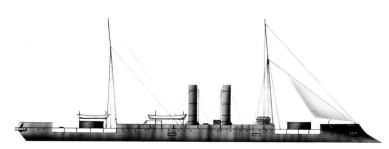

Type: Italian turret battleship
Displacement: 4,393 tonnes (4,324 tons)
Dimensions: 93.9m x 12m x 6.3m (308ft x 39ft 4in x 20ft 8in)
Machinery: Single screw
Top speed: 12 knots
Main armament: Two 254mm (10in) muzzle-loading rifled (MLR) guns
Armour: 127mm (5in) belt and turrets
Launched: November 1865

An iron-hulled schooner rigged vessel, *Affondatore* had a pronounced wrought iron ram. She had two turrets, each designed by the British Navy's Captain Cowper Coles. She acted as the flagship of Admiral Persano's fleet at the Battle of Lissa in July 1866, and remained in service with the Italian Navy for a further 41 years.

Agincourt

Type: British battleship
Displacement: 10,812 tonnes (10,642 tons) full load
Dimensions: 124m x 18.2m x 85m (406ft 10in x 59ft 9in x 278ft 10in)
Top speed: 14.8 knots
Main armament: Four 229mm (9in) guns and 24 178mm (7in) muzzle-loading rifled guns
Launched: 1862

Agincourt had all her guns in one long armoured battery, and her two sister ships were the longest single-screw warships ever built. She was one of the last British ships to be fitted with muzzle-loading guns, which were replaced in the 1860s with breach-loading weapons. She was not broken up until 1960.

Akagi

Type: Japanese aircraft carrier
Displacement: 29,580 tonnes (29,114 tons)
Dimensions: 249m x 30.5m x 8.1m (816ft 11 in x 100ft x 26ft 7in)
Machinery: Turbines, four shafts
Top speed: 32.5 knots
Main armament: Ten 203mm (8in), 12 119mm (4.7in) guns

Armour: 152mm (6in) belt
Launched: 1925

Akagi was designed as a 41,820 tonne (41,161 ton) battle cruiser but, while still on the stocks, the Washington Naval Treaty of 1922 (whereby Japan was forced to restrict her naval programme)

caused the design to be altered. Built to dispatch up to 60 aircraft, she was modified to carry heavier aircraft and more light guns. *Akagi* led the Japanese carrier assault on

Pearl Harbor on 7 December 1941, but was destroyed seven months later by bombs dropped by US divebombers at the decisive Battle of Midway.

Alabama

Type: Confederate raider
Displacement: 1,071 tonnes (1,054 tons) full load
Dimensions: 67m x 9.6m x 4.3m (219ft 10in x 31ft 6in x 14ft 1in)
Machinery: Single screw, auxiliary steam power
Top speed: 13 knots
Main armament: One 50kg (110lb) gun
Launched: 1862

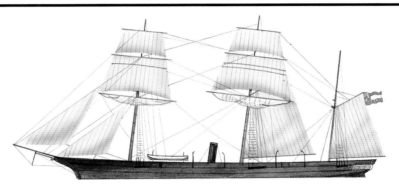

Laid down in Britain in 1862, *Alabama* was probably the most famous vessel of the US Civil War because her commerce-raiding activities almost destroyed the Union's mercantile marine. Captained by Raphael Semmes, she was sunk by USS *Kearsage* in the English Channel in June 1864.

Albemarle

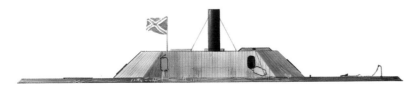

Type: Confederate ironclad
Dimensions: 46.4m x 10.4m x 2.7m (152ft 3in x 34ft 1in x 8ft 10in)
Main armament: Two 203mm (8in) guns

Because of its limited industrial capacity, the Confederacy could not

outbuild the Union Navy, so it concentrated on assembling a fleet of ironclads capable of deflecting Union attacks. *Albemarle* operated successfully off North Carolina, but was disposed of by a torpedo fired by one Lieutenant Cushing on 28 October 1864.

Alberto da Giussano

Type: Italian fast destroyer
Displacement: 5,170 tonnes (5,089 tons) full load
Dimensions: 169.4m x 15.2m x 4.3m (555ft 9in x 49ft 10in x 14ft 1in)
Main armament: Eight 152mm (6in) guns

One of a class of four units built to counter the powerful French Lion class destroyers, *Alberto di Giussano* represented an extremely efficient ship. Lightly armoured, she was one of the fastest destroyers in the world at the time of her launch – one of her class achieved a speed of 42 knots during trials and maintained a steady 40 knots for eight hours.

Alecto

Type: British gun boat
Displacement: 816 tonnes (803 tons) full load
Machinery: 200hp engine driving two paddles

A wooden paddle wheel frigate, *Alecto* underwent trials against *Rattler* to discover whether propeller propulsion was superior to that of paddles. *Rattler* was identical to *Alecto,* but with a 200hp engine driving a propeller.

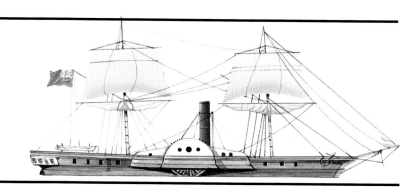

Almirante Cochrane

Type: Chilean battleship
Displacement: 3,631 tonnes (3,574 tons)
Dimensions: 64m x 13.9m x 6.7m (210ft x 45ft 7in x 22ft)
Main armament: Six 209mm (8.2in) guns
Armour: 229mm (9in) belt, 203 to 152mm (8 to 6in) on central battery
Launched: 1874

Admirante Cochrane and her sister, *Blanco Encalada,* combined good protection with powerful armament on a small displacement. Her guns were in an armoured box. Both took part in the war with Peru when Chile seized large parts of the Peruvian coastline. *Blanco Encalada* was the first battleship to be sunk by a modern torpedo.

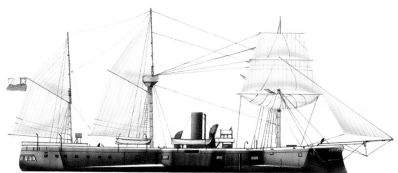

Aluminaut

Type: Deep sea exploration vessel
Weight: 81 tonnes (80 tons)
Cruising speed: 3 knots

Built in 1965, *Aluminaut* is capable of exploring to depths of 4,475m (14,682 ft). She is equipped with a side scan sonar which builds up a map of the terrain on either side. *Aluminaut* was used in searching out the H-bomb lost off Spain in 1966.

America

Type: American racing yacht
Displacement: 103.6 tonnes (102 tons)
Dimensions: 33.8m x 7.6m x 3.7m (110ft 11in x 25ft x 12ft 2in)

The America's Cup was named after this yacht, which won the first race between the USA and Britain in 1851. A very graceful schooner, *America* was designed by George Steers. During the American Civil War she was bought by the Confederates, then captured by the Unionists, and used by the American Navy until 1873. In 1942 her hull split in a huge snow storm and she was finally broken up in 1945.

America

Type: Italian Royal Yacht
Displacement: 5,729 tonnes (5639 tons)
Dimensions: 135m x 15.5m (442ft 11in x 50ft 10in)
Top speed: 18 knots
Launched: 1884

America was first a cruise ship on the Liverpool to New York route. She was sold to Italy in 1887 and rechristened *Trinacria*.

America

Type: US aircraft carrier
Displacement: 81,090 tonnes (79,813 tons) full load, 61,000 tonnes (60,039 tons) standard
Dimensions: 324m x 77m x 10.7m (1063ft x 252ft 7in x 35ft)
Machinery: Four-shaft (four Westinghouse geared turbines), 280,000hp
Top speed: 33 knots
Main armaments: Three Mark 29 launchers for NATO Sea Sparrow SAMs, three 20mm (0.79in) Phalanx CIWS (Close-in Weapons System)
Launched: 1964

The Kitty Hawk class were the first aircraft carriers not to carry conventional guns. Intended to be larger and improved versions of the earlier Forrestal class, *Kitty Hawk* (CV 63) and *Constellation* (CV 64) were the first two built. The third, *America* (CV 66), was launched in 1964, and incorporated further improvements based on operational experience. Her dimensions are slightly different to those of her sisters, with a narrower smokestack. She was the first carrier to be equipped with an integrated Combat Information Centre (CIC) and is also fitted with a bow-mounted sonar. A fourth ship, *John F. Kennedy* (CV 67), was built after the US Congress refused to sanction a nuclear-powered vessel in 1964. Policy has since changed, and all large US carriers since then have used nuclear propulsion, leaving *America* and her sisters as the largest conventionally-driven vessels in service. Her own armament is limited to short-range self defence weapons, and she relies instead on her aircraft and the weapons of her escorts. The composition of her air wing has varied through the years, but she is capable of operating some 82 machines. In the early 1990s, the air wing comprised 20 F-14 Tomcats, 24 F/A-18 Hornets, 10 A-6E Intruders, 4 KA-6D Intruders, 4 EA-6B Prowlers, 4 E-2C Hawkeyes, 10 S-3A Vikings and 6 SH-3H Sea Kings. A complement of more than 5,000 is needed to operate her at sea. *America* saw action during the Vietnam War and during the Gulf War.

Ammiraglio di Saint Bon

Type: Italian battleship
Displacement: 10,156 tonnes (9,996 tons)
Dimensions: 105m x 21m x 7.6m (344ft 6in x 69ft x 25ft)
Top speed: 18 knots
Main armament: Four 254mm (10in), eight 152mm (6in) guns
Launched: 1897

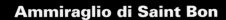

Ammiraglio di Saint Bon was a compact, heavily protected ship. A flagship of the Italian navy, she was a fine example of the emphasis that Italian naval planners of the time put on armour. For example, her 152mm (6in) guns were housed in an armoured central battery.

Improvements in metallurgical technology in the late 1800s meant that the ship's speed was not impaired by her solid build. The *Saint Bon* took part in the Italo-Turkish War, and was stationed at Venice during World War I. She was decommissioned in June 1920.

Andrea Doria

Type: Italian battleship
Displacement: 26,115 tonnes (25,704 tons)
Dimensions: 176m x 28m x 8.8m (577ft 5in x 91ft 10in x 28ft 10in)
Machinery: Turbines
Main armament: 13 305mm (12in), 16 152mm (6in) guns
Armour: 229mm belt, 229mm turrets, 127mm on guns

From 1937 to 1940 *Andrea Doria*, and her sister ship, *Caio Duilio*, underwent a very rigorous reconstruction programme. The *Andrea Doria*'s top speed was increased from 21.5 to 27 knots and she was given improved armour on her turrets and engine rooms. Both ships remained in service until 1958.

Aoba

Type: Japanese cruiser
Displacement: 8,900 tonnes (8,760 tons)
Dimensions: 185m x 15.8m x 5.7m (607ft x 51ft 10in x 18ft 8in)
Machinery: Four shaft geared turbines generating 102,000 shp
Main armament: Six 203mm, 4 120mm guns
Launched: Sept 1926

Aoba and her sister *Kinugasa* were improved versions of the previous Kago class of heavy cruisers, and were the first Japanese cruisers to be fitted with catapults. Modernisation brought their displacement to 10,820 tonnes (10,650 tons). *Aoba* was sunk at Kure in July 1945 by US aircraft.

Appalachian

Type: US command ship
Displacement: 14,133 tonnes
(13,910 tons)
Dimensions: 132.6m x 19.2m x 7.3m
(435ft x 63ft x 24ft)
Machinery: Single-shaft turbine
Speed: 17 knots
Main armament: Two 127mm (5in),
eight 40mm (1.6in) guns

Appalachian was one of an
important group of ships that acted
as HQ and air control for the
amphibious assaults on Japanese-
held islands during World War II.
She later served briefly as Pacific
Fleet flagship in 1947, before being
removed from the active list that
year. She was broken up in 1960.

Aquila

Type: Italian aircraft carrier
Displacement: 28,810 tonnes (28,356
tons)
Dimensions: 231.5m x 29.4m x 7.3m
(759ft 6in x 96ft 5in x 24ft)
Top speed: 32 knots
Main armament: Eight 135mm
(5.3in) guns, 36 aircraft

Launched: 1926

Aquila began her life as the 33,764-tonne (33,232 ton) cruise
ship *Roma*. She was requisitioned by the Italian Navy in 1941
for conversion into the first Italian aircraft carrier. More
powerful engines were installed as well as an enormous
second underwater keel, into which cement was poured to
increase stability. *Aquila*
never saw service and
was broken up in 1951.

Arabia

Type: UK passenger liner
Displacement: 2,440 tonnes (4202
tons)
Dimensions: 89.6m (284ft) x
12.5m(41ft)
Machinery: Sidewheel
Launched: 1851

The last of the wooden-hulled
paddle-steamers built for the
Cunard Line, *Arabia* boasted steam
central heating, a cupola over the
saloon to give increased height and
two well-stocked libraries. She was
a transport during the Crimean War
of 1854. In 1858 she was damaged
in a collision with *Europa* and was
sold in 1864.

Aradam

Aradam was one of a class of 17
short-range vessels. These had a
double hull with blisters and were
a repeat of the previous Perla
class. They gave good service
during World War II, and although
their surface speed was low they
were strong and very
manoeuvrable. The early boats
of the class took part in the
Spanish Civil War

and all operated in the
Mediterranean Sea during World
War II, except *Macallé*, which
served in the Red Sea. Only one
boat, *Alagi*, survived World War II.
Aradam was scuttled in September
1943 in Genoa harbour to avoid
capture, but was later raised by the
Germans. She was finally sunk by
bombing the following year.

Type: Italian submarine
Displacement: 691 tonnes (680 tons) on
surface, 880 tonnes (866 tins) submerged
Dimensions: 60.2m x 6.5m x 4.6m (197ft 6in x
21ft 4in x 15ft)
Machinery: Diesel for surface work, electric
twin screw for underwater propulsion
Top speed: 14 knots (surface), 7 knots
(submerged)
Main armament: Six
530mm (21in) torpedo
tubes, one 100mm (4in)
gun

Arago

Type: US passenger liner
Displacement: 2,296 tonnes
(2,260 tons)
Dimensions: 85.6m x
12.5m (281ft x 41ft)
Machinery: Sidewheel
Launched: 1855

Arago entered service in 1855 and
sailed on the New York-Europe run
until taken over as a transport by
the US Government in 1861 for
service in the Civil War. She
resumed a monthly service in 1865,
but was then suspended in 1867
owing to high operating costs
incurred because of the coal-
hungry nature of her engines.
Arago was sold to Peru in 1869.

Aragon

Type: Spanish cruiser
Displacement: 3,342 tonnes (3,289 tons)
Dimensions: 71.9m x 13.4m x 7.2m (236ft x 44ft x 23ft 7in)
Machinery: Single-screw horizontal compound
Top speed: 14 knots
Main armament: Six 163mm (6.4in) guns

Aragon was one of a class of three wooden-hulled warships originally planned as ironclads and so very strongly built. Her main guns were mounted on the broadside, and her end guns carried on sponsons to give fire ahead or astern. A sister ship, *Castilla*, was sunk by US forces at Manila on 1 May 1898.

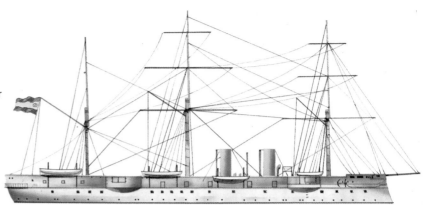

Araguaya

Type: Brazilian destroyer
Displacement: 1,829 tonnes (1,800 tons)
Dimensions: 98.5m x 10.7m x 2.6m (323ft x 35ft x 8ft 6in)
Machinery: Two shaft geared turbines
Top speed: 35.5 knots
Main armament: Four 127mm (5in), two

40mm (1.6in) guns
Launched: 1946

Araguaya and her five sisters were built to replace the six H class vessels taken over by the Royal Navy at the outbreak of World War II. They followed the same original design but used American equipment. All were built between 1943 and 1946 at the Ilha das Cobras Navy Yard. *Araguaya* was discarded in 1974.

Arapiles

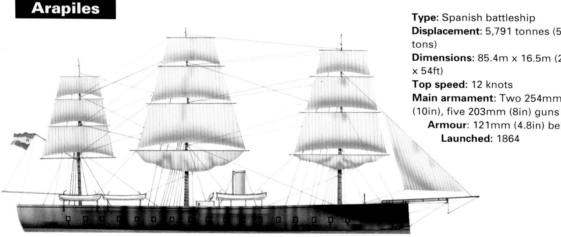

Type: Spanish battleship
Displacement: 5,791 tonnes (5,700 tons)
Dimensions: 85.4m x 16.5m (280ft x 54ft)
Top speed: 12 knots
Main armament: Two 254mm (10in), five 203mm (8in) guns
Armour: 121mm (4.8in) belt
Launched: 1864

Arapiles was originally planned as a wooden screw frigate but was altered while still on the stocks to a broadside ironclad with a midship armour belt that added over 200 tonnes (203 tons) to the displacement. In 1873 she grounded off Venezuela and was sent to New York for repairs. This coincided with the crisis between Spain and the USA over the seizure of the American steamer *Virginius* by a Spanish cruiser off Cuba. In the end, the poor state of *Arapiles'* wooden hull meant that it was uneconomic to carry out repairs.

Archibald Russel

Type: British barque
Displacement: 2,423 tonnes (2,385 tons)
Dimensions: 88.7m x 13.1m x 7.3m (291ft x 43ft x 24ft)
Launched: 1905

Archibald Russel was a steel four-masted barque able to carry nearly 4,064 tonnes (4,000 tons) of cargo. She was one of the few sailing vessels with bilge keels that greatly added to her steadiness in a heavy sea. She was also fitted with many labour-saving devices and although not fast was very steady, often giving good runs in spite of her size. After World War I *Archibald Russel* was sold to a Danish firm who used her as a training ship while on regular cargo voyages. By 1930 *Archibald Russel* was employed in the Australian grain trade.

Archimede

Type: Italian submarine
Displacement: 1,032 tonnes (1,016 tons) on surface, 1,286 tonnes (1,266 tons) submerged
Dimensions: 72.4m x 6.7m x 4.5m (237ft 6in x 22ft x 15ft)
Machinery: Diesel for surface work, electric twin screw for underwater propulsion
Top speed: 17 knots (surface), 8 knots (submerged)

Main armament: Eight 533mm (21in) torpedo tubes, one 100mm (4in) gun
Launched: March 1939

The Italian Navy operated five submarines in the Brin class, which were all completed from 1938 to 1939. The last two, *Archimede* and *Torricelli,* were built in secret to replace two submarines of the same name which had been transferred covertly to Nationalist forces during the Spanish Civil War. The Brin class were efficient, streamlined vessels, which had a long range. They had a partial double hull, with four torpedo tubes in the bow and four in the stern. An unusual feature of this design was the 100mm (4in) gun

mounted in the conning tower, but after a year or so it was replaced by a 120mm (4.7in) weapon on the foredeck. At the outbreak of World War II, *Archimede* was operating in the Red Sea and the Indian Ocean, where she remained until May 1941. She then made an epic journey around the Cape of Good Hope to Bordeaux, from where she began operations in the Atlantic. She was sunk by Allied aircraft off the coast of Brazil on 14 April 1943. Her sister vessels *Torricelli*, *Guglielmotti* and *Galvani* were also sunk during the war, while the *Brin* survived, to be used by the Allies as an ASW target until 1948.

Arctic

Type: US passenger liner
Displacement: 2,896 tonnes (2,850 tons)
Dimensions: 86m x 13.7m x 9.6m (282ft x 45ft x 31ft 6in)
Machinery: Sidewheel
Top speed: 12.5 knots
Launched: 1849

Arctic was one of a group of four paddle-wheel steamers belonging to the Collins Line that were well in advance of any

steam vessels then serving on the North Atlantic run. On 21 September 1854, *Arctic* left the UK bound for New York with 246 passengers and 135 crew. On the 27th, while steaming through thick fog, she collided with the French steamer *Vesta*. *Arctic* was holed in three places and sank with the loss of 322 drowned, including the wife and children of Collins, the line's owner. The Collins Line collapsed in 1858, when the US government withdrew its mail subsidy.

Ardent

Type: British destroyer
Displacement: 2,022 tonnes (1,990 tons)
Dimensions: 95.1m x 9.8m x 3.7m (312ft x 32ft 3in x 12ft 3in)
Machinery: Twin shaft geared turbines

Main armament: Four 120mm (4.7in) guns, eight 533mm (21in) torpedo tubes
Top speed: 35 knots
Launched: 1929

Ardent was one of a class of eight units with which the Royal Navy began a new era of destroyer construction, after a lapse of eight

years from the end of World War I. *Ardent* was sunk in June 1940 by *Scharnhorst* and *Gneisenau*, while escorting the aircraft carrier *Glorious*, which also fell prey to the German guns. Three other 'A' class ships were lost during the war, and a further one was damaged and never repaired.

Arethusa

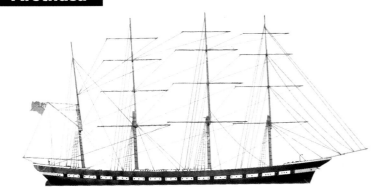

Type: British sail training ship
Displacement: 3,242 tonnes (3,191 tons)
Dimensions: 97.5m x 13.5m x 7.3m (320ft x 44ft 3in x 24ft)

In 1932, *Arethusa* took up her duties as a sail training ship. *Arethusa* was formerly the four-masted steel barque *Peking,* a German ship belonging to Laeisz's 'Flying P' Line; she was captured in World War I. *Arethusa* was well equipped, with three decks giving

plenty of space for accommodation and drill, and she was closely connected with the Shaftesbury Homes for Poor Boys. She replaced a training ship of the same name, which, while in service with the Royal Navy, gained the distinction of being the last warship to go into battle under sail alone.

Arethusa

Type: British cruiser
Displacement: 6,822 tonnes (6,715 tons)
Dimensions: 154m x 15.5m x 5m (506ft x 51ft x 16ft 6in)
Machinery: Four shaft geared turbines
Main armament: Six 152mm (6in), four 102mm (4in) guns
Armour: 51mm (2in) thick waterline belt, 25mm (1in) bulkheads and deck plus 76mm (3in) round magazines

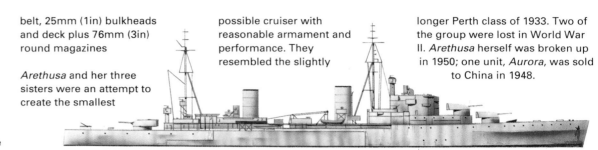

Arethusa and her three sisters were an attempt to create the smallest possible cruiser with reasonable armament and performance. They resembled the slightly longer Perth class of 1933. Two of the group were lost in World War II. *Arethusa* herself was broken up in 1950; one unit, *Aurora*, was sold to China in 1948.

Aretusa

Type: Italian torpedo cruiser
Displacement: 846 tonnes (833 tons)
Dimensions: 70m x 8.2m x 3.5m (229ft 8in x 27ft x 11ft 6in)
Machinery: Twin screw triple expansion
Main armament: One 120mm (4.7in) gun, six 450mm (17.7in) torpedo tubes

Aretusa was one of a class of eight graceful-looking steel-hulled torpedo cruisers. Coal supply was 183 tonnes (180 tons), sufficient to give a range of over 2,890km (1,521 miles) at 10 knots. By the early 1900s their top speed had fallen to 16-17 knots, and by 1910 two of the class had been converted to minelayers. *Aretusa* was discarded in 1912.

Argonaut

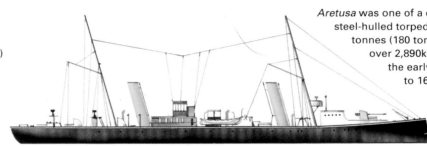

Type: US submarine
Displacement: 60 tonnes (59 tons) submerged
Dimensions: 11m x 2.7m (36ft x 9ft)
Launched: 1897

Argonaut was built by Simon Lake as a salvage vessel for inshore waters. A 30hp gasoline engine drove the single screw, and the engine could be connected to the twin front wheels for movement along the sea bed; the third wheel aft steered the craft. There was an air chamber forward so that divers could enter or leave. The vessel was rebuilt in 1899 and once made a trip of around 3,200km (1,684 miles). A crew of five was carried.

Argonaut

Type: US submarine/minelayer
Displacement: 2,753 tonnes (2,710 tons) on surface, 4,145 tonnes (4,080 tons) submerged
Dimensions: 116m x 10.4m x 4.6m (381ft x 34ft x 15ft 6in)
Machinery: Twin shaft diesels for surface work, electric for underwater propulsion

Main armament: Two 152mm (6in) guns, four 533mm (21in) torpedo tubes, all mounted in the bow; 60 mines

Launched: November 1927

Argonaut was the only purpose-built minelaying submarine to serve in the US Navy. During World War II she was used as a transport in the Pacific. *Argonaut* was lost in 1943.

Ariadne

Type: British cruiser/minelayer
Displacement: 4,064 tonnes (4,000 tons)
Dimensions: 127.4m x 12.2m x 4.5m (418ft x 40ft x 14ft 9in)
Machinery: Twin shaft turbines
Main armament: Six 102mm (4in) guns, 100-156 mines
Top speed: 40 knots
Launched: 1943

Ariadne was one of a class of six successful fast minelayers built under the 1938 Navy programme. They were intended to operate alone in enemy waters and had a small silhouette backed up by a formidable armament for defence against both air and surface attack. During World War II, they were used to run in much-needed ammunition to the beleaguered island of Malta, as their high speed enabled them to make a dash through dangerous waters. All six saw extensive war service, with three of the class being sunk through enemy action. *Ariadne* was broken up in 1965.

Ariel

Type: British sailing ship
Displacement: 866 gross tonnes (852 gross tons), 1,067 tonnes (1050 tons) full load
Dimensions: 59.4m x 10.3m (195ft x 33ft 9in)
Launched: 1865

Ariel was built by Steele of Greenock for the China tea trade. Any vessel used in this trade had to be fast and *Ariel* was no exception: she was able to make up to 16 knots for long periods. She was a handsome vessel with well-proportioned lines. The length of the lower masts was longer than usual in this type of ship and with the deep sail set, *Ariel* made good speed in light winds. After six successful years, she left London in January 1872 bound for Sydney, Australia, but disappeared without trace.

Arizona

Type: British passenger liner
Displacement: 5,247 tonnes (5,164 tons)
Dimensions: 137m x 13.7m (450ft x 40ft)
Machinery: Compound, single screw

In 1879, *Arizona* won the Atlantic Blue Ribbon by making the eastbound crossing in seven days and eight hours. In November of that year she ran head on into an iceberg in dense fog off Newfoundland, but the bow bulkhead held and she did not sink.

Ark Royal

Type: British galleon
Displacement: 813 tonnes (800 tons)
Dimensions: 88.7m x 13.1m x 7.3m (291ft x 43ft x 24ft)
Launched: 1587

Built for Sir Walter Raleigh in 1587, and originally named *Anne Royal*, this ship was purchased by Queen Elizabeth I for £5,000 and renamed

Ark Royal. She was the flagship of Lord Howard of Effingham at the battle against the Spanish Armada of 1588 and was one of the largest vessels in the English fleet. *Ark Royal* had two gun decks, a double forecastle, a quarter deck and a poop deck right aft. She had an

elegant outline and none of the cluttered superstructure then common on such large vessels. Her armament ranged from 19 to 2.7kg (41.8 to 5.9lb) guns. Britain was the first nation to adopt the galleon, during the reign of Henry VIII, while Spain was the last great maritime nation to adopt the type. *Ark Royal* was accidentally burnt while in dock.

Ark Royal

Type: British aircraft carrier
Displacement: 28,164 tonnes (27,720 tons)
Dimensions: 243.8m x 28.9m x 8.5m (800ft x 94ft 9in x 27ft 9in)
Machinery: Triple shaft Parsons geared turbine

Top speed: 31 knots
Main armament: sixteen 114mm (4.5in) guns
Armour: 114mm (4.5in) belt, 7.6mm (3in) bulkheads
Launched: April 1937

Ark Royal was the first large purpose-built aircraft carrier constructed for the Royal Navy, with a long flight deck some 18m (60ft)

above the deep water load line. Her full complement was 60 aircraft, although she never actually carried this many. *Ark Royal* was sunk in November 1941 by the German submarine *U81*.

Arleigh Burke

Type: US guided missile destroyer
Displacement: 8,534 tonnes (8,400 tons)
Dimensions: 142.1m x 18.3m x 9.1m (266ft 3in x 60ft x 30ft)
Machinery: Twin shaft gas turbine
Main armament: Harpoon and

Tomahawk missiles, 127mm (5in) gun
Top speed: 30+ knots

This large class (yet to be completed) was designed to replace the ageing Adams and Coontz class destroyers, which entered

service in the early 1960s. *Arleigh Burke* and her numerous sisters' main

mission is to provide effective anti-aircraft cover, for which they have the SPY 1D version of the Aegis system. They also have powerful anti-surface and anti-submarine weapons. Each ship costs well over $1,000 million.

Armando Diaz

Type: Italian destroyer
Displacement: 5,406 tonnes (5,321 tons)
Dimensions: 169.3m x 15.5m x 5.5m (555ft 6in x 50ft 10in x 18ft)
Machinery: Twin shaft geared turbines
Top speed: 36.5 knots
Main armament: Eight 152mm (6in) guns
Armour: 24mm (1in) belt, 20mm (0.8in) bulkheads and deck
Launched: 1932

Armando Diaz and her sister ship *Luigi Cadorna* were part of the Italian Navy's 1929-30 building programme. They bore a strong resemblance to the previous group of swift cruisers, but they did not have the slight tumble-home of the earlier ships. This gave them more internal space, which in turn permitted reduced upper works and a smaller bridge. These improvements helped to enhance the vessels' stability in heavy seas. Both ships had a fixed seaplane catapult on the rear superstructure, while improved 152mm (6in) guns were carried in the spacious gun housings. These vessels could also carry a useful quantity of mines; anything from 84 to 138, depending on the type. *Armando Diaz* and *Luigi Cadorna* were fast, effective destroyers, reasonably well-armed and with good sea-keeping characteristics. *Armando Diaz* proved this when she almost reached 40 knots on her sea trials (with an installed power of 121,407hp). Her fuel tanks were capacious and able to carry some 1,016 tonnes (1,000 tons) of oil, giving her a not inconsiderable range of over 4,750km (2,500 miles) at an average speed of 25 knots. Both ships operated extensively in the Mediterranean Sea during World War II. *Armando Diaz* was sunk in February 1941, when the British submarine *HMS Upholder* torpedoed her while she was escorting a convoy.

Armide

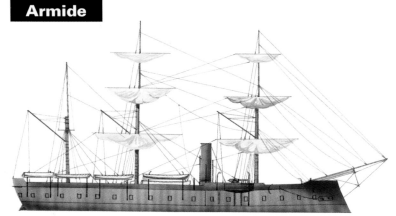

Type: French battleship (Alma class)
Displacement: 3,569 tonnes (3,513 tons)
Dimensions: 70m x 14 x 7m (229ft 8in x 46ft x 23ft)
Machinery: Single shaft horizontal compound
Top speed: 11.9 knots
Main armament: Six 193mm (7.6in) guns
Armour: 152mm (6in) belt, 120mm (4.7in) on battery
Launched: November 1867

Armide and her six sisters were designed as central battery ships for service on far flung foreign stations. The larger battleships then in service were too costly to build and maintain away from Europe, so *Armide* was ideally suited to arenas where she was unlikely to meet an opponent stronger than herself. *Armide* had a wooden hull and was barque-rigged, with a sail area of 1,450m2 (14,500ft2). Alma class were 'handy' ships, able to turn in 330m (360yd) diameter.

Arminius

Type: German battleship
Displacement: 1,917 tonnes (1,887 tons)
Dimensions: 63.2m x 10.9m x 4.6m (207ft 5in x 35ft 9in x 15ft)
Machinery: Single screw, single horizontal two-cylinder engine
Top speed: 11.2 knots
Main armament: Four 208mm (8.2in) guns
Armour: 114mm (4.5in) belt

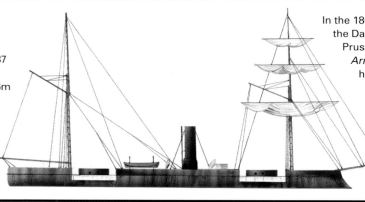

In the 1860s Prussia was anxious to defend herself against the Danes. Unable to build suitable warships herself, Prussia looked further afield and purchased the *Arminius,* a ship being built in England. She was hastily completed, but too late to take part in the war with Denmark in the Baltic. One of a type designed by Captain Cowper Coles of the Royal Navy, *Arminius* became the first battleship to join what was to become the German Navy. She became a coastal defence vessel, helping to protect the River Elbe in the Franco-Prussian war of 1870. She was discarded in 1921.

Arpad

Type: Austrian battleship
Displacement: 8,965 tonnes (8,823 tons)
Dimensions: 114.8m x 19.9m x 7.5m (376ft 6in x 65ft 2in x 24ft 6in)
Machinery: Twin screw triple expansion engines
Top speed: 19.6 knots
Main armament: Three 240mm (9.5in), twelve 150mm (6in) guns
Armour: 220mm (8.6in)

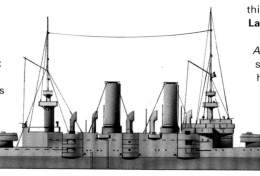

thick belt, 280mm (11in) turrets and centre casement
Launched: 1901

Arpad was developed as a small battleship type for service in the Adriatic. Although fairly well protected, her main armament was weak, but her secondary battery was as powerful as any battleship in service. *Arpad* was one of the first warships to rely heavily on electricity for working the main guns, hoists and ventilators. Scrapped in 1921.

Artevelde

Type: Belgian fishery protection vessel, minelayer and royal yacht
Displacement: 2,306 tonnes (2,270 tons)
Dimensions: 98.5m x 10.5m x 3.3m (323ft 2in x 34ft 5in x 10ft 10in)
Machinery: Twin screw geared turbines
Top Speed: 28.5 knots

Main armament: Four 104mm (4.1in) guns

The *Artevelde* was laid down at Antwerp to replace the *Zinnia*, and was intended for service as a fishery protection vessel, doubling as a royal yacht as required. This multi-purpose vessel could also act as a minelayer and

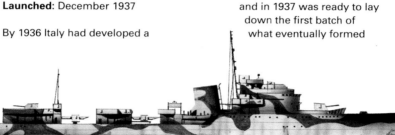

could stow up to 120 mines. In May 1940 the Germans captured *Artevelde* while she was still on the stocks. She was completed by them and renamed the *Lorelei*. At the

end of World War II she returned to Belgium where she served until the early 1950s. She was broken up in 1954/55. *Artevelde*'s original cost was estimated at 30 million francs.

Artigliere

Type: Italian destroyer
Displacement: 2,540 tonnes (2,500 tons)
Dimensions: 106.7m x 10.2m x 3.5m (350ft x 33ft 4in x 11ft 6in)
Machinery: Twin screw geared turbines
Top speed: 38 knots
Main armament: Four

120mm (4.7in) guns
Launched: December 1937

By 1936 Italy had developed a

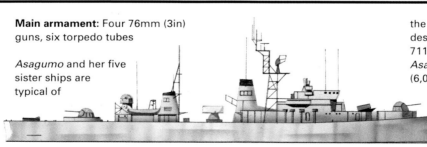

successful destroyer design and in 1937 was ready to lay down the first batch of what eventually formed

the largest single class of destroyer built for the Italian Navy. Twenty one units were built, all of which saw extensive war service as effective escorts capable of taking a great deal of punishment. As with pre-war destroyers, the anti-aircraft guns proved inadequate and were soon improved. *Artigliere* was lost in action in October 1940.

Artiglio II

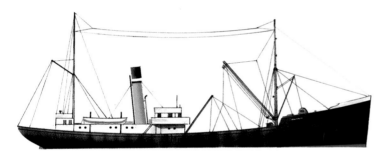

Type: Italian salvage vessel
Displacement: 305 tonnes (300 tons) (approx)
Dimensions: 42.6m x 7.6m x 2.1m (139ft 9in x 25ft x 7ft) (approx)
Top speed: 14 knots (approx)

Artiglio II was a small coaster bought by the Italian Society for Marine Recovery who, in 1929, were called in to recover gold from the liner *Egypt*, which had sunk in

1922. *Artiglio II* replaced *Artiglio* which had been accidentally blown up while laying charges on the wreck. The recovery marked a new era in underwater salvage, as the liner had sunk to a depth of 110m (120yd) – far deeper than conventional diving gear could cope with – necessitating the use of a new type of diving suit. Most of the gold, valued at £1,054,000, was successfully recovered.

Asagumo

Type: Japanese destroyer
Displacement: 2,083 tonnes (2,050 tons)
Dimensions: 114m x 11.8m x 4m (374ft x 38ft 9in x 13ft)
Machinery: Twin shaft diesel engines

Main armament: Four 76mm (3in) guns, six torpedo tubes

Asagumo and her five sister ships are typical of

the mid period of Japanese destroyers after World War II. With 711 tonnes (700 tons) of oil fuel, *Asagumo* has a range of 11,400km (6,000 miles) at 20 knots. The gunnery, radar and sensors were all supplied by the USA.

Asahi

Type: Japanese battleship
Displacement: 15,443 tonnes (15,2000 tons)
Dimensions: 133.5m x 23m x 8.4m (438ft x 75ft 6in x 27ft 6in)
Machinery: Twin screw vertical triple expansion
Top speed: 18 knots
Main armament: Four 305mm (12in), 14 152mm (6in) guns

Launched: November 1898

In 1896 Japan began a naval expansion programme. Because her own shipyards were not yet ready, the *Asahi* and her three sisters were ordered from British yards and designed by G.C. Macrow along the lines of the Royal Navy's Majestic class. *Asahi* saw extensive service in the 1904-05 war with Russia, but in 1921 was re-classified as a coast defence ship and in 1923 became a training ship. She was broken up in 1947.

Asama

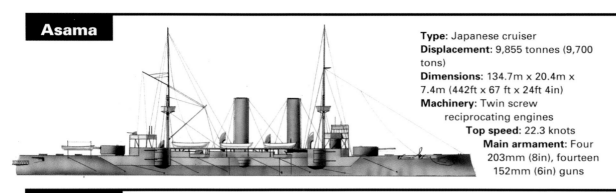

Type: Japanese cruiser
Displacement: 9,855 tonnes (9,700 tons)
Dimensions: 134.7m x 20.4m x 7.4m (442ft x 67 ft x 24ft 4in)
Machinery: Twin screw reciprocating engines
Top speed: 22.3 knots
Main armament: Four 203mm (8in), fourteen 152mm (6in) guns

Armour: 179mm (7in) thick main belt, 127mm (5in) thick upper belt with a 51mm (2in) deck
Launched: March 1898

Asama was designed by Philip Watts, later to become the chief designer for the Royal Navy. After World War I she became a training ship and was eventually scrapped in 1947.

Asashio

Type: Japanese destroyer
Displacement: 2,367 tonnes (2,330 tons)
Dimensions: 118.2m x 10.4m x 3.7m (388ft x 34ft x 12ft)
Machinery: Twin shaft geared turbines
Top speed: 35 knots
Main armament: Six 127mm (5in) guns
Launched: December 1936

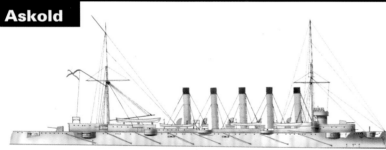

The Asashio class of ten units were larger versions of the two preceding classes of destroyers and marked Japan's abandonment of any treaty limitations. New steam turbines proved unreliable at first, and poor handling of the defective steering gear was not corrected until December 1941. All ten ships were lost during World War II, the *Asashio* falling victim to US aircraft.

Askold

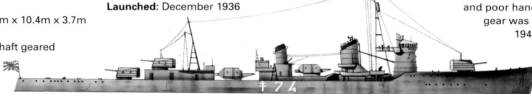

Type: Russian cruiser
Displacement: 6,198 tonnes (6,100 tons)
Dimensions: 133.2m x 15m x 6.2m (437ft x 16ft 5in x 20ft 4in)
Machinery: Triple screw vertical triple expansion
Top speed: 23.8 knots
Main armament: Twelve 152mm (6in), twelve 76mm

(3in) guns

Askold was laid down in the Krupp yard in 1898. She was fitted with nine of the newly-developed Schulz-Thornycroft boilers. In 1904 *Askold* was flagship to the cruiser squadron at Port Arthur during the Russo-Japanese war. She was broken up in 1921.

Assari Tewfik

Type: Turkish battleship
Displacement: 4,762 tonnes (4,687 tons)
Dimensions: 83m x 16m x 6.5m (272ft 4in x 52ft 6in x 21ft 4in)
Machinery: Single shaft compound engines
Top speed: 13 knots
Main armament: Eight 228mm (9in) muzzle-loading guns
Launched: 1868

The iron-hulled *Assari Tewfik* had six of her heavy guns concentrated in an armoured battery, which also protected the funnel base. Two more guns were mounted directly above the battery. This arrangement helped reduce the average size of battleships, resulting in greater manoeuvrability. In February 1913, during the Balkan wars, *Assari Tewfik* ran on a rock and had to be abandoned.

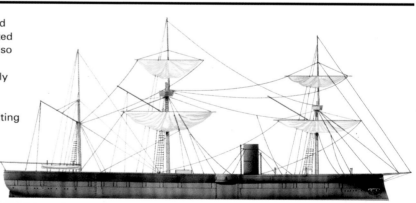

Aster

Type: Belgian minehunter
Displacement: 605 tonnes (595 tons)
Dimensions: 51.5m x 8.9m x 2.5m (169ft x 29ft x 8ft)
Machinery: Single screw diesel engine, two manoeuvring propellors and one bow thruster
Top speed: 15 knots
Main armament: One 20mm (0.8 in) anti-aircraft gun
Launched: 1981

Since World War II mine warfare has been neglected in the West, unlike in Russia where mining capabilities continued to be developed. In the late 1970s, France, Belgium and the Netherlands agreed to build a new class of 35 vessels. Each country builds its own hulls which were fitted out in Belgium with French electronics and Dutch machinery. All vessels carry full nuclear, biological and chemical (NBC) protection and minesweeping equipment.

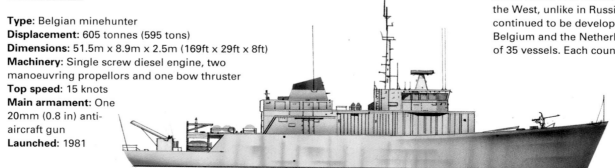

Astore

Type: Italian torpedo boat
Displacement: 220 tonnes (216 tons)
Dimensions: 50.3m x 5.3m x 1.75m (165ft 2in x 17ft 5in x 5ft 9in)
Machinery: Twin screw triple expansion engines
Top speed: 25.8 knots
Main armament: Three 47mm (1.8in) guns, three 450mm (17.7in) torpedo tubes
Launched: June 1907

Astore was one of a group of

six torpedo boats completed during 1907 and 1908 as a follow-on design to the eight-strong Cigno class. She was classified as a high seas torpedo boat, and was intended for service in the Adriatic. Apart from

the three torpedo tubes she was lightly armed, and had a range of some 590km at full speed. The Italian Navy had 19 such high seas boats in service, laid down from 1905 onwards. They all had

distinguished active careers throughout World War I. *Astore* and her five sister ships served mostly in the Adriatic, where their main task was convoy escort. Two of these vessels were later converted into fast minesweepers, but the reminder stayed substantially in the same configuration throughout their service career. All ships in the class survived the war, and were finally discarded in 1923.

Astoria

Type: US cruiser
Displacement: 12,662 tonnes (12,463 tons)
Dimensions: 179.2m x 18.8m x 6.9m (588ft x 61ft 9in x 22ft 9in)
Machinery: Four shaft geared turbines
Top speed: 32.7 knots
Main armament:

Nine 203mm (8in), eight 127mm (5in) guns
Launched: December 1933

Astoria was one of a group of seven heavy cruisers that improved upon the previous Salt Lake City group. She was sunk in action off Savo Island in 1942.

Athabaskan

Type: Canadian destroyer
Displacement: 4,267 tonnes (4,200 tons)
Dimensions: 129.8m x 15.5m x 4.5m (426ft x 51ft x 15ft)
Machinery: Twin screw, gas turbines
Top speed: 30 knots
Main armament: One 127mm (5in) gun, one triple mortar
Launched: 1970

Athabaskan and her three sisters were designed for anti-submarine warfare. Two hangars house Sea King helicopters, giving the ships greater flexibility than other anti-submarine vessels of the period. A comprehensive electronics system includes an effective long-range radar warning device.

Atlanta

Type: Confederate ironclad
Displacement: 1,022 tonnes (1,006 tons)
Dimensions: 62m x 12.5m x 4.7m (204ft x 41ft x 15ft 9in)
Machinery: Single screw

Top speed: 7 knots
Main armament: Two 178mm (7in), two 165mm (6.4in) guns

In November 1861, the blockade runner *Fingal* arrived at Savannah

with a large cargo of war material. Unable to escape, she was bought by the Confederate Navy in January 1862, converted into an ironclad and renamed *Atlanta*. The re-building was supervised by J. A.

Tift, who had previously constructed another large ironclad for the Confederacy. In June 1863, after a brief battle, *Atlanta* ran aground and surrendered to the Union.

Atlanta

Type: US cruiser
Displacement: 8,473 tonnes (8,340 tons)
Dimensions: 165m x 16.2m x 6.2m (541ft 6in x 53ft 2in x 20ft 6in)
Machinery: Twin shaft turbines
Top speed: 32.5 knots
Main armament: Sixteen 127mm (5in) guns

Atlanta was the lead ship in a class of 11 small US cruisers. As originally designed, they were intended to patrol the exposed areas of the battle fleet as effective anti-aircraft vessels. Later vessels in the class carried improvements, including better splinter protection, more guns and good sonar capability. In 1942 Atlanta was torpedoed and disabled by the Japanese and finally sunk by US forces.

Atlantis

Type: German raider
Displacement: 7,987 tonnes (7,862 tons)
Dimensions: 148m x 18.5m x 9.5m (486ft x 61ft x 31ft)
Machinery: Twin screw diesel engines
Top speed: 18 knots
Main armament: Six 146mm (5.9in) guns, four torpedo tubes
Launched: 1937

Formerly Goldenfels of the Hansa Line, Atlantis was a fast cargo vessel ideally suited to commerce raiding far from German shores. In 1940 she was equipped with two scout planes and 93 mines. She also acted as supply ship to patrolling U-boats. Spotted by a scout plane while re-fuelling a submarine, she was blown up by the British cruiser Devonshire in 1941.

Atropo

Type: Italian submarine
Displacement: 234.6 tonnes (231 tons) on surface, 325 tonnes (320 tons) submerged
Dimensions: 44.5m x 4.4m x 2.7m (146ft x 14ft 5in x 8ft 10in)
Machinery: Twin screw diesels on surface, electric motors underwater
Main armament: Two 450mm (17.7in) torpedo tubes

German-designed Atropo had two periscopes, one in the conning tower and one in the central control room, both of which had tapered ends to reduce their visibility to the enemy.

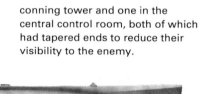

Attentive

Type: British cruiser
Displacement: 2,712 tonnes (2,670 tons)
Dimensions: 114m x 11.6m x 4.2m (374ft x 38ft 3in x 13ft 6in)
Machinery: Twin screw triple expansion engines
Top speed: 25.6 knots
Main armament: Ten 76mm (3in) guns

In 1902 the British Admiralty gave outline specifications for a group of lightly protected cruisers to act as scouts. Attentive was one such vessel subsequently built. The ships had light draught to enable them to operate in shallow waters, but in service they were also used as destroyer leaders and their light armament proved insufficient. As a result of this, Attentive and her eight sister ships were re-armed with nine 102mm (9in) guns in 1911-12. All ships in the class saw extensive action during World War I, with two being sunk in action. Attentive was sold in 1920.

Attilio Regolo

Type: Italian cruiser
Displacement: 5,419 tonnes (5,334 tons)
Dimensions: 142.9m x 14.4m x 4.9m (469ft x 47ft 3in x 16ft)
Machinery: Twin screw turbines
Main armament: Eight 135mm (5.4in) guns
Armour: 20mm (0.8in) over guns
Launched: August 1940

Attilio Regolo was one of a group of 12 fast cruisers of the Capitani Romani class laid down in 1939 in answer to the large, powerful French destroyers then entering service. To keep costs down, an original displacement limit of 3,454 tonnes (3,400 tons) was placed on the design, but this was later increased. Five of the class were never completed, being broken up on the stocks; three were lost in action; and one was scuttled to avoid capture. Attilio Regolo was transferred to France in 1948.

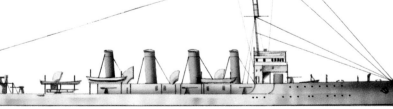

Attu

Type: US escort carrier
Displacement: 11,076 tonnes (10,902 tons)
Dimensions: 156.1m x 32.9m x 6.3m (512ft 3in x 108ft x 20ft 9in)
Machinery: Twin screw reciprocating engines

Main armament: One 127mm (5in) gun

In 1942 shipbuilder Henry J. Kaiser was

mass producing cargo vessels to replace those lost in war, and it was decided to complete 50 of the unfinished hulls as escort

carriers. *Attu* and her 49 sisters were completed within one year. She served in the Pacific until 1946.

Audace

Type: Italian torpedo boat
Displacement: 1,016 tonnes (1000 tons)
Dimensions: 86m x 8.3m x 2.8m (283ft x 27ft 6in x 9ft 6in)
Machinery: Twin screw geared turbines

Main armament: Seven 102mm (4in) guns
Launched: 1915

Originally the Japanese vessel *Kawakaze*, bought by the Italians after World War I, *Audace* served as control vessel to the target ship *San Marcos* in the 1930s. In 1944 she was sunk by British destroyers.

Audace

Type: Italian destroyer
Displacement: 4,470 tonnes (4,400 tons)
Dimensions: 135.9 x 14.6m x 4.5m (446ft x 48ft x 15ft)
Machinery: Two shaft geared turbines
Top speed: 33 knots
Main armament: Two

127mm (5in) guns, one SAM launcher
Launched: 1971

Audace and her sister

Ardito are fine examples of multi-function fleet escorts with the prime task of neutralising enemy submarines. Two helicopters with

comprehensive weapons kit and sensors are carried. *Audace* has a flush-decked hull of high freeload with uncluttered superstructure, but some of the weapons have a poor arc of fire due to the height of the superstructure. The double hangar is housed aft, while the fore bridge houses the communications and sensor equipment.

Audacious

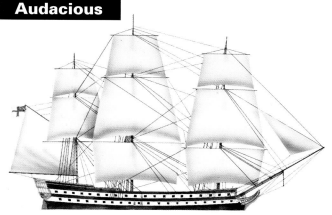

Type: British 74-gun sailing ship-of-the-line
Displacement: 1,422 tonnes (1,400 tons)
Dimensions: 54.8m x 14.9m (180ft x 49ft)
Main armament: 36 x 32-pounders on the lower deck, 34 x 24-pounders on the main gun deck, ten 18-pounders on the upper deck

Audacious saw extensive service in the almost continuous war that raged at the turn of the 18th century. Her type was considered to be the best balance

between offensive power and sailing ability, and formed the backbone of the battleline. *Audacious* took part in many actions, including the Battle of the Nile in August 1798, when she fought and overcame the French ship *Conquérant*. However, British vessels of the period were built to a standard pattern and were considered too small for the number of guns carried. French vessels had a better underwater hull form and were usually able to outsail their British counterparts.

Audacious

Type: British battleship
Displacement: 26,111 tonnes (25,700 tons)
Dimensions: 182.1m x 27.1m x 8.7m (597ft 6in x 89ft x 28ft 6in)
Machinery: Four shaft geared turbines
Top speed: 21 knots
Main armament: Ten 342mm

(13.5in), 16 x 102mm (4in) (guns
Armour: 305-203mm (12-8in) main belt with 280mm (11in) on turrets
Launched: October 1911

Built in answer to the growing strength and ambition of the German navy, *Audacious* was part of

the 1911 British battleship expansion programme. She carried the foremast before the funnels, giving better vision

to fire control when underway, a standard arrangement on all subsequent dreadnoughts. While on patrol in 1914 *Audacious* struck a mine and all attempts to tow her to safety failed. She was the first major ship lost in World War I.

Audacity

Type: British escort carrier
Displacement: 11,176 tonnes
(11,000 tons)
Dimensions: 142.4m x 17.4m x 7.5m
(467ft 3in x 57ft x 24ft 6in)
Machinery: Single shaft diesel
Main armament: One 102mm (4in)
gun

Audacity was the first escort carrier
to enter service with the Royal

Navy, and was formerly the German
merchant ship *Hannover,* which had
been captured in the West Indies in
1940. The superstructure was
removed and a flight deck 140m x
18m (400ft x 60ft) was built above
the hull. There was no hangar or
elevator, so her aircraft had to
remain on the deck, exposed to the
weather. She normally carried six
Martlet fighters, which she operated
against Condor reconnaissance
aircraft who until then had almost a

free hand against British convoys to
the Middle and Far East. *Audacity*
retained most of her cargo-carrying
capacity, so could also help deliver
much needed supplies along with
the ships she was escorting. She
served in this unique role for only
six months, until she was
torpedoed and sunk by *U-751* in
December 1941. Although her
service life was short, *Audacity*
contributed greatly to the
defence of Allied merchant

shipping and helped prove the
worth of the escort carrier concept.
She was the first in a long line of
such emergency constructions, able
to provide a measure of air power
in mid-ocean where land-based
aircraft could not reach. Her
successors, and the later Merchant
Aircraft Carriers (MAC), were also
based on merchant ship hulls, and
most carried Swordfish biplanes for
anti-submarine duties on the
Atlantic convoy routes.

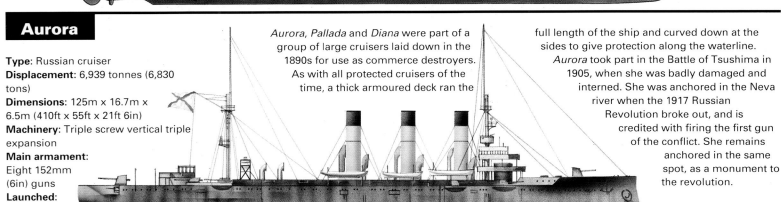

Augusta Victoria

Type: Passenger liner/auxiliary
cruiser
Displacement: 7,783 tonnes (7,661
tons)
Dimensions: 140m x 17m (459ft x
56ft)
Machinery: Twin screw triple
expansion engines

In 1887 the German Hamburg
American Line decided to start an
express liner service between

Hamburg and New York and
commissioned the *Augusta
Victoria*. Her maiden
voyage in 1889 was a
record-breaking
crossing, taking
just seven
days, two
and a

half hours. In 1897 her displacement
was increased to 8,614 tonnes
(8,479 tons) and in 1904 she was
sold to the Russian Navy as an
auxiliary cruiser for service in
the Russo-Japanese War of
1904-5. Re-named *Kuban*,

she acted as a decoy vessel for the
ill-fated fleet heading for the Straits
of Tsushima and, after cruising
briefly in the area, returned to
Russia. She was
scrapped in
1907.

Augusto Riboty

Type: Italian flotilla leader
Displacement: 2,003 tonnes (1,972
tons)
Dimensions: 103.7m x 9.7m x
3.6m (340ft x 32ft x 12ft)
Machinery: Twin shaft turbines
Main armament: Eight
102mm (4in) guns

Augusto Riboty and her two sister
ships were originally planned to be
lightly armoured light cruisers to be
laid down in 1913. However, they
emerged as flotilla leaders with
heavy armament. *Carlo Alberto
Racchia* and *Carlo Mirabello*
were both sunk by mines,
but *Augusto Riboty*
survived World War
II, to be scrapped
shortly thereafter.

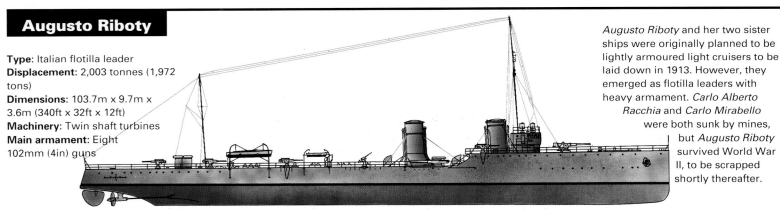

Aurora

Type: Russian cruiser
Displacement: 6,939 tonnes (6,830
tons)
Dimensions: 125m x 16.7m x
6.5m (410ft x 55ft x 21ft 6in)
Machinery: Triple screw vertical triple
expansion
Main armament:
Eight 152mm
(6in) guns
Launched:
1900

Aurora, Pallada and *Diana* were part of a
group of large cruisers laid down in the
1890s for use as commerce destroyers.
As with all protected cruisers of the
time, a thick armoured deck ran the

full length of the ship and curved down at the
sides to give protection along the waterline.
Aurora took part in the Battle of Tsushima in
1905, when she was badly damaged and
interned. She was anchored in the Neva
river when the 1917 Russian
Revolution broke out, and is
credited with firing the first gun
of the conflict. She remains
anchored in the same
spot, as a monument to
the revolution.

Australia

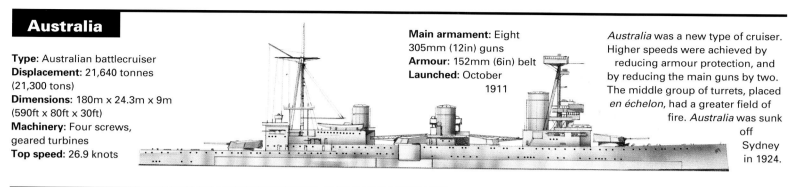

Type: Australian battlecruiser
Displacement: 21,640 tonnes (21,300 tons)
Dimensions: 180m x 24.3m x 9m (590ft x 80ft x 30ft)
Machinery: Four screws, geared turbines
Top speed: 26.9 knots

Main armament: Eight 305mm (12in) guns
Armour: 152mm (6in) belt
Launched: October 1911

Australia was a new type of cruiser. Higher speeds were achieved by reducing armour protection, and by reducing the main guns by two. The middle group of turrets, placed *en échelon*, had a greater field of fire. *Australia* was sunk off Sydney in 1924.

Averroff

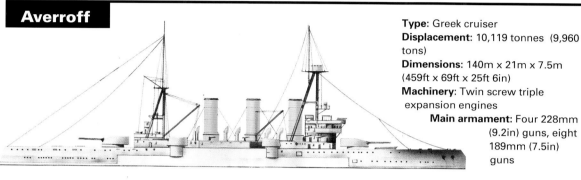

Type: Greek cruiser
Displacement: 10,119 tonnes (9,960 tons)
Dimensions: 140m x 21m x 7.5m (459ft x 69ft x 25ft 6in)
Machinery: Twin screw triple expansion engines
Main armament: Four 228mm (9.2in) guns, eight 189mm (7.5in) guns

Launched: March 1910

Averoff, the most powerful ship in the Greek Navy, was built in Italy as an armoured cruiser. Bought for the Greeks under the will of millionaire Giorgios Averoff, she served in the Balkan war prior to World War I. After a complete refit in the 1920s, *Averoff* served until the 1970s.

Avon

Type: British frigate
Displacement: 2,133 tonnes (2,100 tons)
Dimensions: 91.8m x 11m x 3.8m (301ft 4in x 36ft 8in x 12ft 9in)
Machinery: Twin screw vertical triple expansion
Main armament: Two 102mm (4in) guns

Avon was one of over 90 ships laid down in the River class between 1941-43 and completed during 1942-44. They were ocean-going, anti-submarine escorts and proved better vessels than the smaller Flower class corvettes. Two sets of engines

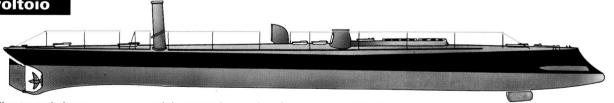

were installed and in later vessels the fuel capacity was increased from 447 to 656 tonnes (440 to 646 tons). The original

light armament was also increased. After World War II many ships of the class passed to other navies, where they continued to give good service until the 1960s. *Avon* was sold to Portugal in 1949.

Avvoltoio

Type: Italian torpedo boat
Displacement: 25 tonnes (25 tons)
Dimensions: 26m x 3.3m x 1.3m (86ft x 11ft x 4ft 6in)
Machinery: Single screw vertical

triple expansion engine. Steam supplied by a single locomotive boiler developing 420hp
Top speed: 21.3 knots
Main armament: Two 356mm

(14in) torpedo tubes, one 1-pounder revolving cannon
Launched: 1879

Surprise was the main weapon of

the torpedo boat, and early types were fast and small, lightly built and unprotected. *Avvoltoio* was the second such type adopted by the Italians. Discarded in 1904.

Avvoltoio

Type: Italian torpedo boat
Displacement: 132 tonnes (130 tons)
Dimensions: 46.3m x 5.2m x 2.3m (152ft x 17ft 2in x 7ft 9in)
Machinery: Twin screw vertical triple expansion engine
Top speed: 26.6 knots
Main armament: Three 356mm (14in) torpedo

tubes, two 3-pounder guns

By the mid 1880s the small torpedo craft of the 1870s had become large ocean-going vessels. *Avvoltoio* and her four sister ships were first class boats able to keep up with the fleet and with a good range. All ships were discarded between 1912-1914.

B1 Submarine

Type: British submarine
Displacement: 284 tonnes (280 tons) on surface, 319 tonnes (314 tons) submerged
Dimensions: 41m x 4.1m x 3m (135ft x 13ft 6in x 10ft)
Machinery: Single screw petrol on surface, electric motor for underwater propulsion

Main armament: Two 457mm (18in) torpedo tubes
Launched: October 1904

Before the completion of the A class submarines, the improved B class was underway. The extended superstructure on top of the hull gave improved surface performance, while small hydroplanes on the conning tower improved underwater handling. *B1* was broken up in 1921.

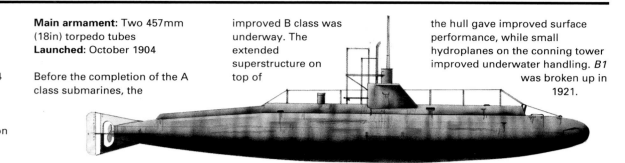

Bacchante

Type: British cruiser
Displacement: 4,139 tonnes (4,070 tons)
Dimensions: 85.3m x 13.8m x 7.2m (280ft x 45ft 6in x 23ft 9in)
Machinery: Single screw horizontal compound engine
Top speed: 15 knots
Main armament: Fourteen 178mm (7in) guns

Launched: October 1876

Bacchante class cruisers were the halfway stage between the existing iron-hulled broadside cruiser and the steel-hulled type that entered service in the 1880s. They were also the last iron ships built for the Royal Navy. When built, *Bacchante* and her two sisters were the largest vessels to carry compound engines. *Bacchante* was sold in 1897.

Bahia

Type: Brazilian cruiser
Displacement: 3,200 tonnes (3,150 tons)
Dimensions: 122.5m x 11.9m x 4.2m (401ft 6in x 39ft x 14ft)
Machinery: Three shaft turbines
Main armament: Ten 114mm (4.7in) guns
Launched: April 1909

Bahia and her sister ship *Rio Grande Do Sul* were built by Armstrong and completed in 1910, when they were the world's fastest small cruisers. They saw extensive service in World War I, operating off the north west coast of Africa. In 1925-26 both ships were re-boilered and re-engineered, increasing their speed to nearly 29 knots. Both ships served with the Allies in World War II, but in July 1945 *Bahia* exploded after being torpedoed by a German submarine while on patrol between Brazil and Africa. She sank within three minutes.

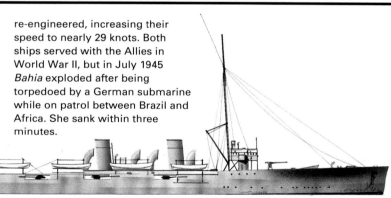

Baikal

Type: Russian train ferry
Displacement: 2,844 tonnes (2,800 tons)
Dimensions: 76.2m x 19.2m (250ft x 63ft)
Launched: June 1900

Baikal was built to connect the eastern and western sections of the Trans-Siberian railway across Lake Baikal, where she was also used as an ice-breaker during the winter. Built on the Tyne in the 1890s, she was then taken to pieces for transportation to the lake where she was re-assembled. *Baikal* was invaluable during the Russo-Japanese War. She served on the lake until the railway was extended round the shore.

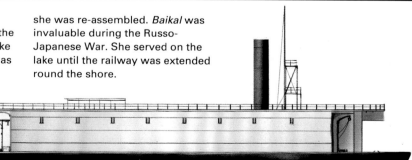

Baleares

Type: Spanish cruiser
Displacement: 13,279 tonnes (13,070 tons)
Dimensions: 193.5m x 19.5m x 5.2m (635ft x 64ft x 17ft 4in)
Machinery: Four shaft geared turbines
Main armament: Eight 203mm (8in) guns
Armour: 51mm (2in) thick belt with 114mm (4.5in) round magazines

Designed by Sir Philip Watts as part of the 1926 programme, *Baleares* followed the Kent class but had better speed and improved anti-aircraft armament. In the Spanish Civil War she formed part of the Nationalist force and in 1938 came into conflict with Government ships off Cape Palos, where she was torpedoed and sunk, with heavy loss of life.

Baleno

Type: Italian destroyer
Displacement: 2,123 tonnes (2,090 tons)
Dimensions: 94.3m x 9.2m x 3.3m (309ft 6in x 30ft x 10ft 9in)
Machinery: Twin screw geared turbines
Top speed: 39 knots
Main armament: Four 119mm (4.7in) guns, six 533mm (21in) torpedo tubes
Launched: March 1931

Baleno was one of a class of four fast destroyers built for the Italian Navy in the early 1930s. These sleek ships were made with a slimmer hull than earlier Italian destroyers, a feature which reduced drag and gave them a higher speed than previous designs. This narrow profile meant that internal storage was reduced, which limited fuel capacity and kept the ships' range to some 6,910km (4,163 miles) at 12 knots.

Combat experience in the early days of World War II showed the need for some improvements. Warships had shown themselves to be more vulnerable to air attack than had been anticipated, so *Baleno* and her sister ships were quickly fitted with extra anti-aircraft weapons. These destroyers saw hard service in the Mediterranean, and none survived the war; all being sunk in action. On 16 April 1941,

Baleno and another destroyer, *Luca Tarigo,* were escorting five merchant ships from Sicily to Tripoli. The convoy was spotted by four British destroyers, who attacked immediately. In spite of a gallant fight, the *Luca Tarigo* and the merchantmen were sunk with heavy loss of life. *Baleno* managed to limp away with a severe list, heavily damaged and taking on water. Her crew were unable to carry out enough repairs to keep her afloat, and she capsized and sank the following day.

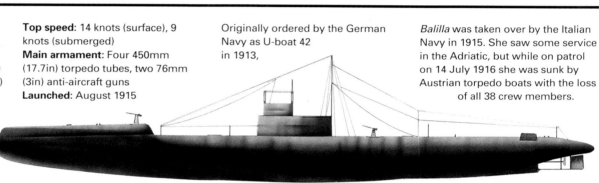

Balilla

Type: Italian submarine
Displacement: 740 tonnes (728 tons) on the surface, 890 tonnes (876 tons) submerged
Dimensions: 65m x 6m x 4m (213ft 3in x 19ft 8in x 13ft)
Machinery: Twin shaft diesel (surface), electric motor (submerged)

Top speed: 14 knots (surface), 9 knots (submerged)
Main armament: Four 450mm (17.7in) torpedo tubes, two 76mm (3in) anti-aircraft guns
Launched: August 1915

Originally ordered by the German Navy as U-boat 42 in 1913,

Balilla was taken over by the Italian Navy in 1915. She saw some service in the Adriatic, but while on patrol on 14 July 1916 she was sunk by Austrian torpedo boats with the loss of all 38 crew members.

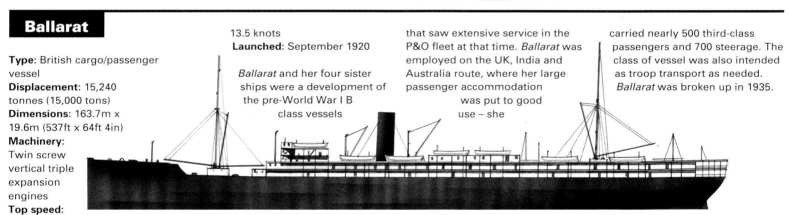

Ballarat

Type: British cargo/passenger vessel
Displacement: 15,240 tonnes (15,000 tons)
Dimensions: 163.7m x 19.6m (537ft x 64ft 4in)
Machinery: Twin screw vertical triple expansion engines
Top speed:

13.5 knots
Launched: September 1920

Ballarat and her four sister ships were a development of the pre-World War I B class vessels

that saw extensive service in the P&O fleet at that time. *Ballarat* was employed on the UK, India and Australia route, where her large passenger accommodation was put to good use – she

carried nearly 500 third-class passengers and 700 steerage. The class of vessel was also intended as troop transport as needed. *Ballarat* was broken up in 1935.

Balmoral Castle

Type: British liner
Displacement: 13,574 tonnes (13,360 tons)
Dimensions: 180m x 19.6m x 9.6m (590ft 6in x 64ft 4in x 31ft 6in)
Machinery: Twin screw quadruple expansion engines
Top speed: 17 knots
Launched: November 1909

Balmoral Castle and her sister *Edinburgh Castle* belonged to the Union-Castle line. *Balmoral Castle*

operated on the South African route and was the first Cape liner to be fitted with wireless. She had accommodation for 317 first-class, 220 second-class and 268 third-class passengers. In 1910 *Balmoral Castle* served as a royal

yacht during celebrations for the Union of South Africa, and during World War I she served as a troop transport. She was sold for scrap in 1939.

Balny

Type: French torpedo boat
Displacement: 66 tonnes (65 tons)
Dimensions: 40.8m x 3.4m x 1m (134ft x 11ft x 3ft 3in)
Machinery: Single screw compound engine
Top speed: 19 knots
Armament: Two 355mm (14in)

torpedo tubes in the bow
Launched: 1886

Balny was one of a group of 10 ocean-going torpedo boats designed by Normand as a development of existing launches.

However, the ships were not really big enough for their task and rolled badly in heavy seas. In 1890 all were restricted to coastal defence.

Baloeran

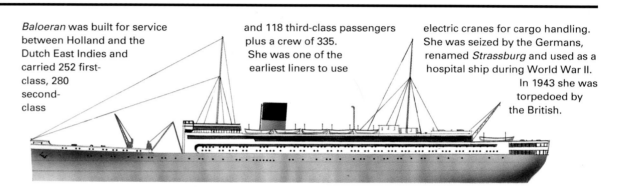

Type: Dutch liner
Displacement: 21,336 tonnes (21,000 tons)
Dimensions: 175m x 21.3m x 8.6m (574ft x 70ft x 28ft 3in)
Machinery: Twin screw diesel engines
Top speed: 18.5 knots
Launched: 1929

Baloeran was built for service between Holland and the Dutch East Indies and carried 252 first-class, 280 second-class

and 118 third-class passengers plus a crew of 335. She was one of the earliest liners to use

electric cranes for cargo handling. She was seized by the Germans, renamed *Strassburg* and used as a hospital ship during World War II. In 1943 she was torpedoed by the British.

Baltic

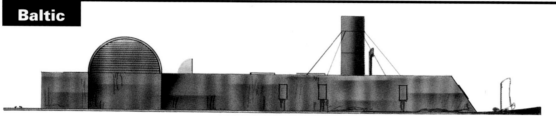

Type: Confederate ironclad
Displacement: 652 tonnes (642 tons)

Dimensions: 56.5m x 11.5m x 2m (185ft 4in x 37ft 9in x 6ft 6in)
Machinery: Inclined engines

driving 8m (26ft 3in) diameter paddle wheels
Top speed: 6 knots

Main armament: One 42-pounder, two 32-pounder guns
Launched: 1860

Baltic was a wooden-hulled sidewheel steamer built as a tow boat and adopted by the State of Alabama for conversion into an ironclad during the American Civil War. She was captured in 1865 and sold at auction.

Baltic

Type: British merchant vessel
Displacement: 24,258 tonnes (23,876 tons)
Dimensions: 221m x 23m (725ft x 75ft 6in)
Machinery: Twin screw triple expansion engines
Top speed: 17 knots
Launched: November 1903

Baltic was one of the 'big four' steamships built by Harland and Wolff of Belfast for the White Star Line. She was capable of carrying nearly 900 passengers plus 2000 steerage, and when launched was the

world's largest ship. *Baltic* was used as a troop transport during World War I, was re-boilered in

1924 and laid up in 1932. She was broken up in 1933.

Baltimore

Type: US cruiser
Displacement: 17,303 tonnes (17,030 tons)
Dimensions: 205.7m x 21.5m x 7.3m (675ft x 70ft 6in x 24ft)
Machinery: Four shaft geared turbines
Top speed: 33 knots

Main armament: Nine 203mm (8in) guns
Launched: July 1942

The Baltimore class of 24 units was the first to be built after the lifting of size limitations

imposed by the Washington and London Naval Treaties. The increase in size permitted improvements in both protection

and sea-keeping qualities, and the class was authorised in 1940. Two of the class became the first guided missile cruisers in the US Navy, others later served as fire support vessels in Vietnam. *Baltimore* was decommissioned in 1971.

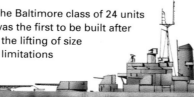

Bande Nere

Type: Italian coastal minesweeper
Displacement: 375 tonnes (370 tons)
Dimensions: 44.1m x 8.5m x 2.6m
(144ft 8in x 28ft x 8ft 6in)
Machinery: two Fiat-G.M. 8-268A
diesels
Top speed: 13 knots
Main armament: Two
20mm (0.8in) anti-aircraft
guns

The *Bambu* is one of four
converted American
Adjutant-class minesweepers,

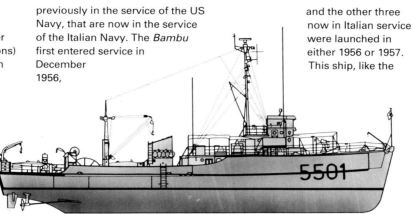

previously in the service of the US
Navy, that are now in the service
of the Italian Navy. The *Bambu*
first entered service in
December
1956,

and the other three
now in Italian service
were launched in
either 1956 or 1957.
This ship, like the

other in its class, has a crew of two
officers and 29 enlisted men, and is
equipped with both radar and
sonar. These ships, like many
minesweepers, are wooden-hulled
to defeat magnetic mines, and they
are powered by two propellers
developing 1200 bhp. Capable of
carrying up to 40 tonnes (40 tons) of
fuel, they are well suited to coastal
patrol work. Indeed, these ships are
now assigned to the United Nations
patrol force in the Red Sea for just
such a purpose. They will undertake
these duties in the immediate
future.

Banshee

Type: Confederate blockade runner
Displacement: 508 tonnes (500
tons)
Dimensions: 64m x 7m x 2.4m
(210ft x 23ft x 8ft)
Machinery: Two cylinder engine
driving paddle wheels
Top speed: 11 knots
Launched: 1863

Banshee was typical of the high
speed vessels that ran vital

supplies through to the
Southern armies during
the latter part of the
American Civil War. To
help her avoid detection
she had a low silhouette,
short pole masts and a
minimum of rigging.
She also had a
shallow draft to

enable her to slip in over sand
bars. Further camouflage was
afforded by the light grey
paintwork, and Welsh coal was
used because it gave off very little
smoke and therefore did not give
away her

position to the enemy. *Banshee*
was one of the first vessels built
of steel and ran economically
on coal. She was captured
by the Union on her
ninth blockade-
busting trip.

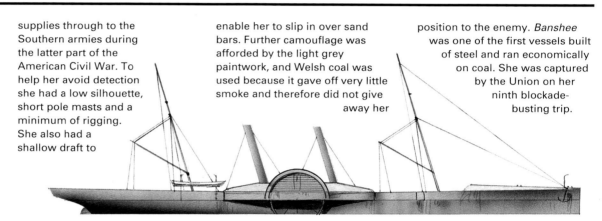

Barbara

Type: German merchant vessel
Displacement: 2,110 tonnes (2,077
tons)
Dimensions: 90m x 13m x
5.6m (295ft 3in x 42ft 8in x
18ft 4in)
Machinery: Single screw
diesel engines
Top speed: 13 knots

The *Barbara* was
designed to test the

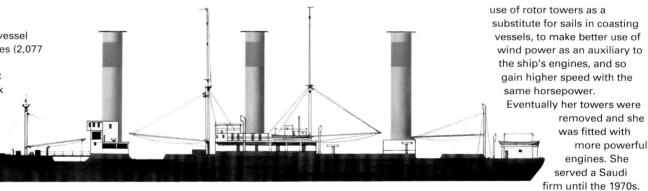

use of rotor towers as a
substitute for sails in coasting
vessels, to make better use of
wind power as an auxiliary to
the ship's engines, and so
gain higher speed with the
same horsepower.
Eventually her towers were
removed and she
was fitted with
more powerful
engines. She
served a Saudi
firm until the 1970s.

Barbarigo

Type: Italian submarine
Displacement: 774 tonnes (762
tons) on the surface, 938
tonnes (923 tons)
submerged
Dimensions: 67m x 6m x
3.8m (220ft x 19ft 8in x
12ft 6in)
Machinery: Twin shaft diesel
(surface), electric motors
(submerged)
Top speed: 16 knots (surface), 9.8
knots (submerged)

Main armament: Six 450mm
(17.7in) torpedo tubes, two 76mm
(3in) guns
Launched: November 1917

Barbarigo was one of a group of
four medium-sized submarines laid
down in October 1915 but not
completed until the end of World
War I. The batteries were placed in

four watertight compartments
under the horizontal deck that
ran the full length of the
vessel. This was a new
arrangement, as the
batteries were usually
concentrated in one
large compartment for
easy access. The
Barbarigo class had a range of just
over 3,218km (1,694 miles) at 11
knots, but they could not submerge
deeper than 50m (164ft). However,
underwater manoeuvrability was
good. *Barbarigo* was sold in 1928.

Barbarigo

Type: Italian submarine
Displacement: 1,059 tonnes (1,043 tons) on the surface, 1,310 tonnes (1,290 tons) submerged
Dimensions: 73m x 7m x 5m (239ft 6in x 23ft x 16ft 6in)
Machinery: Twin shaft diesel (surface), electric motors (submerged)
Top speed: 17.4 knots (surface), 8 knots (submerged)
Main armament: Eight 533mm (21in) torpedo tubes

Barbarigo was one of a class of 11 units, only one of which

survived World War II. These vessels were built with a partial double hull and internal ballast tanks. They were reasonably fast and manoeuvrable, but had poor transverse stability. This characteristic was aggravated by the long conning tower, a common feature of Italian submarines in this period. The class also had a relatively short range, some 1,425km (750 miles) on the surface, or 228km (120 miles) submerged at

three knots. This was deemed adequate for Mediterranean operations, although like other Italian submarines, they often ranged remarkably far from home. The maximum dive limit was about 100m (330ft). *Barbarigo* herself was laid down in 1937 and completed during 1939. After more than four years of active service, she was

converted into a submersible transport. The intention was for her to carry essential supplies on a series of round trips to Japan. This was a hopelessly inefficient method of delivering such supplies, but Allied air and naval power in the Pacific called for desperate measures. Her first such voyage was in June 1943, but she was spotted on the surface by Allied aircraft in the Bay of Biscay, who attacked and sunk her.

Barham

Type: British battleship
Displacement: 32,004 tonnes (31,500 tons)
Dimensions: 196m x 27.6m x 8.8m (643ft x 90ft 6in x 29ft)
Machinery: Four shaft turbines
Top speed: 24 knots
Main armament: Eight 381mm (15in), fourteen 152mm (6in)guns
Launched: October 1914

The *Barham* and her three sisters were designed to compete with the new battleships (with 355mm (14in) guns) being designed by Germany, Japan and the USA. The class was equipped with newly designed 381mm (15in) guns, which proved

more accurate than the previous 343mm (13.5in) guns, and also

carried a much bigger bursting charge. *Barham* served at Jutland in 1916, where she was severely damaged. All ships in the class underwent modernisation in the early 1930s. *Barham* was sunk with heavy loss of life off Salum in the Mediterranean by *U-331* on 25 November 1941.

Barrozo

Type: Brazilian coastal defence battleship
Displacement: 1,375 tonnes (1,354 tons)
Dimensions: 57m x 11.2m x 2.4m (186ft x 37ft x 8ft)
Machinery: Single screw single expansion engine
Top speed: 9 knots
Main armament: Two 178mm (7in), three 120mm (4.7in) guns
Launched: 1864

Barrozo was an armoured central battery ship with a wooden hull which served extensively in the 1865-1870 war with Paraguay. Towards the end of the war in July 1870, the Paraguayans tried to capture *Barrozo* and *Rio Grande* by

drifting down river in canoes and then boarding the ships. *Rio Grande* was boarded first, and most of her crew were killed. Meanwhile, *Barrozo* had steamed alongside and was able to kill all on *Rio Grande*'s deck with grape shot. *Barrozo* was discarded in 1885.

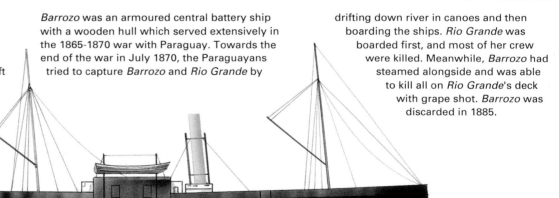

Basento

Type: Italian naval water tanker
Displacement: 1,944 tonnes (1,914 tons)
Dimensions: 66m x 10m x 4m (216ft 6in x 33ft x 13ft)
Machinery: Twin screw diesels
Top speed: 12.5 knots
Launched: 1970

Basento and her two sister ships form part of the essential auxiliary service that supplies fresh water to the Italian fleet. Each ship has a capacity of 1,016 tonnes (1,000 tons) and has a range of nearly 5,700km (3,000 miles) at 7 knots. Armament consists of two anti-aircraft guns. The machinery space is

concentrated aft, with a combined funnel and mast placed immediately behind the bridge. The fore and aft parts of the hull are connected by a companionway supported on raised pumping stations. *Basento* and her sisters were built to

replace the ageing auxiliary vessels that were originally donated to the Italians by the USA.

Basileus Georgios

Type: Greek battleship
Displacement: 1,802 tonnes (1,774 tons)
Dimensions: 61m x 10m x 4.8m (200ft x 33ft x 16ft)
Machinery: Twin screw compound engines
Main armament: Two 228mm (9in) guns

Launched: December 1867

Basileus Georgios was a small central battery ship with a full length armour belt. The armour made up 340 tonnes (335 tons) of the

displacement, giving the diminutive battleship greater offensive and defensive

capabilities on a small displacement than any other battleship of her time. The battery was placed forward of centre and ahead of the funnel, with end ports in the corners to enable firing ahead or astern.

Basilicata

Type: Italian cruiser
Displacement: 2,519 tonnes (2,480 tons)
Dimensions: 83m x 12.7m x 5m (272ft x 41ft 8in x 16ft 6in)
Machinery: Twin screws, two sets of vertical triple expansion engines
Main armament: Six 152mm (6in) guns
Launched: July 1914

Basilicata and her sister ship *Campania* were cruisers built for colonial service, and were intended as an improvement on the *Calabria*, launched in 1894. Both ships were

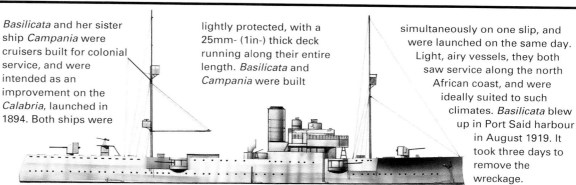

lightly protected, with a 25mm- (1in-) thick deck running along their entire length. *Basilicata* and *Campania* were built

simultaneously on one slip, and were launched on the same day. Light, airy vessels, they both saw service along the north African coast, and were ideally suited to such climates. *Basilicata* blew up in Port Said harbour in August 1919. It took three days to remove the wreckage.

Batavia

Type: British liner
Displacement: 2,594 tonnes (2,553 tons)
Dimensions: 99m x 12m (327ft x 39ft)
Machinery: Single screw compound engines

Batavia was sold on the stocks to the Cunard Steamship Company for service on their Atlantic run,

although it was hoped that she would also sail from Liverpool to Bombay via Suez. However, after one trip this route was abandoned. In 1888 *Batavia* was sold to new owners. She was chartered by the Canadian Pacific and worked the Vancouver, Yokohama, Hong Kong route. In 1904, while transporting goods to Russia during the Russo-Japanese war, she was captured by Japanese warships and re-named *Shikotan Maru*. She was wrecked in 1924.

Batcombe

Type: British fire-fighting tug
Dimensions: 18m x 5.4m (60ft x 18ft)
Launched: 1970

Batcombe is a typical tugboat specially equipped for fire-fighting duties and carrying high pressure

hoses with which she is able to quickly cover any burning vessel with a blanket of foam and water. The foam and water hoses are mounted on the bridge, which has good all round visibility because of its curved structure. When not in use as a fire-fighter, *Batcombe* performs as a normal tugboat.

Bayan

Type: Russian cruiser
Displacement: 7,924 tonnes (7,800 tons)
Dimensions: 135m x 17m x 6.7m (443ft x 55ft 9in x 22ft)
Machinery: Twin screw vertical triple expansion engines
Main armament: Two 203mm (8in),

eight 152mm (6in) guns
Armour: 203mm (8in) belt reducing to 76mm (3in) at bow and stern, 178mm (7in) on turrets
Launched: June 1900

Bayan was a medium-sized cruiser with good protection. Fast in trials, she could not maintain maximum speed in service due to problems

getting the coal from the bunkers to the furnaces. She served in various roles during the Russo-Japanese war, until captured in January 1905. She was sunk as a target in 1932.

Bayano

Type: British escort vessel
Displacement: 6,896 tonnes (6,788 tons)
Main armament: Four 152mm (6in), two 102mm (4in) guns
Launched: June 1917

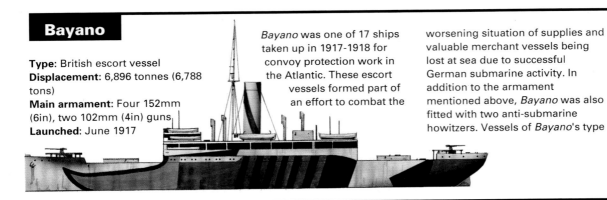

Bayano was one of 17 ships taken up in 1917-1918 for convoy protection work in the Atlantic. These escort vessels formed part of an effort to combat the worsening situation of supplies and valuable merchant vessels being lost at sea due to successful German submarine activity. In addition to the armament mentioned above, *Bayano* was also fitted with two anti-submarine howitzers. Vessels of *Bayano*'s type – medium-sized merchant vessels with moderate speed – were economic to run and more efficient to operate than the armed merchant cruisers. *Bayano* served in the Royal Navy from December 1917 to March 1919.

Bayern

Type: German battleship
Displacement: 32,412 tonnes (32,000 tons)
Dimensions: 182.4m x 30m x 8m (598ft 5in x 99ft x 27ft 10in)
Machinery: Triple screw geared turbines
Main armament: Eight 380mm (15in), sixteen 150mm (5.9in) guns

Armour: 350mm (13.8in) lower waterline belt, 170-249mm (6.7-9.8in) upper belt, 350mm (13.8in) on turrets

Bayern and her three sisters were the last German battleships laid down before World War I and marked a major change in policy because, for the first time, German designers opted to equal the gunpower of the British 380mm (15in) gunned battleships. *Bayern* was a very stable vessel in short seas, and so was a good gun platform, but she rolled badly in long seas. Internal subdivision was good and some of the design features were later incorporated into the *Bismarck* of World War II. *Bayern* was sunk at Scapa Flow in 1919.

Béarn

Type: French aircraft carrier
Displacement: 28,854 tonnes (28,400 tons)
Dimensions: 182.5m x 27m x 9m (599ft x 88ft 11in x 30ft 6in)
Machinery: Four screws, geared turbines, triple expansion engines
Top speed: 21.5 knots
Main armament: Eight 152mm (6in) guns
Launched: April 1920

During World War II *Béarn* was not employed as a front line carrier because of her low speed, but she gave valuable service as an aircraft ferry. After the fall of France in 1940, *Béarn* was held at Martinique to prevent her return to France. After the war she served off Indo-China (Vietnam). Scrapped in 1949.

Belfast

Type: British cruiser
Displacement: 15,138 tonnes (14,900 tons)
Dimensions: 187m x 20m x 7m (613ft 6in x 66ft 4in x 23ft 2in)
Machinery: Four shaft geared turbines
Top speed: 32.5 knots

Main armament: Twelve 152mm (6in) guns
Armour: 114mm (4.5in) waterline belt

Belfast and her sister *Edinburgh* were originally planned as 10,160-tonne (10,000-ton) follow on units to the Southampton class. *Belfast* had triple-mounted 152mm (6in) guns in four turrets that were able to elevate up to 45 degrees. *Belfast* struck a mine four months after completion, breaking her back. She returned to service in October 1944, having been given added underwater protection. She is now on display at Tower Bridge.

Belgic

Type: British passenger liner
Displacement: 24,940 tonnes (24,547 tons)
Dimensions: 212m x 23.8m x 11m (696ft 6in x 78ft x 36ft 3in)
Machinery: Triple screw geared turbines

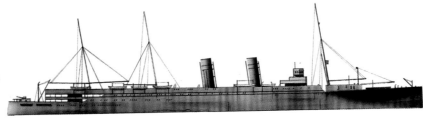

Belgic was originally intended for the Belgian International Liner service running between Antwerp and New York. Had she been completed for the company she would have been the largest liner to ever fly the Belgian flag. However, at the start of World War I there was a severe shortage of merchant shipping and *Belgic* was hurriedly completed in 1917 as a large cargo carrier. Later she became a troopship. At the end of the war she underwent a major refit, emerging as the graceful liner *Belgenland*, with two promenade decks, three funnels and accommodation for 2,700 passengers. She was broken up in 1936.

Belleisle

Type: British battleship
Displacement: 4,948 tonnes (4,870 tons)
Dimensions: 74.6m x 16m x 6.5m (245ft x 52ft x 21ft 6in)
Machinery: Twin screws, two cylinder direct acting engines
Top speed: 13 knots
Main armament: Four 305mm (12in) guns
Launched: February 1876

Belleisle and her sister ship *Orion* were originally laid down for the Turkish Navy at Samuda's yard on the Thames. British neutrality during the Russo-Turkish war of 1878

meant that these ships could not be delivered, so they were bought by the Royal Navy, mainly to prevent the collapse of their builder. Their 305mm (12in) guns were mounted in a large central battery, where they could fire ahead and astern as well as in broadside. They were the last ships of this type to enter British service. Poor sea-keeping capabilities combined with a low freeboard meant that the two vessels could not serve with a deep-water fleet, so they

were used in the coastal defence role. Their thick armour and heavy armament made them powerful ships for this task. The armour belt ran the full length of the hull, and supported a 2.4m (8ft) solid-forged ram, already an anachronism in 1876. *Belleisle* spent most of her service life as a home-based coastal protection ship, while *Orion* carried out the same task in the Far East and later from Malta. In

1886 they were fitted with extra light guns and a torpedo net. From 1900, *Belleisle* was used as a target hulk for testing the new Lyddite shells. She was broken up in 1904. *Orion* was converted to a store ship in 1910, being finally disposed of in 1913.

Bellona

Type: British cruiser
Displacement: 7,518 tonnes (7,400 tons)
Dimensions: 156m x 15m x 5.4m (512ft x 50ft 6in x 18ft)
Machinery: Four screws, geared turbines
Main armament: Eight 133mm (5.25in) guns
Armour: 76mm (3in) side

Bellona was one of five simplified Dido class cruisers. They formed part of the expanding naval programme that gathered momentum as war with Germany

became inevitable – in 1939 the British laid down 14 cruisers, two battleships and two large cruisers, plus many smaller units. As World

War II progressed, additional anti-aircraft weapons were added. All ships in the class saw active war service. After the war *Bellona* and her sister ship *Black Prince* were lent to the Royal New Zealand Navy, but *Bellona* was returned in 1956 in exchange for another in the class, the modernised *Royalist*.

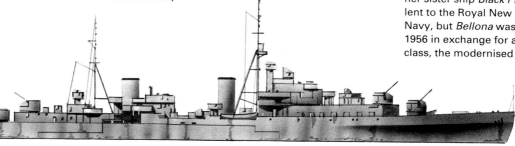

Ben-My-Chree

Type: British aircraft carrier
Displacement: 3,942 tonnes (3,880 tons)
Dimensions: 114m x 14m x 5.3m (375ft x 46ft x 17ft 6in)
Machinery: Twin screw turbines
Top speed: 24.5 knots
Launched: March 1908

Ben-My-Chree, a former passenger vessel on the Isle of Man route, was converted into an aircraft carrier in 1915. She was fitted with a large

hangar aft, plus a flying-off ramp on the fore deck. *Ben-My-Chree* served in the Dardanelles campaign, her aircraft sinking two Turkish vessels. While anchored in Kastelorgio harbour in 1917, *Ben-My-Chree* was attacked by Turkish shore batteries and sank.

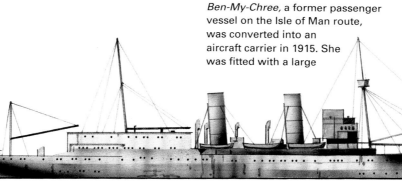

Benbow

Type: British battleship
Displacement: 10,770 tonnes (10,600 tons)
Dimensions: 99m x 21m x 8.2m (325ft x 68ft x 27ft 10in)
Machinery: Twin screw, inverted compound engines
Top speed: 17.5 knots
Main armament: Two 412mm (16.25in), ten 152mm (6in) guns

Launched: June 1885

Benbow was one of the Rodney class of battleship built in answer to the French Formidable class then under construction. Original armament was to have been four 343mm (13.5in) and eight 152mm (6in) guns, but the Woolwich Arsenal was unable to deliver these and so two 112-tonne (111-ton) guns were mounted

instead, in large open barbettes, one fore and one aft. The weight so saved was used to install an extra pair of 152mm (6in) guns. There were many problems with the main armament, and the entire battleship class was delayed, *Benbow* herself taking six years to complete. She was scrapped in 1909.

Benedetto Brin

Type: Italian battleship
Displacement: 13,426 tonnes (13,215 tons)
Dimensions: 138.6m x 23.8m x 8.8m (449ft 6in x 78ft 3in x 29ft)
Machinery: Twin screw triple expansion engines
Top speed: 20.3 knots
Main armament: Four 304mm

(12in), four 203mm (8in), twelve 152mm (6in) guns

Benedetto Brin was designed by one of the world's leading designers and took his name. Her design was a compromise, with protection reduced in favour of speed

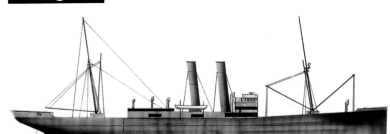

and firepower. *Benedetto Brin* and her sister *Regina Margherita* were unique ships with good sea-keeping capabilities. *Benedetto Brin* was lost at Brindisi harbour, as a result of Austrian sabotage, on 27 September 1915.

Bengasi

Type: Italian naval transport
Displacement: 3,617 tonnes (3,560 tons)
Dimensions: 87.3m x 11.2m x 5.8m (286ft 8in x 37ft x 19ft)
Machinery: Single screw vertical triple expansion engines
Main armament: Two 76mm (3in) guns

Bengasi was originally the Turkish

transport *Derna*, running the Italian blockade of Tripoli. She briefly flew the German flag as *Eitel Friedrich*. With the fall of Tripoli, *Derna* was sunk in harbour by the retreating Turks but was raised in 1911 and taken into the Italian Navy, serving as a transport along the coast of the Mediterranean. As *Bengasi*, she was sold into private ownership in November 1925.

Benton

Type: American ironclad gunboat
Displacement: 643 tonnes (633 tons)
Dimensions: 61.5m x 22m (202ft x 72ft 9in)
Machinery: Inclined engines driving a single stern wheel
Main armament: Two 279mm

(11in) guns
Converted: 1861

Benton was originally the catamaran-hulled salvage vessel *Submarine No. 7*. She was converted by planking over the space between the hulls, adding a new bow and building a two-tier casement

housing the main armament over most of her hull. Her

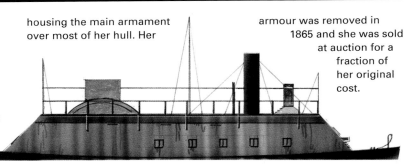

armour was removed in 1865 and she was sold at auction for a fraction of her original cost.

Berlin

Type: German frigate
Displacement: 1,016 tonnes (1,000 tons)
Dimensions: 48.7m x 11.5m (160ft x 38ft)
Main armament: Twenty 24-pounders
Launched: 1674

Berlin was a Brandenburg frigate of medium size developed from the larger and slower ships of the line. These ships were built as the result of a growing need for a special vessel to scout and force its way through a group of small sloops, acting as lookout for the main fleet. Frigates were never

intended to fight the standard ships of the line, but were better employed cruising the world's oceans, protecting the commercial trade of their own country and attacking that of the enemy. *Berlin* was a good sea boat, and the experience gained from her performance enabled other countries to develop their own frigates along similar lines. These vessels grew from ships carrying around 20 cannon, to larger types mounting over 40 guns on a single deck.

Berlin

Type: German cruiser
Displacement: 3,816 tonnes (3,756 tons)
Dimensions: 111m x 13m x 5.6m (364ft 9in x 43ft 8in x 18ft 5in)
Machinery: Twin screw triple expansion engines
Main armament: Ten 102mm (4.1in) guns

Berlin was one of a class of seven units named after major German cities. The class was a development of the previous Gazelle class and had more powerful engines and a thicker protective deck. However, the lightweight shells from the rapid-fire 102mm (4in) guns later proved inadequate in action. *Berlin* was hulked in 1935.

Bermuda

Type: Confederate blockade runner
Displacement: 1,019 tonnes (1,003 tons)
Dimensions: 64m x 9m (211ft x 30ft)
Machinery: Single screw vertical direct acting engines
Top speed: 8 knots
Launched: 1861

At the start of the American Civil War *Bermuda* ran supplies through the Union blockade to the Confederate army and took cotton back to the UK. By 1862 the blockade had tightened, and *Bermuda* was transferring supplies to a faster vessel in

Bermuda when she was captured by a Union gunboat. She was bought by a Bostonian company for service on their New York to New Orleans line and was re-named *General Meade*.

Beta

Type: Italian submarine
Displacement: 40 tonnes (40 tons) on surface, 46 tonnes (46 tons)

submerged
Dimensions: 15m x 2.3m x 2.5m (49ft 7in x 7ft 8in x 8ft 5in)

Machinery: Single screw petrol engine on surface, electric motor submerged
Main armament: Two 444mm (17.7in) torpedo tubes
Launched: July 1916

In 1912 two small experimental submarines were built in the Venice Naval Yard for harbour surveillance and defence. They did

not serve in the Italian Navy but were given the temporary names of *Alfa* and *Beta*. Next came the 31.4-tonne (31-ton) A class of 1915/16, closely followed by the B class of which this *Beta* was one. She was better known as *B1*. Only three of the class became operative, as harbour defence vessels, with three being broken up in 1920 before completion.

Bettino Ricasoli

Type: Italian destroyer
Displacement: 1,480 tonnes (1,457 tons)
Dimensions: 85m x 8.5m x 2.8m (278ft 6in x 28ft 2in x 8ft 10in)
Machinery: Twin screw geared turbines
Main armament: Three 119mm (4.7in) guns

The *Bettino Ricasoli* was one of a group of four vessels built to update the World War I Palestro class. The armament was unusual in that there were two guns mounted aft on a platform with the third on the forecastle. The crew numbered 120, increasing to 152 for times

of war. *Bettino Ricasoli*'s machinery proved unreliable in service, and by 1940 her speed had

fallen to 33 knots. She was sold to Sweden and renamed *Puke*, but her machinery continued to give trouble and she was stricken in 1947.

Birmingham

Type: British cruiser
Displacement: 6,136 tonnes (6,040 tons)
Dimensions: 140m x 15.2m x 4.8m (457ft x 50ft x 16ft)
Machinery: Four shaft geared turbines
Top speed: 25.5 knots

Main armament: Nine 152mm (6in) guns

Birmingham, one of a class of four cruisers which updated the previous Chatham class, was one of the first British warships to see service in World War I.

She sank two German merchant vessels in early August 1914, and sank the German submarine *U15*, the first U-boat to be destroyed by a British warship, on 9 August.

Birmingham's class formed part of the logical development of the cruiser type in the Royal Navy, possessing high speed with a good armament.

Bismarck

Type: German cruiser
Displacement: 3,385 tonnes (3,332 tons)
Dimensions: 82m x 13.7m x 6m (270ft x 45ft x 20ft 3in)
Machinery: Single screw horizontal engine
Top speed: 12.5 knots
Main armament: Sixteen 152mm (6in) guns
Launched: July 1877

Bismarck and her five sister ships were iron-hulled, flush-decked corvettes intended for service on foreign stations. They were supplied with a full rig of canvas plus a lifting screw to provide better sailing qualities when the engine was not in use. The class proved ideal for policing distant seas, and Germany added ten of the type to her navy in the 1870s alone. Later *Bismarck* was fitted with two torpedo tubes. She was hulked in 1891 and broken up in 1920.

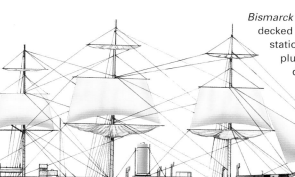

Bismarck

Type: German battleship
Displacement: 50,955 tonnes
(50,153 tons)
Dimensions: 250m x 36m x 9m
(823ft 6in x 118ft x 29ft 6in)
Machinery: Three shaft geared
turbines
Main armament: Eight 380mm
(15in) guns
Launched: February 1939

The 1919 Treaty of Versailles
imposed tight
restrictions on
German naval

developments, and caused a hiatus
in the design and construction of
capital ships. In spite of this, the
Germans managed to carry out
numerous secret design studies,
and when the Anglo-German Naval
Treaty of 1935 came into force,
were able to respond quickly.
They began the construction of
two battleships, the *Bismark* and
the *Tirpitz*. As they had been
unable to properly test new
hull forms, they used the

World War I Baden design as the
basis of the new ships. They were
equipped with powerful modern
engines, 380mm (15in) main guns,
and large numbers of anti-aircraft
guns. While they were fine, effective
warships, the dated armour
configuration meant that the
steering gear and
much of the

communications and control
systems were poorly protected. In
May 1941, *Bismark* was sent on a
raiding mission into the Atlantic,
where after a massive search
operation, the Royal Navy caught
up with her. In the ensuing battles
she sunk *Hood,* before suffering so
much damage from shell and
torpedo fire that she was scuttled
by her own crew. *Tirpitz* spent most
of the war in dock, and was finally
sunk in a Norwegian fjord by aerial
bombing.

Black Prince

Type: British cruiser
Displacement: 13,716 tonnes (13,500 tons)
Dimensions: 154m x 23m x 8m (505ft 6in x 73ft
6in x 26ft)
Machinery: Twin screw triple expansion
engines
Top speed: 23 knots
Main armament: Six 228mm (9.2in), ten
152mm (6in) guns
Armour: 76-152mm (3-6in) armoured
waterline belt

Launched: November 1904

Black Prince and her sister ship *Duke of
Edinburgh* were the first vessels
designed for the Royal Navy by Phillip
Watts. The 228mm (9.2in) guns were
grouped in single turrets with three
forward and three aft, while the
large battery of 152mm (6in) guns
were housed amidships.

Unfortunately they were carried too low down,
and consequently were almost unworkable at
sea. Also, in an attempt to reduce the usual high
upper decks by eliminating bulwarks, the vessels
proved very wet amidships. *Black Prince* was
sunk at Jutland in May 1916 when she ran
into the German battle fleet in the confusion
of the night.

Blake

Type: British cruiser
Displacement: 9,296 tonnes
(9,150 tons)
Dimensions: 122m x 20m x
7.3m (399ft 9in x 65ft x 24ft)
Machinery: Twin screw triple
expansion engines
Main armament: Two

228mm (9.2in), ten 152mm (6in) guns
Launched: November 1889

Blake and her sister *Blenheim* were two of the
largest protected cruisers of the period. They
performed well at sea, and in service were able
to maintain a speed of 19 knots for considerable
periods. Endurance should have been 28,500km
(15,000 miles) at ten knots, but this was later
reduced to an estimated 19,000km (10,000
miles). *Blake* was re-boilered in
1899, and sold in
1920.

Blenheim

Type: British depot ship
Displacement: 16,865 tonnes
(16,600 tons)
Dimensions: 160m x 19m
x 7.6m (528ft 6in x 63ft

3in x 25ft 3in)
Machinery: Twin screw geared
turbines
Main armament: Four
102mm (4in) guns

Launched: December 1919

Blenheim was the
ex-Blue Funnel
liner *Achilles.*
Early in

World War II she was converted
into a depot ship for destroyers
and fitted with eight 20mm (0.8in)
anti-aircraft guns. *Blenheim* carried
out all the maintenance work
needed by the destroyer fleet, as
well as providing additional
casualty facilities as required. She
was scrapped
in 1948.

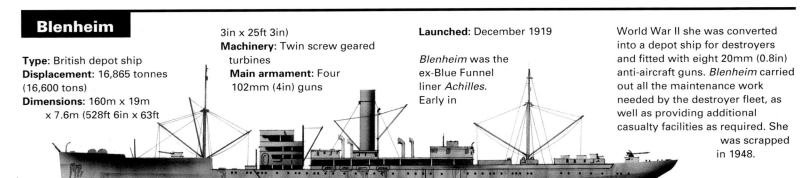

Blitz

Type: Austrian torpedo gunboat
Displacement: 433 tonnes (426 tons)
Dimensions: 59m x 7m x 2m (193ft 6in x 22ft 8in x 6ft 10in)
Machinery: Single screw triple expansion engines
Main armament: Nine 3-pounders, Four 355mm (14in) torpedo tubes

Blitz and her sister ship *Komet* were designed to combat the much improved type of torpedo boats then entering service worldwide. Normal gunboats were too slow to keep up with the fleet, so the torpedo gunboat seemed to be the answer – with its high speed and large number of light guns. Torpedo tubes were positioned with one in the bow, one firing aft and two on a turntable amidships. Both ships were allocated to Italy in 1920 and were later broken up there.

Blücher

Type: German liner
Displacement: 12,531 tonnes (12,334 tons)
Dimensions: 168m x 19m (549ft 6in x 62ft)
Machinery: Twin screw quadruple expansion engines

Blücher was built for the Hamburg-Amerika Line and on completion in 1902 was assigned to the Atlantic route. In 1917 she was taken over by the Allies, and in 1919 resumed her New York run as a French passenger liner. *Blücher* was laid up from 1921-23 and on her return to service was re-named *Suffren*. She was broken up in Italy in 1929.

Blücher

Type: German cruiser
Displacement: 17,526 tonnes (17,250 tons)
Dimensions: 162m x 24m x 8m (530ft 6in x 80ft 3in x 26ft 3in)
Machinery: Three shaft vertical triple expansion engines
Main armament: Twelve 203mm (8.2in) guns
Armour: Waterline belt 63.5-178mm (2.4-7in) thick, same on turrets

Launched: April 1908

Blücher was a logical development of the previous Scharnhorst class, and was built in answer to the newest large British cruiser type. Unfortunately, the British cruiser in question was the *Invincible* which, during building, was still listed as an armoured cruiser; by the time of her completion she was listed as a battlecruiser and carried 305mm (12in) guns as part of her armament. This information came too late for *Blücher*, as she was too far advanced to be altered. The *Blücher* had a complete belt up to the second deck, with horizontal protection provided by a sloping deck about 51mm (2in) thick plus a lighter protective deck on top of the belt. *Blücher* was sunk at the Dogger Bank on 24 January 1915.

Bodryi

Type: Russian destroyer
Displacement: 2,072 tonnes (2,039 tons)
Dimensions: 113m x 10m x 4m (370ft 3in x 33ft 6in x 12ft 6in)
Machinery: Twin screw geared
Main armament: Four 127mm (5.1in) guns

By the early 1930s the weakness of the Russian destroyer force was obvious. In 1932 an improved type of destroyer was designed, with the help of Italy. The class was known as the Type 7, but it was not until 1935 that the first ship was laid down.

Bodryi was one of the first group of 28 ships, and was found to lack seaworthiness under the conditions of the Arctic and Northern Pacific in which she was intended to serve. A revised design was produced, and by the start of World War II 46 ships were complete, of which 20 were later lost. *Bodryi* was scrapped in 1958.

Bogatyr

Type: Russian cruiser
Displacement: 6,751 tonnes (6,645 tons)
Dimensions: 134m x 17m x 6m (439ft 8in x 54ft 6in x 20ft 8in)
Machinery: Twin screw vertical triple expansion engines

Main armament: Twelve 152mm (6in) guns

Upon completion *Bogatyr* was one of the finest cruisers in the world. *Bogatyr* served with the armoured cruiser squadron during the Russo-Japanese war, but ran aground in May 1904 and was badly damaged. During World War I she was re-armed with 127mm (5in) guns and fitted out to carry 100 mines. She was scrapped in 1922.

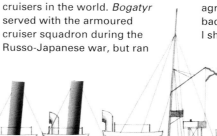

Bombarda

Type: Italian escort vessel/corvette
Displacement: 740 tonnes (728 tons)
Dimensions: 64m x 9m x 2.5m (211ft x 28ft 7in x 8ft 4in)
Machinery: Twin screw diesel engines

Main armament: One 102mm (4in) gun

Bombarda was one of a class of 59 escorts built under a wartime specification that called for a cheap, quick-to-build anti-submarine escort vessel for service in the

Mediterranean. When Italy surrendered, Germany seized many of her ships. *Bombarda* was re-named

Uj206 and was scuttled in April 1945. She was later salvaged and repaired, and remained in service until 1975.

Bombardiere

Type: Italian destroyer
Displacement: 2,540 tonnes (2,500 tons)
Dimensions: 107m x 10m x 4m (350ft x 33ft 7in x 11ft 6in)
Machinery: Twin screw turbines
Top speed: 38 knots

Main armament: Five 120mm (4.7in) guns
Launched: March 1942

Bombardiere was one

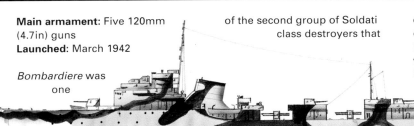

of the second group of Soldati class destroyers that

eventually formed the largest class of destroyer built for the Italian Navy. Their anti-aircraft armament was poor, but this was later improved. *Bombardiere* was sunk by the British submarine *Splendid* on 17 January 1943.

Bombe

Type: French torpedo gunboat
Displacement: 375 tonnes (369 tons)
Dimensions: 60m x 6m x 3m (194ft 3in x 19ft 7in x 10ft 5in)
Machinery: Twin screw vertical compound engines
Main armament: Two 355mm (14in) torpedo tubes, two 3-pounders

Launched: April 1885

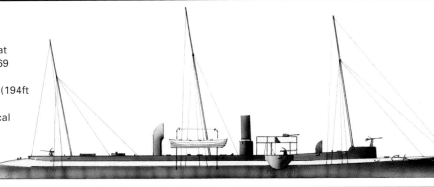

Bombe and her sisters were produced to counter the threat from torpedo boats, and were designed with sufficient speed to keep up with the battle fleet. Displacement was kept to a minimum, though none of the ships possessed sufficient seaworthiness. *Bombe* was broken up in 1921.

Bonhomme Richard

Type: American frigate
Displacement: 1,014 tonnes (998 tons)
Dimensions: 46m x 2m x 5.7m (152ft x 40ft x 19ft)
Main armament: Twenty-eight 12-pounder cannon
Launched: 1765

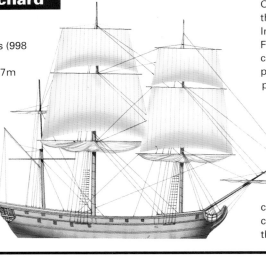

Originally *Bonhomme Richard* was the *Duc de Duras*, built for the East India Company for service between France and the Far East. She had a crew of 375 and, as well as the 12-pounder cannon, carried six 18-pounders and eight 9-pounders. In 1779 the *Duc de Duras* was placed at the disposal of the legendary American naval officer John Paul Jones and re-named *Bonhomme Richard*. Under his command she first escorted French troop convoys, then began a raiding cruise against British commerce in the Bay of Biscay. On 23 September

1779 she encountered a Baltic convoy, escorted by HMS *Serapis* and the *Countess of Scarborough*, and there ensued the Battle of Flamborough Head, one of the fiercest naval conflicts of the century. *Bonhomme Richard* engaged *Serapis* in bitter fighting and, after several hours' combat at close quarters, *Serapis* was forced to surrender when fire broke out on board. However, *Bonhomme Richard* was also severely damaged – on fire and leaking badly. She was abandoned and sank two days later on 25 September 1779. One hundred and fifty of her crew had been lost during the battle.

Borea

Type: Italian destroyer
Displacement: 386 tonnes (380 tons)
Dimensions: 64m x 6m x 2.3m (210ft x 19ft 6in x 7ft 6in)
Machinery: Twin screw triple

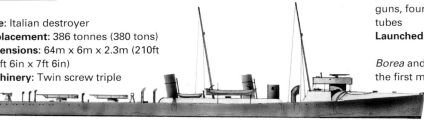

Main armament: Five 76mm (3in) guns, four 355mm (14in) torpedo tubes
Launched: December 1902

Borea and her five sisters formed the first major class of torpedo craft to be built in Italy. All ships were later re-

boilered, and the armament was modified. In 1915 minelaying equipment was added. *Nembo* was sunk in 1916 by the Austrian submarine *U16* which, in turn, was sunk by the exploding depth charges on the sinking ship. *Borea* was sunk by Austrian destroyers *Csepel* and *Balaton* on 14 May 1917.

Borea

Type: Italian destroyer
Displacement: 1,697 tonnes (1,670 tons)
Dimensions: 93m x 9m x 4m (305ft 9in x 30ft x 9ft 10in)
Machinery: Twin screw geared turbines
Top speed: 36 knots
Main armament: Four 120mm (4.7in) guns
Launched: January 1927

This class of eight fast destroyers were actually improved versions of the previous Sauro class. They were slightly longer than the earlier vessels, and had more powerful machinery, which was supposed to add an extra knot to the top speed. In sea trials, the design speed of 36 knots was often exceeded. One of the class, *Turbine*, produced over 51,000hp, and managed to maintain a startling 40 knots for more than four hours. Under service conditions, these ships actually averaged some 33 knots, although this was still a creditable figure. After a few years of operational use, *Borea* was modified in the light of this experience. Her secondary armament of light guns was altered, and she was also adapted to carry anti-shipping mines. She could hold up to 52 of these weapons, depending on type and size. All of these ships served in the Italian Navy in World War II, although none survived the war. Most were sunk by Allied air attack, and *Borea* met her end in this way. On 17 September 1940, she was just off the north African coast, near Benghazi, when she was pounced upon and sunk by Royal Navy Swordfish aircraft which had been launched from the fleet aircraft carrier *Illustrious*. As an interesting footnote, one of the class ended her career in a slightly different way. She was sunk by the German Luftwaffe after the Italian surrender in 1943.

Bosna

Type: Austrian river monitor
Displacement: 590 tonnes (580 tons)
Dimensions: 62m x 10m x 1m (203ft 5in x 33ft 9in x 4ft 3in)
Machinery: Twin screw triple expansion engines
Top speed: 13.5 knots
Main armament: Two 120mm (4.7in) guns, two 120mm (4.7in) howitzers

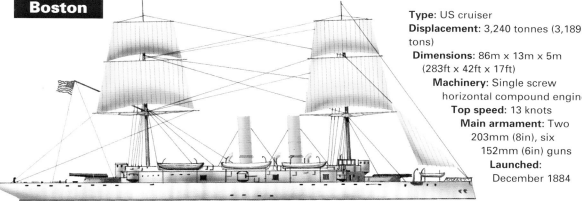

Bosna was one of a growing group of monitors built for service on the River Danube and its tributaries. They carried heavy armament on a shallow draught, and were well protected against light weapons. *Bosna*'s guns were mounted in a single turret forward, while the howitzers were placed aft, with a good field of fire. *Bosna* was re-named *Temes* soon after being laid down in 1914 (in honour of the original *Temes* sunk that year). The original ship was later raised and returned to service, and *Temes* reverted to her original name in 1917. In 1920 *Bosna* became the Yugoslav *Vardar*.

Boston

Type: US cruiser
Displacement: 3,240 tonnes (3,189 tons)
Dimensions: 86m x 13m x 5m (283ft x 42ft x 17ft)
Machinery: Single screw horizontal compound engine
Top speed: 13 knots
Main armament: Two 203mm (8in), six 152mm (6in) guns
Launched: December 1884

Boston carried heavy armament on a relatively small displacement but was slow. *Boston* and her sister *Atlanta* were brig rigged with a large superstructure amidships. Two 203mm (8in) guns were mounted singly in open barbettes fore and aft. The 152mm (6in) guns were sited inside the superstructure. Four 3-pounder guns were carried in small cylindrical mountings at each corner of the superstructure. *Boston* was scuttled in May 1946.

Boudeuse

Type: French frigate
Displacement: 559 tonnes (550 tons)
Dimensions: 40m (131ft) long on the gun deck
Top speed: 11 knots
Main armament: Twenty-six 18-pounder cannons
Launched: 1763

Boudeuse was a small frigate that proved fast and handy, carrying a large spread of canvas on light spars. Her hull was lightly sheathed and covered with flat-headed iron nails which rusted together forming a solid, yet easy to repair, layer. With the end of the Seven Years War (1756-63), Frenchman Louis de Bougainville established a colony on the Falkland Islands. When the Spanish forced the French to evacuate the islands, Bougainville set out across the Pacific in command of *Boudeuse* and eventually arrived at Tahiti, which he formally annexed in 1767.

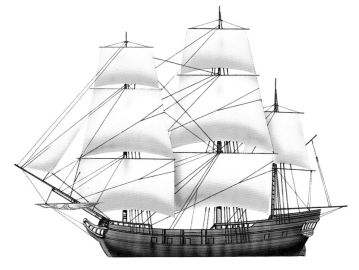

Bounty

Type: British merchant ship
Displacement: 218 tonnes (215 tons)
Dimensions: 28m x 6m x 3m (91ft x 20ft x 10ft)
Top speed: 9 knots
Launched: 1780

Bounty was originally the merchant ship *Bethia*. In 1787 *Bethia* was sold, re-named *Bounty* and fitted out to transport breadfruit

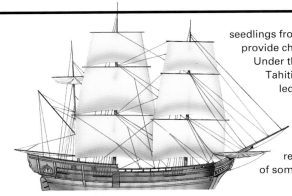

seedlings from Tahiti to the West Indies as part of a plan to provide cheap food for the slaves on the sugar plantations. Under the command of Captain Bligh, *Bounty* set sail for Tahiti in late 1787. On the return trip in 1788 the crew, led by second mate Fletcher Christian, mutinied, set Bligh and 18 men adrift in a small launch and returned to Tahiti in *Bounty*. Christian then sailed her to Pitcairn Island where she was run ashore and burnt. Bligh and his men managed to reach Timor, in the East Indies, after an epic voyage of some 7,600km (4,000 miles).

Bourrasque

Type: French destroyer
Displacement: 1,930 tonnes (1,900 tons)
Dimensions: 106m x 10m x 4.2m (347ft x 31ft 9in x 14ft)
Machinery: Twin screw geared turbines
Main armament: Four 127mm (5in) guns

The 12 vessels in the Bourrasque class formed part of the 1922 programme by which France planned to upgrade her navy. *Bourrasque* was well armed and compared favourably

with her contemporaries. However, any advantage to be gained from using a large-calibre gun was lost because the rate of fire was only four to five rounds per minute.

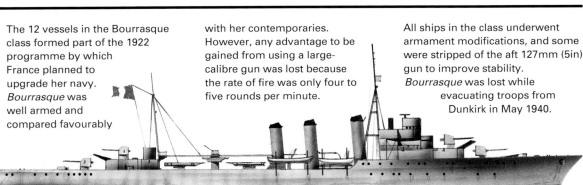

All ships in the class underwent armament modifications, and some were stripped of the aft 127mm (5in) gun to improve stability. *Bourrasque* was lost while evacuating troops from Dunkirk in May 1940.

Bouvet

Type: French battleship
Displacement: 12,200 tonnes (12,007 tons)
Dimensions: 118m x 21m x 8.3m (386ft 6in x 70ft 2in x 27ft 6in)
Machinery: Triple screw vertical expansion engines
Top speed: 18 knots
Main armament: Two 304mm

(12in), two 275mm (10.8in) guns
Launched: April 1896

Bouvet was the last of the basic Charles Martel design and was thought to be the best of the group. She lacked the massive superstructure of the preceding group, and had a built-up stern which

improved seaworthiness. In March 1915 *Bouvet* took part in an attack on the

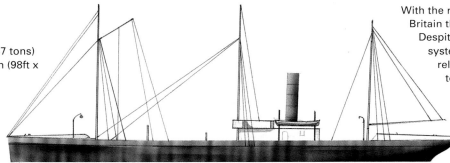

Dardanelles, during which she was seriously damaged by Turkish guns before running onto a mine. She rapidly filled with water, her bulkheads collapsed and she sank within two minutes with the loss of 660 lives.

Bowes

Type: British cargo vessel
Displacement: 444 tonnes (437 tons)
Dimensions: 30m x 5.5m x 3m (98ft x 18ft x 9ft 6in)
Machinery: Single screw compound engines
Top speed: 9 knots
Launched: 1852

With the rapid growth of industrialisation in Britain the demand for coal escalated. Despite the expansion of the railway system, areas such as the Tyne still relied upon an active coasting trade to transport its coal to London. *Bowes* was one of the many iron-hulled colliers involved in the trade. She had a single funnel but could carry a light rig if steadying sails were required.

Boyarin

Type: Russian cruiser
Displacement: 3,251 tonnes (3,200 tons)
Dimensions: 105m x 12m x 4.8m (345ft x 41ft x 16ft)
Machinery: Twin screw vertical triple expansion engines
Top speed: 24 knots

Main armament: Six 120mm (4.7in) guns

Boyarin was built for the Russians by Burmeister and Wain, Copenhagen. She was a scout cruiser, and also acted as a destroyer cruiser. Completed in 1903, *Boyarin*

was stationed at Port Arthur and in 1904, on the outbreak of war with Japan, she was sent on a scouting mission, struck a newly laid Russian mine and was abandoned.

Although a returning Russian force found *Boyarin* still afloat no serious salvage attempt was made. Instead, she was torpedoed by Russian vessels in an effort to sink her, but this failed. She finally sank in a storm two days later.

Boyky

Type: Russian destroyer
Displacement: 4,826 tonnes (4,750 tons)
Dimensions: 140m x 15m x 5m (458ft 9in x 49ft 5in x 16ft 6in)
Machinery: Twin screw geared turbines
Top speed: 35 knots

Main armament: Eight 57mm (2.25in) guns, plus missiles
Launched: 1960

Boyky was one of a group of destroyers forming the middle

development period of Russian destroyer construction. She was originally completed as a missile ship armed with SS-N-1 launchers for anti-ship

missiles. When these became obsolete in the mid 1960s, the whole group was converted into anti-submarine vessels. These conversions were done between 1968 and 1977. *Boyky* served in the North Atlantic and the North Pacific and found time to visit the USA, in spite of strained relations during the Cold War.

Bremen

Type: German liner
Displacement: 2,717 tonnes (2,674 tons)
Dimensions: 97m x 12m (318ft x 41ft)
Machinery: Single screw compound engine
Top speed: 10 knots

In June 1858 the *Bremen* opened the

North Atlantic route for the North German Lloyd Line. She carried 22 cabin and 93 steerage passengers, as well as 152 tonnes of cargo. She reached New York in just over 12 days, a performance which helped establish the company's reputation. In 1874 *Bremen* was sold to a British company. Her engines were removed and she served as a sailing ship until she was wrecked in 1882.

Bremen

Type: German liner
Displacement: 52,482 tonnes (51,656 tons)
Dimensions: 286m x 31m (938ft x 102ft)
Machinery: Quadruple screw geared turbines

Bremen was built for the North German Lloyd Line and had accommodation for around 2000 passengers plus a crew of 960. In 1933 *Bremen* set a new Atlantic record, later lost to *Rex*.

During World War II *Bremen* served as a German naval accommodation ship and was given dazzle-painted camouflage. In 1941 a fire was

started in a storeroom by a cabin boy and *Bremen was* burnt out.

Bremse

Type: German cruiser/minelayer
Displacement: 5,950 tonnes (5,856 tons)
Dimensions: 140m x 13m x 6m (460ft 7in x 43ft 4in x 19ft 8in)
Machinery: Twin

screw turbines
Main armament: Four 152mm (6in) guns

At the start of World War I, Germany had a severe shortage of minelaying vessels. *Bremse* and *Brummer* filled the gap. The building of the Greek battleship *Salamis*, then being constructed in Germany, was put on hold

and her two sets of turbines were used as the basis for the two new ships. *Bremse* was completed in 1916 and served as a minelayer, able to escape action thanks to its superior turn of speed. At the end of the war *Bremse* was scuttled, along with the rest of the German High Seas Fleet, at Scapa Flow in June 1919, but was later salvaged.

Breslau

Type: German cruiser
Displacement: 5,676 tonnes (5,587 tons)
Dimensions: 138m x 14m x 5m (455ft 44ft x 16ft 10in)
Machinery: Quadruple screw turbine engines
Main armament: Twelve 102mm (4in) guns

Launched: May 1911

At first glance *Breslau* and her three sisters appeared to follow the conventional design for German cruisers. However, they featured numerous imported

improvements, including, for the first time on light cruisers, an armoured belt of nickel steel that ran along most of the ship's length and formed part of the structure, so

saving weight yet providing added strength to the hull. In World War I *Breslau* served in the Meditteranean and was taken over as the Turkish ship *Midilli*. She sank after striking mines in 1918.

Bretagne

Type: French battleship
Displacement: 6,878 tonnes (6,770 tons)
Dimensions: 12m x 18m (265ft 8in x 59ft 4in)
Machinery: Single screw compound engine
Top speed: 12 knots
Main armament: One hundred and thirty 32-pounders plus various other weapons
Launched: February 1855

French naval weakness had become brutally apparent in 1840, when she was forced to back down over the Syrian confrontation. French battleships at that time were steam-powered with sail assistance, and tended to suffer from poor sailing qualities. British ships of the same period were designed with sail as their main motive force, and steam as an auxiliary source of power. Their sea-keeping qualities were thus usually much better than those of their French counterparts. During the 1850s, attempts were made to build up a strong French Navy, but these were countered by the British, who could outbuild any other nation at that time. *Bretagne* was one of the new-style of French steam battleships of the period. She had three decks housing 130 of the new pattern of long gun, and a full rig of canvas with boiler rooms placed either side of the huge main mast. Built at Brest, *Bretagne* was the second largest wooden three-decker ever built. In 1866 she was removed from the French Navy list.

Bretagne

Type: French battleship
Displacement: 29,420 tonnes (28,956 tons)
Dimensions: 166m x 27m x 10m (544ft 8in x 88ft 3in x 32ft 2in)
Machinery: Quadruple screw geared turbines
Top speed: 20 knots
Main armament: Ten 340mm (13.4in) guns
Launched: April 1913

Because France found herself falling behind in the dreadnought naval race, *Bretagne* and her sisters *Provence* and *Lorraine* were based on the design of the preceding Courbet class to cut down construction time. *Bretagne* served in the Mediterranean from 1916-1918, then underwent a series of extensive modernisations in 1921-23, 1927-30 and 1932-35. With the surrender of France in 1940,

Bretagne and other French naval warships were called upon to join a British alliance, but the French admiral Gensoul refused. British aircraft from the aircraft carrier *Ark Royal* opened fire on the anchored vessels, and within ten minutes *Bretagne* had been blown up and capsized.

Brin

Type: Italian submarine
Displacement: 1,032 tonnes (1,016 tons) on the surface, 1,286 tonnes (1,266 tons) submerged
Dimensions: 70m x 7m x 4.2m (231ft 4in x 22ft 6in x 13ft 6in)
Machinery: Twin screw diesel engines on surface, two electric motors submerged
Main armament: Eight 533mm (21in) torpedo tubes

Brin was one of a class of long-range submarines with a partial double hull developed from the Archimede class. Early in World War II, *Brin* served in the Mediterranean and Atlantic. In 1943 she was stationed in Ceylon, helping to train British anti-submarine units in the Indian Ocean.

Brindisi

Type: Italian cruiser
Displacement: 4,074 tonnes (4,010 tons)
Dimensions: 130m x 13m x 5m (428ft 8in x 41ft 11in x 17ft 4in)
Machinery: Twin screw turbines
Main armament: Nine 99mm (3.9in) guns

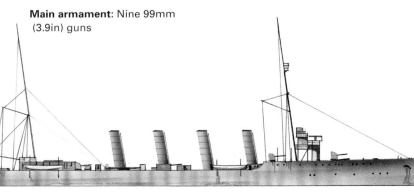

Brindisi was originally the Austrian scout *Helgoland*, which was ceded to Italy in 1920. She was one of the last fast, lightly armed scouts to enter service, and saw action in World War I. It was planned to re-arm *Brindisi* and her two sisters with heavier weapons, but this was never carried out. During service for the Italians, *Brindisi* was equipped to carry 170 mines. She was discarded in 1937.

Britannia

Type: British liner
Displacement: 2,083 tonnes (2,050 tons)
Dimensions: 70m x 17m (over paddle boxes) x 5m (228ft x 56ft x 16ft 10in)
Machinery: Side wheels driven by side lever engines
Top speed: 8.5 knots
Launched: February 1840

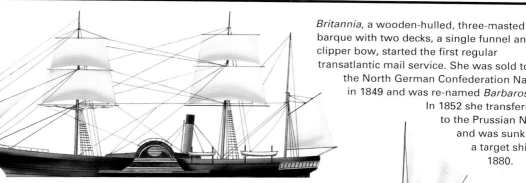

Britannia, a wooden-hulled, three-masted barque with two decks, a single funnel and a clipper bow, started the first regular transatlantic mail service. She was sold to the North German Confederation Navy in 1849 and was re-named *Barbarossa*. In 1852 she transferred to the Prussian Navy and was sunk as a target ship in 1880.

Britannia

Type: British yacht
Displacement: 264 tonnes (260 tons)
Dimensions: 36.5m x 7m (120ft x 24ft)
Launched: 1890

By the end of the 1880s the USA had produced a number of successful yachts for competition in the America's cup. The hull design was of a cutter, and stability was achieved by using a thin metal plate fin as

well as concentrating the ballast as low as possible. This class of yacht gained great favour in Britain as well as in America, and by the end of the 1880s *Britannia*, a cutter-rigged yacht based on the American design, was ordered for the Prince of Wales, later to be Edward VII. Upon his death *Britannia* was handed over to George V, who successfully took part in some 624 regattas, winning 360 prizes with her. In the 1920s the rig was altered to resemble a J-class yacht. *Britannia* was sunk off Cowes upon George V's death in 1936.

Britannia

Type: Swedish liner
Displacement: 4,283 tonnes (4,216 tons)
Dimensions: 114.6m x 15m x 6m (376ft 4in x 50ft x 20ft 4in)
Machinery: Single screw geared turbine engines

Britannia was one of the most successful passenger vessels to serve on the North Sea, where she operated from 1929-1966 (only discontinuing service for the duration of World War II). She was sold in 1966 for service as a cruise liner in the Mediterranean.

Britannic

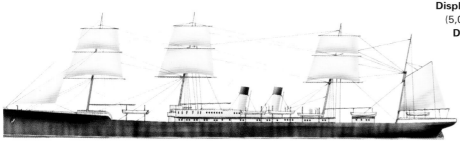

Type: British liner
Displacement: 5,084 tonnes (5,004 tons)
Dimensions: 139m x 14m (455ft x 45ft 3in)
Machinery: Single screw compound engines
Top speed: 16 knots
Launched: February 1874

Britannic and her sister *Germanic* were built for the White Star Line and soon established a reputation for regularity and speed on the North Atlantic route. In 1887 *Britannic* collided with fellow liner *Celtic* off Sandy Hook and both vessels were damaged. During the Boer War at the end of the 1890s, *Britannic* became a transport. She was scrapped in 1903.

Britannic

Type: British liner
Displacement: 48,928 tonnes (48,158 tons)
Dimensions: 275m x 27m (903ft x 94ft)
Machinery: Triple screw geared turbines

Britannic was the largest of a trio of large liners ordered by the White Star Line from Harland and Wolff, her sisters being *Olympic* and *Titanic*. In 1915 the Admiralty ordered completion of *Britannic* as a hospital ship, and she was assigned to the Mediterranean. In 1916 she ran onto a German mine in the Aegean, and an hour after the explosion she keeled over and sank.

British Skill

Type: British tanker
Displacement: 67,090 tonnes (66,034 tons) gross, 129,822 tonnes (127,778 tons) deadweight
Dimensions: 261m x 40m (856ft 3in x 131ft 3in)
Machinery: Twin screw diesel engines

British Skill is one of the newest large-sized oil tankers, and was one of a number of similar units built to replace the ageing supertankers of the previous decade. Crew numbers vary between 30 and 40, and control of the engines is largely automatic – except when manoeuvring into and out of dock. Steering such a long vessel at low speed is difficult, but is made easier with Doppler radar, which measures speed and angle of turn.

Broadsword

Type: British frigate
Displacement: 4,470 tonnes (4,400 tons)
Dimensions: 131m x 15m x 4m (430ft 5in x 48ft 8in x 14ft)
Machinery: Twin screw gas turbine engines
Main armament: Four M38 Exocet launchers, two 40mm (1.6in guns

Broadsword was the first of a batch of general-purpose frigates designed to follow on from the Leander class. It was planned to build 26 units armed with missiles only, their main anti-submarine weapon being the Lynx helicopter. Later groups were fitted with extra weapons and sensors.

Bronte

Type: Italian Navy fuel carrier
Displacement: 9,611 tonnes (9,460 tons)
Dimensions: 119m x 14.3m x 7.5m (391ft x 47ft x 25ft)
Machinery: Twin screw vertical triple expansion engines
Top speed: 14.5 knots
Main armament: Four 6-pounder guns

Bronte was one of two purpose-built fleet collier/oil carriers constructed for the Italian fleet. They followed the usual turn-of-the-century design for such vessels, with capacious holds and a forest of derricks and kingposts to enable rapid re-fuelling of the fleet at sea. *Bronte* was captured by the British on 21 August 1941 and re-named *Empire Peri*. She returned to Italy in 1946 and was discarded in the same year.

Bronzo

Type: Italian submarine
Displacement: 726 tonnes (715 tons) on the surface, 884 tonnes (870 tons) submerged
Dimensions: 60m x 6.5m x 4.5m (197ft x 21ft 4in x 14ft 9in)
Machinery: Twin screw diesel engines on surface, electric motors

submerged
Main armament: Six 533mm (21in) torpedo tubes, one 99mm (93.9in) gun

Bronzo was captured by the British in July 1943 after surfacing off Syracuse, not knowing the base had been captured. She was handed over to France in 1944, re-named *Naral* and scrapped in 1948.

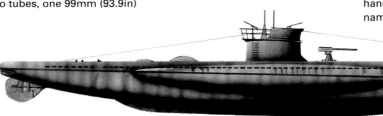

Brooklyn

Type: American sloop
Displacement: 2,572 tonnes (2,532 tons)
Dimensions: 71m x 13m x 5m (233ft x 43ft x 16ft 3in)
Machinery: Single screw, two horizontal condensing engines
Main armament: One 100-pounder, twenty-two 228mm (9in) guns

Brooklyn was a graceful-looking wooden-hulled vessel, and carried a large spread of sail as she was intended to cruise under sail for most of her time at sea. She saw extensive service during the American Civil War, and led the Union attack into Mobile Bay. After the war, *Brooklyn* served on numerous foreign stations and remained in service until 1889.

Brooklyn

Type: US cruiser
Displacement: 10,229 tonnes (10,068 tons)
Dimensions: 123m x 20m x 7.3m (402ft 7in x 64ft 8in x 24ft)
Machinery: Twin screw vertical triple expansion engines
Top speed: 22 knots
Main armament: Eight 203mm (8in) guns
Armour: 76mm (3in) belt, 140mm (5.5in) on turrets
Launched: October 1895

The US Navy cruiser *Brooklyn* was authorised in 1892 and her design followed many French concepts of the time. Her main guns were mounted in four twin turrets, which were distributed around the ship in a lozenge pattern. One turret was positioned high up in the bow, with another directly aft. The two remaining turrets were mounted on each side. Her bow protruded above an iron ram, while a raised forecastle helped give her good sea-keeping qualities. *Brooklyn* had a relatively thin armoured belt and deck, so her protection was further increased by the use of a cellular system to minimise the effects of a penetrating hit. Her unusual propulsion system used two engines in tandem. Only

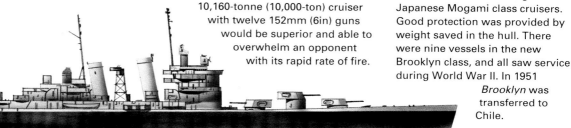

one was needed for cruising, but when high speed steaming was required the ship had to be stopped while the second unit was coupled up. Even so, she could still make 16 knots on one engine. *Brooklyn* fought in the Battle of Santiago, off Cuba, in July 1898. She was sold off in 1921.

Brooklyn

Type: US cruiser
Displacement: 12,395 tonnes (12,200 tons)
Dimensions: 185m x 19m x 7m (608ft 4in x 61ft 9in x 22ft 9in)
Machinery: Four shaft geared turbines
Main armament: Fifteen 152mm (6in) guns
Launched: November 1936

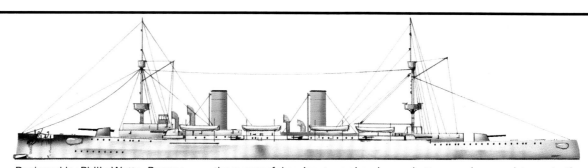

The 1930 London Treaty had imposed severe restrictions on the large 203mm (8in) gun cruiser type, design studies showing that a 10,160-tonne (10,000-ton) cruiser with twelve 152mm (6in) guns would be superior and able to overwhelm an opponent with its rapid rate of fire.

During the early 1930s the US Navy upgraded the existing Brooklyn class in response to the new fifteen 152mm (6in) gun Japanese Mogami class cruisers. Good protection was provided by weight saved in the hull. There were nine vessels in the new Brooklyn class, and all saw service during World War II. In 1951 *Brooklyn* was transferred to Chile.

Bucintoro

Type: Venetian galley
Dimensions: 30m x 6m (100ft x 20ft)

The galley was the traditional vessel used for centuries in the Mediterranean. It served both as a warship and merchant vessel, although its cargo capacity compares unfavourably with that of the short, rounded hull form of the carrack from the same period. Galleys were widely used to transport soldiers on short journeys, and Venetian galleys provided the bulk of the Christian army transport during the Crusades. The *Bucintoro* was the Doge's state galley, and was brought out for ceremonial occasions. She had two decks, was ornately carved and gilded and was propelled by 42 oars. There were several state galleys named *Bucintoro* during the lifetime of the Venetian Republic. The last one was broken up in 1824.

Buenos Aires

Type: Argentinian cruiser
Displacement: 4,864 tonnes (4,788 tons)
Dimensions: 124m x 14m x 6.7m (408ft x 47ft 29n x 22ft)
Machinery: Twin screw vertical triple expansion engines
Main armament: Two 203mm (8in), four 152mm (6in) guns

Designed by Philip Watts, *Buenos Aires* was a steel-hulled, wood-sheathed cruiser along the lines of the successful cruiser type already in use by other navies. She had a flush deck with a complete double bottom, and a complete protective deck ran the full length of the ship. *Buenos Aires* was scrapped in 1931.

Bullfinch

Type: British destroyer
Displacement: 396 tonnes (390 tons)
Dimensions: 65m x 6m x 2.5m (214ft 6in x 20ft 6in x 7ft 10in)
Machinery: Twin screw triple expansion engines
Top speed: 30 knots
Main armament: One 12-pounder, five 6-pounders, two 457mm (18in) torpedo tubes
Launched: February 1898

After the success of the previous group of destroyers, the British Admiralty decided, in 1894, to build a further group, increasing their top speed by three knots to 30 knots. Although a basic design was followed, the individual builders were allowed some degree of latitude, so some ships featured two, three or four funnels depending on machinery layout. All ships conformed to a standard armament and a crew of 63. *Bullfinch* was not completed until June 1901 as her builders, Earle, went bankrupt after her launch. *Bullfinch* was scrapped in 1919.

Byedovi

Type: Russian destroyer
Displacement: 355 tonnes (349 tons)
Dimensions: 56.6m x 6m x 3m (185ft 6in x 19ft 6in x 9ft 8in)
Machinery: Twin screw vertical triple expansion engines
Top speed: 26.5 knots
Main armament: One 12-pounder, five 3-pounders, three 380mm (15in) torpedo tubes
Launched: 1902

Byedovi was one of a group of 22 destroyers laid down in Russian yards between 1900 and 1903 that followed the successful British-built *Sokol* of 1895 in general design. Many of the class served in the Russo-Japanese War of 1904-05, and gave good service. After the Battle of Tsushima in 1905 *Byedovi* was captured by the Japanese while trying to escape with the injured Admiral Rozhestvenski, commander-in-chief of the Russian fleet, aboard. She was scrapped in 1922.

C Class Submarine

Type: British submarines
Displacement: 295 tonnes (290 tons) on surface, 325 tonnes (320 tons) submerged
Dimensions: 43m x 4m x 3.5m (141ft x 13ft 1in x 11ft 4in)
Machinery: Single screw petrol engine (surface), electric motor (submerged)
Top speed: 12 knots on surface, 7.5 knots submerged
Main armament: Two 457mm (18in) torpedo tubes
Launched: 1906

All the C Class gave good service. *C3* was used to blow up the viaduct at Zeebrugge in 1918, and four were sent to Russia, but were deliberately sunk to prevent them falling into German hands.

C1

Type: Japanese submarine
Displacement: 2,605 tonnes (2,564 tons) on surface, 3,702 (3,761 tons) submerged
Dimensions: 108.6m x 9m x 5m (256ft 3in x 29ft 5in x 16ft 4in)
Machinery: Twin screw diesel engines on surface, electric motors submerged
Top speed: 17.7 knots on surface, 6 knots submerged
Main armament: One140mm (5.5in) gun, six 533mm (21in) torpedo tubes
Launched: 1943

C1 was one of a large group of submarines that were laid down in the early 1940s. Some became supply transports, carrying supplies to beleaguered Japanese forces on numerous Pacific islands. Later, a few of the class were converted so that they could carry four of the small Kaiten, or suicide boats, on the rear hull casing just aft of the conning tower.

Cabotia

Type: British cargo boat
Displacement: 5,243 tonnes (5,160 tons)
Dimensions: 125.5m x 15.5m (411ft 7in x 50ft 8in)
Machinery: Single screw triple expansion engines
Top speed: 11 knots
Launched: 1917

Cabotia, originally called *War Viper*, was one of a group of standard cargo vessels built to replace the ever-increasing number of merchant ships lost due to German submarine attacks during World War I. *Cabotia* served on the North Atlantic route. In 1925 she was sold to new owners and saw service worldwide as a tramp (general cargo) steamer. *Cabotia* was sunk by a mine off the British coast in January 1940.

Caimen

Type: French battleship
Displacement: 7,650 tonnes
(7,259 tons)
Dimensions: 82.6m x 18m x 8m
(271ft x 59ft x 26ft 2in)
Machinery: Twin screw vertical
compound engines
Top speed: 15 knots
Main armament: Two 420mm

(16.5in) guns
Armour: 203-500mm (8-19in)
shallow armour belt at
waterline
Launched: May 1885

At the end of the 1870s, France
abandoned the broadside
ironclad battleships and

adopted the barbette system of
mounting the heavy guns high
above the waterline away from
harm caused by rough seas.
Caimen was laid down in 1878. She
was one of four large coast
defence vessels noted for their
heavy armour and ordnance, with
two heavy guns
placed in towers.

Caio Duilio

Type: Italian cruiser
Displacement: 6,604 tonnes (6,506
tons)
Dimensions: 144m x 17m x 4.7m
(472ft 4in x 55ft 7in x 15ft 4in)
Machinery: Twin screw geared
turbines
Top speed: 31 knots
Main armament: Eight 76mm

(3in), plus Terrier surface-to-air
missiles
Launched: December 1962

Caio Duilio and her sister *Andrea
Doria* were designed as escort

cruisers of an entirely new type,
having a wide beam in relation to
their length. Both could carry four
armed helicopters. In 1980 *Caio
Duilio* became a training cruiser,

Caio Mario

Type: Italian cruiser
Displacement: 5,419 tonnes
(5,334 tons)
Dimensions: 143m x 14m x 4.8m
(469ft 1in x 46ft x 15ft 7in)

Machinery: Twin screw turbines
Top speed: 40 knots
Main armament: Eight 135mm
(5.3in) guns

Launched: August 1941

Caio Mario was part of a class of
12 extremely fast cruisers
designed to act as anti-
destroyer escorts as well as

fast scouts. Their high speed was
achieved at the expense of
protection, and only a light splinter-
proof deck covered the machinery.
The guns were mounted in twin
turrets, and fired six rounds per
minute. *Caio Mario* was not fully
completed for service when she was
scuttled at La Spezia in 1943 to
prevent her capture by the Germans.

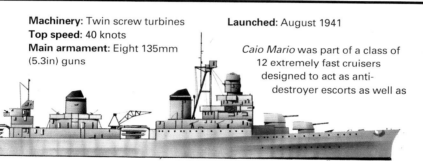

Cairo

Type: US gunboat
Displacement: 902 tonnes
(887 tons)
Dimensions: 53m x 16m x 2m
(173ft 9in x 4ft 9in x 6ft 6in)
Machinery: Single stern wheel
driven by two non-condensing
reciprocating engines
Top speed: 8 knots

Main armament: Three 203mm
(8in), three 178mm (7in) guns
Launched: December 1861

The Union ship *Cairo* had a low
wooden hull surmounted by a large
armoured casement with sloping
sides. Additional armour was
constructed round the engines.
Cairo was sunk by a mine
on 2 December 1862.

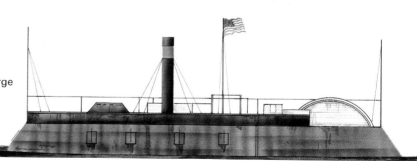

Calatafimi

Type: Italian destroyer
Displacement: 894 tonnes
(880 tons)
Dimensions: 85m x 8m x 3m
(278ft 9in x 26ft 3in x 9ft 9in)
Machinery: Twin screw turbines
Top speed: 34 knots
**Main
armament:**

Four 102mm (4in) guns, six 444mm
(17.5in) torpedo tubes
Launched: March 1923

Originally ordered in 1915,
Calatafimi and her three

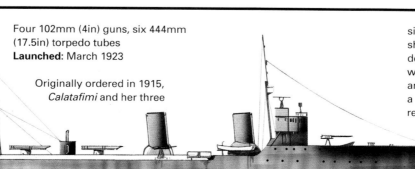

sisters were delayed due to the
shortage of materials caused by the
demands of the army. In 1938 they
were re-classified as torpedo boats
and the armament was altered, with
a single 102mm (4in) weapon
replacing the twin mount aft. In 1943
Calatafimi was captured by
the Germans and re-
named *TA19*. She was
sunk in 1944 .

Caledonia

Type: British liner
Displacement: 17,319 tonnes (17,046 tons)
Dimensions: 168m x 22m x 9m (552ft x 72ft x 29ft)
Machinery: Twin screw geared turbines
Top speed: 17 knots
Launched: April 1925
Date of profile: 1925

Caledonia was a large turbine steamer built for the Anchor Line, who intended to use her on their New York to London service. She was built with five decks, and had

her lifeboats double-banked above the top deck. Her accommodation was luxurious and she had space for 205-first class, 403-second class and 800 third-class passengers. There were also two holds, fore and aft, for carrying cargo, but she was primarily intended as a fast passenger ship. She worked the North Atlantic route regularly until the outbreak of

World War II put a stop to passenger services. In September 1939 she was requisitioned by the British authorities, who pressed her into service as a hastily converted stopgap auxiliary cruiser. She was given eight obsolete 152mm (6in) guns, plus two 76mm (3in) guns for antiaircraft defence. In this configuration she was renamed *Scotstoun*. Most combatant nations pressed such

conversions into service, equipped with a selection of inadequate and obsolete guns. Their main weakness was a complete lack of protection. They offered large and vulnerable targets, as proven by *Scotstoun*, when she was torpedoed and sunk on 13 June 1940 by the German submarine *U-25*.

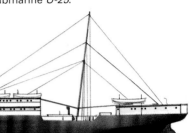

Californian

Type: British cargo/liner
Displacement: 6,322 tonnes (6,223 tons)
Dimensions: 146m x 14m (480ft x 46ft)
Machinery: Single screw reciprocating engines
Top speed: 13 knots
Launched: 1901
Date of profile: 1912

Californian was a mixed cargo and passenger liner. She had four masts, each equipped with several derricks for handling her large cargo

capacity. Passenger accommodation was amidships. In 1912, *Californian* became embroiled in the *Titanic* controversy when she was named as the mystery ship that failed to respond to calls for help from the sinking ship. The British Court of Enquiry deemed that *Californian* had only been 19km (10 miles) away from the doomed liner, but later evidence suggests that this was not the case. The matter remains unresolved to this day.

Calliope

Type: British cruiser
Displacement: 2,814 tonnes (2,770 tons)
Dimensions: 72m x 13m x 6m (235ft x 44ft 6in x 20ft)
Machinery: Single screw compound engines
Main armament: Four 152mm (6in), twelve 127mm (5in) guns
Launched: July 1884

Calliope was a typical sail and steam cruising vessel of the period.

She had a protective steel deck over the machinery and the screw could be adjusted so that it revolved freely when the ship was proceeding under sail alone, thereby minimising drag. The Rennie engines had two low- and two high-pressure cylinders fed by six locomotive boilers. The 152mm (6in) guns were mounted on sponsons at each end of the battery. *Calliope* was one of the last of her type to enter service.

Calliope

Type: Italian torpedo boat
Displacement: 220 tonnes (216 tons)
Dimensions: 53m x 5m x 2m (173ft 11in x 17ft 5in x 5ft 10in)
Machinery: Twin screw vertical triple expansion engines
Top speed: 26.5 knots
Main armament: Three 47mm (1.85in) guns, three 450mm (17.7in) torpedo tubes
Launched: August 1906

Calliope was one of a group of eight torpedo boats based upon the design of Thornycroft, who were among the world's leading builders of torpedo craft. Built by Pattison of Naples, the last of the class were launched in 1909 and were intended for service in the Adriatic. They were good, stoutly

built seagoing vessels, their hull plates being thicker than the previous Perseo class. Two of the class were fitted with oilburning boilers which slightly reduced the displacement and

gave greater endurance. *Calliope*'s armament was later changed to two 76mm (3in) guns and one machine gun. All ships in the class gave good service during World War I. *Calliope* was stricken in 1924.

Calliope

Type: British cruiser
Displacement: 4,770 tonnes (4,695 tons)
Dimensions: 136m x 12.6m x 5m (446ft x 41ft 6in x 14ft 9in)
Machinery: Quadruple screw geared turbines
Main armament: Two 152mm (6in) guns
Armour: 25-102mm (1in-4in) belt
Launched: December 1914

From 1905, after the introduction of the dreadnought battleship, there were generally only two types of cruiser being constructed – very large battlecruisers, or small cruisers of high speed intended as scouts. *Calliope* and her sister *Champion* were the first two vessels of the 22-strong C class of light cruiser laid down between 1914 and 1917. Previous cruiser types had three or four funnels, but by re-arranging the boiler rooms this was reduced to two in the C class. *Calliope* was broken up in 1931.

Calshot Spit

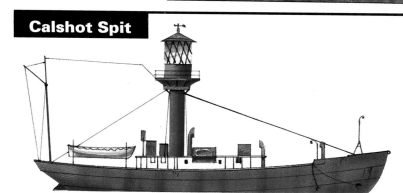

Type: British lightship
Displacement: 213 tonnes (210 tons)
Dimensions: 21m x 5m (70ft x 17ft)
Launch date: 1920

Calshot Spit is a lightship that serves in the English Channel. She is permanently anchored to mark the passage between the River Bramble and the shore near Southampton's busy waterways. The constricted waters here race between the Isle of Wight and the mainland at speeds of up to 5.5 knots, creating a dangerous navigation area for shipping. *Calshot Spit* has one powerful light mounted on top of a tall tower, and this flashes every 15 seconds. It can be seen for a radius of up to 19km (10 miles).

Campania

Type: British liner
Displacement: 18,288 tonnes (18,000 tons)
Dimensions: 189m x 20m (620ft x 65ft 3in)
Machinery: Twin screw triple expansion engines
Top speed: 22 knots
Date of profile: 1895

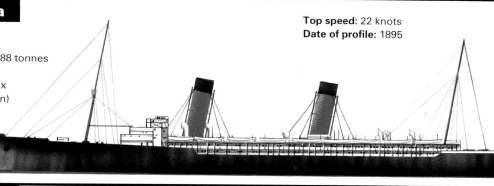

Cunard's *Campania* and her sister *Lucania* were the largest ships in the world when they were introduced on to the North Atlantic route in 1893. *Campania* carried 1,700 passengers plus 416 crew. In 1915 she was taken over for service as an aircraft carrier. She sank in 1918 after drifting into the battleship *Revenge*.

Campania

Type: Italian cruiser
Displacement: 3,238 tonnes (3,187 tons)
Dimensions: 83m x 12.7m x 5m (272ft 4in x 41ft 8 in x 16ft 7in)
Machinery: Twin screw vertical triple expansion engines
Main armament: Six 152mm (6in) guns

Campania was laid down in 1913 and entered service in 1917. She served as a colonial patrol boat and training ship and was able to carry 100 cadets plus officers. Her armament was reduced in the 1920s, and in 1921 she was re-classified as a gunboat. From 1932 she served as a full-time training ship. *Campania* was broken up in 1937.

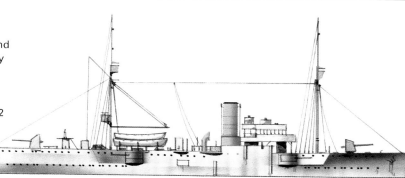

Canada

Type: French liner
Displacement: 3,251 tonnes (3,200 tons)
Dimensions: 108m x 13m (355ft x 44ft)
Machinery: Paddle wheels, side lever engines
Launched: 1866

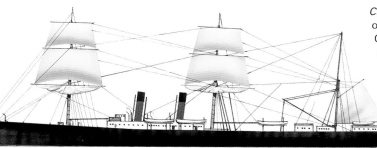

Canada, originally named *Panama*, was one of the first French-built ships to join the Compagnie Generale Transatlantique for service on their New York route. Between 1872 and 1876 all the company's paddle vessels, including *Canada*, were converted to screw propulsion and fitted with compound engines. *Canada* was scrapped in 1908.

Canada

Type: British battleship
Displacement: 32,634 tonnes (32,120 tons)
Dimensions: 202m x 28m x 9m (660ft 9in x 92ft x 29ft)
Machinery: Quadruple screw geared turbines
Main armament: Ten 355mm (14in) guns
Launched: November 1913
Date of profile: 1918

In 1911 Chile had two new battleships under construction, but work ceased in 1914 and *Almirante Latorre*, the most advanced of the two, was bought by the Royal Navy and re-named *Canada*. Completed in 1915, she was one of the most effective battleships in the fleet and saw action at the Battle of Jutland in 1916. She was returned to Chile in 1920.

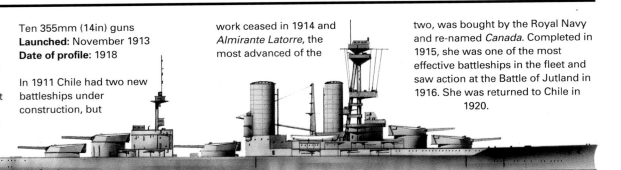

Canadian

Type: British liner
Displacement: 1,792 tonnes (1,764 tons)
Dimensions: 85m x 10m (278ft x 34ft)
Machinery: Single screw compound engines
Launched: 1854
Date of profile: 1854

Canadian was one of the first screw steamers – and the first two-funnelled steamer – on the North Atlantic run between Liverpool and Quebec-Montreal. In 1855 she served as a transport during the Crimean War, but returned to service on the Canadian route in 1856. In June 1857 *Canadian* was wrecked a few kilometres south of Quebec.

Canberra

Type: British liner
Displacement: 45,524 tonnes (44,807 tons)
Dimensions: 249m x 31m (817ft x 101ft 8in)
Machinery: Twin screw steam turbines, electric drive
Launched: March 1960
Date of profile: 1964

carry 2,186 passengers and 938 crew and was lavishly fitted out. After a three-month world cruise in 1982 *Canberra* was requisitioned as a troop transport for service in the Falkland Islands, during which time she narrowly escaped disaster on several occasions. She returned to the UK in July 1982 and, after a refit, resumed normal service in the Pacific.

Canberra was built for the P&O Steam Navigation Company and entered service in May 1961 for service on the Pacific route. She could

Candiope

Type: Italian cargo vessel
Displacement: 3,353 tonnes (3,300 tons)
Dimensions: 76m x 13m (251ft x 43ft 6in)
Machinery: Single screw triple expansion engines
Launched: 1918

Originally named *War Mingan*, *Candiope* was one of a group of cargo vessels hastily built for the British Merchant Marine during World War I. She was built in Canada because Britain's yards were fully occupied with the war programme, and was constructed from wood due to the shortage of available steel. She was completed too late to see much service with the British Merchant Marine, and was sold to Credito Industriale di Venezia in 1919. Broken up in 1923.

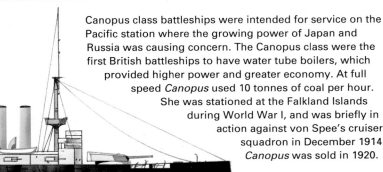

Canopus

Type: British battleship
Displacement: 13,360 tonnes (13,150 tons)
Dimensions: 128m x 23m x 8m (421ft 6in x 74ft x 26ft)
Machinery: Twin screw triple expansion engines
Top speed: 18.3 knots
Main armament: Four 305mm (12in) guns
Armour: 152mm (6in) belt
Launched: October 1897
Date of profile: 1899

Canopus class battleships were intended for service on the Pacific station where the growing power of Japan and Russia was causing concern. The Canopus class were the first British battleships to have water tube boilers, which provided higher power and greater economy. At full speed *Canopus* used 10 tonnes of coal per hour. She was stationed at the Falkland Islands during World War I, and was briefly in action against von Spee's cruiser squadron in December 1914. *Canopus* was sold in 1920.

Caorle

Type: Italian landing ship
Displacement: 8,128 tonnes (8,000 tons)
Dimensions: 135m x 19m x 5m (444ft x 62ft x 16ft 6in)
Machinery: Twin screw diesel engines
Top speed: 17.5 knots
Main armament: Six 76mm (3in) guns
Launched: March 1957
Date of profile: 1983

This ship was originally one of the US

Suffolk County class, which were a group of seven vessels built for the US Navy in the 1950s as tank and troop landing ships. They were a popular and effective design, with greater speed and carrying capacity than previous ships of this type. Equipped with air-conditioning, they were regarded as pleasant ships to serve on compared to other

troop transports. In 1972, the *USS York County* was sold to the Italian Navy, who renamed her *Caorle*. She was capable of carrying up to 575 fully-equipped assault troops, or a mixture of troops, tanks or other vehicles. She was built with a flat bottom and shallow draught, which allowed her bow to be grounded on a shallow beach. Men and equipment could then be unloaded directly on to the beach

through the large bow doors. Her engines developed over 14,000hp and she had an unrefuelled range of over 31,350km (16,500 miles) at 13 knots. This could, of course, be extended by refuelling at sea. She was fitted with twin variable-pitch propellers which allowed precise manoeuvring in confined spaces, such as harbours and crowded beacheads. The Italian Navy has retained a maritime landing capability, and in the San Marco Marine battalion has a highly-regarded assault force.

Cap Trafalgar

Type: German liner
Displacement: 19,106 tonnes (18,805 tons)
Dimensions: 187m x 22m (613ft x 72ft 3in)
Machinery: Triple screw turbines
Top speed: 17.8 knots
Launched: July 1913
Date of profile: 1914

Cap Trafalgar was built for the

Hamburg to South America route and could carry 400 first-class, 274 second-class and 912 third-class passengers plus 436 crew. When World War I broke out she was anchored at

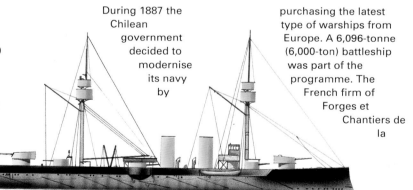

Buenos Aires. During August 1914 she underwent conversion into an armed raider. Her third funnel was removed, and she was armed with two 102mm (4in) guns, plus smaller weapons. On 13 September *Cap*

Trafalgar was re-fuelling at Trinidada when she was engaged in action by the British armed merchant liner *Carmania*. *Cap Trafalgar* was sunk and her survivors were rescued by the German collier that had been re-fuelling her.

Capitan Prat

Type: Chilean battleship
Displacement: 7,011 tonnes (6,910 tons)
Dimensions: 100m x 18.5m x 7m (328ft x 60ft 8in x 22ft 10in)
Machinery: Twin screw horizontal triple expansion engines
Top speed: 18.3 knots
Main armament: Four 239mm (9.4in) guns

During 1887 the Chilean government decided to modernise its navy by

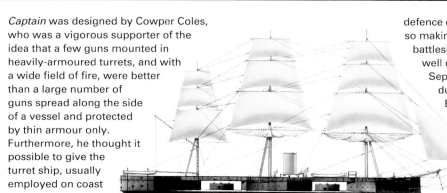

purchasing the latest type of warships from Europe. A 6,096-tonne (6,000-ton) battleship was part of the programme. The French firm of Forges et Chantiers de la

Méditerranee won the contract, and *Capitan Prat* was laid down in 1889. Her 239mm (9.4in) guns were mounted singly in turrets, one at each end of the vessel and one on each side of the hull. A secondary battery of eight 120mm (4.7in) guns was mounted in twin turrets on the upper deck. Armour alone took up one third of her displacement. Until World War I, *Capitan Prat* was Chile's most powerful warship. She was scrapped in 1930.

Captain

Type: British battleship
Displacement: 7,892 tonnes (7,767 tons)
Dimensions: 98m x 16m x 7.8m (320ft x 53ft 3in x 25ft 6in)
Machinery: Twin screw horizontal truck engines
Top speed: 14 knots
Main armament: Four 305mm (12in) guns
Launched: March 1869

Captain was designed by Cowper Coles, who was a vigorous supporter of the idea that a few guns mounted in heavily-armoured turrets, and with a wide field of fire, were better than a large number of guns spread along the side of a vessel and protected by thin armour only. Furthermore, he thought it possible to give the turret ship, usually employed on coast

defence duties, a full set of canvas, so making it a true ocean-going battleship. *Captain* performed well during trials. However, in September 1870 she sank during a storm in the Bay of Biscay with the loss of 473 men, including Coles who was aboard to observe how his brainchild performed at sea.

Carabiniere

Type: Italian frigate
Displacement: 2,743 tonnes (2,700 tons)
Dimensions: 113m x 13m x 4m (371ft x 43ft 6in x 12ft 7in)
Machinery: Twin screw, diesels, gas turbines
Top speed: 20 knots (diesel), 28 knots (diesel and gas)

Main armament: Six 76mm (3in) guns
Launched: September 1967
Date of profile: 1968

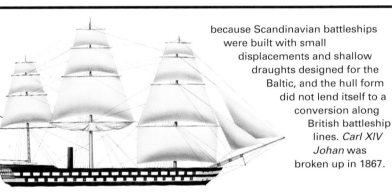

Anti submarine weapons aboard *Carabiniere* comprise a single semi-automatic depth charge mortar and six torpedo tubes plus two helicopters. Anti-missile defence is provided by SCLAR rockets. She also has full radar equipment.

Cardenal Cisneros

Type: Spanish cruiser
Displacement: 6,998 tonnes (6,888 tons)
Dimensions: 111m x 19m x 7m (364ft 1in x 61ft x 21ft 7in)

Machinery: Twin screw horizontal triple expansion engines
Top speed: 20 knots
Main armament: Two 240mm (9.5in) guns
Armour: 300mm (11.8in) belt amidships
Launched: March 1897
Date of profile: 1908

Cardenal Cisneros was laid down in 1890 and completed in 1904, by which time her design was already dated. Her guns were mounted in turrets fore and aft, with eight 140mm (5.5in) guns spread over the upper deck, protected behind shields. A year after completion, *Cardenal Cisneros* struck a submerged rock in the Bay of Muros and sank within 40 minutes.

Carl XIV Johan

Type: Swedish battleship
Displacement: 26,424 tonnes (26,008 tons)
Dimensions: 54m x 14m (176ft 11in x 48ft 2in)
Main armament: Sixty-eight guns
Launched: 1824

The Swedes were impressed with the performance of British steam battleships during the 1854-55 Baltic campaign against Russian forces. Fearing that Russia would improve her fleet, Sweden sought assistance from Britain in late 1855. The existing sailing battleship *Carl XIV Johan* had already been undergoing conversion, but her final transformation was not a success,

because Scandinavian battleships were built with small displacements and shallow draughts designed for the Baltic, and the hull form did not lend itself to a conversion along British battleship lines. *Carl XIV Johan* was broken up in 1867.

Carlo Alberto

Type: Italian cruiser
Displacement: 7,170 tonnes (7,957 tons)
Dimensions: 106m x 18m x 7m (346ft 9in x 59ft 2in x 23ft 7in)
Machinery: Twin screw triple expansion engines
Top speed: 19 knots
Main armament: Twelve 152mm

(6in), six 120mm (4.7in) guns
Launched: September 1896

The *Carlo Alberto* belonged to the second group of armoured cruisers built for the Italian Navy. Although her protection was good, not having a gun heavier than

152mm (6in) was a drawback. The armoured belt ran the full length of the ship, rising up amidships to provide protection for the battery. In 1902 *Carlo Alberto* took part in experiments to test Marconi's long-range radio equipment at sea. She was discarded in 1920.

Carlo Bergamini

Type: Italian frigate
Displacement: 1,676 tonnes (1,650 tons)
Dimensions: 94m x 11m x 3m (308ft 3in x 37ft 3in x 10ft 6in)
Machinery: Twin screw diesel motors
Main armament: Three 76mm (3in)

guns
Launched: June 1960

The overall design of the vessel underwent many changes, but upon completion *Carlo Bergamini* was regarded as an excellent ship. As well as fully automatic 76mm (3in) guns, she

carried a new type of single-barrelled mortar automatic depth charge discharger capable

of firing 15 rounds per minute to a range of 920m (1,000yd), and two types of 304mm (12in) torpedo tubes. A single helicopter is housed aft behind the exhaust funnel.

Carmania

Type: British liner
Displacement: 19,836 tonnes
(19,524 tons)
Dimensions: 205.7m x 22m (674ft
10in x 72ft 2in)
Machinery: Triple screw turbines
Top speed: 20 knots
Launched: February 1905
Date of profile: 1906

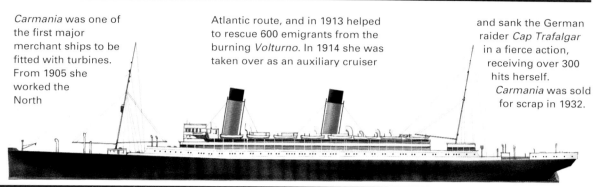

Carmania was one of
the first major
merchant ships to be
fitted with turbines.
From 1905 she
worked the
North

Atlantic route, and in 1913 helped
to rescue 600 emigrants from the
burning *Volturno*. In 1914 she was
taken over as an auxiliary cruiser

and sank the German
raider *Cap Trafalgar*
in a fierce action,
receiving over 300
hits herself.
Carmania was sold
for scrap in 1932.

Carola

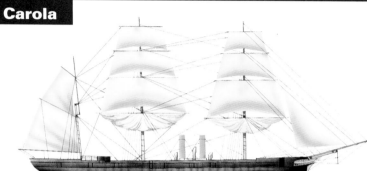

Type: German cruiser
Displacement: 2,425 tonnes (2,387
tons)
Dimensions: 76m x 12m x 6m (250ft
6in x 41ft x 20ft)
Machinery: Single screw horizontal
compound engines
Top speed: 13.5 knots
Main armament: Ten 152mm (6in)
guns
Launched: November 1880

Carola was an iron-hulled, flush-
decked cruiser forming part of a
four-strong class that followed the
Bismarck group. She carried a
barque rig, and the battery was
carried on one deck with the
forward gun recessed in the hull. In
1893 *Carola* became a gunnery
training ship, was given a new
raised armament and was re-rigged
with two military masts.

Caroline

Type: British cruiser
Displacement: 5,017 tonnes (4,733
tons)
Dimensions: 136m x 13m x 160m
(446ft x 41ft 6in x 16ft)
Machinery: Quadruple screws,
geared turbines
Main armament: Two 152mm (6in),
eight 102mm (4in) guns

Armour: 25-76mm belt
Launched: September 1914

Caroline was one of a six-vessel
light cruiser class. As the type
developed over the years the
armament was increased, but
Caroline suffered from a mixed

armament. However, she was
a stable and generally
successful cruiser. In 1917
she was given an extended
fighter plane flying-off
platform so that she

could engage one of the many
Zeppelins then raiding Britain. The
platform was removed in 1918.
Caroline was still in use during the
1980s, serving as a Royal Navy
Volunteer Reserve (RNVR) drill
ship on the River
Thames.

Carpathia

Type: British cargo/liner
Displacement: 13,781 tonnes
(13,564 tons)
Dimensions: 170m x 20m (558ft x
64ft 4in)
Machinery: Twin screw quadruple
engines
Launched: August 1902

Carpathia was built for Cunard's
Atlantic route and was typical of the
large mixed cargo/passenger vessels
of the period. In 1912 she picked up
many of the survivors from the
sunken *Titanic*. In 1918
Carpathia was sunk by
the German *U55*
while on her way
to New York.

Carthage

Type: British liner
Displacement: 14,533 tonnes (14,304 tons)
Dimensions: 165m x 22m (540ft x 71ft)
Machinery: Twin screw geared
turbines
Top speed: 19.5 knots
Launched: August 1931
Date of profile: 1934

Originally named *Canton*, *Carthage* entered
service between London and Hong Kong in
1931. She carried 175 first-class and 196 second-
class passengers, plus an extensive range of

cargo. The Royal Navy took her over as
an armed merchant cruiser in 1940,
and equipped her with 152mm (6in)
guns and anti-aircraft weapons. In
1943 she served as a troop
transport. Between 1947 and 1948
she underwent extensive
renovation and returned to
service as a passenger
liner. She was broken up
in Japan in 1961.

Casco

Type: US ironclad
Displacement: 1,189 tonnes (1,170 tons)
Dimensions: 68m x 14m x 2m (225ft x 45ft x 6ft 9in)
Machinery: Twin screw direct acting engines
Top speed: 9 knots
Main armament: Two 280mm (11in) guns
Launched: 1865
Date of profile: 1865

During the summer of 1862 the gunboats of the Union Navy were finding it increasingly difficult to deal with the strength of the Confederate defences along the Mississippi and its tributaries. The existing Union gunboats were finding it difficult to deal with the strong Confederate naval forces, while the river was too shallow to employ any of the then serving ironclads. Designs were hastily prepared for a new group of ironclads with only 1.2m (4ft) draught and carrying the lightest armour of any monitor built for the Union Navy. The initial work was carried out by Ericsson, but actual construction was overseen by Alban Stimers. *Casco* and her sisters were built with two large Dahlgren guns mounted in a single central armoured turret. They also had ballast tanks, which could be used to reduce the height of the ship. High quality materials were scarce, and the hulls of these ships were made using unseasoned timber. Stimers was also too busy to manage construction in detail, and all 19 ships of the class ended up being significantly over their design weight. *Casco* and four others of the class were soon modified for use as torpedo (the term then used for mines) boats, with one of the main guns removed. Overall, the programme was regarded as a failure, for which Stimers took the blame. In spite of this, he should be remembered for contributing a great deal to the successful development of the ironclad.

Castalia

Type: British ferry
Displacement: 1,558 tonnes (1,533 tons)
Dimensions: 89m x 15m x 2m (290ft x 50ft x 6ft)
Machinery: Paddle wheels, compound engines
Top speed: 6 knots
Launched: 1874
Date of profile: 1874

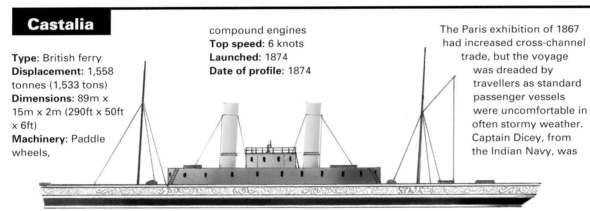

The Paris exhibition of 1867 had increased cross-channel trade, but the voyage was dreaded by travellers as standard passenger vessels were uncomfortable in often stormy weather. Captain Dicey, from the Indian Navy, was impressed by the steadiness of catamarans able to sail in heavy seas because of their double hulls, and so came up with designs for the double-hulled *Castalia*. Although stability and comfort were greatly improved she was slow, and the paddle floats had to be repaired after each trip. *Castalia* served as a ferry for only two summer seasons, and was then taken out of service and used as a hospital ship. She was eventually broken up in Holland.

Castelfidardo

Type: Italian battleship
Displacement: 4,560 tonnes (4,527 tons)
Dimensions: 82m x 15m x 6m (268ft 4in x 49ft 9in x 20ft 10in)
Machinery: Single screw reciprocating engine
Main armament: Four 203mm (8in), twenty-two 164mm (6.5in) guns
Armour: 109mm (4.3in) belt
Launched: August 1863

Castelfidardo was originally completed with a schooner rig. This was later altered to a barque rig, and finally to two military masts towards the end of her career. She took part in the attack upon the island of Lissa in July 1866 and was part of Rear Admiral Vacca's squadron. During the later action against the Austrian fleet she was set on fire aft but survived the blaze. At the end of her long career, *Castelfidardo* became a coast defence ship. She was broken up in 1910.

CB12

Type: Italian submarine
Displacement: 25 tonnes (24.9 tons) on surface, 36 tonnes (35.9 tons) submerged
Dimensions: 15m x 3m x 2m (49ft 3in x 9ft 10in x 6ft 9in)
Machinery: Single screw diesel (surface), electric drive (submerged)
Main armament: Two 450mm (17.7in) torpedoes in exterior cages
Launched: August 1943
Date of profile: 1945

The CB programme of miniature submarines begun in 1941 was intended to comprise 72 vessels, but only 22 were ever laid down. They could be transported by railway and were designed for local defence. Range was 2,660km (1,400 miles) at 5 knots on diesel engines, and 95km (50 miles) at 3 knots submerged. Complement was one officer and three crew. All 22 units that entered service were built by Caproni Taliedo of Milan and designed by Major Engineer Spinelli. Maximum diving depth was 55m (180ft 5in).

Cécille

Type: French cruiser
Displacement: 5,932 tonnes (5,839 tons)
Dimensions: 115m x 15m x 6m (378ft 9in x 49ft 3in x 19ft 9in)
Machinery: Twin screw vertical compound engines
Top speed: 19 knots
Main armament: Eight 162mm

(6.4in), ten 140mm (5.5in) guns
Launched: May 1888
Date of profile: 1894

Upon her completion in 1890, *Cécille* was the second-largest cruiser in the French Navy. The hull was of iron and steel, and was divided into 15 airtight

compartments stretching from the armoured deck, which ran the whole length of the vessel, to the side plating. *Cécille* had two separate engine rooms with 12 cylindrical boilers. Her crew numbered 517. She was broken up in 1919.

Centauro

Type: Italian destroyer
Displacement: 2,255 tonnes (2,220 tons)
Dimensions: 104m x 11m x 4m (339ft x 38ft x 11ft 6in)
Machinery: Twin

screw geared turbines
Main armament: Four 76mm (3in) guns
Launched: April 1954

Centauro was one of a class of four vessels built to Italian plans and

specifications and funded under the US off-shore programme of the 1950s which aimed to increase the military power of friendly nations. All units had automatic anti-submarine and medium anti-aircraft armament, plus US sonar equipment. The guns were mounted one above the other in twin gun houses and could fire 60 rounds per minute. All vessels later underwent armament modification.

Centennial State

Type: US cargo vessel
Displacement: 10,727 tonnes (10,558 tons)
Dimensions: 157m x 19m (516ft x 62ft 4in)
Machinery: Twin screw triple expansion engines
Top speed: 14 knots
Launched: December 1920

Centennial State made her maiden voyage in 1921. Although primarily a cargo vessel, she could also carry 80 passengers. In 1923 she was sold and

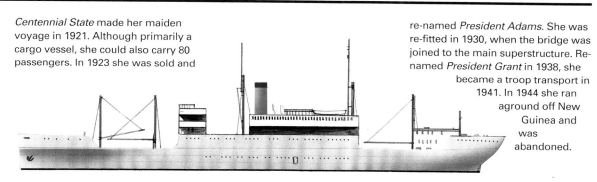

re-named *President Adams*. She was re-fitted in 1930, when the bridge was joined to the main superstructure. Re-named *President Grant* in 1938, she became a troop transport in 1941. In 1944 she ran aground off New Guinea and was abandoned.

Centurion

Type: British battleship
Displacement: 1,021 tonnes (1,005 tons)
Dimensions: 44m x 12m x 5m (144ft 1in x 40ft 1in x 16ft 5in)
Armament: Sixty guns
Launched: 1732
Date of profile: 1740

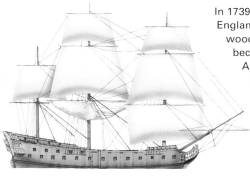

In 1739 war broke out between England and Spain. *Centurion*, a wooden third-rate battleship, became flagship of George Anson who had orders to engage the Spanish in the South Atlantic and Pacific. The squadron set out in September 1740 but the voyage was a disaster, over 1,300 men

dying, though only four died through enemy action. During the long voyage *Centurion* fought many actions against the Spanish, and captured the *Nostra Signora de Cabadonga*. *Centurion* was badly damaged while rounding Cape Horn, but in June 1744 she arrived back in Britain. She later underwent a major re-fit during which her armament was reduced to 50 guns.

Centurion

Type: British battleship
Displacement: 10,668 tonnes (10,500 tons)
Dimensions: 110m x 21m x 7.7m (360ft x 70ft x 25ft 6in)
Machinery: Twin screw triple expansion engines
Top speed: 18.5 knots

Main armament: Four 254mm (10in) guns
Launched: August 1892

Centurion and her sister *Barfleur* were second-class battleships that formed part of the large expansion programme for the Royal Navy begun in 1889. They were intended to counteract the powerful

armoured cruisers of the Russian Navy in the Pacific. The relatively light draught of the vessels enabled

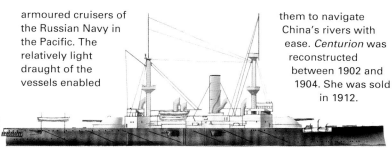

them to navigate China's rivers with ease. *Centurion* was reconstructed between 1902 and 1904. She was sold in 1912.

Chamäleon

Type: Austrian minelayer
Displacement: 1,184 tonnes (1,165 tons)
Dimensions: 88m x 9m x 3m (288ft 8in x 30ft 2in x 8ft 10in)
Machinery: Twin screw

vertical triple expansion engines
Main armament: Four 90mm (3.5in) guns
Launched: December 1913

A purpose-built minelayer carrying 300

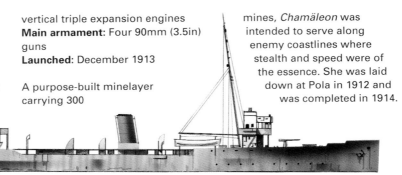

mines, Chamäleon was intended to serve along enemy coastlines where stealth and speed were of the essence. She was laid down at Pola in 1912 and was completed in 1914.

Chamäleon carried light armament for use against the torpedo craft and aircraft then coming into play in the Adriatic, and proved to be the most successful minelayer in the Austrian Navy. She had a long, sleek hull with rails set into the main deck for handling the mines. In 1920 she was handed over to the British, and later sold to a firm of Italian shipbreakers.

Chao Yung

Type: Chinese cruiser
Displacement: 1,566 tonnes (1,542 tons)
Dimensions: 64m x 10m x 5m (210ft x 32ft x 15ft)
Machinery: Twin screw horizontal compound reciprocating engines
Main armament: Two 254mm (10in) guns

Launched: November 1880

In the 1800s China did not possess a unified fleet. Instead, separate squadrons ordered their own warships as required. It was only in times of emergency that the squadrons united to form a

single battle fleet. Chao Yung and her sister were ordered for the Peiyang fleet and laid down in 1880. Chao Yung was exceptionally fast for her day and carried a powerful armament on a small displacement. In 1894, in action against the Japanese at the Battle of the Yalu, she was set on fire and, listing badly, was later sunk.

Chaperon

Type: American stern wheel steamer
Displacement: 812 tonnes (800 tons)
Dimensions: 37m x 6m x 2m (121ft x 21ft x 4ft)
Machinery: Stern wheel, compound engine
Top speed: 8 knots
Launched: 1884

Chaperon was one of over 5,000 paddle steamers built for service on the Mississippi and its tributaries during the 19th century. She was built entirely of wood and, as was usual with this type of craft, had a long, low hull with minimum draught. Like all Mississippi steamers, she was strengthened fore and aft with sturdy

supporting trusses stretched over spars above the upper deck.

Charlemagne

Type: French battleship
Displacement: 11,277 tonnes (11,100 tons)
Dimensions: 114m x 20m x 8m (374ft x 66ft 5in x 27ft 6in)
Machinery: Triple screw triple expansion engines
Top speed: 18 knots

Main armament: Four 305mm (12in) guns
Armour: 203-368mm (8-14.5in) belt, 380mm (15in) on turrets
Launched: October 1895

In Charlemagne and her two sisters, France followed

the design trend of other powers and adopted twin mountings for

the main armament. Her design tried to achieve too much on a small displacement, but even so she was a good economical steamer. She burnt less than 10 tonnes (10 tons) of coal per hour at full speed. Charlemagne was broken up in 1920.

Charles

Type: French frigate galley
Displacement: 1,016 tonnes (1,000 tons)
Dimensions: 45m x 11m x 4m (150ft x 38ft x14ft)
Armament: Forty guns
Launched: 1776
Date of profile: 1776

Charles was one of the more unusual vessels built during the 18th century, being a large frigate equipped with a full set of sails plus oars, or sweeps, for use when the ship was becalmed. The oars were used from the lower deck and could drive the vessel along at an approximate speed of 6 knots. Charles was used

successfully in the battle against the Barbary Pirates, who repeatedly attacked trade in the Mediterranean to deadly effect. Charles had two full decks running her entire length, and the deck below the sweep deck was devoted to stores. Crew quarters were forward, officers' aft. Charles handled well under sail, but this type of frigate galley was not generally a popular design.

Charles Martel

Type: French battleship
Displacement: 11,880 tonnes (11,693 tons)
Dimensions: 115m x 22m x 8m (378ft 11in x 71ft 2in x 27ft 6in)
Machinery: Twin screw triple expansion engines
Top speed: 18 knots
Main armament: Two 304mm (12in), two 274mm (10.8in) guns
Armour: 254-457mm (10-18 in) belt
Launched: August 1893
Date of profile: 1893

Laid down in 1891, *Charles Martel* was part of the French naval programme which was intended to replace all their wooden-hulled ironclads by 1900. She followed the usual French practice of having her main armament laid out in lozenge or diamond fashion. The two 304mm (12in) guns were mounted fore and aft in armoured turrets, while the two 274mm (10.8in) weapons were in smaller turrets, on sponsons which protruded from each side of the hull. Her secondary armament was eight 140mm (5.5in) guns in electrically-driven turrets on the main and upper deck. Lighter anti-torpedo boat guns were mounted on the superstructure and the heavy military-pattern masts. She had a distinctive appearance, with a high forecastle, and a covered flying bridge linking both masts.The main armoured deck rested on top of her armour belt, and there was another splinter-proof deck below this. Her interior was also broken up into dozens of separate watertight compartments, which helped reduce the chance of catastrophic damage from a penetrating hit. Problems with her boilers delayed completion, but once she reached service *Charles Martel* proved to be a good sea boat, able to maintain a high speed in heavy seas. She remained in service throughout World War I, although she took no active part in the conflict. She was finally stricken and scrapped in 1922.

Charleston

Type: US cruiser
Displacement: 4,267 tonnes (4,200 tons)
Dimensions: 97.4m x 14m x 6m (319ft 6in x 46ft x 18ft 4in)
Machinery: Twin screw horizontal compound engines
Top speed: 18.9 knots
Main armament: Two 203mm (8in), six 152mm (6in) guns
Launched: July 1888
Date of profile: 1897

During the mid 1880s the building of US warships was suspended, but by 1887 this suspension was lifted, and plans for a new type of cruiser were purchased in Britain from Sir William Armstrong. All the materials for building the vessels were to be of US origin.

Charleston was the first of the group, and followed the design of previous cruisers already built by Armstrong for Japan and Chile. She had a full protective deck 51-76mm (2-3in) thick. A 203mm (8in) gun was positioned at each end of the superstructure, and the 152mm (6in) guns were carried amidships on the main deck. *Charleston* was the first US cruiser built without sail power. She was wrecked in November 1899.

Charlie class

Type: Russian missile submarine
Displacement: 4,064 tonnes (4,000 tons) on surface, 4,877 tonnes (4,800 tons) submerged
Dimensions: 95m x 10m (311ft 8in x 32ft 10in)
Machinery: Single screw nuclear powered
Top speed: 24 knots
Main armament: Eight cruise missiles, six 533mm torpedo tubes
Launched: 1967

The SS-N-7 anti-ship cruise missile outdated the anti-ship torpedo. It was the first Russian anti-ship missile that could be fired underwater, which made it possible to approach the target undetected, fire and then escape unchallenged. Twelve of the Charlie class were completed between 1968 and 1972, but the programme was stopped in the late 1970s because of the threat posed by the new US Los Angeles attack submarines.

Charlotte Dundas

Type: British paddle steamboat
Displacement: unrecorded
Dimensions: 17m x 5m x 2m (56ft x 18ft x 8ft)
Machinery: Paddle wheel, horizontal double acting engine
Top speed: 4 knots
Launched: 1801
Date of profile: 1802

Charlotte Dundas was the first practical steamboat, and was used in experiments to test the viability of steamboats in place of horse-propelled vessels. She was built of wood and had a single engine of 10hp with a single cylinder. Steam was provided by a boiler next to the engine. The paddle wheel was at the stern, and she had two rudders. In March 1802 *Charlotte Dundas* took six hours to tow two loaded 70-tonne (70-ton) barges along 37km (19.5 miles) of the Forth and Clyde canal against a strong wind. Although a success, the drainage problems caused by the wash to the canal banks forced her to be abandoned, and she was left to rot up a creek for many years before finally being broken up in 1861. Her designer, William Symington, was a talented engineer well ahead of his time, but he died a pauper in London in 1831.

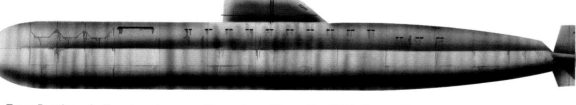

Châteaurenault

Type: French commerce raider
Displacement: 8,024 tonnes (7,898 tons)
Dimensions: 135m x 17m x 7m (443ft x 55ft 9in x 24ft 3in)
Machinery: Triple screw vertical triple expansion engines
Main armament: Two

162mm (6.4in), six 140mm (5.5in) guns
Launched: May 1898

Châteaurenault was intended to be a commerce destroyer, her long hull and

four funnels designed to deceive a likely victim into identifying her as a liner of unknown origin. On 14 December 1917 she was transporting nearly 1,000 troops across the Ionian Sea when she was struck by a torpedo from the German submarine *UC38*. *Châteaurenault* returned fire, but on submerging *UC38* fired again and sank her. All on board were rescued.

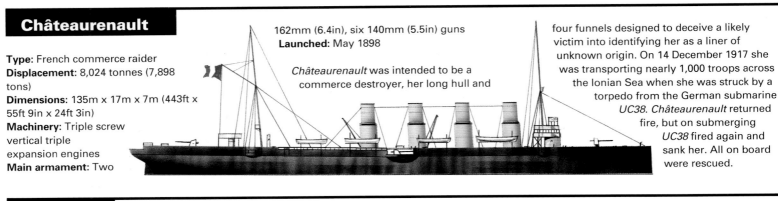

Chazhma

Type: Russian missile range ship
Displacement: 13,716 tonnes (13,500 tons)
Dimensions: 140m x 18m x 8m (458ft x 59ft x 26ft)
Machinery: Twin screw diesel engines
Top speed: 15 knots

Launched: 1959
Date of profile: 1970
Formerly a 7,381-tonne (7,265-ton) bulk ore carrier of the Dshankoy class, *Chazhma* was converted into a missile range

ship in 1963 for service in the Pacific. A Ship Globe radar was mounted in the huge dome on top of the bridge amidships. A helicopter platform and hangar, built into the aft superstructure, enable her to operate one Hormone helicopter.

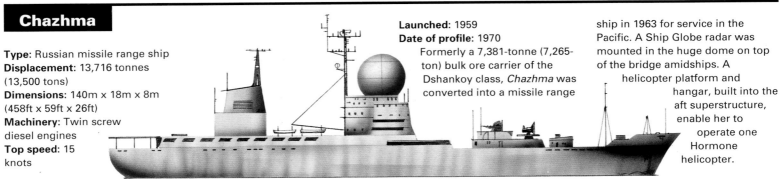

Chen Yuan

Type: Chinese battleship
Displacement: 7,792 tonnes (7,670 tons)
Dimensions: 94m x 18m x 6m (307ft 9in x 59ft x 20ft)
Machinery: Twin screw horizontal compound engines
Top speed: 15.7 knots
Main armament: Four 304mm (12in),

two 152mm (6in) guns
Launched: November 1882

By the end of the 1870s the Chinese decided to modernise their navy along western lines. A major programme was begun in the 1880s, and *Chen*

Yuan and her sister *Ting Yuan* were China's only battleships. Both were steel-hulled, and featured a strongly armoured central citadel which covered the engines,

boilers and magazines. *Chen Yuan* survived the 1894 Battle of Yalu, but was captured by the Japanese in 1895. Scrapped in 1914.

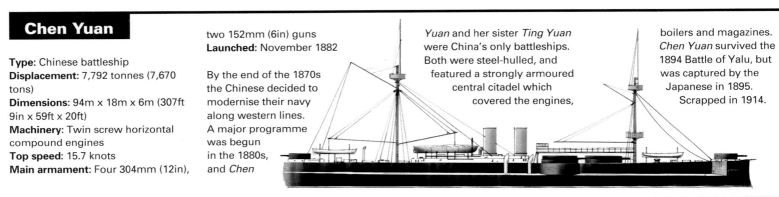

Chester

Type: US cruiser
Displacement: 4,762 tonnes (4,687 tons)
Dimensions: 129m x 14m x 5m (423ft x 47ft x 16ft 9in)
Machinery: Quadruple screw turbines
Top speed: 24 knots
Main armament: Two

127mm (5in), six 76mm (3in) guns
Launched: June 1907

By 1903 the US Navy required a new type of fast scout with high speed and good sea-

keeping qualities to work directly with the battlefleet. Three vessels were laid down in 1904 and were used as test-beds for different types of propulsion. *Chester* was equipped with Parsons turbines, a means of propulsion that proved relatively successful. She was sold in 1930.

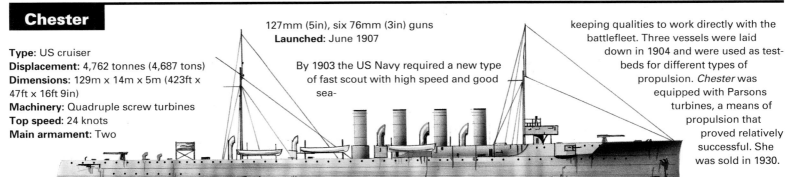

Chicago

Type: US cruiser
Displacement: 4,942 tonnes (4,864 tons)
Dimensions: 104m x 15m x 6m (342ft 2in x 48ft 3in x 19ft)
Machinery: Twin screw compound overhead beam engines
Main armament: Four 203mm (8in),

eight 152mm (6in) guns
Launched: December 1885

Chicago was the largest vessel in the 1883 naval programme. Completed in 1889, she underwent a re-fit from 1895-98 and later became an accommodation ship at Pearl Harbor until 1935. She foundered while under tow to the USA in 1936.

Chicora

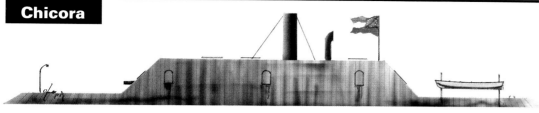

Type: Confederate ironclad
Displacement: unrecorded
Dimensions: 45m x 10m x 4m (150ft x 35ft x 14ft)
Machinery: Single screw direct acting engine
Top speed: 5 knots
Main armament: Two 228mm (9in), two 178mm (7in) guns

Launched: 1862

Chicora and *Palmetto State* followed the usual Confederate design, a raised central armoured casement housing the four guns on a low freeboard hull. Both vessels played a major role in the defence of Charleston against Union attack. Upon the fall of Charleston, both vessels were sunk to avoid capture.

Chidori

Type: Japanese torpedo boat
Displacement: 749 tonnes (737 tons)
Dimensions: 82m x 7m x 3m (269ft x 24ft 3in x 82ft)
Machinery: Twin screw turbines
Top speed: 30 knots
Main armament: Three 127mm (5in) guns

Launched: April 1933

Chidori was one of a class of four vessels laid down between 1931 and 1933. With their armament of 127mm (5in) guns and four 533mm (21in) torpedo tubes they were virtually small destroyers, but it soon became apparent that they were all badly top heavy. All ships in the class were re-built to correct the defect, and had a lighter armament mounted, plus the addition of 61 tonnes (60 tons) of permanent ballast to increase displacement. After a further re-fit in 1942, *Chidori* was sunk by a US submarine in 1944.

Chin Yuan

Type: Chinese cruiser
Displacement: 2,337 tonnes (2,300 tons)
Dimensions: 76m x 12m x 6m (250ft x 38ft x 15ft)
Machinery: Twin screw horizontal triple expansion engines
Main armament: Three 203mm (8.2in), two 152mm (6in) guns

Launched: September 1886

Chih Yuan and her sister *Ching Yuan* were built by Armstrong in the UK and were designed by William White, who later designed all the British battleships of the 1890s. Both fast cruisers were of an outstanding design, able to mount a heavy armament on a relatively small displacement. *Chih Yuan* was sunk at the Battle of Yalu in September 1894. *Ching Yuan* was sunk at Wei-Hai-Wei in 1895.

Chikugo

Type: Japanese frigate
Displacement: 1,493 tonnes (1,470 tons)
Dimensions: 93m x 11m x 4m (305ft 5in x 35ft 5in x 11ft 6in)
Machinery: Twin screw diesels
Main armament: Two 76mm (3in) guns

Launched in 1970, *Chikugo* was one of eleven units laid down in 1968. They were the smallest ships in the world to carry the anti-submarine weapon ASROC. Anti-aircraft armament is weak, as the ships are intended for service inshore under cover of land-based fighter aircraft.

China

Type: British liner
Displacement: 2,680 tonnes (2,638 tons)
Dimensions: 99m x 12m (326ft x 40ft)
Machinery: Single screw geared oscillating engines
Top speed: 12 knots
Launched: March 1862
Date of profile: 1862

The iron-hulled Cunard liner *China* was able to carry 150 'cabin' passengers, 770 steerage and 1,422 tonnes (1,400 tons) of cargo. She was the first screw steamer built for Cunard's mail service, and proved very economical. *China* was re-fitted with compound engines in 1873. She became the *Theodor*, a four-masted barque, in 1883, and disappeared at sea in 1906.

Chishima

Type: Japanese cruiser
Displacement: 762 tonnes (750 tons)
Dimensions: 70m x 8m x 3m (229ft 8in x 26ft 3in x 9ft 10in)
Machinery: Twin screw vertical triple expansion engines
Top speed: 22 knots
Main armament: Five 76mm (3in) guns
Launched: November 1890
Date of profile: 1892

Chishima was laid down in St. Nazaire in January 1890 as a

light cruiser intended for the Japanese Navy. She was part of the Japanese 1882 building programme. She had a long, unarmoured, graceful hull with two broad funnels, plus three masts

carrying a light rig. Four of her main guns were mounted in sponsons, two on each beam. The fifth was placed in the bow. Secondary armament consisted of six 1-pounder light guns, which

were sited on the bridge, on the poop and amidships. There were also two 380mm (15in) torpedo tubes on the upper deck, and a single one in the bow, above the waterline. She was completed and handed over to the Japanese Navy on 24 November 1892, but never entered service. On her delivery voyage from Europe to Japan, she collided in the Inland Sea with the P&O steamer *Ravenna*. *Chishima* sank with the loss of 75 crew.

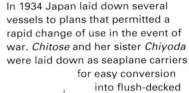

Chitose

Type: Japanese seaplane carrier
Displacement: 13,716 tonnes (13,500 tons)
Dimensions: 193m x 19m x 7m (631ft 7in x 61ft 8in x 23ft 8in)
Machinery: Twin screw turbines

and diesel engines
Top speed: 29 knots
Main armament: Four 127mm (5in) guns
Launched: November 1936

In 1934 Japan laid down several vessels to plans that permitted a rapid change of use in the event of war. *Chitose* and her sister *Chiyoda* were laid down as seaplane carriers for easy conversion into flush-decked aircraft carriers.

In 1941 the sterns of both vessels were altered to enable the launching of midget submarines. Between 1942 and 1944 the ships were re-fitted as conventional carriers, with a 91m (300ft) hangar housing 30 aircraft on the upper deck. *Chitose* first saw action in 1942. She was sunk in October 1944 by aircraft from USS *Essex* and *Lexington*.

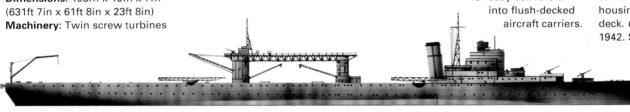

Chiyoda

Type: Japanese cruiser
Displacement: 2,489 tonnes (2,450 tons)
Dimensions: 94m x 13.1m x 5.2m (308ft x 43ft x 17ft)
Machinery: Twin screw triple expansion engines
Top speed: 19 knots
Main armament: Ten 120mm (4.7 in) guns

Armour: 114mm (4.5in) thick waterline belt
Launched: June 1890
Date of profile: 1892

Chiyoda was a replacement for the French-built *Unebi* which was lost while on the delivery voyage to

Japan in October 1887. Japan's first modern-type armoured cruiser, *Chiyoda* took part in the battle of the Yalu in 1894 and the war against Russia. She was discarded in 1922.

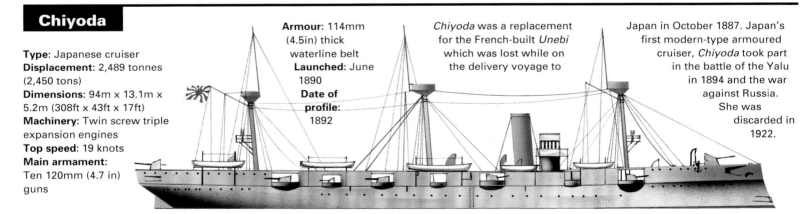

Choctaw

Type: US ironclad
Displacement: 1,020 tonnes (1,004 tons)
Dimensions: 79m x 13.7m x 2.4m (260ft x 45ft x 8ft)
Machinery: Paddle wheels driven by compound engines
Top speed: 6 knots
Main armament: Three 228mm (9in) guns
Launched: 1855

Choctaw was one of a second group of powerful ironclads that followed on from the successful Cairo class. She was converted from a merchant ship that had independent wheels that

provided better steering and greater control in the waters of the Mississippi. She was given a massive casemate forward that housed three 228mm (9in) guns plus

one 100-pounder rifle. Just forward of the paddle boxes, a second casemate contained two howitzers pointing forward. The after part of the ship housed two 30-pounder rifles. Alterations were made in 1862 and *Choctaw* saw action around Vicksburg in the Civil War. She was sold in 1866.

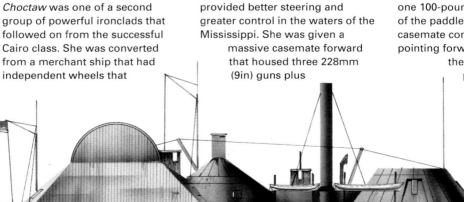

Cigno

Type: Italian frigate
Displacement: 2,455 tonnes (2,220 tons)
Dimensions: 103m x 12m x 4m (339ft 3in x 38ft x 11ft 6in)
Machinery: Twin screw geared turbines
Main armament: Four 76mm (3in) guns

Launched: March 1955

Cigno and her three sister ships were built for the Italian Navy to Italian designs, but were financed by the US offshore programme. All had US sonar equipment and carried automatic anti-submarine and medium anti-aircraft armament. The Italian-made 76mm (3in) guns were mounted in twin turrets and could fire 60 rounds per minute. In the 1960s the gun turrets were replaced by three single 76mm (3in) mounts. All four vessels in the class had retired from service by the late 1980s.

Circé

Type: French cruiser
Displacement: 2,784 tonnes (2,740 tons)
Dimensions: 76m x 13.6m x 5.9m (249ft x 44ft 7in x 19ft 4in)
Machinery: Single screw compound engine

Top speed: 11 knots
Main armament: Twenty-four 163mm (6.4 in) guns
Launched: 1860
Date of profile: 1862

Originally laid down as a sailing frigate in April 1850, *Circé* was lengthened amidships while still on the stocks and converted to screw propulsion under the French expansion programme of 1858. Originally she had been intended to carry 46 guns on a gun deck running the full length of the vessel. There were ten other units in the class and all were treated in the same way. *Circé* was completed in 1863 and finally stricken in 1875 after only 12 years' service.

Città di Catania

Type: Italian auxiliary cruiser
Displacement: 3,313 tonnes (3,261 tons)
Dimensions: 110.8m x 12.8m x 5.7m (363ft 6in x 42ft x 18ft 9in)
Machinery: Triple screw turbines
Main armament: Four 120mm (4.7in) guns
Launched: 1910

Città di Catania was built by Ansaldo for the Italian State Railway as a fast passenger liner. Passenger accommodation was situated amidships on the upper deck in a built-up superstructure. She was taken over in World War I as an auxiliary cruiser, and armed with 120mm (4.7in) guns plus two 76mm (3in) weapons. She was handed back to her owners in December 1918. She also served in World War II, as a naval transport, until sunk by a British submarine off Brindisi in August 1943.

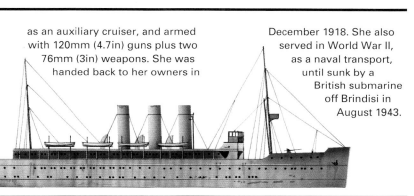

City of Berlin

Type: British liner
Displacement: 5,579 tonnes (5,491 tons)
Dimensions: 149m x 13.4m (489ft x 44ft)
Machinery: Single screw compound engine
Top speed: 15 knots
Launched: 1875

City of Berlin entered service on the North Atlantic in May 1875. She had 202 cabins plus room for 1,500 third-class passengers. In 1879 she had electric light installed, the first vessel to be so fitted. She was given triple expansion engines in 1887. In 1893, she transferred to the American Line as *Berlin*. In the 1898 US war with Spain she became the *Meade*. She was scrapped in 1921.

City of Brussels

Type: British liner
Displacement: 3,130 tonnes (3,081 tons)
Dimensions: 118.8m x 12.2m (390ft x 40ft)
Machinery: Single screw horizontal trunk engines
Launched: 1869

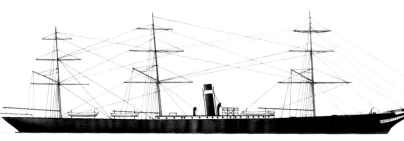

The Inman liner *City of Brussels* was one of the first North Atlantic liners, to have steam steering gear, and in 1876 received compound engines. On 7 January 1883 she was stationary in bad weather 30km (20 miles) off Liverpool when she was hit by the steamer *Kirby Hall*. All but ten of the 167 on board were saved.

City of Glasgow

Type: British liner
Displacement: 1,635 tonnes (1,609 tons)
Dimensions: 69.2m x 10.4m (227ft x 34ft)
Machinery: Single screw geared engines
Top speed: 9 knots
Launched: 1850

City of Glasgow was originally run in the North Atlantic by her builders, the Glasgow firm of Tod and McGregor, but they later sold her to what became the Inman Line. She had a bathroom that used sea water and the main deck had plenty of space with better facilities than those usually found on the sailing packets with which she competed. In March 1854, she vanished en route from Liverpool to Philadelphia.

City of New York

Type: US liner
Displacement: 10,667 tonnes (10,499 tons)
Dimensions: 170.7m x 19m (560ft x 62ft 4in)
Machinery: Twin screw triple expansion engines
Top speed: 21 knots
Launched: March 1888

In 1887, the Inman Line, by now part of the International Navigation Company, had City of New York and City of Paris built in Britain. The former served briefly as the scout Harvard in the Spanish-American War of 1898, and in World War I as the armed transport Plattsburg. She was broken up in 1923.

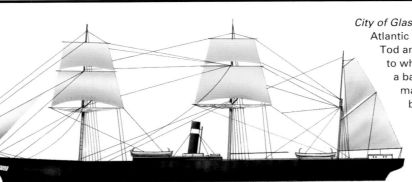

City of Rome

Type: British liner
Displacement: 8,550 tonnes (8,415 tons)
Dimensions: 171m x 15.8m (560ft x 52ft)
Machinery: Single screw compound engines
Top speed: 16 knots
Launched: 1881
Date of profile: 1881

This graceful three-funnelled liner was acclaimed as one of the most beautiful vessels to serve anywhere. She was built by the Barrow Shipbuilding Company for the Inman Line, but upon entering service in 1881 she failed to reach her designed speed and was returned to her builders; they then sold her on to the Anchor Line. City of Rome was designed to carry a mix of 520 first- and second-class passengers plus 810 third-class. There was a large dining saloon forward of the bridge, lavish public rooms, as well as luxurious first-class cabins. City of Rome was scrapped in 1902.

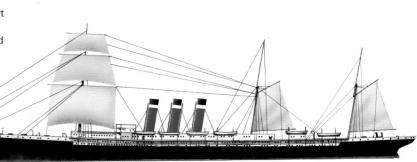

Clan Macalister

Type: British cargo vessel
Displacement: 6,896 tonnes (6,787 tons)
Dimensions: 138m x 19m (453ft 8in x 62ft 3in)
Machinery: Twin screw triple expansion engines
Launched: 1930

This general-purpose cargo liner was built for the Clan Line. In May 1940 she was lying at Southampton when she was commandeered to carry eight landing craft to Dunkirk to assist in the evacuation of British troops. Arriving on 29 May, Clan Macalister unloaded her landing craft and was then, unaccountably, ordered to anchor, making this highly vulnerable vessel a target for German aircraft. She was soon hit and caught fire. Efforts to control the blaze failed, and she was abandoned.

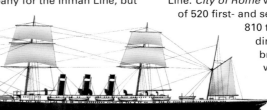

Clémenceau

Type: French battleship
Displacement: 48,260 tonnes (47,500 tons)
Dimensions: 247.9m x 33m x 9.6m (813ft 2in x 108ft 3in x 31ft 7in)
Machinery: Four screws, geared turbines
Main armament: Eight 381mm (15in) guns

Launched: 1943

Clémenceau was one of three French battleships laid down between 1935 and 1939. The others were Richelieu and Jean Bart; a fourth – Gascoigne – was ordered but later cancelled. When France fell, the Germans found Clémenceau's incomplete hull in dock at Brest. When the Allies invaded France, the Germans considered using it to block the harbour entrance, but before this could be done she was sunk during a bombing raid in August 1944. The illustration shows her as she would have looked if completed according to the 1940 plans.

Clémenceau

Type: French aircraft carrier
Displacement: 33,304 tonnes (32,780 tons)
Dimensions: 257m x 46m x 9m (843ft 2in x 150ft x 28ft 3in)
Machinery: Twin screw geared turbines
Main armament: Eight 100mm (3.9in) guns
Aircraft: 40
Launched: December 1957

Clémenceau (R98) and her sister *Foch* (R99) were originally intended as part of class of six fleet carriers, but in the event, only two were built. They were the first French purpose-built carriers, and *Clémenceau* underwent constant modification during design and construction. Changes included an extended flight deck with an 8° angle, new steam catapults, and the sophisticated deck landing aids developed in the 1950s. Enlarged fuel tanks for her air wing also contributed to a significant weight gain, causing more powerful machinery than originally required to be fitted. Her armament was also reduced from that planned. She has served the French Navy well, operating in the Pacific, off the coast of Lebanon, and taking part in the 1991 Gulf War. During her career she has been extensively modernised, with new defensive weapons and command systems added. Her air wing has normally comprised 16 Super Étendards, 3 Étendard IVP, 10 F-8 Crusaders, 7 Alizé, plus helicopters. In recent years she has operated more helicopters at the expense of fixed-wing aircraft. She is due to be replaced by the nuclear-powered *Charles de Gaulle* in the late 1990s.

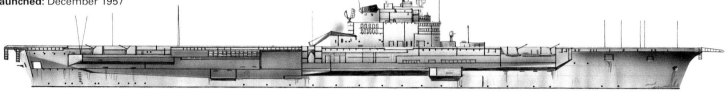

Cleopatra

Type: British transport
Displacement: 274 tonnes (270 tons)
Dimensions: 28m x 4.5m (92ft x 15ft)
Launched: September 1877

Cleopatra was purpose-built to carry 'Cleopatra's Needle' from Alexandria to London. The iron hull had stout bulkheads inside at 3m (10ft) intervals to strengthen the sides, and also to hold the 189-tonne (186-ton), 20m (68ft 6in) long monument securely in place. The crew were housed in a cabin on the upper deck. In late September 1877 *Cleopatra* left Alexandria in tow of the 1,350-tonne (1,329-ton) *Olga*. The two vessels were joined by a 365m (400yd) long, 89mm (3.5in) diameter cable. During a severe storm in the Bay of Biscay a huge wave rolled *Cleopatra* onto her side and the *Olga* was forced to release the tow cable. *Cleopatra*'s crew was rescued by *Olga*, and the foundering vessel was left to her fate. She was eventually towed to Spain by the passing cargo vessel *Fitzmaurice*. In early 1878 *Cleopatra* was finally towed into Britain by the tug *Anglia*, and 'Cleopatra's Needle' was erected on the Thames Embankment in London.

Clermont

Type: US passenger steamship
Displacement: 101 tonnes (100 tons)
Dimensions: 40m x 4m x 0.6m (133ft x 13ft x 2ft)
Machinery: Paddle wheels, single cylinder engine
Top speed: 5 knots
Launched: 1807

Clermont was the first steamboat to achieve commerical success in service. Registered as the *North River Steamboat of Clermont*, she was built to a design by Robert Fulton in the wake of his successful experiments carried out in 1803 on the River Seine in Paris. The diminutive vessel made a successful trial run on the Hudson River on 7 August 1807, and then entered service as a steam packet for the remainder of the 1807 season. *Clermont* continued in service on the Hudson for the next seven years.

Cleveland

Type: British destroyer
Displacement: 1,473 tonnes (1,450 tons)
Dimensions: 85m x 9m x 4m (280ft x 29ft x 12ft 6in)
Machinery: Twin screw turbines
Top speed: 28 knots
Main armament: Four 102mm (4in) guns
Launched: April 1940

In 1938 the worsening world situation caused alarm in Britain, and efforts were made to increase the strength of the navy. However, when World War II broke out Britain was still short of destroyers to escort the Atlantic convoys. By 1940 the Royal Navy decided to put in hand a programme of small destroyers that could be quickly and easily constructed. *Cleveland* was one of the first group of 1,016-tonne (1,000-ton) Hunt class escort destroyers subsequently built. Originally they were designed to carry six 102mm (4in) guns, but this armament proved too top heavy, and the number of guns was reduced to four. Although ballast and stabilisers were added to reduce roll in a seaway, movement was jerky. *Cleveland* was wrecked in June 1957.

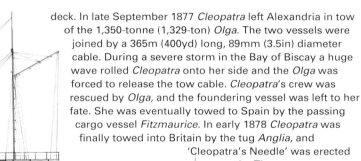

Coatit

Type: Italian cruiser
Displacement: 1,313 tonnes
(1,292 tons)
Dimensions: 92m x 9m x 4m
(300ft 6in x 30ft 6in x 14ft)
Machinery: Twin screw triple
expansion engines
Top speed: 23
knots

Main armament: Twelve 76mm (3in) guns
Launched: November 1899

Coatit was one of a batch of 16 torpedo cruisers built for
the Italian Navy. Her heavy coal consumption
reduced her effective range at high speed, and
she was soon eclipsed by larger cruisers.
Coatit was classified as a scout during
World War I, and in 1919 was fitted out
as a minelayer. She was discarded a
year later.

Cockerill

Type: Belgian cargo boat
Displacement: 2,480 tonnes (2,441 tons)
Dimensions: 88m x 14m (288ft 9in x 45ft)
Machinery: Single screw vertical compound
engine
Top speed: 8 knots
Launched: 1901
Date of profile: 1901

Until 1900, the vast majority of merchant
vessels were sailing ships. With the
completion of *Cockerill* in 1901, the

era of the sailing ship was nearing its end;
Cockerill was a new type of steam cargo
boat soon to be copied by all nations. Her
two major cargo areas were separated
by the boilers and engine room, and
she also carried a light rig to act as
steadying sails. *Cockerill* belonged
to the steamship line of the same
name, and carried
perishables from
Belgium to London.

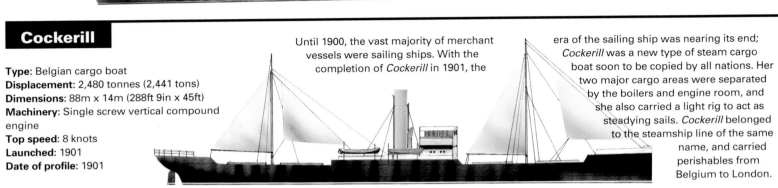

Colbert

Type: French battleship
Displacement: 8,890 tonnes (8,750
tons)
Dimensions: 97m x 17m x 9m (317ft
7in x 57ft 3in x 29ft)
Machinery: Single screw horizontal
return engines
Main armament: Eight 274mm
(10.8in), two 238mm (9.4in), eight

140mm (5.5in) guns
Launched: September 1875

Colbert and her sister ship *Trident*
were the last wooden-hulled French
capital ships. Partly to save coal,
and also to safeguard against
machinery breakdown, *Colbert* was
fully rigged with 2,044sq metres
(22,000sq ft) of sail. She was
removed from the list in 1900.

Collingwood

Type: British battleship
Displacement: 9,652 tonnes (9,500
tons)
Dimensions: 99m x 21m x 8m (324ft
10in x 68ft x 26ft 3in)
Machinery: Twin screw inverted
compound engines
Top speed: 17 knots
Main armament: Four

304mm(12in), six 152mm (6in)
guns
Armour: 203-457mm (8-
18in) waterline belt
Launched: November
1882

Collingwood was the
prototype of

the new British battleship class laid
down in the summer of 1880. Later
units varied, especially in the fitting
of heavier guns, but she was to set
the overall design for
British battleships for
the next 20 years.
A transverse

water chamber was fitted at each
end of the vessel to steady her when
rolling. The main deck ran from end
to end of the hull, upon which were
carried the four heavy guns
mounted in pairs in two barbettes
on the centreline. Because of her
low freeboard, *Collingwood* was
very wet in a seaway. She was
placed in reserve in 1902
and scrapped in 1909.

Colossus

Type: British battleship
Displacement: 23,419 tonnes (23,050
tons)
Dimensions: 166m x 26m x 9m (546ft
x 85ft x 28ft 9in)
Machinery: Four
shaft

turbines
Top speed: 21 knots
Main armament: Ten 304mm
(12in) guns
Launched: April 1910

Colossus and her sister *Hercules*
formed part of the rapid British
naval expansion programme of
1909. She had improved
armour protection over
previous dreadnoughts.
To save weight the
after mast was

omitted, but the foremast, with its
vital fire control centre, was placed
behind the first funnel and suffered
severely from smoke interference.
Colossus was one of the last British
battleships to mount 304mm (12in)
guns; the next major group would
carry the new 343mm (13.5in)
weapons.

Columbia

Type: US cruiser
Displacement: 8,402 tonnes (8,270 tons)
Dimensions: 126m x 18m x 7m (413ft x 58ft x 22ft 7in)

Machinery: Triple srew vertical triple expansion engines
Top speed: 22.8 knots
Main armament: One 203mm (8in), two 152mm (6in) guns

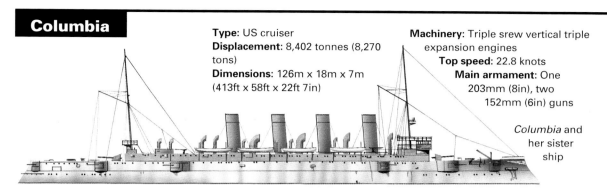

Columbia and her sister ship *Minneapolis* were the only large protected cruisers built for the US Navy during the 1880s and 1890s. They were designed as commerce destroyers and upon completion were among the fastest cruisers in the world. Both ships served during the 1898 war with Spain. *Columbia* was de-commissioned from 1907-1915, when she was recalled. Sold in 1922.

Columbia

Type: British liner
Displacement: 8,424 tonnes (8,292 tons)
Dimensions: 148m x 17m (485ft x 56ft)
Machinery: Twin screw triple expansion engines
Top speed: 16 knots

Launched: 1902

Built for the Anchor line, *Columbia* served on the North Atlantic until World War I, when she was taken over as an armed merchant cruiser and re-named *Columbella*. She was returned to her owners in 1919, became the *Moreas* of the Byron line in 1926, was sold to Greece in 1928, and was scrapped in Italy in 1929.

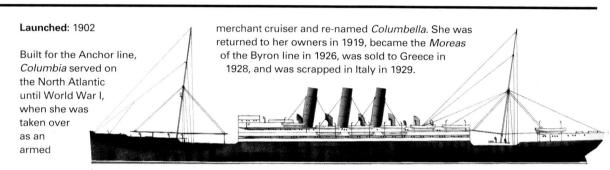

Columbus

Type: German liner
Displacement: 32,871 tonnes (32,354 tons)
Dimensions: 236m x 25m (775ft x 83ft)
Machinery: Twin screw turbines
Launched: August 1922

Columbus was laid down in 1914 for Norddeutscher Lloyd. Construction was halted until 1920, and she was ready for launching in June 1922. By November 1923 she was complete and ready to take her 513 first-class, 574 second-class and 705 third-class passengers on the maiden voyage to New York.

In 1929 new turbines increased her speed to 23 knots. She was scuttled in December 1939 to prevent her capture by the British.

Comet

Type: British steamboat
Displacement: 28 tonnes (28 tons)
Dimensions: 15m x 3.4m x 1.2m (51ft x 11ft 3in x 4ft)
Machinery: Paddle wheels, single cylinder engine
Top speed: 6.7 knots
Launched: July 1812
Date of profile: 1812

Comet was built on the Clyde by John Wood and Company. When first completed she had two small paddle wheels on each side, but later these were replaced by larger wheels which raised her speed from 5 knots to 6.7 knots. *Comet* operated on the Clyde until 1816, when she was transferred to the Firth of Forth. Here she continued her successful career until she ran aground in December 1820 and became a total loss.

Comet

Type: British destroyer
Displacement: 2,575 tonnes (2,535 tons)
Dimensions: 111m x 11m x 4m (362ft 9in x 35ft 8in x 14ft 5in)
Machinery: Twin screw turbines
Top speed: 36.7 knots
Main armament: Four 114mm (4.5in) guns

Launched: June 1944

Comet belonged to a 24-unit class of large destroyers built during World War II. They all followed the same basic pattern, with two guns firing ahead and two aft. There was a single sloping funnel behind the bridge. Additional anti-aircraft guns were added as the vessels entered service, and one of the class, the *Contest*, was the first British destroyer with an all-welded hull. All vessels in the class survived the war. Four went to Norway in 1946, and four were handed over to Pakistan in the 1950s. *Comet* was broken up in 1962.

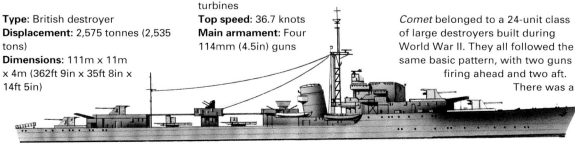

Comète

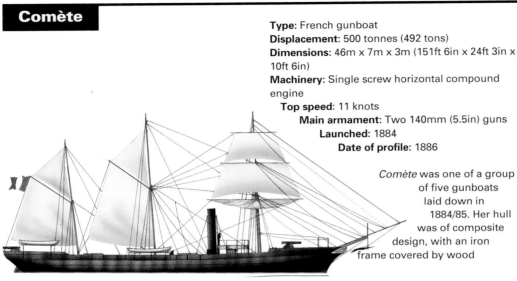

Type: French gunboat
Displacement: 500 tonnes (492 tons)
Dimensions: 46m x 7m x 3m (151ft 6in x 24ft 3in x 10ft 6in)
Machinery: Single screw horizontal compound engine
Top speed: 11 knots
Main armament: Two 140mm (5.5in) guns
Launched: 1884
Date of profile: 1886

Comète was one of a group of five gunboats laid down in 1884/85. Her hull was of composite design, with an iron frame covered by wood

planking. This was a cheap method of construction which also enabled repairs to be carried out in far-flung colonial stations without proper dock facilities. She had a single coal-fired engine which only developed some 500hp, so great reliance was placed on her sails. Her 140mm (5.5in) main guns were muzzle loaders, and were supplemented by two 100mm (3.9in) guns and a pair of machine guns. Gunboats of *Comète*'s type played a useful policing role in French colonial possessions. Although lightly armed, they were powerful enough to deal with most native unrest. They were also valuable training vessels for the navy. If conflict with a major power had broken out, most of the boats of this type would have been laid up and their crews sent to man larger deep-sea vessels. *Comète* was stricken in 1909.

Commandant de Rose

Type: French steam schooner
Displacement: 3,556 tonnes (3,500 tons)
Dimensions: 85m x 14m x 7m (280ft x 45ft 6in x 23ft)
Machinery: Twin screw triple expansion engines
Top speed: Not recorded (about 10 knots)
Launched: July 1918

Commandant de Rose was one of 40 wooden schooners ordered from a major US shipbuilder by France during World War I. They were five-masted vessels with a pair of small auxiliary steam engines. *Commandant de Rose* and her sisters proved commercial failures, but had the war continued into 1919, the vessels would have realised their worth. *Commandant de Rose* was scrapped in 1923.

Commandant Teste

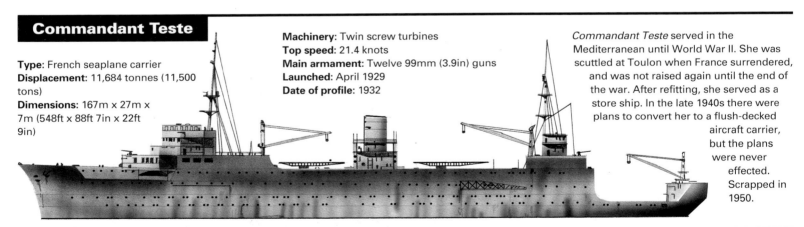

Type: French seaplane carrier
Displacement: 11,684 tonnes (11,500 tons)
Dimensions: 167m x 27m x 7m (548ft x 88ft 7in x 22ft 9in)

Machinery: Twin screw turbines
Top speed: 21.4 knots
Main armament: Twelve 99mm (3.9in) guns
Launched: April 1929
Date of profile: 1932

Commandant Teste served in the Mediterranean until World War II. She was scuttled at Toulon when France surrendered, and was not raised again until the end of the war. After refitting, she served as a store ship. In the late 1940s there were plans to convert her to a flush-decked aircraft carrier, but the plans were never effected. Scrapped in 1950.

Comus

Type: British cruiser
Displacement: 2,418 tonnes (2,380 tons)
Dimensions: 68m x 14m x 5.8m (225ft x 44ft 6in x 19ft 3in)
Machinery: Single screw horizontal compound engines
Top speed: 12.9 knots
Main armament: Four 152mm (6in) guns
Launched: April 1878

Comus was the first cruiser in the Royal Navy to adopt the Italian method of armour – a 38mm (1.5in) thick protective deck placed some metres below the waterline. *Comus* was ship rigged, and her class were the first cruisers of less than 3,048 tonnes (3,000 tons) to be given metal hulls. They were either iron- or steel-framed, with steel plating and timber cladding up to the upper deck. *Comus* was scrapped in 1904.

Condé

Two 193mm (7.6in), eight 162mm (6.4in) guns
Armour: 58-152mm (2.3-6in) waterline belt
Launched: March 1902

Condé was a logical follow-on from the successful *Jeanne D'Arc*, laid down in 1896 and based upon

a concept of Admiral Fournier who advocated the use of large, well protected vessels against the commerce of an enemy. There was extensive waterline protection, and two armoured decks bonded the upper and lower edges of the belt, forming an armoured box. *Condé* was broken up in 1933.

Type: French cruiser
Displacement: 10,396 tonnes (10,233 tons)
Dimensions: 140m x 20m x 8m (458ft 8in x 66ft 3in x 25ft 2in)
Machinery: Triple screw vertical triple expansion engines
Top speed: 21.5 knots
Main armament:

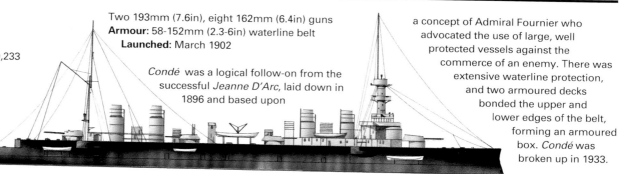

Confienza

Type: Italian cruiser
Displacement: 984 tonnes (969 tons)
Dimensions: 73m x 8m x 3m (240ft 9in x 26ft 5in x 10ft)
Machinery: Twin screw double expansion engines
Top speed: 17 knots
Main armament: One 120mm (4.7in) gun

Confienza formed part of a group of experimental steel-hulled cruisers designed to fill the gap between the smaller torpedo cruiser and the standard 3,048-tonne (3,000-ton) cruiser. All vessels in the group had different equipment and hull

forms, and all reached 18 knots on trials, with the exception of *Confienza*. As well as a light fore-and-aft rig, *Confienza* also had six 57mm

(2.2in) guns and five 355mm (14in) torpedo tubes. She was discarded in 1901.

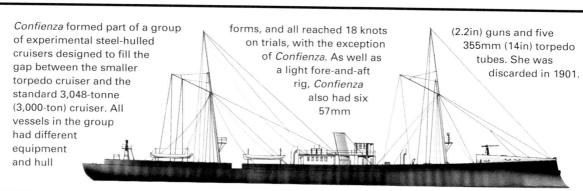

Confienza

Type: Italian destroyer
Displacement: 1,093 tonnes (1,076 tons)
Dimensions: 82m x 8m x 3m (268ft 8in x 26ft 3in x 9ft 2in)
Machinery: Twin screw turbines
Main armament: Four 102mm (4in) guns
Launched: December 1920

One of a class of four vessels that were an improved version of the *Audace* launched in 1913. In 1938 all vessels in *Confienza*'s class were re-classified as torpedo boats, but plans to revise the

armament were never followed through. The smaller weapons carried included two 76mm (3in) anti-aircraft guns plus two machine guns and four 450mm (17.7in)

torpedo tubes. Three of the group were war losses, while *Confienza* was sunk in collision with the naval auxiliary vessel *Capitano Cecchi* off Brindisi on 20 November 1940.

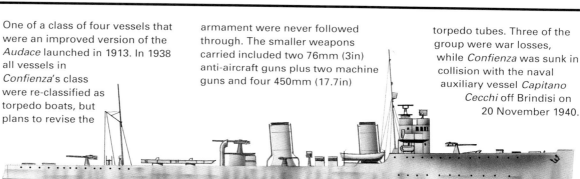

Connecticut

Type: US battleship
Displacement: 17,948 tonnes (17,666 tons)
Dimensions: 140m x 23m x 7m (456ft 4in x 76ft 10in x 24ft 6in)
Machinery: Twin screw vertical triple expansion engines
Main armament: Four 305mm (12in), eight 203mm (8in) and twelve

178mm (7in) guns
Launched: September 1904

Part of a six-strong class, *Connecticut* was an enlarged

version of the previous Virginia class and repeated the use of three different calibres

for the main armament, except that the 152mm (6in) weapons were updated to 178mm (7in). *Connecticut* compared very favourably with British and Japanese capital ships of the same period.

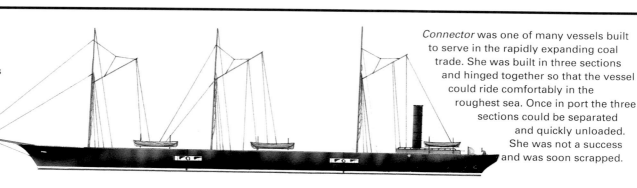

Connector

Type: British cargo vessel
Displacement: 2,032 tonnes (2,000 tons)
Dimensions: 52m x 9m (170ft x 30ft)
Machinery: Single screw compound engines
Launched: 1852

Connector was one of many vessels built to serve in the rapidly expanding coal trade. She was built in three sections and hinged together so that the vessel could ride comfortably in the roughest sea. Once in port the three sections could be separated and quickly unloaded. She was not a success and was soon scrapped.

Conqueror

Type: British battleship
Displacement: 6,299 tonnes (6,200 tons)
Dimensions: 88m x 18m x 7m (288ft x 58ft x 23ft 6in)
Machinery: Twin screw inverted compound engines
Main armament: Two 305mm (12in) guns

Armour: 203-305mm (8-12in) waterline belt, 280mm (11in) on turret
Launched: September 1881

Conqueror was an unusual design that combined the gun with the ram. She and her sister *Hero* were larger versions of

the Rams of the 1870s. *Conqueror* was the last coast defence vessel built for the Royal Navy and proved too small for ocean-going operations. She was broken up in 1907, while her sister *Hero* was sunk as a gunnery target the following year.

Conqueror

Type: British battleship
Displacement: 26,284 tonnes (25,870 tons)
Dimensions: 177m x 27m x 9m (581ft x 88ft 7in x 28ft)
Machinery: Quadruple shaft turbines
Top speed: 21 knots
Main armament: Ten 342mm (13.5 in) guns
Armour: 203-305

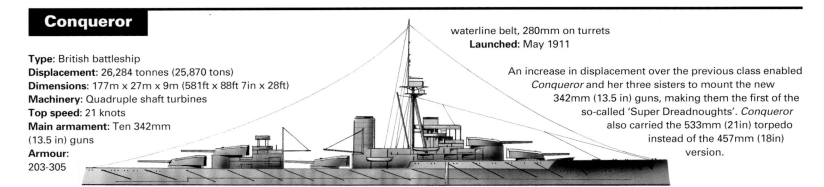

waterline belt, 280mm on turrets
Launched: May 1911

An increase in displacement over the previous class enabled *Conqueror* and her three sisters to mount the new 342mm (13.5 in) guns, making them the first of the so-called 'Super Dreadnoughts'. *Conqueror* also carried the 533mm (21in) torpedo instead of the 457mm (18in) version.

Constitution

Type: US sailing frigate
Displacement: 2,236 tonnes (2,200 tons)
Dimensions: 53m x 13m x 4m (175ft x 43ft 6in x 14ft 3in)
Top speed: 13 knots
Main armament: Twenty-eight 24-pounders, ten 12-pounders
Launched: October 1797

Constitution was designed by Joshua Humphreys and built at Boston. Commissioned in 1798, she served in the war against France, and in 1799 captured two privateers. She was then taken out of service, but with the outbreak of a new conflict against the Barbary pirates in 1803, *Constitution* was recommissioned. In 1812 she narrowly avoided

capture by the British, and then underwent extensive repairs from 1812-15. She was rebuilt in 1833, 1871-77, 1906 and again in 1927-30. Numerous plans to scrap the ship were thwarted by popular demand, and *Constitution* is now stationed at Boston. She is the oldest commissioned warship afloat.

Conte Biancamano

Type: Italian liner
Displacement: 24,806 tonnes (24,416 tons)
Dimensions: 199m x 23m (652ft 7in x 76ft)
Machinery: Twin screw turbines
Top speed: 21 knots
Launched: April 1925

Conte Biancamano was one of a number of large Italian liners built in Britain during the 1920s for service on the North Atlantic route. She was a spacious vessel and could carry 280 first-, 420 second-, 390 third- and 660 fourth-class passengers,

plus a crew of 500. In 1941 she was seized by the US and became the navy transport *Hermitage*. In 1947 she was returned to Italy. After re-

fitting she served on the South Atlantic route until she was broken up in 1960.

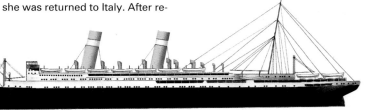

Conte di Cavour

Type: Italian battleship
Displacement: 29,496 tonnes (29,032 tons)
Dimensions: 186m x 28m x 9m (611ft 6in x 91ft 10in x 30ft)
Machinery: Twin screw turbines
Top speed: 28.2 knots

Main armament: Ten 320mm (12.6in), twelve 120mm (4.7in) guns
Launched: October 1911

Conte di Cavour was designed in 1908 as an improved version of the *Dante Alighieri*. Completed in 1914, *Conte di Cavour* was extensively rebuilt between 1933 and 1937 and emerged as a virtually new ship. She had new machinery and her hull was

lengthened. Sunk at Taranto by torpedoes fired from British aircraft, *Conte di Cavour* was later refloated and towed to Trieste. She was rebuilt but was captured by the Germans in September 1943, and eventually sunk during an air raid in 1945. Her wreckage was broken up at the end of World War II.

Conte di Savoia

Type: Italian liner
Displacement: 49,278 tonnes (48,502 tons)
Dimensions: 248.3m x 30m (814ft 8in x 96ft 2in)
Machinery: Quadruple screw turbines
Top speed: 29.5 knots
Launched: October 1931
Date of profile: 1932

By the beginning of the 1930s, tourist traffic across the Atlantic had increased enormously.

Germany, France and Great Britain all introduced large luxury ocean liners within the space of a few years, and Italy was not slow to follow. *Conte di Savoia* and her near-sister *Rex* began serving on the Atlantic route in 1932. At that time they were the largest merchant ships built in Italy, and were also the first liners specifically designed to win the coveted Blue Riband, awarded to the fastest crossing of the Atlantic. *Conte di Savoia* was able to carry up to 2,060 passengers, and was operated by a crew of 750. Her passenger accommodation was sumptuous, a special feature being the large colonna hall, which was nearly 7.3m

(24ft) high, and had an area of over 560sq.m (6,028sq ft). She was also equipped with a gyro-driven stabiliser, the first to be fitted to so large a ship. She worked the Genoa to New York route from 1932, but was laid up in 1939. She remained in dock until September 1943, when she was set on fire and eventually sunk by Allied bombing. In 1946 she was raised to the surface, and serious consideration was given to restoration. In the end this was thought to be too expensive, and she was broken up in 1950.

Conte Grande

Type: Italian liner
Displacement: 26,071 tonnes (25,661 tons)
Dimensions: 200m x 23m (654ft 10in x 76ft)
Machinery: Twin screw turbines
Launched: June 1927

Conte Grande was designed to carry 578 first-, 420 second- and 720 third-class passengers, plus 532 crew. She

began service on the Genoa-New York run, and joined the Italia Line in 1932 for service on the South American route. *Conte Grande* was laid up in Brazil

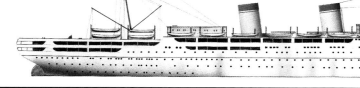

when Italy entered World War II in 1940, and was sold to the US government in 1942. They re-named her *Monticello* and used her as a troop transport. She returned to Italy in 1947, resumed her old name and

underwent an extensive re-fit. In 1949 she was back on the South American run, and until 1956 was used on the New York route during the summer months. She was broken up in 1961.

Conte Verde

Type: Italian liner
Displacement: 19,065 tonnes (18,765 tons)
Dimensions: 170m x 23m (559ft 5in x 74ft 2in)
Machinery: Twin screw turbines
Top speed: 20 knots
Launched: October 1922

Conte Verde was a graceful vessel with

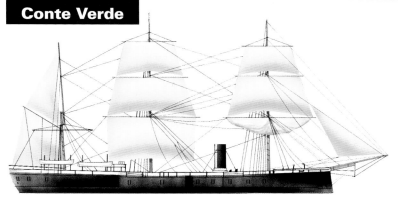

Type: Italian battleship
Displacement: 3,928 tonnes (3,866 tons)
Dimensions: 74m x 15m x 6.5m (241ft 10in x 50ft x 21ft 4in)
Machinery: Single screw single expansion engine
Main armament: Eighteen 160-pounders, four 72-pounders
Launched: July 1867

Conte Verde was an unusual wooden-hulled broadside battleship

in that only parts of the bow and stern were armoured with iron plates, the rest of the hull being protected by thick wooden timbers. She was one of a group of three vessels originally laid down as frigates, but converted into ironclads while still on the stocks. *Conte Verde*'s armament was altered to six 254mm (10in) guns and one 203mm (8in) gun on or near her completion in 1871. She was discarded in 1880 and scrapped in 1898.

Conte Verde

accommodation for 230 first-, 290 second- and 1,880 third-class passengers, plus 440 crew. Her maiden voyage was between Genoa and Buenos Aires, and she transferred to the New York route in June

1923. In 1926 she transferred back to the La Plata ports in South America, and joined the Italia fleet in early 1932. From 1940 to 1942 she was laid up at Shanghai, and then made a few voyages as a prisoner-of-war exchange ship between China and

Japan on charter to the Japanese government. In 1943 Italy withdrew from the Axis, and *Conte Verde* was scuttled to prevent her capture by the Japanese. They raised her, and after re-fitting in Japan, she was used as a troop transport. She was sunk by US forces in 1944, the wreck raised in 1949, and scrapped in 1951.

Corallo

Type: Italian submarine
Displacement: 707 tonnes (696 tons) (surface), 865 tonnes (852 tons) (submerged)
Dimensions: 60m x 6.5m x 5m 9197ft

5in x 21ft 2in x 15ft 3in)
Machinery: Twin screw diesel (surface), electric motors (submerged)

Main armament: One 100mm (3.9in) gun, six 533mm (21in) torpedo tubes
Launched: August 1936
Date of profile: 1941

Corallo was a short-range submarine of the ten-strong Perla class. All submarines in the class took an active part in the Spanish Civil War, where two were ceded to the Nationalist forces for several months. They also took an active role in World War II, carrying out lengthy patrols and sinking the British cruiser *Bonaventure*. Five of the class were lost to enemy action. *Corallo* was sunk off Bougie on 13 December 1942 by the British sloop *Enchantress*.

Cormorant

Type: British gunboat
Displacement: 891 tonnes (877 tons)
Dimensions: 56m x 8.5m x 3.6m (185ft x 28ft 2in x 12ft)
Machinery: Single screw reciprocating engines
Top speed: 10 knots
Main armament: One 110-pounder, one 68-pounder
Launched: February 1860

The wooden-hulled *Cormorant* was designed to provide the fire-power of two vessels, but her deep draught limited her use in very shallow waters. Her crew numbered around 90. *Cormorant's* armament was later changed to one 178mm (7in) muzzle-loader. She was broken up in 1870.

Cornwall

Type: British cruiser
Displacement: 10,007 tonnes (9,850 tons)
Dimensions: 192m x 21m x 5m (630ft x 68ft 4in x 16ft 3in)
Machinery: Four shaft turbines

Top speed: 34 knots
Main armament: Eight 203mm (8in) guns, four 102mm (4in) anti-aircraft guns
Armour: 38-76mm (1.5-3in) protected deck over vitals
Launched: March 1926

Cornwall was built for operations in the Pacific, and

had good range and seakeeping qualities. In early 1941 she sank the German raider *Pinguin*. On 4 April 1942 *Cornwall*, together with another cruiser, left Colombo. On the following day they were without air protection when a wave of Japanese dive bombers attacked them. Both ships were sunk with heavy loss of life.

Coronel Bolognesi

Type: Peruvian cruiser
Displacement: 3,251 tonnes (3,200 tons)
Dimensions: 116m x 12m x 4m (380ft x 40ft 4in x 14ft)
Machinery: Twin screw triple expansion engines
Top speed: 24.6 knots
Main armament: Two 152mm (6in) guns
Launched: November 1906
Date of profile: 1908

Coronel Bolognesi and her sister *Almirante Grau* were named after Peruvian heroes of the war against Chile in 1879-83. During *Coronel Bolognesi*'s delivery trip her boilers were allowed to run dry, causing extensive damage. Both vessels underwent extensive re-

fitting between 1923 and 1925. One of the longest-serving warships in the world, *Coronel Bolognesi* was stricken from the Peruvian Navy list in 1958.

Coronel Bolognesi

Type: Peruvian destroyer
Displacement: 3,150 tonnes (3,100 tons)
Dimensions: 116m x 12m x 5m (380ft 7in x 38ft 5in x 17ft)
Machinery: Twin screw turbines
Top speed: 36 knots
Main armament: Four 120mm (4.7in)

guns
Launched: August 1955
Date of profile: 1984

Coronel Bolognesi was formerly one of the Freisland class of

destroyers built in Holland for the Royal Dutch Navy. They constituted the backbone of the Dutch anti-submarine groups

until the late 1970s, when they were replaced by the newer Standaard class frigate. Between 1980 and 1982 the former class were transferred to the Peruvian Navy, who planned to fit them out with Exocet missiles and other new weapons systems and sensors. *Coronel Bolognesi* arrived in Peru in July 1982 for another long spell of service.

Corrientes

Type: Argentinian destroyer
Displacement: 284 tonnes (280 tons)
Dimensions: 58m x 6m x 2m (190ft x 19ft 6in x 7ft 4in)
Machinery: Twin screw triple expansion engines

Main armament: One 14-pounder, three 6-pounders, three 457mm (18in) torpedo tubes
Launched: 1896

This type of ship was an attempt to

protect battleships from the threat posed by torpedo boats. In 1893 Yarrow built the *Havock*, the forerunner of all later destroyer types. Argentina, quick to appreciate its qualities and, seeing it as the answer to the torpedo craft used by other South American navies, ordered four from Yarrow. *Corrientes* was taken off the effective list in 1925.

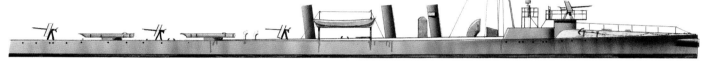

Corsican

Type: British liner
Displacement: 11,619 tonnes (11,436 tons)
Dimensions: 157m x 19m (516ft x 61ft 4in)
Machinery: Twin screw triple expansion engines

Top speed: 16 knots
Launched: April 1907

Corsican was completed in November 1907 with accommodation for 208

first-, 298 second- and 1,000 third-class passengers. In 1912 she collided with an iceberg, but was only slightly

damaged. She plied the Glasgow-Montreal route in 1914, but was taken over as a troop transport when World War I broke out. Re-named *Marvale*, she was fitted out as a cabin class vessel for the Canadian Pacific Line in 1922. In 1923 she was stranded on Freel Rock off Cape Race and became a loss.

Cosmao

Type: French cruiser
Displacement: 1,954 tonnes (1,923 tons)
Dimensions: 95m x 9m x 5m (311ft 8in x 29ft 6in x 17ft)
Machinery: Twin screw horizontal compound engines
Main armament: Four 140mm (5.5 in) guns
Launched: 1889

Cosmao and her two sisters had three sharply raked masts and two funnels. The guns were closely grouped amidships on sponsons, and had a good field of fire. Upon completion, *Cosmao* had four 355mm (14in) torpedo tubes, but these were later removed. There were also four 3-pounders and four 1-pounder machine guns. *Cosmao* could also carry 150 mines. All three vessels were good sea boats, but suffered from excessive vibration above 20 knots. *Cosmao* was broken up in 1922.

Cossack

Type: British cruiser
Displacement: 1,981 tonnes (1,950 tons)
Dimensions: 73m x 11m x 4.5m (240ft x 36ft x 14ft 6in)
Machinery: Twin screw horizontal compound direct-acting engines
Main armament: Six 152mm (6in) guns
Launched: June 1886

Cossack and her seven sisters were modified versions of the small Scout class cruiser, with increased dimensions enabling a main battery of six 152mm (6in) guns to be carried. In service they were good sea boats, but tended to pitch badly in a heavy sea. *Cossack* was completed in 1889 and saw extensive service as a third-class cruiser until she was sold in 1905.

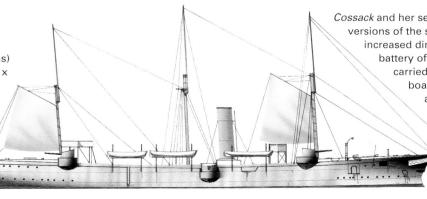

Courageous

Type: British aircraft carrier
Displacement: 26,517 tonnes (26,100 tons)
Dimensions: 240m x 27m x 8m (786ft 5in x 90ft 6in x 27ft 3in)
Machinery: Quadruple screw turbines
Top speed: 31.5 knots
Main armament: Sixteen 120mm (4.7in) guns
Aircraft carried: 48
Launched: February 1916
Date of profile: 1937

Courageous and her sister *Glorious* were completed in 1917 as fast cruisers for World War I service in the Baltic. They were heavily armed with four 380mm (15in) guns, but had very little armour. By the 1920s, Britain was anxious to increase her carrier strength, so both vessels, together with their near sister *Furious*, were converted to aircraft carriers. The conversion of *Courageous* was completed in March 1928. Her superstructure and armament were removed and replaced by an aircraft hangar running almost the full length of the ship. The forward 18m (59ft) of this hangar was an open deck, which could be used to fly off slow flying aircraft such as Swordfish. Above this was an open flight deck, with two large elevators set into it. She had a small navigation and operating island on the starboard side of the flightdeck, which also held the funnel updraughts. All three ships served through the 1930s, and formed the backbone of the British carrier force at the outbreak of World War II. In the opening days of the war, *Courageous* was torpedoed and sunk by *U-20*. *Glorious* was sunk in June 1940 by *Scharnhorst* and *Gneisenau*, while *Furious* survived the war, being scrapped in 1948.

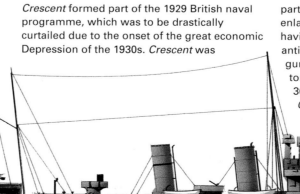

Courbet

Type: French battleship
Displacement: 9,855 tonnes (9,700 tons)
Dimensions: 95m x 20m x 7.6m (312ft x 67ft x 25ft)
Machinery: Twin screw vertical compound engines
Top speed: 15 knots
Main armament: Four 340mm (13.4in), four 266mm (10.5in) guns
Launched: April 1882
Date of profile: 1890

The largest central battery ships ever built, *Courbet* and her sister *Dévastation* were laid down by the French immediately after the Franco-Prussian War of 1870 in order to strengthen the navy. They were powerful fighting units and were usually handy. Two funnels set side-by-side rose up through the main battery. By the 1890s *Courbet*'s rig had been modified, with each mast carrying two fighting tops. She was removed from the navy list in 1910.

Couronne

Type: French battleship
Displacement: 6,173 tonnes (6,076 tons)
Dimensions: 80m x 17m x 8m (262ft 5in x 54ft 9in x 27ft)
Machinery: Single screw horizontal return engines
Top speed: 13 knots
Main armament: Thirty 163mm (6.4in) guns
Launched: March 1861
Date of profile: 1863

Couronne was the first iron-hulled capital ship to be laid down. Upon completion in 1862 she proved a better seaboat than her wooden-hulled contemporaries, and she was still afloat some 70 years after her launch. She underwent several armament changes during her career, and in 1885 she became a gunnery training ship, having had all her armour removed. *Couronne* was hulked in 1910, and was still afloat in the 1930s.

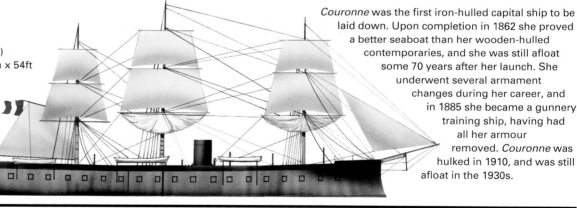

Crescent

Type: British destroyer
Displacement: 1,927 tonnes (1,897 tons)
Dimensions: 97m x 10m x 3m (317ft 9in x 33ft x 8ft 6in)
Machinery: Twin screw turbines
Top speed: 36.4 knots
Main armament: Four 120mm (4.7in) guns
Launched: September 1931
Date of profile: 1932

Crescent formed part of the 1929 British naval programme, which was to be drastically curtailed due to the onset of the great economic Depression of the 1930s. *Crescent* was part of the C and D classes, which were slightly enlarged versions of the B class destroyer, having increased fuel capacity and a 76mm (3in) anti-aircraft gun, as well as the 120mm (4.7in) guns. *Crescent* also had eight 533mm (21in) torpedo tubes. The machinery developed 36,000hp for a designed speed of 35.5 knots. *Crescent* was transferred to the Royal Canadian Navy in 1937, and was sunk in a collision on 25 June 1940.

Cretecable

Type: British tug
Displacement: 266 tonnes (262 tons)
Dimensions: 38m x 8.5m x 4m
(125ft x 27ft 6in x 13ft 4in)
Machinery: Single screw triple
expansion engines
Top speed: 10 knots
Launched: July 1919
Date of profile: 1919

Due to the shortage of materials at the end of World War I, it was decided to use ferro-concrete in the construction of tugs and small transports. There was also a shortage of skilled labour, but it was found that concrete ships could be built by largely unskilled labour in new, open sites and so the British Admiralty put in hand a

comprehensive programme of new tugs and barges. *Cretecable* was completed four months after her launch and proved successful in trials. Unfortunately her career was brief, as she was wrecked in October 1920.

Cricket

Type: US gunboat
Displacement: 180 tonnes (178 tons)
Dimensions: 47m x 8.5m x 1.2m (154ft x
28ft 2in x 4ft)
Machinery: Stern wheel paddle compound
engine
Top speed: 6 knots
Armament: Six 24-pounder
howitzers

Launched: 1856

Cricket, a small river steamer, was purchased by the Union Navy in November 1862 and converted by January 1863. She patrolled the Mississippi and captured the last two Confederate army transports in the Little Red River area. She narrowly escaped capture herself in 1864, and was sold in 1865.

Cricket

Type: British river gunboat
Displacement: 655 tonnes (645 tons)
Dimensions: 72m x 11m x 1.2m (237ft 6in x 36ft x 4ft)
Machinery: Twin screw triple expansion engines
Top speed: 14 knots
Main armament: Two 152mm (6in) guns
Launched: 1916
Date of profile: 1917

In 1915 twelve large gunboats were ordered from Yarrow, who designed and built them. The shallow draught was achieved by placing the propellers in 'tunnels', and the vessels were well armed for their displacement. *Cricket* formed part of the Insect class, and was intended for service on China's rivers. However, initially she served off the east coast of Britain as part of the country's defence against persistent airship attacks during World War I. Later she was sent to Russia for service on the Dvina River. *Cricket* was towed to the Mediterranean in 1920, but was laid up in Port Said in 1941 after being damaged in a bombing raid.

Cristóbal Colon

Type: Spanish armoured cruiser
Displacement: 8,100 tonnes (7,972 tons)
Dimensions: 111.7m x 18m x 7m
(366ft 8in x 59ft 10in x 23ft 4in)
Machinery: Twin screw vertical triple
expansion engines
Top speed: 20 knots
Main armament: Two 254mm (10in),

ten 152mm (6in) and six 120mm
(4.7in) guns
Launched: 1896

During the 1890s Spain was expanding her navy and purchased many vessels then under construction in Europe. Italy

supplied the armoured cruiser *Giuseppe Garibaldi* and she was re-named *Cristóbal Colon*. In action with US forces in July 1898 she was run ashore after escaping from *Santiago de Cuba*. She later slid into deep water before she could be salvaged.

Cristoforo Colombo

Type: Italian cruiser
Displacement: 2,362 tonnes (2,325 tons)
Dimensions: 75m x 11m x 5m (248ft 5in x
37ft x 17ft 2in)
Machinery: Single screw
reciprocating engine
Main armament: Eight 120mm
(4.7in) guns

Launched: September 1875

In February 1873 the first modern cruiser was laid down for the Italian Navy at the Venice Naval Dockyard to the plans of Benedetto Brin. She was named *Cristoforo Colombo* and was a graceful wooden-hulled, barquentine-rigged vessel. She was completed during November 1875 and was discarded in 1891.

Cristoforo Colombo

Launched: September 1892

Type: Italian cruiser
Displacement: 2,756 tonnes (2,713 tons)
Dimensions: 76m x 11m x 5.7m (250ft 8in x 37ft x 18ft 8in)
Machinery: Single screw reciprocating engine
Main armament: Eight 120mm (4.7in) guns

This ship is often listed as a rebuilt version of the 1875 *Cristoforo Colombo*. In fact she is a duplicate steel-hulled vessel, laid down in September 1890. She was intended as a station ship for the Red Sea, and was barque rigged with a copper-sheathed hull. She was discarded in early 1907.

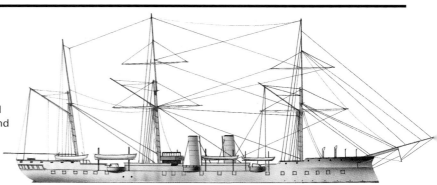

Cunene

Type: Portuguese cargo vessel
Displacement: 8,966 tonnes (8,825 tons)
Dimensions: 137m x 17.6m x 7.7m (450ft x 58ft x 25ft 3in)
Machinery: Single screw

triple expansion engine
Top speed: 12 knots
Launched: 1911
Date of profile: 1917

At the end of World War I all German merchant vessels over 1,625 tonnes (1,600 tons) were seized by the Allies. *Cunene*, formerly the *Adelaide*, was taken over by Portugal in 1916 and saw service until 1925. After five years of idleness, she was brought back into service in 1930. She was scrapped in 1955.

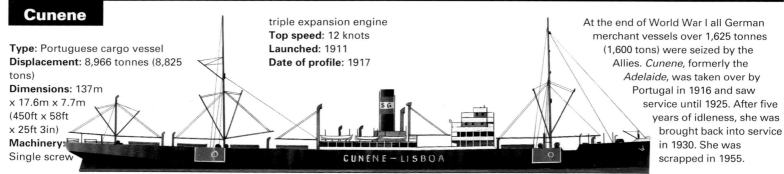

Curacoa

Type: British cruiser
Displacement: 5,100 tonnes (5,020 tons)
Dimensions: 137m x 13m x 4.5m (450ft 2in x 43ft 8in x 14ft 9in)
Machinery: Twin screw turbines
Top speed: 29 knots
Main

armament: Five 152mm (6in) guns
Launched: 1917

Curacoa was part of a group of new Cardiff-class cruisers built under the aegis of Britain's 1916 Emergency War Programme. In early 1939 she was converted into an anti-aircraft cruiser and had her 152mm (6in) guns replaced with eight 102mm (4in) anti-aircraft weapons. In October 1942 the liner *Queen Mary*, in her wartime role as a troopship, was being escorted across the Atlantic by *Curacoa* when she thought she detected a submarine nearby. The 81,280-tonne (80,000-ton) liner took evasive action just as *Curacoa* was about to cross her bows and, unable to avoid a collision, the cruiser was cut in two with the loss of 338 lives.

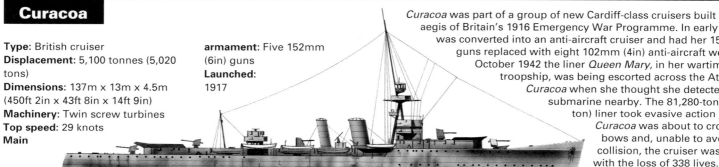

Curlew

Type: British gunboat
Displacement: 965 tonnes (950 tons)
Dimensions: 60m x 8.5m x 3m (195ft x 28ft x 10ft 6in)
Machinery: Twin screw horizontal direct acting compound engines
Top speed: 14.5 knots
Main armament: One 152mm (6in),

three 127mm (5in) guns
Launched: October 1885

Classified as first-class gun vessels, *Curlew* and her sister *Landrail* were the last of the old-style gunboats that had filled the British Navy lists over

the years. *Curlew* was a steel-hulled vessel with fine lines and a relatively shallow draught. Unfortunately, *Curlew* and her sister proved unsuitable as gunboats and were too slow to be cruisers. *Curlew* served in British waters until she was sold in 1906.

Curtatone

Launched: August 1888

Type: Italian gunboat
Displacement: 1,292 tonnes (1,272 tons)
Dimensions: 54m x 10m x 4.5m (177ft 2in x 32ft 10in x 14ft 10in)
Machinery: Single screw compound engine
Main armament: Four 120mm (4.7in) guns

Steel-hulled, three-masted and barque-rigged, *Curtatone* was a typical small gunboat of the period, built to police overseas possessions and supply trained crew for larger warships. The three boilers developed just over 1,000hp, though during cruises reliance was usually placed on sail power alone.

Cushing

Type: US torpedo boat
Displacement: 118 tonnes (116 tons)
Dimensions: 42m x 4.5m x 1.5m
(140ft x 15ft 1in x 4ft 10in)
Machinery: Twin screw vertical
quadruple expansion engines
Top speed: 23 knots
Main armament: Three 457mm
(18in) torpedo tubes, three 6-
pounders
Launched: January 1890
Date of profile: 1890

By the 1870s, the self-propelled torpedo had become accepted as an effective weapon of naval warfare. Most of the major powers had small, fast torpedo boats in service, although the Americans didn't follow suit until somewhat later. *Cushing* was the US Navy's first true purpose-designed torpedo boat, and she was not laid down until April 1888. She was built by the Herreshoff company, and unlike *Stiletto*, her wooden-hulled predecessor, she was built of steel. *Cushing* had a long, slim hull with a curved deck and an anachronistic ram bow. She was designed with a low silhouette, and had two conning towers, one at each end, and two widely spaced funnels. Once in service, *Cushing* was used initially on experimental torpedo development work at the Newport Naval Torpedo Station. In 1897, once the technology was regarded as being well proven, she was used as a despatch boat off the coast of Cuba. She saw active service during the American war with Spain in 1898. In a single action in the August of that year, she came across and captured four small Spanish transports. After the war she returned to Newport, where she eventually ended up as a target hulk. She was finally sunk in September 1920. *Cushing* was the first in a long line of US torpedo boats and fast attack craft.

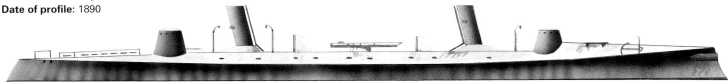

Cushing

Type: US destroyer
Displacement: 7,924 tonnes (7,800
tons)
Dimensions: 161m x 17m x 9m
(529ft 2in x 55ft 1in x 28ft 10in)
Machinery: Twin screw gas turbines
Top speed: 30 knots
Main armament: Two 127mm (5in)
guns, six 322mm (12.75in) torpedo
tubes
Launched: June 1978

Cushing and her 30 sister ships formed the largest destroyer class built by any western navy since World War II, and were developed as replacements for the large number of existing general-purpose destroyers then reaching the end of active service.

Designed as anti-submarine vessels, the Cushing class also carry two

helicopters each, plus the effective rapid-fire Phalanx for air defence, and Harpoon and Sparrow missiles. The ships of the class were the first US Navy surface vessels to be fitted with gas turbines. Designed top speed using both engines is in excess of 30 knots, while one engine can achieve 19 knots.

Custoza

Type: Austrian battleship
Displacement: 7,730 tonnes (7,609
tons)
Dimensions: 95m x 17.6m x 8m
(311ft 8in x 58ft x 26ft)
Machinery: Single screw
horizontal compound engines
Top speed: 13.7 knots
Main armament: Eight
260mm (10.2in), six 89mm
(3.5in) guns
Launched: August 1872
Date of profile: 1878

Custoza was the second Austrian iron-hulled capital ship and was designed to make effective use of the ram. She was one of the largest central battery ships ever built, and had a long career. In 1877 her full rig was reduced, and in the early 1880s additional smaller weapons were added, plus three 350mm (13.8in) torpedo tubes. *Custoza* was converted into a barracks ship in 1914. In 1920 she was handed over to Italy and scrapped soon after.

Cutty Sark

Type: British clipper
Displacement: 978 tonnes (963 tons)
Dimensions: 65m x 11m (212ft 5in x
36ft)
Top speed: 21 knots
Launched: 1869
Date of profile: 1869

The *Cutty Sark* was composite-built, with an iron framework and wooden hull. Although designed specifically

for the tea trade by Hercules Linton, *Cutty Sark* only made eight voyages as a tea clipper before the trade was lost to faster steamships using the newly-opened Suez Canal. In 1872 she narrowly lost the annual China Tea Race to rival tea clipper *Thermopylae*. From 1877 to 1883 *Cutty Sark* worked as a general tramp ship, and was then transferred to the Australian wool route. Her last wool voyage was in 1894-95, after which she was

sold to the Portuguese. Re-rigged as a barquentine, she served as a Portuguese vessel for 27 years before returning to England as a training ship. *Cutty Sark* is the only surviving tea clipper and is now preserved, fully restored, in a dry dock at Greenwich, London.

Cyclop

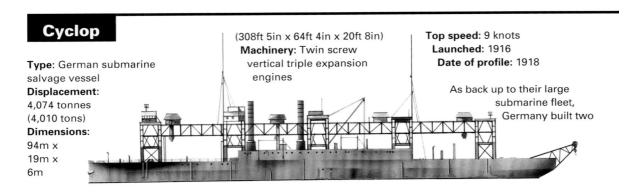

Type: German submarine salvage vessel
Displacement: 4,074 tonnes (4,010 tons)
Dimensions: 94m x 19m x 6m

(308ft 5in x 64ft 4in x 20ft 8in)
Machinery: Twin screw vertical triple expansion engines

Top speed: 9 knots
Launched: 1916
Date of profile: 1918

As back up to their large submarine fleet, Germany built two submarine salvage ships – *Vulkan* and *Cyclop*. *Cyclop* had twin hulls which had massive gantries running their full length with a designed lift of 1,219 tonnes (1,200 tons). Submarines were lifted up between the two hulls and repaired in situ, or carried to a repair basin. *Cyclop* entered service in 1918. She was handed over to Britain at the end of World War I, and scrapped in 1923.

Cyclops

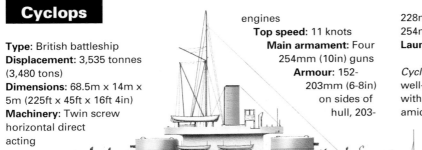

Type: British battleship
Displacement: 3,535 tonnes (3,480 tons)
Dimensions: 68.5m x 14m x 5m (225ft x 45ft x 16ft 4in)
Machinery: Twin screw horizontal direct acting

engines
Top speed: 11 knots
Main armament: Four 254mm (10in) guns
Armour: 152-203mm (6-8in) on sides of hull, 203-

228mm (8-9in) on upper hull, 228-254mm (9-10in) on turrets
Launched: July 1871

Cyclops and her three sisters were well-armoured, low freeboard ships with an upper hull structure amidships that protected the base of the two turrets. The overhanging bridge carried the ship's boats which were

handled by a single boom attached to the mast. Although designed specifically for harbour defence, the vessels were also used for general coastline protection. Between 1887 and 1889 all four vessels underwent extensive refits. Although launched in 1871, *Cyclops* was not completed until 1877, after which time she spent most of her career in reserve until she was sold in 1903.

Czar

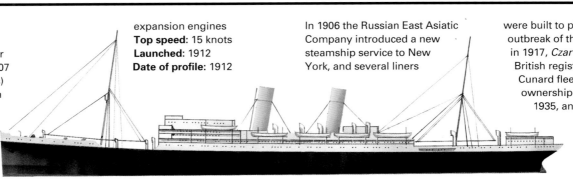

Type: Russian liner
Displacement: 6,607 tonnes (6,503 tons)
Dimensions: 130m x 16m (426ft x 53ft)
Machinery: Twin screw quadruple

expansion engines
Top speed: 15 knots
Launched: 1912
Date of profile: 1912

In 1906 the Russian East Asiatic Company introduced a new steamship service to New York, and several liners

were built to ply the route. With the outbreak of the Russian Revolution in 1917, *Czar* was transferred to the British registry and joined the Cunard fleet. She changed ownership in 1921, 1930 and 1935, and in 1946 she became the British *Empire Penryn*. She was scrapped in 1949.

D1

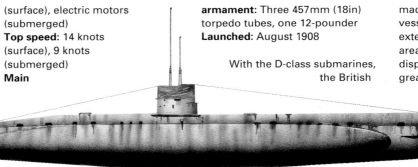

Type: British submarine
Displacement: 490 tonnes (483 tons) (surface), 604 tonnes (595 tons) (submerged)
Dimensions: 50m x 6m x 3m (163ft x 20ft 6in x 10ft 5in)
Machinery: Twin screw diesel engines

(surface), electric motors (submerged)
Top speed: 14 knots (surface), 9 knots (submerged)
Main

armament: Three 457mm (18in) torpedo tubes, one 12-pounder
Launched: August 1908

With the D-class submarines, the British

made their first attempt to produce vessels that could be used on extended patrols away from coastal areas. The D class had increased displacement, diesel engines and greater internal space. Unlike earlier classes, the D class could also send wireless messages as well as receive them. *D1* was sunk as a target in 1918.

Daffodil

Type: British minesweeper/sloop
Displacement: 1,219 tonnes (1,200 tons)
Dimensions: 80m x 10m x 3m (262ft 6in x 33ft x 11ft)
Machinery: Single screw triple expansion engines
Top speed: 16.5 knots

Main armament: Two 76mm (3in) guns
Launched: August 1915

With the outbreak of World War I the Admiralty authorised the building of 12 multi-purpose surface vessels capable of serving as minesweepers, touring and carrying out escort duties. Steadying

sails were carried to help keep their heads to the wind. A single screw gave them a large turning circle. Initially *Daffodil* was used as a minesweeper, but she was transferred to escort duties

in 1917. She was sold in 1935.

Daga

Type: Italian escort ship
Displacement: 1,138 tonnes (1,120 tons)
Dimensions: 82m x 8.6m x 3m (270ft x 28ft 3in x 9ft 2in)
Machinery: Twin screw turbines

Top speed: 31.5 knots
Main armament: Two 100mm (3.9in) guns, six 450mm (17.7in) torpedo tubes
Launched: July 1943

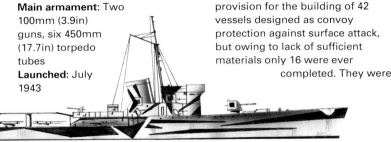

Italian naval war estimates made provision for the building of 42 vessels designed as convoy protection against surface attack, but owing to lack of sufficient materials only 16 were ever completed. They were enlarged versions of the Spica class launched between 1933 and 1938, and carried a larger torpedo armament and more anti-aircraft weapons. However, only one ship actually served in the Italian Navy as the rest were seized by the Germans in 1943. Of the 15 vessels pressed into German service, 13 were sunk, including *Daga* which was mined in October 1944.

Dagabur

Type: Italian submarine
Displacement: 690 tonnes (680 tons) (surface), 861 tonnes (848 tons) (submerged)
Dimensions: 60m x 6.5m x 4m (197ft 6in x 21ft x 13ft)
Machinery: Twin screw diesel engines (surface), electric motors (submerged)
Main armament: one 100mm (3.9in) gun, six 533mm (21in) torpedo tubes

Launched: November 1936
Date of profile: 1940

Dagabur was one of a class of 17. During the Spanish Civil War two of the class were modified to carry small assault craft, which were used to inflict serious damage on British vessels *Valiant* and *Queen Elizabeth* in 1941. *Dagabur* was sunk by the British destroyer *Wolverine* in 1942.

Dahlgren

Type: US torpedo boat
Displacement: 148 tonnes (146 tons)
Dimensions: 46m x 5m x 1.5m (151ft 4in x 16ft 5in x 4ft 8in)
Machinery: Twin screw vertical triple expansion engines

Top speed: 31 knots
Main armament: Four 1-pounders, two 457mm (18in) torpedo tubes
Launched: May 1899
Date of profile: 1899

Dahlgren and her sister *Craven* were authorised in 1896, laid down in March 1897 and completed in 1899. They had closely-spaced funnels, a single light pole mast and two single torpedo tubes mounted aft. The crew numbered 29. *Dahlgren* was sold in 1920.

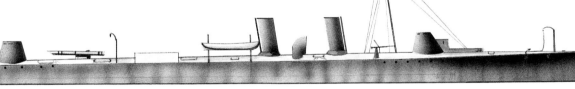

Daino

Type: Italian survey vessel
Displacement: 850 tonnes (838 tons)
Dimensions: 68m x 9m x 2m (224ft x 29ft 6in x 7ft 3in)
Machinery: Twin screw triple expansion
Top speed: 14 knots
Launched: 1945

Daino was formerly a German coal-burning minesweeper known as *B2* and, later, *M802*. She was part of a group of vessels laid down in 1943-44 and built from prefabricated sections supplied by various European sub-contractors. At the end of World War II, *M802* served with the German Minesweeping Administration clearing mines from the North Sea and the Baltic. She was transferred to Italy in 1949 and was converted to oil fuel. As *Daino*, she served as a minesweeper and then as an escort. In 1960 her 100mm (3.9in) and three 40mm (1.6in) guns were removed and she became a survey vessel.

Dalmazia

Type: Italian oiler
Displacement: 5,080 tonnes (5,000 tons)
Dimensions: 80m x 10m x 4.6m (260ft x 32ft 6in x 15ft 3in)
Machinery: Twin screw triple expansion engines
Main armament: One 120mm (4.7in) gun

Launched: 1922
Date of profile: 1966

Formerly a water carrier, *Dalmazia* served the Italian Navy as an oil carrier for many years. Her engines developed 1,450hp at full speed. Cargo capacity was 1,829 tonnes (1,800 tons). As well as carrying a 120mm (4.7in) gun, she was armed with two 20mm (0.8in) anti-aircraft weapons.

Danaide

Type: Italian corvette
Displacement: 812 tonnes (800 tons)
Dimensions: 64m x 8.5m x 2.5m
(211ft 3in x 28ft 3in x 8ft 6in)
Machinery: Twin screw diesel
engines
Top speed: 18.5 knots
Main armament: Four 40mm (1.6in)
anti-aircraft guns
Launched: October 1942
Date of profile: 1966

From 1942 onwards, the Italian Navy laid down a class of some 60 small escort vessels. The last in the class was not completed until 1948. Pressures of war caused the early ships in the class to be built extremely quickly. *Danaide* was one of the first, and was completed only four months after launching and less than a year after being laid down. She was originally fitted out for minesweeping, and operated extensively in the Mediterranean during World War II. Like her sister ships, she was extensively modified throughout her life, with new weapons and equipment being added. Changes to the class included the addition of a navigating bridge. *Danaide* was further converted to the corvette leader role, which entailed a small command deckhouse being installed in front of the bridge. To make space for this, the multi-barrelled depth charge thrower carried on the foredeck by most of her sisters was removed. These were capable and effective boats, well suited to patrol and escort duties. Many survived the war, and by the mid-1960s there were still 17 in service. Range was a creditable 5,320 kilometres (2,800 miles) at 15 knots. She could carry 65 tonnes (64 tons) of fuel on board. Her diesels could develop 3,500hp to achieve a top speed of 18 knots, but by the 1960s, hard service had reduced her speed to 15 knots.

Dandolo

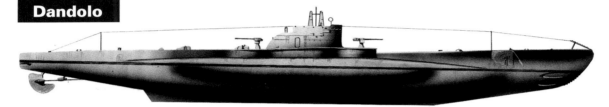

Type: Italian submarine
Displacement: 1,080 tonnes (1,063 tons) (surface), 1,338 tonnes (1,317 tons) (submerged)
Dimensions: 73m x 7.2m x 5m
(239ft 6in x 23ft 8in x 16ft 5in)
Machinery: Twin screw diesel engines (surface), electric motors (submerged)
Top speed: 17.4 knots (surface), 8 knots (submerged)
Main armament: Two 100mm (3.9in) guns, eight 533mm (21in) torpedo tubes
Launched: November 1937

Dandolo, a long-range, single hull boat with internal ballast tanks, was one of a class of nine vessels that were among the best Italian ocean-going submarines during World War II. Surface range at 17 knots was 4,750 kilometres (2,500 miles), and submerged range at 9 knots was 14,250 kilometres (7,500 miles). Maximum operational depth was 100 metres (328ft). All but *Dandolo* were lost in action. *Dandolo* herself was scrapped in 1947.

Daniel Boone

Type: US submarine
Displacement: 7,366 tonnes (7,250 tons) (surface), 8,382 tonnes (8,250 tons) (submerged)
Dimensions: 130m x 10m x 10m
(425ft x 33ft x 33ft)
Machinery: Single screw, single water-cooled nuclear reactor, turbines
Top speed: 20 knots (surface), 35 knots (submerged)
Main armament: Sixteen Polaris missiles, four 533mm (21in) torpedo tubes
Launched: June 1962

Daniel Boone

and her 30 sisters are equipped with Polaris missile with a range of 2,850 kilometres (1,500 miles). Launching tubes are carried behind the large fin. *Daniel Boone* and her sisters cost over $109,000,000 each.

Danmark

Date of profile: 1865

Type: Danish battleship
Displacement: 4,823 tonnes (4,747 tons)
Dimensions: 82m x 15m x 6m (270ft x 50ft x 19ft 2in)
Machinery: Single screw compound engines
Top speed: 8.5 knots
Main armament: Twelve 152mm (6in), twelve 203mm (8in) guns
Launched: February 1864

Originally *Danmark* was the *Santa Maria*, an ironclad ordered from Thompson of Glasgow by Lieutenant North of the US Confederate Navy. Unfortunately Confederate funds were low, and delays in paying the installments postponed her completion. She was finally sold to Denmark, which was at war with Prussia, and was re-named *Danmark*.

Dante Alighieri

Type: Italian battleship
Displacement: 22,149 tonnes (21,800 tons)
Dimensions: 168m x 26.5m x 10m (551ft 2in x 87ft 3in x 31ft 10in)
Machinery: Quadruple screw turbines

Armour: 152-249mm (6-9.8in) on belt
Launched: August 1910
Date of profile: 1923

Designed by Engineering Admiral Masdea, the *Dante Alighieri* was the first battleship to mount triple turrets on the centreline. She was reconstructed in 1923 and given a tripod mast. Scrapped in 1928.

Danton

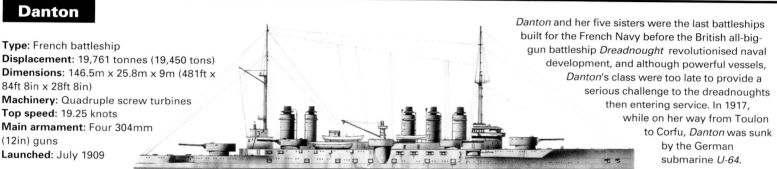

Type: French battleship
Displacement: 19,761 tonnes (19,450 tons)
Dimensions: 146.5m x 25.8m x 9m (481ft x 84ft 8in x 28ft 8in)
Machinery: Quadruple screw turbines
Top speed: 19.25 knots
Main armament: Four 304mm (12in) guns
Launched: July 1909

Danton and her five sisters were the last battleships built for the French Navy before the British all-big-gun battleship *Dreadnought* revolutionised naval development, and although powerful vessels, *Danton*'s class were too late to provide a serious challenge to the dreadnoughts then entering service. In 1917, while on her way from Toulon to Corfu, *Danton* was sunk by the German submarine *U-64*.

Daphné

Type: French submarine
Displacement: 884 tonnes (870 tons) (surface), 1,062 tonnes (1,045 tons) (submerged)
Dimensions: 58m x 7m x 4.6m (189ft 8in x 22ft 4in x 15ft)
Machinery: Twin screw diesel (surface), electric drive (submerged)
Top speed: 13.5 knots (surface), 16 knots (submerged)
Main armament: Twelve 552mm (21.7in) torpedo tubes
Launched: June 1959
Date of profile: 1959

Completed in 1964, *Daphné* was one of a new type of submarine developed during the early 1950s that had low noise, good manoeuvrability, a small crew and were easy to maintain. The hull form had a deep keel that improved stability. One type of torpedo carried can be fired at a depth of 300 m (985ft), twice that of standard torpedoes.

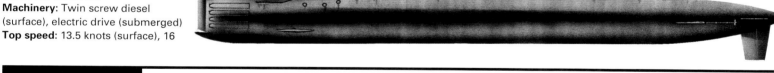

Dar Pomorza

Type: Polish sailing ship
Displacement: 1,646 tonnes (1,620 tons)
Dimensions: 73m x 12m x 6.4m (239ft x 41ft x 21ft)
Machinery: Auxiliary motors developing 360hp
Top speed: 6 knots
Launched: 1909
Date of profile: 1909

It was not until the introduction of the triple expansion engine that sail power gave way completely to steam, and as late as the 1880s many steamships still carried auxiliary sails. Accordingly, a great number of sailing vessels continued to be built after 1900, and were often fitted with small auxiliary motors to aid passage in times of calm. *Dar Pomorza* was one such vessel. Built at Hamburg, she was taken over by the Polish Merchant Navy after World War I for service as a training ship.

Dardo

Type: Italian motor gunboat
Displacement: 218 tonnes (215 tons)
Dimensions: 46m x 7m x 1.7m (150ft x 23ft 9in x 5ft 6in)
Machinery: Twin screw diesels and gas turbines
Top speed: 40+ knots

Main armament: One 40mm (1.6in) gun, four 533mm (21in) torpedo tubes
Launched: 1964
Date of profile: 1966

Dardo was one of four motor gunboats laid down at Taranto in 1964. The design specification called for a fast vessel that was capable of being rapidly converted into an armed gunboat for use as a fast minelayer (with an anti-aircraft gun and eight mines) or as a torpedo boat (with one 40mm (1.6in) gun and 21 x 533mm (21in) torpedoes). The necessary conversions could be completed in under 24 hours as and when required. All vessels in the class proved good seaboats and were well suited to the needs of the Italian Navy.

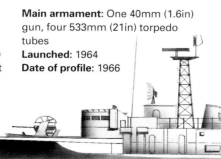

Daring

Type: British destroyer
Displacement: 264 tonnes (260 tons)
Dimensions: 56.6m x 5.7m (185ft 6in x 19ft)
Machinery: Twin screw three-stage compound engines
Main armament: One 12-pounder, three 6-

pounders, three torpedo tubes
Launched: November 1893
Date of profile: 1894

During the early 1890s, the British Admiralty requested designs for small destroyers that would be

faster than the rapidly growing fleet of French torpedo boats. Thornycroft and Yarrow subsequently came up with the design for *Daring*, based upon their successful sea-going

torpedo boats. The hull at the stern had a flat floor at the waterline, so enabling the screws to be lifted to allow for navigation in relatively shallow waters. *Daring* was broken up in 1912.

Daring

Type: British destroyer
Displacement: 3,636 tonnes (3,579 tons)
Dimensions: 114m x 13m x 4m (375ft x 43ft x 13ft)
Machinery: Twin screw
Top speed: 31.5 knots
Main armament: Six

120mm (4.5in) guns
Launched: August 1949
Date of profile: 1949

Daring and her seven sisters were expanded and improved versions of Battle-class and Weapon-class vessels, and were able to perform a number of tasks, including anti-submarine

and reconnaissance duties. They were the largest destroyers built for the Royal Navy and had an all-welded hull construction. The 120mm (4.5in) guns were automatic and radar controlled. The lattice fore mast was built around the fore funnel, giving *Daring* an unusual and distinctive appearance.

Darino

Type: British cargo boat
Displacement: 2,090 tonnes (2,057 tons)
Dimensions: 72m x 11m x 5.3m (236ft 3in x 36ft 6in x 17ft 4in)
Machinery: Twin screw triple expansion engines
Top speed: 10 knots
Launched: October 1917
Date of profile: 1917

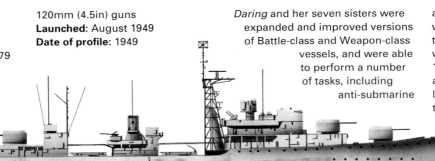

Darino was a typical medium-sized trader of the period, but she had much higher standards of comfort for

the few passengers she carried than was generally the rule. She had two continuous decks with three holds served by five steam winches, and most of her trade was between Britain, Portugal and Spain. She served on this route until she was torpedoed by a German submarine and sunk off Cape Finisterre while *en route* to Liverpool from Oporto on 19 November 1939.

D'Assas

Type: French cruiser
Displacement: 4,015 tonnes (3,952 tons)
Dimensions: 96m x 13.6m x 6m (315ft 5in x 44ft 10in x 20ft 6in)
Machinery: Twin screw vertical triple expansion engines
Main armament: Six 162mm (6.4in) guns

Launched: March 1896
Date of profile: 1898

By the 1890s France had begun to expand her fleet. The

programme of new construction included *D'Assas* and two sister ships. They were second-class cruisers with good armour protection comprising a steel armoured deck, and the hull had a pronounced tumble-home with four of the 162mm (6.4in) guns mounted on large sponsons. The remaining guns were carried aft and on the forecastle. *D'Assas* was completed in March 1898, and served until 1914.

Dauphin Royale

Type: French sailing line of battleship
Displacement: 1,077 tonnes (1,060 tons) approx
Top speed: 8 knots approx
Main armament: 104 guns
Launched: 1658
Date of profile: 1658

When Richelieu came to power in 1624, he set about improving the sorry state of France's once powerful

navy. He ordered five ships from Holland and from these beginnings grew the large fleet, which included *Dauphin Royale*, that fought the Anglo-Dutch fleet off Beachy Head in June 1690. *Dauphin Royale* was a large vessel with two main gundecks and one upper deck. The French fleet at Beachy Head totalled 70 ships of the line, with 4,600 guns and 28,000 crew. However, the weaker Allied force succeeded in repelling their stronger opponents.

Davidson

Type: US frigate
Displacement: 3,454 tonnes (3,400 tons)
Dimensions: 126m x 13.5m x 7m (414ft 8in x 44ft 3in x 24ft)
Machinery: Single screw, turbines
Top speed: 27 knots
Main armament: Two 127mm (5in) dual-purpose guns
Launched: 1964
Date of profile: 1966

The Garcia class of anti-submarine ships was built between 1962 and 1968. Ten were launched and were originally classed as ocean escorts, but their designation and role was soon changed to that of frigate. Gyro-driven stabilisers enable *Davidson* to operate effectively in heavy seas, and her anti-submarine capabilities are significantly improved over earlier frigate designs. As well as the two single gun mounts, she carries a large box launcher which holds eight Asroc anti-submarine missiles. She was also originally equipped with twin torpedo tubes in the stern, but these have since been removed. Her combat effectiveness is increased by the SH-2 Seasprite helicopter housed in a hanger towards the stern. She is flush-decked, with a radically raked stem and combined mast and exhaust stack, to give her a distinctive silhouette. *Davidson*'s range is 7,600 kilometres (4,000 miles) at 20 knots, and she has a full complement of 270. The same hull design and layout was also used for the contemporary Brooke class, though these had the rear 127mm (5in) gun turret removed and replaced by a single Mk22 Terrier/-Standard long range surface-to-air missile launcher.

Davout

Type: French cruiser
Displacement: 3,080 tonnes (3,031 tons)
Dimensions: 88m x 12m x 6.6m (288ft 9in x 39ft 4in x 21ft 8in)
Machinery: Twin screw inverted triple expansion engines
Top speed: 20.7 knots
Main armament: Six 162mm (6.4in) guns
Launched: October 1889

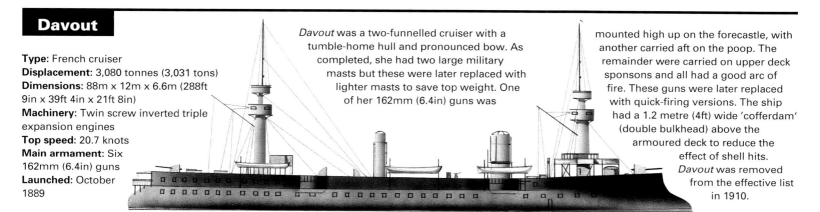

Davout was a two-funnelled cruiser with a tumble-home hull and pronounced bow. As completed, she had two large military masts but these were later replaced with lighter masts to save top weight. One of her 162mm (6.4in) guns was mounted high up on the forecastle, with another carried aft on the poop. The remainder were carried on upper deck sponsons and all had a good arc of fire. These guns were later replaced with quick-firing versions. The ship had a 1.2 metre (4ft) wide 'cofferdam' (double bulkhead) above the armoured deck to reduce the effect of shell hits. *Davout* was removed from the effective list in 1910.

D'Bataviase

Type: Dutch merchant ship
Displacement: 711 tonnes (700 tons)
Dimensions: 37m x 10m (121ft 5in x 33ft 6in)
Main armament: Twenty cannon
Launched: 1620
Date of profile: 1620

Within a few decades of their declaration of independence in 1581, the Dutch had replaced the Portuguese as masters of the far eastern trade routes. Dutch merchant ships carried a powerful armament and were easily converted into warships, as vessels of the Dutch East India Company were often called upon to defend themselves against pirates. *D'Bataviase Eeuw* was a Dutch East India Company ship and had a single gundeck running her full length, with a large cargo area below. The upper deck could carry more guns as and when required.

De Grasse

Type: French cruiser
Displacement: 11,730 tonnes (11,545 tons)
Dimensions: 188m x 18.5m x 5.4m (617ft 2in x 61ft x 18ft 2in)
Machinery: Twin screw, turbines
Top speed: 33.5 knots
Main armament: Twelve 127mm (5in) dual-purpose guns
Launched: 1946

Date of profile: 1956

Ordered under the 1937 French naval estimates, *De Grasse* and her two sister ships were designed as faster versions of the previous cruiser class, with improved aircraft-carrying ability. They had two catapults and a hangar amidships. Of the three ships ordered, only *De Grasse* was ever laid down. Her construction was suspended during the German occupation of Lorient, resumed in 1946, then halted again. It began once more in January 1951 and she was completed at Brest dockyard as an anti-aircraft cruiser, equipped as a fleet command ship for radar-controlled air strikes. In 1966 *De Grasse* was re-fitted as a flagship of the Pacific Experimental Nuclear Centre, and had several of her gun turrets removed. A tall lattice mast was fitted aft.

De Ruyter

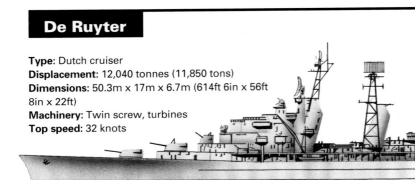

Type: Dutch cruiser
Displacement: 12,040 tonnes (11,850 tons)
Dimensions: 50.3m x 17m x 6.7m (614ft 6in x 56ft 8in x 22ft)
Machinery: Twin screw, turbines
Top speed: 32 knots

Main armament: Eight 152mm (6in) guns
Launched: December 1944
Date of profile: 1966

De Ruyter, originally *De Zeven Provincien*, was authorised in 1938. Her design was to have been an enlarged version of the 7,620-tonne (7,500-ton) *De Ruyter*, launched in 1935 and later sunk by Japanese warships in 1942. Construction on the new *De Ruyter* had not progressed far when World War II halted it completely. She was eventually completed in 1953. In 1973 the ship was sold to Peru, where she became the *Almirante Grau*.

Decatur

Type: US destroyer
Displacement: 426 tonnes (420 tons)
Dimensions: 77m x 7m x 2m (252ft 7in x 23ft 6in x 6ft 6in)
Machinery: Twin screw vertical triple expansion

engines
Top speed: 29 knots
Main armament: Two 76mm (3in) guns, five 6-pounders, two 457mm (18in) torpedo tubes
Launched: September 1900

The Decatur class of five units was the largest destroyer class laid down before 1899. All previous destroyers had been 'one-off' vessels of between 238 and 283 tonnes (235 and 279 tons). The Decaturs were authorised in 1898 and served mainly in the Philippines. In 1917 *Chauncey* was rammed and sunk by the steamer *Rose*, but all remaining vessels in the class survived World War I and were sold in 1920.

Dédalo

Type: Spanish seaplane carrier
Displacement: 10,972 tonnes (10,800 tons)
Dimensions: 182m x 16.7m x 6m (597ft x 55ft x 20ft 6in)
Machinery: Single screw triple expansion engines
Main armament: Two 102mm (4in) guns
Launched: 1901
Date of profile: 1933

Dédalo had space for one small airship forward, with its own mooring mast and complete hydrogen plant. Aft was the seaplane deck with extensive workshops. The ship was sunk in 1935 by Nationalist aircraft. In 1940 the wreck was raised and scrapped.

Dédalo

Type: Spanish aircraft carrier
Displacement: 16,678 tonnes (16,416 tons)
Dimensions: 190m x 22m x 8m (622ft 4in x 73ft x 26ft)
Machinery: Quadruple screws, turbines
Top speed: 30 knots
Main armament:

Twenty-six 40mm (1.6in) guns
Aircraft: Twenty
Launched: April 1943
Date of profile: 1980

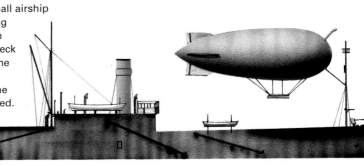

Dédalo was formerly the US carrier *Cabot*, laid down in 1942 and completed the following year. After service in World War II, she was decommissioned in 1947. In 1967 she was lent to Spain, who purchased her in 1972, re-naming her *Dédalo*. She remained in service until the carrier *Principe de Asturias* (1982) entered service.

Deep Quest

Type: US commercial submarine
Displacement: 5 tonnes (5 tons)
Dimensions: 12m long (39ft 4in)
Machinery: Twin reversible thrust motors
Top speed: 4.5 knots
Launched: June 1967
Date of profile: 1980

Deep Quest was the first submersible built with fairing around a double sphere, one for the crew, the other for the propulsion unit. She works as a deep search and recovery submarine, and can descend down to 2,438 metres (8,000 ft). Such vessels are vital when examining the seabed for cable-laying and pipelines.

Deepstar 4000

Type: Commercial submarine
Dimensions: 5.4m x 3.5m x 2m (17ft 9in x 11ft 6in x 6ft 6in)
Machinery: Two fixed, reversible five horsepower AC motors
Top speed: 3 knots
Launched: 1965

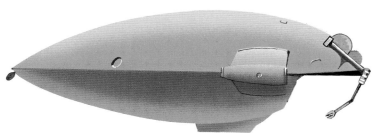

The *Deepstar 4000* was built between 1962 and 1964 by the Westinghouse Electric Corporation and the Jacques Cousteau group OFRS. The hull consists of a steel sphere with 11 openings, and she carries a wide range of scientific equipment.

Defence

Type: British cruiser
Displacement: 14,833 tonnes (14,600 tons)
Dimensions: 158m x 22m x 8m (519ft x 74ft 6in x 26ft)
Machinery: Twin screw triple expansion engines
Main armament: Four 228mm (9.2in), ten 190mm (7.5in) guns
Launched: May 1907

Date of profile: 1909

Defence was laid down in 1905 as part of the 1904 Defence Programme. She and her two sisters were

enlarged versions of the previous Warrior armoured cruiser class, and had an extra 1,016 tonnes (1,000 tons) displacement to enable them to carry heavier armament. Unfortunately, the level of protection was slightly reduced. At the start of World War I the Defence class formed part of a squadron searching for the elusive German battleship *Goeben*. *Defence* was sunk at Jutland in 1916, with the loss of 893 lives.

Delfino

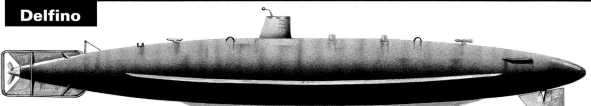

Type: Italian submarine
Displacement: 96 tonnes (95 tons) (surface), 108 tonnes(107 tons) (submerged)

Dimensions: 24m x 3m x 2.5m (78ft 9in x 9ft 5in x 8ft 4in)
Machinery: Single screw (surface),

electric motor (submerged)
Main armament: Two 355mm (14in) torpedo tubes

Launched: 1892
Date of profile: 1896

Constructed at La Spezia Naval Dockyard, *Delfino* was the first submarine built for the Italian Navy. She was rebuilt in 1902-04 with increased dimensions and displacement. A petrol motor was added and the conning tower enlarged. She was discarded in 1918.

Delfino

Type: Italian submarine
Displacement: 948 tonnes (933 tons) (surface), 1,160 tonnes (1,142 tons) (submerged)
Dimensions: 70m x 7m x 7m (229ft x 23ft 7in x 24ft)
Machinery: Twin screw diesel (surface), electric motors

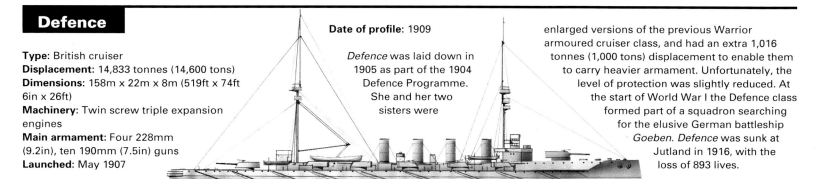

(submerged)
Main armament: Eight 533mm (21in) torpedo tubes, one 102mm (4in) gun

Launched: April 1930
Date of profile: 1942

Delfino was completed in 1931. She was used for training and transport duties from 1942. Sunk in 1943.

Delhi

Type: Indian cruiser
Displacement: 9,895 tonnes (9,740 tons)
Dimensions: 166m x 16.7m x 6m (544ft 6in x 55ft 2in x 20ft)
Machinery: Quadruple screws, turbines
Top speed: 32 knots
Main armament: Six 152mm (6in)

guns, four 102mm (4in) anti-aircraft guns
Launched: September 1932
Date of profile: 1966

Delhi, formerly the British *Achilles* of the Leander class, was lent to the New

Zealand Navy in 1937. She helped to defeat the German battleship *Admiral Graf Spee* in December 1939, and was returned to service with the

Royal Navy in 1943. In 1948 she was sold to the Indian Navy where she served as flagship until 1957. By 1959 India had developed her own shipbuilding capability, and *Delhi* was downgraded and put into general service. She was put on the reserve list and scrapped in 1978.

Delta

Type: Chinese gunboat
Displacement: 426 tonnes (420 tons)
Dimensions: 36.5m x 9m x 2.5m (120ft x 30ft x 8ft)
Machinery: Twin screw horizontal compound engines
Top speed: 9.6 knots
Main armament: One 317mm(12.5in) gun
Launched: 1876
Date of profile: 1876

George Rendell designed a number of successful gunboats from 1868 to 1879, starting with the British 183-tonne (180-ton) vessel, *Staunch*. Their common feature was the use of a single extremely large gun mounted on a small, low profile hull with shallow draught. Italy also used

four of the type, equipped with a 121-ton (119-ton) 400mm (15.7in) Krupp gun. *Delta* was one of a four units ordered by China in 1875 and completed in 1877. They were effectively floating gun platforms rather than warships, but were useful for coastal defence. *Delta* was equipped with a single 36-tonne (35-ton) 317mm (12.5in) gun, which could only be traversed a few degrees from dead ahead. To aim the gun, the whole boat had to be pointed at the target, and she was fitted with twin screws to enable her to manoeuvre quickly. Seemingly a vulnerable target, her small size and low profile actually made her very difficult to hit. Her armament also made her a danger to ironclad ships of the line some 10 times her size. All four of the Chinese Rendell gunboats were captured by the Japanese in 1895. They were broken up between 1906 and 1907.

Delta I

Type: Russian submarine
Displacement: 11,176 tonnes (11,000 tons) submerged
Dimensions: 150m x 12m x 10.2m (492ft x 39ft 4in x 33ft 6in)
Machinery: Twin screw, two nuclear reactors, turbines
Main armament: Twelve SS-N-48 missile tubes, six 457mm (18in) torpedo tubes
Launched: 1971
Date of profile: 1980

Until the early 1970s, the USA led the world in highly-sophisticated and effective nuclear missile submarines. However, in 1973 Russia introduced the first of a new series of missiles that could out-range Poseidon. Initial tests showed a range of over 7,600 kilometres (4,000 miles), and the missiles soon appeared in the new large Delta-class vessels that entered service between 1972 and 1977.

Demologos

Type: US battleship
Displacement: 2,514 tonnes (2,475 tons)
Dimensions: 47.5m x 17m x 3m (156ft x 56ft x 10ft)
Machinery: Paddle wheel, inclined steam cylinder, compound engines
Top speed: 7 knots
Main armament: Twenty 32-pounders
Launched: October 1814
Date of profile: 1815

Demologos was the first steam-powered warship in the world. She was designed for coast-defence service during the war then in progress against Britain. Originally named *Fulton the First*, the twin-hulled ship was laid down in June 1814. A single paddle wheel was positioned in the gap between the two hulls, where it was well protected against enemy fire. The ship was completed with two masts carrying lateen sails, plus a set of jibs. The war with Britain ended before she saw action, and *Demologos* was laid up in New York as a store ship. On 4 June 1829 she was destroyed by an internal explosion.

D'Entrecasteaux

Type: French cruiser
Displacement: 8,142 tonnes (8,014 tons)
Dimensions: 120m x 18m x 8m (393ft 6in x 58ft 6in x 26ft)
Machinery: Twin screw triple expansion engines
Top speed: 19.2 knots
Main armament: Two 238mm (9.4in) , twelve 140mm (5.5in) guns
Launched: June 1896

D'Entrecasteaux was designed by Lagane for service on foreign station. A graceful, flush-decked cruiser, her hull had a pronounced tumble home with eight of the 140mm (5.5in) guns on the main deck and four more on the upper deck. Protection was afforded by a sloping deck 100mm (3.9in) thick on the

slopes, plus a splinter-proof deck below. Coal supply was 660 tonnes (650 tons) normal and 1,016 tonnes (1,000 tons) maximum, plus 203 tonnes (200 tons) of oil used to increase combustion. Electricity was used extensively to work the guns, ammunition hoists and auxiliary machinery.

D'Entrecasteaux was handed over to Belgium in 1922.

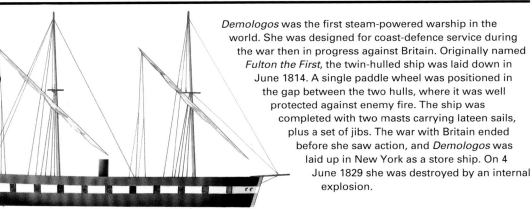

Denver

Launched: June 1902

Type: US cruiser
Displacement: 3,570 tonnes (3,514 tons)
Dimensions: 94m x 13m x 4.8m (308ft 10in x 44ft x 15ft 9in)
Machinery: Twin screw vertical triple expansion engines
Top speed: 16.7 knots
Main armament: Ten 127mm (5in) guns

The six vessels of the Denver cruiser class were flush-decked ships, which made for larger interiors so that the ships could carry troops. They were well supplied with electricity to power the fans needed when serving in the tropics. The Denver class compared unfavourably with similar cruisers in foreign navies because of their low speed, but armament was good.

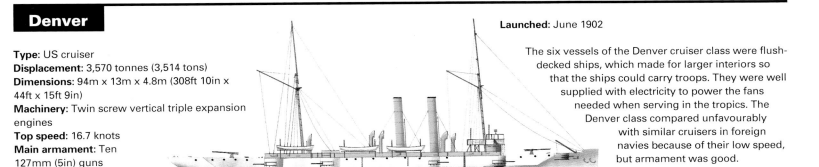

Denver

Date of profile: 1983

Type: US Navy command ship
Displacement: 9,477 tonnes (9,328 tons)
Dimensions: 174m x 30.5m x 7m (570ft 3in x 100ft x 23ft)
Machinery: Twin screw, turbines
Main armament: Eight 76mm (3in) guns
Launched: January 1965

This class of 11 ships are enlarged versions of the previous Raleigh group, with increased troop and vehicle capacity and a comprehensive docking facility forming the stern of the vessel. Access to the dock is via massive lock gates in the stern.

Derbyshire

Type: British liner
Displacement: 11,836 tonnes (11,650 tons)
Dimensions: 153m x 20m (502ft x 66ft 4in)
Machinery: Twin screw diesel engines
Top speed: 15 knots
Launched: June 1935
Date of profile: 1936

employees travelling to and from British stations overseas. From 1939-1942 she served as an armed merchant cruiser, and then became a troopship. In 1946 *Derbyshire* was released from transport duties and underwent an extensive re-fit. She served as a passenger/cargo liner on the Rangoon route from 1948-1963, and was then sold for scrap.

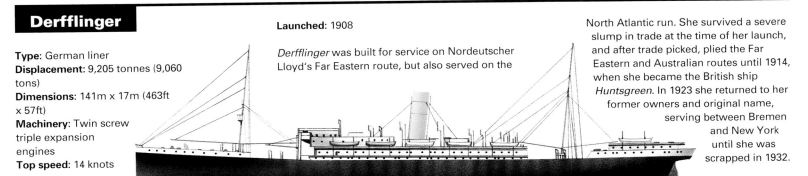

Derbyshire was a one-class liner that could carry 291 passengers. These were usually government

Derfflinger

Launched: 1908

Derfflinger was built for service on Nordeutscher Lloyd's Far Eastern route, but also served on the

Type: German liner
Displacement: 9,205 tonnes (9,060 tons)
Dimensions: 141m x 17m (463ft x 57ft)
Machinery: Twin screw triple expansion engines
Top speed: 14 knots

North Atlantic run. She survived a severe slump in trade at the time of her launch, and after trade picked, plied the Far Eastern and Australian routes until 1914, when she became the British ship *Huntsgreen*. In 1923 she returned to her former owners and original name, serving between Bremen and New York until she was scrapped in 1932.

Derfflinger

Type: German battlecruiser
Displacement: 30,706 tonnes (30,223 tons)
Dimensions: 210m x 29m x 8m (689ft x 95ft 2in x 27ft 3in)
Machinery: Quadruple screws, turbines
Top speed: 28 knots

Main armament: Eight 304mm (12in) guns
Armour: 300mm (11.8in) waterline belt
Launched: July 1913
Date of profile: 1914

In 1916 *Derfflinger* inflicted severe damage on the *Queen Mary* but was hit by ten 380mm (15in) and ten 304mm (12in) shells. Despite severe damage she survived. She was scuttled at Scapa Flow in 1919.

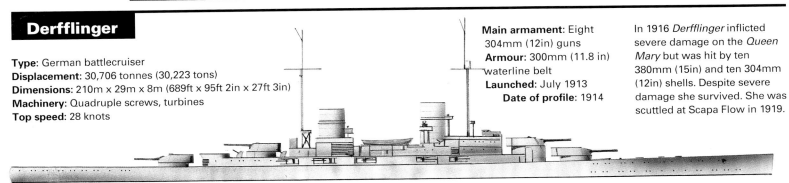

Des Geneys

Type: Italian frigate
Displacement: 1,532 tonnes (1,508 tons)
Dimensions: 47m x 12.6m x 5.7m (154ft 6in x 41ft 4in x 18ft 8in)
Machinery: Thirty six cannon
Launched: December 1827
Date of profile: 1828

Des Geneys was originally named *Haute Combe* and was part of the Sardinian fleet until 1839. She formed part of the early Italian Navy. She was a typical frigate of the period, with a single gundeck running her full length. In 1854 she became a transport and her armament was reduced to four cannon. *Des Geneys* was removed from service in 1865.

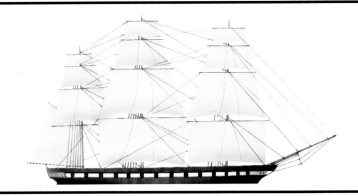

Des Moines

Type: US cruiser
Displacement: 21,844 tonnes (21,500 tons)
Dimensions: 218m x 23m x 8m (717ft x 75ft 6in x 26ft)
Machinery: Quadruple screw, turbines
Top speed: 33 knots
Main armament: Nine 203mm (8in), twelve 127mm (5in) guns
Launched: September 1946
Date of profile: 1948

The three units of the Des Moines class were the first ships to mount the complete automatic rapid-fire 203mm (8in) guns. *Des Moines*' two sisters were also the first warships to have air conditioning. *Des Moines* was placed in reserve in 1980.

D'Estienne d'Orves

Type: French frigate
Displacement: 1,351 tonnes (1,330 tons)
Dimensions: 80m x 10m x 3m (262ft 6in x 33ft 10in x 9ft 10in)
Machinery: Twin screw diesel engines
Top speed: 23.3 knots
Main armament: Four Exocet launchers, one 100mm (3.9in) dual-purpose gun

Launched: June 1973
Date of profile: 1992

D'Estienne d'Orves is one of a group of 20 frigates that followed on from the previous class of larger ships, the Commandant Riviére group. The new class are mainly designed for anti-submarine work in coastal waters, although they can also operate in foreign waters.

Destructor

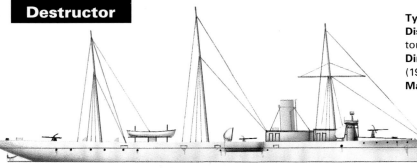

Type: Spanish torpedo gunboat
Displacement: 465 tonnes (458 tons)
Dimensions: 58m x 7.6m x 2m (192ft 6in x 25ft x 7ft)
Machinery: Twin screw triple expansion engines
Main armament: One 89mm (3.5in) gun, five 380mm (15in) torpedo tubes

Launched: July 1886

Destructor was one of the first vessels fitted with triple expansion engines. She had twin funnels, three hinged masts, and light plating on the conning tower forward and by the machinery spaces. She carried an armament of light weapons and a single 89mm (3.5in) gun.

Deutschland

Type: German battleship
Displacement: 8,939 tonnes (8,799 tons)
Dimensions: 90m x 19m x 8m (293ft x 62ft 4in x 26ft)
Machinery: Single screw horizontal single expansion engine
Main armament: Eight 254mm (10in) guns

Launched: September 1874
Date of profile: 1876

Deutschland was a powerful central battery ship with the main armament concentrated in an armoured box amidships. In 1882 her armament was altered, and in 1895 she was rebuilt as a heavy cruiser with military masts replacing her original rig. She was broken up in 1909.

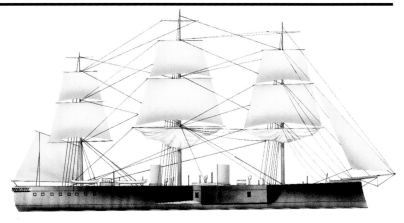

Deutschland

Type: German liner
Displacement: 16,766 tonnes (16,502 tons)
Dimensions: 208.5m x 20.4m (684ft x 67ft)
Machinery: Twin screw quadruple expansion engines
Top speed: 23.6 knots
Launched: January 1900
Date of profile: 1900

When she was launched, *Deutschland* was the largest and finest liner in the world. Fitted with

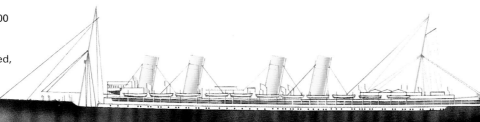

four funnels arranged in pairs, she presented a graceful and powerful image, and set the standard for the later luxury liners that plied the Atlantic route. Her passenger accommodation was superb, especially for those travelling first class. She could carry a maximum of 700 first-class, 300 second-class and

280 third-class passengers. Her only fault was a strong vibration which became obvious when she was driven at high speed, and efforts were made to cure this during her sea trials. Her machinery could develop some 33,000hp, and on her maiden voyage to New York she captured the coveted Blue Riband

with an average speed of 22.4 knots. She was to retain this record for the next six years. In 1910 she was docked near Stettin for conversion to a cruise liner. In this configuration she was renamed *Victoria Luise*, although she only served as such for a few years. In 1914 she was fitted out as an auxiliary cruiser, although her boilers were in such poor condition that she never saw service in this form. After World War I, Germany was permitted to keep her, making her the largest ship in the German Merchant Marine. She was finally broken up in 1925.

Deutschland

Type: German battleship
Displacement: 14,216 tonnes (13,993 tons)
Dimensions: 127.6m x 22m x 8m (418ft 8in x 73ft x 27ft)
Machinery: Twin screw triple expansion engines
Top speed: 18.5 knots
Main armament: Fourteen 170mm (6.7in), four 280mm (11in) guns
Armour: 248mm (9.75in) belt, 280mm (11in) on main turrets
Launched: November 1904
Date of profile: 1908

Deutschland was part of Germany's last pre-dreadnought class laid down between 1903 and 1905. They differed slightly from the previous class in that they had more 89mm (3.5in) guns plus improved protection, but other weaknesses remained – as was shown at the Battle of Jutland when one in the class, *Pommern*, suffered a magazine explosion after only one hit from a torpedo. Small tube boilers were used for the Deutschland class, and these became standard for all vessels of the German Navy. Two ships of the class survived to serve in World War II and were lost in action. *Deutschland* was scrapped in 1922.

Deutschland

Type: German submarine
Displacement: 1,536 tonnes (1,512 tons) (surface), 1,905 tonnes (1,875 tons) (submerged)
Dimensions: 65m x 8.9m x 5.3m (213ft 3in x 29ft 2in x 17ft 5in)
Machinery: Twin screw diesel engines (surface), electric motors (submerged)
Top speed: 12.4 knots (surface),

5.2 knots (submerged)
Launched: March 1916

Deutschland was a cargo-carrying submarine of the U151 class and made two trips to the USA for rubber, nickel and other cargo before America entered World War I. *Deutschland* was then armed as *U155*. She was later ceded to Britain and was scrapped in 1922.

Deutschland

Type: German training ship
Displacement: 5,588 tonnes (5,500 tons)
Dimensions: 145m x 18m x 4.5m (475ft 9in x 59ft x 14ft 9in)
Machinery: Triple screw diesel motors, turbines
Main armament: Four 100mm (3.9in) guns
Launched: 1960

Deutschland was the first West German naval ship to exceed the post-war limit of 3,048 tonnes (3,000 tons), and entered service in May 1963. She was a light cruiser that could also operate as a

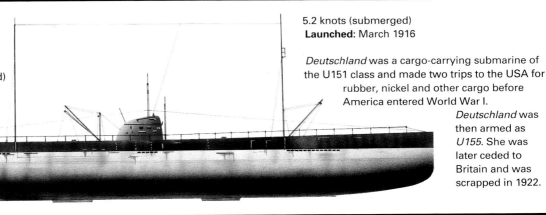

minelayer, and she carried a varied armament for training purposes, including 100mm (3.9in) and 40mm (1.6in) guns, depth charge launchers and torpedo tubes. Two types of machinery were also installed to maximise training opportunities for the 267 cadets. Her total complement numbered 550.

Devastation

Type: British battleship
Displacement: 9,448 tonnes (9,300 tons)
Dimensions: 87m x 20m x 8m (285ft x 65ft 3in x 26ft 8in)
Machinery: Twin screw trunk engines
Main armament: Four 304mm (12in) guns

Launched: July 1871
Date of profile: 1873

The 1868 design for the breastwork turret ship *Devastation* was a major step in the evolution of the battleship, producing a good

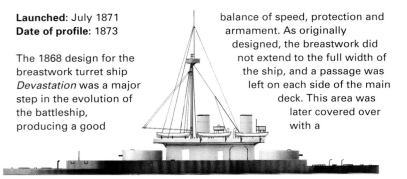

balance of speed, protection and armament. As originally designed, the breastwork did not extend to the full width of the ship, and a passage was left on each side of the main deck. This area was later covered over with a

superstructure that extended to the sides of the ship and continued aft halfway to the stern. A recess in the aft superstructure allowed theguns to fire with maximum depression over the stern. No sails were carried and there was only one mast. *Devastation* was re-fitted in 1879, and between 1891 and 1892 she was given triple expansion engines. She was sold in 1908.

Dévastation

Type: French battleship
Displacement: 10,617 tonnes (10,450 tons)
Dimensions: 95m x 21m x 8m (311ft 6in x 69ft 9in x 27ft)
Machinery: Twin screw vertical compound engines
Main armament: Four 274mm (10.8in), four 340mm (13.4in) guns

Launched: April 1879
Date of profile: 1889

The massive central battery ship *Dévastation* was among the first vessels completed after France's war with Prussia in 1870. The main battery was never satisfactory and was continually updated. New machinery was installed 1901. *Dévastation* was scrapped in 1922.

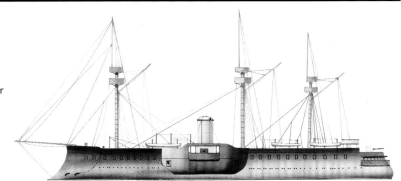

Devonshire

Type: British cruiser
Displacement: 11,023 tonnes (10,850 tons)
Dimensions: 144m x 21m x 7.3m (473ft 6in x 68ft 6in x 24ft)
Machinery: Twin screw triple expansion engines
Top speed: 22 knots
Main armament: Six 152mm

(6in), four 190mm (7.5in) guns
Armour: 51-152mm (2-6in) belt, 127mm (5in) on turrets, 152mm (6in) on casemate, 51mm (2in) on armoured deck
Launched: April 1904

Devonshire was one of a class of six vessels that were an attempt to improve upon the previous 9,956-tonne (9,800-ton) Monmouth class without an excessive increase in size. At that time great advances were being made in the quality of armour, making it possible to protect the vitals of cruisers against 152mm (6in) fire using relatively thin armour. This also kept displacement to a minimum. *Devonshire* was sold for scrapping in 1921.

Devonshire

Type: British destroyer
Displacement: 6,299 tonnes (6,200 tons)
Dimensions: 158m x 16m x 6m (520ft 6in x 54ft x 20ft)
Machinery: Twin screw, turbines plus four gas turbines
Top speed: 32.5 knots
Main armament: Four 114mm (4.5in) guns, twin launcher for

long-range Seaslug missile
Launched: June 1960
Date of profile: 1966

Designed at the end of the 1950s, *Devonshire* and her seven sisters were intended to operate in the 'fall-out' area of a nuclear explosion. Deck installations were under cover and the ships had clean lines to facilitate the 'washing down' process in the event of nuclear attack. The class has now been superseded by the Type 42 destroyer.

Diablo

Type: US submarine
Displacement: 1,890 tonnes (1,860 tons) (surface), 2,467 tonnes (2,420 tons) (submerged)
Machinery: Twin screw diesel

engines (surface), electric motors (submerged)
Main armament: Two 150mm (5.9in) guns, ten 533mm (21in) torpedo tubes
Launched: 1944

Date of profile: 1945

Diablo was a double-hulled ocean-going submarine

developed from the previous Gato class, but was more strongly built with an improved internal layout which increased the displacement by about 40 tonnes (40 tons). *Diablo* was transferred to Pakistan and re-named *Ghazi* in 1964. She was sunk in 1971 during the war with India.

Diana

Type: Italian sloop
Displacement: 2,590 tonnes (2,550 tons)
Dimensions: 114m x 12m x 3.5m (373ft 8in x 38ft 5in x 11ft 6in)
Machinery: Twin screw turbines
Main armament: Two 102mm (4in) guns, six 20mm (0.8in) weapons
Launched: May 1940

Diana was designed as the prime minister's yacht, but could also be used as a fast transport for valuable cargoes. In this capacity she carried 11 motor boats to the central Mediterranean for an attack on Malta in July 1941. *Diana* was sunk by two torpedoes fired from the British submarine *Thrasher* on 29 June 1942.

Diaspro

Type: Italian submarine
Displacement: 711 tonnes (700 tons) (surface), 873 tonnes (860 tons) (submerged)
Dimensions: 60m x 6.4m x 4.6m (197ft 5in x 21ft 2in x 15ft)
Machinery: Twin screw diesel engines (surface), electric motors (submerged)
Main armament: One 100mm (3.9in) gun, six 533mm (21in) torpedo tubes
Launched: July 1936

Diaspro was a short-range boat of the Perla class, with a maximum operational depth of 70-80 m (230-262ft). All ten units served in World War II and the Spanish Civil War. *Diaspro* was removed from the Navy List in 1948.

Dictator

Type: US battleship
Displacement: 4,509 tonnes (4,438 tons)
Dimensions: 95m x 15m x 6m (312ft x 50ft x 20ft 6in)
Machinery: Single screw vibrating lever engines
Main armament: Two 380mm (15in) guns
Launched: December 1863

The huge monitor *Dictator* was a true ocean-going vessel unlike the earlier smaller monitors then in service with the Union Navy. As designed, she was to have had a speed of 16 knots, combined with a large radius of action due to her 1,016-tonne (1,000-ton) coal capacity. But in practice, she could only carry half that amount at half the designed speed.

Dido

Type: British cruiser
Displacement: 5,690 tonnes (5,600 tons)
Dimensions: 114m x 16m x 6m (373ft x 53ft 6in x 20ft 6in)
Machinery: Twin screw triple expansion engines
Main armament: Six 120mm (4.7in), five 152mm (6in) guns
Launched: March 1896

Dido had two 152mm (6in) guns on the aft deck, one on the foredeck and one each broadside aft of the bridge. The 120mm (4.7in) guns were positioned on the broadside between the fore and aft bridge structures. Sold in 1926.

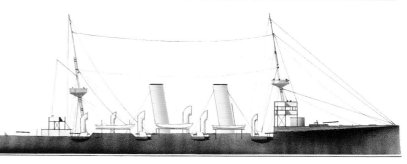

Dido

Type: British cruiser
Displacement: 6,960 tonnes (6,850 tons)
Dimensions: 156m x 15m x 5m (511ft 10in x 50ft 6in x 16ft 9in)
Machinery: Quadruple screws, turbines
Main armament: Eight 127mm (5.25in) guns
Launched: July 1939

Dido was one of 11 cruisers designed as anti-aircraft vessels carrying semi-automatic 127mm (5.25in) guns on power-loaded mountings with a 70° elevation. Four of the class were lost in action during World War II, but *Dido* survived and was broken up in 1958.

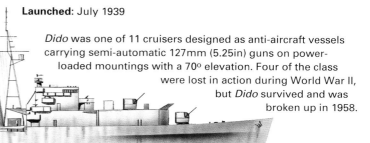

Dido

Type: British frigate
Displacement: 2,844 tonnes (2,800 tons)
Dimensions: 113m x 12m x 5.4m (372ft x 41ft x 18ft)
Machinery: Twin screw turbines
Top speed: 30 knots
Main armament: Two 114mm (4.5in) guns, one quad launcher for Seacat missiles
Launched: December 1961
Date of profile: 1966

The 26-strong Leander class became the backbone of the British frigate force during the 1960s and early 1970s. They followed the basic pattern of the earlier Rothesay/Whitby class, but were more versatile and had improved fighting capabilities. *Dido* was one of the first ships in the class, and was equipped with a powerful early-warning radar, a bow-mounted sonar and a variable depth sonar. As constructed, her armament was a single twin 114mm (4.5in) gun turret, a triple-barrelled anti-submarine mortar and a Seacat point defence missile launcher. She also carried a Wasp (later replaced by a Lynx) light helicopter which could carry anti-submarine homing torpedoes. In an improvement over earlier frigates, *Dido* had air conditioning plus comfortable living

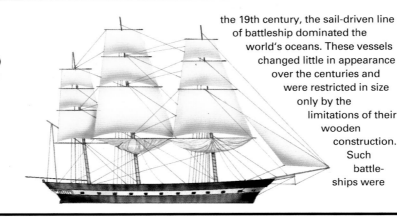

accommodation. Later ships of the class were built with an extra 1m (3ft 3in) in the beam to increase stability and internal stowage. In later years, many of this class had their armament modified. Some had their guns replaced by four Exocet surface-to-surface missile launchers, while others, including *Dido*, had them replaced by an Ikara long-range anti-submarine missile launcher. Chile and New Zealand used two British-built Leanders each, while the Dutch and the Indians built six each themselves.

Diligente

Type: French corvette
Displacement: 508 tonnes (500 tons)
Dimensions: 25.6m x 7m (84ft x 23ft 6in)
Main armament: Twenty 18-pounders
Launched: 1803
Date of profile: 1803

From the time of the Spanish Armada in 1588 until the middle of the 19th century, the sail-driven line of battleship dominated the world's oceans. These vessels changed little in appearance over the centuries and were restricted in size only by the limitations of their wooden construction. Such battle-ships were supported by a whole range of smaller warships designed for specific duties such as scouting, escorting and independent patrolling. The corvette was one level below that of the 36-gun frigate and was usually employed on scouting or raiding missions. The corvette was a relatively new rate of warship and had evolved slowly from the smaller sloop and brig. The main armament was carried on the main deck, or on the upper deck.

Discovery

Type: British exploration ship
Displacement: 1,646 tonnes (1,620 tons)
Dimensions: 52m x 10m (172ft x 34ft)
Machinery: Single screw compound engines
Launched: March 1901
Date of profile: 1901

Built in Dundee, Scotland, *Discovery* was the first purpose-built vessel designed for research work. She was built of wood at a time when the art of wooden shipbuilding was beginning to disappear, but this was essential as it was better able to withstand the pressure of ice. *Discovery* had a magnetic laboratory, so no iron or steel could be used within 9 metres (30ft) of it. Specially woven hemp was used in the rigging immediately around the laboratory. In 1901 she left Britain for the Antarctic under the command of Captain Scott. She was later used on other research trips and was then berthed on the Thames for many years before finally returning to her home port of Dundee.

Dixmude

Type: French aircraft carrier
Displacement: 11,989 tonnes (11,800 tons)
Dimensions: 150m x 23m x 7.6m (490ft 10in x 78ft x 25ft 2in)
Machinery: Single screw diesel engines
Main armament: Three 102mm (4in) guns
Launched: December 1940
Date of profile: 1952

Dixmude was one of three vessels built in the US for lease to Britain. Her original name was *Rio Parana*. On arrival in Britain the flight deck was increased to 134 metres (440ft) and in 1942 her US weapons were replaced with British 102mm (4in) Mk V weapons. Re-named *Biter*, she served almost exclusively on convoy escort duties. She was returned to the US in 1945 and was then handed over to France where she became the *Dixmude* and served as an aircraft transport. In the early 1950s she was disarmed, and in 1960 she was hulked as an accommodation ship. She was returned to the US in 1966 and later scrapped.

Dmitri Donskoi

Type: Russian cruiser
Displacement: 5,987 tonnes (5,893 tons)
Dimensions: 90m x 15.8m x 7m (296ft 5in x 52ft x 24ft 4in)
Machinery: Twin screw vertical compound engines
Top speed: 15.5 knots
Main armament: Two

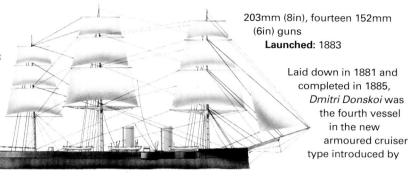

203mm (8in), fourteen 152mm (6in) guns
Launched: 1883

Laid down in 1881 and completed in 1885, *Dmitri Donskoi* was the fourth vessel in the new armoured cruiser type introduced by

Russia in 1870. The 152mm (6in) guns were carried in a battery on the main deck, while the 203mm (8in) guns were carried on sponsons. Her heavy sail rig was reduced in 1895 when she underwent a major refit, and her armament was altered to six 152mm (6in) and ten 120mm (4.7in) guns. *Dmitri Donskoi* was scuttled following the Battle of Tsushima in May 1905.

Dmitri Donskoi

Type: Russian cruiser
Displacement: 19,507 tonnes (19,200 tons)
Dimensions: 210m x 21m x 7m (689ft x 70ft x 24ft 6in)
Machinery: Twin screw turbines

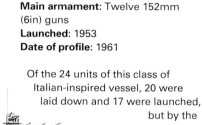

Main armament: Twelve 152mm (6in) guns
Launched: 1953
Date of profile: 1961

Of the 24 units of this class of Italian-inspired vessel, 20 were laid down and 17 were launched, but by the

end of 1960 only 14 were completed and operational. Nearly all the units were fitted for minelaying duties, mine stowage being on the main deck. The 152mm (6in) guns were mounted in triple turrets, two fore and two aft, with each group having its own range finders. Two units were fitted with guided weapons in place of the two aft gun turrets.

Dogali

Type: Italian cruiser
Displacement: 2,235 tonnes (2,200 tons)
Dimensions: 76m x 11m x 4.5m (250ft x 37ft x 14ft 6in)

Machinery: Twin screw triple expansion engines
Main armament: Six 152mm (6in) guns

Launched: December 1885
Date of profile: 1890

Dogali was originally the lightly constructed steel cruiser *Salaminia*, built for the Greek Navy. Purchased by Italy in 1887, she was then re-named *Angelo Emo*

but soon became *Dogali*. In 1908 she was sold to Uruguay and was re-named *24 De Agosta*. In 1910 she became the *Montevideo*. *Dogali* was the first warship to be built with triple expansion engines, which developed 7,600 horsepower. Crew numbered 224, and they were housed under a raised forecastle and poop. The vessel was discarded in 1914 and scrapped in about 1930.

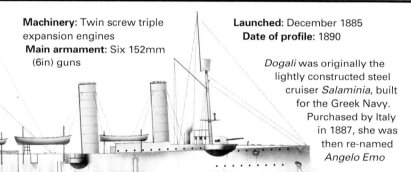

Dolfijn

Type: Dutch submarine
Displacement: 1,518 tonnes (1,494 tons) (surface), 1,855 tonnes (1,826 tons) (submerged)
Dimensions: 80m x 8m x 4.8m (260ft 10in x 25ft 9in x 15ft 9in)
Machinery: Twin screw diesel (surface), electric motors (submerged)
Main armament: Eight

533mm (21in) torpedo tubes
Launched: May 1959
Date of profile: 1966

Dolfijn and her three sisters are of a triple-hulled design with a maximum diving depth of nearly

304 metres (1,000ft). The design was a unique solution to the problem of internal space, the hull consisting of three cylinders arranged in a triangular shape. The upper cylinder houses the crew, navigational equipment and armament, while the lower cylinders house the powerplant.

Dolphin

Type: US gunboat
Displacement: 1,509 tonnes (1,486 tons)
Dimensions: 78m x 9.7m x 4m (256ft 6in x 32ft x 15ft 3in)
Machinery: Single screw vertical compound engines
Main armament: One 152mm (6in)

gun
Launched: April 1884

Dolphin was the first all-steel warship in the US Navy. She originally had a light barque rig, but was re-rigged as a three-masted schooner before a

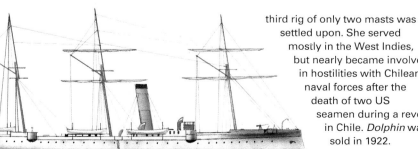

third rig of only two masts was settled upon. She served mostly in the West Indies, but nearly became involved in hostilities with Chilean naval forces after the death of two US seamen during a revolt in Chile. *Dolphin* was sold in 1922.

Dolphin

Type: US submarine
Displacement: 1,585 tonnes (1,560 tons) (surface), 2,275 tonnes (2,240 tons) (submerged)
Dimensions: 97m x 8.5m x 4m (319ft 3in x 27ft 9in x 13ft 3in)
Machinery: Twin screw diesel (surface), electric motors (submerged)

Top speed: 17 knots (surface), 18 knots (submerged)
Main armament: One 102mm (4in) gun, six 533mm (21in) torpedo tubes
Launched: March 1932
Date of profile: 1933

Dolphin was an experimental boat, originally designated V7, then given the serial number SS169. She was a distinct move away from the large ocean-going boats

then popular, but was not considered a success because of the attempt to incorporate most of the features of the preceding class in a hull half the size. During World War II she was assigned to training duties. She was broken up in 1946.

Domenico Millelire

Type: Italian submarine
Displacement: 1,473 tonnes (1,450 tons) (surface), 1,934 tonnes (1,904 tons) (submerged)
Dimensions: 86m x 7.4m x 4.2m (282ft x 24ft 6in x 14ft)
Machinery: Twin screw diesel (surface), electric motors (submerged)

Top speed: 17.5 knots with diesel engines, 7 knots on ancillary motors (surface), 8.9 knots (submerged)
Main armament: One 120mm (4.7in) gun, six 533mm (21in) torpedo tubes
Launched: September 1927

Domenico Millelire was one of four boats that were the first large displacement submarines built by the Italian Navy. They all made

numerous ocean cruises and underwent modernisation in 1934. In 1936-37 they took part in the Spanish Civil War. *Domenico Millelire* was laid up in 1941 and used as floating oil depot ship GR248.

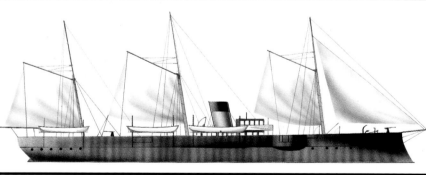

Don

Type: Russian auxiliary cruiser
Displacement: 10,668 tonnes (10,500 tons)
Dimensions: 153m x 17.6m (503ft x 58ft)

Machinery: Triple screw triple expansion engines
Launched: 1890

Date of profile: 1905

Originally the German

liner *Fürst Bismarck*, the ship was sold to Russia in 1904 and re-named *Don*. After the war she was named *Moskva* and was later sold to Austria where she served as the depot ship *GAA*. After World War I she became the Italian *San Giusto* and served on the Atlantic. She was scrapped in 1924.

Donetz

Type: Russian gunboat
Displacement: 1,219 tonnes (1,200 tons)
Dimensions: 64m x 10m x 3m (210ft x 35ft x 10ft)
Machinery: Twin screw horizontal compound engines

Main armament: One 152mm (6in), two 203mm (8in) guns
Launched: November 1887

Donetz and her five sisters all served in the Black Sea Fleet. In October 1914 *Donetz* was torpedoed and sunk, but she was later raised and repaired. She was irretrievably sunk in May 1919.

Doric

Type: British liner
Displacement: 28,935 tonnes (28,480 tons)
Dimensions: 183m x 20.6m (600ft 6in x 67ft 6in)
Machinery: Twin screw turbines
Top speed: 16 knots
Launched: 1922

Doric was the only turbine-driven liner to be built for the White Star Line. She was built for service on

their Liverpool-St Lawrence, Canada route and could carry 583 cabin class and 1,688 third-class

passengers. By 1930 her accommodation had been modified to take 320 cabin class, 657 tourist class, and 537 third-class passengers. In 1935 she was in collision with the freighter *Formigny*, and was so badly damaged she was sold for scrap.

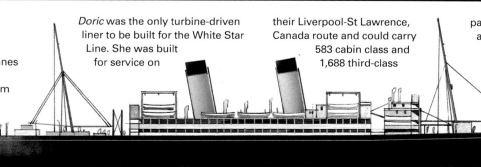

Doudart de la Grée

Type: French frigate
Displacement: 2,235 tonnes (2,200 tons)
Dimensions: 102m x 11.5m x 3.8m (334ft x 37ft 9in x 12ft 6in)
Machinery: Twin screw diesels
Top speed: 25 knots
Main armament: Three 100mm (3.9in) guns, twin anti-aircraft weapons
Launched: April 1961
Date of profile: 1963

Nine vessels of the Commandant Riviére class were built under the French 1956 and 1957 navy

estimates by the Lorient Naval Dockyard. They were good general-purpose, anti-submarine vessels of small displacement, and were intended for patrol work or escort duties Their speed was not particularly high, but they packed a reasonable amount of equipment in a light hull. The standard machinery was four diesels coupled to the twin screws, which

provided 16,000hp, and gave a range of over 8,500km (4,500 miles) at 15 knots, or 11,400km (6,000 miles) at 12 knots. One vessel in this class was instead fitted with an experimental combined gas turbine/diesel

installation, which gave a dramatic increase in maximum range. *Doudart de la Grée* had a wartime crew complement of 210, and could also carry some 80 commandos. In later life, one of her 100mm (3.9in) gun turrets was replaced by four Exocet missile launchers. New developments in construction techniques and equipment design meant that production of this class was quickly superseded by more modern frigate designs.

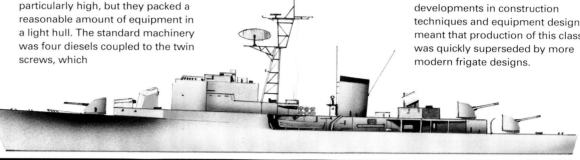

Downes

Type: US frigate
Displacement: 4,165 tonnes (4,100 tons)
Dimensions: 126.6m x 14m x 7.5m (415ft 4in x 46ft 9in x 24ft 7in)
Machinery: Single screw, turbines

Main armament: One 127mm (5in) gun, one eight-tube Sea Sparrow missile launcher plus Phalanx
Launched: December 1969

The Doyle class frigates were comparable to the destroyers of World War II, although they were criticised for having limited manoeuvrability and anti-submarine capability. The tower

amidships houses funnel exhausts and was originally intended to carry an advanced electrical array. However, this was not developed and *Downes* carries standard sea and air search radars instead. Forty-six of this class were built, forming a major part of NATO's defence capability.

Doyle

Type: US destroyer
Displacement: 2,621 tonnes (2,580 tons)
Dimensions: 106m x 11m x 5.4m (348ft 6in x 36ft x 18ft)
Machinery: Twin screw, turbines
Main armament: Four 127mm (5in) guns, five 533mm (21in) torpedo tubes
Launched: March 1942

Developed from the Sims class, the large class to which *Doyle* belonged was the last destroyer class to be designed and built for the US Navy before the Americans entered World War II. Production was sped up by the elimination of unnecessary

curves in the superstructure, and many in the class were completed with straight-fronted bridge structures. Many ships in the class were transferred to other navies after World War II, where they continued to give good service. *Doyle* was scrapped in 1970.

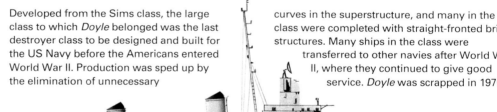

Doyle

Type: US frigate
Displacement: 3,708 tonnes (3,650 tons)
Dimensions: 135.6m x 14m x 7.5m (444ft 10in x 45ft x 24ft 7in)
Machinery: Single screw, gas turbines
Top speed: 28 knots +

Main armament: One 76mm (3in) gun plus Harpoon missile launcher
Launched: May 1982
Date of profile: 1990

Doyle belongs to the largest class of major surface warship built in the West since World War II. The only anti-submarine weapons carried are torpedo tubes as *Doyle* carries two helicopters to fulfil this role. All vessels carry full radar systems.

Dragone

Type: Italian destroyer/escort
Displacement: 1,117 tonnes (1,100 tons)
Dimensions: 83.5m x 8.6m x 3m (274ft x 28ft 3in x 10ft 4in)
Machinery: Twin screw, turbines
Main armament: Two 102mm (4in) guns, six 450mm (17.7in)

torpedo tubes, plus smaller weapons
Launched: August 1943
Date of profile: 1944

Dragone and her sisters were enlarged versions of the previous Spica class, but were slower in spite of an increase in machinery power. Seized by the Germans and numbered *TA30*, *Dragone* was sunk on 15 June 1944 by torpedoes fired from British MTBs. Her career had lasted only nine weeks.

Dragonfly

Type: British gunboat
Displacement: 726 tonnes (715 tons)
Dimensions: 60m x 10m x 1.8m (196ft 6in x 33ft 8in x 6ft 2in)
Machinery: Twin screw, turbines
Main armament: Two 102mm (4in) guns
Launched: 1938

Dragonfly was similar to the 1937 *Scorpion*, but was slightly smaller. Originally five vessels were planned for this class of river gunboat but one was cancelled. Engines developed 3,800hp and they carried 90 tonnes (90 tons) of fuel oil. Crew complement was 74. The vessels were primarily intended for river patrols in the Far East. Small and compact with a shallow draught, they were able to navigate up most of the shallow rivers, policing areas often unsettled by warring local chieftains. *Dragonfly* was sunk by Japanese dive bombers while attempting to escape from Singapore on 14 February 1942.

Drake

Type: British cruiser
Displacement: 14,376 tonnes (14,150 tons)
Dimensions: 162m x 22m x 8m533ft 6in x 71ft 4in x 26ft)
Machinery: Twin screw triple expansion engines
Main armament: Sixteen 152mm (6in), two 233mm (9.2in) guns
Launched: March 1901

When first completed, *Drake* and her four sisters were the fastest group of ships in the world. Engines developed 30,000hp and they had excellent seakeeping qualities due to the high freeboard. *Drake* was torpedoed and sunk in October 1917 by the German submarine *U79*.

Dreadnought

Type: British battleship
Displacement: 11,060 tonnes (10,886 tons)
Dimensions: 104.5m x 19.4m x 8m (343ft x 63ft 10in x 26ft 3in)
Machinery: Twin screw vertical compound engines
Main armament: Four 317mm (12.5in) guns
Launched: March 1875
Date of profile: 1885

This vessel was originally designed by Reed as a unit of the Devastation class to be called *Fury*. Work was suspended while she was on the stocks pending a report on stability, protection and armament that was being prepared by the Committee of Designs. As *Dreadnought*, the ship was eventually completed in 1879 as a larger version of *Devastation*, and she incorporated many modifications on the earlier design. The 317mm (12.5in), 25-tonne (25-ton) guns were of a new specification, and were carried by *Dreadnought* throughout her entire career. The complete armour belt was the thickest continuous protection carried by a British warship. She was broken up in 1908.

Dreadnought

Type: British battleship
Displacement: 22,194 tonnes (21,845 tons)
Dimensions: 160.4m x 25m x 8m (526ft 3in x 82ft x 26ft 3in)
Machinery: Quadruple screws, turbines
Top speed: 21.6 knots
Main armament: Ten 304mm (12in) guns
Armour: 203-280mm (8-11in) waterline belt, 280mm (11in) on turrets
Launched: February 1906

With the launching of *Dreadnought* a new, more advanced era of warship construction began. She was the first 'all big gun' battleship, and made all previous battleships obsolete. *Dreadnought* saw active service in World War I, being surpassed only by even larger ships of her type, to which she gave the generic name dreadnought. She was scrapped in 1923.

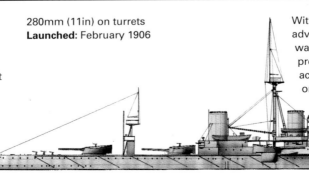

Dreadnought

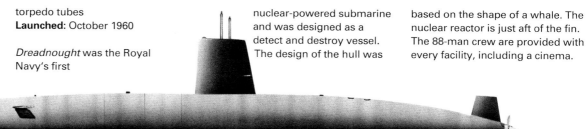

Type: British submarine
Displacement: 3,556 (3,500 tons) tonnes (surface), 4,064 tonnes (4,000 tons) (submerged)
Dimensions: 81m x 9.8m x 8m (265ft 9in x 32ft 3in x 26ft)
Machinery: Single screw, nuclear reactor, steam turbines
Main armament: Six 533mm (21in)

torpedo tubes
Launched: October 1960

Dreadnought was the Royal Navy's first nuclear-powered submarine and was designed as a detect and destroy vessel. The design of the hull was based on the shape of a whale. The nuclear reactor is just aft of the fin. The 88-man crew are provided with every facility, including a cinema.

Dristigheten

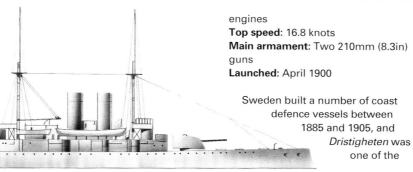

Type: Swedish coast defence ship
Displacement: 3,500 (3,445 tons) tonnes
Dimensions: 86.8m x 15m x 4.8m (285ft x 48ft 6in x 16ft)
Machinery: Twin screw triple expansion

engines
Top speed: 16.8 knots
Main armament: Two 210mm (8.3in) guns
Launched: April 1900

Sweden built a number of coast defence vessels between 1885 and 1905, and *Dristigheten* was one of the last of the group. She was designed to operate in the Baltic and Kattegat and had a relatively high speed which was needed to cover the length of the Swedish coastline. Main armament was housed in turrets, one aft and one forward. The secondary battery was concentrated amidships. Coal supply was enough for six days at top speed. *Dristigheten* was scrapped in 1961.

Dromia

Type: Italian minesweeper
Displacement: 132 tonnes (130 tons)
Dimensions: 32m x 6.4m x 1.8m (106ft x 21ft x 6ft)
Machinery: Twin screw diesel engines
Top speed: 14 knots
Main armament: One 20mm (0.8in) gun
Launched: 1957
Date of profile: 1964

Dromia was one of a group of 20 inshore minesweepers of the British Ham class built in Italy between 1955 and 1957. All vessels in the class were ordered by NATO and were named after small sea creatures. They were designed to operate in shallow waters, rivers and estuaries, and when first built they were an entirely new type of minesweeper, embodying many of the lessons learned during World War II and subsequent hostilities.

Drottning Victoria

Type: Swedish coast defence ship
Displacement: 7,234 tonnes (7,120 tons)
Dimensions: 121m x 18.5m x 6.8m (397ft x 61ft x 22ft 6in)
Machinery: Twin screw turbines
Top speed: 22.5 knots
Main armament: Six 152mm (6in),

four 280mm (11in) guns
Launched: September 1917
Date of profile: 1946

Drottning Victoria was a compact, powerful vessel designed to provide mobile defence for likely targets of enemy forces. She was originally completed in 1921 with a light tripod mast, but she underwent a major re-fit between 1935 and 1937 and her upper works were re-modelled. Coal supply was 365 tonnes (360 tons), and she carried 277 tonnes (273 tons) of oil. *Drottning Victoria* was scrapped in 1959.

Drum

Type: US submarine
Displacement: 1,854 tonnes (1,825 tons) (surface), 2,448 tonnes (2,410 tons) (submerged)

Dimensions: 95m x 8.3m x 4.6m (311ft 9in x 27ft 3in x 15ft 3in)
Machinery: Twin screw diesel (surface), electric motors (submerged)
Main armament: One 76mm (3in) gun, ten 533mm (21in) torpedo tubes

Launched: May 1941
Date of profile: 1941

Developed from the Tambor class, *Drum* was a double hull, ocean-going submarine with good seakeeping qualities and range. She was one of a class of over 300 boats, and as such was part of the largest warship project undertaken by the USA. She became a museum exhibit in 1968.

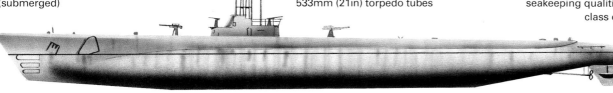

Dubourdieu

Type: French cruiser
Displacement: 3,760 tonnes (3,700 tons)
Dimensions: 77m x 14m x 6.6m (253ft 6in x 46ft x 21ft 8in)
Machinery: Single screw horizontal compound engines
Top speed: 13.9 knots
Main armament: Twelve 140mm (5.5in), four 162.5mm (6.4in) guns
Launched: 1884
Date of profile: 1886

In the 1870s and 1880s, France was

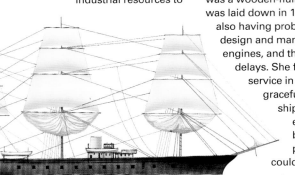

still building many cruisers in wood. This was regarded as more economical than steel construction, and also allowed the devotion of most of her valuable steel and industrial resources to the production of ironclads. America was the only other major power still building cruisers in this way, but this was because she suffered from a shortage of steel mills. Dubourdieu was a wooden-hulled cruiser that was laid down in 1880. France was also having problems with the design and manufacture of engines, and this led to long delays. She finally entered service in 1886. She was a graceful vessel, with a full ship rig of sail and an elegant clipper bow. Her coal-fired propulsion system could generate some 3,000hp, but she was intended to spend much of her time cruising under sail alone. Dubourdieu was designed for overseas and colonial duties, where she might have to spend long periods of time with no access to sophisticated dockyard facilities, and where coaling stations would be few and far between. She had a powerful armament for a ship of this size. Her 162mm (6.4in) main guns were on sponsons on the upper deck, while the 140mm (5.5in) secondary armament was mounted in broadside on the main deck. Her design was quickly superseded by dramatic advances in technology, and she was scrapped in 1899.

Duca di Genova

Type: Italian cruiser
Displacement: 3,962 tonnes (3,900 tons)
Dimensions: 68m x 15m x 7m (223 ft x 49ft 3in x 23ft)
Machinery: Single screw direct acting engine
Top speed: 9 knots
Main armament: 50 cannon (varied)
Launched: 1860
Date of profile: 1866

Duca di Genova was originally a Sardinian wooden-hulled frigate with a good spread of canvas. From the 1820s, Sardinia had steadily built up her navy to a reputable size, and the Duca di Genova was one of the Sardinian Navy's major vessels. Her engines were of the first simple expansion type, and developed just over 1,000hp. Her complement numbered

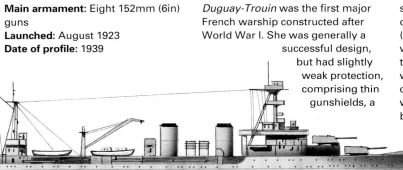

490. While in the Sardinian Navy, Duca di Genova served on the South American station, overseeing Italian interests in the area. She was absorbed into the newly formed Italian Navy in 1861. The vessel was eventually laid up in 1875.

Duguay-Trouin

Type: French cruiser
Displacement: 9,500 tonnes (9,350 tons)
Dimensions: 184m x 17m x 6m (604ft x 56ft 3in x 17ft 3in)
Machinery: Quadruple screws, turbines
Top speed: 34.5 knots
Main armament: Eight 152mm (6in) guns
Launched: August 1923
Date of profile: 1939

Duguay-Trouin was the first major French warship constructed after World War I. She was generally a successful design, but had slightly weak protection, comprising thin gunshields, a splinter-proof conning tower and a double armoured deck. The 152mm (6in) guns were of a new pattern which brought them into line with the French Army's 152mm (6in) weapon. All three vessels in the class were economical on trials. She was disarmed at Alexandria in 1940, but later rejoined Allied forces. She was broken up in 1952.

Duguay-Trouin

Type: French destroyer
Displacement: 5,892 tonnes (5,800 tons)
Dimensions: 152.5m x 15.3m x 6.5m (500ft 4in x 50ft 2in x 21ft 4in)
Machinery: Twin screw, turbines
Main armament: Two 100mm (3.9in) guns, one eight-cell Crotale launcher
Launched: June 1973

Duguay-Trouin was one of three vessels in a class that were designed to follow on from the earlier Aconit-class destroyer. The single-screw propulsion of the earlier class had been unsuccessful, leading to a doubling up of the machinery in Duguay-Trouin. This resulted in an increase in speed of four knots. Helicopter facilities were included, plus essential backup, making the Duguay-Trouin and her sisters the first French warships of destroyer size to operate anti-submarine helicopters. The missile launcher is mounted forward of the funnel, which also carries the mast, with extensive magazines below.

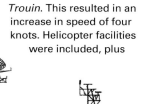

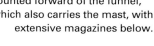

Duguesclin

Type: French battleship
Displacement: 6,210 tonnes (6,112 tons)
Dimensions: 81m x 17.4m x 7.6m (265ft 9in x 57ft 3in x 25ft)
Machinery: Twin screw vertical compound engines
Top speed: 14.5 knots
Main armament: Six 140mm (5.5in), one 193mm (7.6in), four 240mm (9.4in) guns

Armour: 152-254mm (6-10in) on waterline belt, 203mm (8in) on barbettes
Launched: 1883

Duguesclin had a wooden hull sheathed in copper, and standard wrought iron armour. She originally carried a heavy brig rig, but was later given two masts with military tops. Crew numbered 440. *Duguesclin* had one sister, the *Vauban*. *Duguesclin* was stricken in 1904.

Duilio

Type: Italian battleship
Displacement: 12,264 tonnes (12,071 tons)
Dimensions: 109m x 19.7m x 8.3m (358ft 2in x 64ft 8in x 27ft 3in)
Machinery: Twin screw vertical compound engines
Top speed: 15 knots
Main armament: Four 450mm (17.7in) guns

Launched: May 1876
Date of profile: 1885

Duilio and her sister *Enrico Dandolo* were designed by Benedetto Brin, and upon completion were the most powerful warships in the world. Although laid down in 1873, *Duilio* was not completed until 1880. She was modernised in 1890, and again in 1900. After providing good service, *Duilio* was stripped of her armament in 1909 and became a floating oil tank.

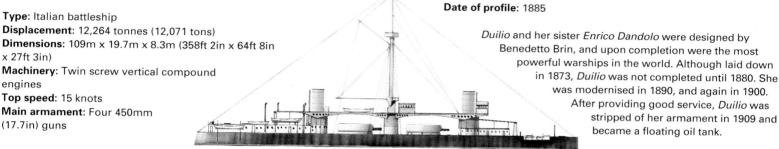

Duilio

Type: Italian battleship
Displacement: 29,861 tonnes (29,391 tons)
Dimensions: 187m x 28m x 8.5m (613ft 2in x 91ft 10in x 28ft 2in)
Machinery: Twin screw, turbines
Top speed: 27 knots
Main armament: Ten 320mm (12.6in) guns
Launched: April 1913
Date of profile: 1942

Between 1937 and 1940 *Duilio* and her sister *Andrea Doria* underwent extensive modernisation and emerged as virtually new ships. *Duilio* was employed on convoy escort duty and interception raids. She was scrapped in 1957-58.

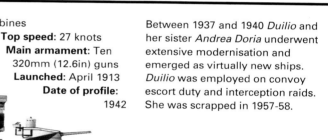

Duilio

Type: Italian liner
Displacement: 24,670 tonnes (24,281 tons)
Dimensions: 193.5m x 23.2m (634ft 10in x 76ft)
Machinery: Quadruple screws, turbines
Launched: 1916

The construction of *Duilio*, Italy's first home-built merchant vessel to exceed 20,320 tonnes (20,000 tons) was delayed for the duration of World War I. She was eventually completed in October 1923.

Her maiden voyage between Genoa and New York took place that same month, and in 1928 she was transferred to the South American route. In 1933 she made her first voyage to Cape Town to start a new South African service. She was laid up in 1940, but was chartered in 1942 by the International Red Cross. *Duilio* was sunk in 1944, and was raised and scrapped in 1948.

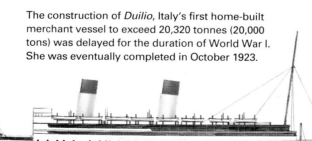

Duke of Wellington

Type: British steam line of battleship
Displacement: 5,922 tonnes (5,829 tons)
Dimensions: 73m x 18m x 7.5m (240ft x 60ft x 25ft)
Machinery: Single screw compound engines
Top speed: 10 knots
Main armament: Ten 203mm (8in) guns plus 121 smaller weapons
Launched: September 1852

Date of profile: 1855

The *Duke of Wellington* was laid down at Pembroke Dock in May 1849. In early 1852, with the growing threat of war with France, a hurried conversion programme was put in hand and she was converted into a steam vessel with engines that developed 900hp. However, it would be nearly another 30 years before sails completely disappeared from warships in favour of engine power alone.

Duncan

Type: British destroyer
Displacement: 1,973 tonnes (1,942 tons)
Dimensions: 100m x 10m x 4m (329ft x 32ft 10in x 12ft 10in)
Machinery: Twin screw, turbines
Main armament: Four 120mm (4.7in) guns
Launched: July 1932

Date of profile: 1940

Duncan formed part of the C and D class destroyers laid down in 1931 and 1932 respectively. They were slightly enlarged versions of the B class. *Duncan* was fitted out as a destroyer leader. During World War II, after the class had been greatly reduced by losses, the remaining vessels were converted into escort carriers. Of the vessels lost, one was wrecked, three were sunk in collision and six were sunk in action. *Duncan* was broken up in 1945, the rest were broken up between 1945 and 1947.

Duncan

Type: US destroyer
Displacement: 3,606 tonnes (3,550 tons)
Dimensions: 120m x 12.4m x 5.8m (390ft 6in x 41ft x 19ft)
Machinery: Twin screw, turbines
Main armament: Six 127mm (5in) guns, six torpedo tubes

Launched: October 1944

Duncan formed part of an extensive World War II building programme of ocean-going destroyers with a powerful armament and good radius. Thirty-six of the original group, known as the Gearing class, were converted in 1949 and fitted with enemy-aircraft early warning systems. Of the nearly 100-unit class, several were still in service as late as 1980. *Duncan* was stricken from the list in 1973.

Dunderberg

Type: US battleship
Displacement: 7,173 tonnes (7,060 tons)
Dimensions: 115m x 22m x 6.4m (377ft 4in x 72ft 10in x 21ft)
Machinery: Single screw back-acting engines
Top speed: 12 knots
Main armament: Eight 280mm (11in), two 380mm (15in) guns
Launched: July 1865

Dunderberg was a brigantine rigged casemate vessel with a double bottom, collision bulkhead and a massive solid oak ram. Although laid down in late 1862, she was not completed in time for service in the Civil War due to a shortage of materials and skilled labour. Upon completion she was one of the largest and most powerful vessels built for the US Navy. Her builder bought her back from the US Navy and sold her on to France, where she was renamed *Rochambeau*. She was stricken in 1872.

Dunkerque

Type: French battlecruiser
Displacement: 36,068 tonnes (35,500 tons)
Dimensions: 214.5m x 31m x 8.6m (703ft 9in x 102ft 3in x 28ft 6in)
Machinery: Quadruple screws, turbines
Top speed: 29.5 knots
Main armament: Sixteen 127mm (5in), eight 330mm (13in) guns
Launched: October 1935

Dunkerque was the first French warship to be laid down after the Washington Treaty of 1922. She was the culmination of a series of design studies that resulted in an answer to the German *Deutschland*s of the early 1930s. A hangar and catapult were provided for the four scout planes. She was scuttled in 1942.

Dunois

Type: French gunboat
Displacement: 903 tonnes (889 tons)
Dimensions: 78m x 8.4m x 3.8m (256ft x 27ft 10in x 12ft 8in)
Machinery: Twin screw vertical triple expansion engines
Top speed: 21.7 knots
Main armament: Six 9-pounders
Launched: October 1897

Dunois was a two-funnelled vessel with two pole masts, a straight stem and a turtle-backed foredeck. No torpedoes were fitted in this group, and the main armament was situated on the upper deck near the funnels. In service, neither *Dunois* nor her sister ship made the designed speed, but they were able to make 20 knots for lengthy periods. *Dunois* was removed from the effective list in 1920.

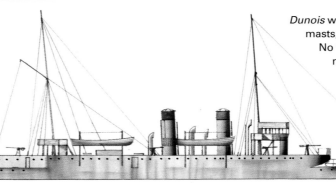

Dupetit-Thouars

Type: French cruiser
Displacement: 2,032 tonnes (2,000 tons)
Dimensions: 78m x 10.8m x 4.8m (257ft x 35ft 5in x 16ft)
Machinery: Single screw vertical compound engines
Top speed: 15 knots
Main armament: Ten 140mm (5.5in) guns
Launched: 1874
Date of profile: 1876

The French Navy built large numbers of wooden-hulled cruisers at this time, intended for independent operations on colonial service. Economy, simplicity of construction and ease of maintenance were more important than being at the cutting edge of naval technology. Dupetit-Thouars was one of a class of four such vessels, barque-rigged with a wooden hull. Her engines developed 2,018hp and steam was supplied by four coal-fired boilers. Even so, she was intended to spend much of her time cruising under sail power. Her 140mm (5.5in) main guns were muzzle loaders, and were mounted in broadside, with one on the bow and one aft. Later a few light guns were added. Each vessel in the class had a slightly different armament configuration, while one vessel was equipped with tripod masts in an unsuccessful attempt to reduce the amount of rigging. These ships were really at the end of a line of development, and Dupetit-Thouars was stricken in 1897.

Dupleix

Type: French cruiser
Displacement: 12,984 tonnes (12,780 tons)
Dimensions: 194m x 19.8m x 7m (636ft 6in x 65ft x 23ft 7in)
Machinery: Triple screw turbines
Top speed: 34 knots
Main armament: Eight 89mm (3.5in), eight 203mm (8in) guns
Armour: 51-57mm (2-2.25in) main belt
Launched: October 1930
Date of profile: 1937

Dupleix was the last of a group of four cruisers laid down at yearly intervals from 1926 to 1929. All were slightly different, and improvements were included as experience was gained during construction. The ships were modified versions of the Tourville class, and about two knots were sacrificed in favour of better protection. Seventeen watertight bulkheads carried right up to the upper deck, and coal bunkers were arranged to give extra protection. Dupleix was scuttled at Toulon in 1942, but was raised in 1943 only to be sunk by Allied bombing.

Dupleix

Type: French destroyer
Displacement: 4,236 tonnes (4,170 tons)
Dimensions: 139m x 14m x 5.7m (456ft x 46ft x 18ft 8in)
Machinery: Twin screw gas turbines, plus diesels
Main armament: One 100mm (3.9in) gun, two fixed torpedo launchers
Launched: October 1975

Dupleix was one of eight ships built at Brest Naval Dockyard for service as anti-submarine vessels. A major innovation was the use of gas turbine engines. These can develop 52,000hp for a speed of 30 knots, compared with her diesels, which develop 10,400hp for 18 knots. The use of gas turbines, however, produced severe limitations on the available space amidships due to the requirement for extensive intake and uptake trunking. This forced a choice between the Malafon anti-submarine missile and helicopters. The latter were chosen, and all in the class carry a double hangar aft. The helicopters can also be fitted out for surface work, as well as the standard ASW role. In wartime an extra set of four Exocet missiles can be fitted.

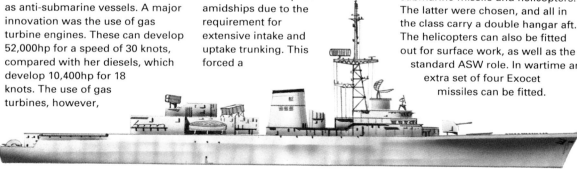

Dupuy de Lôme

Type: French cruiser
Displacement: 6,676 tonnes (6,670 tons)
Dimensions: 114m x 15.8m x 8m (374ft x 52ft x 26ft 2in)
Machinery: Triple screw, vertical and horizontal expansion engines
Top speed: 19.8 knots
Main armament: Six 162mm (6.4in), two 193mm (7.6in) guns
Launched: 1890
Date of profile: 1892

Although launched in 1890, Dupuy de Lôme was not completed until 1895 due to delays caused by an accident to her boilers. She was the first cruiser with triple screws. The ship was reconstructed in 1905 and given three funnels, and the military masts were removed. She was sold to Peru in 1912, and re-sold to Belgium in 1920, where she was converted into a cargo ship and re-named Peruvier.

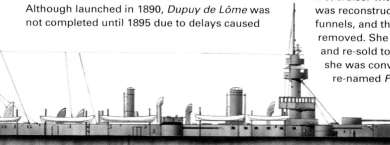

Dupuy de Lôme

Type: French submarine
Displacement: 846 tonnes (833 tons) (surface), 1,307 tonnes (1,287 tons) (submerged)
Dimensions: 75m x 6.4m x 3.6m

(246ft x 21ft x 11ft 10in)
Machinery: Twin screw three cylinder reciprocating steam engine (surface), electric motors

(submerged)
Main armament: Two 76mm (3in) guns, eight 450mm (17.7in) torpedo tubes

Launched: September 1915

Dupuy de Lôme was part of the 1913 naval programme. She served with the Morocco Flotilla from 1917 until the end of World War I, and was then reconstructed. Her steam engines were replaced by diesels taken from German submarines which developed 2,900hp. *Dupuy de Lôme* was discarded in 1935.

Duquesne

Type: French cruiser
Displacement: 6,000 tonnes (5,905 tons)
Dimensions: 100m x 15m x 7.9m (329ft 5in x 50ft x 26ft)
Machinery: Single screw horizontal compound engines
Main armament: Fourteen 140mm (5.5in), seven 193mm (7.6in) guns
Launched: 1876

Duquesne was ship rigged and iron-hulled with a coppered wood sheathing. She had nine watertight compartments plus a collision bulkhead. The vessel was completed in 1878. She was reboiled in 1894 and given the new horizontal compound engines. In 1895 her armament was updated to quick-fire weapons. *Duquesne* was removed from the effective list in 1901.

Duquesne

Type: French destroyer
Displacement: 6,187 tonnes (6,090 tons)
Dimensions: 157.6m x 15.5m x 7m (517ft x 50ft 10in x 23ft 9in)
Machinery: Twin screw turbines
Main armament: Two 100mm (3.9in) guns, one Malafon anti-

submarine missile launcher, four torpedo launchers
Launched: February 1966

Duquesne and her sister *Suffren* were the first French

destroyers specially designed to carry surface-to-air missiles. They were intended to provide both air and anti-submarine defence for the new generation of French aircraft carriers. *Duquesne* is also fitted with four Exocet missile launchers.

Durandal

Type: French destroyer
Displacement: 300 tonnes (296 tons)
Dimensions: 57.5m x 6.3m x 3m 188ft 8in x 20ft 8in x 10ft 5in)
Machinery: Twin screw triple expansion engines
Main armament: One 65mm (2.6in) , six 47mm (1.85in) guns, two 380mm (15in) torpedo tubes
Launched: February 1899
Date of profile: 1908

Durandal was France's first destroyer, and the lead ship of a four-strong class ordered in 1896 as prototypes for a new type of anti-torpedo-boat vessel. The ships were built by Normand, who already had wide experience in building torpedo craft. Two Norman water tube boilers supplied the

engines, which developed 4,800hp. Coal supply was approximately 38 tonnes (38 tons). *Durandal* had a flying deck which ran nearly her entire length, with funnels and gun mounts passing up through it. As originally completed, she had two masts. All vessels in the class could make 26 knots in bad weather and were generally good sea boats.

Durbo

Type: Italian submarine
Displacement: 710 tonnes (698 tons) (surface), 880 tonnes (866

tons) (submerged)
Dimensions: 60m x 6.4m x 4m (197ft 6in x 21ft 13ft)

Machinery: Twin screw diesel (surface), electric motors (submerged)

Top speed: 14 knots (surface), 7.5 knots (submerged)
Main armament: One 100mm (3.9in) gun, six 533mm (21in) torpedo tubes
Launched: March 1938

All 17 vessels in *Durbo*'s class gave good service in World War II, but only one survived it. In 1940 *Durbo* was depth-charged off Gibralter by British destroyers and was eventually scuttled.

Dykkeren

Type: Danish submarine
Displacement: 107 tonnes (105 tons) (surface), 134 tonnes (132 tons) (submerged)

Dimensions: 34.7m x 3.3m x 2m (113ft 10in x 10ft 10in x 7ft 3in)
Machinery: Twin screw petrol engine (surface),

electric motor (submerged)
Main armament: Two 457mm (18in) torpedo tubes
Launched: June 1909
Date of profile: 1910

Dykkeren was built in Italy by Fiat-San Giorgio, La Spezia. She was sold to the Danish Navy in October 1909. In 1916 she was in collision with the Norwegian steamer *Vesta* and sank. She was salvaged in 1917, and broken up in 1918.

E 20

Type: British submarine
Displacement: 677 tonnes (667 tons) (surface), 820 tonnes (807 tons) (submerged)
Dimensions: 55.6m x 4.6m x 3.8m (182ft 5in x 15ft x 12ft 6in)
Machinery: Twin screw diesel (surface), electric motors (submerged)

Main armament: One 76mm (3in) gun, five 457mm (18in) torpedo tubes
Launched: June 1915

One of a class of over 50 that included the first submarines capable of extended overseas patrols, the first

to mount a deck gun. *E 20* was sunk in 1915 in the Sea of Marmora by the German *UB14*, becoming the first submarine to be sunk by another.

Eagle

Type: British aircraft carrier
Displacement: 27,664 tonnes (27,229 tons)
Dimensions: 203.4m x 32m x 8m (667ft 6in x 105ft x 26ft 3in)

Machinery: Quadruple screw, turbines
Main armament: Five 102mm (4in), nine 152mm (6in) guns
Aircraft: 24
Launched: June 1918
Date of profile: 1932

Eagle was originally laid down as the Chilean Navy super-dreadnought *Almirante Cochrane*, but on the outbreak of World War I work began to turn her into an aircraft carrier for the Royal Navy. She eventually entered service in 1924. In August 1942, *Eagle* was sunk in the Mediterranean by *U73*, while attempting to deliver aircraft to Malta.

Eagle

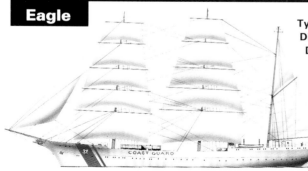

Type: US training ship
Displacement: 1,845 tonnes (1,816tons)
Dimensions: 90m x 11m x 5m (295ft x 39ft x 17ft)
Machinery: Single screw, diesel engines
Launched: June 1936
Date of profile: 1982

Built by Blohm and Voss, Hamburg, and originally named *Horst Wessel*,

Eagle is a steel-hulled vessel that served as a naval training barque, before being taken into service by the USA in January 1946 as part of the World War II reparations. She was assigned to the US Coast Guard and is used to train Coast Guard cadets on summer cruises. The crew numbers 65 plus 195 cadets. *Eagle* is one of four similar German-built training ships, another of which was also taken over by the USA and later sold on to Brazil.

Eagle

Type: British aircraft carrier
Displacement: 47,200 tonnes (46,452 tons)
Dimensions: 245m x 34m x 11m (803ft 9in x 112ft 9in x 36ft)
Machinery: Quadruple screw, turbines
Main armament: Sixteen 114mm (4.5in) guns

Aircraft: 80
Launched: March 1946

With the completion of the programmes of 1936 and 1937 and with the construction

of the Illustrious class of 1938 in progress, designs were prepared in 1942 for their successors. These designs allowed for two complete hangars and the ability

to handle the heavier aircraft that were expected to be introduced. *Eagle* entered service in October 1951, was decommissioned in January 1972, and was sent for breaking-up in 1978. She was the sister ship of HMS *Ark Royal*.

Eagle 17

Type: US patrol boat
Displacement: 624 tonnes (615 tons)
Dimensions: 60m x 8m x 2.6m (200ft x 25ft 6in x 8ft 6in)
Machinery: Single screw, turbines
Top speed: 18 knots
Main armament: Two 76mm (3in), two 102mm (4in) guns
Launched: 1919

During World War I, American destroyers were operating at full stretch, while her shipyards were also at full capacity. The Eagles were intended to be cheaper, simpler alternatives to full-blown destroyers, capable of anti-submarine operations in open water. Plans were made for the construction of 112 units, but in the event only 60 were made. They were designed to be fabricated quickly and easily, and by companies not normally involved in naval construction. Their profile comprised mainly flat surfaces, with as few complex curves as possible. Rather than tie down existing resources, a special plant was erected by Henry Ford. Their machinery developed 2,500hp, and they could carry some 106 tonnes (105 tons) of fuel oil. They had a reasonable range of 5,600km (3,500 miles) at 10 knots. The tips of the propeller blades turned just three feet (1m) below the load draught line. The initial plans provided for higher top speed, of more than 20 knots, as well as an armament fit which included a single 127mm (5in) gun. In the event the design was simplified further to the austere configuration that was finally produced. The first Eagle was commissioned in October 1918, but she and her sisters entered service too late to have much effect on the war. They served through the 1920s and 1930s, and six were transferred to the US Coast Guard. Eight of the remaining boats survived to serve in World War II.

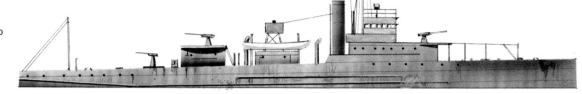

Eber

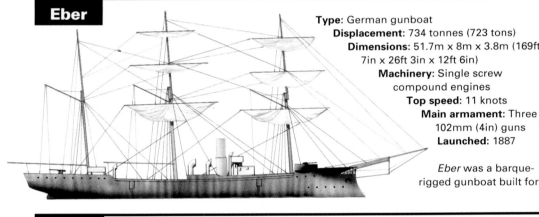

Type: German gunboat
Displacement: 734 tonnes (723 tons)
Dimensions: 51.7m x 8m x 3.8m (169ft 7in x 26ft 3in x 12ft 6in)
Machinery: Single screw compound engines
Top speed: 11 knots
Main armament: Three 102mm (4in) guns
Launched: 1887

Eber was a barque-rigged gunboat built for colonial service. She differed from previous gunboats in that she had a ram bow. Two of her 102mm (4in) guns were mounted on sponsons on either side of the forecastle, with a third aft. Her engines developed 760hp, and the screw could be hoisted out of the way when she was under sail power alone. In 1889 Eber was in the Pacific when she was ordered to Apia harbour in Samoa to join the German Squadron assembling to face a US force of three cruisers. However, a fierce typhoon struck the island in the early hours of 16 March 1889. Unable to use her engines, Eber was driven aground and wrecked.

Eber

Type: German gunboat
Displacement: 1,212 tonnes (1,193 tons)
Dimensions: 63.9m x 9m x 3.6m (209ft 8in x 29ft 6in x 12ft)
Machinery: Twin screw triple expansion engines
Top speed: 14 knots
Main armament: Three 102mm (4in) guns
Launched: 1903
Date of profile: 1905

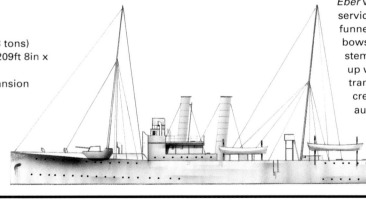

Eber was one of four units designed for overseas service. They resembled small cruisers, with tall funnels and raking masts. Two of the class had ram bows, but Eber and the remaining unit had straight stems. Upon the outbreak of World War I, Eber met up with the liner Cap Trafalgar in mid-Atlantic and transferred her armament and a large part of her crew so that Cap Trafalgar could become an auxiliary cruiser. The unarmed Eber then proceeded to Brazil where she was interned. Brazil later joined the Allies, and on 16 October 1917 Eber was blown up by her crew.

Edera

Type: Italian minesweeper
Displacement: 411 tonnes (405 tons)
Dimensions: 44m x 8m x 2.6m (144ft x 26ft 6in x 8ft 6in)
Machinery: Twin screw, diesel engines
Top speed: 14 knots
Main armament: Two 20mm (0.8in) anti-aircraft guns
Launched: 1955

Edera was one of the 19-strong Agave class of minesweepers. Built in Italian yards, the vessels were similar to the minesweepers that had already been transferred to the Italian Navy from the US Navy. The last ship in the Agave class was completed in 1956. The vessels were of non-magnetic wood and alloy composite construction, and were designed for inshore minesweeping duties, including rivers and estuaries. During the 1960s the class formed part of Italy's effective counter-mining force. Two diesel engines developed 1,200hp. Fuel carried was 25 tonnes (25 tons), enough for 4,750 kilometres (2,500 miles) at 10 knots. Crew numbered 38.

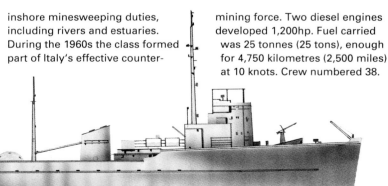

Edgar

Type: British cruiser
Displacement: 7,467 tonnes (7,350 tons)
Dimensions: 118m x 18.2m x 7.2m (387ft 6in x 60ft x 23ft 9in)
Machinery: Twin screw triple expansion engines
Top speed: 18 knots
Main armament: Ten 152mm (6in), two 233mm (9.2in) guns
Launched: November 1890

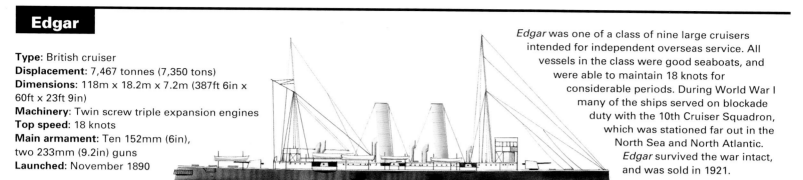

Edgar was one of a class of nine large cruisers intended for independent overseas service. All vessels in the class were good seaboats, and were able to maintain 18 knots for considerable periods. During World War I many of the ships served on blockade duty with the 10th Cruiser Squadron, which was stationed far out in the North Sea and North Atlantic. *Edgar* survived the war intact, and was sold in 1921.

Edgar Quinet

Type: French cruiser
Displacement: 14,068 tonnes (13,847 tons)
Dimensions: 159m x 21.5m x 8.4m (521ft 4in x 70ft 6in x 27ft 7in)
Machinery: Triple screw vertical triple expansion engines
Top speed: 23.9 knots

Main armament: Fourteen 193mm (7.6in) guns
Launched: September 1907
Date of profile: 1912

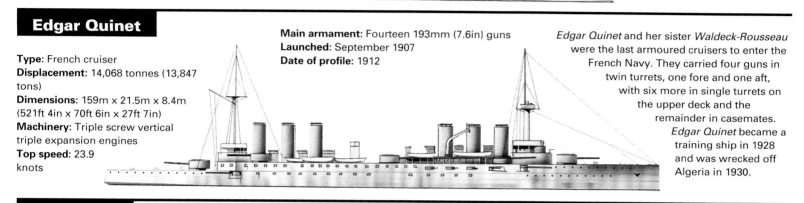

Edgar Quinet and her sister *Waldeck-Rousseau* were the last armoured cruisers to enter the French Navy. They carried four guns in twin turrets, one fore and one aft, with six more in single turrets on the upper deck and the remainder in casemates. *Edgar Quinet* became a training ship in 1928 and was wrecked off Algeria in 1930.

Edinburgh

Type: British destroyer
Displacement: 4,851 tonnes (4,775 tons)
Dimensions: 141m x 14.9m x 5.8m (463ft x 48ft x

19ft)
Machinery: Twin screw, gas turbines
Main armament: One 114mm (4.5in) gun, helicopter-launched Mk44 torpedoes, two triple

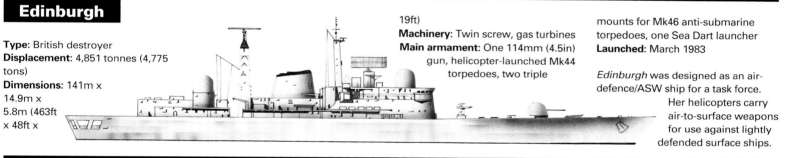

mounts for Mk46 anti-submarine torpedoes, one Sea Dart launcher
Launched: March 1983

Edinburgh was designed as an air-defence/ASW ship for a task force. Her helicopters carry air-to-surface weapons for use against lightly defended surface ships.

Eendracht

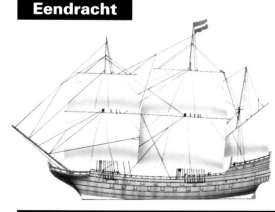

Type: Dutch sailing ship
Displacement: 365 tonnes (360 tons)
Dimensions: 30m x 8.6m (98ft 5in x 28ft 5in)
Main armament: 19 cannon and 12 swivel guns
Launched: 1600
Date of profile: 1600

Within a few years of their declaration of independence in the early 1580s, the Dutch had become the predominant trading power in the East. The rapid ascendency of the Dutch as a trading nation was due largely to their single-minded pursuit of commerce alone, unlike their

rivals who spent a great deal of time trying to 'convert' the peoples with whom they traded. The Dutch East India Company soon controlled the Cape of Good Hope route, and in 1615 an expedition was launched to find a new route to the East. The *Hoorn* and the *Eendracht* set out westward, but *Hoorn* caught fire and *Eendracht* was left to complete the voyage alone. The expedition rounded the cape of South America in January 1916, the explorers naming it Cape Horn after their ship and home town of Hoorn. The *Eendracht* had two decks plus an upper deck that carried the 12 swivel guns.

Effingham

Type: British cruiser
Displacement: 9,906 tonnes (9,750 tons)
Dimensions: 184m x 20m x 6.2m (605ft x 65ft x 20ft 6in)
Machinery: Quadruple screws, turbines

Top speed: 30.5 knots
Main armament: Seven 190mm (7.5in) guns
Armour: 38-76mm (1.5-3in) belt
Launched: June 1921

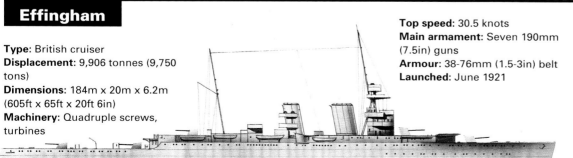

In 1915 a new class of large cruiser, which included *Effingham*, was designed as an answer to the small number of German raiders that were then preying upon British commerce all over the world. *Effingham* was wrecked on an uncharted rock off Norway on 18 May 1940 while escorting troops for the failed 'Norwegian campaign'.

Egeria

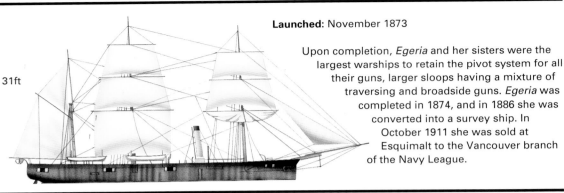

Launched: November 1873

Type: British sloop
Displacement: 964 tonnes (949 tons)
Dimensions: 48.7m x 9.4m x 3.8m (160ft x 31ft x 12ft 6in)
Machinery: Single screw compound reciprocating engine
Top speed: 11.3 knots
Main armament: Two 178mm (7in) guns, two 64-pounders

Upon completion, *Egeria* and her sisters were the largest warships to retain the pivot system for all their guns, larger sloops having a mixture of traversing and broadside guns. *Egeria* was completed in 1874, and in 1886 she was converted into a survey ship. In October 1911 she was sold at Esquimalt to the Vancouver branch of the Navy League.

Egypt

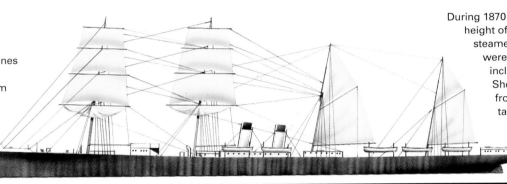

Type: British liner
Displacement: 4,744 tonnes (4,670 tons)
Dimensions: 134m x 13m (440ft x 44ft)
Machinery: Single screw compound engines
Launched: 1871

During 1870 the National Line was at the height of its fame and had ten large steamers to its name. Two more were ordered to expand the fleet, including the luxury liner *Egypt*. She served on the Atlantic run from 1871-1890, being briefly taken over as a troop transport during the Zulu War of 1879. *Egypt* was burnt at sea in July 1890.

Ekaterina II

Type: Russian battleship
Displacement: 11,224 tonnes (11,048 tons)
Dimensions: 100.9m x 21m x 8.5m (331ft x 68ft 11in x 27ft 11in)
Machinery: Twin screw vertical triple expansion engines
Top speed: 16 knots
Main armament: Six 304mm (12in)

guns
Launched: May 1886
Date of profile: 1890

Ekaterina II was built for the Black Sea Fleet, and was one of the first major warships to have triple

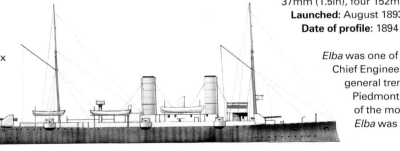

expansion engines. She and her sisters were among the most powerful battleships of their day, with their six guns mounted on a pear-shaped redoubt amidships. *Ekaterina II* was re-classified as a second-class battleship in 1906, and a year later became a target ship. She was sunk during target practice off Tendra harbour in 1907.

Elba

Type: Italian cruiser
Displacement: 2,773 tonnes (2,730 tons)
Dimensions: 84m x 13m x 5.4m (278ft 2in x 42ft 8in x 18ft)
Machinery: Twin screw horizontal triple expansion engines
Top speed: 17.9 knots
Main armament: Six

37mm (1.5in), four 152mm (6in) guns
Launched: August 1893
Date of profile: 1894

Elba was one of a class of six cruisers designed by Chief Engineer Masdea. They followed the general trend of the British-built Dogali and Piedmont classes, and were among the first of the modern cruiser types to be developed. *Elba* was discarded in 1920.

Elisabeta

Launched: 1887

Type: Romanian cruiser
Displacement: 1,341 tonnes (1,320 tons)
Dimensions: 73m x 10.2m x 3.6m (239ft 6in x 33ft 6in x 12ft)
Machinery: Twin screw horizontal triple expansion engines
Main armament: Four 152mm (6in) guns

In 1878 Romania gained independence from Turkey and soon had a small army and a navy of about 1,500 men was .The main unit of this force was *Elisabeta*, built in Britain. She served for many years, and was the Royal Yacht for much of her life.

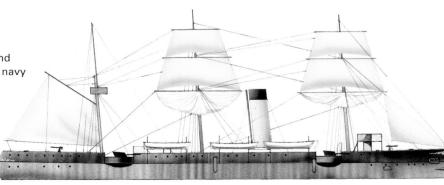

Emanuele Filiberto

Type: Italian battleship
Displacement: 10,058 tonnes (,900 tons)
Dimensions: 111.8m x 21m x 7.2m (366ft 10in x 69ft 3in x 23ft 10in)
Machinery: Twin screw, triple expansion engines
Top speed: 18 knots
Main armament: Eight 152mm (6in), four 254mm (10in) guns
Armour: 102-248mm (4-9.8in) thick waterline belt
Launched: 1897

By the end of the 1880s, the Italian Navy were becoming concerned by the cost and size of their battleships, as the most recent class laid down was displacing more than 15,240 tonnes (15,000 tons). The Minister of the Navy, Vice-admiral Saint Bon, proposed the construction of two cheaper, medium-sized ships with a simple armament layout. *Emanuele Filiberto* was laid down in 1893, launched in 1897, and completed in 1902. She was somewhat of a disappointment in service, with firepower too light for a battleship of the line. Her speed and sea-keeping qualities were also inadequate, due to the low 4.4m (14ft 6in) freeboard forward and 3m (10ft) clearance aft. She had a high superstructure amidships, holding the twin funnels, a single military mast and her boats. Her four 254mm (10in) main guns were mounted in two armoured turrets, placed above barbettes to give clearance in heavy seas. Her secondary armament of eight 152mm (6in) guns were mounted in broadside on the main superstructure. Her propulsion system could develop 13,500hp, and more than 610 tonnes (600 tons) of coal gave her a range of over 6,460km (3,400 miles) at 10 knots. Despite her weaknesses, she had a reasonably long service life, only being discarded in 1920.

Emanuele Filiberto Duca D'Aosta

Type: Italian cruiser
Displacement: 10,540 tonnes (10,374 tons)
Dimensions: 187m x 17.5m x 6.5m (613ft 2in x 57ft 5in x 21ft 4in)
Machinery: Twin screw, turbines
Top speed: 37.3 knots
Main armament: Eight 152mm (6in) guns
Launched: July 1935

Emanuele Filiberto Duca D'Aosta was one of two enlarged versions of the Montecuccol class that formed part of the 1931-33 building programme. The new vessels had the same armament as the smaller ships, but had slightly more powerful machinery and improved armour protection. *Emanuele Filiberto Duca D'Aosta* saw extensive service in World War II, often running much needed supplies to North Africa. In March 1949 she was ceded to Russia and was re-named *Stalingrad*. In the 1950s she was re-named *Kerch* and was discarded shortly thereafter. Her sister ship, *Eugenio Di Savoia*, was ceded to Greece in 1951 and was scrapped in 1964.

Emanuele Pessagno

Type: Italian destroyer
Displacement: 2,621 tonnes (2,580 tons)
Dimensions: 107.3m x 10m x 3.4m (352ft 6in x 33ft x 11ft 2in)
Machinery: Twin screw, turbines
Top speed: 38 knots
Main armament: Six 120mm (4.7in) guns, six 533mm (21in) torpedo tubes
Launched: August 1929
Date of profile: 1932

Emanuele Pessagno was ordered in 1926 and laid down in 1927-28. She and the 11 other vessels that made up her class all saw extensive service in World War II. Although smaller than their French rivals of the Guepard and Jaguar classes, the Italian vessels carried the same powerful armament and had a three-knot speed advantage over them. During trials, one of *Emanuele Pessagno*'s sisters was reported to have achieved 45 knots. When first completed, the vessels were re-classified as scouts, but by 1938 they were listed as destroyers. Only one vessel survived the war; eight were sunk in action, two were scuttled and one was mined. *Emanuele Pessagno* was torpedoed by a British submarine in May 1942.

Emanuele Russo

Type: Italian gunboat
Displacement: 288 tonnes (284 tons)
Dimensions: 52m x 5.7m x 1.8m (170ft 7in x 18ft 8in x 6ft)
Machinery: Twin screw, vertical triple expansion engines
Top speed: 25.8 knots
Main armament: Two 102mm (4in) guns
Launched: January 1922
Date of profile: 1927

Emanuele Russo was one of six vessels in the improved 'PN' torpedo-gunboat class built between 1910 and 1918 and intended as escorts for coastal convoys. *Emanuele Russo*'s engines developed 3,462hp and range was 1,786 kilometres (1,100 miles) at 11 knots and 1,086 kilometres (675 miles) at 15 knots. Four vessels in the class were discarded in 1939, one scrapped in 1950 and *Emanuele Russo* caught fire at Naples in March 1923 and was scrapped.

Emden

Type: German cruiser
Displacement: 4,336 tonnes (4,628 tons)
Dimensions: 118m x 13m x 4.8m
(389ft x 44ft x 16ft)
Machinery: Twin screw vertical
triple expansion engines
Top speed: 25 knots
Main armament: Ten
102mm (4in) guns

Armour: 76-100mm-thick waterline belt
Launched: May 1908
Date of profile: 1910

Emden served in Asiatic waters until the
outbreak of World War I, when she was sent
on a raiding cruise in the Indian Ocean.
She destroyed 16 British vessels before
being wrecked on a reef in
November 1914. Her wreck was
partially dismantled in 1950.

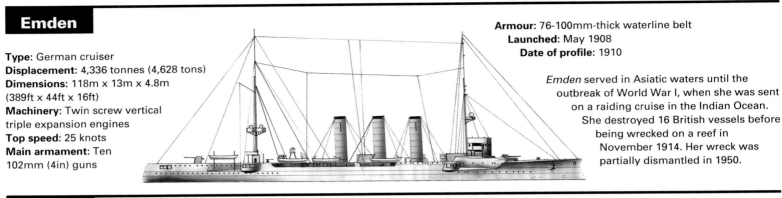

Emden

Type: German cruiser
Displacement: 7,102 tonnes
(6,990 tons)
Dimensions: 155m x 14m x
6.6m (509ft x 47ft x 21ft 8in)
Machinery: Twin screw,
turbines

Top speed: 29.4 knots
Main armament: Eight 152mm
(6in) guns
Launched: January 1925

The 1919 Treaty of Versailles

stipulated that Germany could only
retain six old cruisers, and that
they could not be replaced until
the existing vessels were 20
years old. The first new cruiser
built for the German Navy was
based on the old
wartime

cruiser design. *Emden* was intended
for overseas service, and combined
fuel supply was 1,138 tonnes (1,120
tons) of coal and oil, giving her a
range of 10,460 kilometres (6,500
miles). She took part in the attack on
Norway early in World War II. After
suffering bomb damage at Kiel, she
was scuttled in May 1945
and the wreck was broken
up in 1948.

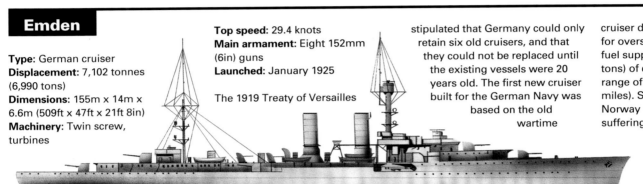

Emerald

Type: British cruiser
Displacement: 9,601 tonnes (9,450
tons)
Dimensions: 173.7m x 16.6m x 5.6m
(570ft x 54ft 6in x 18ft 4in)
Machinery: Quadruple screws,
turbines
Main armament: Seven 152mm (6in)
guns

Launched: May 1920

In 1917 designs were drawn up for a
group of fast cruisers
capable of catching
the high-speed light
cruisers which
Britain feared

were being built by the Germans. A
high length-to-beam ratio
was used

to achieve a designed maximum
speed of 33 knots, and a nine-metre
(30-ft) freeboard forward helped
Emerald to maintain her speed in
bad weather. *Emerald* was re-
fitted in 1931, saw service in World
War II, and was sold for scrap
in 1948.

Emperador Carlos V

Type: Spanish cruiser
Displacement: 9,235 tonnes (9,090 tons)
Dimensions: 115.8m x 20.5m x 7.6m
(380ft x 67ft x 25ft)
Machinery: Twin screw, vertical
triple expansion engines
Top speed: 20 knots
Main armament: Eight
140mm (5.5in), two
280mm (11in) guns
Armour: 51mm

(2in) thick belt, 165mm (6.5in) thick
protective deck
Launched: March 1895

Emperador Carlos V was one of the
last armoured cruisers built for the
Spanish Navy. In 1898 she was part
of a squadron formed to re-take the
Philippine Islands from the USA.
She was removed from the
effective list in 1931.

Empire Windrush

Type: British liner
Displacement: 14,104 tonnes (13,882
tons)
Dimensions: 160m x 20m (524ft x
66ft)
Machinery: Twin screw, geared
diesels
Launched: 1930

Date of profile: 1946

Empire Windrush was
formerly the German

ship *Monte Rosa*, built
for the Hamburg-South
America Line. In 1942
she transported troops

between Denmark and Norway, and then served
as a repair workshop for the battleship *Tirpitz*. In
1944 she struck a mine. After repairs,
she became a hospital ship. After
World War II she became the British
liner *Empire Windrush* and was
managed by the New Zealand Line.
In March 1954 an explosion in the
engine room set the liner on fire
and she sank.

Empress of Britain

Type: British liner
Displacement: 14,416 tonnes (14189 tons)
Dimensions: 167m x 20m (549ft x 66ft)
Machinery: Twin screw, quadruple expansion engines

Top speed: 20 knots
Launched: November 1905

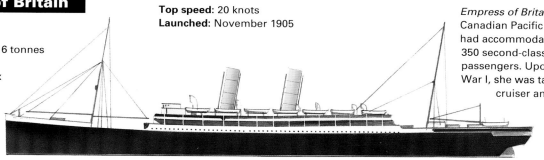

Empress of Britain entered service for the Canadian Pacific Company in 1906. She had accommodation for 310 first-class, 350 second-class and 800 third-class passengers. Upon the outbreak of World War I, she was taken over as an auxiliary cruiser and later served as a troop transport. In 1924 she underwent a re-fit, and was scrapped in 1930.

Empress of Britain

Type: British liner
Displacement: 43,025 tonnes (42,348 tons)
Dimensions: 231.8m x 29.7m (760ft 6in x 97ft 5in)
Machinery: Quadruple screws, turbines
Top speed: 25.5 knots
Launched: June 1930

Date of profile: 1931

Empress of Britain was the largest

pasenger vessel built for the Canadian Pacific Company. She could carry 465 first-class, 260 tourist-class and 470 third-class passengers. In 1939 she was taken over as a troop transport. She was attacked by a lone German bomber just off the coast of Ireland on 26 October 1940, and the Polish destroyer *Burza* took the burning liner in tow. However, on 28 October she was sunk by torpedoes from the German submarine *U32*.

Empress of Canada

Type: British liner
Displacement: 20,342 tonnes (20,022 tons)
Dimensions: 183m x 22.9m (601ft x 75ft)
Machinery: Twin screw, turbines
Top speed: 19 knots
Launched: June 1928
Date of profile: 1947

The *Empress of Canada*

was formerly the *Duchess of Richmond*, and entered service for the Canadian Pacific Company in 1929. She could carry 580 cabin-class, 480 tourist-class and 510 third-class passengers,

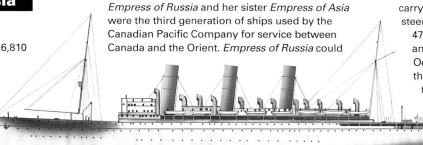

as well as a crew of 510. In 1939 the vessel was taken over as a troop transport. She was re-named *Empress of Canada* in 1947, and plied the Liverpool to Montreal route. In January 1953 she caught fire at her berth and sank. She was righted in March of the same year, but was considered beyond repair. In August 1953 she was sold for breaking up.

Empress of Russia

Type: British liner
Displacement: 17,079 tonnes (16,810 tons)
Dimensions: 180m x 20m x 8.8m (590ft x 68ft x 29ft)
Machinery: Quadruple screws, turbines
Launched: August 1912

Empress of Russia and her sister *Empress of Asia* were the third generation of ships used by the Canadian Pacific Company for service between Canada and the Orient. *Empress of Russia* could

carry 200 first-class, 100 second-class and 800 steerage-class passengers. Crew numbered 475. During World War I the ship became an armed merchant cruiser in the Indian Ocean. She resumed normal service after the war, but was taken over as a troop transport in World War II. In 1945 she was gutted by fire during a post-war re-fit and was subsequently broken up.

Endeavour

Type: British merchant ship
Displacement: 376 tonnes (370 tons)
Dimensions: 31m x 8.7m (101ft 7in x 28ft 7in)
Launched: 1760
Date of profile: 1768

Endeavour was originally a collier out of Whitby, but in 1768 she was chartered for Captain Cook's expedition to the Pacific. *Endeavour* proceeded

from Tahiti to the uncharted waters of the southwest Pacific in order to circumnavigate the main islands of New Zealand. The expedition then travelled on to the east coast of Australia, landing at Botany Bay. During this part of the voyage *Endeavour* was nearly lost on the Great Barrier Reef, but she was floated off successfully and was repaired in a nearby river. *Endeavour* returned to Britain by way of Batavia and the Cape of Good Hope. In 1771 she was sent to the Falkland Islands as a store ship.

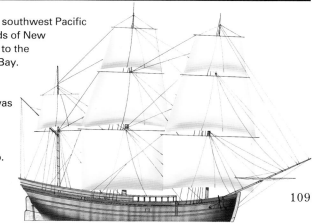

Endurance

Type: British ice patrol ship
Displacement: 3,657 tonnes (3,600 tons)
Dimensions: 91.5m x 14m x 5.5m (300ft x 46ft x 18ft)
Machinery: Single screw diesel engine
Top speed: 14.5 knots
Main armament: Two 20mm (0.8in) guns
Launched: May 1956
Date of profile: 1982

Endurance, originally named *Anita Dan*, was built by Krögerwerft, Rendsburg, for the Lauritzen Line. In

1967 she was purchased by the British Government for use as an ice patrol vessel in the South Atlantic, and was converted at the Harland and Wolff yard in Belfast, Ireland. As well as having extra equipment fitted, her hull was strengthened for operations in icy waters. Her propulsion system was a single Burmeister and Wain diesel engine

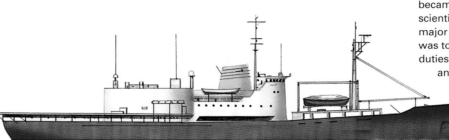

developing 3,220hp, giving a range of some 22,800km (12,000 miles). She entered service as a support ship to the British Atlantic Survey in 1968, and her red-painted hull became a welcome sight to the scientists and explorers. She had a major refit in 1978. One of her tasks was to carry out guard and patrol duties around the Falkland Islands, and the announcement of her withdrawal in the early 1980s helped give the Argentinian Government the incorrect impression that the British were no longer willing or able to protect their interests there.

Engadine

Type: British seaplane carrier
Displacement: 1,702 tonnes (1,676 tons)
Dimensions: 96.3m x 12.5m (316 ft x 41ft)
Machinery: Triple screw, turbines
Top speed: 21 knots
Launched: September 1911
Date of profile: 1915

Upon the outbreak of World War I, the British Admiralty took over a

number of fast cross-channel steamers for conversion into seaplane carriers. *Engadine* and her sister *Riviera* were two such ships and both were quickly converted to carry three aircraft. By December 1914 they were in action against the

German airship sheds at Cuxhaven. *Engadine* was modified in 1915. She then served with the Grand Fleet, carrying out North sea sweeps and anti-submarine patrols, and pursuing the German airships then beginning to increase their attacks upon the British mainland. *Engadine* later served in the Mediterranean. She was returned to her owners in 1919.

Engadine

Type: British helicopter support ship
Displacement: 9,144 tonnes (9,000 tons)
Dimensions: 129.3m x 17.8m x 6.7m (424ft 3in x 58ft 5in x 22ft)
Machinery: Single screw diesel engines
Launched: 1966

Engadine was laid down in August 1965 and was designed for the training of helicopter crews in deep-water operations.

Although she does not carry her own aircraft, these can be embarked as necessary and housed in the

large hangar aft of the funnel. At any one time, *Engadine* can carry four Wessex and two WASP helicopters, or two of the larger Sea Kings. Complement is 81, plus an additional 113 training crew. *Engadine* can also operate pilotless target aircraft. She is a unique vessel, giving a thorough training to the helicopter crews that form a major part of the anti-submarine defence of surface ships.

Enrico Dandolo

Type: Italian battleship
Displacement: 12,461 tonnes (12,265 tons)
Dimensions: 109.2m x 19.7m x 8.8m (358ft 3in x 64ft 8in x 28ft 10in)
Machinery: Twin screw vertical triple expansion engines
Top speed: 15.6 knots
Main armament: Four 450mm (17.7in) guns
Armour: 550mm (21.7in) thick belt amidships, 400mm (15.75in) on turrets and central citadel
Launched: July 1878
Date of profile: 1882

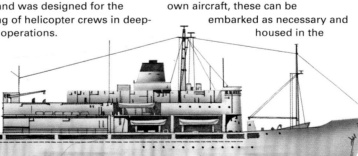

After the Battle of Lissa in 1866, Italian Navy budgets were severely cut, but during the second administration of Augusto Riboty the situation improved, and funds were made available for the construction of thoroughly modern vessels. Riboty was succeeded by Saint Bon, who allowed Benedetto Brin full rein to develop heavily-armed, well-protected, fast capital ships. *Enrico Dandolo* and her sister *Duilio* were the first of such vessels, and were the first battleships with giant guns and no provision for sailing. *Enrico Dandolo* served as a floating battery in World War I, and was discarded in 1920.

Enrico Tazzoli

Type: Italian submarine
Displacement: 1,574 tonnes (1,550 tons) (surface), 2,092 tonnes (2,060 tons) (submerged)

Dimensions: 84.3m x 7.7m x 5.2m (276ft 6in x 25ft 3in x 17ft)
Machinery: Twin screw diesel (surface), electric motors

(submerged)
Main armament: Two 120mm (4.7in) guns, eight 533mm (21mm) torpedo tubes

Launched: October 1935

Enrico Tazzoli was completed in 1936. She took part in the Spanish Civil War, and served in the Mediterranean for the early part of World War II. In 1940 she transferred to the Atlantic. In 1942 she was re-fitted to transport supplies to Japan, but on her first trip in 1943 she was inexplicably lost in the Bay of Biscay.

Enrico Tazzoli

Type: Italian submarine
Displacement: 1,845 tonnes (1,816 tons) (surface), 2,463 tonnes (2,425 tons) (submerged)
Dimensions: 94m x 8.2m x 5m (311ft 3in x 27ft x 17ft)
Machinery: Twin screw diesel (surface), electric motors (submerged)

Top speed: 20 knots (surface), 10 knots (submerged)
Main armament: Ten 533mm (21in) torpedo tubes
Launched: April 1942

Enrico Tazzoli was formerly the USA vessel *Barb*, completed in 1943 as part of the vast World War II Gato class. She transferred to the Italian Navy in 1955 after conversion to the

Guppy snorkel, which included a modified structure and 'fairwater' for better underwater performance. She carried 254 tonnes (250 tons) of oil fuel, enough for 19,311 kilometres (12,000 miles) at 10 knots.

Enrico Toti

Type: Italian submarine
Displacement: 1,473 tonnes (1,450 tons) (surface), 1,934 tonnes (1,904 tons) (submerged)

Dimensions: 87.7m x 7.8m x 4.7m (288ft x 25ft 7in x 15ft 5in)
Machinery: Twin screw diesel (surface), electric

motors (submerged)
Top speed: 17.5 knots (surface), 8.9 knots (submerged)
Main armament: One 120mm (4.7in) gun, six 533mm (21in) torpedo tubes
Launched: April 1928

Enrico Toti was a long-range vessel with a diving depth of 90 metres (295ft). She served in the Spanish Civil War, but was too large to be effective in the Mediterranean and was laid up in 1943.

Enrico Toti

Type: Italian submarine
Displacement: 532 tonnes (524 tons) (surface), 591 tonnes (582 tons) (submerged)
Dimensions: 46.2m x 4.7m x 4m (151ft 7in x 15ft 5in x 13ft)
Machinery: Single screw diesel (surface), electric motors (submerged)

Main armament: Four 533mm (21in) torpedo tubes
Launched: March 1967
Date of profile: 1968

Enrico Toti was the lead boat in a class of four which were the first submarines to be built in Italy since World

War II. The design was revised several times, and a coastal hunter/killer type intended for shallow and confined waters was finally approved.

Entemedor

Type: US submarine
Displacement: 1,854 tonnes (1,825 tons) (surface), 2,458 tonnes (2,420 tons) (submerged)

Dimensions: 95m x 8.3m x 4.6m (311ft 9in x 27ft 3in x 15ft 3in)
Machinery: Twin screw diesel (surface), electric motors (submerged)
Top speed: 20.2 knots

(surface), 8.7 knots (submerged)
Main armament: Ten 533mm (21in) torpedo tubes
Launched: December 1944

Entemedor was a double-hulled, ocean-going submarine belongong to the large World War II Gato class. Fuel tanks, containing up to 480 tonnes (472 tons), were situated in the central double hull section. Maximum diving depth was 95 metres (312ft). She was transferred to Turkey in 1973.

Enterprise

Type: US sloop
Displacement: 1,397 tonnes (1,375 tons)
Dimensions: 56.3m x 10.6m x 4.3m (185ft x 35ft x 14ft 3in)
Machinery: Single screw horizontal compound return connecting rod engines
Main armament: One 134mm (5.3in), four 228mm (9in), one 280mm (11in) guns
Launched: June 1874

By 1873 no major new US vessels had been laid down for nearly ten years. That same year authorisation was given for the construction of eight new warships, one of which was the *Enterprise*. She was a barque-rigged, wooden-hulled vessel. Her 228mm (9in) and 280mm (11in) guns were smooth-bored, while her 134mm (5.3in) gun was a Parrott rifled muzzle-loader. She saw relatively long service, in spite of her somewhat dated design, becoming a training ship in 1892 and not being sold until 1909.

Enterprise

Type: US aircraft carrier
Displacement: 25,908 tonnes (25,500 tons)
Dimensions: 246.7m x 26.2m x 7.9m (809ft 6in x 86ft x 26ft)
Machinery: Quadruple screws, turbines
Main armament: Eight 127mm (5in) guns

Aircraft: 96
Launched: October 1936

Early *Enterprise* designs had a flush deck, but this was thought to pose a smoke threat to landing aircraft, and an island structure to carry

funnel uptakes and provide control centres was devised. The hangars were light structures indpendent

from the hull, that could be closed off with rolling shutters. *Enterprise* was re-fitted in 1942 while in action at the Battle of Midway, during which her dive bombers helped sink three Japanese carriers. She was sold in 1958, despite efforts to preserve her as a memorial.

Enterprise

Type: US aircraft carrier
Displacement: 91,033 tonnes (89,600 tons)
Dimensions: 335.2m x 76.8m x 10.9m (1,100ft x 252ft x 36ft)
Machinery: Quadruple screws, turbines, steam

supplied by eight nuclear reactors
Top speed: 35 knots
Aircraft: 99
Launched: September 1960

Nuclear-powered aircraft carriers had been suggested as far back as 1946, but

cost delayed development of the project. *Enterprise* had a range of 643,720 kilometres (400,000 miles) at 20 knots. When completed in 1961 she was the largest vessel in the world, and was the second nuclear-powered warship to enter service. Her crew numbered 5,500. She was re-fitted between 1979 and 1982 and given a revised island structure.

Erato

Type: Italian torpedo boat
Displacement: 13.7 tonnes (13.5 tons)
Dimensions: 19.2m x 2.2m x 1.1m

(63ft x 7ft 6in x 3ft 9in)
Machinery: Single screw vertical triple expansion engine
Armament: One 25mm (1in) revolver,

two 355mm (14in) torpedo tubes
Launched: 1883

Erato was one of a class of light units built by Thornycroft. She was

designed for inshore service. Upon completion, *Erato* and her sisters were classified as fourth-class torpedo boats. They were discarded between 1896 and 1899, two being transferred to the Customs Service in 1898.

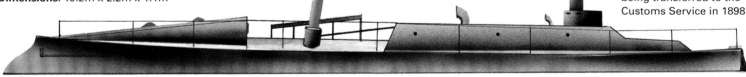

Erebus

Type: British sailing ship
Displacement: 375 tonnes (370 tons)
Dimensions: 30m x 8.7m (98ft 5in x 28ft 6in)
Launched: Date unknown
Date of profile: 1840

Erebus, together with the sailing ship *Terror*, was an exploration ship used by Captain Sir James Ross in his attempts to reach the South

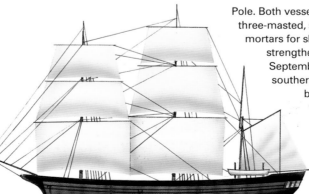

Pole. Both vessels started life as bomb ketches, which were three-masted, stoutly-built vessels used to mount heavy mortars for shore bombardment. *Erebus* and *Terror* were strengthened for the first voyage, which began in September 1839. In 1841 they reached the southernmost point of any expedition before turning back. Tragedy nearly struck during the second voyage when the two ships collided while negotiating icebergs. Both vessels lost their rudders on a third voyage, and were eventually paid off in September 1843.

Erebus

Type: British monitor
Displacement: 8,585 tonnes (8,450 tons)
Dimensions: 123.4m x 26.9m x 3.6m (404ft 10in x 88ft 3in x 11ft 10in)
Machinery: Twin screw triple expansion engines
Top speed: 14 knots
Main armament: Two 152mm (6in), two 380mm (15in) guns
Armour: 102mm (4in) internal belt, 102mm (4in) over magazine, 330mm (13in) on turret face
Launched: 1916
Date of profile: 1916

The monitor was a shallow-draught class of vessel especially designed for shore bombardment. A large building programme was begun in Britain during the early years of World War I, as the obsolescent battleships then used for the task were too cumbersome and vulnerable to submarine attack. Monitors, with their flat bottom, low profile and effective armour would be able to sail safely in much shallower waters, yet would be able to bring heavy fire to bear on coastal installations and defences. Some were also equipped with thick bulges at the waterline to further enhance torpedo protection. In late 1915, the Royal Navy were keen to increase the numbers of such vessels in service, especially as too many of their battleships were at that time operating in the shore bombardment role in the Dardanelles action. *Erebus* and her sister were laid down at that time, and launched the following June. Her two 380mm (15in) main guns were mounted in an armoured turret, itself placed on a tall barbette slightly forward of centre. The two 152mm (6in) guns were installed amidships. She had a low conning tower placed just forward of the main guns, and which must have suffered from muzzle blast. There was also a spotting station on the tripod mast. *Erebus* was broken up in 1946.

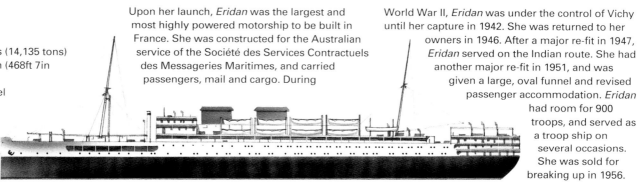

Eridan

Type: French liner
Displacement: 14,361 tonnes (14,135 tons)
Dimensions: 142.6m x 18.5m (468ft 7in x 61ft)
Machinery: Twin screw diesel engines
Top speed: 16 knots
Launched: June 1928
Date of profile: 1929

Upon her launch, *Eridan* was the largest and most highly powered motorship to be built in France. She was constructed for the Australian service of the Société des Services Contractuels des Messageries Maritimes, and carried passengers, mail and cargo. During World War II, *Eridan* was under the control of Vichy until her capture in 1942. She was returned to her owners in 1946. After a major re-fit in 1947, *Eridan* served on the Indian route. She had another major re-fit in 1951, and was given a large, oval funnel and revised passenger accommodation. *Eridan* had room for 900 troops, and served as a troop ship on several occasions. She was sold for breaking up in 1956.

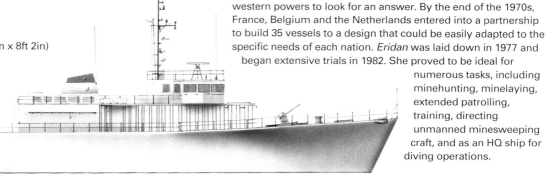

Eridan

Type: French minehunter
Displacement: 552 tonnes (544 tons)
Dimensions: 49m x 8.9m x 2.5m (161ft x 29ft 2in x 8ft 2in)
Machinery: Single screw diesel engine
Top speed: 15 knots
Main armament: One 20mm (0.8in) gun
Launched: February 1979
Date of profile: 1992

During the 1970s, the threat of Russian minelaying capability forced the western powers to look for an answer. By the end of the 1970s, France, Belgium and the Netherlands entered into a partnership to build 35 vessels to a design that could be easily adapted to the specific needs of each nation. *Eridan* was laid down in 1977 and began extensive trials in 1982. She proved to be ideal for numerous tasks, including minehunting, minelaying, extended patrolling, training, directing unmanned minesweeping craft, and as an HQ ship for diving operations.

Erie

Type: US gunboat
Displacement: 2,376 tonnes (2,339 tons)
Dimensions: 100m x 12.5m x 3.4m (328ft 6in x 41ft 3in x 11ft 4in)
Machinery: Twin screw turbines
Top speed: 20.4 knots
Main armament: Four 152mm (6in) guns
Launched: 1936

Erie was built to an unusual design in which the needs for peacetime patrols and wartime missions were successfully combined in a vessel that also provided adequate accommodation for its crew and marine contingent, as well as being economical to run. *Erie*'s unique hull design enabled her relatively low 5,941hp to drive her along at 20 knots, and her long bow helped to keep the vessel dry. A scouting plane was carried, but it was not possible to fit a catapult and so the aircraft was handled by crane. *Erie* and her sister *Charleston* were the first US ships to carry the new 152mm (6in), 47-calibre weapon with its combined shell and powder. *Erie* was torpedoed and sunk by a German U-boat off Curaçao in 1942.

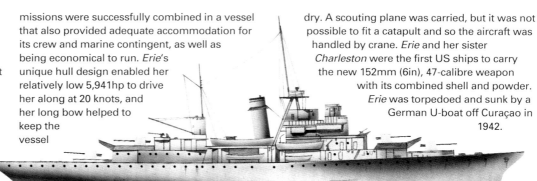

Erin

Type: British battleship
Displacement: 25,654 tonnes (25,250 tons)
Dimensions: 170.5m x 27.9m x 8.6m (559ft 5in x 91ft 6in x 28ft 3in)

Machinery: Quadruple screws, turbines
Main armament: Ten 343mm (13.5in) guns
Launched: September 1913

Built as the *Reshadieh* for the Turkish Navy,

Erin was taken over by the Royal Navy prior to completion, and served with the Grand Fleet for the duration of World War I. Her reduced coal capacity, 1,148 tonnes (1,130 tons) less than that of a contemporary British battleship of the King George V class, did not detract from her performance. She was re-fitted in 1917, placed in reserve in 1919 and scrapped in 1921.

Erinpura

Type: British liner
Displacement: 5,224 tonnes (5,142 tons)
Dimensions: 125m x 16m x 7m (411ft x 52ft 6in x 23ft 5in)
Machinery: Twin screw triple expansion engines
Launched: 1911

Erinpura was built for The British India Steamship Company's Far Eastern routes. During World War I she served as a hospital ship, and in this capacity ran aground on a reef during a sandstorm in 1919. She remained there for over a year. She was finally cut in half and the stern section was towed to Bombay where a new forward section was fitted. In 1923 she resumed normal service. In May 1943 she was part of the Malta supply convoy, but suffered a direct hit from enemy aircraft. She sank in four minutes, her 12-pounder gun still firing as she went down.

Eritrea

Type: Italian sloop
Displacement: 3,117 tonnes (3,068 tons)
Dimensions: 96.9m x 13.3m x 4.7m (318ft x 43ft 8in x 15ft 5in)
Machinery: Twin screw diesel engines, plus electric drive
Main armament: Four 120mm (4.7in) guns

Launched: September 1936

Eritrea was an elegant warship. Her diesel and electric motors could be used independently or together. Maximum speed with diesels was 18 knots, and range was

9,500 kilometres (5,000 miles) at 15.3 knots. Range with diesel and electric was nearly 7,112 kilometres (7,000 miles) at 11.8 knots. *Eritrea* was re-fitted for minelaying duties in 1940-41. She was captured in 1943 and handed over to France in early 1948, where she was re-named *Francis Garnier*. She was stricken in 1966.

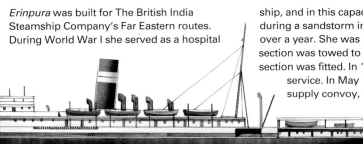

Ermanno Carlotto

Type: Italian gunboat
Displacement: 221 tonnes (218 tons)
Dimensions: 48.8m x 7.5m x 0.9m (160ft x 24ft 7in x 3ft)
Machinery: Twin screw vertical triple expansion engines
Main armament: Two 76mm (3in) guns

Launched: 1918
Date of profile: 1933

Ermanno Carlotto was a shallow-draught river gunboat built by the Shanghai Dock and Engineering Company. Two Yarrow boilers provided steam for the 1,100hp engines, and the twin screws operated in tunnels to achieve maximum benefit from the shallow draught. On 9 September 1943 she was scuttled in Shanghai to prevent her falling into Japanese hands. However, the Japanese re-floated her and named her *Naromi*. In 1945 she was taken over by China and re-named *Kiang Kun*. She was scrapped in 1960.

Erne

Type: British destroyer
Displacement: 630 tonnes (620 tons)
Dimensions: 71m x 7m x 2.9m (233ft 6in x 23ft 6in x 9ft 9in)
Machinery: Twin screw, triple expansion engines
Top speed: 25.6 knots

Main armament: One 12-pounder, two 457mm (18in) torpedo tubes
Launched: January 1903

Part of the 1901-1904 naval building programme included a large group of destroyers known as the E, or

River, class. *Erne* was the first of the 34-strong class to be launched. Although successful trials with turbines had already been

carried out in *Cobra* and *Viper*, *Erne* was given triple expansion engines. *Erne* was wrecked in 1915, but the successful class set the trend for future British destroyer development.

Ersh (SHCH 303)

Type: Russian submarine
Displacement: 595 tonnes (586 tons) (surface), 713 tonnes (702 tons) (submerged)

Dimensions: 58.5m x 6.2m x 4.2m (192ft x 20ft 4in x 13ft 9in)
Machinery: Twin screw diesel engines (surface), electric motors

(submerged)
Main armament: Two 45mm (1.8in) guns, six 533mm (21in) torpedo tubes

Launched: 1931
Date of profile: 1940

Ersh belonged to a class of 88 boats, coastal submarines with a single hull and a maximum diving depth of 90 metres (295ft). Thirty-two were lost during World War II, but the survivors remained in service with the Russian Navy until the mid 1950s. *Ersh* was scrapped in 1958.

Erzherzog Albrecht

Type: Austrian battleship
Displacement: 6,075 tonnes (5,980 tons)
Dimensions: 89.6m x 17m x 6.7m (294ft 3in x 56ft 3in x 22ft)
Machinery: Single screw two-cylinder horizontal engine
Top speed: 12.8 knots
Main armament: Eight 240mm (9.5in) guns
Armour: 203mm (8in) belt

Launched: April 1872

Erzherzog Albrecht was the Austro-Hungarian Navy's first iron-hulled warship. She was designed with offensive power and speed reduced to allow for better protection. She served until 1908, when she was re-named *Feuerspeier* and became a tender to a gunnery training ship. In 1920 she was handed over to Italy and became the *Buttafuaco Custoza*. She was scrapped in 1946.

Erzherzog Friedrich

Type: Austrian cruiser
Displacement: 1,724 tonnes (1,697 tons)
Dimensions: 67.8m x 12m x 5m (222ft 5in x 40ft x 16ft 5in)
Machinery: Single screw horizontal engines
Top speed: 8.9 knots
Main armament: Seventeen 30-pounders
Launched: April 1857
Date of profile: 1868

As originally completed in 1858, *Erzherzog Friedrich* and her sister *Dandolo* were flush-decked, wooden-hulled cruisers with the main deck housing most of the battery. *Erzherzog Friedrich* was rebuilt between 1877 and 1880 to include a topgallant forecastle with added poop to provide extra accommodation for cadets. The ship was taken out of active service in 1897, and was used for transporting boilers from Pola to Trieste. She was scrapped in 1899.

Erzherzog Karl

Type: Austrian battleship
Displacement: 10,640 tonnes (10,472 tons)
Dimensions: 126.2m x 21.7m x 7.5m (414ft 2in x 71ft 6in x 24ft 8in)
Machinery: Twin screw triple expansion engines
Top speed: 20.5 knots
Main armament: Twelve 190mm (7.5in), four 240mm

(9.45in) guns
Launched: October 1903
Date of profile: 1906

Erzherzog Karl was one of three units that formed the last of the pre-dreadnought type built for the Austrian Navy. She served in the Adriatic in World War I, and was taken over by Yugoslavia in 1919. In 1920 she was handed over to France and scrapped.

Esk

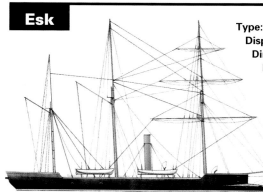

Type: British gunboat
Displacement: 270 tonnes (265 tons)
Dimensions: 26.6m x 8m x 2m (87ft 4in x 26ft x 6ft 6in)
Machinery: Twin screw two-cylinder reciprocating engine
Top speed: 8.5 knots
Main armament: Three 64-pounders
Launched: April 1877
Date of profile: 1880

Esk formed part of a different class of gunboats from previous groups, and was a development of the Ant class, which was designed for inshore work. *Esk* and her ten sisters were given a light rig for service on overseas stations, and a bow rudder was provided to improve handling. They were iron-hulled vessels with engines that developed 410hp. The class were ideal for river work, and several served in China. The *Dee* and *Medina* were sent to the Suez Canal during the Egyptian revolt of 1882. *Esk* was sold in Hong Kong in April 1903.

Esmeralda

Type: Chilean cruiser
Displacement: 2,997 tonnes (2,950 tons)
Dimensions: 82.3m x 12.8m x 5.6m (270ft x 42ft x 18ft 6in)
Machinery: Twin screw horizontal compound engines
Top speed: 18.3 knots
Main armament: Six 152mm (6in), two 254mm (10in) guns
Launched: June 1883
Date of profile: 1891

Up until the early 1880s, cruisers had only a partially armoured main deck, extending from a watertight bulkhead near the bow to another one towards the stern. This configuration kept cost and weight down, but left the ends of the ship totally unprotected. The concept of a continuous protective deck was first introduced by Lord Armstrong in the *Esmeralda*, designed for the Chilean Navy by George Rendell. She had an armoured main deck which was more than 25mm (1in) thick, and which vaulted steeply from 0.3m (1ft) above the waterline to 1.2m (4ft) below it. This was supplemented by a cellular layer which held her coal supplies, and which further reduced the risk of damage. Above this was the roomy and well-ventilated crew area. Her 254mm (10in) main guns were mounted singly in barbettes at each end of the vessel, while the 152mm (6in) weapons were mounted in sponsons amidships. In 1894 she was sold to Japan, and served in the Russo-Japanese war of 1904-05. She was struck off in 1912.

Esmeralda

Type: Chilean cruiser
Displacement: 7,112 tonnes (7,000 tons)
Dimensions: 132.8m x 16.2m x 6m (436ft x 53ft 2in x 20ft 3in)
Machinery: Twin screw vertical triple expansion engines
Main armament: Sixteen 152mm (6in), two 203mm (8in) guns
Armour: 152mm (6in) belt waterline belt, 38-51mm (1.5-2in) on deck
Launched: April 1894

Esmeralda was a steel-hulled, wood and copper-sheathed belted cruiser designed by Philip Watts and built by Lord Armstrong's yard for the Chilean Navy. She had a ram bow and a flush deck, and carried her 152mm (6in) guns on the main deck with the 203mm (8in) guns mounted one fore and one aft. Blast screens were fitted to protect the 203mm (8in) gun crews from the blast of the other guns nearby. She was re-fitted in 1910 and discarded in 1929.

Esmeralda

Type: Chilean training ship
Displacement: 3,731 tonnes (3,673 tons)
Dimensions: 94m x 13m x 7m (308ft 6in x 43ft x 23ft)
Machinery: Single screw diesel engine
Top speed: 11 knots
Main armament: Two 57mm (2.25in) guns
Launched: 1951
Date of profile: 1954

Esmeralda was a purpose-built sail training ship completed in 1952. She was built at Cadiz for the Spanish Navy, and was originally to have been named *Don Juan de Austria*. However, on 12 May 1953 the new vessel was transferred to the Chilean Navy and re-named *Esmeralda*. She served as a training ship for cadets, as well as taking part in several tall ships races. Eighty cadets could be carried, as well as a crew of 271. Her single Fiat diesel engine developed 1,400hp and range under engine alone was 15,200 kilometres (8,000 miles). Her four-masted schooner rig carried 2,392 square metres (26,910 sq ft) of canvas.

Espadon

Type: French submarine
Displacement: 159 tonnes (157 tons) (surface), 216 tonnes (213 tons) (submerged)
Dimensions: 32.5m x 3.9m x 2.5m (106ft 8in x 12ft 10in x 8ft 2in)
Machinery: Single screw triple expansion steam engine (surface), electric motor (submerged)
Main armament: Four 450mm (17.7in) torpedoes
Launched: September 1901
Date of profile: 1902

The big problem facing early submarine designers was how to propel the boat. Trials with compressed air were successful, but the storage space this required was too great to achieve reasonable speed and range. By the 1880s steam power was being used on the surface, the machinery being shut down in order to switch to the newly introduced electric motors for submersion. *Espadon* was one of this type of submarine. She was removed from the effective list in 1919.

Espadon

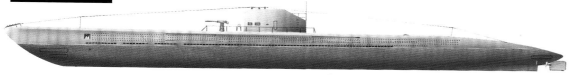

Type: French submarine
Displacement: 1,168 tonnes (1,150 tons) (surface), 1,464 tonnes (1,441 tons) (submerged)
Dimensions: 78.2m x 6.8m x 5m

(256ft 9in x 22ft 5in x 16ft 9in)
Machinery: Twin screw diesel engines (surface), electric motors (submerged)
Main armament: One 100mm

(3.9in) gun, ten 533mm (21in) torpedo tubes
Launched: May 1926
Date of profile: 1930

Espadon belonged to a group of minelaying submarines that were the first interwar first class submarines. They were heavily armed, with four bow, two stern and two twin torpedo tubes mounted in containers in the upper hull. Eight of the group were lost during World War II, including *Espadon* which was scuttled in September 1943.

España

Type: Spanish battleship
Displacement: 15,991 tonnes (15,740 tons)
Dimensions: 140m x 24m x 7.8m (459ft x 78ft 9in x 25ft 7in)
Machinery: Quadruple screws, turbines
Top speed: 19.5 knots
Main armament: Twenty 102mm (4in), eight 304mm (12in) guns

Armour: 76-203mm (3-8in) belt, plus 76mm (3in) on battery, 203mm (8in) on turrets
Launched: February 1912

España and her two sisters combined dreadnought armament with pre-dreadnought dimensions. *España* ran aground in 1923 and could not be salvaged. *Alfonso XIII*, one of *España*'s sisters, took her name in 1931, but was sunk by a mine in 1937.

Esperance Bay

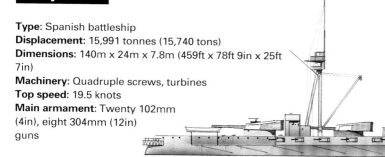

Type: British passenger/cargo ship
Displacement: 14,074 tonnes (13,853 tons)
Dimensions: 168.3m x 20.8m (552ft 2in x 68ft 3in)
Machinery: Twin screw, turbines
Top speed: 15 knots
Launched: December 1921

Esperance Bay was a large turbine steamer built for the Commonwealth Government Line of Freemantle by Beardmore of Glasgow. She was one of a class of three ships designed for mixed passenger and cargo service between Britain and Australia. In 1928 *Esperance Bay* was sold to the White Star Line, but was managed by the Aberdeen Line. She changed ownership in 1933, and again in 1936. In 1939 she was taken over as an armed merchant cruiser, and in 1941 was converted into a troop transport. Her first post-war voyage was to New Zealand in 1946. She was sold for scrap in 1955.

Esperia

Type: Italian liner
Displacement: 11,580 tonnes (11,398 tons)
Dimensions: 161m x 18.8m (528ft 3in x 61ft 8in)
Machinery: Twin screw, turbines
Launched: 1918
Date of profile: 1930

Esperia was completed in 1921 for service on the Genoa-Alexandria route. She had accommodation for 205 first-class, 118 second-class and 56 third-class passengers, plus 100 steerage. Crew numbered 275. Her engines developed 19,680hp and her service speed was 18 knots. On 20 August 1941, *Esperia* was sailing with a convoy of reinforcements from Italy to North Africa when she was sunk by three torpedoes from the British submarine *Unique*.

Espero

Type: Italian destroyer
Displacement: 386 tonnes (380 tons)
Dimensions: 64m x 5.9m x 2.2m (210ft x 19ft 6in x 7ft 6in)
Machinery: Triple expansion engines

Main armament: Five 57mm (2.24in) guns, four 355mm (14in) torpedo tubes
Launched: July 1904

Espero was one of a class of six vessels built for the Italian Navy by Pattison of Naples. Three of the class were sunk in action during World War I. In 1921 the three remaining vessels were re-classified as torpedo boats. Two years later *Espero* was discarded.

Espero

Type: Italian destroyer
Displacement: 1,696 tonnes (1,670 tons)
Dimensions: 93.2m x 9.2m x 2m (305ft 9in x 30ft 2in x 9ft 10in)
Machinery: Twin screw, turbines
Top speed: 36 knots
Main armament: Four 120mm (4.7in) guns
Launched: 1927

Date of profile: 1930

All eight units in the Espero class were laid down in 1925 and were slightly larger and

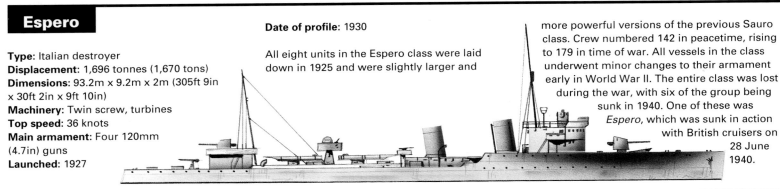

more powerful versions of the previous Sauro class. Crew numbered 142 in peacetime, rising to 179 in time of war. All vessels in the class underwent minor changes to their armament early in World War II. The entire class was lost during the war, with six of the group being sunk in 1940. One of these was *Espero*, which was sunk in action with British cruisers on 28 June 1940.

Esploratore

Type: Italian despatch boat
Displacement: 1,239 tonnes (1,220 tons)
Dimensions: 71.7m x 9m x 3.6m (235ft 6in x 30ft x 11ft 10in)
Machinery: Paddle wheels, reciprocating engines
Top speed: 17 knots
Main armament: Two 120mm (4.7in) guns
Launched: 1863

Esploratore was a wooden ship with a light schooner rig. She was one of the fastest vessels in the world, with an endurance of about 3,420km (1,800 miles) at full speed. From 1888 she was employed as a local defence ship at Venice. She was discarded in 1895 and re-designated as GM10 depot ship. Her sister vessel's machinery was used in a new ship named *Esploratore*, launched in 1885.

Espora

Type: Argentinian torpedo gunboat
Displacement: 528 tonnes (520 tons)
Dimensions: 60.9m x 7.6m x 2.5m (200ft x 25ft x 8ft 3in)
Machinery: Twin screw triple expansion engines
Top speed: 19.5 knots
Main armament: Two 14-

pounders, five 457mm (18in) torpedo tubes
Launched: 1890
Date of profile: 1896

Built by Lairds of Birkenhead, *Espora* and her sister *Rosales* were steel-hulled boats with a raised forecastle and poop. Two sets of twin torpedo tubes were carried amidships, with the fifth tube in the bows. *Espora* proved successful in action during the Chilean and Brazilian civil wars. Her boilers and armament were changed in 1905. *Espora* was discarded in 1920. *Rosales* sank in 1892.

Essex

Type: US sailing frigate
Displacement: 863 tonnes (850 tons)
Dimensions: 43m x 11m (141ft 9in x 36ft 6in)
Main armament: Twenty-six 12-pounders and ten 6-pounders
Launched: September 1799
Date of profile: 1799

Essex was a large sailing frigate paid for by popular subscription. Although she and four other frigates, also paid for by popular subscription, were

completed too late to see much action in the war with France, they proved valuable additions to the newly formed US Navy. As built, *Essex* was a very fast frigate, but numerous changes made to her by different commanders greatly reduced her speed. She first saw action in early 1800, and became the first US warship to round the Cape of Good Hope. In early 1814 *Essex* was captured by two British frigates after an action lasting nearly three hours. From 1833 *Essex* served as a prison ship at Kingston, Jamaica, until she was sold at auction in 1837.

Essex

Type: US aircraft carrier
Displacement: 35,438 tonnes (34,880 tons)
Dimensions: 265.7m x 29.2m x 8.3m (871ft 9in x 96ft x 27ft 6in)
Machinery: Quadruple screws, turbines
Top speed: 32.7 knots
Main armament:

Twelve 127mm (5in) guns
Launched: July 1942

By the end of the 1930s, the increased needs of the navy for air cover led

to an explosion in the size of aircraft carriers, and a larger hull was introduced to stow the aviation fuel required for the 91 aircraft now carried. There were 24 vessels in the Essex class, *Essex* entering service in 1942. She was removed from the effective list in 1969 and scrapped in 1973.

Étendard

Type: French gunboat
Displacement: 508 tonnes (500 tons)
Dimensions: 43.4m x 7.3m x 2.7m (142ft 6in x24ft 3in x 8ft 10in)
Machinery: Twin screw vertical compound engines
Top speed: 9 knots
Main armament: One 120mm (4.7in) gun, one 140mm (5.5in) gun
Launched: 1868
Date of profile: 1869

Both France and Britain had large colonial empires in the second half of the nineteenth century which required policing to keep in order. Both nations produced large numbers of gunboats; cheap and simple vessels able to operate for long periods away from sophisticated bases and logistic support, but powerful enough to deal with most small incidents in far flung colonies. *Étendard* was one of an eight-strong class of gunboats built in Bordeaux. Her hull was of wooden construction, and came complete with a full brigantine rig of sail and twin screw coal-fired engines. Her bunkers could only carry a maximum of 56 tonnes (55 tons) of coal, and she was thus expected to rely on sail power for most of the time. She had a single 140mm (5.5in) gun mounted on the forecastle, just in front of the foremast, while her 120mm (4.7in) gun was carried aft. Her full complement numbered 69. *Étendard* was one of the longest serving boats in the group, and was only removed from the effective list in 1892.

Etna

Type: Italian cruiser
Displacement: 3,881 tonnes (3,820 tons)
Dimensions: 91.4m x 13.2m x 6.2m (300ft x 43ft 4in x 20ft 4in)
Machinery: Twin screw double expansion engines
Top speed: 17.8 knots
Main armament: Six 152mm (6in), two 254mm (10in) guns

Launched: September 1885
Date of profile: 1887

Etna and her two sister ships were the first major group of modern warships built for the Italian Navy. The basic design was successful, and set the pattern for many later cruisers worldwide, combining good speed and heavy armament with good protection and reasonable seakeeping qualities. *Etna* was laid down in January 1883 and completed in 1887. In 1907 she was converted into a training ship and served as such until 1914, when she became a harbour defence ship and later a depot ship at Taranto. She was discarded in 1921.

Etna

Type: Italian cruiser
Displacement: 5,994 tonnes (5,900 tons)
Dimensions: 153.8m x 14.4m x 5.9m (504ft 7in x 47ft 6in x 19ft 6in)
Machinery: Twin screw, turbines
Main armament: Six 135mm (5.3in) guns

Launched: May 1942

Etna was originally ordered for Siam in 1938 and was to have been called *Taksin*. She was laid down at Trieste in 1939, but work ceased in December 1941, and in 1942 she was taken over by the Italian Navy. Major design changes were introduced to complete *Etna* as an anti-aircraft cruiser. Work continued slowly and she was only about 60 per cent complete when she was seized by German forces in 1943. They tried to complete the vessel for their own use, but she was scuttled in Trieste harbour.

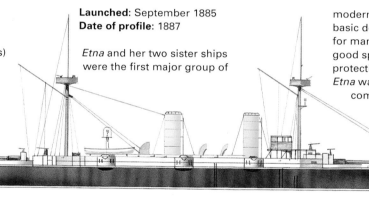

Etna

Type: Italian naval cargo ship
Displacement: 14,427 tonnes (14,200 tons)
Dimensions: 140m x 19m x 8m (495ft 6in x 63ft x 26ft 4in)
Machinery: Single screw, turbines
Top speed: 16.5 knots
Launched: June 1944
Date of profile: 1963

Etna was formerly the US attack cargo ship *Whitley*. She entered service in September 1944 and took part in the landing of US forces on Iwo Jima. She then served on transport duties until the end of World War II. In February 1962 she was transferred to the Italian Navy and re-named *Etna*. She carries a powerful set of heavy lifting gear, including a double gantry housing the tank landing craft. *Etna* was one of many such vessels supplied to allies in the 1950s and 1960s. They were used for cargo, or were the support for infantry landings where rapid cargo handling facilities were vital.

Etruria

Type: British liner
Displacement: 7,841 tonnes
(7,718 tons)
Dimensions: 153m x 17m
(502ft x 57ft)
Machinery: Single
screw compound
engines
Top speed: 19.9
knots
Launched: 1885

Etruria and *Umbria* were the last major steamships
built for the Cunard Line. Luxurious
accommodation was provided for
550 saloon passengers, and the
magnificent decor and fittings
introduced the concept of the
'floating hotel' for the first time. In
May 1885 *Etruria* took the Blue
Riband of the Atlantic for her
record-breaking
westbound passage.
She was scrapped in
1909.

Etruria

Type: Italian cruiser
Displacement: 2,317 tonnes (2,281 tons)
Dimensions: 84.8m x 12m x 4.8m (278ft
3in x 39ft 4in x 15ft 9in)
Machinery: Twin screw horizontal triple
expansion engines
Top speed: 17 knots
Main armament: Six 120mm (4.7in),
four 152mm (6in)
guns
Launched:
April 1891
Date of profile: 1894

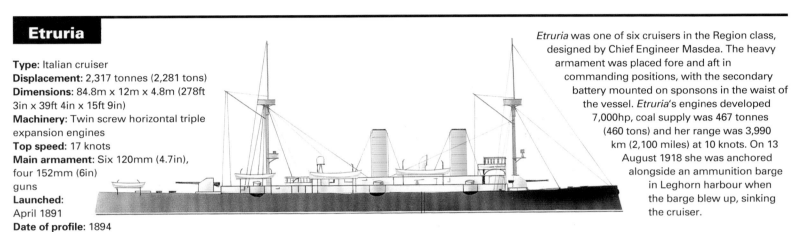

Etruria was one of six cruisers in the Region class,
designed by Chief Engineer Masdea. The heavy
armament was placed fore and aft in
commanding positions, with the secondary
battery mounted on sponsons in the waist of
the vessel. *Etruria*'s engines developed
7,000hp, coal supply was 467 tonnes
(460 tons) and her range was 3,990
km (2,100 miles) at 10 knots. On 13
August 1918 she was anchored
alongside an ammunition barge
in Leghorn harbour when
the barge blew up, sinking
the cruiser.

Ettore Fieramosca

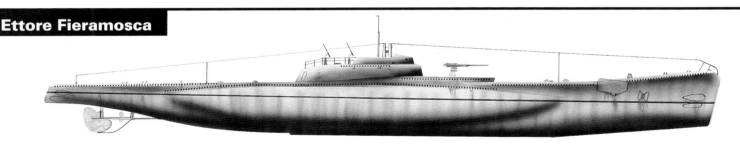

Type: Italian submarine
Displacement: 1,580 tonnes (1,556
tons) (surface), 1,996 tonnes (1,965
tons) (submerged)
Dimensions: 84m x 8.3m x 5.3m

(275ft 7in x 27ft 3in x 17ft 5in)
Machinery: Twin screw diesel
engines (surface), electric motors
(submerged)
Main armament: One 120mm (4.7in)

gun, eight 533mm (21in) torpedo
tubes
Launched: April 1929

Ettore Fieramosca had room for a
small plane in a hangar at the rear of
the conning tower, but the aircraft
was never embarked. The submarine
was laid up in March 1941.

Eugenio Di Savoia

Type: Italian cruiser
Displacement: 10,842 tonnes (10,672 tons)
Dimensions: 186.9m x 17.5m x 6.5m (613ft 2in x 57ft
5in x 21ft 4in)
Machinery: Twin screw, turbines
Top speed: 36.5 knots
Main armament: Six 100mm (3.9in)
anti-aircraft guns, eight 152mm

(6in) guns, six 533mm (21in)torpedo tubes
Launched: March 1935
Date of profile: 1938

Eugenio di Savoia was one of two vessels provided for under
the Italian naval programme of 1931-33, and was
laid down at Ansaldo's yard in Genoa in July 1933. She was
completed in January 1936. In 1951 *Eugenio di Savoia* was
removed from the effective list and transferred to Greece,
where she was re-named *Hella*. She remained in
service until 1964.

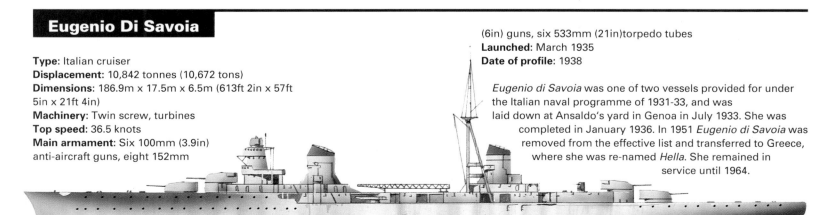

Euler

Type: French submarine
Displacement: 403 tonnes (397 tons)
(surface), 560 tonnes (551 tons)
(submerged)

Dimensions: 52m x 5.4m x 3m
(171ft x 17ft 9in x 10ft 3 in)
Machinery: Twin screw diesel
engines (surface), electric motors

(submerged)
Main armament: One 450mm (17.7in)
torpedo tube, four drop collars, plus
two external cradles

Launched: October 1912

France had built up a formidable submarine fleet when World War I broke out. *Euler* formed part of a large class of 16 boats. Range was 3,230 kilometres (1,700 miles) at 10 knots on the surface, and 160 kilometres (84 miles) at 5 knots submerged. *Euler* was removed from the effective list in the 1920s.

Euridice

Type: Italian cruiser
Displacement: 918 tonnes (904 tons)
Dimensions: 73.9m x 8.2m x 3.7m
(242 ft 6in x 27ft x 12ft 2in)
Machinery: Twin screw triple expansion engines
Top speed: 20 knots
Main armament: One 120mm

(4.7in) gun, six 430mm (17in) torpedo tubes
Launched: 1890

Euridice was laid down in February 1889 and completed in May 1891. She was one of

a class of eight torpedo cruisers that were improved versions of the Tripoli torpedo cruiser. The new class had steel hulls and originally carried a light fore and aft rig. They were

intended to act as fast scouts on the fringes of the fleet, as well as acting independently. *Euridice* was discarded in 1907.

Euro

Type: Italian destroyer
Displacement: 353 tonnes (348 tons)
Dimensions: 62m x 6.5m x 2.6m
(203ft 5in x 21ft 4in x 8ft 6in)
Machinery: Twin screw triple expansion engines
Main armament: One 76mm

(3in) gun, two 355mm (14in) torpedo tubes
Launched: August 1900
Euro was one of six vessels in the first major destroyer class to be built for the Italian Navy.

They were fast, strongly built ships, with a range of 551 kilometres (290 miles) at 26 knots, increasing to 3,800 kilometres (2,000 miles) at 12 knots. During World War II five ships in the class were converted into minelayers. From 1922 and 1923, *Euro* served as a target ship, and in September 1924 she was re-named *Strale* so that her original name could be given to a new boat then under construction. *Strale* was discarded soon afterwards.

Euro

Type: Italian destroyer
Displacement: 1,696 tonnes (1,670 tons)
Dimensions: 93.2m x 9.2m x 3m
(305ft 9in x 30ft 2in x 9ft 10in)
Machinery: Twin

screw turbines
Top speed: 36 knots
Main armament: Four 120mm (4.7in) guns, six 533mm (21in) torpedo tubes
Launched: July 1927

Euro was part of a class of six vessels that were slightly largers versions of the previous Sauro class. All were laid down in 1925, the last unit being launched in 1928. Designed for a speed of 36 knots with 40,000hp, *Euro* actually achieved 38.9 knots during a four-hour full power trial. However, in service her best sea speed was about 35 knots. *Euro* was sunk by German bombers on 1 October 1943.

Euro

Type: Italian destroyer
Displacement: 3,088 tonnes (3,040 tons)
Dimensions: 122.7m x 12.9m x 8.4m (402ft 6in x 42ft 4in x 27ft 6in)
Machinery: Twin screw diesels and gas turbines
Top speed: 29 knots (diesel), 32 knots (turbines)
Main armament: One 127mm (5in) gun plus missiles
Launched: December 1982

Following the success of the Lupo-class frigate, Italy decided to build an enlarged version to carry a fixed hangar for two helicopters. *Euro* entered service in 1983. The aft flight deck is 27m (88ft 6in) long and 12m 39ft 4in) wide, and there is a stern well for a new

Variable Depth Sonar which is streamed out on a 600-m (1,968-ft) long cable. Plans are in hand to increase this to 900m (2,953ft). The vessels of the Lupo class will need replacing by the year 2000, and it is intended that *Euro* and her sisters will then be suitably updated.

Europa

Type: Italian seaplane carrier
Displacement: 8,945 tonnes (8,805 tons)
Dimensions: 123m x 14m x 7.6m (403ft 10in x 46ft x 25ft)
Machinery: Single screw vertical triple expansion engines
Top speed: 12 knots
Main armament: Two 30mm (1.2in) anti-aircraft guns
Launched: August 1895
Date of profile: 1915

Europa started life as the British merchant ship *Manila*, with a gross displacement of only 4,200 tonnes (4,134 tons). In 1898 her name was changed to *Salacia*. In 1911 she was sold to Germany. She then took the Italian flag under the name *Quarto*. In 1915 she was finally purchased by the Italian Navy and converted to a seaplane carrier, becoming the first Italian ship to operate fixed wing aircraft. This conversion work took three months to complete, after which *Europa* emerged with two large aircraft hangars, one ahead and one aft of the low superstructure. There was a large davit mounted on the bow, which acted as a winch for launching and retrieving the aircraft. These were normally stored with wings folded in the hangars. They would have to be rolled forward, their wings locked open, then winched down to the surface one-by-one before they could take off under their own power. This process had to be reversed after landing, and flight operations could only be carried out in calm seas. She could carry eight seaplanes, and normally operated a group of six fighters and two reconnaissance machines. She was based at Brindisi from October 1915 until January 1916, then transferred to Velona until 1918. She survived World War I, but was discarded and scrapped in 1920. *Europa* was typical of the hasty seaplane carrier conversions introduced by most navies at the time, vessels which were the forerunners of the aircraft carrier.

Europa

Type: German liner
Displacement: 50,542 tonnes (49,746 tons)
Dimensions: 285m x 31m (93ft 9in x 102ft 1in)
Machinery: Quadruple screws, turbines
Top speed: 27.9 knots
Launched: July 1928

Europa was a luxury liner built for the Norddeutscher Lloyd Line's rapidly expanding North Atlantic routes. She could carry 600 first-class, 500 second-class, 300 tourist-class and 600 third-class passengers, as well as a crew of 960. She had an unusual raked bow running down to a bulbous forefoot which made for an easier passage through the water. In 1929 she was badly damaged by fire while being fitted out, but was eventually completed in 1930. She maintained a regular service until 1939, when she was taken over as an accommodation ship. In 1946 she became the French ship *Liberté*, but while she was laid up she broke away from her moorings, collided with the sunken wreck of the liner *Paris* and sank. She was raised, but a serious fire delayed her reconstruction. *Europa* finally resumed service in 1950. She was sold in 1961 and was broken up in 1962.

Europa

Type: Danish liner
Displacement: 10,387 tonnes (10,224 tons)
Dimensions: 147.6m x 19m (484ft 3in x 62ft 4in)
Machinery: Single screw diesel engines
Top speed: 17.2 knots
Launched: February 1931

Europa was one of two motor ships built by Burmeister and Wain of Copenhagen for the East Asiatic Company's service between Copenhagen and North America. During the 1920s and 1930s the motor ship was popular with small companies because they were economical to run, requiring fewer engine-room staff. The single-class system and good quality service made *Europa* popular with passengers, of which she carried 64. When the Germans occupied Denmark in 1940, *Europa* transferred to the British flag. On 3 May 1941, she was burnt out at Liverpool following a German air raid. Her sister ship *Amerika* was also lost during World War II, torpedoed and sunk in the North Atlantic by the German submarine *U-306*.

Euryalus

Type: British cruiser
Displacement: 3,175 tonnes (3,125 tons)
Dimensions: 61m x 15.8m x 6.7m (200ft x 51ft 10in x 22ft)
Machinery: Single screw simple compound engine
Top speed: 12 knots
Main armament: 51 guns
Launched: 1853
Date of profile: 1853

Designed by Sir Baldwin Walker, *Euryalus* was a wooden-hulled 60-gun battleship which was converted to a 51-gun steam frigate while still completing. Her single gun deck ran the full length of the vessel, with only a few internal structures and the casing of the single telescopic funnel. Her engines developed 400hp. By the 1860s screw propulsion had largely replaced the paddle wheel, and in order to protect the machinery from enemy fire the engines were placed below the waterline. However, as these early engines generally proved unreliable in service, reliance on sail power was to continue for some time. *Euryalus* was sold in 1865.

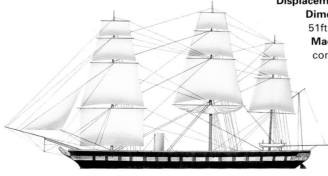

Euryalus

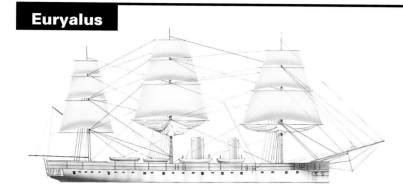

Type: British cruiser
Displacement: 3,995 tonnes (3,932 tons)
Dimensions: 85.3m x 13.8m x 7m (280ft x 45ft 6in x 23ft 3in)
Machinery: Single screw horizontal compound engines
Top speed: 14.7 knots
Main armament: Two 152mm (6in), fourteen 178mm (7in) guns
Launched: January 1877

Euryalus was an iron-hulled cruiser designed by Nathaniel Barnaby. Upon completion in 1878, *Euryalus* and her two sisters were the largest vessels to have compound engines, and their greatly improved reliability gave the ships a cruising range of 7,600 kilometres (4,000 miles) at 10 knots. However, under sail power alone the performance of the vessels was poor. *Euryalus* was sold in 1897.

Eurydice

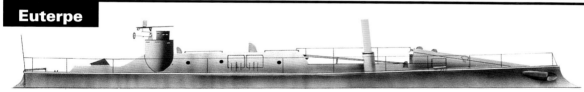

Type: French submarine
Displacement: 636 tonnes (626 tons) (surface), 800 (787 tons) tonnes (submerged)
Dimensions: 65.9m x 4.9m x 4m (216ft 2in x 16ft x 13ft 5in)
Machinery: Twin screw diesel (surface), electric motors (submerged)

Main armament: Seven 533mm (21in) torpedo tubes
Launched: May 1927
Date of profile: 1928

Eurydice was a double-hulled, medium displacement submarine with an operational diving depth of 80 metres (262ft). She was one of a

class of 26 boats built between 1925 and 1934. *Eurydice* was scuttled at Toulon in June 1944, but was raised and later sunk by Allied bombing.

Euterpe

Type: Italian torpedo boat
Displacement: 13.5 tonnes (13.3 tons)
Dimensions: 19.2m x 2.2m x 1.1m (63ft x 7ft 6in x 3ft 9in)

Machinery: Single screw vertical triple expansion engines
Main armament: One 25mm (1in) machine gun, two 355mm (14in) torpedo tubes

Launched: 1883

Designed and built by Thornycroft, *Euterpe* was one of eight small torpedo boats intended for coast

defence. During the time of her building, torpedo boats were growing in importance and were posing a serious threat to battlefleets, especially at night. *Euterpe*'s torpedo tubes were carried in the bow and were loaded from a ramp behind the turtle-backed foredeck. *Euterpe* was re-numbered *37* in 1886, and was discarded around 1897.

Evangelista Torricelli

Type: Italian submarine
Displacement: 1,845 tonnes ((1,816 tons) (surface), 2,463 tonnes (2,425 tons) (submerged)
Dimensions: 95m x 8.2m x 5m (311ft 6in x 27ft x 17ft)
Machinery: Twin screw diesel engines (surface), electric motors (submerged)

Top speed: 20 knots (surface), 10 knots (submerged)
Main armament: Ten 533mm (21in) torpedo tubes
Launched: July 1944

Evangelista Torricelli was formerly the US ocean-going submarine *Lizardfish* of the vast Balao class. She was handed over to Italy on 5 March 1966, along with two sister vessels.

Ever Globe

Type: Taiwanese container ship
Displacement: 43,978 tonnes (43,285 tons)
Dimensions: 231m x 32m (757ft 10in x 105ft)
Machinery: Single screw diesel engine
Launched: 1984

Ever Globe is one of a large, expanding fleet of container ships owned by the Evergreen Marine Corporation which is based in Taiwan and registered in

Panama. She has three holds for containers, plus a massive deck area where more can be stacked. Container ships of this type, which

revolutionised cargo handling, were first introduced in the 1960s.

Exeter

Armour: 76mm (3in) side armour, plus 25.4mm (1in) deck
Launched: July 1929
Date of profile: 1939

Type: British cruiser
Displacement: 10,657 tonnes (10,490 tons)
Dimensions: 175m x 17.6m x 6m (575ft x 58ft x 20ft 3in)
Machinery: Quadruple screw turbines
Top speed: 32 knots
Main armament: Six 203mm (8in) guns

In late 1939 *Exeter* was in action against the German battleship *Admiral Graf Spee*. *Exeter* was re-built in 1940-41. She was sunk in action at the Battle of the Java Sea in 1942.

Exmoor

Type: British destroyer
Displacement: 1,651 tonnes (1,625 tons)
Dimensions: 85.3m x 9.6m x 3.7m (280ft x 31ft 6in x 12ft 5in)
Machinery: Twin screw turbines
Top speed: 26.7 knots
Main armament: Six 102mm (4in) guns
Launched: March 1941

Exmoor was part of a massive emergency programme, begun in late 1938, to meet the need for a destroyer class that could carry out general duties and escort work. By the outbreak of World War II, 20 of the vessels in the new Hunt class were already being built. All the ships proved excellent escorts, their 102mm (4in) anti-aircraft guns providing good protection against air attack. They also had fast acceleration and were generally handy vessels. *Exmoor* was transferred to Denmark after the war, in 1953.

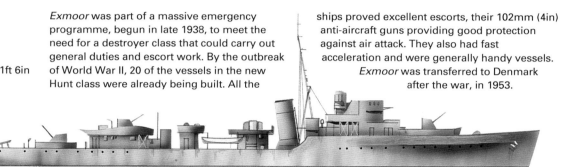

Exmouth

Type: British destroyer leader
Displacement: 2,041 tonnes (2,009 tons)
Dimensions: 104.5m x 10.2m x 3.8m (342ft 10in x 33ft 9in x 12ft 6in)
Machinery: Twin screw turbines
Main armament: Five 120mm (4.7in) guns
Launched: February 1934

Exmouth was one of the E-class destroyers that were improved versions of the C- and D-class vessels. The E-class had increased fuel capacity and higher speed, plus extra stowage. Two of *Exmouth*'s sisters were fitted out to carry mines, but *Exmouth* was an enlarged version of the flotilla destroyer, with one more 120mm (4.7in) gun and a higher speed. In spite of poor weather conditions, trials run in September 1934 were good. At 20 knots, just over two tonnes (two tons) of oil fuel was used every hour. *Exmouth* was sunk with all hands in Moray Firth in January 1940, the likely victim of a German U-boat.

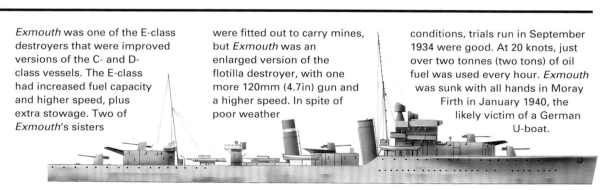

Explorateur Grandidier

Date of profile: 1926

Type: French liner
Displacement: 10,432 tonnes (10,268 tons)
Dimensions: 145m x 18.5m (475ft 9in x 60ft 8in)
Machinery: Twin screw triple expansion engines
Top speed: 14 knots
Launched: 1924

Completed in December 1925, *Explorateur Grandidier* was one of two ships built for the Far Eastern service, and she ran a regular service to Madagascar until she was laid up in Marseilles when France fell to the Germans in 1940. When the Germans evacuated Marseilles, *Explorateur Grandidier* was sunk to block the harbour entrance. She was broken up after 1945.

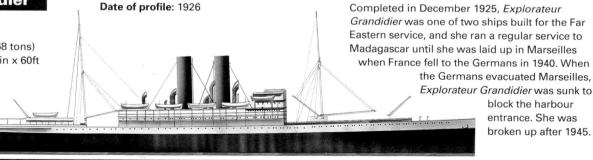

Explorer

Launched: March 1954

Type: British submarine
Displacement: 792 tonnes (780 tons) (surface), 1,016 tonnes (1,000 tons) (submerged)
Dimensions: 68m x 4.8m (225ft 6in x 15ft 8in)
Machinery: Twin screw diesel engines (surface), hydrogen peroxide (submerged)

Explorer and her sister *Excalibur* were two experimental submarines ordered from Vickers-Armstrong by the Royal Navy. The streamlined hull was designed to operate at high underwater speeds, which were made possible by using 'high test' peroxide similar to that used in the effective German type XXI submarines built towards the end of World War II. *Explorer* was the first submarine to be launched for the Royal Navy since the completion of the A class of 1948.

Extremadura

Type: Spanish cruiser
Displacement: 2,168 tonnes (2,134 tons)
Dimensions: 87m x 11m x 4.5m (288ft x 36ft x 14ft 6in)
Machinery: Twin screw triple expansion engines
Top speed: 20.5 knots
Main armament: Four 120mm (4.7in), four 162mm (6.4in) guns
Launched: 1900
Date of profile: 1906

Extremadura was one of a class of two small twin-funnelled cruisers. She

was laid down at Cadiz in 1899, and was launched in 1900. Her sister ship, *Puerto Rico*, was launched in 1902. *Extremadura* was originally intended to carry Hontoria 140mm (5.5in) guns plus Krupp 102mm (4in)

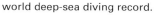

weapons. However, Armstrong quick-firing guns were eventually fitted instead. Her two 162mm (6.4in) main guns were carried amidships on the broadside, and were almost level with her twin funnels. The lighter 120mm (4.7in) weapons were mounted side-by-side in

pairs, two in the bow and two pointing directly aft. Her propulsion machinery was powered by four coal-fired boilers, and generated some 2600hp. She normally carried some 107 tonnes (106 tons) of coal, but in wartime could squeeze a maximum of 212 tonnes (210 tons) into her bunkers. Protection was enhanced by a 13mm (0.5in) armoured deck which ran the full length of her hull, with a raised crown covering the engine room. Beneath this were 11 separate watertight, compartments, two of which were for the engine room. *Extremadura* was discarded and scrapped in 1930.

F1

Type: British submarine
Displacement: 368 tonnes (363 tons) (surface), 533 tonnes (525 tons) (submerged)
Dimensions: 46m x 4.9m x 3.2m (151ft x 16ft x 10ft 6in)
Machinery: Twin screw diesels (surface), electric motors (submerged)
Top speed: 14 knots (surface), 8.7 knots (submerged)

Main armament: Three 457mm (18in) torpedo tubes
Launched: March 1915

F1 was one of a class of three vessels which were among the last coast-defence submarines built for the Royal Navy due to the Admiralty's decision to

adopt an offensive policy by building ocean-going submarines of great range. *F1* was laid down

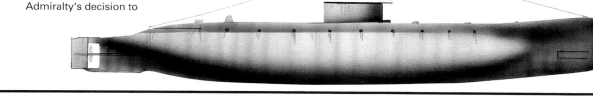

in 1913. All vessels in the class saw extensive service during World War I. A proposed group of boats in the same class was cancelled in 1914. *F1* was broken up in 1920.

F1

Type: Italian submarine
Displacement: 226 tonnes (262 tons) (surface), 324

tonnes (319 tons) (submerged)
Dimensions: 45.6m x 4.2m x 3m (149ft 7in x 13ft 9in x 10ft)
Machinery: Twin screw diesels

(surface), electric motors (submerged)
Main armament: One 76mm (3in) anti-aircraft gun, two 450mm (17.7in) torpedo tubes
Launched: April 1916
Date of profile: 1916

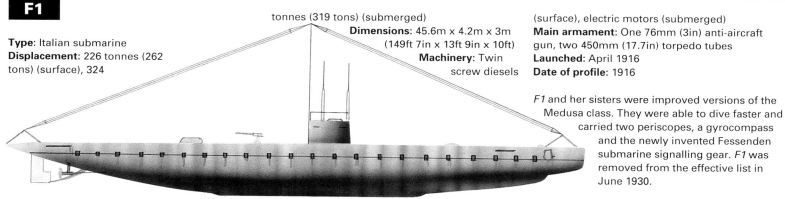

F1 and her sisters were improved versions of the Medusa class. They were able to dive faster and carried two periscopes, a gyrocompass and the newly invented Fessenden submarine signalling gear. *F1* was removed from the effective list in June 1930.

F4

Type: US submarine
Displacement: 335 tonnes (330 tons) (surface), 406 tonnes (400 tons) (submerged)
Dimensions: 43.5m x 4.7m x 3.7m (142ft 9in x 15ft 5in x 12ft 2in)
Machinery: Twin screw diesels (surface), electric motors (submerged)
Top speed: 11 knots (surface), 5 knots (submerged)
Main armament: Four torpedo tubes
Launched: January 1912

F4 and her three sisters were contemporaries of, and similar to, the E class, where the tendency towards a smaller type of submarine had originated. All the E and F class boats were withdrawn from service in 1915 for re-engineering. *F4* left

Honolulu harbour on 25 March 1915 for a short trial run, but she never returned. She was located at a depth of 91 metres (300ft) just off Pearl Harbor, well beyond the depth from which such a vessel had hitherto been successfully raised. Five months later, however, *F4* was successfully raised for salvage, thereby setting up a new world deep-sea diving record.

Faà Di Bruno

Type: Italian coast defense ship
Displacement: 2,899 tonnes (2,854 tons)
Dimensions: 55.5m x 27m x 2.2m (182ft 3in x 88ft 7in x 7ft 4in)
Machinery: Twin screw connected to two old engines previously used by discarded torpedo boats
Top speed: 3.3 knots
Main armament: Two 380mm (15in) guns
Launched: January 1916
Date of profile: 1917

Originally the GA43, *Faà di Bruno* was designed by General Engineer Rota and was laid down at the Royal Naval Yard, Venice, in October 1915. Her trial speed was 3.3 knots, with a service speed of 2.5 knots. Her 380mm (15in) guns were originally intended for the battleship *Cristoforo Colombo*, which was also laid down in 1915 but which was never completed. *Faà di Bruno* was discarded in November 1924, but remained in naval service although she was not listed. She was numbered GM194 and was used as a floating battery for the defence of Genoa harbour during World War II.

Faà Di Bruno

Type: Italian submarine
Displacement: 1,076 tonnes (1,060 tons) (surface), 1,334 tonnes (1,313 tons) (submerged)
Dimensions: 73m x 7m x 5m (239ft 6in x 23ft 7in x 16ft 9in)
Machinery: Twin screw diesels (surface), electric motors (submerged)
Top speed: 17.4 knots (surface), 8 knots (submerged)
Main armament: Two (3.9in) 100mm guns, eight 533mm (21in) torpedo tubes
Launched: June 1939
Date of profile: 1939

Derived from the Glauco class, *Faà di Bruno* was a long-range, single-hulled, ocean-going boat with internal ballast tanks designed by Bernardis. In 1940 she was sunk in the North Atlantic by HMS *Havelock*.

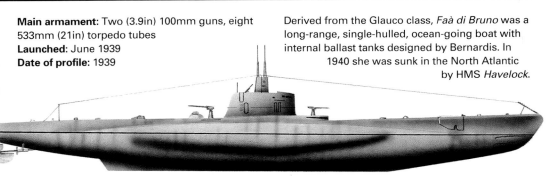

Fabert

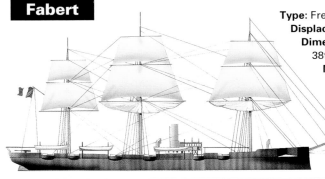

Type: French cruiser
Displacement: 2,133 tonnes (2,100 tons)
Dimensions: 76m x 11m x 5.6m (249ft 4in x 38ft x 18ft 4in)
Machinery: Single screw horizontal compound engines
Top speed: 12.4 knots
Main armament: Eight 140mm (5.5in) guns
Launched: 1874
Date of profile: 1880

Fabert was wooden-hulled and barque-rigged. She was laid down in 1868 and completed in 1876. Six of her guns were mounted on sponsons on the upper deck, with one gun in the bow as a chaser which was able to fire through ports in each side of the hull just aft of the straight stem. This gun was mounted on a slide carriage which ran on rails so that the gun could be moved quickly from one side to the other. The remaining gun was mounted aft. *Fabert* was removed from service in 1899.

Falco

Type: Italian flotilla leader
Displacement: 1,788 tonnes (1,760 tons)
Dimensions: 94.7m x 9.5m x 3.6m (310ft 8in x 31ft 2in x 11ft 10in)
Machinery: Twin screw turbines
Top speed: 35.2 knots
Main armament: Three 152mm (6in) guns
Launched: August 1919
Date of profile: 1920

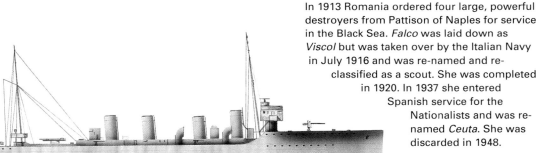

In 1913 Romania ordered four large, powerful destroyers from Pattison of Naples for service in the Black Sea. *Falco* was laid down as *Viscol* but was taken over by the Italian Navy in July 1916 and was re-named and re-classified as a scout. She was completed in 1920. In 1937 she entered Spanish service for the Nationalists and was re-named *Ceuta*. She was discarded in 1948.

Farfadet

Type: French submarine
Displacement: 188 tonnes (185 tons) (surface), 205 tonnes (202 tons) (submerged)
Dimensions: 41.3m x 2.9m x 2.6m (135ft 6in x 9ft 6in x 8ft 6in)
Machinery: Single screw electric motors
Top speed: 6 knots (surface), 4.3 knots (submerged)
Main armament: Four 450mm (17.7in) torpedo tubes
Launched: May 1901

Farfadet and her three sisters relied solely on a set of accumulators for power, which gave them a range of only 218.5km (115 miles) at 5.3 knots surfaced, and 53km (28 miles) at 4.3 knots submerged. The four torpedoes were carried outside in cradles aft of the conning tower. As a result of the conning tower being left open, *Farfadet* sank at Bizerta on 6 July 1905, with the loss of 14 lives. She was subsequently raised and re-commissioned as *Follet* in 1909. She was removed from the effective list in 1913.

Farragut

Type: US destroyer
Displacement: 283 tonnes (279 tons)
Dimensions: 65m x 6.3m x 1.8m
(214ft x 20ft 8in x 6ft)
Machinery: Twin screw vertical triple
expansion engines
Top speed: 33.7 knots
Main armament: Six 6-
pounder guns, two

457mm (18in) torpedo tubes
Launched: July 1898

Farragut was the US Navy's first
destroyer, although when originally
authorised she was described as a
torpedo boat. She was laid down in

July 1897 at the Union Iron Works,
and was completed in March 1899.
Her engines developed 5,878hp, and
steam was supplied by three

Thornycroft boilers. Coal supply
was 96 tonnes (95 tons).Her
crew numbered 66. In August
1918 Farragut was re-named
Coast Torpedo Boat Nº 5. She
was sold in 1919.

Fasana

Type: Italian destroyer
Displacement: 1,052 tonnes (1,036 tons)
Dimensions: 83.5m x 7.8m x 3m (274ft x 25ft7in
x 9ft 10in)
Machinery: Twin screw turbines
Top speed: 32.6 knots
Main armament: Two 100mm (3.9in) guns
Launched: November 1912
Date of profile: 1922

Fasana was formerly the Austrian *Tátra*, one of
a class of seven vessels that were the best and
most powerful destroyers in the Austro-
Hungarian Navy. *Fasana* was transferred to the
Italian Navy in August 1920, and once in
Italian service her armament was
changed, her 533mm (21in) torpedo
tubes being reduced to the
standard 450mm (17.7in).
She was removed from
the effective list in 1923.

Faulknor

Type: British flotilla leader
Displacement: 2,024 tonnes
(1,993 tons)
Dimensions: 100m x 10m x
6.4m (330ft 10in x 32ft 6in x
21ft 1in)

Machinery: Triple screw turbines
Top speed: 29 knots
Main armament: Six 102mm (4in)
guns, four 533mm (21in) torpedo
tubes
Launched: February 1914

Designed by J. S. White in 1912,
Faulknor was one of four large,
powerful destroyers ordered by
the Chilean Navy. Previously
named *Almirante Simpson*, the
ship was taken over by the
British Navy in August
1914, whereupon

the fore funnel was raised and a
more powerful radio outfit installed.
Unlike other British destroyers at
the time which had a single gun
firing forward, *Faulknor* and her
sisters were heavily armed with
three or four guns firing forward.
After World War I, *Faulknor* was re-
fitted and returned to Chile where
she served until she was removed
from the effective list in 1933.

Fenian Ram

Type: US submarine
Displacement: 19 tonnes (19
tons)
Dimensions: 9.4m x 1.8m x
2.2m (31ft x 6ft x 7ft 3in)
Machinery: Single screw
petroleum engine
Main armament: One 228mm (9in)

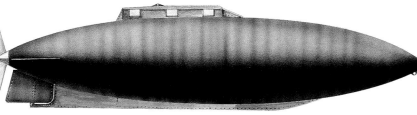

gun
Launched: May 1881

Fenian Ram was built for the Fenian
Society by the Delamater Iron Works,

New York. In 1883 she was towed to
Newhaven under great secrecy, so
that her crew of three could
familiarise themselves with her
handling. The vessel was
exhibited at Madison Square
Gardens in 1916 in order to raise
funds for the Irish uprising that took
place that year. In 1927 she was
housed in West Side Park, New York.

Ferdinando Palasciano

Type: Italian hospital ship
Displacement: 10,651 tonnes (10,484 tons)
Dimensions: 152m x 18.3m (499ft 3in x
60ft 2in)
Machinery: Twin screw
quadruple expansion engines
Top speed: 15.3 knots
Launched: June 1899
Date of profile: 1916

Ferdinando Palasciano was built for the
German Norddeutscher Lloyd line and was
originally named *König Albert*. She carried 257
first class, 119 second class and 1,799 steerage

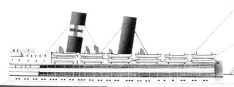

plus 230 crew. She was interned in Italy at
the start of World War I, and was then taken
over, re-named *Ferdinando Palasciano* and
converted into a hospital ship. After the
war she was bought by the Navigazione
Generale Italiana of Genoa, and began a
regular passenger service to New York.
In 1923 she was re-named *Italia*
and became a naval
transport. She was
scrapped in 1926.

Ferdinando Primo

Type: Italian passenger ship
Displacement: 250 tonnes (247 tons)
Dimensions: 38m x 6m (9m over paddle boxes) x 1.9m (127ft 4in x 20ft 2in (32ft) x 6ft 5in)
Machinery: Paddle wheels, side lever twin cylinder engine
Top speed: 6 knots
Launched: June 1818
Date of profile: 1818

Ferdinando Primo was the first passenger steamer to operate in the Mediterranean. She was built in Naples for the newly formed

Societa Napoletana Pietro Andriel. The founder of the new company, Captain Pierre Andriel, was a steam pioneer who had commanded the first steamship to cross the English Channel in 1816. *Ferdinando Primo* was a wooden three-masted vessel, with two paddle wheels. Her engine was a side-lever unit built by James Cook of Tradeston, Scotland, and developed a mighty 32hp. It comprised two metal cylinders 686mm (12ft) in diameter, with a 1m (3ft) stroke. These operated using steam at the remarkably low pressure of approximately 1kg (2lb) from a flat-sided iron boiler. This engine drove the two 4m (13ft)

diameter paddle wheels, each of which had eight paddles 1.5m (5ft) wide by .5m (1ft 7in) deep. She had good passenger accommodation for a ship of her size, with 16 private cabins and a spacious public saloon able to seat 50 people. Her maiden voyage was in October 1818, when she sailed from Naples to Genoa. Her arrival caused a

sensation. On 30 October she left Genoa with 10 passengers on board, arriving at Marseilles on 3 November. She again caused a stir, and was the first steam vessel to enter that port.

Ferraris

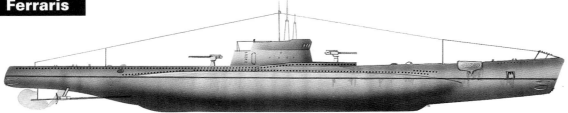

Type: Italian submarine
Displacement: 1,000 tonnes (985 tons) (surface), 1,279 tonnes (1,259 tons) (submerged)

Dimensions: 70.5m x 6.8m x 4m (231ft 4in x 22ft 4in x 13ft 5in)
Machinery: Twin screw diesel (surface), electric motors

(submerged)
Main armament: Eight 533mm (21in) torpedo tubes, two 100mm (3.9in) guns

Launched: August 1934

Ferraris and her sister *Galileo* were long range vessels with a partial double hull. Both boats took part in the Spanish Civil War, and were stationed in the Red Sea during World War II. *Galileo* was lost in the Red Sea during a surface battle with the British trawler *Moonstone*. *Ferraris* was sunk in the North Adriatic by the British destroyer *Lamerton* in October 1941.

Ferret

Type: British destroyer
Displacement: 762 tonnes (750 tons)
Dimensions: 75m x 7.8m x 2.7m (246ft x 25ft 8in x 8ft 9in)
Machinery: Twin screw turbines
Top speed: 33 knots

Main armament: Two 102mm guns
Launched: April 1911

Ferret was the lead ship in a group of destroyers that were originally intended to be repeats

of the previous Acorn class. She was laid down in September 1910 and was completed in October 1911. Twenty other ships of the class were also begun in 1910, but

six others were put out to private firms to see if they could improve upon the Acorn design. On trials, *Ferret* maintained slightly over 30 knots for eight hours, a credit to her builder J. S. White. However, although the fore funnel was set well back from the bridge, the exhaust fumes still caused problems for those on the bridge. This was rectified later when her funnel was raised. *Ferret* was scrapped in 1921.

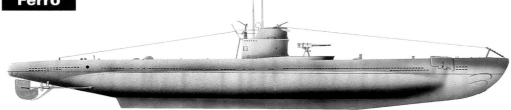

Ferro

Type: Italian submarine
Displacement: 1,130 tonnes (1,113 tons) (surface), 1,188 tonnes (1,170 tons) (submerged)
Dimensions: 64m x 6.9m x 4.9m (210ft 7in x 22ft

11in x 16ft 2in)
Machinery: Twin screw diesel (surface), electric motors (submerged)
Main armament: One 100mm (3.9in) gun, six

533mm (21in) torpedo tubes
Launched: Not completed

Ferro was designed as a medium-sized boat with a partial double hull, and was a development of the Argo class with slightly increased dimensions and a reduced conning tower. She was laid down on 2 June 1943 at Cantieri Riuniti Dell'Adriatico, Monfalcone, but was seized by German forces during September 1943 and designated *UIT 12*. The vessel was never launched, as she was destroyed while still on the slips in May 1945.

Ferry Lavender

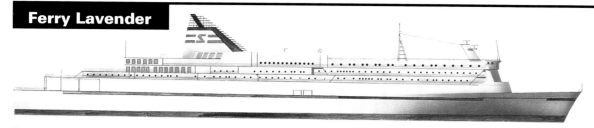

Type: Japanese ferry
Displacement: 20,222 tonnes (19,904 tons)
Dimensions: 193m x 29.4m x 6.7m (632ft x 96ft 5in x 22ft 2in)
Machinery: Twin screw diesel engines
Top speed: 21.8 knots
Launched: March 1991

Ferry Lavender is a roll-on, roll-off passenger ferry which was ordered by the Shin Nihonkai Ferry Company Limited in 1990, and was delivered in September 1991. She operates in Japanese waters and can carry 796 passengers. She has two vehicle decks, with access through bow and stern ramps. Her engines develop 13,200hp, and she uses just over 60 tonnes (60 tons) of oil per day.

Fervent

Type: British destroyer
Displacement: 280 tonnes (275 tons)
Dimensions: 60m x 5.7m x 2.5m (200ft 4in x 19ft 1in x 8ft)
Machinery: Twin screw triple expansion engines
Main armament: Three 6-pounders, one 12-pounder
Launched: March 1895

Fervent was part of the building programme of 1894-95, designed to combat the strength of the French Navy. *Fervent* followed the design of earlier destroyers, but was fitted with old-style locomotive boilers and had only one funnel. She was scrapped in 1920.

Feth-I-Bulend

Type: Turkish battleship
Displacement: 2,805 tonnes (2,761 tons)
Dimensions: 72m x 12m x 5.5m (236ft 3in x 39ft 4in x 18ft)
Machinery: Single screw horizontal compound engines
Top speed: 13 knots
Main armament: Four 228mm (9in) guns
Armour: 152-228mm (6-9in) waterline belt
Launched: 1870

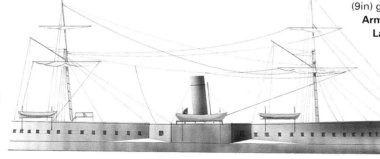

Feth-I-Bulend was an iron-hulled, central battery ship built at Blackwall in London. She was laid down in 1868 and completed in 1872. She was reconstructed between 1903 and 1907. In 1912, *Feth-I-Bulend* was sunk by the Greek torpedo vessel *№ 11*.

Fieramosca

Type: Italian cruiser
Displacement: 3,804 tonnes (3,745 tons)
Dimensions: 93m x 13m x 5.7m (305ft 9in x 43ft 4in x 18ft 8in)
Machinery: Twin screw double expansion engines
Main armament: Six 152mm (6in), two 254mm (10in) guns
Launched: August 1888

Fieramosca was almost identical to the Enta class cruisers built during the same period. The two heavy guns were carried in low barbettes, one forward and one aft, and each had a good arc of fire. The 152mm (6in) weapons were carried in the waist on sponsons. *Fieramosca* was removed from the effective list in 1909.

Filicudi

Type: Italian net layer
Displacement: 847 tonnes (834 tons)
Dimensions: 50m x 10m x 3.2m (165ft 4in x 33ft 6in x 10ft 6in)
Machinery: Twin screw diesel-electric motors
Top speed: 12 knots
Main armament: One 40mm (1.6in) gun
Launched: September 1954

Filicudi and her sister *Alicudi* were laid down in 1954 at the Ansaldockyard, Leghorn. They were based on a standard NATO design and were ordered by NATO to serve as vessels that could protect harbours by laying nets of various depths across their entrances. A large, open deck for handling the nets is situated in the low bow section. A boom attached to the foremast controls the positioning of nets as they are raised or laid. A compact combined bridge and control centre is situated above the superstructure.

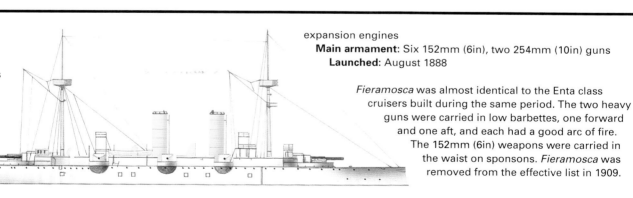

Filippo Corridoni

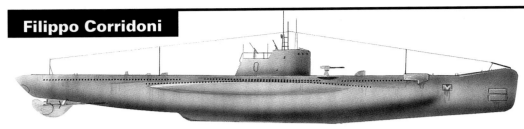

Type: Italian submarine
Displacement: 996 tonnes (981 tons) (surface), 1,185 tonnes (1,167 tons) (submerged)
Dimensions: 71.5m x 6m x 4.8m (234ft 7in x 20ft 2in x 15ft 9in)
Machinery: Twin screw diesel (surface), electric motors (submerged)
Top speed: 11.5 knots (surface) 7 knots (submerged)
Main armament: One 102mm (4in) gun, four 533mm (21in) torpedo tubes, 16-24 mines
Launched: March 1930

Filippo Corridoni was a short-range, minelayer developed from the Pisani class. She was used mainly to transport supplies during World War II. She was removed from the effective list in 1948.

Fionda

Type: Italian destroyer
Displacement: 1,138 tonnes (1,120 tons) approx
Dimensions: 82.2m x 8.6m x 2.8m (270 ft x 28ft 3in x 9ft 2in)
Machinery: Twin screw turbines
Main armament: Two 100mm (3.9in) guns
Launched: Not completed

Italian war estimates provided for the building of 42 boats in *Fionda*'s class. Only 16 were laid down, with the lead ship *Ariete* being the only vessel actually delivered to the Italian Navy. *Fionda* was laid down in 1942, but she was captured by the Germans while on the slips and designated *TA 46*. In February 1945 she was damaged in an air raid. Construction began again and she was renamed *Velebit,* but she was never completed.

Fisalia

Type: Italian submarine
Displacement: 256 tonnes (252 tons) (surface), 310 tonnes (305 tons) (submerged)
Dimensions: 45m x 4.2m x 3m (148ft 2in x 13ft 9in x 9ft 10in)
Machinery: Twin screw diesel (surface), electric motors (submerged)
Top speed: 12 knots (surface), 8 knots (submerged)
Main armament: Two 450mm (17.7in) torpedo tubes
Launched: February 1912

Fisalia was one of a class of eight boats that were the first Italian submarines to have diesel engines. They were good sea boats with excellent underwater manoeuvrability. *Fisalia* was laid down in October 1910 and completed in September 1912. She served in the Adriatic during World War I, and was discarded in 1918.

Fiume

Type: Italian cruiser
Displacement: 14,394 tonnes (14,168 tons)
Dimensions: 182.8m x 20.6m x 7.2m (599ft 9in x 67ft 7in x 23ft 7in)
Machinery: Twin screw turbines
Top speed: 32 knots
Main armament: Eight 203mm (8in) guns
Launched: April 1930
Date of profile: 1932

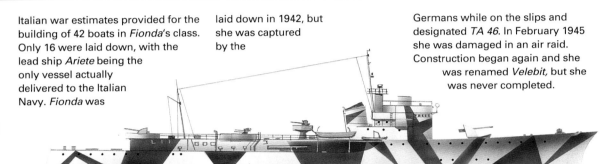

Modifications were made to the original design of *Fiume* to make her comply with the 10,160-tonne (10,000-ton) limit imposed by the Washington Treaty. On trials, *Fiume* made 33 knots with 120,000hp. She had three sister vessels, *Gorzia, Pola* and *Zara.* All four vessels were lost in World War II. *Fiume* was sunk in action with a British battleship in March 1941 while aiding the damaged *Pola. Pola* was eventually scuttled to prevent her from falling into British hands.

Flamingo

Type: Confederate blockade runner
Displacement: 508 tonnes (500 tons)
Dimensions: 65m x 6m x 2m (214ft x 20ft x 7ft)
Machinery: Paddle wheels, diagonal oscillating engines
Launched: 1864

Flamingo was typical of the later, more sophisticated blockade runners used during the American Civil War. Her hull was long and low, and only a light rig was carried on pole masts to reduce her silhouette against the skyline. These purpose-built blockade runners were usually built in Britain and manned by British crews. Speed was essential, and some runners made 18 knots, making them the fastest vessels in the world at the time. They were lightly built, and several built in around 1864 had steel hulls to reduce weight further. Many vessels fell victim to the Union blockaders, and others disappeared during bad weather.

Flamingo

Type: Austrian torpedo boat
Displacement: 91.4 tonnes (90 tons)
Dimensions: 39.9m x 4.8m x 1.9m
(130ft 11in x 15ft 9in x 6ft 3in)
Machinery: Single screw triple
expansion engine
Top speed: 19 knots
Main armament: Two 350mm
(13.8in) torpedo tubes
Launched: 1889

Flamingo was one of a group of 20
small torpedo boats built for the
Austrian Navy in the late 1880s and
1890s. They were based on the
earlier and successful Schichau

design, and incorporated a number
of improvements. *Flamingo* herself
was laid down in 1888 and
completed in 1889. She and one
sister ship were built in Trieste by
the Stabilimento Tecnico Triestino.
The other 16 of the class were built
at other yards. All of this series had
excellent sea-keeping qualities,
which were enhanced by the use of
a covered whale-backed foredeck.
Her twin torpedo tubes were
mounted on a turntable amidships,
just aft of her steeply raked funnel.
Secondary armament was confined
to lightweight quick-firing
guns
mounted fore

and aft. Her single engine was
originally fed from a single
locomotive boiler. It could develop
around 1,000hp, and gave
Flamingo an operating range of
about 2,280km (1,200 miles) at 10
knots. All these boats underwent
major reconstruction between

1900 and 1910. During this refit,
Flamingo had her boiler replaced
by two Yarrow units, and eventually
re-entered service bearing pennant
number 26. She was mined and
sunk off Pola on 23 August 1914. 18
remaining boats were converted to
minesweepers in 1917, and 16 of
these were transferred to Italy in
1920. Most were scrapped soon
after, but four became Italian
customs patrol boats and
operated in this role until 1925.

Flandre

Type: French battleship
Displacement: 5,791 tonnes (5,700
tons)
Dimensions: 80m x 17m x 8.2m
(262ft 5in x 55ft 9in x 26ft 10in)
Machinery: Single screw
horizontal compound
engines
Top speed: 13.9 knots
Main armament:
Twenty-two 152mm
(6in), ten 55-pounder
guns

Launched: June 1864

Flandre and her nine sisters were authorised in
1860, and became the largest single group of
French battleships built. They were originally
envisaged as iron ships, but, because of the
massive resources put into building armoured
floating batteries for the Crimean War, nine of the
ten in fact had wooden hulls. The ships were
closely modelled on *La Gloire* but had thicker
armour. All except four guns were carried on the
broadside on the main deck. *Flandre* was stricken
in 1886.

Flandre

Type: French battleship
Displacement: 25,230 tonnes
(24,833 tons)
Dimensions: 176.4m x 27m x 8.7m
(578ft 9in x 88ft 7in x 28ft 6in)
Machinery: Four screws, two for
turbines and two for vertical triple
expansion engines
Top speed: 21 knots
(designed)
Main armament:

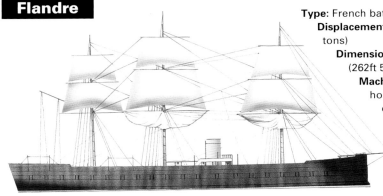

Twelve 340mm (13.4in),
twenty-four 140mm (5.5 in)
guns
Launched: October
1914

Flandre was laid down in
October 1913 as one of a class of
five units in response to the
increased gun calibres being
used by other countries. It
was decided to

fit the 340mm (13.4in) guns in three
quadruple turrets, which were in
reality two twin mounts placed side
by side in a single well-armoured
barbette. Work halted on the class in
1914 and they were launched to
clear the docks. Four were scrapped
in 1924-25; *Béarn* was completed as
an aircraft carrier.

Flandria

Type: Dutch liner
Displacement: 10,334 tonnes (10,171 tons)
Dimensions: 143.9m x 18m (472ft x 59ft)
Machinery: Twin screw turbines
Top speed: 14.5 knots
Launched: June 1922

Built by Barclay,
Curle and Company
in Scotland for
Royal Holland Lloyd,

Flandria was completed in September 1922 for
service on the Amsterdam-South American
route. She had accommodation for 215 first-
class, 110 second-class and 1,000 third-class
passengers After 14 years on the South

American run *Flandria* was sold to Cie.
Transatlantique. She was renamed *Bretagne*,
and her accommodation was refitted to take
440 cabin-class passengers from French
ports to the West Indies, a route she took
over in 1937. On 14 October 1939, *Bretagne*
was torpedoed and sunk by the German
submarine *U 45* while only 570 km(300
miles) from the English Channel.
As originally built,
Flandria was a typical
passenger liner of the
post-World War I period.

Flavio Gioia

Type: Italian cruiser
Displacement: 2,533 tonnes (2,493 tons)
Dimensions: 78m x 12.8m x 5.2m (256ft x 42ft x 17ft)
Machinery: Single screw horizontal compound engine
Main armament: Eight 149mm (5.9in) guns
Launched: 1881

Flavio Gioia was a medium-sized steel-hulled barque-rigged cruiser completed in January 1883. She had a sloping protective deck under a cellular layer made up of small compartments to reduce the effect of shell fire by confining it to a small space usually used for stores or coal. In 1892 she was converted to a training ship, with a new armament. In 1922 she was discarded but still used to train boy seamen at Naples as *CM 181* (unoffical name *Caracciolo*). She was disposed of in 1923.

Florida

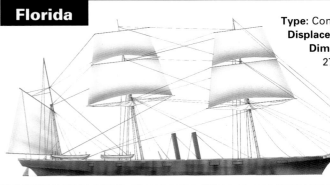

Type: Confederate cruiser
Displacement: 711 tonnes (700 tons)
Dimensions: 60m x 8.3m x 4m (192ft x 27ft 2in x 13ft)
Machinery: Single screw reciprocating engine
Top speed: 12 knots
Main armament: Two 178mm(7in), six 152mm (6in) guns
Launched: 1861

Florida was built for the Confederacy by Miller and Sons of Liverpool, England. She was about to be seized by Britain when the Confederate representative managed to get her to sea. Yellow fever forced her to head for Mobile for more crew and supplies, but she was back at sea in January 1863. *Florida* made two cruises, capturing a total of over four million dollars worth of ships and cargoes. Finally she was seized in a Brazilian port, taken to the USA and 'accidentally' sunk by a Union transport in November 1864.

Florida

Type: US cruiser
Displacement: 4,282 tonnes (4,215 tons)
Dimensions: 108m x 13.8m x 6m (355ft x 45ft 2in x 19ft 10in)
Machinery: Single screw horizontal back-acting engines
Main armament: Ten 228mm (9in), three 60-pounder guns

Florida was originally *Wampanoag*, one of five in a class of fast, wooden-hulled vessels authorised in 1863 to act as commerce raiders in case of a war with Britain, which looked likely at the time. She was the fastest steamship in the world in 1868, but came in for harsh criticism from Admiral Porter and was never allowed to fulfill her promise. She was sold in 1885.

Florida

Type: US monitor
Displacement: 3,277 tonnes (3,225 tons)
Dimensions: 77.75m x

15.25m x 3.8m (255ft x 50ft x 12ft 6in)
Machinery: Twin screw vertical triple expansion engines
Top speed: 12.5 knots
Main armament: Two 306mm (12in) guns
Launched: November 1901

One of a class of four that were the last of the big-gun monitors built for the US Navy. The maximum thickness of the belt armour was at the 38mm (1.5in) armoured-deck level only, tapering to 127mm 5in) at the lower edge and at the ends. The 306mm (12in) guns were in a single turret forward. Four 102mm (4in) guns were also carried, two at the rear of the superstructure and two under the bridge firing. All at some time served as submarine tenders. *Florida* was sold in 1922, but *Wyoming* was not sold until 1939.

Flutto

Type: Italian submarine
Displacement: 973 tonnes (958 tons) (surface), 1,189 tonnes (1,170 tons) (submerged)
Dimensions: 63.2m x 7m x 4.9m (207ft x 23ft x 16ft)
Machinery: Twin screw diesel engines (surface),

electric motors (submerged)
Top speed: 16 knots (surface), 7 knots (submerged)
Main armament: Six 533mm (21in)

torpedo tubes
Launched: November 1942

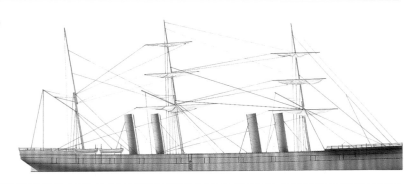

Flutto was one of a class of 48 medium submarines planned in three groups, all to be completed by the end of 1944. In the end only eight of the first group were finished. *Flutto* was sunk of the coast of Sicily on 11 July 1943 by British motor torpedo boats *640, 651* and *670*.

Flying Cloud

Type: US sailing ship
Displacement: 1,812 tonnes (1,783 tons)
Dimensions: 71.6m x 12.4m (235ft x 40ft 8in)
Top speed: 14+ knots
Launched: 1851

Of all the famous American clipper ships builtbetween 1850 and 1860, *Flying Cloud* had the best record. She was designed and built by Donald McKay of Boston for the White Diamond Line but she was sold whilst still building to the Swallow Tail Line. In whole sail wind conditions, *Flying Cloud* could not be beaten, but she was not a fast ship in light winds. Like all soft-wood clippers, she soon became strained and water soaked, and her best speeds were in her first five years. In 1874 she went aground at New Brunswick, and then caught fire while under repair in St John.

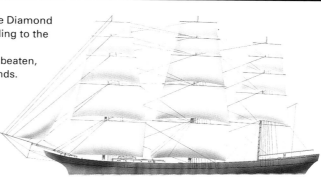

Foca

Type: Italian submarine
Displacement: 188 tonnes (185 tons) (surface), 284 tonnes (280 tons) (submerged)
Dimensions: 42.5m x 4.3m x 2.6m (139ft 5in x 14ft x 8ft 7in)
Machinery: Triple screw petrol engines (surface), electric motors (submerged)
Main armament: Two 450mm (17.7in) torpedo tubes
Launched: September 1908

Foca was the only Italian submarine to have three shafts driven by three sets of FIAT petrol engines. On 26 April 1909 *Foca* caught fire and she was scuttled to prevent the blaze spreading; she was later raised. She was finally discarded in September 1918 as World War I drew to a close.

Foca

Type: Italian submarine
Displacement: 1,354 tonnes (1,333 tons) (surface), 1,685 tonnes (1,659 tons) (submerged)
Dimensions: 82.8m x 7.2m x 5.3m (271ft 8in x 23ft 6in x 17ft 5in)
Machinery: Twin screw diesel engines (surface), electric motors (submerged)
Main armament: Six 533mm (21in) torpedo tubes
Launched: June 1937

Foca and her two sisters were long-range torpedo and minelaying boats with a maximum diving depth of 90 metres (295ft). Mine capacity was originally 20, later increased to 36, and there was a 100mm (3.9in) gun. *Foca* was sunk off Haifa by British mines in October 1940.

Folaga

Type: Italian corvette
Displacement: 740 tonnes (728 tons)
Dimensions: 64m x 8.7m x 2.5m (210ft x 28ft 7in x 8ft 4in)
Machinery: Twin screw diesel engines
Top speed: 19 knots
Main armament: One 100mm (3.9in) gun
Launched: November 1942

Folaga was one of a class of 60 vessels designed early in World War II as cheap anti-submarine escorts for service in the Mediterranean. They could be quickly built, some being completed in less than seven months, and had a good range of 5,700km (3,000 miles). To allow for silent running during anti-submarine operations, two electric motors were carried. Range in this mode was 30km (16 miles). *Folaga* survived the war and was stricken in 1965.

Folgore

Type: Italian despatch boat
Displacement: 370 tonnes (364 tons)
Dimensions: 56.7m x 6.3m x 2.2m (186ft x 20ft 8in x 7ft)
Machinery: Twin screw double expansion engines
Main armament: Two 57mm (2.25in) guns, three 356mm (14in) torpedo tubes
Launched: 1886

Folgore was designed by Benedetto Brin and built at Castelammare Naval Dockyard. She was completed in 1887 and originally listed as a torpedo despatch vessel. She and her sister, *Saetta*, were among the first of this type of fast torpedo-armed vessel built for the Italian Navy. On 5 July 1889, *Folgore* was damaged in a collision off Capri with the cruiser *Bausan*; she was put in reserve and eventually sold in 1900. *Saetta* was used in oil fuel experiments and discarded in 1908.

Folgore

Type: Italian destroyer
Displacement: 2,123 tonnes (2,090 tons)
Dimensions: 96m x 9.2m x 3.3m (315ft x 30ft 2in x 10ft 10in)
Machinery: Twin screw turbines
Top speed: 38.8 knots
Main armament: Four 119mm (4.7in) guns, six 533mm (21in) torpedo tubes
Launched: April 1931

Folgore was one of a class of four fast destroyers which were developed from the earlier Freccia class. The new ships had a narrower beam than before, which reduced hull drag and ensured a high sustained speed. The penalty for this was less internal storage space, which reduced the amount of weapons, equipment and fuel they could carry. Their maximum range was 6,840km (3,600 miles) at 12 knots, but this was considered adequate for operations in the Mediterranean. These were graceful looking vessels, with a high foredeck and a single low funnel. All four ships had their armament upgraded at various times, and were eventually modified to carry up to 52 mines. They were popular minelaying vessels, as their high speed enabled them to transit to and from the mining area quicker than most other ships, leaving them less vulnerable to detection and interception. The whole class saw extensive active service during World War II and none survived that conflict. Three were sunk in action, including *Folgore*, who met her end under the guns of British destroyers and cruisers in December 1942. The fourth, *Baleno*, capsized in April 1941, the day after she was severely damaged while defending a merchant convoy from British destroyers.

Forban

Type: French torpedo boat
Displacement: 152 tonnes (150 tons)
Dimensions: 44m x 4.6m x 1.4m (144ft 4in x 15ft 3in x 4ft 5in)
Machinery: Twin screw triple expansion engines
Top speed: 31 knots
Main armament:
Two 356mm (14in) torpedo tubes
Launched: July 1895

Forban was a major milestone in torpedo boat development – she was the first vessel to exceed 30 knots. Ordered in 1893, she was designed and built by Normand, and followed on from the three vessels in the Filibustier class, which possessed fine sea-keeping qualities and were ideal for service in the English Channel. Indeed the threat of these vessels caused the British to build the first true destroyers in reply. *Forban* was also a superb sea boat, with more powerful engines than the Filibustiers. In 1907 her torpedo tubes were replaced by 457mm (18in) ones and she was sold in 1920.

Forbin

Type: French cruiser
Displacement: 1,880 tonnes (1,850 tons)
Dimensions: 95m x 9m x 5.2m (311ft 8in x 29ft 6in x 17ft 2in)
Machinery: Twin screw horizontal compound engines
Top speed: 19.5 knots
Main armament: Four 140mm (5.5in) guns
Launched: January 1888

Forbin was one of a class of three medium-sized cruisers with fine lines and a pronounced plough bow. Originally she carried two 140mm (5.5in) guns, but this was increased to four, mounted on the broadside in upper deck sponsons with a good field of fire. The hull had a very marked tumblehome. The curved 41mm (1.6in) armoured deck ran the full length of the ship. Range was 4,560km (2,400 miles) at 10 knots with a 203-tonne (200-ton) coal supply. *Forbin* became a collier in 1913.

Foresight

Type: British cruiser
Displacement: 2896 tonnes (2,850 tons)
Dimensions: 109.7m x 11.9m x 4.3m (360ft x 39ft x 14ft)
Machinery: Twin screw triple expansion engines
Top speed: 25.3 knots
Main armament: Ten 12-pounder guns
Launched: October 1904

Foresight was laid down in late 1903 as one of eight similar scout cruisers ordered by the Admiralty to act as destroyer group leaders. All were built in private yards, following a broad specification provided by the Admiralty, but with the design details left to the builder. The requirement called for a 25-knot vessel with a 38mm (1.5in) thick protective deck plus a shallow draft for inshore operations. *Foresight* and her sister *Forward* followed the usual practice of the period of having a forecastle and poop; the remaining six had no poop and had a clear run aft. *Foresight* had three guns forward, three guns aft and her remaining guns in the waist; later additional guns were added. *Foresight* was sold in 1921.

Forfait

Type: French cruiser
Displacement: 2,438 tonnes (2,400 tons)
Dimensions: 76m x 11.6m x 5.5m (249ft 4in x 38ft x 18ft)
Machinery: Single screw, horizontal compound engines
Top speed: 13.4 knots
Main armament: Fifteen 140mm (5.5in) guns
Launched: 1879

Forfait was a wooden-hulled cruiser with a partial double bottom made possible by an intricate network of iron beams, as it was not possible to fit a fully leakproof double bottom in a wooden ship. She carried her main armament on the upper deck with the two forward guns recessed to provide ahead fire. *Forfait* was laid down in 1876 and completed in 1880, the remaining three ships in the class following between 1881 and 1885. She was removed from the effective list in 1897.

Formidabile

Type: Italian battleship
Displacement: 2,769 tonnes (2,725 tons)
Dimensions: 65.8m x 13.6m x 5.4m (215ft 10in x 44ft 7in x 17ft 9in)
Machinery: Single screw single expansion engines
Top speed: 10 knots
Main armament: Sixteen 164mm (6.5in), four 203mm (8in) 72-pounder guns
Launched: October 1861

Formidabile and *Terribile* were originally designed as 30-gun floating batteries but became instead ocean-going broadside ironclads with 20 guns and were rearmed with eight 203mm (8in) guns. *Formadibile* was removed from the effective list in 1903.

Formidable

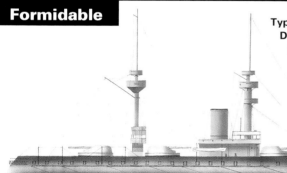

Type: French battleship
Displacement: 11,908 tonnes (11,720 tons)
Dimensions: 101.4m x 21.3m x 8.5m (332ft 8in x 70ft x 27ft 9in)
Machinery: Twin screw vertical compound engines
Main armament: Three 371mm(14.6in), four 160mm (6.3in), ten 140mm (5.5in) guns
Armour: 356-559mm (14-22in) thick waterline belt, 405mm (15.95in) on the bartbettes
Launched: April 1885

From 1877 to 1879, France laid down seven barbette ships, of which *Formidable* was the last. *Formidable* had her three 371mm (14.6in) guns in single barbettes on the centreline, with the secondary battery on the main deck. The steel belt ran the full length but only 306mm (12in) of it was above water. Formidable was deleted from the navy list in 1911.

Formidable

Type: British aircraft carrier
Displacement: 28,661 tonnes (28,210 tons)
Dimensions: 226.7m x 29.1m x 8.5m (743ft 9in x 95ft 9in x 28ft)
Machinery: Triple screws, turbines
Top speed: 30.5 knots
Main armament: Sixteen 114mm (4.5in) guns, 36 aircraft
Launched: August 1939

The 1936 programme called for the construction of two 23,368-tonne (23,000-ton) carriers and at first plans were drawn up based on *Ark Royal*. With the realisation that war

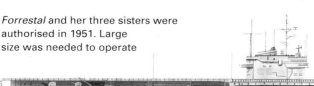

in Europe was coming ever closer, and that such carriers would be subject to constant air attack, armour protection and defensive armament was seen as important. The aircraft hangar was set in an armoured box intended to be proof against 227kg (500lb) bombs and 152mm (6in) gunfire. *Formidable* was scrapped in 1953.

Forrestal

Type: US aircraft carrier
Displacement: 80,516 tonnes (79,248 tons)
Dimensions: 309.4m x 73.2m x 11.3m (1,015ft x 240ft x 37ft)
Machinery: Four screws, turbines
Top speed: 33 knots
Main armament: Eight 127mm (5in) guns, 90 aircraft
Launched: Decmeber 1954

Forrestal and her three sisters were authorised in 1951. Large size was needed to operate fast combat jets, which needed more fuel than their piston-engined predecessors. Designed around the A3D, *Forrestal* had space for around 3.4 million litres (750,000 gallons) of aviation fuel. She is scheduled for frontline service until the turn of the century.

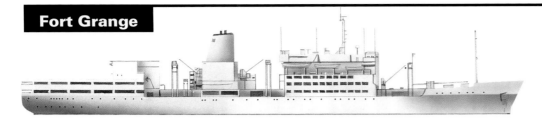

F | The Encyclopedia of Ships

Fort Grange

Type: British replenishment ship
Displacement: 23,165 tonnes (22,800 tons)
Dimensions: 183.9m x 24.1m x 8.6m (603ft 4in x 79ft x 28ft 3in)
Machinery: Single screw, diesel engine
Launched: December 1976

One of two sister ships ordered in 1971, *Fort Grange* was completed in April 1978. She is fitted with a helicopter flight deck aft that can be used for replenishment operations or as an extra base for fleet aint-submarine helicopters. Both vessels carry an extensive supply of anti-submarine stores, and have a total capacity of 3,556 tonnes (3,500 tons) of armament, naval and general stores in four holds. The engine gives a 19,000-km (10,000-mile) range at 20 knots. Bow thrusters are fitted for easier manoeuvrability.

Forte

Type: British cruiser
Displacement: 4,430 tonnes (4,360 tons)
Dimensions: 103.5m x 15.1m x 5.8m (339ft 6in x 49ft 6in x 19ft)
Machinery: Twin screw triple expansion engines
Main armament: Two 152mm(6in), eight 119mm (4.7in) guns

Forte was one of a class of eight provided under the massive expansion programme of the Naval Defence Act of 1889. She was an improved Apollo with 1,016 tonnes (1,000 tons) more displacement, a heavier armament and better seaworthiness. *Forte* was laid down at Chatham in 1891. One 152mm (6in) gun was mounted forward, the other aft. *Forte* was sold in 1914; her sister *Hermione* not until 1940.

Forth

Type: British cruiser
Displacement: 4,115 tonnes (4,050 tons)
Dimensions: 96m x 14m x 5.9m (315ft x 46ft x 19ft 6in)
Machinery: Twin screw, horizontal direct-acting compound engines
Main armament: Two 203mm (8in), ten 152mm (6in) guns
Launched: October 1886

Forth and her sisters were a complete break from previous second class cruisers. The 203mm (8in) guns were mounted behind shields, one fore and one aft. Two pole masts with light rigging were fitted but for the first time all sail power was done away with. Another first was the fitting of a full-length protective deck between 51 and 76mm (2 and 3in) thick. *Forth* was sold in 1921.

Foudre

Type: French torpedo depot ship
Displacement: 6,186 tonnes (6,089 tons)
Dimensions: 118.7m x 17.2m x 7.2m (389ft 5in x 56ft 5in x 23ft 7in)
Machinery: Twin screw triple expansion engines
Main armament: Eight 99mm (3.9in) guns
Launched: October 1895

Foudre was built as a special depot ship for ten small torpedo boats each fitted with one 380mm (15in) torpedo tube. These boats were carried on cradles positioned in groups either side of the centre superstructure. *Foudre* underwent many conversions – to repair ship, minelayer, aircraft depot ship, seaplane carrier, in which role she served in World War I. She was scrapped in 1921.

Foudroyante

Type: French floating battery
Displacement: 1,600 tonnes (1,575 tons)
Dimensions: 51.1m x 13.1m x2.5m (167ft 6in x 43ft x 8ft 4in)
Machinery: Single screw, high-pressure engines
Top speed: 5 knots
Main armament: Sixteen 60-pounder guns
Armour: 102mm (4in) thick on battery and hull
Launched: June 1855

With the outbreak of war with Russia in 1854, Napoleon III of France was not prepared to risk his wooden warships against the shell fire of the Baltic forts. *Foudroyante* was one of five ungainly-looking but extremely practical warships designed to withstand the sustained fire of powerful shore forts and batteries while delivering their own attack.

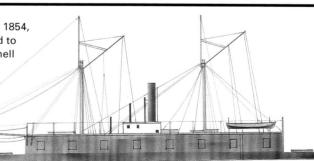

136

Framée

Type: French destroyer
Displacement: 354 tonnes (348 tons)
Dimensions: 58.1m x 6.3m x 3m (190ft 7in x 20ft 8in x 9ft10in)
Machinery: Twin screw triple expansion engines
Top speed: 26 knots
Main armament: One 65mm (2.56in) gun
Launched: October 1899

The threat that small torpedo boats posed was the catalyst for the

development of a new class of warship, the destroyer. These were supposed to be powerful enough to overcome such boats, while still being light and fast enough to catch them. They used the new pattern of watertube boiler to feed fast-running engines, but full design speed was rarely achieved. A more critical problem was that of weight distribution. In trying to pack the necessary weapons and equipment into a narrow hull, the designers had ended up with a ship that was top-heavy and which rolled excessively. Later modifications included removal of the main mast and aft control area, but the problem was never cured. The class was never repeated, although lessons learnt were incorporated in later designs. *Framée* was accidentally rammed and sunk on 11 August 1900 by the battleship *Brennus*.

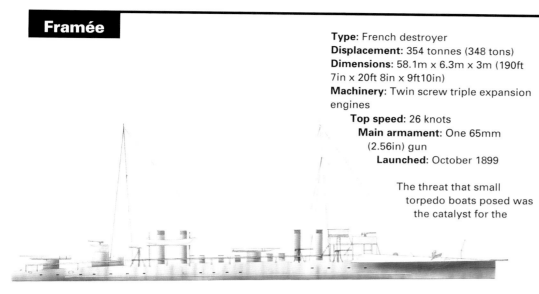

France

Type: French liner
Displacement: 27,188 tonnes (26,760 tons)
Dimensions: 217.2m x 23m (712ft 7in x 75ft 6in)
Machinery: Four screws, turbines
Top speed: 25.9 knots
Launched: September 1910

When *France* joined the North Atlantic route for the Companie Generale Transatlantique in 1912, she was one of the smallest

express liners on the service, but except for the *Lusitania* and *Mauretania* she was the fastest merchant ship afloat. In 1914, *France* became an auxiliary cruiser, then a troop transport (as *France IV*). In 1916 she became a hospital ship and in 1917 a troop transport once more. In 1919 she returned to the Atlantic route, when because of her popularity, passengers had to bid for their cabins. She made her last crossing in 1932 and was broken up in 1934/35.

France

Type: French liner
Displacement: 67,406 tonnes (66,344 tons)
Dimensions: 315.5m x 33.5m (1,035ft x110ft)
Machinery: Four screws, turbines
Top speed: 30+ knots
Launched: 1961

France was built by Chantiers de L'Atlantique de St Nazaire for the

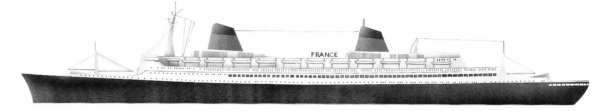

Companie Generale Transatlantique for their Le Havre-New York route. At the time of her launch, she was the world's longest merchant ship. *France* made her maiden voyage in

February 1962, and was well able to maintain a service speed of 30 knots, but that was not enough to fend off the growing influence of transatlantic air travel, then getting

into its stride. In 1974, the subsidy that kept her in service was stopped and she was withdrawn. In 1979 she was sold to Norwegian Caribbean Lines and renamed *Norway*.

Francesco Caracciolo

Type: Italian battleship
Displacement: 34,544 tonnes (34,000 tons)
Dimensions: 212m x 29.6m x 9.5m (695ft 6in x 97ft x 31ft 2in)
Machinery: Four screws, turbines
Top speed: 28 knots
Main armament: Eight 381mm (15in), twelve 152mm (6in) guns
Launched: 1920

Work started on *Francesco Carraciolo* and three sister units in 1914 but was halted in 1916 so that materials and labour could be devoted to building destroyers, submarines and light craft. Work recommenced in October 1919, but after the

launch, the hull was sold, in October 1920, to the Navigazione Generale Italiana who intended to convert her into a merchant ship. Lack of funds stopped this and a plan to turn her into an aircraft carrier was also

dropped, and she was scrapped in 1921. The three sister ships were less advanced when work was halted and they were scrapped on the stocks. *Francesco Carracciolo*'s design gave her four widely spaced turrets, with the 152mm (6in) guns in two groups near the centre of the vessel.

Francesco Ferruccio

Type: Italian cruiser
Displacement: 8,230 tonnes (8,100 tons)
Dimensions: 111.8m x 18.2m x 7.3m (366ft 10in x 59ft 9in x 24ft)
Machinery: Twin screw vertical triple expansion engines
Main armament: One 254mm (10in), two 203mm (8in), fourteen 152mm (6in) guns
Armour: Complete belt 102-152mm (4-6in) thick, with same on turrets
Launched: 1902

Francesco Ferruccio was one of a successful type designed during the early to mid-1890s and supplied to the navies of Argentina, Spain and Japan as well as Italy. They were heavily armed vessels with good speed. Overall they were a well-balanced design and were able to withstand the fire of most battleships and defeat any standard cruiser. *Francesco Ferruccio* was commissioned in September 1905.

Francesco Morosini

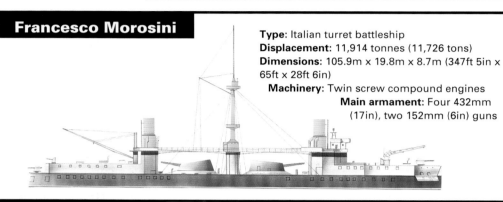

Type: Italian turret battleship
Displacement: 11,914 tonnes (11,726 tons)
Dimensions: 105.9m x 19.8m x 8.7m (347ft 5in x 65ft x 28ft 6in)
Machinery: Twin screw compound engines
Main armament: Four 432mm (17in), two 152mm (6in) guns
Armour: 451mm (17.75in) thick belt amidships
Launched: July 1885

Francesco Morosini was authorised under the 1880 programme, laid down in 1881 at the Naval Arsenal, Venice, and completed in April 1889. The design for her and her two sisters was based on the turret ship *Duilio*, but included improvements, such as a raised forecastle and breechloading guns. *Francesco Morosini* was sunk as a target in September 1909.

Francesco Nullo

Type: Italian destroyer
Displacement: 914 tonnes (900 tons)
Dimensions: 73m x 7.3m x 2.7m (239ft 6in x 24ft x 9ft)
Machinery: Twin screws, turbines
Main armament: Five 76mm (3in) guns
Launched: November 1914

Francesco Nullo was one of a class of eight laid down in 1913/14 and was the first Italian destroyer to have a single-calibre gun armament. She was built by Pattison of Naples and completed in 1915. The design set the pattern for the next major destroyer groups. The armament of these ships underwent several changes and during World War I all were fitted out as minelayers. They were reclassified as torpedo boats in 1929 and *Francesco Nullo* was renamed *Fratelli Cairoli* so the original name could be used for a destroyer. *Nullo/ Cairoli* was sunk by an enemy mine in December 1940.

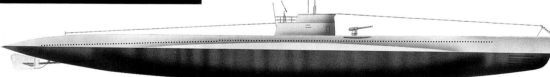

Francesco Rismondo

Type: Italian submarine
Displacement: 676 tonnes (665 tons) (surface), 835 tonnes (822 tons) (submerged)
Dimensions: 66.5m x 5.4m x 3.8m (218ft 2in x 17ft 9in x 12ft 4in)
Machinery: Twin screw, diesel (surface), electric motors (submerged)
Main armament: One 99mm (3.9in) gun, six 551mm (21.7in) torpedo tubes
Launched: December 1928

Francesco Rismondo was the former Yugoslav submarine *N1*, captured in April 1941 along with her sister *N2* at Cattaro by the Italian Navy. *Francesco Rismondo* was captured by German forces at Bonifacio on 14 September 1943 and sunk by them four days later off the same port.

Franconia

Type: British liner
Displacement: 18,440 tonnes (18,150 tons)
Dimensions: 190.5m x 21.7m (625ft x 71ft)
Machinery: Twin screw, quadruple expansion engines
Launched: July 1910

Franconia was building for the Thompson Line when she was bought by Cunard for service on the Boston route and winter Mediterranean cruising. She could hold 2,850 passengers and, with her sister, was the first Cunarder to have a gym. *Franconia* was sunk 370km (195 miles) off Malta on 4 October 1916 by the German UB 47.

Frank Cable

Type: US submarine tender
Displacement: 23,368 tonnes (23,000 tons)
Dimensions: 196.9m x 25.9m x 7.6m
(646ft x 85ft x 25ft)
Machinery: Single screw, turbine
Top speed: 18 knots
Main armament: Two
40mm (1.6in) guns
Launched: 1978

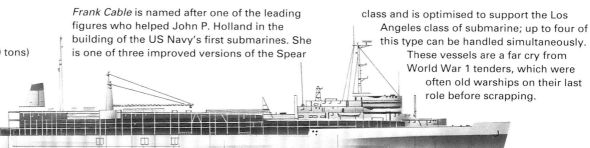

Frank Cable is named after one of the leading figures who helped John P. Holland in the building of the US Navy's first submarines. She is one of three improved versions of the Spear class and is optimised to support the Los Angeles class of submarine; up to four of this type can be handled simultaneously. These vessels are a far cry from World War 1 tenders, which were often old warships on their last role before scrapping.

Frans Suell

Type: Swedish ferry
Displacement: 35,850 tonnes
(35,285 tons)
Dimensions: 169.4m x 27.6m x
6.25m (556ft x 90ft 6in x 20ft 6in)
Machinery: Twin screw, diesel engines
Launched: January 1991

Frans Suell is a super car ferry built in Split,

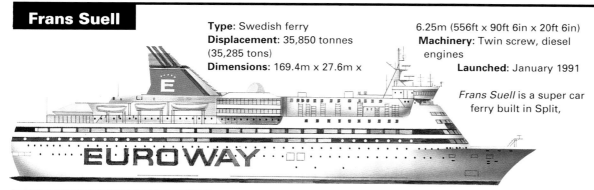

Croatia, and operated by Sea Link Shipping of Sweden in the Baltic. The basic hull design is the same as that used on two large ferries built for the Viking Line in the late 1980s. From the lowest part of the vessel to the top of the wheelhouse there are 12 decks, two of which are used for road vehicles. Accommodation is for 2,300 passengers, with some cabins having balconies.

Fratelli Bandiera

Type: Italian submarine
Displacement: 880 tonnes (866 tons) (surface),
1,114 tonnes (1,096 tons) (submerged)

Dimensions: 69.8m x 7.2m x 5.2m (229ft x 23ft 8in x 17ft)
Machinery: Twin screw, diesel engines (surface),

electric motors (submerged)
Top speed: 15.1 knots (surface), 8.2 knots (submerged)
Main armament: One 99mm (3.9in) gun, eight 533mm (21in) torpedo tubes
Launched: August 1929

Fratelli Bandiera was one of a class of four. Soon after completion the bow was raised and by 1942 the conning tower had been reduced in size. During the war she was used for training and transporting supplies; she was scrapped in 1948.

Freccia

Type: Italian destroyer
Displacement: 354 tonnes (348 tons)
Dimensions: 62.1m x 6.5m x 2.6m (203ft 7in x 21ft 4in x 8ft 6in)
Machinery: Twin screw, triple expansion engines
Top speed: 31+ knots
Main armament: One 76mm (3in) gun
Launched: November 1899

Laid down in 1899 and completed in 1902, *Freccia* was designed and constructed by the German builders

Schichau. She and her five sisters formed the first major group of destroyers built for the Italian Navy. She was lost on 12 October 1911, in the Italo-Turkish

War, when she went aground at the entrance to Tripoli harbour.

Freccia

Type: Italian destroyer
Displacement: 2,134 tonnes
92,100 tons)
Dimensions: 96mm x 9.75m x
3.2m (315ft x 32ft x 10ft 4in)
Machinery: Twin screw,

turbines
Main armament: Four 119mm
(4.7in) guns
Launched: August 1930

Freccia was one of class of four units,

which were a complete break with the previous classes of two- and three-funnelled destroyers in the Italian Navy, and set the pattern for destroyer design in Italy for several years. Two sets of triple 533mm (21in) torpedo tubes were carried between the single, raked funnel and the main mast. *Freccia* was sunk during an air raid while lying off Genoa on 9 August 1943.

Fremantle

Type: Australian fast patrol boat
Displacement: 214 tonnes (211 tons)
Dimensions: 41.8m x 7.1m x 1.8m (137ft 2in x 23ft 4in x 6ft)
Machinery: Triple screw diesel engines
Main armament: One 40mm (1.6in) gun
Launched: 1979

In December 1977, the Australian government decided to purchase 15 large patrol boats. *Fremantle* was the lead ship of the class and was laid down in the December of that year. Launched in 1979, she was commissioned on 17 March 1980. She was built by Brooke Marine of Lowestoft, England, while the remaining boats were built by North Queensland Engineers at Cairn, Australia. These are fairly large patrol boats, and faster than the Attack-class vessels which previously fulfilled this role. The Royal Australian Navy uses them for long-range coastal patrols to prevent smuggling and the landing of illegal immigrants. Their armament is thus comparatively light, being confined to a single 40mm (1.6in) Bofors dual purpose gun, a pair of single 12.7mm (0.5in) heavy machine guns, and an 81mm (3.2in) mortar capable of firing parachute flares. The reasonable size of these ships, however, would permit the installation of extra sensors and light missile systems should they be required. They have a flush-decked hull, with a monobloc superstructure that houses the bridge, the command centre and the exhaust uptake. Two MTU diesel engines develop a total of more than 6,000hp, while a supplementary Doorman diesel allows long range cruising at eight knots. *Fremantle* has a range of 2,755km (1,450 miles) at 30 knots, but can achieve nearly 9,120km (4,800 miles) at eight knots. She has a full crew complement of 22 officers and men.

Freya

Type: German cruiser
Displacement: 2,444 tonnes (2,406 tons)
Dimensions: 85.4m x 10.8m x 5.6m (280ft x 35ft 5in x 18ft 4in)
Machinery: Single screw, compound expansion engines
Top speed: 15.2 knots
Main armament: Eight 150mm (5.9in) guns
Launched: December 1874

Freya was a wooden-hulled cruiser with a ram bow and a full spread of canvas. She was laid down at the Danzig Naval Dockyard and completed in 1876. Two slightly smaller vessels of the same type were built at Danzig at the same time. *Freya*'s armament was carried on slide carriages on the upper deck on the broadside, with the bridge positioned aft between the main and mizzen masts. Most of *Freya*'s service was spent abroad; she was broken up in 1896.

Friant

Type: French cruiser
Displacement: 3,861 tonnes (3,800 tons)
Dimensions: 95m x 13m x 6.4m (311ft 8in x 42ft 8in x 21ft)
Machinery: Twin screw triple expansion engines
Main armament: Six 163mm (6.4in), four 102mm (4in) guns
Launched: April 1893

Friant was a three-funnelled cruiser with a pronounced tumblehome to the hull and a ram bow. Though the sides were unarmoured, internal protection was quite thorough. The armoured deck was 30mm (1.2in) thick on the flat and 81mm (3.2in) thick on the slopes. Above this was a cellular layer plus a splinter deck just above the machinery spaces, should anything pierce the main armoured deck. During the Russo-Japanese War of 1904/5, cruisers similar to *Friant* absorbed a huge amount of punishment. *Friant* was an escort in the Mediterranean during World War I becoming a submarine tender in 1918. She was removed from the effective list in 1920.

Friedrich der Grosse

Type: German battleship
Displacement: 7,718 tonnes (7,596 tons)
Dimensions: 96.6m x 16.2m x 7.2m (316ft 10in x 53ft x 23ft 6in)
Machinery: single screw, horizontal compound engine
Top speed: 14 knots
Main armament: Four 259mm (10.2in) guns
Launched: September 1874

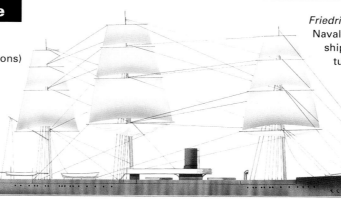

Friedrich der Grosse was laid down in 1859 at the Royal Naval Dockyard, Kiel, as one of a class of three turret ships; she was completed in November 1877. The two turrets were carried amidships behind two-metre (7ft) bulwarks that were lowered in battle. Her sister *Grosser Kurfurst* was accidentally rammed and sunk 26 days after commissioning. *Friedrich der Grosse* and *Preussen* were modernised in 1889/90. They served as guard ships until the end of the 1890s and later became coal hulks. *Friedrich der Grosse* was sold for scrapping in 1919.

Friedrich Carl

Type: German battleship
Displacement: 7,043 tonnes (6,932 tons)
Dimensions: 94.1m x 16.6m x 8m (308ft 10in x 54ft 6in x 26ft 3in)
Machinery: Single screw, horizontal single expansion engine
Top speed: 13.6 knots
Main armament: Sixteen 210mm

(8.25in) guns
Launched: January 1867

The ship-rigged central-battery vessel *Friedrich Carl* was the first battleship specifically ordered for the German Navy. During the 1870 war with France, she was stationed in the Jade. In 1892, *Friedrich Carl* became a torpedo school ship. She was renamed *Neptun* and sold in 1905.

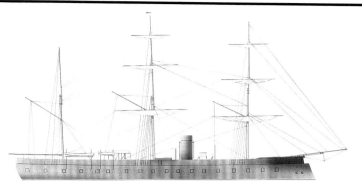

Friendship

Type: British sailing brig
Displacement: 278 tonnes (274 tons)
Dimensions: 28m x 6m (91ft 10in x 19ft 8in)
Top speed: 10 knots
Launched: 1780

In 1788, *Friendship* was part of

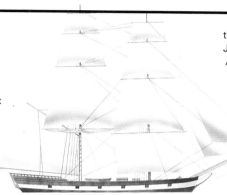

the fleet that arrived at Port Jackson, New South Wales, Australia, with the first cargo of British convicts. Nine vessels in all made up the fleet, carrying 759 convicts, 40 of whom died on the voyage.

Friendship was a two-masted brig, with one main deck running the full length of the vessel and

with headroom of less than 1.4 metres (4ft 6in), making life very uncomfortable for the convicts. A light armament was carried. In July 1788, *Friendship* left Port Jackson with three other vessels to make the return journey to Britain, but soon scurvy reduced the crew to such an extent that the ship had to be scuttled near Macassar and the survivors put on another ship.

Frithjof

Type: German battleship
Displacement: 3,750 tonnes (3,691 tons)
Dimensions: 78.9m x 14.9m x 5.8m (258ft 10in x 48ft 11in x 19ft)
Machinery: Twin screw triple expansion engines
Main armament: Three 239mm (9.4in) guns
Armament: 178-241mm (7-9.5in) thick belt, 203mm (8in) on the turrets
Launched: July 1891

Frithjof was one of a class of eight vessels designed for coastal defence in the Baltic Sea. The main guns were carried in three turrets – two forward side by side on a raised barbette, with the third aft on the centreline. The 86mm (3.4in) secondary weapons were carried, all behind shields, at the corners of the superstructure and in the waist on sponsons. The class underwent a rebuild between 1900 and 1904, which included reboilering, the vessels receiving two funnels. *Frithjof* was sold in 1919, becoming a cargo ship, and was broken up in 1930.

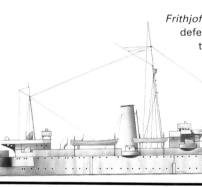

Frithjof

Type: Norwegian cruiser
Displacement: 1,392 tonnes (1,370 tons)
Dimensions: 65.8m x 10m x 4.1m (216ft x 32ft 10in x 13ft 5in)
Machinery: Twin screw, triple expansion engines
Main armament: Two 119mm (4.7in) guns
Launched: 1896

Before the advent of the submarine, *Norway* protected her coastline and fjords first with a force of small, powerful monitors, which in the 1880s and 1890s gave way to small coast-defence battleships backed up by cruisers and torpedo boats. *Frithjof* fell between small cruiser and torpedo boat in type. In 1908, she was rebuilt as a cadet training ship and was stricken in 1928.

Front Driver

Type: Swedish cargo vessel
Displacement: 195,733 tonnes (192,651 tons)
Dimensions: 285m x 45m (935ft x 147ft 8in)
Machinery: Single screw, diesel

engine
Launched: January 1991

Front Driver is a dual-purpose oil/bulk ore carrier owned by Bonfield Shipping of Sweden. She

has nine holds with wing tanks and can handle three types of oil cargo. The hull has a double bottom and is made up of 52 per cent high-tensile steel for extra strength. She entered service in April 1991.

Frunze

Type: Russian destroyer
Displacement: 1,321 tonnes (1,300 tons)
Dimensions: 93m x 9.3m x 2.8m (305ft x 30ft 6in x 9ft 2in)
Machinery: Twin screw, turbines
Top speed: 34 knots
Main armament: Four 102mm (4in) guns, one 75mm (3in) gun
Launched: 1915

Frunze was based on the highly successful Russian destroyer *Novik* and was originally named *Bistry*. Two sets of triple 450mm (17.7in) torpedo tubes were carried on the centreline abaft the superstructure, with another triple set carried in front. During her lifetime her armament underwent several changes. *Frunze* was sunk by German aircraft in 1941.

Fu Ch'ing

Type: Chinese cruiser
Displacement: 2,235 tonnes (2,200 tons)
Dimensions: 77m x 11m x 5.5m (252ft 6in x 36ft x 18ft)
Machinery: Single screw, reciprocating engine
Top speed: 15 knots
Main armament: Two 208mm (8.2in), eight 119mm (4.7in) guns
Launched: 1893

Fu Ch'ing was a steel-hulled barque-rigged cruiser with a ram bow. The 208mm (8.2in) guns were carried forward on sponsons. Two 119mm (4.7in) guns were carried aft on sponsons, four were carried on the broadside, one was carried on the forecastle and one on the poop. *Fu Ch'ing* was sunk in 1898.

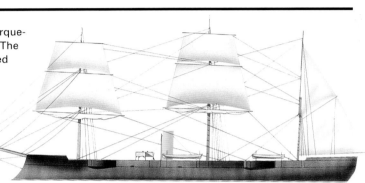

Fu Lung

Type: Chinese torpedo boat
Displacement: 130 tonnes (128 tons)
Dimensions: 44m x 5m x 2.3 m 144ft 4in x 16ft

5in x 7ft 6in)
Machinery: Single screw, triple expansion engine
Main armament: Two 356mm (14in) torpedo tubes

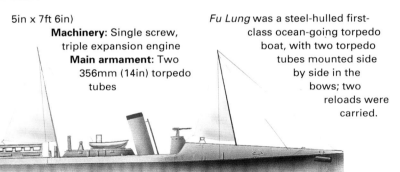

Fu Lung was a steel-hulled first-class ocean-going torpedo boat, with two torpedo tubes mounted side by side in the bows; two reloads were carried.

She was one of two torpedo boats with Ping Yuen and Kwang Ping in the Chinese Inshore Squadron at the Yalu in 1894, and the presence of such vessels contributed to the Japanese decision not to carry the action on into the night. *Fu Lung* was captured by the Japanese on 8 February 1895 at the fall of Wei-Hai-Wei and renamed *Fukuryu*. She was broken up in 1908.

Fuad

Type: Turkish despatch vessel
Displacement: 1,075 tonnes (1,058 tons)
Dimensions: 76.2m x 9.1m x 3.7m (250ft x 30ft x 12ft)
Machinery: Paddle wheels
Top speed: 12.5 knots
Main armament: One 119mm

(4.7in) gun plus three smaller guns
Launched: 1864

Fuad and her three sisters were iron-hulled vessels with a light rig and two raking

funnels. As despatch boats they were ideal, having speed and a good range. They were among the last paddle-driven warships. *Fuad* was discarded in 1898.

Fugas

Type: Russian minesweeper
Displacement: 152 tonnes (150 tons)
Dimensions: 45.1m x 6.1m x 1.9m (148ft x 20ft x 6ft)

Machinery: Twin screw, double expansion engines
Main armament: One 63mm (2.5in) gun
Launched: 1910

Following the success of Russian minesweeping activities around Port Arthur in 1904 during the war with Japan, it was decided to build a group of boats designed for minesweeping but which could also be minelayers. *Fugas* was mined off Saurop in November 1916; three of her four sisters were also mined during World War I, the fourth surviving to be scrapped in 1930.

Fuji

Type: Japanese battleship
Displacement: 12,737 tonnes (12,533 tons)
Dimensions: 125.28m x 22.25m x 8.1m (411ft x 73ft x 26ft7in)
Machinery: Twin screw vertical triple expansion engines
Top speed: 18 knots
Main armament: Four 305mm (12in), ten 152mm (6in) guns
Armour: 356-457mm (14-18in) on main belt, 102mm (4in) on upper belt and 229-356mm (9-14in) on barbettes.
Launched: March 1896

In the early 1890s, Japan anticipated war with China, and placed an order with Britain for two modern battleships designed by G. Macrow of the Thames Ironworks. *Fuji*, and her sister ship *Yashima*, were improved versions of the Royal Sovereign class, although they carried lighter but equally

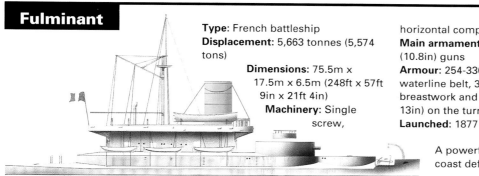

effective 305mm (12in) guns instead of the 344mm (13.5in) weapons of the British ships. The weight saved was used to improve the armour protection, especially around the barbettes. Their main armament was placed at the fore and aft ends of the vessel, while four of the 152mm (6in) guns were mounted in casements on the main deck. The rest of these guns were behind shields on the upper deck. These were fine, capable ships, and the first modern battleships in the Japanese Navy. They were completed too late for the 1894-1895 Sino-Japanese war, but took part in the 1904-1905 Russo-Japanese conflict. *Yashima* was sunk by a Russian mine in May 1904, but *Fuji* survived the war. She fought in the Battle of the Yellow Sea in August 1904 and sunk the Russian battleship *Borodino* at the Battle of Tsushima on 25 May 1905. She was finally stricken in 1923.

Fulminant

Type: French battleship
Displacement: 5,663 tonnes (5,574 tons)
Dimensions: 75.5m x 17.5m x 6.5m (248ft x 57ft 9in x 21ft 4in)
Machinery: Single screw, horizontal compound engines
Main armament: Two 274mm (10.8in) guns
Armour: 254-330mm (10-13in on the waterline belt, 330mm (13in) on the breastwork and 305-330mm (12-13in) on the turret
Launched: 1877

A powerful, single-turreted, coast defence ship, with the main armament concentrated in the large, 876mm (4ft 6in) diameter turret forward. The superstructure aft was narrow and supported a wide flying bridge intended to be narrow enough for the widely-spaced guns in the turret to fire directly aft. Her hull was built mainly of steel. *Fulminant* was laid down in 1875, completed in 1882 and stricken in 1908.

Fulmine

Type: Italian destroyer
Displacement: 347 tonnes (342 tons)
Dimensions: 62m x 6.5m x 2.25m (204ft x 21ft x 7ft 6in)
Machinery: Twin screw triple expansion engines
Top speed: 24 knots
Main armament: Five 57mm (2.25in) guns, three 356mm (14in) torpedo tubes
Launched: 1898

In July 1897, at the Odero yard at Sestri Ponente, Italy laid down the first destroyer to join the Italian Navy. Designed by Eng. Insp. Gen. Martinez, it followed the standard destroyer design of the period, with a long, sleek hull and a turtleback forecastle. The design speed was 26.5 knots, but initially only 24 knots was achieved. By 1908 *Fulmine* had been credited with 28 knots. Much experience was gained with this vessel and Italy went on to produce the fastest destroyers in the world, though Italy purchased her next batch from Germany. The ship underwent some changes during her career. The number of torpedo tubes was reduced to two and her gun armament was changed to one 76mm (3in) and three 57mm (2.25in) guns.

Fulmine

Type: Italian destroyer
Displacement: 2,124 tonnes (2,090 tons)
Dimensions: 94.5m x 9.25m x 3.25m (309ft 6in x 30ft 6in x 11ft)
Machinery: Twin screw turbines
Top speed: 38 knots
Main armament: Four 119mm (4.7in) guns
Launched: August 1931

One of a class of eight vessels divided into two groups, one ordered in 1928 and the second, to which *Fulmine* belonged, ordered a year later. Six were lost in action during World War II, including *Fulmine*, which was sunk during an action with British forces. They were amongst the few single funnel destroyers built prior to World War II and all were good sea boats with a splendid turn of speed. As originally designed, these boats had two funnels and a straight bow. But during construction this was changed to one wider funnel and an overhang on the bow to improve sea-keeping.

Fulton

Type: French steamboat
Displacement: 25.5 tonnes (25 tons)

Dimensions: 20.25m x 5.5m x 0.5m (66ft 6in x 17ft 6in x 1ft 8in)
Machinery: Paddle wheels, single cylinder beam engine

Top speed: 4.5 knots
Launched: 1803

The famous American steamboat pioneer, Robert Fulton, had started experimenting with an engine suitable for propelling a small boat in 1794. Four years later, he had developed a screw propeller, although all his later boats were driven by paddles. With financial support from the US Ambassador in Paris, he constructed a small steamboat.

Fulton

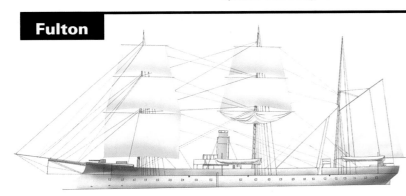

Type: French gunboat
Displacement: 838 tonnes (825 tons)
Dimensions: 60.8m x 8.7m x 3.9m (199ft 5in x 28ft 5in x 12ft 8in)
Machinery: Single screw horizontal compound engine
Top speed: 13 knots
Main armament: Three 140mm (5.5in) guns, one 99mm (3.9in) gun
Launched: January 1887

Laid down in 1882, *Fulton* was not completed until 1888, the delay caused by problems over the supply of engines. This occurred at a time when naval development was making rapid, dramatic strides and a long construction time could lead to vessels becoming dated before completion. *Fulton* was scrapped in 1900, but sister vessels *Inconstant* and *Papin* served in Ecuador's Navy from 1901-1920.

Fulton

Main armament: Two 75mm (3in) guns, eight 450mm (17.7in) torpedo tubes
Launched: April 1919

Type: French submarine
Displacement: 884 tonnes (870 tons) (surface), 1,267 tonnes (1,247 tons) (submerged)
Dimensions: 74m x 6.4m x 3.6m (242ft 9in x 21ft x 11ft 10in)

Machinery: Twin screw, diesel engines (surface), electric motors (submerged)

Laid down at Cherbourg in late 1913, but not completed until July 1920 because of the low priority in France for certain types of warships during World War I. Designed with two 2,000hp turbines, which were altered to diesel while being built.

Fulton

Type: American submarine tender
Displacement: 18,288 tonnes (18,000 tons)
Dimensions: 161.5m x 22.4m x 7.8m (529ft 10in x 73ft 6in x 25ft 7in)
Machinery: Twin screw diesel electric engines
Top speed: 15 knots
Launched: December 1940

One of a class that originally totalled seven units, *Fulton* was commissioned in September 1941. In December of that year she established seaplane bases in the Panama Canal, a prelude to the setting up of a defence zone around the canal. She served as a submarine ship at Midway during 1942. Her facilities have been updated so she can support nuclear attack submarines.

Furieux

Type: French battleship
Displacement: 6,020 tonnes (5,925 tons)
Dimensions: 72.5m x 17.8m x 7.1m (238ft x 58ft 6in x 23ft)
Machinery: Twin screw vertical compound engines
Top speed: 14 knots
Main armament: Two 340mm (13.4in) guns
Armour: 330-457mm (13-18in) thick waterline belt with 457mm (18in) on the barbettes
Launched: July 1883

France's powerful coastal defence force was made up of second-class battleships such as *Furieux*. These would not only deter assaults on the French coast but would act as a second line of defence after both French and enemy forces had sustained heavy losses in a major battle. *Furieux* was completed in 1887, and rebuilt in 1902-4.

Furious

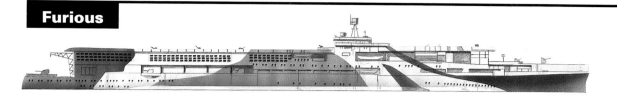

Type: British aircraft carrier
Displacement: 22,758 tonnes
(22,400 tons)
Dimensions: 239.6m x 27.4m x 7.3m

(786ft 4in x 90ft x 24ft)
Machinery: Four screws, turbines
Main armament: Six 102mm (4in)
guns

Aircraft: 36
Launched: August 1916

The origin of one of the best-known

British aircraft carriers of World War II dates back to pre-1914 when Fisher, then First Sea Lord, planned for a fleet of fast, powerful cruisers with shallow draught to operate in the Baltic against Germany's northern coast. *Furious* was one of three such vessels built. She served with the Home and Mediterranean fleets in World War II. Her aircraft attacked the *Tirpitz* in 1944. She was scrapped in 1948.

Furnessia

Type: British liner
Displacement: 5,583 tonnes (5,495 tons)
Dimensions: 135.6m x 13.7m (445ft x 45ft)
Machinery: Single screw compound engines
Top speed: 14 knots
Launched: 1880

For a period of just nine months *Furnessia* was the largest Atlantic liner in service. Her passenger accommodation was of a high standard when she made her

maiden voyage from Glasgow to New York in January 1881. She underwent a major rebuild in 1891, when the passenger accommodation was revised. By 1909, she was taking second- and third-class passengers only, as she had long since been superseded by newer, faster liners. *Furnessia* was eventually scrapped in 1912, having remained in service until the previous year and having given 30 years of almost continuous service.

Furor

Type: Spanish destroyer
Displacement: 376 tonnes (370 tons)

Dimensions: 67m x 6.7m x 1.7m
(219ft 10in x 22ft x 5ft 7in)
Machinery: Twin screw triple

expansion engines
Top speed: 28 knots
Main armament: Two 14-pounder

guns, two 356mm (14in) torpedo tubes
Launched: 1896

Built at Clydebank, Scotland, *Furor* was the first destroyer to enter the Spanish Navy. She was part of Admiral Ceveras's squadron sent to Cuba in 1898. On 3 July, she followed the armoured cruisers out of Santiago and was sunk by the US Fleet that was lying in wait.

Fürst Bismarck

Type: German cruiser
Displacement: 11,461 tonnes (11,281 tons)
Dimensions: 127m x 20.4m x 8.5m (416ft 8in x 67ft x 27ft 9in)
Machinery: Twin screw triple expansion engines
Main armament: Four 239mm (9.4in), twelve 150mm (5.9in) guns

Launched: September 1897

Fürst Bismarck was Germany's first armoured cruiser, and her 203mm (8in) belt was among the thickest on any contemporary ship of the type. She served overseas until 1909 and later became a coast defence ship. Disarmed in 1916, she was scrapped in 1921.

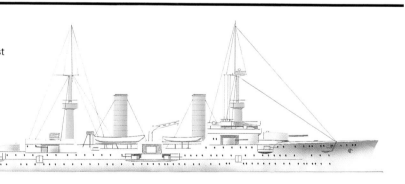

Furutaka

Type: Japanese cruiser
Displacement: 10,506 tonnes (10,341 tons)
Dimensions: 185.2m x 15.8m x 5.6m (607ft 6in x 51ft 9in x 18ft 3in)

Machinery: Four screws turbines
Main armament: Six 203mm (8in) guns
Launched: February 1925

The first large Japanese cruiser to be launched after the signing of the 1922 Washington Treaty that limited displacement to

10,160 tonnes (10,000 tons), *Furutaka* was hastily authorised to compensate for the cancellation of capital ships. As originally completed in 1926, her 203mm (8in) guns were in single turrets, but were later rearranged in three twins. *Furutaka* was sunk in October 1942.

Fusée

Type: French gunboat
Displacement: 1,062 tonnes (1,045 tons)
Dimensions: 50.3m x 9.9m x 3.1m (165ft x 32ft 6in x 10ft)
Machinery: Twin screw vertical compound engines
Top speed: 13 knots
Main armament: One 236mm (9in) gun
Armour: 254mm (10in) thick belt
Launched: May 1884

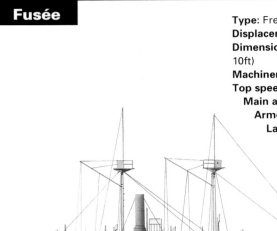

Fusée and her three sisters were designed as armoured gunboats, intended for overseas service or coastal defence. At the time of her completion in 1885, she represented France's policy of having a third line of coastal defence vessels, ready to fight enemy forces

even if the first two lines of defence had suffered losses. *Fusée*'s hull was turtle-backed with considerable tumble home, and in places her sides reached an angle of 45º from vertical. She had a shallow superstructure, at the front of which was mounted the 236mm (9in) main gun, protected by a 100mm (4in) curved armoured shield. Her hull was wood sheathed with copper, but was well-protected by a 254mm (10in) thick belt. This tapered into a sloping ram at the bow. She also had a thick armoured deck which sat on top of this belt. *Fusée*'s armour was made from steel, which was just coming into wider use at that time. Two of her sisters were less well protected, only having compound metal/wood armour. Her engines developed 1,500hp, and she could carry a maximum of 116 tonnes (114 tons) of coal in her bunkers.

Fuso

Type: Japanese battleship
Displacement: 3,777 tonnes (3,837 tons)
Dimensions: 67m x 14.6m x 5.6m (220ft x 48ft x 18ft 3in)
Machinery: Twin screw compound horizontal surface condensing engines
Top speed: 13 knots
Main armament: Four 236mm (9in) guns
Armour: 102-229mm (4-9in) thick

waterline belt with 203mm on the central battery
Launched: April 1877

In 1875, Japan ordered three armoured vessels. Two were armoured broadside cruisers; one was a powerful central battery ironclad named *Fuso*. All were designed by Sir Edward Reed, one of the world's leading naval architects. Rebuilt in 1894, *Fuso* emerged with eight 152mm guns and two military masts, and fought at the Battle of the Yalu. She was broken up in 1910.

Fuso

Type: Japanese battleship
Displacement: 36,474 tonnes (35,900 tons)
Dimensions: 205m x 28.7m x 8.6m (672ft 6in x 94ft x 28ft)
Machinery: Four screws, turbines
Top speed: 23 knots
Main

armament: Twelve 357mm (14in), sixteen 152mm (6in) guns
Armour: 102-306mm (4-12in) thick belt, 119-306mm (4.5-12in) on the turrets with 204mm (8in) barbettes
Launched: March 1914

With the laying down of this vessel in March 1912 in a home yard, Japan confirmed her position as a leading naval power in the Pacific. Up until then, all Japanese battleships had been built in British yards. Although *Fuso* and her sister *Yamarisho* were less heavily armoured than contemporary

US battleships, they carried a heavier armament and were 2 knots faster. As originally completed in 1915, *Fuso* had two funnels, with the first between the bridge and third turret. In an extensive refit in the 1930s, this was removed and replaced by a massive bridge structure. Underwater protection was greatly improved and new machinery fitted. Both ships were sunk by gunfire and torpedoes from US battleships in October 1944.

Fuso Maru

Type: Japanese liner
Displacement: 9,364 tonnes (9,216 tons)
Dimensions: 149.4m x 17.6m (480ft 3in x 57ft 9in)
Machinery: Twin screw triple expansion engines
Top speed: 17 knots
Launched: 1908

Fuso Maru started life as the Russian-American Line's *Russia*, completed in 1908, and was the first liner ordered by that company, which had previously used vessels purchased from other lines. Fitted out for the US immigration trade, by

1923 immigration restrictions into the USA made the *Russia*, now renamed *Latvia*, surplus to requirements, and she was sold to Osaka Shoshen Kaisha, who gave her a major refit. Renamed *Fuso Maru*, she then served in the China Sea trade for 14 years, filling a gap in the Japanese merchant marine until newer vessels entered service. She was removed from the effective list about 1939.

Futura

Type: Dutch bulk carrier
Displacement: 76,127 tonnes (74,928 tons)
Dimensions: 228.6m x 32.2m x 14.5m (750ft x 105ft 6in x 47ft 6in)

Machinery: Single screw diesel engine
Top speed: 14.8 knots
Launched: April 1992
Designed and built by Burmeister and Wain,

Futura is a development of the standard bulk cargo or oil carrier and is one of the first of a series to enter service that include improved safety standards, such as a double hull, gas ventilating of tanks and the ability to ventilate tanks selectively as needed via an extensive layout of ballast pipes. Pumping facilities within the double hull eliminate the need for separate spaces to house this equipment in the cargo-carrying area.

Fuyutsuki

Type: Japanese destroyer
Displacement: 3,759 tonnes (3,700 tons)

Dimensions: 134.2m x 11.6m x 4.2m (440ft 3in x 38ft 13ft 9in)
Machinery: Twin screw turbines

Top speed: 33 knots
Main armament: Eight 96mm (3.8in) guns, four 607mm (23.9in)

torpedo tubes in one quadruple mount
Launched: January 1944

Ordered in 1939 as part of a large class of ocean-going destroyers, originally planned as fast anti-aircraft escorts for working with the Japanese carrier task forces. However the design was modified to carry one quad torpedo tube.

Fylgia

Type: Swedish cruiser
Displacement: 4,810 tonnes (3,670 tons)
Dimensions: 115.1m x 14.8m x 6.3m (377ft 6in x 48ft 6in x 20ft 7in)
Machinery: Twin screw triple expansion engines
Top speed: 22.8 knots
Main armament: Eight 152mm (6in) guns
Launched: December 1905

At the time of *Fylgia*'s completion in 1906 she was the world's smallest armoured cruiser. The armoured waterline belt was concentrated amidships and ran from the fore to the aft turret, ending in a curved bulkhead that protected the vessel from end-on fire. The armoured deck was 51mm (2in) thick on the slopes and curved down at each end of the hull beyond the belt. Built by Finnbodia, she was the ideal fighting ship for Sweden's policy of neutrality, possessing good armament and protection.

G1

Type: British submarine
Displacement: 704 tonnes (693 tons) (surface), 850 tonnes (836 tons) (submerged)
Dimensions: 57m x 6.9m x 4.1m (187ft x 22ft x 13ft 6in)
Machinery: Twin screw diesel-electric motors
Top speed: 14.25

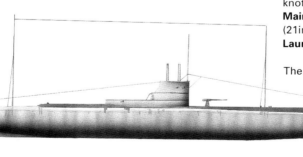

knots (surface), 9 knots (submerged).
Main armament: One 76mm (3in) gun, one 533mm (21in) and four 457mm (18in) torpedo tubes
Launched: August 1915

The G class of 15 boats, based on the E class design, were ordered in 1914 in response to the rumour that Germany was going to build a fleet of double-hulled, ocean-going submarines.

G5

Type: Russian torpedo gunboat
Displacement: 14 tonnes (13.7 tons)
Dimensions: 19.1m x 3.4m x 0.75m (62ft 6in x 11ft x 2ft 6in)
Machinery: Twin screw petrol engines
Top speed: 45 knots
Main armament: Two 12.7mm (.5in) guns, two 533mm (21in) torpedo tubes

One in a class of about 295 vessels, first conceived in the early 1930s. As the series progressed their displacement grew, ending up at 17 tonnes (16.7 tons). Some units achieved a claimed 60 knots. Many had Isotta Fraschini engines, which were very reliable, but those fitted with Russian-built versions had a poorer

record. Torpedoes were launched from the aft, and as they struck the water the vessel had to veer sideways out of their way.

G40

Type: German destroyer
Displacement: 1,068 tonnes
(1,051 tons)
Dimensions: 79.5m x 8.36m x 3.74m
(261ft x 27ft 6in x 12ft 1in)
Machinery: Twin screw turbines
Top speed: 34.5 knots
Main armament:
Three 85mm (3.3in)

guns, six 508mm (20in) torpedo tubes
Launched: February 1915

Although successful, boats such as *G40* and her three sisters were regarded as too big to act in

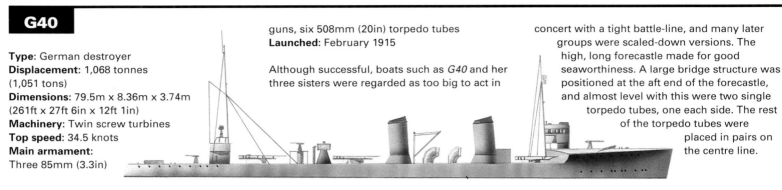

concert with a tight battle-line, and many later groups were scaled-down versions. The high, long forecastle made for good seaworthiness. A large bridge structure was positioned at the aft end of the forecastle, and almost level with this were two single torpedo tubes, one each side. The rest of the torpedo tubes were placed in pairs on the centre line.

G101

Type: German destroyer
Displacement: 1,873 tonnes
(1,843 tons)
Dimensions: 98m x 9.4m x 3.9m
(321ft 6in x 30ft 9in x 12ft 9in)
Machinery: Twin screw
turbines

Top speed: 36.5 knots
Main armament: Four
85mm (3.3in) guns, six
508mm (20in) torpedo
tubes
Launched: 1914

One of a quartet laid down for Argentina at the yard of Germaniawerft, Kiel, in 1914 and completed in 1915 but taken over for the German Navy. *G101*

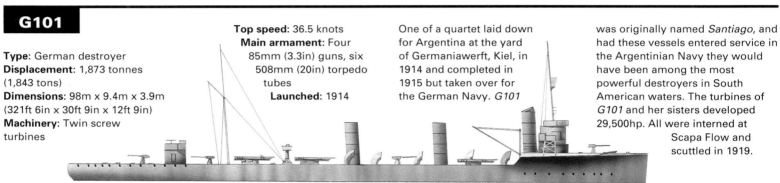

was originally named *Santiago*, and had these vessels entered service in the Argentinian Navy they would have been among the most powerful destroyers in South American waters. The turbines of *G101* and her sisters developed 29,500hp. All were interned at Scapa Flow and scuttled in 1919.

G132

Type: German destroyer
Displacement: 553 tonnes (544 tons)
Dimensions: 65.7m x 7m x 2.6m
(215ft 6in x 2ft x 8ft 6in)
Machinery: Twin screw triple
expansion engines

Top speed: 28 knots
Main armament: Four 51mm
(2in) guns, three 450mm
(17.7in) torpedo tubes
Launched: May 1906

An improved version of the basic German destroyer design, *G132* and her four sisters were built by Germaniawerft, Kiel, between 1905 and 1906. A follow-on boat, *G137*, had a greater displacement and was used in experiments with Parsons turbines, six being

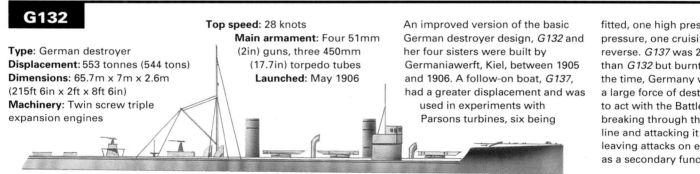

fitted, one high pressure, two low pressure, one cruising and two reverse. *G137* was 2 knots faster than *G132* but burnt more fuel. At the time, Germany was building up a large force of destroyers designed to act with the Battle Fleet by breaking through the enemy battle-line and attacking it with torpedoes, leaving attacks on enemy destroyers as a secondary function.

Gadfly

Type: British destroyer
Displacement: 406 tonnes
(400 tons)
Dimensions: 54.9m x 5.3m x 1.8m

(180ft x 17ft 4in x 5ft 11in)
Machinery: Triple screw turbines
Top speed: 26 knots
Main armament: Two 12 pounders,
three 457mm (18in) torpedo tubes

Launched: June 1906

Gadfly was one of a large class of 36 coastal defence destroyers, built as a cheap alternative to the

Tribal class destroyers, which were primarily intended for service with the fleet. The design followed that of the large first-class torpedo boats of the period, and was an economical way of creating a large fleet of destroyers for coastal defence and local roles. *Gadfly* was renumbered *TB6* soon after completion, and scrapped in 1920.

Galatea

Type: British cruiser
Displacement: 4,761 tonnes
(6,886 tons)
Dimensions: 85.3m x 15.2m x 6.5m
(279ft 9in x 49ft 9in x 21ft 3in)
Machinery: Single screw horizontal
trunk engine
Top speed: 11.8 knots
Main armament: Twenty-four

254mm (10in) guns
Launched: September 1859

One of a group of broadside wooden-hulled cruisers, built as an answer to a group of large and powerful US cruisers authorised in 1854. Completed in 1862, *Galatea* was one of the longest wooden-hulled vessels in the Navy. She was broken up in 1882.

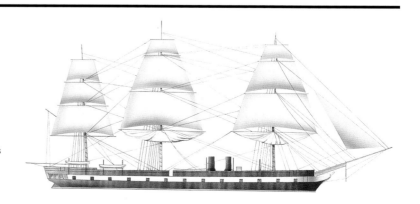

Galatea

Type: British cruiser
Displacement: 5,690 tonnes (5,600 tons)
Dimensions: 91.4m x 17.1m x 6.9m (300ft x 56ft x 22ft 6in)
Machinery: Twin screw triple expansion engines
Top speed: 18.5 knots
Main armament: Two 234mm (9.2in), ten 152mm (6in) guns
Launched: 1887

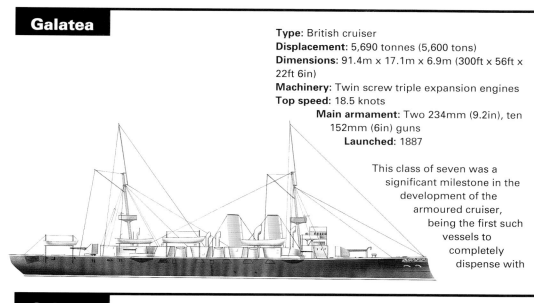

This class of seven was a significant milestone in the development of the armoured cruiser, being the first such vessels to completely dispense with sail power. Galatea had heavy armament for a ship of her size, with her 234mm (9.2in) guns mounted fore and aft and her 152mm (6in) weapons mounted on the beam. She had thick compound wood/metal armour in a 254mm (10in) belt which ran for two-thirds of her length, terminating in 405mm (16in) bulkheads at each end. She also had a 51mm (2in) thick armoured deck, which sloped down to meet the belt. Under this were 130 watertight compartments, and her coal bunkers were also sited to provide extra protection to the machinery spaces. During construction she gained a considerable amount of weight over her design figure, until her draught and performance were greatly affected. After Galatea and her sisters, no more armoured cruisers would be built until lighter and stronger steel armour became available.

Galatea

Type: British cruiser
Displacement: 4,470 tonnes (4,400 tons)
Dimensions: 132.9m x 11.9m x 4.1m (436ft x 39ft x 13ft 5in)
Machinery: Four screws, turbines
Main armament: Two 152mm (6in), six 102mm (4in) guns

With the increasing speeds being achieved by new destroyers prior to World War I, it was no longer possible for existing cruisers to act as effective flotilla leaders. The situation was made worse by the lack of adequate cruisers to work with the main Battle Fleet. So in 1911 the British Navy decided to produce a new class of light cruiser, and eight vessels were laid down from 1912-14. The armour was worked into the structure to form part of the hull strength, helping reduce weight and providing extra thickness amidships alongside the locker and machinery rooms. Early designs showed a vessel with ten 102mm (4in) or five 152mm (6in) guns, but in the event mixed armament was fitted. Four of the class were the first naval vessels to take aircraft to sea, launching them from a platform over the bows. Galatea was scrapped in 1921.

Galatea

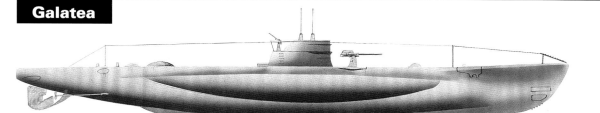

Type: Italian submarine
Displacement: 690 tonnes 679 tons) (surface), 775 tonnes (701 tons) (submerged)

Dimensions: 60.2m x 6.5m x 4.6m (197ft 5in x 21ft 2in x 15ft)
Machinery: Twin screw diesel/electric motors

Main armament: One 99mm (3.9in) gun, six 533mm (21in) torpedo tubes
Launched: October 1933

Galatea was an improved version of the basic '600' design with improved seakeeping qualities, higher speed and better handling when submerged. Many of the 12 in the class underwent modification during their careers and in the Spanish Civil War boats of this class carried out 18 extended patrols. From 1940-43 they saw service in the Mediterranean and all but Galatea were war losses. She was removed from the Navy list in 1948.

Galatea

Type: British frigate
Displacement: 2,906 tonnes (2,860 tons)
Dimensions: 113.4m x 12.5m x 4.5m (372ft x 41ft x 14ft 9in)
Machinery: Twin screws, turbines
Top speed: 28 knots
Main armament: One anti-submarine Ikara missile launcher
Launched: May 1963

One of a class designed in the late 1950s, planned as improved versions of the Type 12 Rothsay class, and intended to be built in five batches spread over ten years, Galatea was part of the first group of seven vessels. In all, 24 were to be constructed with the later ships increasing in size and carrying a greater amount of equipment, including Exocet and updated electronics. The hull has a long unbroken form, with a raised forecastle. Aft is situated the hangar for one or two ASW helicopters. The Ikara missile system in Galatea is housed forward on the extended superstructure in front of the bridge. This class was updated in groups during the 1970s and 1980s. Costs rose as each batch was completed, as more equipment of a greater sophistication was being carried.

Galathée

Type: French submarine
Displacement: 619 tonnes (609 tons) (surface), 769 tonnes (757 tons) (submerged)

Dimensions: 64m x 5.2m x 4.3m (210ft x 17ft x 14ft)
Machinery: Twin screw diesel/electric motors

Main armament: One 76mm (3in) gun, seven 551mm (21.7in) torpedo tubes
Launched: December 1925

On the outbreak of World War II, the group of medium-range submarines to which *Galathée* belonged was the largest class of such vessels in the French Navy, and they operated extensively until 1940. In spite of having a complex torpedo layout, *Galathée* and her consorts were successful ships. She was sunk in June 1944, while two others were captured by Italian forces.

Galena

Type: American ironclad
Displacement: 965 tonnes (950 tons)
Dimensions: 55.2m x 11.3m x 4m (181ft x 37ft x 13ft)
Machinery: Single screw, vibrating lever engines
Top speed: 8 knots
Main armament: Four 229mm (9in), two 200 pounder guns
Launched: February 1862

In 1863, *Galena*'s armour was removed as a result of experience on the James River when her interlocking armour was pierced on many occasions, forcing her out of action. The displacement fell to 738 and she was rerated as a gunboat. *Galena* served on the James

River when Union forces tried to reach the Confederate capital Richmond. Under the guise of repairs to *Galena* in 1862, funds were diverted to build a new sloop – also named *Galena*: the US Congress had refused to vote funds for new construction. The original *Galena* was broken up in 1871.

Galerna

Type: Spanish submarine
Displacement: 1473 tonnes (1,450 tons) (surface), 1753 tonnes (1,725 tons) (submerged)

Dimensions: 67.6m x 6.8m x 5.4m (221ft 9in x 22ft 4in x 17ft 9in)
Machinery: Single screw diesel/electric motors

Main armament: Four 551mm (21.7in) torpedo tubes
Launched: December 1981

Galerna was a medium-range submarine built to the design of the French Agosta class. She marked a major step forward in Spanish submarine technology. This submarine and her three sisters can carry 16 reload torpedoes or nine torpedoes and 19 mines. A full sonar kit is carried of one active and one passive set.

Galician

Type: British liner
Displacement: 13,716 tonnes (13,500 tons)
Dimensions: 134.2m x 16.2m x 8m (440ft 4in x 53ft 1in x 26ft 4in)
Machinery: Twin screw triple expansion engines
Launched: 1901

Galician was the tenth 'G' class liner ordered by the Union Company, which traded with South Africa, and the only one not to appear in Union Line colours, as that company merged with the Castle Line before *Galician* was completed. Accommodation was provided for 90 first-class and 120 second-class passengers. Renamed *Glenart Castle*, she served as a hospital ship in World War I and was sunk by a German submarine in February 1918.

Galilei

Type: Italian submarine
Displacement: 1,001 tonnes (985 tons) (surface), 1,279 tonnes (1,259 tons) (submerged)
Dimensions: 70.5m x 6.8m x 4.1m (231ft 4in x 22ft 4in x 13ft 5in)
Machinery: Twin screw diesel/electric motors
Main armament: Two 99mm (3.9in) guns, eight 533mm (21in) torpedo tubes

Launched: March 1934

Galilei and her sister, *Ferraris*, both served in the Spanish Civil War.

By June 1940 they were stationed in the Red Sea, where *Galilei* was captured in June 1940 by the armed trawler *Moonstone*. She became *X2* in the British Navy and was scrapped in 1946.

Galileo Galilei

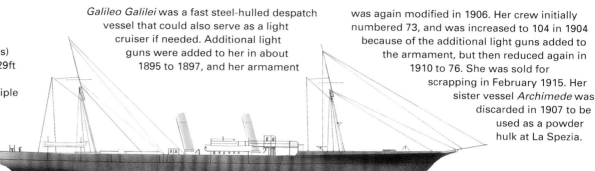

Type: Italian despatch boat
Displacement: 900 tonnes (886 tons)
Dimensions: 70m x 8m x 3.75m (229ft 8in x 26ft 4in x 12ft 4in)
Machinery: Single screw vertical triple expansion engine
Main armament: Four 119mm (4.7in) guns
Launched: May 1887

Galileo Galilei was a fast steel-hulled despatch vessel that could also serve as a light cruiser if needed. Additional light guns were added to her in about 1895 to 1897, and her armament was again modified in 1906. Her crew initially numbered 73, and was increased to 104 in 1904 because of the additional light guns added to the armament, but then reduced again in 1910 to 76. She was sold for scrapping in February 1915. Her sister vessel *Archimede* was discarded in 1907 to be used as a powder hulk at La Spezia.

Gallia

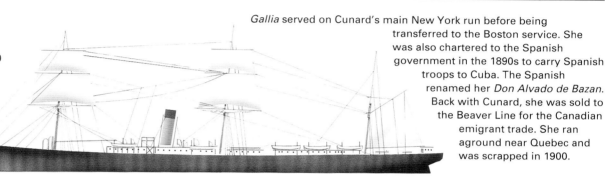

Type: British liner
Displacement: 9,144 tonnes (9,000 tons)
Dimensions: 136m x 45m x 24.3m (445ft x 44ft x 24ft)
Machinery: Single screw, compound engines
Top speed: 16 knots
Launched: 1879

Gallia served on Cunard's main New York run before being transferred to the Boston service. She was also chartered to the Spanish government in the 1890s to carry Spanish troops to Cuba. The Spanish renamed her *Don Alvado de Bazan*. Back with Cunard, she was sold to the Beaver Line for the Canadian emigrant trade. She ran aground near Quebec and was scrapped in 1900.

Gallia

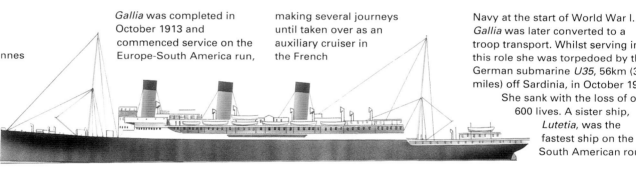

Type: French liner
Displacement: 15,236 tonnes (14,996 tons)
Dimensions: 183m x 20.1m (600ft x 67ft 7in)
Machinery: Triple screw, turbines
Top speed: 20 knots
Launched: 1913

Gallia was completed in October 1913 and commenced service on the Europe-South America run, making several journeys until taken over as an auxiliary cruiser in the French Navy at the start of World War I. *Gallia* was later converted to a troop transport. Whilst serving in this role she was torpedoed by the German submarine *U35*, 56km (35 miles) off Sardinia, in October 1916. She sank with the loss of over 600 lives. A sister ship, *Lutetia*, was the fastest ship on the South American route.

Galvani

Type: Italian submarine
Displacement: 1,032 tonnes (1,016 tons) (surface), 1,286 tonnes ((1,266 tons) submerged)
Dimensions: 72.4m x 6.9m x 4.5m (237ft 6in x 22ft x 14ft 11in)
Machinery: Twin screw diesel/electric motors
Main armament: One 99mm (3.9in) gun, eight 533mm (21in) torpedo tubes
Launched: May 1938

Galvani was one of a successful class of four long-range submarines, developed from the Archimede class. She was sunk in the Persian Gulf by HMS *Falmouth* in 1940.

Galveston

Type: American cruiser
Displacement: 14,357 tonnes (14,131 tons)
Dimensions: 186m x 20.2m x 7.5m (610ft x 66ft 4in x 24ft 6in)
Machinery: Four screw turbines
Top speed: 32.5 knots
Main armament: Twelve 152mm (6in), twelve 127mm (5in) guns
Launched: April 1945

Early designs of *Galveston* were for an anti-aircraft cruiser. She was to be armed with a new 137mm (5.4in) gun, but a mixed armament was accepted in order to get the building programme under way. *Galveston* was laid down in February 1944, and completed in May 1946. Nine earlier members of the class were converted to light fleet carriers in 1942. *Galveston* was stricken in 1973.

Galway Castle

Type: British liner
Displacement: 8,116 tonnes (7,988 tons)
Dimensions: 143.3m x 17.1m x 8.2m (470ft x 56ft 3in x 27ft)
Machinery: Twin screw quadruple expansion engines
Top speed: 13.5 knots
Launched: 1911

Galway Castle was one of a group of intermediate passenger liners known as the 'G castles' that served

the Union-Castle Line on their route to South Africa. Although they were slightly smaller than the preceding 'D-Castles' they were very popular vessels, providing pleasant accommodation for 87 first-class, 130 second-class and 195 third-class passengers. Five holds provided

enough storage space for more than 7,112 tonnes (7,000 tons) of cargo, and the ships displaced more than 15,240 tonnes (15,100 tons) when fully loaded. They may not have been able to match the speed and luxury of the fast mail boats, but they all earned good dividends for

their owners. *Galway Castle* operated on the west coast route to South Africa, and plans were being made to use her on the Mauritius route, when World War I broke out. Painted grey, she then served as a fast troopship. Having survived nearly all of the war, she was torpedoed on 12 September 1918 near the British Isles. By superb seamanship, she was kept afloat in appalling weather long enough for her boats to be launched, even though her back had been broken by the explosion.

Gambia

Type: British cruiser
Displacement: 11,267 tonnes (11,090 tons)
Dimensions: 169.3m x 18.9m x 6.4m (555ft 6in x 62ft x 21ft)
Machinery: Four screws, turbines
Main armament:

Twelve 152mm (6in) guns
Launched: November 1940

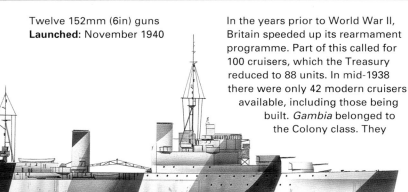

In the years prior to World War II, Britain speeded up its rearmament programme. Part of this called for 100 cruisers, which the Treasury reduced to 88 units. In mid-1938 there were only 42 modern cruisers available, including those being built. *Gambia* belonged to the Colony class. They

were more compact than earlier British cruisers of the same type and formed the basis for subsequent Royal Navy cruisers. An 89mm (3.5in) thick midships belt protected the magazines, with a 51mm (2in) thick deck over the belt, with 38mm (1.5in) over the steering gear. Two of the 11-strong class were sunk in action in World War II, two were sold to Peru in 1959 and one was sold to India in 1957. *Gambia* was broken up in 1968.

Gambier Bay

Type: US aircraft carrier
Displacement: 11,074 tonnes (10,900 ton)
Dimensions: 156.1m x 32.9m x 6.3m (512ft 3in x 108ft x 20ft 9in)
Machinery: Twin screw reciprocating engines
Top speed: 19 knots

Main armament: One 127mm (5in), sixteen 40mm (1.6in) guns
Aircraft: 28
Launched: November 1943

Gambier Bay was one of a 50-strong group of light escort carriers completed from the unfinished hulls of a standard type of

merchant ship. All 50 vessels were completed in under one year. The first mission for the *Gambier Bay* was in early 1944, when she ferried aircraft to USS *Enterprise* and then supported US forces off Saipan, in the Marianas and at Leyte. She was sunk by gunfire during action off Samar in October 1944.

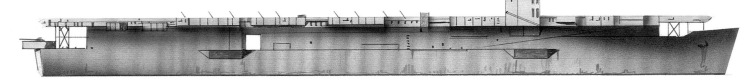

Gangut

Type: Russian battleship
Displacement: 6,697 tonnes (6,592 tons)
Dimensions: 88.3m x 18.9m x 6.4m (289ft 8in x 62ft x 21ft)
Machinery: Twin screw vertical compound engines
Top speed: 14.7 knots
Main armament: One 305mm (12in), four 229mm (9in) and four 152mm (6in) guns

Launched: 1893

Designed at a time when the battle line was likely to be in line abreast, instead of a line ahead, *Gangut* had her single 305mm (12in) gun mounted forward in a centreline turret on the foredeck. The four 229mm (9in)

guns were concentrated in a battery amidships, protected by 127mm (5in) armour. Two 152mm (6in) guns were placed forward on the same level alongside the turret, but

these could only fire straight ahead. Two more 152mm (6in) guns were positioned right aft and these also lacked broadside fire. Laid down in 1889 *Gangut* was completed in 1894. Whilst returning from gunnery practice in 1897 she struck an uncharted rock off Transund harbour and sank.

Gangut

Type: Russian battleship
Displacement: 26,264 tonnes
(25,850 tons)
Dimensions: 182.9m x
26.9m x 8.3m (600ft x 88ft
3in x 27ft 3in)

Machinery: Four screws, turbines
Main armament: Twelve 305mm
(12in), sixteen 119mm (4.7in) guns
Armour: 102-226mm belt (4-8.9in),
127-203mm (5-8in) on turrets and
203mm (8in) on barbettes

Launched: October 1911

Gangut and her three sisters
were Russia's first
dreadnoughts. The contract
was won by Blohm and Voss,
Hamburg, but the Russian
government refused funds

unless they were built in Russia. As
Russian industry could not produce
enough high tensile steel, an
ingenious construction method was
used, based upon the Italian *Dante
Aligheri*. Building time was lengthy,
and *Gangut* was not ready until
1914. Her main guns were the
largest then at sea. She was
renamed *Oktyabrskaya Revolutsia* in
1919 and scrapped in 1956-59.

Garibaldi

Type: Italian cruiser
Displacement: 4,044 tonnes (3,980 tons)
Dimensions: 68.2m x 15.2m x 7.1m (223ft 9in x
50ft x 23ft 4in)
Machinery: Single screw direct acting engines
Top speed: 9 knots
Main armament: Sixteen 200 pounder, sixteen
160 pounder, six 80 pounder guns
Launched: January 1860

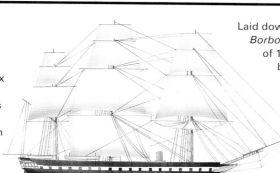

Laid down in August 1857 for the Neapolitan Navy as the
Borbone, and completed in March 1861, *Garibaldi* was one
of 14 large, wooden-hulled frigates that entered service
between 1860 and 1865. These ships formed the
main force of the newly formed Italian Navy
which came into being in 1861, with the far-
sighted Cavour at its head. The main battery
deck housed the heavy weapons with the 80
pounders on the upper deck. *Garibaldi* was
reclassified as a corvette in 1878 and
removed from the effective list in 1894.

Garibaldino

Type: Italian destroyer
Displacement: 419 tonnes (412
tons)
Dimensions: 65m x 6.1m x 2.1m
(213ft 3in x 20ft x 7ft)
Machinery: Twin screw triple
expansion

engines
Top speed: 28 knots
Main armament: Three
76mm (3in) guns, three
450mm (17.7in) torpedo
tubes
Launched: 1910

Originally intended as a follow-up
group to the *Nembo*, launched in
1901, *Garibaldino* incorporated
improvements gained through
operational experience. This class of
six vessels were all laid down in
1905 and completed between 1907
and 1910. *Garibaldino* was

one of the group laid down in 1905.
All were coal burners, but a second
group, known as the Soldato or
Alpino class, were oil burners.
Garibaldino's engines developed
6,000 hp, with a range of 2,850km
(1,500 miles) at 12 knots or 760km
(400 miles) at 23.5 knots. She was
sunk on 16 July 1918, after colliding
with the British destroyer *Cygnet* off
Villefranche in southern France.

Garland

Type: British destroyer
Displacement: 1,005 tonnes (989 tons)
Dimensions: 81.5m x 8.2m x 2.8m (267ft 6in x
27ft x 9ft 3in)
Machinery: Twin screw semi-geared
turbines
Main armament: Three 102mm
(4in) guns, two
533mm (21in)

torpedo tubes
Launched: April 1913

Part of the 1911-12
British

naval programme was a class of 20
destroyers designed to counter the threat of
German destroyers. They were to be
armed with two 102mm (4in) guns plus
four 12 pounders, but three 102mm (4in)
guns were chosen, making them amongst
the most powerful destroyers of
the period. *Garland*
was
broken up
in 1921.

Garnet

Type: British cruiser
Displacement: 2,154 tonnes (2,120 tons)
Dimensions: 67m x 12.2m x 5.5m (219ft 10in
x 40ft x 18ft)
Machinery: Single screw horizontal
compound engines
Top speed: 13.2 knots
Main armament: Twelve 64
pounder guns
Launched: June 1877

Garnet and her five sisters were constructed with
iron framework and wooden hulls. Their
designer, in a bid to improve speed, gave them a
short, full midship section with fine lines at each
end of the hull. Unfortunately this adversely
affected the cruisers' performance when under
sail, as the vessels pitched heavily when driven
hard. All the guns were muzzle loaders and slide
mounted, with five located on each broadside
and two in the bows. *Garnet* was sold in 1904.

Gascon

Type: British liner
Displacement: 12,844 tonnes (12,642 tons)
Dimensions: 135.6m x 15.9m x 7.9m (445ft x 52ft 2in x 26ft)
Machinery: Twin screw triple expansion engines
Top speed: 12 knots
Launched: August 1896

Gascon was the first vessel of the final group of three intermediate liners built for the Union Line for their lucrative South African route. She had

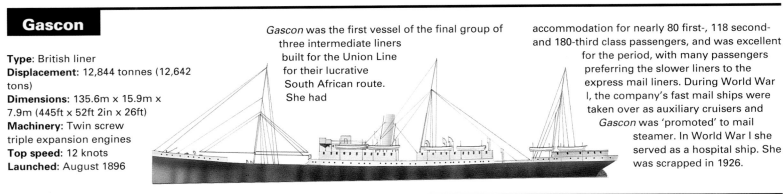

accommodation for nearly 80 first-, 118 second- and 180-third class passengers, and was excellent for the period, with many passengers preferring the slower liners to the express mail liners. During World War I, the company's fast mail ships were taken over as auxiliary cruisers and *Gascon* was 'promoted' to mail steamer. In World War I she served as a hospital ship. She was scrapped in 1926.

Gatling

Type: American destroyer
Displacement: 2,971 tonnes (2,924 tons)
Dimensions: 114.7m x 12m x 4.2m (376ft 5in x 39ft 4in x 13ft 9in)
Machinery: Twin screw

turbines
Main armament: Five 127mm (5in) guns
Launched: June 1943

Gatling was one of the largest classes of destroyers built for the US Navy. By now the London Treaty of 1930 could be ignored and displacement increased by about 1,016 tonnes (1,000 tons), with an armament of 127mm (5in) guns. She was stricken from the Navy list in 1974.

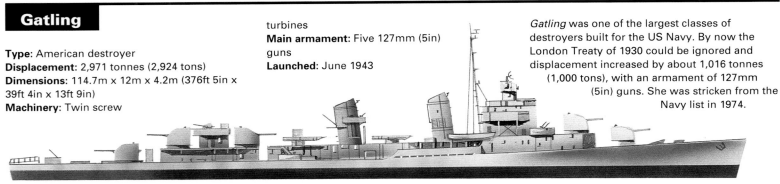

Gefion

Type: German cruiser
Displacement: 4,275 tonnes (4,208 tons)
Dimensions: 110.4m x 13.2m x 6.5m (362ft 2in x 43ft 4in x 21ft 3in)
Machinery: Twin screw triple expansion engines
Top speed: 20.5 knots

Main armament: Ten 104mm (4.1in) guns
Launched: May 1893

Gefion was a distinct change from existing German cruiser design of

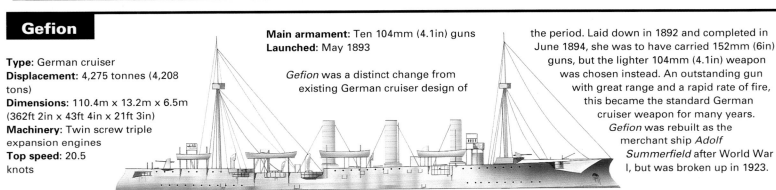

the period. Laid down in 1892 and completed in June 1894, she was to have carried 152mm (6in) guns, but the lighter 104mm (4.1in) weapon was chosen instead. An outstanding gun with great range and a rapid rate of fire, this became the standard German cruiser weapon for many years. *Gefion* was rebuilt as the merchant ship *Adolf Summerfield* after World War I, but was broken up in 1923.

Geiser

Type: Danish cruiser
Displacement: 1,311 tonnes (1,290 tons)
Dimensions: 78.5m x 8.4m x 4m (257ft 6in x 27ft 6in x 13ft)
Machinery: Twin screw vertical triple expansion engines
Main armament: Two 119mm (4.7in) guns

Launched: 1892

After the war with Prussia in 1864, Denmark built up her navy. *Geiser* was amongst the few cruisers acquired. She was the first major warship, apart from torpedo boats, to be fitted with the new Thornycroft watertube boilers, which gave greater efficiency and better performance.

Gelderland

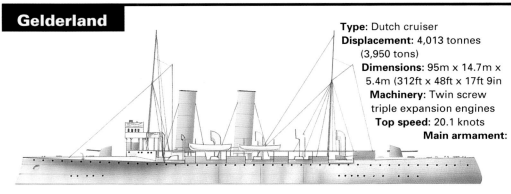

Type: Dutch cruiser
Displacement: 4,013 tonnes (3,950 tons)
Dimensions: 95m x 14.7m x 5.4m (312ft x 48ft x 17ft 9in)
Machinery: Twin screw triple expansion engines
Top speed: 20.1 knots
Main armament:

Two 152mm (6in), six 119mm (4.7in) guns
Launched: 1898

Gelderland served from 1920 as a gunnery training ship, but on the fall of Holland in World War II she was captured by German forces and converted into a flak ship. Renamed *Niobe*, she was fitted with eight 104mm (4.1in) guns plus 20 smaller ones. She was bombed and torpedoed by Russian aircraft, in July 1944, sustaining severe damage and losing 60 of her 300 crew.

Gemlik

Type: Turkish frigate
Displacement: 2,743 tonnes (2,700 tons)
Dimensions: 109.9m x 11m x 5.1m (360ft 7in x 36ft x 16ft 9in)
Machinery: Twin screw gas turbines/diesel engines
Top speed: 28 knots
Main armament: Two 100mm (3.9in) guns, four 533mm (21in) torpedo tubes
Launched: March 1959

Gemlik started life as the *Emden*, a Koln-class

frigate in West German service. She and her sisters were among the first modern warships to be built for the Federal German Navy after World War II. She was laid down in 1958 and completed in October 1961. She has a compact design, and is equipped with a wide range of anti-submarine weapons, sophisticated sensors and electronic counter measures. Her main surface weapons are two 100mm (3.9in)

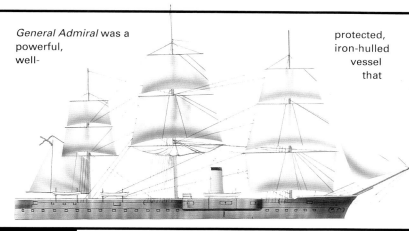

Creusot-Loire dual purpose guns mounted fore and aft in single turrets. They can fire 13.5kg (30lb) shells up to 15km (9 miles) distant, at a maximum rate of 60-80 shells per minute. She has four launch tubes used for anti-submarine acoustic homing torpedoes, supplemented by two four-barrelled anti-submarine mortars. She is also capable of carrying up to 80 anti-ship and anti-submarine mines. Her

main machinery is a combined gas turbine diesel system. For high speed combat operations she has two Brown Boveri gas turbines which develop up to 24,000hp with a range of 1,739km (915 miles) at full speed of 28 knots. She also has four diesels for long-range cruising. These give her a range of 5,662km (2,980 miles) at a maximum speed of 18 knots. In September 1983, *Emden* was transferred to the Turkish Navy, who renamed her *Gemlik*. Another Koln-class vessel was transferred from Germany to Turkey in the same year, and she was renamed *Gelibolu*.

Gemma

Type: Italian submarine
Displacement: 711 tonnes (700 tons) (surface), 843 tonnes (830 tons) (submerged)
Dimensions: 60.2m x 6.5m x 4.6m (197ft 5in x 21ft 2in x 15ft)
Machinery: Twin screw diesel engins (surface), electric motors (submerged)
Top speed: 14 knots

(surface), 7.5 knots (submerged)
Main armament: One 99mm (3.9in) gun, six 533mm (21in) torpedo tubes
Launched: May 1936

Laid down in September 1935 and completed in July 1936, *Gemma* was one of a class of ten short-range boats derived from the Sirena series that had been completed in 1933-34, but

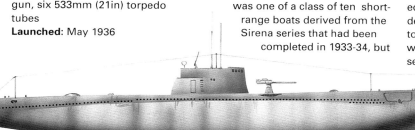

with a slight increase in displacement and more modern equipment. Their maximum diving depth was 70-80m (230-260ft). They took part in the Spanish Civil War with two were ceded to Spain for several months. Five were sunk in World War II, including *Gemma*, accidentally sunk by an Italian submarine.

General Admiral

Type: Russian cruiser
Displacement: 5,112 tonnes (5,031 tons)
Dimensions: 87.1m x 14.6m x 7.3m (285ft 10in x 48ft x 24ft)
Machinery: Single screw vertical compound engines
Top speed: 12.3 knots
Main armament: Six 203mm(8in), two 152mm (6in) guns
Launched: 1873

General Admiral was a powerful, well-

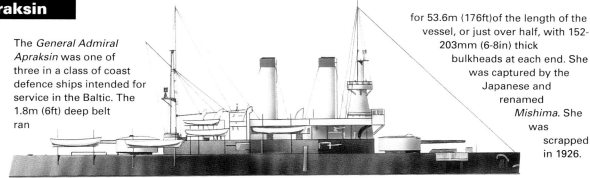

protected, iron-hulled vessel that

was the world's first armoured cruiser and a milestone in naval development. *General Admiral* and her near sister *Gerzog Edinburgski* were provided with a continuous iron belt along the waterline plus a strake of armour over the battery.

General Admiral became a training ship and was then converted to a minelayer, with 600 mines, in 1909. She was removed form the effective list in 1938.

General Admiral Apraksin

Type: Russian battleship
Displacement: 4,192 tonnes (4,126 tons)
Dimensions: 84.6m x 15.8m x 5.2m (277ft 6in x 51ft 10in x 17ft)
Machinery: Twin screw triple expansion engines
Top speed: 16.2 knots
Main armament: Three 254mm (10in), four 119mm (4.7in) guns
Launched: May 1896

The *General Admiral Apraksin* was one of three in a class of coast defence ships intended for service in the Baltic. The 1.8m (6ft) deep belt ran

for 53.6m (176ft)of the length of the vessel, or just over half, with 152-203mm (6-8in) thick bulkheads at each end. She was captured by the Japanese and renamed *Mishima*. She was scrapped in 1926.

General Bragg

Type: Confederate gunboat
Displacement: 853 tonnes (840 tons)
Dimensions: 63.4m x 10m x 3.7m (208ft x 32ft 8in x 12ft)
Machinery: Side wheel paddles, oscillating engine
Top speed: 10 knots
Main armament: One 30 pounder

Parrott rifle, one 32 pounder 42cwt gun and one 12 pounder rifle
Launched: 1851

General Bragg, formerly the *Mexico*, was taken over by the Confederate War Department at New Orleans in 1862 and converted into a gunboat with 102mm (4in) of oak added to the bows and a covering of 25mm (1in) iron. Extra bulkheads were added and the spaces between filled with compressed cotton, making her a formidable ram. She was captured by Union forces in 1862.

General Concha

Type: Spanish gunboat
Displacement: 532 tonnes (524 tons)
Dimensions: 48m x 7.8m x 2.6m (157ft 5in x 25ft 7in x 8ft 7in)
Machinery: Twin screw compound reciprocating engines
Main armament: Three 117mm (4.7in) guns

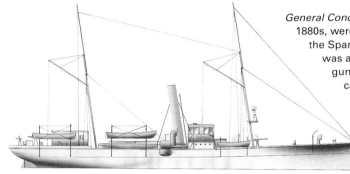

General Concha and her three sisters, built during the 1880s, were among the largest of over 30 gunboats in the Spanish Navy during the late 19th century. She was armed with the newly introduced Hontoria guns. Two of the 117mm (4.7in) weapons were carried one on each broadside, in sponsons. The third was on the foredeck. There were also two smaller guns and a machine gun. Her engines developed 600hp, the coal supply was 81 tonnes (80 tons), and her crew numbered 80.

General Diaz

Type: Italian liner
Displacement: 12,768 tonnes (12,567 tons)
Dimensions: 152.4m x 18.9m (500ft x 62ft)
Machinery: Twin screw quadruple expansion engines
Launched: 1911

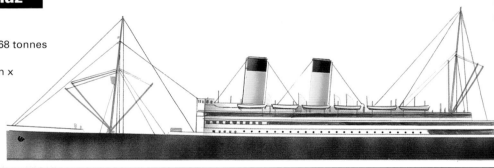

Originally *Kaiser Franz Josef I*, this ship was renamed *General Diaz* in 1919. In 1926, she was converted to oil-firing and in 1929 was renamed *Ganges*. She was refitted in 1936 and renamed *Marco Polo*. In 1943 the Germans took her for use as a transport but she was sunk by them in 1944 as a blockship in La Spezia harbour.

General Garibaldi

Type: Argentinian cruiser
Displacement: 6,949 tonnes (6,840 tons)
Dimensions: 100m x 18.1m x 7.6m (328ft x 59ft 6in x 25ft)
Machinery: Twin screw triple expansion engines
Top speed: 19.9 knots
Main armament: Two 254mm

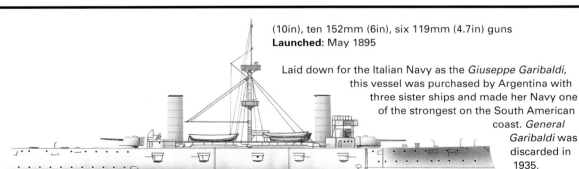

(10in), ten 152mm (6in), six 119mm (4.7in) guns
Launched: May 1895

Laid down for the Italian Navy as the *Giuseppe Garibaldi*, this vessel was purchased by Argentina with three sister ships and made her Navy one of the strongest on the South American coast. *General Garibaldi* was discarded in 1935.

General John Pope

Type: US troop transport
Displacement: 20,498 tonnes (20,175 tons)
Dimensions: 189.9m x 23m x 7.8m (623ft x 75ft x 25ft 7in)
Machinery: Twin turbines

General John Pope was armed with four 127mm (5in) guns plus eight 40mm (1.6in) anti-aircraft guns. She was laid up in 1970.

General Mola

Type: Spanish submarine
Displacement: 986 tonnes (970 tons) (surface), 1,259 tonnes (1,239 tons) (submerged)
Dimensions:
70.5m x
6.9m x 4.1m
(231ft x 22ft
6in x 13ft 6in)

Machinery: Twin screw diesel engines (surface), electric motors (submerged)

Main armament: One 76mm (3in) gun, eight 533mm (21in) torpedo tubes

Formerly the Italian *Evangelista Torricelli*, this submarine was transferred to Spain in 1937.

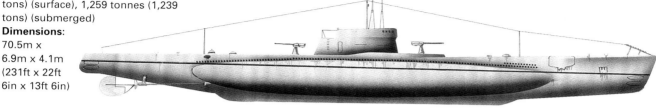

General Pike

Type: American sailing frigate
Displacement: 889 tonnes (875 tons)
Dimensions: 44.2m x 11.3m (145ft x 37ft)
Main armament: Twenty six 24 pounder guns
Launched: June 1813

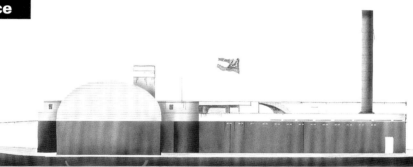

Although the American Navy was not large during the war of 1812, its warships were among the best in the world and *General Pike* is a good example of them. She was a flush-decked frigate with all her guns carried on one deck and she was larger than contemporary British frigates that carried the same armament. She was built by Henry Eckford, a New York shipbuilder, and was laid down in April 1813, but was set on fire by British forces. The unfinished ship was saved and she was soon in action against British forces. She escorted troop transports and was part of the blockading squadron off the British port of Kingston, Ontario. After the war, she was laid up and she was sold in 1825.

General Stirling Price

Type: Confederate gunboat
Displacement: 643 tonnes (633 tons)
Dimensions: 55.5m x 9.1m x 2.8m (182ft x 30ft x 9ft 3in)
Machinery: Side wheel paddles
Top speed: 12 knots
Main armament: One 32 pounder rifle

Launched: 1856

The steamboat *Laurent Millaudon* was taken over by Confederate forces in 1862 and renamed *General Stirling Price*. She was captured by Union forces in the same year and was used in numerous attacks. She was sold in 1865.

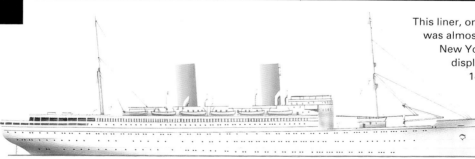

General Von Steuben

Type: German liner
Displacement: 13,538 tonnes (13,325 tons)
Dimensions: 167.8m x 19.8m (550ft 6in x 65ft)
Machinery: Twin screw triple expansion engines
Launched: November 1922

This liner, originally *München*, was almost burnt out in 1930 in New York. Refitted, her displacement rose to 14,925 tonnes (14,690 tons), her top speed to 16.3 knots. She was sunk by a Russian submarine 1945.

George Washington

Type: German liner
Displacement: 25,979 tonnes (25,570 tons)
Dimensions:
220.2m x 23.8m
(722ft 5in x 78ft)
Machinery: Twin screw quadruple expansion

engines
Launched: November 1908

The largest German-built steamer of her time, *George Washington* was taken over by the USA in 1917. In 1951 she was destroyed by fire.

George Washington

Type: US ballistic missile submarine
Displacement: 6,115 tonnes (6,019 tons) (surface), 6,998 tonnes (6,888 tons) (submerged)
Dimensions: 116.3m x 10m x 8.8m (381ft 7in x 33ft x 28ft10in)
Machinery: Single screw, one pressurised water-cooled reactor, turbines
Top speed: 20 knots (surface), 30.5 knots (submerged)
Main armament: Sixteen Polaris missiles, six 533mm (21in) torpedo tubes
Launched: June 1959

In 1955, the Soviet Union began modifying six existing diesel submarines to carry nuclear-tipped ballistic missiles. America was simultaneously developing the Jupiter missile, which was to equip a projected 10,160 tonne (10,000 ton) nuclear-powered submarine. Jupiter used a mix of highly volatile liquids for its propellant, and was posing immense problems of safety and operation. At that time the Polaris A1 missile emerged as an alternative. It was smaller and lighter, and used a much more stable solid propellant. The nuclear submarine *Scorpion*, then building, was chosen as the delivery platform for this new weapon. Her hull was cut in half, and a new 40m (131ft) section added, just aft of her conning tower. Sixteen missiles were carried in the vertical launch tubes, while the submarine retained her normal torpedo tubes for self defence. She could launch her missiles while remaining submerged, and was capable of striking Soviet bases and cities from far out to sea. Renamed *George Washington*, she was the first of a new type of weapons system, and put the USA far ahead in the nuclear arms race.

George Washington

Type: US aircraft carrier
Displacement: 92,950 tonnes (91,487 tons)
Dimensions: 332.9m x 40.8m x 11.3m (1,092ft 2in x 133ft 10in x 37ft)
Machinery: Quadruple screw, two water-cooled nuclear reactors, turbines
Top speed: 30 knots+

Main armament: Four Vulcan 20mm guns plus missiles
Aircraft: 70+
Launched: September 1989
Date of profile: 1993

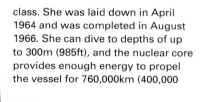

George Washington is one of six Nimitz-class supercarriers that have been built to date. She was laid down in August 1986, some 17 years after *Nimitz*, the first of the class. *George*

Washington carries extensive damage-control systems, including 63mm- (2.5in-) thick armour over parts of the hull, plus box protection over the magazines and machinery spaces. Aviation equipment includes four lifts and four steam catapults. The life of the nuclear reactors is 15 years.

George Washington Carver

Type: US submarine
Displacement: 7,366 tonnes (7,250 tons) (surface), 8,382 tonnes (8,250 tons) (submerged)
Dimensions: 129.5m x 10m x 9.6m (424ft 10in x 33ft 2in x 31ft 6in)
Machinery: Single screw, one pressurised water-cooled nuclear reactor
Main armament: Sixteen Trident C4 missiles, four 533mm (21in)

torpedo tubes
Launched: August 1965

George Washington Carver is one of 29 vessels in the Lafayette class. She was laid down in April 1964 and was completed in August 1966. She can dive to depths of up to 300m (985ft), and the nuclear core provides enough energy to propel the vessel for 760,000km (400,000 miles). *George Washington Carver* has two crews which carry out alternate 70-day patrols. Every six years the vessel undergoes an extensive refit which takes nearly two years to complete.

George Washington Parke Custis

Type: US balloon ship
Displacement: 122 tonnes (120 tons)
Dimensions: 24.3m x 4.4m x 1.7m (80ft x 14ft 6in x 5ft 6in)
Launched: 1855

In 1861 a coal barge was purchased by the US Navy for conversion into a balloon ship, the first in the USA. *George Washington Parke Custis*

was fitted out at the Washington Navy Yard, and carried a gas-generating plant developed by Thaddeus Lowe and modified by John Dahlgren. The gas was produced by mixing iron filings and sulphuric acid,

and this was then pumped into the balloon via a pressure regulator. The newly fitted-out vessel was towed to the Mattawomen Creek (off the Potomac River) in November 1861, where Lowe made a series

of successful ascents, during which he spotted Confederate forces working some 4.8km (3 miles) away. An operational height of 304m (1,000ft) above ground level kept the balloon well out of the range of enemy fire, but it became a sitting target at anything below 90m (300ft). *George Washington Parke Custis* was returned to service as a coal barge in 1865.

Georges Leygues

Type: French destroyer
Displacement: 4,236 tonnes (4,170 tons)
Dimensions: 139m x 14m x 5.7m (456ft x 46ft x 18ft 8in)
Machinery: Twin screw, gas turbines and diesel engines

Main armament: One 100mm gun, Exocet missiles
Launched: December 1976
Date of profile: 1982

Georges Leygues and her seven sisters provide France with a strong anti-submarine force that will serve her well into the next century. Gas turbines develop 52,000hp, diesel engines develop 10,400hp, and range at 18 knots on diesels is 18,050km (9,500 miles). Two Lynx helicopters are carried on board *Georges Leygues*, and she has full hangar facilities in the aft structure.

Georges Philippar

Type: French liner
Displacement: 17,819 tonnes (17,539 tons)
Dimensions: 172.7m x 20.8m (19ft10in x 68ft 3in)
Machinery: Twin screw, diesel engines
Top speed: 17 knots
Launched: November 1930

Georges Philippar was built for the Messageries Maritime Service of Marseille and set out on her maiden voyage to the Far East in February 1932. During the return trip an electrical fire broke out, and *Georges Philippar* sank 233km (145 miles) north east of Cape Guardafui. Fifty-four passengers died in the fire.

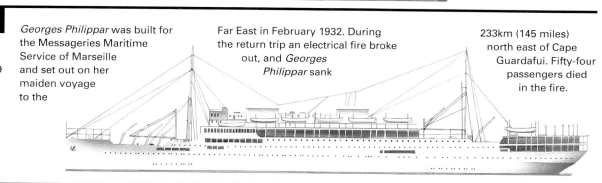

Georgia

Type: Confederate cruiser
Displacement: 711 tonnes (700 tons)
Dimensions: 64.6m x 8.2m x 4.2m (212ft x 27ft x 13ft 9in)
Machinery: Single screw, steeple-geared engine
Main armament: Two 100-pounder guns

Launched: 1863

Built in Scotland, *Georgia* was a fast, iron-hulled, brig-rigged steamer. In 1863 she was bought by Commander Maury for service as an armed raider in the Confederate Navy. After taking on guns and supplies at Ushant, *Georgia* was successful in action against Union ships off the Cape of Good Hope, capturing nine vessels and burning five of them. She was later seized as a prize by the Union cruiser *Niagara*.

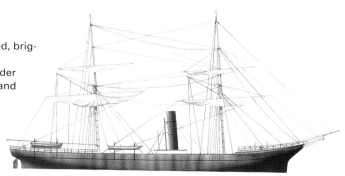

Georgia

Type: US battleship
Displacement: 16,351 tonnes (16,094 tons)
Dimensions: 134.5m x 23.2m x 7.2m (441ft 3in x 76ft 2 in x 23ft 9in)
Machinery: Twin screw, vertical triple expansion engines
Top speed: 19.2 knots
Main armament: Twelve 152mm (6in), eight 203mm (8in), four 305mm (12in) guns turrets
Launched: October 1904
Date of profile: 1906

Georgia and her four sisters were a major development in US battleship design. They were well protected and carried the heaviest possible armament on a relatively modest displacement. To reduce the risk of fire damage, wood was eliminated wherever possible. *Georgia* was given cage masts in 1909-10, and was later re-boilered. She was sold in 1923.

Georgia

Type: US submarine
Displacement: 16,865 tonnes (16,600 tons)(surface), 19,000 tonnes (18,700 tons) (submerged)
Dimensions: 170.7m x 12.8m x 10.8m (560ft x 42ft x 35ft 5in)
Machinery: Single screw, one pressurised water-cooled nuclear reactor, turbines
Top speed: 20+ knots
Main armament: Twenty-four Trident missiles (C4), four 533mm (21in) torpedo tubes
Launched: November 1982

The missile tubes are housed behind the fin. Behind this is the nuclear reactor, shielded from the engine, control centre and living quarters.

Germanic

Type: British liner
Displacement: 5,084 tonnes (5,004 tons)
Dimensions: 138m x 13.8m (455ft x 45ft 6in)
Machinery: Single screw, compound engine
Top speed: 15.7 knots
Launched: July 1874

Date of profile: 1878

The White Star Line's *Germanic* was one of the world's longest-serving and most reliable vessels. In 1905 she was re-named *Ottawa*, and in 1910 she was sold to Turkey and re-named *Gul Djemal*. She was finally scrapped in 1950.

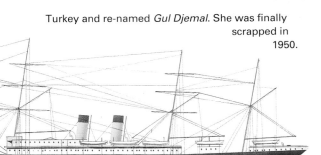

Gerona

Type: Spanish cruiser
Displacement: 3,980 tonnes (3,917 tons)
Dimensions: 80.7m x 15.4m x 6.3m (265ft x 50ft 7in x 20ft 9in)
Machinery: Single-screw, compound engines
Main armament: Thirty-two smooth-bore guns

Launched: 1864

Gerona was one of a class of wooden-hulled frigates built to back up Spain's expanding fleet. Her engines developed 2,400hp and coal supply was 685 tonnes (675 tons). In the 1890s she was a gunnery school. By 1898 she had been removed from the effective list.

Giacinto Pullino

Type: Italian submarine
Displacement: 350 tonnes (345 tons) (surface), 411 tonnes (405 tons) (submerged)
Dimensions: 42.2m x 4m x 3.7m (138ft 6in x 13ft 8in x 12ft 4in)
Machinery: Twin screw, diesel engines (surface), electric motors (submerged)

Main armament: One 47mm (1.85in), one 57mm (2.25in) gun, six 450mm (17.7in) torpedo tubes
Launched: July 1913
Date of profile: 1916

Giacinto Pullino was laid down at La Spezia Dockyard in June 1912 and was completed in December 1913. In July 1916 she was beached on Galiola Island, Quarnaro, and was seized by Austrian forces. She sank while being towed to Pola on 1 August 1917. In 1931 the Italian Navy raised her, and she was later scrapped.

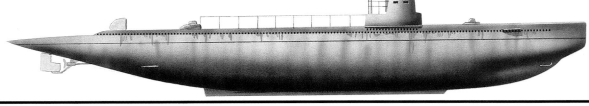

Giacomo Nani

Type: Italian submarine
Displacement: 774 tonnes (762 tons) (surface), 938 tonnes (924 tons) (submerged)
Dimensions: 67m x 5.9m x 3.8m (220ft x 19ft 4in x 12ft 6in)
Machinery: Twin screw, diesel engines (surface), electric motors (submerged)
Main armament: Two 76mm (3in) guns, six 450mm (17.7in) torpedo tubes
Launched: September 1918

Giacomo Nani was laid down in 1915, but was not completed in time to see service in World War I, where her superior speed (both surfaced and submerged) would have been invaluable. She was stricken from the Navy List in August 1935.

Giacomo Nani and her three sisters were fast, medium-sized submarines designed by Laurenti and Cavallini.

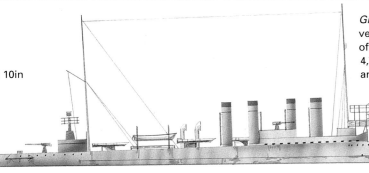

Gillis

Type: US destroyer
Displacement: 1,328 tonnes (1,308 tons)
Dimensions: 95.8m x 9.4m x 3m (314ft 4in x 30ft 10in x 9ft 10in)
Machinery: Twin screw, turbines
Top speed: 35 knots
Main armament: Four 102mm (4in) guns, twelve 533mm (21in) torpedo tubes
Launched: April 1919

Gillis was one of a large class of vessels that were improved versions of the Wickes group. Range was 4,750km (2,500 miles) at 20 knots, and engines developed 27,000hp. *Gillis* was scrapped in 1946.

Giovanni Bausan

Type: Italian cruiser
Displacement: 3,383 tonnes (3,330 tons)
Dimensions: 89.3m x 12.8m x 5.9m (293ft x 42ft x 19ft 4in)
Machinery: Twin screw, double expansion engines
Top speed: 17.4 knots
Main armament: Six 152mm (6in), two 254mm (10in) guns
Launched: December 1883

Giovanni Bausan was originally described as a torpedo ram ship, and was designed by the prolific George Rendell. She was one of the world's first modern cruisers, and one of the first not to rely on sails for her main motive force. She was well-proportioned and powerful, with a 254mm (10in) gun at each end of the vessel, and six 152mm (6in) weapons in the waist, all on one deck. Her armoured deck was 38mm (1.5in) thick and ran the full length of her hull. Beneath this were 10 watertight compartments to help her stay afloat in the event of a penetrating hit. She could carry nearly 570 tonnes (560 tons) of coal, giving her a range of 9,500km (5,000 miles) at 10 knots. In 1899, her 32-calibre 152mm (6in) guns were replaced by more modern 40-calibre weapons. Her armament was again revised in 1905. In 1915 she was regarded as obsolete, and had her 254mm (10in) main guns removed. She was then moored at Tobruk, where she served as a water distilling ship. In July 1916 she was completely disarmed, and became a submarine depot ship based at Brindisi. She was sold for scrap in 1920.

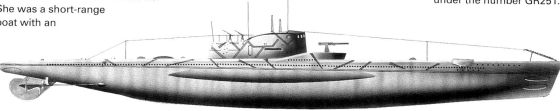

Giovanni Bausan

Type: Italian submarine
Displacement: 894 tonnes (880 tons) (surface), 1,075 tonnes (1,058 tons) (submerged)
Dimensions: 68.2m x 6m x 4.9m (223ft 9in x 20ft x 16ft 2in)
Machinery: Twin screw, diesel engines (surface), electric motors (submerged)
Top speed: 15 knots (surface), 8.2 knots (submerged)
Main armament: One 102mm (4in) gun, six 533mm (21in) torpedo tubes
Launched: March 1928

Giovanni Bausan was one of four submarines laid down in 1925-26. She was a short-range boat with an internal double hull, but because of stability problems when first commissioned, all four boats in the class were fitted with external bulges which reduced their speed by about two knots on the surface and one knot submerged. In 1940 she became a training ship. She was laid up in 1942 and used as a floating oil depot under the number GR251.

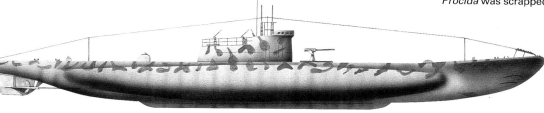

Giovanni da Procida

Type: Italian submarine
Displacement: 843 tonnes (830 tons) (surface), 1,026 tonnes (1,010 tons) (submerged)
Dimensions: 64.6m x 6.5m x 4.3m (212ft x 21ft 4in x 14ft)
Machinery: Twin screw, diesel engines (surface), electric motors (submerged)
Main armament: One 102mm (4in) gun, six 533mm (21in) torpedo tubes
Launched: April 1928

Giovanni da Procida was one of a class of four vessels. In 1942 higher-powered diesels were installed, increasing operational surface speed to 17 knots. She served in the Spanish Civil War. From 1940 to 1943 she patrolled in the Mediterranean. In 1944 she became a training ship. *Giovanni da Procida* was scrapped in 1948.

Giovanni delle Bande Nere

Type: Italian cruiser
Displacement: 6,676 tonnes (6,571 tons)
Dimensions: 169.3m x 15.5m x 5.3m (555ft 6in x 50ft 10in x 17ft 5in)
Machinery: Twin screw, turbines
Main armament: Six 100mm (3.9in), eight 152mm (6in) guns
Launched: April 1930

Giovanni delle Bande Nere was one of Italy's first post-World War I light cruisers which were built to counteract the large, powerful Jaguar-class destroyers of the French Navy. Engines developed over 95,000hp, oil supply was 1,250 tonnes (1,230 tons), and range was 7,220km (3,800 miles) at 18 knots and 1,843km (970 miles) at full speed. *Giovanni delle Bande Nere* was torpedoed and sunk by the British submarine *Urge* on 1 April 1942.

Giulio Cesare

Type: Italian battleship
Displacement: 29,496 tonnes
(29,032 tons)
Dimensions: 186.4m x 28m x 9m
(611ft 6in x 92ft x 30ft)
Machinery: Quadruple screw,
turbines
Top speed: 28.2 knots
Main armament: Twelve

120mm (4.7in), ten 320mm (12.6in)
guns
Launched: October 1911
Date of profile: 1938

Designed in 1908 by
Engineer General
Masdea, *Giulio*

Cesare and her two sisters were the
first large group of Italian
dreadnoughts. *Giulio Cesare* was
completely rebuilt
between 1933 and
1937, and
emerged from

this lengthy transformation with
improved protection, new
machinery and revised armament.
At the end of World War II the ship
was handed over to Russia and was
re-named *Novorossisk*. She served
in the Black Sea until 1955.

Giuseppe Finzi

Type: Italian submarine
Displacement: 1,574 tonnes (1,550
tons) (surface), 2,093 tonnes (2,060
tons) (submerged)
Dimensions: 84.3m x 7.7m x 5.2m
(276ft7in x 25ft 3in x 17ft)
Machinery: Twin screw, diesel
engines (surface), electric motors
(submerged)

Main armament: Two 120mm
(4.7in) guns, eight 533mm (21in)
torpedo tubes
Launched: June 1935

Giuseppe Finzi was a large, long-
range boat developed from a re-
design of the Balilla class. She took
part in the Spanish
Civil War, and

was one of the first Italian
submarines to serve in the Atlantic
during World War II. In 1943 she
was preparing to transport materials
to the Far East when she seized by
the Germans while re-fitting at
Bordeaux,
where she
was scuttled
in 1944.

Giuseppe Garibaldi

Type: Italian cruiser
Displacement: 8,230 tonnes (8,100
tons)
Dimensions: 111m x 18.2m x 7.3m
(366ft 9in x 59ft 9in x 24ft)
Machinery: Twin screw,
vertical triple expansion
engines
Top speed: 19.7 knots

Main armament:
Fourteen 152mm
(6in), two

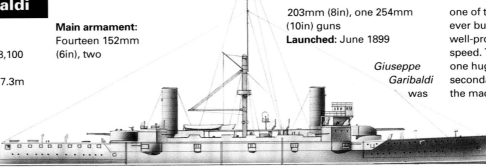

203mm (8in), one 254mm
(10in) guns
Launched: June 1899

*Giuseppe
Garibaldi*
was

one of the most successful cruisers
ever built, combining a powerful,
well-protected armament with good
speed. The centre of the vessel was
one huge armoured box housing the
secondary armament and protecting
the machinery spaces. *Giuseppe
Garibaldi* was
torpedoed and sunk
by an Austrian
submarine in 1915.

Giuseppe Garibaldi

Type: Italian cruiser
Displacement: 11,485 tonnes
(11,305 tons)
Dimensions: 187m x 18.9m x 6.7m
(613ft 6in x 62ft x 22ft)
Machinery: Twin screw, turbines
Top speed: 30
knots
Main armament:

Four 134mm (5.3in) guns, twin
Terrier missile launcher, four
Polaris missile launchers
Launched: April 1934

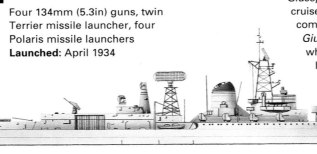

Giuseppe Garibaldi was one of the fifth group of fast, light
cruisers of the Condottieri type which were designed to
combat the powerful French destroyers of the period.
Giuseppe Garibaldi was rebuilt between 1957 and 1962,
when she was given a twin Terrier surface-to-air missile
launcher and tubes for four Polaris ballistic missiles.
Although the missiles were never carried, she was
the only surface vessel
to be so
fitted.

Giuseppe Garibaldi

Type: Italian aircraft carrier
Displacement: 13,500 tonnes (13,370
tons)
Dimensions: 180m
x 33.4m x 6.7m
(590ft 6in x 109ft 6in
x 22ft)
Machinery: Quadruple

screw, gas turbines
Main armament:
Missile
launchers,

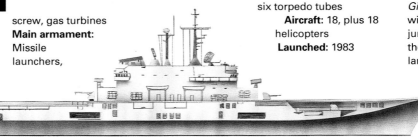

six torpedo tubes
Aircraft: 18, plus 18
helicopters
Launched: 1983

Giuseppe Garibaldi has six decks
with 13 watertight bulkheads. A 'ski-
jump' launch ramp is mounted on
the bows for vertical take-off and
landing aircraft, and this ramp
enables the aircraft
to take off with a
higher gross weight of
fuel and weapons.

Giuseppe la Masa

Type: Italian destroyer
Displacement: 823 tonnes (810 tons)
Dimensions: 72.5m x 7.3m x 2.9m
(238ft x 24ft x 9ft 6in)
Machinery: Twin screw, turbines
Top speed: 34 knots
Main armament: Six
102mm (4in) guns, four
450mm (17.7in) torpedo

tubes
Launched: 1917

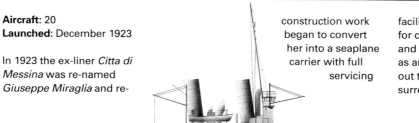

Giuseppe la Masa was one of eight ships that formed the third series of the Indomito-class destroyers. In 1929 she was re-classified as a torpedo boat. During World War II her anti-aircraft armament was increased. Only one ship in the class, the *Giacinto Carini*, survived the war. *Giuseppe la Masa* was scuttled in 1943.

Giuseppe Miraglia

Type: Italian seaplane carrier
Displacement: 5,486 tonnes (5,400 tons)
Dimensions: 115m x 15m x 5.2m
(377ft 4in x 49ft 3in x 17ft)
Machinery: Twin screw, turbines
Top speed: 21.5 knots
Main armament: Four 102mm
(4in) guns

Aircraft: 20
Launched: December 1923

In 1923 the ex-liner *Citta di Messina* was re-named *Giuseppe Miraglia* and re-

construction work began to convert her into a seaplane carrier with full servicing

facilities. She was used extensively for catapult launching experiments, and during World War II she served as an aircraft transport and carried out training duties. In 1943 she was surrendered at Malta.

Gladiator

Type: British corvette
Displacement: 1,229 tonnes (1,210 tons)
Dimensions: 67m x 8.5m x 3m (220ft x 28ft x 10ft)
Machinery: Paddle wheels, oscillating engines
Top speed: 9.5 knots
Main armament: Six 24-pounder

guns
Launched: 1844

By the mid 1850s, the Royal Navy had 77 paddle-wheel warships, 41 of them serving on foreign stations. In 1860 *Gladiator* was part of a combined British and US squadron sent to capture William Walker, the last of the famous US filibusters, who had declared himself President of Nicaragua. His men were taken back to New Orleans on board

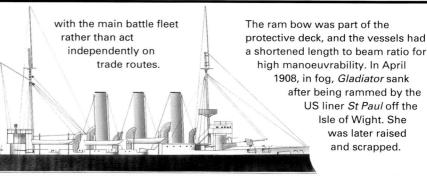

Gladiator. Walker was tried and executed.

Gladiator

Type: British cruiser
Displacement: 5,842 tonnes (5,750 tons)
Dimensions: 104.2m x 17.5m x 6m
(342ft x 57ft 6in x 20ft)
Machinery: Twin screw, triple expansion engines
Top speed: 19 knots

Main armament: Six 120mm
(4.7in), four 152mm (6in) guns
Launched: 1896

Gladiator and her three sisters were designed as ram cruisers, and were intended to operate

with the main battle fleet rather than act independently on trade routes.

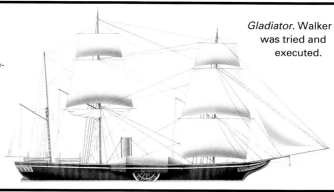

The ram bow was part of the protective deck, and the vessels had a shortened length to beam ratio for high manoeuvrability. In April 1908, in fog, *Gladiator* sank after being rammed by the US liner *St Paul* off the Isle of Wight. She was later raised and scrapped.

Glasgow

Type: British cruiser
Displacement: 4,047 tonnes (3,984 tons)
Dimensions: 76.2m x 16m x 6.8m
(250ft 52ft 6in x 22ft 5in)
Machinery: Single screw, expansion engines
Top speed: 11.5 knots
Main armament: Thirty 203mm (8in),

twenty 32-pounder, one 68-pounder guns
Launched: March 1861

Glasgow was a wooden-hulled frigate that featured a continuous upper deck. Her gun deck was 21m (70ft) longer than that of Nelson's *Victory* due to the use of diagonal framing, a construction method introduced in 1820. *Glasgow* was laid down in 1859 and completed in

1870. She was sold 14 years later.

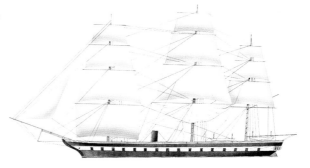

Glasgow

Type: British cruiser
Displacement: 4,876 tonnes (4,800 tons)
Dimensions: 131m x 14m x 5.4m (430 ft x 47ft x 17ft 9in)
Machinery: Quadruple screw, turbines
Top speed: 25.8 knots
Main armament: Ten 102mm (4in), two 152mm (6in) guns
Launched: September1909

Glasgow was the first true British cruiser to be built since the end of the 1890s, and

followed on from the large numbers of lightly armed scouts and heavy armoured cruisers then in service. Well-armed, fast, and with good protection, *Glasgow* and her four sisters were completed in 1910, and their design was to set a precedent for many later successful British cruiser designs. *Glasgow* had a

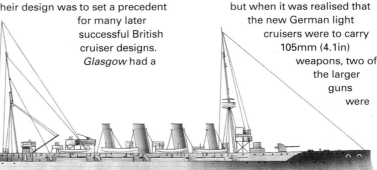

raised forecastle which held one of her 152mm (6in) guns, while the other was mounted aft. Her 102mm (4in) weapons were in the waist. It was originally planned to equip her with 102mm (4in) guns throughout, but when it was realised that the new German light cruisers were to carry 105mm (4.1in) weapons, two of the larger guns were

fitted instead. She had a 51mm (2in) thick armoured deck which thinned down to 19mm (0.75in) at the extreme bow and stern. She could carry up to 1,366 tonnes (1,353 tons) of coal and 263 tonnes (260 tons) of oil. On the outbreak of World War I, *Glasgow* was part of Craddock's ill-fated squadron sent to search for von Spee's powerful German cruiser force in the South Atlantic. The two squadrons met off Coronel, and *Glasgow* was the only British vessel to escape. She later fought in the Battle of the Falkland Islands in December 1914, where she sunk one German cruiser. She was broken up in 1927.

Glasgow

Type: British cruiser
Displacement: 11,652 tonnes (11,470 tons)
Dimensions: 187m x 19m x 5.5m (613ft 6in x 63ft x 18ft)
Machinery: Quadruple screws, turbines
Main armament: Twelve 152mm (6in) guns
Launched: June 1936
Date of profile: 1943

Glasgow and her four sisters were built to match the power of the

Japanese Mogami class. Initial designs attempted to keep the

displacement down to 8,600 tonnes (8,500 tons), the presumed displacement of *Mogami*, but this was not practicable. A catapult was carried between the funnels, and a hangar for two aircraft formed an extension of the bridge. *Glasgow* was broken up in 1958.

Glasgow

Type: British destroyer
Displacement: 4,165 tonnes (4,100 tons)
Dimensions: 125m x 14.3m x 5.8m (410ft x 47ft x 19ft)
Machinery: Twin screw, gas turbines
Main armament: One 115mm (4.5in) gun, one twin Sea Dart mount
Launched: April 1976

Glasgow is one of the first batch of four vessels in the latest class of destroyers built for the British Navy. The long bridge structure carries the air-search

radar, which has a range of 275km (145 miles). A large dome houses the fire control system. The main engines are used for full speed, and are gas turbines

developing 50,000hp. A second set of gas turbines give 9,700hp and are used for cruising. Four diesel generators develop 4,000kw. Range at 18 knots is 7,600km (4,000 miles). A single helicopter is carried aft, with a landing deck on the poop. *Glasgow* has six 324mm (12.75in) torpedo tubes in two triple launchers for anti-submarine torpedoes.

Glatton

Type: British battleship
Displacement: 4,990 tonnes (4,912 tons)
Dimensions: 74.6m x 16.4m x 5.7m (245ft x 54ft x 19ft)
Machinery: Twin screw engines
Top speed: 12 knots
Main armament: Two 304mm (12in) guns
Armour: 245-304mm (9.6-11.9in) waterline belt, 304-

355mm (11.9-13.9in) on turret,

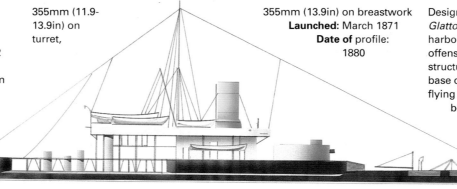

355mm (13.9in) on breastwork
Launched: March 1871
Date of profile: 1880

Designed by Sir Edward Reed, *Glatton* was intended to combine harbour defence with a sea-going offensive role. The raised breastwork structure amidships protected the base of the turret and funnel. A light flying bridge housed the ship's boats, and a deck also ran from the breastwork to a small raised poop aft. *Glatton* only went to sea once, in 1887.

Glatton

Type: British coast defence ship
Displacement: 5,831 tonnes (5,740 tons)
Dimensions: 94.5m x 22.4m x 5m (310ft x 73ft 6in x 16ft 5in)
Machinery: Twin screw, triple expansion engines
Main armament: Four 152mm (6in), two 233mm (9.2in) guns
Armour: 76-178mm belt, 203mm on turrets, 152-203mm on barbettes
Launched: August 1914

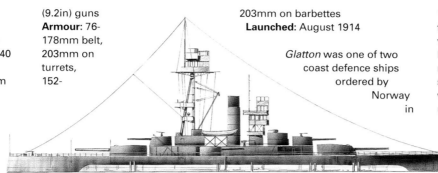

Glatton was one of two coast defence ships ordered by Norway in 1913 and laid down in Britain later that year. In November 1914 both vessels were bought by the Royal Navy for service in World War I, and modified to take standard British shells. Due to more pressing building work, Glatton was not completed until 1918. She was stationed at Dover, but blew up there on 16 September 1918 after only a few days in commission.

Glauco

Type: Italian submarine
Displacement: 160 tonnes (157 tons) (surface), 243 tonnes (9240 tons) (submerged)
Dimensions: 36.8m x 4.3m x 2.6m (120ft 9in x 14ft x 8ft 6in)
Machinery: Twin screw, petrol engines (surface), electric motors (submerged)
Main armament: Three 450mm (17.7in) torpedo tubes
Launched: July 1905

Built at the Venice Naval Dockyard to designs by Engineer Laurenti, Glauco belonged to the first mass-produced group of submarines built for the Italian Navy. When Glauco was laid down in 1903, petrol engines were still being fitted to submarines in spite of the volatile nature of the fuel.

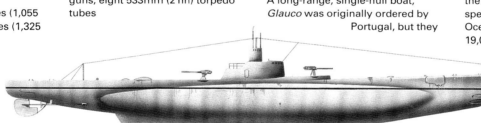

Glauco's engines developed 600hp, giving a surface range of 1,710km (900 miles) at 8 knots. Submerged, her electric motors developed 170hp and range was 65km (40 miles) at 5 knots. Glauco was removed from the effective list in 1916.

Glauco

Type: Italian submarine
Displacement: 1,071 tonnes (1,055 tons) (surface), 1,346 tonnes (1,325 tons) (submerged)
Dimensions: 73m x 7.2m x 5m (239ft 6in x 23ft 8in x 16ft 10in)
Machinery: Twin screw, diesel engines (surface), electric motors (submerged)
Main armament: Two 100mm (3.9in) guns, eight 533mm (21in) torpedo tubes
Launched: January 1935

A long-range, single-hull boat, Glauco was originally ordered by Portugal, but they cancelled her. She was completed for the Italian Navy, and took part in the Spanish Civil War. She then spent time patrolling the Indian Ocean, where her range of some 19,000km (10,000 miles) at 8 knots proved invaluable. She was scuttled off Gibraltar in 1941, having been damaged by HMS Wishart.

Gloire

Type: French battleship
Displacement: 5,720 tonnes (5,630 tons)
Dimensions: 77.8m x 17m x 8.4m (255ft 6in x 55ft 9in x 27ft 10in)
Machinery: Single screw, horizontal return engines
Top speed: 13 knots
Main armament: Thirty-six 162.5mm (6.4in) guns
Launched: November 1859
Date of profile: 1860

Gloire was the world's first 'modern' battleship. Plans showed 68-pounder, smoothbore guns, but she was fitted with rifled versions of the same weapon and was later re-armed with modern guns. Gloire was deleted from the effective list in 1879.

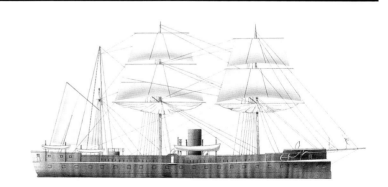

Gloire

Type: French cruiser
Displacement: 10,375 tonnes (10,212 tons)
Dimensions: 139.7m x 20m x 7.6m (458ft 4in x 66ft 3in x 25ft 2in)
Machinery: Triple screw, vertical triple expansion engines
Top speed: 21 knots
Main armament: Six 100mm (3.9in), eight 162mm (6.4in), two 193mm (7.6in) guns
Armour: 102-170mm belt, 203mm over main turrets
Launched: June 1900

Gloire was one of five vessels that fell midway in the development of the French armoured cruiser. Guns were electrically operated, and the hoist machinery was armoured. All ships were good steamers. Gloire was removed from service in 1922.

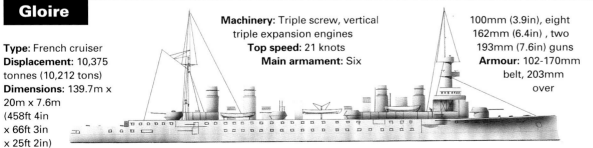

Gloire

Type: French cruiser
Displacement: 9,245 tonnes (9,100 tons)
Dimensions: 179.5m x 17.4m x 5.3m (589ft x 57ft 4in x 117ft 7in)
Machinery: Twin screw, turbines
Top speed: 36 knots
Main

armament: Eight 88mm (3.5in), nine 152mm (6in) guns
Armour: 102mm (4in) waterline belt
Launched: 1935

Gloire's aft superstructure comprised a large hangar with full repair facilities, and she had

a long, open deck which provided adequate space for the handling of four aircraft. A catapult was positioned on top of the aft turret. The 152mm (6in) guns were in triple turrets, two superfiring forward and one aft. *Gloire* was scrapped in 1958.

Glorious

Type: British battlecruiser
Displacement: 23,327 tonnes (22,960 tons)
Dimensions: 239.5m x 24.7m x 6.7m (786ft x 81ft x 22ft 3in)
Machinery: Quadruple screw, turbines
Top speed: 33 knots

Main armament: Eighteen 102mm (4in), four 380mm (15in) guns
Armour: 51-76mm(2-3in) belt along foredeck to end turret, 178-228mm

(7-9in) on turrets
Launched: February 1916
Date of profile: 1918

Glorious, her sister

Courageous, and near sister *Furious* combined maximum firepower with speed. *Glorious* was laid up in 1919, and was converted into an aircraft carrier during the 1920s. She was sunk in June 1940 by the German vessels *Gneiseau* and *Scharnhorst.*

Gneisenau

Type: German cruiser
Displacement: 12,985 tonnes (12,781 tons)
Dimensions: 144.6m x 21.6m x 8.3m (474ft 5in x 70ft 10in x 27ft 6in)
Machinery: Triple screw, triple expansion engines
Main armament: Six 152mm (6in), eight 208mm (8.2in) guns

Armour: 102-152mm (4-6in) waterline belt, 152mm (6in) over battery, 170mm (6.75in) on turrets
Launched: June 1906

Gneisenau and her sister *Scharnhorst* were the

penultimate armoured cruisers built for the German Navy. Both vessels were stationed

in China when World War I broke out. On their way back to Germany they defeated a British squadron off Coronel, but both vessels were sunk by the British off the Falkland Islands in December 1914.

Gneisenau

Type: German battlecruiser
Displacement: 39,522 tonnes (38,900 tons)
Dimensions: 226m x 30m x 9m (741ft 6in x 98ft 5in x 30ft)
Machinery: Triple screw, turbines

Main armament: Fourteen 104mm (4.1in), twelve 150mm (5.9in), nine 280mm (11in) guns

Launched: December 1936
Date of profile: 1938

Gneisenau and her sister *Scharnhorst*

were completed with straight stems, but the bows were later lengthened. Both vessels served in World War II, attacking British commerce and sinking the British aircraft carrier *Glorious. Gneisenau* was broken up between 1947 and 1951.

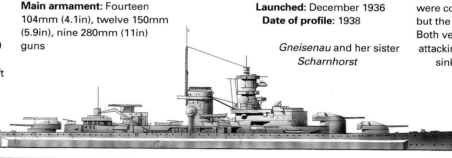

Godavari

Type: Indian frigate
Displacement: 4,064 tonnes (4,000 tons)
Dimensions: 126.5m x 14.5m x 9m (415ft x 47ft 7in x 29ft 6in)
Machinery: Twin screw, turbines
Top speed: 27 knots
Main armament: Two 57mm (2.25in)

guns, four SS-N-2C Styx missiles, plus SA-N-4 Gecko missiles
Launched: May 1980

Godavari is a modified version of the British Leander class. Two helicopters are housed in a large hangar aft, and she carries a unique

range of Russian, European and Indian weapons. The Styx missiles with active radar or infra-red homing capability have a range of 69km (43 miles) at 0.9 Mach with a 500kg (1,100lb) warhead. Gecko has semi-active radar homing to 13km (8 miles) at 2.5 Mach with a 50kg (110lb) warhead.

Goeben

Type: German battlecruiser
Displacement: 25,704 tonnes (25,300 tons)
Dimensions: 186.5m x 29.5m x 9m (611ft 10in x 96ft 9in x 29ft 6in)
Machinery: Quadruple screws, turbines
Top speed: 28 knots
Main armament: Twelve 150mm (5.9in), ten 280mm (11in) guns
Launched: March 1911
Date of profile: 1912

Goeben was one of two ships in a class that formed the second group of battlecruisers built for the rapidly expanding German Imperial Navy before World War I. These ships had five turrets, plus two large boat cranes carried amidships one each side of the second funnel, and their overall protection was equal to that of contemporary battleships. In addition, ventilation to the machinery spaces was provided massive grills in the base of each funnel. Their excellent design and safety features, combined with their heavy armament, made them formidable opponents, and this was borne out during subsequent hostilities with the Royal Navy. With the outbreak of World War I in August, for example, 1914 *Goeben* and *Breslau* were pursued across the Mediterranean by the British ships *Indomitable* and *Indefatigable*, but they managed to easily outrun the British and put into the Turkish port of Constantinople. Both German ships were then transferred to the Turkish Navy, in whose service *Goeben* sanks two British ships in 1918, before being re-named *Yavuz Sultan Selim*. She was modernised between 1926 and 1930 and served until well into the 1960s. She was finally broken up in 1971.

Goito

Type: Italian cruiser
Displacement: 842 tonnes (829 tons)
Dimensions: 73.4m x 7.8m x 3.6m (240ft 10in x 25ft 10in x 11ft 10in)
Machinery: Triple screws, double expansion engines
Main armament: Five 57mm (2.25in) guns
Launched: July 1887

Designed by Benedetto Brin, *Goito* was laid down in 1885 and completed in 1888. She was a sleek, two-funnelled, steel-hulled vessel with engines developing 2,620hp. Range was just over 1,900km (1,000 miles) at 10 knots. She was re-engined in 1897, and was also fitted out to carry 60 mines. From 1909 *Goito* served at Taranto, and in 1913 went on mission to Albania. In 1917 she was stationed at Naples before returning to Taranto in 1918. *Goito* was discarded in March 1920. Her sister, *Montebello*, served her last few years as a training ship, being discarded in 1920. Each vessel was slightly different to her sisters.

Golden Hind

Type: British warship
Displacement: 102 tonnes (100 tons)
Dimensions: 31m x 6m x 2.7m (102ft x 20ft x 9ft)
Main armament: 18 guns
Launched: 1560
Date of profile: 1577

This ship was originally named *Pelican*, and was typical of the small, fast warships of her period. She was of the French pattern, built along Venetian lines, with her poop and forecastle raised significantly above her tiny main deck. Her fore and main masts carried a full rig of square sails, while there was a lateen sail on the mizzen mast. She was made famous as the flagship of Sir Francis Drake's epic voyage of global circumnavigation in 1577-80. Drake had been given secret orders to plunder Spanish ports and shipping in the Americas from Queen Elizabeth of England, and set off from Plymouth on 13 December 1577. This expedition entered the Pacific Ocean September 1578, but here began the worst ordeal of the whole voyage. A series of savage storms lashed the tiny ships, and one sank. Eventually Drake in the *Pelican* voyaged as far north as the present-day location of San Francisco.

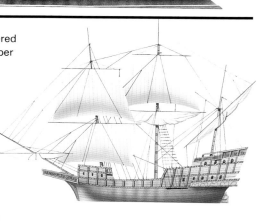

Golf I

Type: Russian submarine
Displacement: 2,336 tonnes (2,300 tons) (surface), 2,743 tonnes (2,700 tons) (submerged)
Dimensions: 100m x 8.5m x 6.6m (328ft x 27ft 11in x 21ft 8in)
Machinery: Triple screws, diesel engine (surface), electric motors (submerged)
Top speed: 17 knots (surface), 12 knots (submerged)
Main armament: Three SS-N-4 ballistic missiles, ten 533mm (21in) torpedo tubes
Launched: 1957

By the 1950s, Russia had embarked upon a massive submarine programme that would initially give her more submarines than any other country. Twenty-three Golf I-class submarines were completed between 1958 and 1962, and entered service at a rate of six to seven per year. The ballistic missiles are housed vertically in the rear section of the extended fin, which produces a great deal of resistance underwater and so reduces speed. Many boats in the class have undergone major changes since their completion.

Gorgon

Type: British coast defence ship
Displacement: 3,535 tonnes (3,480 tons)
Dimensions: 68.5m x 13.7m x 4.9m (225ft x 45ft x 16ft 4in)
Machinery: Twin screws, horizontal direct acting engines
Main armament: Four 254mm (10in) guns

Armour: 152-203mm (6-8in) on hull, 203-228mm (8-9in) on breastwork, 228-254mm (9-10in) on turrets
Launched: October 1871

The threat of war with France in 1870, with its consequent threat to British coastlines, led to the hasty construction of a group of shallow-draught coast defence vessels based on the design of *Cerebus*. However, as the threat of war

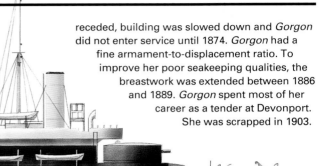

receded, building was slowed down and *Gorgon* did not enter service until 1874. *Gorgon* had a fine armament-to-displacement ratio. To improve her poor seakeeping qualities, the breastwork was extended between 1886 and 1889. *Gorgon* spent most of her career as a tender at Devonport. She was scrapped in 1903.

Gorm

Type: Danish coast defence ship
Displacement: 2,381 tonnes (2,344 tons)
Dimensions: 70m x 15m x 4.3m (231ft x 49ft x 14ft 3in)
Machinery: Single screw, single expansion engines
Main armament: Two 254mm (10in) guns

Armour: 178mm (7in) on hull, 203mm (8in) on turret
Launched: 1870

Gorm was a powerfully armed, shallow-draught coast defence vessel with the Danish Navy. A single turret forward housed the

254mm (10in) Armstrong rifled muzzle-loaders, only 1.6m (5ft 5in) above water level. Armament was altered several times during *Gorm*'s career, including the replacement of the original guns in the turret with 150mm (5.9in) weapons. *Gorm* was scrapped in 1912.

Gossamer

Type: British torpedo gunboat
Displacement: 746 tonnes (735 tons)
Dimensions: 70m x 8.2m x 3.2m (230ft x 27ft x 10ft 6in)
Machinery: Twin screws, triple expansion engines
Top speed: 19 knots
Main armament: Two 120mm (4.7in) guns, five 355mm (14in) torpedo

tubes
Launched: 1890

Gossamer and her 12 sisters were built to combat the growing threat posed by the expanding French

torpedo-boat fleet. To improve seakeeping qualities, the extended forecastle deck ran aft to the main mast. One torpedo tube was carried in the bows. *Gossamer* was sold in 1920.

Göta

Type: Swedish coast defence ship
Displacement: 3,290 tonnes (3,238 tons)
Dimensions: 79.5m x 14.6m x 5m (260ft 10in x 48ft x 16ft 9in)
Machinery: Twin screws, horizontal triple expansion engines
Top speed: 16.3 knots
Main armament: One 208mm (8.2in),

seven 152mm (6in) guns
Launched: 1891
Date of profile: 1908

Göta combined heavy armament with good protection, fair speed and the ability to operate in relatively shallow waters. As originally built, *Göta* carried two

254mm (10in) guns in a single turret forward. However, she was rebuilt between 1900 and 1901 and emerged with a new superstructure and weaponry. She was removed from the list in 1923 and was scrapped in 1944.

Göta Lejon

Type: Swedish cruiser
Displacement: 9,347 tonnes (9,200 tons)
Dimensions: 182m x 6.7m x 6.5m (597ft x 22ft x 21ft 4in)
Machinery: Twin screws, turbines
Main armament: Seven 152mm (6in) guns

Launched: November 1945

Following her policy of maintaining a strong fleet to protect her neutrality during

World War II, Sweden laid down two well-armed and strongly protected cruisers in 1943. Two raked funnels gave *Göta Lejon* and her sister *Tre Kronor* a distinct appearance, enhanced on *Göta Lejon* by the tower bridge structure added during re-building in 1957-58. *Göta Lejon* was sold to Chile in 1971.

THE ENCYCLOPEDIA OF SHIPS

Göteborg

Type: Swedish destroyer
Displacement: 1,219 tonnes (1,200 tons)
Dimensions: 94.6m x 9m x 3.8m (310ft 4in x 29ft 6in x 12ft 6in)
Machinery: Twin screws, turbines
Main armament: Three 120mm (4.7in) guns, six 533mm (21in) torpedo tubes
Launched: October 1935

By 1934 it was obvious that Sweden's destroyer force needed strengthening to preserve her neutrality. A new construction programme was begun and a class of six units began building, to be complete by 1941. The 120mm (4.7in) guns were housed in single mounts, one forward, one aft and one on a raised platform amidships. *Göteborg* was sunk by an internal explosion in 1941. She was raised and served until 1958. She was expended as a target on 14 August 1962.

Gothland

Type: Belgian liner
Displacement: 7,880 tonnes (7,755 tons)
Dimensions: 150m x 16m (491ft x 53ft)
Machinery: Twin screws, triple expansion engines
Top speed: 14 knots
Launched: 1893

Gothland was originally named *Gothic*, and was built for the White Star Line for service on their North Atlantic route. In 1907 she was taken over by the Red Star Line and was re-named. She had a long hull, straight stern and a single funnel topping a short central superstructure that accommodated first-class passengers. Towards the end of her career, *Gothland* served as an emigrant ship. She was scrapped in 1926.

Gotland

Type: Swedish cruiser
Displacement: 5,638 tonnes (5,550 tons)
Dimensions: 134.8m x 15.4m x 5.5m (442ft 3in x 50ft 6in x 18ft)
Machinery: Twin screws, turbines
Top speed: 28 knots
Main armament: Six 152mm (6in) guns
Launched: 1933

Gotland was originally planned as a small aircraft carrier with 12 float planes launched by two catapults. In 1927 the plans were revised to include three twin 152mm (6in) guns, and the vessel's designation changed to that of aircraft cruiser. She usually carried six planes aft, but had room for eight on deck and three below. In 1943-44 *Gotland* was converted into an anti-aircraft cruiser due to the non-availability of modern float planes. She was removed from the effective list in 1960.

Goubet I

Type: French submarine
Displacement: 1.6 tonnes (1.6 tons) (surface), 1.8 tonnes (1.8 tons) (submerged)
Dimensions: 5m x 1.7m x 1m (16ft 5in x 5ft 10in x 3ft 3in)
Machinery: Single screw, electric motor
Top speed: 5 knots
Launched: 1887
Date of profile: 1888

The greatest difficulty facing the early submarine designers was underwater propulsion. Steam power and compressed air were being tested but they had limitations. However, an answer appeared in 1859 when Plante invented the lead accumulator. By 1880, this had been improved by coating the surface with red lead, making available to submarine designers a suitable power source that no longer relied on the atmosphere. *Goubet I* had a pointed, cylindrical hull with an observation dome. She was one of the first successful submarines, but was discarded because of her small size.

Goubet II

Type: French submarine
Displacement: 4.5 tonnes (4.5 tons) (surface), 5 tonnes (5 tons) (submerged)
Dimensions: 8m x 1.8m x 1.8m (26ft 3in x 6ft x 6ft)
Machinery: Single screw, electric motor
Launched: 1889

Goubet II was laid down one year after the launch of *Goubet I*. Motive power was provided by a 4hp Siemens electric road car engine, and range at full speed was about 38km (20 miles). The motor was powered from a battery of Laurent-Cely accumulators carried in the lower portion of the hull. After a series of tests, *Goubet II* was rejected by the French authorities because of her small size. However, she was a well-planned, successful craft and the valuable experience gained during her building and trials was put to good use by later submarine designers.

169

Gouden Leeuw

Type: Dutch minelayer
Displacement: 1,311 tonnes (1,291 tons)
Dimensions: 65.8m x 11m x 3.3m (216ft x 36ft x 11ft)
Machinery: Twin screws, triple expansion engines
Top speed: 15 knots
Main armament: Two 76mm (3in) anti-aircraft guns
Launched: 1931
Date of profile: 1932

Gouden Leeuw was one of two minelayers built by De Maas at Rotterdam for service in the Far

East. Even though industrial and harbour facilities were well-provided for in most Dutch colonies, her twin steam engines were specifically designed to be easy to maintain. They developed 1,750hp, which gave her an average turn of speed. *Gouden Leeuw* had airy and spacious accommodation for 121 officers and

men, and was regarded as comfortable to serve on, even in the hot and humid climate of the Dutch East Indies. Her gun armament was light, and only intended for self-defence. Her main weapon was the

anti-shipping mine, and she was capable of carrying up to 250 of these, depending on the size and type. These were carried in a magazine aft, and were laid by running along rails which led along the poop deck to the stern. Her wartime service was short. She was caught and sunk by Japanese warships off Tarakan on 12 January 1942, less than a month after the start of the war in the Pacific. Her sister ship *Prins van Oranje* survived the conflict, and was then scuttled at Souabaya on 7 March 1942.

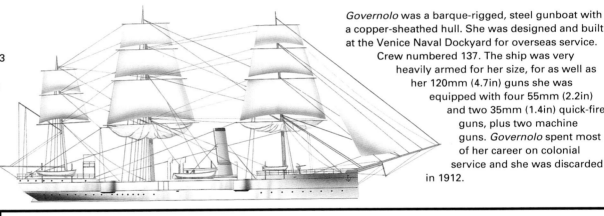

Governolo

Type: Italian gunboat
Displacement: 1,222 tonnes (1,203 tons)
Dimensions: 56.4m x 10m x 4.6m (185ft x 33ft 9in x 15ft)
Machinery: Single screw, compound engines
Top speed: 15 knots
Main armament: Four 120mm (4.7in) guns
Launched: May 1894

Governolo was a barque-rigged, steel gunboat with a copper-sheathed hull. She was designed and built at the Venice Naval Dockyard for overseas service. Crew numbered 137. The ship was very heavily armed for her size, for as well as her 120mm (4.7in) guns she was equipped with four 55mm (2.2in) and two 35mm (1.4in) quick-fire guns, plus two machine guns. *Governolo* spent most of her career on colonial service and she was discarded in 1912.

Governor Moore

Type: Confederate gunboat
Displacement: 1,234 tonnes (1,215 tons)
Dimensions: unknown
Machinery: Paddlewheels, walking beam engine
Top speed: 8 knots
Main armament: Two 32-pounder rifled guns
Launched: 1854
Date of profile: 1854

Formerly the *Charles Morgan* built in New York, the boat was seized at New Orleans in January 1862 and re-named *Governor Moore* after the governor of Louisiana. She was then added to the newly formed Louisiana State Navy, which was later absorbed into the Confederate Navy. The ship saw plenty of action against Union forces. Having successfully rammed the fast Union gunboat *Varuna* off New Orleans, *Governor Moore* was turning to leave her

defeated opponent when she was fired on by the Union vessel *Oneida*. *Governor Moore* ran aground and was destroyed by her own crew.

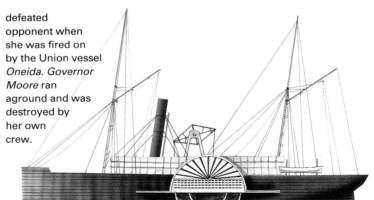

Graf Spee

Type: German battlecruiser
Displacement: 36,576 tonnes (36,000 tons)
Dimensions: 223m x 30.4m x 8.4m (731ft 8in x 99ft 9in x 27ft 7in)
Machinery: Quadruple screws, turbines
Top speed: 28 knots
Main armament: Twelve 150mm (5.9in), eight

350mm (13.8in) guns
Launched: September 1917
Date of profile: 1917

Graf Spee was to have been an improved version of the powerful *Hindenburg*, launched in 1917. The main armament of *Graf Spee* was updated, the weapons being positioned in four twin turrets, two superfiring fore and aft. The secondary armament was concentrated on the upper deck in a long battery that was a continuation of the raised foredeck. The Germans hoped to complete all four vessels in the class by 1918, but although *Graf Spee* was launched in 1917 she was never completed and was scrapped in 1921-23.

Graf Zeppelin

Type: German aircraft carrier
Displacement: 28,540 tonnes (28,090 tons)
Dimensions: 262.5m x 31.5m x 8.5m (861ft 3in x 103ft 4in x 27ft 10in)
Machinery: Quadruple screws, turbines
Main armament: Twelve 104mm (4.1in), sixteen 150mm (5.9in) guns

Aircraft: 42
Launched: December 1938

After World War I Germany was denied any opportunity of developing a carrier force as a result of restrictions imposed upon them in 1919. By 1933 Wilhelm Hadelar had

prepared a basic design for a full deck carrier able to operate 30 aircraft, but lack of construction experience delayed the project. In

1935 work began, but *Graf Zeppelin*'s completion was delayed to make way for the U-boat programme. The incomplete carrier was scuttled a few months before the end of World War II. She was raised by the Russians, but sank on her way to Leningrad.

Grafton

Type: British frigate
Displacement: 1,480 tonnes (1,456 tons)
Dimensions: 94.5m x 10m x 4.7m (310ft x 33ft x 15ft 6in)
Machinery: Single screw, turbines
Top speed: 27.8 knots

Main armament: Two 40mm (1.6in) guns
Launched: September 1954

Grafton was in a class of 12 vessels. All ships in the class were built in pre-

fabricated sections before final assembly on the launching ramp. *Grafton* was very lightly gunned, having only two 40mm (1.6in) guns.

Her anti-submarine weapons consisted of two Limbo three-barrelled depth-charge launchers which could fire a pattern of large depth charges with great accuracy over a wide area. The next class of anti-submarine frigates built for the Royal Navy greatly improved upon the weak gun armament.

Grampian

Type: British liner
Displacement: 11,130 tonnes (10,955 tons)
Dimensions: 148m x 18m (486ft x 60ft)
Machinery: Twin screws, turbines
Top speed: 15 knots
Launched: 1907
Date of profile: 1907

Grampian was a mixed cargo and passenger vessel built for the Allan

Line. She could carry 210 first-class, 250 second-class and 1,000 third-

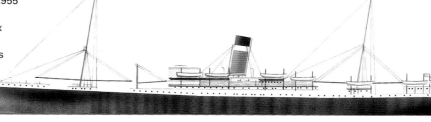

class passengers and plied the Glasgow to Canada route. The ship managed to maintain a fairly regular service throughout World War I. In 1917 the Allan Line, which by then owned 20 transatlantic steamers, was taken over by the Canadian Pacific Line. *Grampian* continued in service until she was scrapped in 1926.

Grasshopper

Type: British torpedo gunboat
Displacement: 558 tonnes (550 tons)
Dimensions: 60.9m x 7m x 3m (200ft x 23ft x 10ft 4in)
Machinery: Twin screws, triple expansion engines
Main armament: One 102mm (4in) gun, four 355mm (14in) torpedo tubes

Launched: August 1887

Grasshopper was one of a new type of gunboat built for the Royal Navy. Unlike existing fast torpedo boats, the new

torpedo gunboats had good range and protection. Engines developed 2,700hp. Range at full speed was 1,140km (600 miles); and at 10 knots, 7,600km (4,000 miles). No sails were carried, the two pole masts being used for signalling. *Grasshopper* was sold in 1905.

Grasshopper

Type: British destroyer
Displacement: 937 tonnes (923 tons)
Dimensions: 82.6m x 27.5m x 9.7m (271ft x 27ft 10in x 9ft 6in)
Machinery: Triple screws, turbines
Top speed: 27 knots
Main armament: One

102mm (4in), three 12-pounder guns
Launched: November 1909

In 1907 the British Admiralty obtained plans of the latest German destroyers and set plans in motion to combat them. Initial designs for *Grasshopper* and her 15 sisters specified oil fuel, but this was soon changed to the more readily available coal fuel. The class carried a new torpedo, which was fitted with a heater to improve performance and had a range of 10,972m (12,000 yd) at 30 knots. *Grasshopper* was sold in 1921.

Graudenz

Type: German cruiser
Displacement: 6,484 tonnes (6,382 tons)
Dimensions: 142.7m x 13.8m x 5.7m (468ft 2in x 45ft 3in x 18ft 10in)
Machinery: Twin screws, turbines
Main armament: Twelve 104mm (4.1in) guns
Launched: October 1913

Graudenz and her sister *Regensburg* belonged to the 1911 German naval programme, and their design reverted to the three-funnel layout of an earlier class, as opposed to the four-funnel design then in favour. Apart from that, both vessels were a continuation of the well-established German light-cruiser type. Both ships were

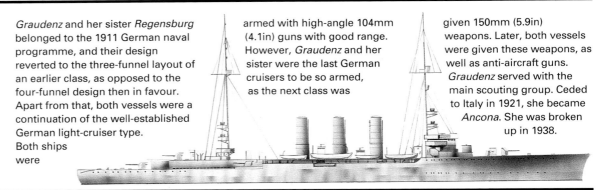

armed with high-angle 104mm (4.1in) guns with good range. However, *Graudenz* and her sister were the last German cruisers to be so armed, as the next class was given 150mm (5.9in) weapons. Later, both vessels were given these weapons, as well as anti-aircraft guns. *Graudenz* served with the main scouting group. Ceded to Italy in 1921, she became *Ancona*. She was broken up in 1938.

Gravina

Type: Spanish cruiser
Displacement: 1,170 tonnes (1,152 tons)
Dimensions: 64m x 9.7m x 4.2m (210ft x 32ft x 13ft 9in)
Machinery: Single screw, horizontal compound engine
Main armament: Two 76mm (3in), two 152mm (6in) guns

Launched: 1881

An iron-hulled, barque-rigged vessel built at Blackwall, London, *Gravina* was part of a large class of eight cruisers built for the Spanish Navy. Six were built in Spain, the other

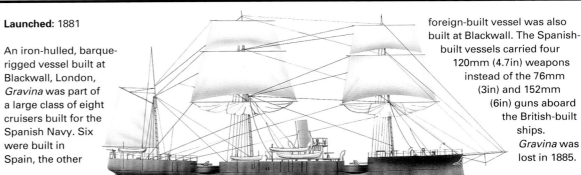

foreign-built vessel was also built at Blackwall. The Spanish-built vessels carried four 120mm (4.7in) weapons instead of the 76mm (3in) and 152mm (6in) guns aboard the British-built ships. *Gravina* was lost in 1885.

Gravina

Type: Spanish destroyer
Displacement: 2,209 tonnes (2,175 tons)
Dimensions: 101.5m x 9.6m x 3.2m (333ft x 31ft 9in x 10ft 6in)
Machinery: Twin screws, turbines
Main armament: Five 120mm (4.7in) guns, six 533mm (21in) torpedo tubes

Launched: December 1931

Gravina belonged to the largest class of destroyers built for the Spanish Navy. The class of 16 vessels was made up of two groups, *Gravina* being part of the second group. The destroyers were virtual copies of the British Scott-class flotilla

leaders. All vessels in *Gravina*'s class were built at Cartegena and launched between 1926 and 1933. The ships of the second group all

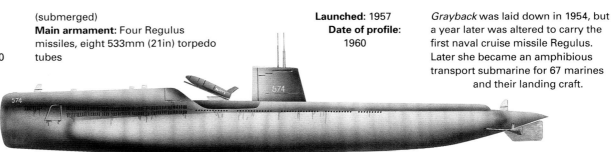

had large gun shields. Engines developed 42,000hp, and oil fuel capacity was 548 tonnes (540 tons). Range at 14 knots was 8,550km (4,500 miles). She was stricken in the 1960s.

Grayback

Type: US submarine
Displacement: 2,712 tonnes (2,670 tons) (surface), 3,708 tonnes (3,650 tons) (submerged)
Dimensions: 102m x 9m (335ft x 30ft)
Machinery: Twin screws, diesel engines (surface), electric motors

(submerged)
Main armament: Four Regulus missiles, eight 533mm (21in) torpedo tubes

Launched: 1957
Date of profile: 1960

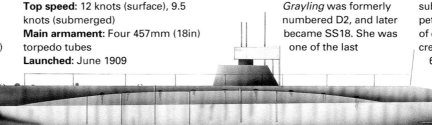

Grayback was laid down in 1954, but a year later was altered to carry the first naval cruise missile Regulus. Later she became an amphibious transport submarine for 67 marines and their landing craft.

Grayling

Type: US submarine
Displacement: 292 tonnes (288 tons) (surface), 342 tonnes (337 tons) (submerged)
Dimensions: 41m x 4.2m x 3.6m (135ft x 13ft 9in x 12ft)
Machinery: Twin screws, petrol engines (surface), electric motors (submerged)

Top speed: 12 knots (surface), 9.5 knots (submerged)
Main armament: Four 457mm (18in) torpedo tubes
Launched: June 1909

Grayling was formerly numbered D2, and later became SS18. She was one of the last

submarines in the US Navy to have petrol engines, which were a source of constant anxiety to her 15-man crew. *Grayling*'s engines developed 600hp, giving her a surface range of 2,356km (1,240 miles) at 10 knots. She was discarded in 1922.

Great Britain

Type: British liner
Displacement: 3,322 tonnes (3,270 tons)
Dimensions: 88m x 15m (289ft x 50ft)
Machinery: Single screw, compound engine
Top speed: 9 knots
Launched: July 1843
Date of profile: 1844

Designed by Brunel, *Great Britain* was the first iron, screw-propelled liner. She was built for the Great Western Steamship Company for their Atlantic service at William Patterson's yard in Bristol. As she

was being built, it became obvious that when fully-equipped she would not be able to pass through the dock gates, so after a year's delay she was towed round to London to have her engines fitted. She took six years to complete, but when she entered service she was still larger than any of her contemporaries. At first she was named *Mammoth*, and was propelled by four

cylinder engines with an overhead crankshaft connected to the propeller via chain gearing. She could carry up to 360 passengers in a good degree of comfort for the time. Her maiden voyage was to New York, where she

made the crossing in 15 days, taking 606 tonnes of cargo and 60 passengers. She was refitted in 1846 with new propellers, and her six masts reduced to five. In 1846 she ran aground near Belfast, and after a year she was refloated and rebuilt with two funnels and four masts. She eventually ended her career as a a hulk in the Falkland Islands, but in 1970 was towed back to Bristol for full restoration before becoming a museum.

Great Eastern

Type: British liner
Displacement: 19,217 tonnes (18,915 tons)
Dimensions: 210m x 25.3m (689ft x 83ft)
Machinery: Single screw, paddle wheels
Top speed: 13.5 knots
Launched: January 1858

Brunel's ship *Great Eastern* was almost five times larger than any ship in the world at

the time of her launch. Constructed on the Thames, she was built parallel to the river as she

was too long to be launched in the conventional manner. She carried 596 passengers, plus 2,400 steerage. Although a celebrated ship, *Great Eastern* proved a failure on the transatlantic run, and in 1865 she was put into service as a cable layer. She was laid up in 1874, and beached for breaking up in 1888.

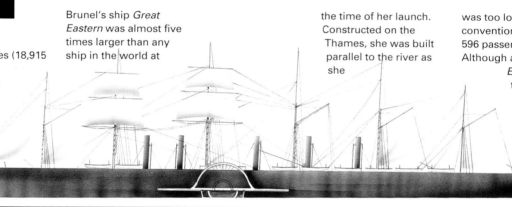

Great Republic

Type: US sailing ship
Displacement: 4,627 tonnes (4,555 tons)
Dimensions: 102m x 16m (335ft x 53ft)
Launched: October 1853

Great Republic was the largest sailing ship of her time. She had four complete decks, the uppermost being flush with the sides of the

ship as in later steamships. She had been designed to carry immense amounts of cargo while only requiring a crew of standard size, so cutting down on running costs.

Sadly, prior to her first voyage to Britain, a fire burnt her down to the water and she was scuttled. The wreck was sold and raised, and she was re-built without an upper deck and with a much reduced cargo capacity and rig. Her original crew of 130 was also halved. The great ship passed through several new owners before sinking in a severe storm in March 1872.

Great Western

Type: British liner
Displacement: 1,341 tonnes (1,320 tons)
Dimensions: 72m x 18m x 5m (236ft x 58ft 3in x 16ft 7in)
Machinery: Paddle wheels, side-lever engines
Top speed: 9 knots
Launched: July 1837

Great Western was a wooden-hulled vessel, and the first of Brunel's trio of liners.

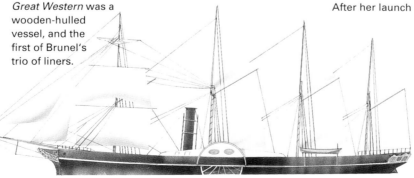

After her launch at Bristol she was towed to London to have her machinery fitted. Her side-lever engines developed 750hp. Coal consumption was 33 tonnes (33 tons) per day. Built for the Great Western Steamship Company, the liner was the first purpose-built passenger liner. In the eight years after her launch she made 64 round voyages across the Atlantic. She was broken up in 1856.

Greif

Type: German cruiser
Displacement: 2,265 tonnes (2,230 tons)
Dimensions: 102.6m x 9.7m x 4.3m (336ft 8in x 32ft x 14ft 3in)
Machinery: Twin screws, horizontal compound engines
Main armament: Two 104mm (4.1in) guns

Launched: July 1886

Greif was based on the *Butz*, but did not have the torpedo armament. One of the 104mm (4.1in) guns was positioned forward on a raised platform behind a breakwater in front of the bridge. The other 104mm (4.1in) gun was positioned aft. Ten 37mm (1.5in) machine guns lined the waist of the vessel. *Greif's* engines developed 5,795hp. Range was 7,524km (3,960 miles) at 10 knots, and 3,800km (2,000 miles) at 18 knots. *Greif* was re-armed in 1891. From 1912 she served as a mine hulk until she was scrapped in 1922.

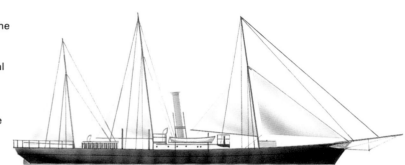

Grille

Type: German royal yacht
Displacement: 499 tonnes (491 tons)
Dimensions: 56.8m x 7.3m x 2.8m (186ft 6in x 24ft 3in x 9ft 4in)
Machinery: Single screw, single expansion engine
Top speed: 13.2 knots
Launched: September 1857
Date of profile: 1858

Grille, Germany's first royal yacht, was laid down in France in 1856. She was a graceful vessel with three masts and one slender sloping funnel. She served until a new royal yacht entered service in the 1890s. *Grille* underwent an extensive refit between 1897 and 1898, and her bowsprit was removed. In 1914 she became a cadet training ship. She was scrapped in 1920.

Grillo

Type: Italian assault craft
Displacement: 8 tonnes (8 tons)
Dimensions: 16m x 3m x 0.7m (52ft 6in x 10ft 2in x 2ft 4in)
Machinery: Single screw, electric motors
Top speed: 4 knots
Main armament: Two 450mm (17.7in) torpedoes

Launched: 1918

Grillo was commissioned in March 1918. She was designed by Engineer Bisio, and was a development of an earlier Bisio design which carried only one torpedo. *Grillo* and her three sister craft were fitted with caterpillar chains to enable them to climb over obstacles. Crew numbered one officer and three in May 1918 but was immediately raised by the Austrians, who used her as a prototype in their attempts to construct a similar vessel.

Grom

Type: Polish destroyer
Displacement: 3,150 tonnes (3,100 tons)
Dimensions: 120.5m x 11.8m x 4.6m (395ft 4in x 38ft 9in x 15ft)
Machinery: Twin screws, turbines
Main armament: Four 130mm (5.1in) guns, two 76mm (3in) anti-aircraft guns

Launched: 1952

Grom was the former Russian destroyer *Smetlivy*, and one in the largest groups of destroyers built for the Russian Navy. The group comprised the first Russian destroyers built after World War II, and their design incorporated several features taken from the successful German destroyers.

Smetlivy transferred from the Russian Navy and became the Polish ship *Grom* in 1957. In 1958 a modernisation programme was put in hand for the remaining Russian vessels in the class.

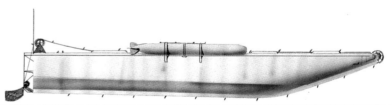

Gromki

Type: Russian destroyer
Displacement: 355 tonnes (350 tons)
Dimensions: 64m x 6.4m x 2.5m (210ft x 21ft x 8ft 6in)
Machinery: Twin screws, vertical triple expansion engines
Top speed: 26 knots
Main armament: One 11-pounder, five three-pounder guns, three 380mm (15in) torpedo tubes
Launched: 1904

Gromki belonged to one of the largest group of destroyers built for the Russian Navy, and formed part of the Second Pacific Squadron. During the Battle of Tsushima in 1905, *Gromki* was set upon by a group of Japanese vessels. After a two-hour running battle, *Gromki* was crippled. She sank at midday on 28 May 1905, two-thirds of her crew having been killed or wounded.

Gromki

Type: Russian destroyer
Displacement: 1,483 tonnes (1,460 tons)
Dimensions: 98m x 9.3m x 3.2m (321ft 6in x 30ft 6in x 10ft 6in)
Machinery: Twin screws, turbines
Main armament: Three 102mm

(4in) guns, ten 457mm (18in) orpedo tubes
Launched: December 1913

Gromki was one of a class of nine destroyers that were reduced versions of the 1,300-tonne (1,280-ton) *Novik*. *Gromki*

formed part of the 1911 naval programme intended to increase the Black Sea Fleet. Design studies had begun in 1907, and revised designs showed a 50-tonne (50-ton) increase in displacement to enable the vessel to carry more armament. Five twin torpedo tubes were carried on the centreline, with one 102mm (4in) gun forward and two aft. Engines developed 25,500hp, but not all the vessels in *Gromki*'s class reached the designed top speed. All ships served in World War I. *Gromki* was scuttled at Sevastopol in June 1918.

Gromki

Type: Russian destroyer
Displacement: 2,070 tonnes (2,039 tons)
Dimensions: 112.8m x 10.2m x 3.8m (370ft 3in x 33ft 6in x 12ft 6in)
Machinery: Twin screws, turbines
Main armament: Two 76mm (3in), four 130mm (5.1in) guns, six 533mm (21in) torpedo tubes

Launched: 1936

Gromki was one of the Russian Type 7 destroyers designed with Italian assistance. As with all pre-World War II designs, the anti-aircraft armament was inadequate, but this was

updated during the war. *Gromki* was laid down at Leningrad in 1936 and completed in 1939.

Engines developed 48,000hp, and oil fuel capacity was 548 tonnes (540 tons), enough for 1,533km (807 miles) at full speed and 4,955km (2,608 miles) at 19 knots. *Gromki* survived the war and was discarded in the 1950s.

Gromoboi

Type: Russian cruiser
Displacement: 12,564 tonnes (12,367 tons)
Dimensions: 144m x 20.7m x 8.8m (472ft 6in x 68ft x 29ft)
Machinery: Triple screws, triple expansion engines
Top speed: 20 knots

Main armament: Sixteen 152mm (6in), four 203mm (8in), twenty 12-pounder guns
Armour: 152mm-thick belt
Launched: May 1899

Gromoboi was a powerful, well-protected vessel. In 1904 she outran a group of Japanese cruisers, making a speed of 18 knots despite being seriously damaged. She was scrapped in 1922.

Grondeur

Type: French torpedo boat
Displacement: 133 tonnes (131 tons)
Dimensions: 45m x 4.4m x 1.3m (147ft 10in x 14ft 6in x 4ft 6in)
Machinery: Twin screws, triple expansion engines
Top speed: 23.5

knots
Main armament: Two 47mm (1.85in) guns, two 355mm (14in) torpedo tubes
Launched: February 1892

Grondeur was a development of the *Coureur*, launched in 1888 to test the new Thornycroft Watertube Boiler which gave the vessel a very high power output compared to weight. *Grondeur* was slightly larger and more strongly constructed than *Coureur*, and living accommodation for the crew was greatly improved. The torpedo tubes were positioned forward and aft. She was sold in 1926.

Grongo

Type: Italian submarine
Displacement: 960 tonnes (945 tons) (surface), 1,130 tonnes (1,113 tons) (submerged)
Dimensions: 63m x 6.9m x 4.8m (207ft 2in x 23ft x 16ft)
Machinery: Twin screws, diesel engines (surface), electric motors (submerged)

Top speed: 16 knots (surface), 7 knots (submerged)
Main armament: One 99mm (3.9in) gun, six 533mm (21in) torpedo tubes
Launched: May 1943

Grongo was one of the first series of boats developed from the Argo class, which had been launched in 1936. *Grongo*'s diesel engines developed 2,400hp, and

surfaced range was 10,260km (5,400 miles) at eight knots. Her electric motors developed 800hp, and submerged range was 128km (80 miles) at four knots or 13 kilometres at seven knots. *Grongo* was scuttled at La Spezia in 1943, but the Germans raised her. She was sunk during an air raid on Genoa in September 1944.

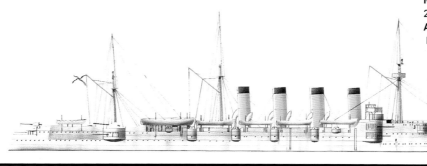
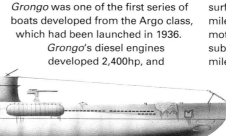
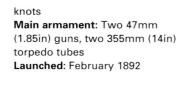

Gröningen

Type: Dutch destroyer
Displacement: 3,119 tonnes (3,070 tons)
Dimensions: 116m x 11.7m x 3.9m (380ft 3in x 38ft 6in x 13ft)
Machinery: Twin screws, turbines
Top speed: 36 knots
Main armament: Four 120mm (4.7in) guns
Launched: January 1954
Date of profile: 1966

Completed in September 1956, *Gröningen* was one of a class of eight post-war vessels that resembled the light cruisers of the war years. They were some of the few destroyers to be built with some side armour as well as deck protection. *Gröningen*'s bridge superstructure ran into her forefunnel, which was surrounded by a cage mast. This held a radar antenna and some electronic warning equipment. Another lattice mast aft held the large rotating antenna for the main surface warning radar. Her armament consisted mainly of conventional dual purpose guns, although they were mounted in fully-automated turrets, and controlled by a radar director. They had a maximum rate of fire of 50 rounds per minute, which demanded sophisticated automatic ammunition winching and handling systems. The large size of this class was partly a result of the increased magazine space needed to take full advantage of these weapons' capabilities. Originally, two of the class were fitted with eight tubes for anti-submarine torpedoes, but these were removed in 1961. *Gröningen* and most of her sisters were never equipped with these weapons, and were thus some of the first destroyers ever built with no torpedo capability. Their anti-submarine capability was limited to two short-range ASW rocket launchers. These ships represent the final development of the gun-armed destroyer, as missiles were just around the corner for this class of ship.

Grosser Kurfürst

Type: German liner
Displacement: 13,392 tonnes (13,182 tons)
Dimensions: 177m x 19m (581ft x 62ft 4in)
Machinery: Twin screws, quadruple expansion engines
Top speed: 16 knots
Launched: December 1899
Date of profile: 1899

Grosser Kurfürst was built for the North German Lloyd Line for service on their North Atlantic and Australian trade routes. She had accommodation for 299 first-class, 317 second-class and 172 third-class passengers plus 2,201 steerage. Her maiden voyage took place in May 1900. In November she began work on the Australian trade route. She was interned in New York upon the outbreak of World War I, and in 1917 was seized, renamed *Aeolus* and entered service for the US Navy. She was handed over to the US Shipping Board in 1919, and in 1922 was renamed *City of Los Angeles*. In 1923 she was fitted out as a luxury cruise liner. She was laid up in 1933 and scrapped in 1937.

Grosser Kurfürst

Type: German battleship
Displacement: 28,598 tonnes (28,148 tons)
Dimensions: 175.7m x 29.5m x 8.3m (576ft 5in x 96ft 9in x 27ft 3in)
Machinery: Triple screws, turbines
Main armament: Eight 86mm (3.4in), fourteen 150mm (5.9in), ten 305mm (12in) guns
Launched: May 1913

Turbines were used in German battleships for the first time on *Grosser Kurfürst* and her three sisters. The ships were greatly improved versions of the Helgolands, and had superfiring guns aft, allowing the broadside to be increased from six to ten 305mm (12in) guns. The vessels in this class were contemporaries of the first British 342mm (13.5in) gunned battleships with similar displacement, but where the British had decided to adopt the heavier guns and have only moderate protection, *Grosser Kurfürst* and her sisters retained the 305mm (12in) guns and used the saving in displacement for greater armour protection. *Grosser Kurfürst* served at Jutland. She surrendered at the end of World War I, and was scuttled at Scapa Flow, along with the rest of the German fleet, in 1919. She was raised and scrapped in 1936.

Grouper

Type: US submarine
Displacement: 1,845 tonnes (1,816 tons) (surface), 2,463 tonnes (2,425 tons) (submerged)
Dimensions: 94.8m x 8.2m x 4.5m (311ft 3in x 27ft 15in)
Machinery: Twin screws, diesel engines (surface), electric motors (submerged)
Launched: October 1941
Date of profile: 1960

Grouper was originally completed as one of the Gato class, and was then converted into one of the first hunter/killer submarines dedicated specifically to destroying enemy missile submarines. The concept required that the hunter/killer submarine be very quiet and carry long-range listening sonar with high bearing accuracy. So equipped, the submarine could lie in wait off enemy bases, or in narrow straits, and intercept the enemy boats as they moved out to patrol.

Grouper was converted in 1951, and in 1958 she became the sonar test submarine for the Underwater Sound Laboratory at New London. The submarine was decommissioned in 1968, and was scrapped in 1970.

Grozyaschi

Type: Russian gunboat
Displacement: 1,653 tonnes (1,627 tons)
Dimensions: 72.2m x 12.6m x 3.7m (237ft x 41ft 6in x 12ft 2in)
Machinery: Twin screws, vertical triple expansion engines
Top speed: 15 knots
Main armament: One

152mm (6in), one 228mm (9in) gun
Launched: May 1890
Date of profile: 1898

Grozyaschi was an armoured gunboat with a well-balanced design for a small ironclad. During World War I, the vessel was re-armed with four 152mm (6in) guns, one firing ahead and three aft. Two sister vessels were lost during the Russo-Japanese War of 1904-05. Grozyaschi was scrapped in 1922.

Guadiana

Type: Portuguese destroyer
Displacement: 670 tonnes (660 tons)
Dimensions: 73.2m x 7.2m x 2.3m (240ft 2in x 23ft 8in x 7ft 6in)
Machinery: Twin screws, turbines
Main armament: One 102mm (4in), two 76mm (3in) guns, four 457mm (18in) torpedo tubes

Launched: September 1914

Guadiana was one of four Yarrow-type destroyers that were assembled in Portugal. At the time the group comprised the largest number of ships ordered by the Portuguese Navy for many years. The 102mm (4in) gun was mounted on a platform on the forecastle, with the two twin torpedo mounts located aft on the centreline separated by two small structures, one of which carried a 76mm (3in) gun. Engines developed 11,000hp, and range at 15 knots was 3,040km (1,600 miles). She was discarded in 1934.

Guadiaro

Type: Spanish minesweeper
Displacement: 782 tonnes (770 tons)
Dimensions: 74.3m x 10.2m x 3.7m (243ft 9in x 33ft 6in x 12ft)
Machinery: Twin screws, triple expansion engines plus exhaust turbines
Top speed: 16 knots

Main armament: Two 20mm (0.8in) anti-aircraft guns
Launched: June 1950

Guadiaro was in the first group of minesweepers built for the Spanish Navy after World War II. The design was modelled on the successful German-designed Bidasoa, launched in 1943. Guadiaro and her six sisters were all modernised between 1959 and 1960.

Guam

Type: US battlecruiser
Displacement: 34,801 tonnes (34,253 tons)
Dimensions: 246m x 27.6m x 9.6m (807ft 5in x 90ft 9in x 31ft 9in)
Machinery: Quadruple screws, turbines
Top speed: 33 knots

Main armament: Twelve 127mm (5in), nine 305mm (12in) guns
Launched: November 1943

Guam and her sister Alaska were built to combat the fast raiders of the German Scharnhorst type then believed to be under construction for the Japanese Navy. Guam was an enlarged version of the cruiser Baltimore, with three triple turrets housing specially designed 305mm (12in) guns and upgraded armour. She was flush-decked, with a single funnel flanked by the cranes for the two catapults which launched the scout planes. Range at 15 knots was 22,800km (12,000 miles). Guam was scrapped in 1961.

Guerriera

Type: Italian armoured battery
Displacement: 2,389 tonnes (2,352 tons)
Dimensions: 56m x 14.4m x 4.2m (183ft 9in x 47ft 4in x 14ft)
Machinery: Single screws, single expansion engines
Main armament: Twelve guns

Launched: May 1866

Guerriera was a wooden-hulled, three-masted ironclad battery laid down in 1864 and completed in 1868. The central battery had sloping sides, and the vessel had a very low freeboard. Engines developed 454hp, and the masts carried steadying sails. The ship was designed for harbour defence and was never intended for sea service. Guerriera was discarded in 1875.

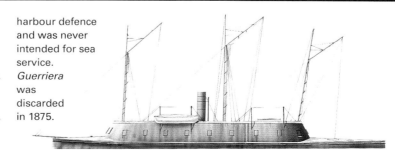

Guerriere

Type: US cruiser
Displacement: 4,017 tonnes (3,954 tons)
Dimensions: 95m x 14m x 6.5m (312ft 6in x 46ft x 21ft 5in)
Machinery: Single screw, horizontal back acting engines
Top speed: 13 knots
Main armament: Two 134mm

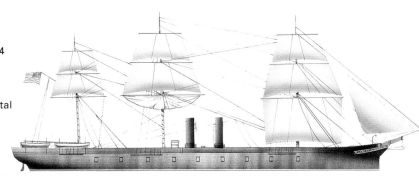

(5.3in), one 162.5mm (6.4in) rifled guns, six 228mm (9in) smoothbores
Launched: September 1865

Guerriere's hull was built of unseasoned oak which quickly deteriorated, all the seasoned timber having been used up during the American Civil War. *Guerriere* was completed as a corvette in 1867, had a spar deck added in 1869-70, and was scrapped in 1872.

Guglielmo Marconi

Type: Italian submarine
Displacement: 1,214 tonnes (1,195 tons) (surface), 1,513 tonnes (1,490 tons) (submerged)
Dimensions: 76.5m x 6.8m x 4.7m (251ft x 22ft 4in x 15ft 5in)
Machinery: Twin screws, diesel engines

(surface), electric motors (submerged)
Main armament: One 100mm

(3.9in) gun, eight 533mm (21in) torpedo tubes
Launched: July 1939

Guglielmo Marconi had a range of some 5,700km (3,000 miles) at 17 knots surfaced, and 19,950km (10,500 miles) at eight knots submerged. Maximum diving depth was 90m (295ft). She was sunk by the German *U-67* while patrolling the Atlantic in late 1941.

Guglielmo Pepe

Type: Italian destroyer
Displacement: 1,235 tonnes (1,216 tons)
Dimensions: 85m x 8m x 2.8m (278ft 10in x 26ft 3in x 9ft 2in)
Machinery: Twin screws, turbines
Top speed: 31.5 knots
Main armament: Six 102mm (4in) guns,

four 450mm (17.7in) torpedo tubes
Launched: September 1914

Guglielmo Pepe was a large, powerful flotilla leader

designed and built by Ansaldo, Genoa. She was one of three units laid down in 1913 and was to have been given eight torpedo tubes, but on completion she was fitted with only four. In 1916 she was given two 76mm (3in) anti-aircraft guns, but these were removed the following year. In 1921 the ship was re-classified as a destroyer and in June 1938 she was transferred to Spain where she was re-named *Teruel* and served until she was scrapped in 1947.

Guichen

Type: French cruiser
Displacement: 8,409 tonnes (8,277 tons)
Dimensions: 133m x 16.7m x 8.2m (436ft 4in x 55ft x 27ft)
Machinery: Triple screws, triple expansion engines

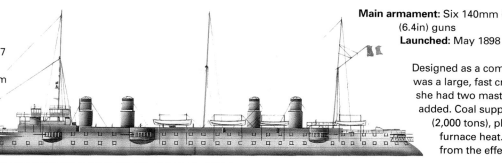

Main armament: Six 140mm (5.5in), two 162mm (6.4in) guns
Launched: May 1898

Designed as a commerce raider, *Guichen* was a large, fast cruiser. As completed she had two masts, but a third was later added. Coal supply was 2,032 tonnes (2,000 tons), plus oil fuel to increase furnace heat. She was removed from the effective list in 1922.

Gurkha

Type: British frigate
Displacement: 2,743 tonnes (2,700 tons)
Dimensions: 109m x 12.9m x 5.3m (360ft x 42ft 4in x 17ft 6in)
Machinery: Single screw, turbine and gas turbine
Top speed: 28 knots
Main armament: Two 114mm (4.5in)

guns, one Limbo three-barrelled anti-submarine mortar
Launched: July 1960

Gurkha was one of seven all-purpose

frigates in the Tribal class. These vessels were among the first ships to be fully air-conditioned in all crew areas and most working spaces. The standard steam turbine developed 12,500hp, and could be boosted by a gas turbine which increased output to 20,000hp. She was very seaworthy, and made good speed even in poor weather.

Gus

Type: Russian hovercraft
Displacement: 27 tonnes (27 tons)
Dimensions: 21.3m x 7.1m (69ft 11in x 23ft 4in)
Machinery: Two aircraft propellers, three gas turbines
Top speed: 60 knots
Launched: 1970

Russia operates the world's largest fleet of commercial hovercraft, and in the 1970s began development and deployment of a large fleet of military vessels. The first model to enter service (and the first air cushion vehicle to enter service in large numbers anywhere in the world) was this small 27-tonne (27-ton) machine with the NATO code-name Gus. This design was actually a development of the civilian machine known to NATO as Skate. The Gus is only able to carry troops, and a full load comprises some 25 marines (Naval Infantry in Russian parlance). Vehicles would have to be carried by the larger Aist or Pomornik classes of hovercraft. The Gus can only carry light weapons for self defence, and instead relies on speed and the area defence systems of an assault task force for protection. Her three gas turbines produce 2340hp, and drive two tractor airscrews via reduction gear. Range is 351km (185 miles) at 50 knots, increasing to 380km (200 miles) at 43 knots. Her main sensor is a simple navigation radar. While vulnerable to bad weather, these vehicles have some advantages for amphibious assaults. They are able to operate in extremely shallow water, and can ride straight onto dry land if the beach is flat enough. Their speed gives them the ability to launch surprise attacks from over the horizon, giving the defenders very little time to react. During the Cold War, the Soviet Navy had large numbers of such vessels available for operations in the Baltic and in the Black Sea.

Gustave Zédé

Type: French submarine
Displacement: 265 tonnes (261 tons) (surface), 274 tonnes (270 tons) (submerged)
Dimensions: 48.5m x 3.2m x 3.2m (159ft x 10ft 6in x 10ft 6in)
Machinery: Single screws, electric motor
Top speed: 9.2 knots (surface), 6.5 knots (submerged)
Main armament: One 450mm (17.7in) torpedo tube
Launched: June 1893

After overcoming some initial problems of inadequate power from the 720-celled batteries, together with their excessive weight which gave her uneven diving qualities, Gustave Zédé became one of the world's first successful submarines. She completed over 2,500 dives without incident. During trials she made the 66km (41 mile) journey from Toulon to Marseille underwater. Gustave Zédé was the first submarine to be fitted with a periscope, and this innovation put France at the forefront of submarine technology. The hull was made up from 76 sections of Roma-bronze, and all the controls in the boat were placed centrally under the conning tower. Gustave Zédé was stricken from the Navy List in 1909.

Gustave Zédé

Type: French submarine
Displacement: 862 tonnes (849 tons) (surface), 1,115 tonnes (1,098 tons) (submerged)
Dimensions: 74m x 6m x 3.7m (242ft 9in x 19ft 8in x 12ft 2in)
Machinery: Twin screws, reciprocating engines (surface), electric motors (submerged)
Top speed: 17.5 knots (surface), 11 knots (submerged)
Main armament: Eight 450mm (17.7in) torpedo tubes
Launched: May 1913
Date of profile: 1914

Gustave Zédé was one of the last steam-driven submarines built for the French Navy, and at the time of her completion in October 1914 she was one of the fastest submarines in the world. Her two reciprocating engines developed 3,500hp, and her electric motors developed 1,640hp. Range was 2,660km (1,400 miles) at 10 knots surfaced, and 256km (135 miles) at 5 knots submerged. In 1921-22 the boat was fitted with diesel engines taken from the ex-German submarine U-165. At the same time Gustave Zédé was fitted with a new bridge, and two of the aft buoyancy tanks were converted to carry diesel fuel. She was stricken from the Navy List in 1937.

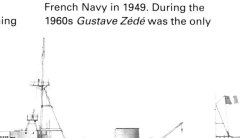

Gustave Zédé

Type: French command ship
Displacement: 3,282 tonnes (3,230 tons)
Dimensions: 93.8m x 13.5m x 4.2m (308ft x 44ft 3in x 14ft)
Machinery: Twin screws, diesel engines
Top speed: 16 knots
Main armament: Three 104mm (4.1in) guns
Launched: April 1934

Gustave Zédé was the former German submarine depot training ship Saar. France acquired her from the USA in October 1947, and after a major refit she was commissioned into the French Navy in 1949. During the 1960s Gustave Zédé was the only ship in the French Navy to carry a fully comprehensive command system. By 1967 the vessel had become the flagship of the Fleet Training Centre.

Gustavo Sampaio

Type: Brazilian torpedo gunboat
Displacement: 487 tonnes (480 tons)
Dimensions: 59.9m x 6.1m x 2.5m (196ft 9in x 20ft x 8ft 6in)
Machinery: Twin screws, triple expansion engines
Main armament: Two 89mm (3.5in) guns, three 406mm (16in) torpedo

tubes
Launched: 1893

Aurora was bought from Britain by Brazil in October 1893 and re-named *Gustavo Sampaio*. She was the second warship to sink a battleship with a torpedo when, on the night of 16 April 1894, she attacked the

ship *Aquidaban* and sank her. Despite sustaining 38 hits, *Gustavo Sampaio* survived. She was discarded in 1920.

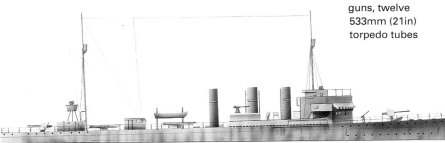

Gwin

Type: US destroyer
Displacement: 1,205 tonnes (1,187 tons)
Dimensions: 96.2m x 9.3m x 2.7m (315ft 7in x 30ft x 9ft)
Machinery: Twin screws, turbines
Top speed: 32 knots
Main armament: Four

102mm (4in) guns, twelve 533mm (21in) torpedo tubes

Launched: December 1917
Date of profile: 1918

Gwin was an early 'flush-decker', many of which served alongside modern counterparts during World War II. She had three funnels and a raised structure amidships that carried two of the 102mm (4in) guns. She was sold in 1939.

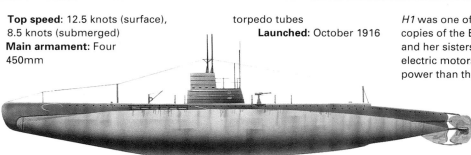

Gymnôte

Type: French submarine
Displacement: 30 tonnes (30 tons) (surface), 31 tonnes (31 tons) (submerged)
Dimensions: 7.3m x 1.8m x 1.6m (58ft 5in x 6ft x 5ft 6in)
Machinery: Single screw, electric motor
Top speed: 7.3 knots (surface), 4.2

knots (submerged)
Main armament: Two 355mm (14in) torpedo tubes
Launched: September 1888

prepared initial designs for *Gymnôte*, but with his death, the plans were revised by Gustave Zédé, who produced a single-hull steel submarine with a detachable lead

keel. Electric power was provided by 204 cells spread along the lower part of the hull. Ordered in 1886, *Gymnôte* made over 2,000 dives in al. She sank in dock at Toulon in 1907, was raised, and scrapped in 1908.

Dupuy de Lôme

H L Hunley

Type: Confederate submarine
Displacement: approx 2 tonnes (2 tons)
Dimensions: 12m x 1m x 1.2m (40ft x 3ft 6in x 4ft)
Machinery: Single screw, hand-propelled
Top speed: 2.5 knots
Main armament: One spar torpedo
Launched: 1863
Date of profile: 1864

H L Hunley was the first true

submarine to be successfully used against an enemy. The main part of the hull was shaped from a cylindrical steam boiler, with the tapered ends added. The craft had a nine-man crew: eight to turn the hand-cranked propeller; one to steer. On 17 February 1864, she sank the Union ship *Housatonic*, but was dragged down with her.

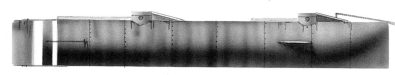

H1

Type: Italian submarine
Displacement: 370 tonnes (365 tons) (surface), 481 tonnes (474 tons)(submerged)
Dimensions: 45.8m x 4.6m x 3.7m (150ft 3in x 15ft 4in x 12ft 5in)
Machinery: Twin screws, diesel engines (surface), electric motors

Top speed: 12.5 knots (surface), 8.5 knots (submerged)
Main armament: Four 450mm

torpedo tubes
Launched: October 1916

H1 was one of eight that were exact copies of the British H class. She and her sisters were unique - their electric motors developed more power than their diesels. *H1* received a 76mm (3in) gun in 1941, served in World War II, and was scrapped in 1947.

H4

Type: US submarine
Displacement: 398 tonnes (392 tons) (surface), 529 tonnes (521 tons) (submerged)
Dimensions: 45.8m x 4.8m x 3.8m (150ft 3in x 15ft 9in x 12ft 6in)
Machinery: Twin screws, diesel engines (surface), electric motors (submerged)

Top speed: 14 knots (surface), 10 knots (submerged)
Main armament: Four 457mm (18in) torpedoes
Launched: October 1918

H4 was ordered for the Russian Tsarist navy but was purchased for the US Navy in 1918.

She was built by the Electric Boat Company. In 1920, H4 was

renumbered SS147. The US H class had a designed depth limit of 6m (20ft) and were very successful boats. H4 was scrapped in 1931.

Haai

Type: Dutch coast defence ship
Displacement: 1,580 tonnes (1,555 tons)
Dimensions: 59.6m x 13.4m x 2.9m (195ft 5in x 44ft x 9ft 9in)
Machinery: Twin screws, compound engines
Top speed: 8 knots
Main armament: Two 228mm (9in)

guns
Launched: 1871

Haai was a monitor with a single turret with two 228mm (9in) guns; she also had a ram bow. She and

four sister vessels, plus a near-sister, formed the first large class of coast-defence ships built for the Dutch Navy. Haai was later rearmed with one 279mm (11in) gun plus lighter guns.

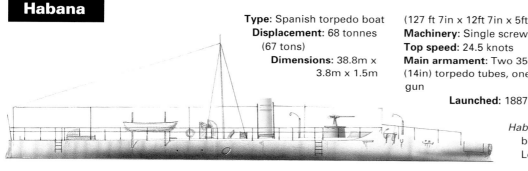

Habana

Type: Spanish torpedo boat
Displacement: 68 tonnes (67 tons)
Dimensions: 38.8m x 3.8m x 1.5m

(127 ft 7in x 12ft 7in x 5ft)
Machinery: Single screw
Top speed: 24.5 knots
Main armament: Two 355mm (14in) torpedo tubes, one machine gun
Launched: 1887

Habana was built in London by

Thornycroft, and was one of 13 first-class boats constructed up to 1887 for the Spanish Navy. Spain had always been in the forefront of naval development, especially in the 1880s, when she possessed a powerful fleet of ironclads that placed her navy sixth in the world. Habana carried her machine gun on the conning tower; the two torpedo tubes were mounted in the bow.

Habsburg

Type: Austrian battleship
Displacement: 8,964 tonnes (8,823 tons)
Dimensions: 114.5m x 19.8m x 7.4m (376ft x 65ft 2in x 24ft 6in)
Machinery: Twin screws, vertical triple expansion engines
Top speed: 19.6 knots

Main armament: Twelve 150mm(5.9in), three 240mm (9.4in) guns
Launched: September 1900

Habsburg was one of a trio of vessels that were the first true Austrian ocean-going battleships since the

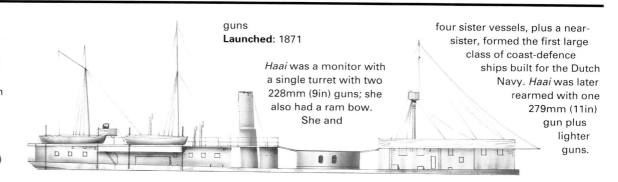

launching of Tegetthoff in 1878. Her top superstructure was removed in 1910/11. After World War I, all three were handed over to Britain and scrapped in 1921.

Hachijo

Type: Japanese escort
Displacement: 1,020 tonnes (1,004 tons)

Dimensions: 77.7m x 9m x 3m (255ft x 29ft 10in x 9ft 10in)
Machinery: Twin screws, diesel engines

Main armament: Three 120mm (4.7in) guns
Launched: April 1940

Hachijo was a prototype for successive classes of Japanese escort. During World War II, her AA armament of four 25mm (1in) guns was increased to 15; her depth-charge load of 12 increased to 25, then 60. She was broken up in 1948.

Hai Lung

Type: Taiwanese submarine
Displacement: 2,414 tonnes (2,376 tons) (surface), 2,702 tonnes (2,660 tons) (submerged)
Machinery: Single screw, diesel engines (surface), electric motors (submerged)
Top speed: 11 knots (surface), 20 knots (submerged)
Main armament: Six 533mm (21in) torpedo tubes
Launched: October 1986
Date of profile: 1989

The small Taiwanese Navy was set up in the 1950s to combat the threat of invasion from mainland China. Two of their most modern and effective warships are the diesel-electric submarines of the Hai Lung (Sea Dragon) class. They are modified Zwaardvis-class submarines sold to Taiwan by the Dutch, and were probably the most efficient conventional submarine design of the 1970s. The Zwaardvis boats were themselves based on the US Barbel class, but had many differences in detail and equipment. They are extremely quiet boats, with all machinery mounted on noise reducing anti-vibration mountings. They have a full range of sophisticated sensors and navigation equipment, and carry up to 28 heavyweight Tigerfish acoustic

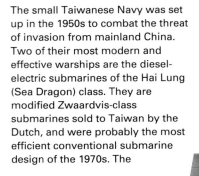

homing torpedoes. They have three diesel engines which provide some 4,200hp, while the single Holec electric motor develops 5,100hp. Their range is over 19,000km (10,000 miles) at 9 knots on the surface, but submerged range is significantly less than this. They have a maximum crew of 67. *Hai Lung* and her sister *Hai Hu* were commissioned in December 1987, and were the first export orders for the Dutch submarine industry. Their delivery was made in the face of strong protests from the Peoples' Republic of China, and a further order for two more boats was barred by the Dutch government.

Hajen

Type: Swedish submarine
Displacement: 108 tonnes (107 tons) (surface), 130 tonnes (127 tons) (submerged)
Dimensions: 19.8m x 3.6m x 3m (65ft x 11ft 10in x 9ft 10in)
Machinery: Single screw, paraffin engine (surface), electric motor (submerged)
Top speed: 9.5 knots (surface), 7 knots (submerged)
Main armament: One 457mm (18in) torpedo tube
Launched: July 1904

Hajen was the first submarine built for the Swedish Navy. She was designed by naval engineer Carl Richson, who had been sent to the USA to study submarine development in 1900. *Hajen* was laid down at Stockholm in 1902. In 1916 she underwent a major rebuild, and her length was increased by 1.8m (6ft). She was withdrawn from service in 1922 and became a museum exhibit.

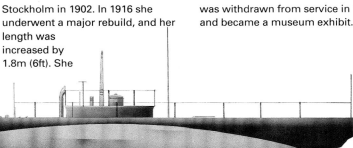

Hakuryu Maru

Type: Japanese steel carrier
Displacement: 5,278 tonnes (5,195 tons)
Dimensions: 115m x 18m x 5m (377ft 4in x 59ft x 16ft 5in)
Machinery: Single screw, diesel engines
Top speed: 15 knots
Launched: 1991

Hakuryu Maru is unusual in that she was built specifically to carry steel coils from the steelworks at Fukuyama to transit ports. The steel cable is transferred to a lift table suspended from four hydraulic cylinders. The table is then lowered to pallet carriers, each with a 90-tonne (88-ton) load capacity, and the steel coils are then stowed in the appropriate cargo spaces. To maximise cargo capacity, one load is left on the table lift while the ship is in transit. Her hull is of a special design, with a deep double bottom and a total of 1,400 tonnes (1,378 tons) of permanent iron and concrete ballast, which is distributed to provide stable sea motion and, most importantly considering the loads involved, to limit heel to three degrees while loading and unloading.

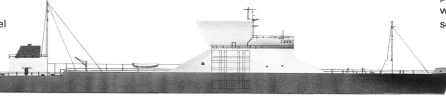

Halla

Type: Korean cement carrier
Displacement: 10,427 tonnes (10,427 tons)
Dimensions: 111.8m x 17.8m x 7m (367ft x 58ft 5in x 23ft)
Machinery: Single screw, diesel engines
Top speed: 13 knots
Launched: January 1991

Halla No 2 is a self-unloading carrier. The cement is carried in two enclosed holds, which are separated by the unloading machinery room. Air is pumped through the cement to move it to the chain conveyors which carry it to the machinery room. There the cement is transferred to a bucket elevator and is lifted to the overside discharge boom, which is suspended from the lattice tower some 22m (72ft) above the main deck. To load the cargo, cement passes from the shore facility into a distribution tank on deck. It is then piped by four air slides into both holds. 1,000 tonnes (984 tons) of cement can be loaded in one hour. Unloading 500 tonnes (492 tons) of cement also takes one hour. It only requires a crew of 27 to handle this very complex vessel.

Hamakaze

Type: Japanese destroyer
Displacement: 2,489 tonnes (2,450 tons)
Dimensions: 118.5m x 10.8m x 3.7m (388ft 9in x 35ft 5in x 12ft 4in)
Machinery: Twin screws, turbines
Main armament: Four 152mm (6in) guns, eight 610mm (24in) torpedo tubes

Launched: November 1940

Hamakaze was the first Japanese destroyer to be fitted with radar. When completed in 1941, she and her 17 sisters were armed with six 152mm (6in)

guns in twin turrets, but in 1943-44 the aft turret on top of the aft superstructure was removed and replaced with additional anti-aircraft guns. The torpedo tubes were

positioned amidships in enclosed quadruple mounts. Only one vessel in the class survived World War II. *Hamakaze* was sunk by US surface ships on 7 April 1945.

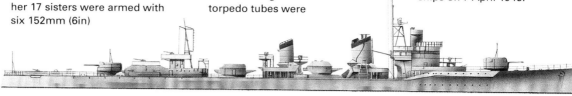

Hamayuki

Type: Japanese destroyer
Displacement: 3,760 tonnes (3,700 tons)
Dimensions: 131.7m x 13.7m x 4.3m (432ft x 45ft x 14ft)
Machinery: Twin screws, gas

turbines
Top speed: 30 knots
Main armament: One 76mm (3in) gun, one eight-cell Sea Sparrow launcher, two Phalanx
Launched: September 1983

Hamayuki was a radical departure from previous Japanese anti-submarine destroyer designs. Although the weapons systems are of US origin, the concept and general layout closely resemble the successful French George Leygues class. The British propulsion machinery consists of two groups of gas turbines, one set developing 56,780hp, and the other 10,680hp.

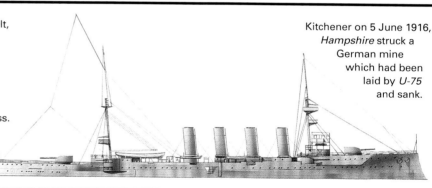

Hampshire

Type: British cruiser
Displacement: 11,023 tonnes (10,850 tons)
Dimensions: 144.3m x 20.8m x 7.3m (473ft 6in x 68ft 6in x 24ft)
Machinery: Twin screws, triple expansion engines
Main armament: Six 152 mm (6in), four 190mm (7.5in) guns

Armour: 51-152mm (2-6in) belt, 127mm (5in) on turrets, 152mm (6in) on casemates, 51mm (2in) on main deck
Launched: September 1903

Hampshire was an improved version of the Monmouth class. Her engines developed 21,508hp. While en route to Russia with Lord

Kitchener on 5 June 1916, *Hampshire* struck a German mine which had been laid by *U-75* and sank.

Han

Type: Chinese submarine
Displacement: 5,080 tonnes (5,000 tons) submerged, surface

displacement tonnage unknown
Dimensions: 90m x 8m x 8.2m (295ft 3in x 26ft 3in x 27ft)

Machinery: Single screw, one pressurised-water nuclear reactor with turbine drive
Top speed: 25 knots submerged
Main armament: Six 533mm (21in) torpedo tubes
Launched: 1972

The Chinese Navy took a

massive leap forward in the early 1970s with its Han-class attack submarines. The highly streamlined hull shape is based upon that of the American vessel *Albacore*, and is a radical departure from previous Chinese submarine designs. Four boats were completed by 1991.

Hancock

Type: American frigate
Displacement: 762 tonnes (750 tons)
Dimensions: 43.8m x 10.8m (144ft x 35ft 6in)
Main armament: Ten six-pounder, twenty-four 12-pounder guns
Launched: 1776

Hancock was the fastest sailing frigate of her era, and was one of the 13 frigates of the Continental Navy authorised by Congress in December 1775. By 1777 *Hancock* was in action against British commerce, and in June of that year she and her fellow frigate *Boston* forced the British frigate *Fox* to surrender. In July *Hancock* was

captured by the British and re-named *Iris*. She served her new owners well until she was captured by the French and used as a cruiser. By 1793 the once-proud ship had become a powder hulk at Toulon. She was blown up there by the British.

Hannover Express

Type: German container ship
Displacement: 76,330 tonnes (75,128 tons)
Dimensions: 294m x

32.2m x 13.5m (964ft 6in x 105ft 10in x 44ft 4in)
Machinery: Single screw, diesel engines
Top speed: 23.8 knots
Launched: October 1990
Date of profile: 1992

Hannover Express was the first in a class of five container ships that were improvements on an already successful design. *Hannover Express* has an increased container-carrying capacity which was made possible, in part, by using high-tensile steel in her construction. The resulting saving in weight allows 11 rows of containers to be stowed in the hull instead of ten. Additionally, re-arranging the longitudinal beams made it possible for the vessel to carry heavy-lift cargoes, which is not usually possible with this type of vessel. Only 21 crew are needed to operate the ship.

Hanoverian

Type: British liner
Displacement: 13,723 tonnes (13,507 tons)
Dimensions: 183.2m x 18.4m (601ft x 60ft 4in)
Machinery: Twin screws, triple expansion engines

Top speed: 15 knots
Launched: February 1902

Date of profile: 1902

Hanoverian served on the North Atlantic, carrying 245 first-class, 250 second-class and 1,000 steerage passengers. In 1904 she transferred to the Mediterranean and was re-named *Mayflower*, then *Cretic*. From 1915 to 1919 she was a troop transport, before resuming her original role as *Devonian*. She was sold for breaking up in 1929.

Hansa

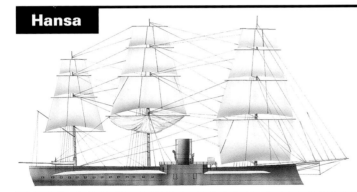

Type: German battleship
Displacement: 4,403 tonnes (4,334 tons)
Dimensions: 73.4m x 14.1m x 6.7m (241ft x 46ft 3in x 22ft 3in)
Machinery: Single screw, horizontal single expansion engines
Top speed: 12.5 knots
Main armament: Eight 210mm (8.25in) guns
Armour: 114-152mm (4.5-6in) main belt, 114mm (4.5in) on central battery
Launched: October 1872

Hansa was the first battleship to be built in Germany. She was laid down at the Danzig Dockyard in 1868 and took seven years to complete. The 210mm (8.25in) guns were carried in a two-tier casemate, with two guns on each side in the lower level, and four firing from corner positions in the upper level. *Hansa* became a training hulk in 1888 and was scrapped in 1906.

Harald Haarfagre

Type: Norwegian coast-defence ship
Displacement: 3,919 tonnes (3,858 tons)
Dimensions: 92.6m x 14.7m x 5.3m (304ft x 48ft 6in x 17ft 8in)
Machinery: Twin screws, triple expansion engines
Main armament: Six 120mm (4.7in), two 208mm (8.2in) guns

Armour: 102-178mm (4-7in) belt, 127-203mm (5-8in) on main turrets
Launched: January 1897

Harald Haarfagre was Norway's first major warship. Built in Britain by Armstrong, she was a compact vessel with engines that developed 3,700hp. Taken over by Germany during World War I, she was converted into a floating anti-aircraft battery re-named *Thetis*.

Harriet Lane

Type: American gunboat
Displacement: 610 tonnes (600 tons)
Machinery: Paddle wheels
Top speed: 9 knots
Main armament: Three 228mm (9in) guns
Launched: November 1857
Date of profile: 1863

Harriet Lane was the first steamer built for the US Treasury Department, and was named after President Buchanan's niece, who had been his main aide at the White House. A wooden-hulled, side-wheel steamer, she was built by William Webb of New York and took part in numerous actions against Confederate forces. She was captured by the Confederates during the struggle for Galveston, and then served in the short-lived Texas Marine Department. She was converted into a blockade runner in 1864. In 1867 she was handed over to the US, sold and re-named *Elliot Richie*. She was abandoned in 1884 off Brazil.

Hartford

Type: American cruiser
Displacement: 2,946 tonnes (2,900 tons)
Dimensions: 68.5m x 13.4m x 5.2m (225ft x 44ft x 17ft 2in)
Machinery: Single screw, twin horizontal condensing engines
Top speed: 13.5 knots
Main armament: Twenty 228mm (9in) guns
Launched: November 1858
Date of profile: 1861

Hartford was laid down in Boston Navy Yard in 1858, and was completed in June

1859. She was given engines that were lighter and more efficient than those in earlier vessels, while burning less coal. She proved to be a good sailor, and was capable of making 7.3 knots under sail and steam in poor

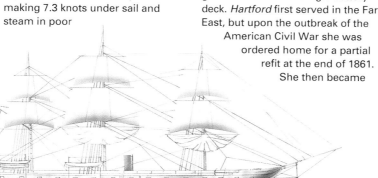

weather. She could managed 9.5 knots for extended periods while in better weather. She was wooden hulled, with a ship rig, and all her guns mounted on a single battery deck. *Hartford* first served in the Far East, but upon the outbreak of the American Civil War she was ordered home for a partial refit at the end of 1861. She then became

the flagship of the Union Admiral Farragut in his drive up the Mississippi, and was permanently on active duty apart from a short break for repairs. It was from this ship that Farragut commanded the raid on Mobile Bay, in his legendary "Damn the Torpedoes" attack. *Hartford* remained in service after the war, and was given new machinery in 1880, and then again in 1887. She then served as a training ship. Finally, she was moved to Norfolk Navy Yard, where she sank at her berth on 20 November 1956.

Haruna

Type: Japanese battlecruiser
Displacement: 32,715 tonnes (32,200 tons)
Dimensions: 214.5m x 28m x 8.4m (703ft 9in x 91ft 10in x 27ft 6in)
Machinery: Quadruple screws, turbines
Main armament: Sixteeen 152mm (6in), eight 355mm (14in) guns
Armour: 76-

203mm (3-8in) belt, 228mm (9in) on turrets
Launched: November 1912

Haruna was one of the first dreadnought-type warships to be laid down in a Japanese yard, and her sister *Kongo* was the last

major Japanese warship to be built abroad. The four ships in *Haruna*'s class originallly had three funnels and light military masts. In 1927-28 *Haruna* underwent a major refit and emerged re-

classified as a battleship. The fore funnel was removed, and the second was enlarged and heightened. Sixteen new boilers were installed, bulges were fitted and the thickness of the armour was increased, thereby increasing the overall total weight from 6,606 tonnes (6,502 tons) to 10,478 tonnes (10,313 tons). *Haruna* was sunk by US aircraft in July 1945. She was broken up in 1946.

Haruna

Type: Japanese destroyer
Displacement: 5,029 tonnes (4,950 tons)
Dimensions: 153m x 17.5m x 5.2m (502ft x 57ft 5in x 17ft)
Machinery: Twin screws, turbines
Main armament: Two 127mm (5in) guns, Sea Sparrow missile

launcher, six 324mm (12.75in) torpedo tubes
Launched: February 1972

Haruna was laid down in March 1970 and completed in February 1973. She and her sister ship *Hiei* are intended to serve as command ships for anti-submarine escort groups. They are unusual vessels, with the entire aft part of the ship devoted to operating facilities for the three large Sea King

anti-submarine helicopters. The midships section is dominated by the hangar, which occupies the full beam of the vessel and extends forward alongside the single broad funnel. The 127mm (5in) guns are mounted forward and are fully automatic, firing up to 40 rounds per minute. Between 1986 and 1987 *Haruna* underwent a major refit to improve her anti-aircraft defensive system.

Hatteras

Type: American gunboat
Displacement: 1,144 tonnes (1,126 tons)
Dimensions: 64m x 10.3m x 5.4m (210ft x 34ft x 18ft)
Machinery: Sidewheel, oscillating (walking beam) engine
Top speed: 8 knots
Main armament: One 20-pounder, four 32-pounder guns
Launched: Unknown
Date of profile: 1862

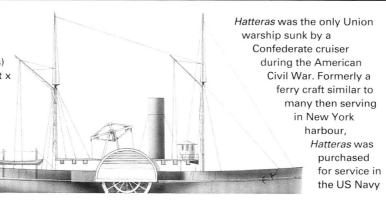

Hatteras was the only Union warship sunk by a Confederate cruiser during the American Civil War. Formerly a ferry craft similar to many then serving in New York harbour, *Hatteras* was purchased for service in the US Navy

in 1861. She had a large, upright frame that supported the arms connected to the steam drum. She also carried a light steadying rig. In 1863 *Hatteras* was on blockade duty off Galveston when she sighted the Confederate raider *Alabama*. Giving chase, *Hatteras* soon found herself well ahead of her supporting force and was defenceless when *Alabama* turned on her and opened fire. *Hatteras* was sunk after a ferocious 13-minute battle.

Havel

Type: German liner
Displacement: 6,985 tonnes (6,875 tons)

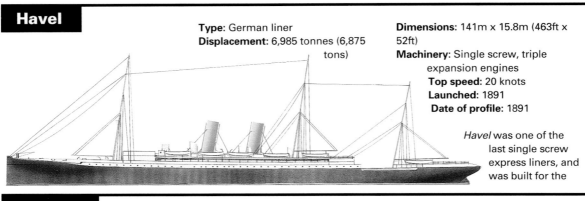

Dimensions: 141m x 15.8m (463ft x 52ft)
Machinery: Single screw, triple expansion engines
Top speed: 20 knots
Launched: 1891
Date of profile: 1891

Havel was one of the last single screw express liners, and was built for the

Norddeutscher Lloyd Line's North Atlantic route. She could carry 244 first-class, 122 second-class and 460 third-class passengers. In 1898 *Havel* was sold to Spain for service as an armed merchant cruiser. Re-named *Meteoro*, she was part of the squadron assigned to re-capture the Philippines. In 1899 she transferred to the Spanish CIA Trasatlantica and was re-named *Alfonso XII*. She was scrapped in Italy in 1926.

Havock

Type: British destroyer
Displacement: 243.8 tonnes (240 tons)
Dimensions: 54.8m x 5.6m x 3.3m (180ft x 18ft 6in x 11ft)
Machinery: Twin screws, triple expansion engines
Top speed: 26 knots
Main armament: One 12-

pounder, three six-pounder guns, three torpedo tubes
Launched: August 1893

Havock was the world's first true destroyer. In 1892 Alfred Yarrow was asked to prepare an answer to

the French torpedo craft then being built. *Havock* was completed in 1894. Ten watertight bulkheads divided the vessel into 11 compartments. Her 12-pounder gun

was carried on a platform forward, and there were two six-pounders in the waist and one aft. On trials, *Havock* proved to be a good, fast sea vessel with very little vibration or heel under full helm. She was scrapped in 1912.

Helena

Type: Swedish cargo vessel
Displacement: 22,548 tonnes (22,193 tons)
Dimensions: 169m x 25.6m x 7m (554ft 6in x 84ft x 23ft)
Machinery: Single screw, diesel engines
Top speed: 14.6 knots
Launched: 1990

Helena is one of a new generation of roll-on, roll-off freighters designed to carry a mixed cargo consisting of paper products, trailers, small cars and containers. She has a full-length double bottom, plus a double skin in the lower cargo areas and engine room. Traffic when loading is two-way, and all her four decks are inter-

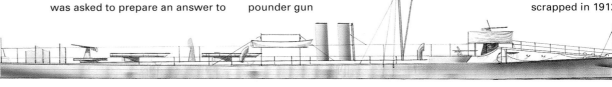

connected by ramps. All cargo-handling operations are monitored by closed-circuit on display units in the wheelhouse and in the engine room control centre. *Helena* entered service in August 1991 and operates between Sweden and other European countries.

Helgoland

Type: Danish battleship
Displacement: 5,417 tonnes (5,332 tons)
Dimensions: 79m x 18m x 5.8m (259ft 7in x 59ft x 19ft 4in)

Machinery: Twin screws
Top speed: 13.7 knots
Main armament: One 304mm (12in), four 260mm (10.2in) guns
Armour: 203-304mm (8-12in) belt, 254mm (10in) on turret and central battery
Launched: May 1878

For many years, *Helgoland* was Denmark's largest

warship. The battery housing the four 260mm (10.2in) guns was situated amidships, with the sides of the hull on each side of the battery recessed to allow for end-on fire. Forward was a single turret housing the 304mm (12in) gun. Two 127mm (5in) guns were also carried, one fore and one aft. A small outfit of sails could be carried on the two masts. *Helgoland* was removed from the effective list in about 1907.

Helgoland

Type: German battleship
Displacement: 24,700 tonnes (24,312 tons)
Dimensions: 166.4m x 28.5m x 8.3m (546ft x 93ft 6in x 27ft 6in)
Machinery: Triple screws, triple expansion engines
Main armament: Fourteen 150mm

(5.9in), twelve 304mm (12in) guns
Armour: 102-300mm (4-11.8in) belt, 280mm (11in) on turrets, 76-170 (3-6.7in) on casemates
Launched: 1909

Helgoland was the last three-funnelled German battleship,

and the first to adopt the 304mm (12in) gun as a main armament. All ships in her class served in World War I, two being damaged at the Battle of Jutland in 1916. *Helgoland* was broken up in 1924.

Helice

Type: Norwegian cargo vessel
Displacement: 50,292 tonnes (49,500 tons)
Dimensions: 205m x 32.2m x 13m (672ft 7in x 105ft 8in x 42ft 8in)
Machinery: Single screw, diesel engines

Top speed: 16 knots
Launched: September 1990

Helice has four cargo holds in which free-standing

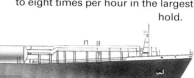

prismatic tanks constructed from carbo-manganese steel have been built. In addition, two control, or purge, tanks are situated on deck. The engine room is fully automated

for unmanned operation. *Helice* carries mixed cargo, and each tank is cooled by two huge fans. If necessary, the air can be changed up to eight times per hour in the largest hold.

Henri IV

Type: French battleship
Displacement: 8,948 tonnes (8,807 tons)
Dimensions: 108m x 22.2m x 6.9m (354ft 4in x 73ft x 23ft)
Machinery: Triple screws, triple expansion engines

Main armament: Seven 140mm (5.5in), two 274mm (10.8in) guns
Armour: 76-390mm (3-11in) belt, 305mm (12in) on main turrets
Launched: August 1899

Henri IV was unusual in that weight was saved by cutting down the aft hull leaving very little freeboard. The 274mm (10.8in) guns were carried one forward on

the raised superstructure 8.5m (28ft) above the water, and one in the aft turret 4.8m (16ft) above the water. The belt was 2m (7ft) deep, with just over half the depth below the waterline. The decks were flat and armoured. She also had lateral armoured bulkheads. Total weight of armour was about 3,556 tonnes (3,500 tons). *Henri IV* was stricken in 1921.

Henri Grâce à Dieu

Type: British battleship
Displacement: 1,016 tonnes (1,000 tons) (approx)
Dimensions: Unknown
Main armament: Twenty-one heavy bronze guns, 130 iron guns, 100 hand guns
Launched: 1514
Date of profile: 1545

Henri Grâce à Dieu was commissioned by Henry VIII as a replacement for the 6010-tonne (600-ton) *Regent,* which was lost in action in 1512. Upon completion, the new ship was the largest warship in the world, with only the Portuguese *Santa Catarina Do Monte Sinai* coming anywhere near her in size. *Henri Grâce à Dieu* was built at Deptford on the River Thames. She was carrack-built with

a very high forecastle and poop. She had four masts and carried a large spread of heavily ornate golden sails. Square sails were carried on the fore and main masts, with lateen sails on the two mizzen masts. She was re-built between 1536 and 1539. *Henri Grâce à Dieu* was accidentally destroyed by fire in 1553.

Henri Poincaré

Type: French submarine
Displacement: 1,595 tonnes (1,570 tons) (surface), 2,117 tonnes (2,084 tons) (submerged)
Dimensions: 92.3m x 8.2m x 4.7m (302ft 10in x 27ft x 15ft 5in)
Machinery: Twin screws, diesel engines (surface), electric motors

(submerged)
Main armament: One 82mm (3.2in) gun, plus two 400mm (15.7in) and nine 550mm (21.7in) torpedo tubes
Launched: April 1929
Date of profile: 1933

Henri Poincaré was one of 29 double-hulled ocean-going submarines laid down between 1925 and 1931. The vessel was scuttled at

Toulon in 1942, but was salvaged by the Italians and returned to Genoa for overhaul. As *FR118*, she was sunk in September 1943 after being seized by German forces.

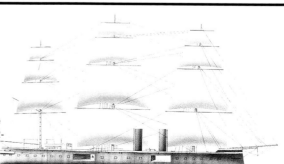

Hercules

Type: British battleship
Displacement: 8,971 tonnes (8,830 tons)
Dimensions: 99m x 18m x 7.6m (324ft 10in x 59ft x 25ft)
Machinery: Single screw, horizontal truck engines
Main armament: Four 178mm (7in), two 228mm (9in), eight 254mm

(10in) muzzle-loading guns
Armour: 152-228mm belt, 203mm on battery
Launched: February 1868

Hercules was a 'one-off' design developed from the *Bellerophon*, but with better armour and weight distribution that made her much steadier in bad weather. She had a pointed ram and no poop, the upper line of the hull being a complete sweep. She was re-engined in 1892-93 after which re-fit she was placed in reserve and then served as a training ship until she was sold in 1932.

Hermes

Type: British aircraft carrier
Displacement: 13,208 tonnes (13,000 tons)
Dimensions: 182.9m x 21.4m x 6.5m (600ft x 70ft2in x 21ft 6in)
Machinery: Twin screws, turbines
Top speed: 25 knots
Main armament: Three 102mm (4in), six 140mm (5.5in) guns
Aircraft: 20
Launched: 1919
Date of profile: 1933

Hermes was the first true purpose-designed aircraft carrier to be ordered by any navy, and her configuration became the accepted pattern for future ships. She was laid down in 1917, but was not completed until 1924, and was thus beaten into service by the Japanese carrier *Hosho*. The Royal Navy intended to operate her alongside a cruiser squadron, with her aircraft providing reconnaissance at long ranges. To meet this requirement, she was built along cruiser lines, with similar powerful machinery enabling her to make high speeds. Her hull had a cruiser form, with the main deck providing the strength. Above this was a 122m (400ft) hangar deck, surmounted by the full length open flight deck, which had a considerable rise aft. Her bridge, funnel, command centre and masts were all grouped in a large island on the starboard side of the flight deck, leaving it clear for its whole length. Her 150mm (5.9in) guns were set in the hull, while the smaller weapons were mounted on the starboard edge of the flight deck. She could not carry many aircraft, and in 1940 her air wing comprised only 12 fighters. For 15 years she was the only true carrier in Royal Navy service, and gained a great deal of experience that would be vital in the war to come. Her wartime career was actually relatively short, as she was attacked and sunk by Japanese aircraft off Ceylon on 9 April 1942.

Hermes

Type: British aircraft carrier
Displacement: 25,290 tonnes (24,892 tons)
Dimensions: 224.6m x 30.4m x 8.2m (737ft x 100ft x 27ft)
Machinery: Twin screws, turbines
Top speed: 29.5 knots
Main armament: Thirty-two 40mm (1.6in) guns
Aircraft: 42
Launched: February 1953

In 1943 designs were drawn up for a class of eight carriers with machinery twice as powerful as that installed in the earlier Colossus class. Armour was to be improved, and a stronger flight deck was planned to handle the new, heavier aircraft then entering service. Eventually, only four ships in the class were laid down and the Admiralty decided to scrap these while they were still on the stocks at the end of World War II.

However, due to the inability of many existing carriers to handle the new jet aircraft, construction was continued. After several design changes, *Hermes* was finally completed in 1959. By 1979 she was handling the new Harrier vertical take-off jets. In 1982 she served as flagship in the Falklands. She was put on reserve in 1984.

Heroine

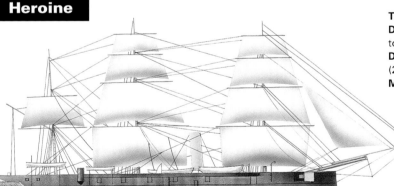

Type: British cruiser
Displacement: 1,442 tonnes (1,420 tons)
Dimensions: 60.9m x 11.5m x 4.8m (200ft x 38ft x 15ft 9in)
Machinery: Single screw, horizontal compound engines
Main armament: Eight 152mm (6in) guns
Launched: December 1881

Designed by Nathaniel Barnaby, *Heroine* was one of a class of seven vessels built in the Naval Dockyards. They were originally classed as sloops, but in 1884 they were uprated to corvettes. All the ships in *Heroine*'s class were wooden-hulled, but uniquely for such vessels, they were given a 19-25.4mm (10in) thick protective steel deck which extended 22m (72ft) and covered the vitals. *Heroine*'s engines developed 1,470hp, and her range at 10 knots was 11,400km (6,000 miles). She was sold in 1902.

Hibernian

Type: British liner
Displacement: 1,918 tonnes (1,888 tons)
Dimensions: 85m x 11.5m (280ft x 38ft)
Machinery: Single screw, inverted engines
Launched: 1861

By the late 1850s, the number of passengers travelling to America had greatly increased, and all the major steamship companies were building additional vessels to cater for the growing trade. Built for the Allan Line, *Hibernian* served on the Liverpool to Canada route. Accommodation was for 80 first-class and 450 third-class passengers. In 1884 she was given compound engines and her masts were reduced to two. She was scrapped in 1921.

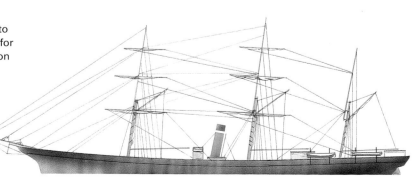

Hiei

Type: Japanese cruiser
Displacement: 2,235 tonnes (2,200 tons)
Dimensions: 70m x 12.4m x 5.3m (229ft 8in x 40ft 8in x 17ft 4in)
Machinery: Single screw, reciprocating horizontal compound engine
Main armament: Six 150mm (5.9in), three 170mm (6.7in) guns

Armour: 89-114mm (3.5-4.5in) belt
Launched: June 1877

Designed and built in Britain, *Hiei* was one of three vessels that formed the foundation of the Japanese battle fleet. In 1895, after suffering severe damage in action with Chinese battleships at the Battle of Yalu in 1894, *Hiei's* topmasts were removed and her barque rig was reduced. From 1898 she was a survey ship, until she was discarded in 1911.

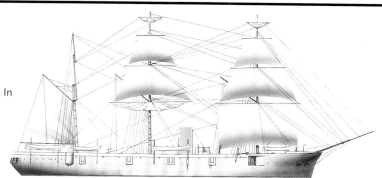

Highland Chieftain

Type: British liner
Displacement: 14,357 tonnes (14,131 tons)
Dimensions: 166m x 21m x 8.5m (544ft 6in x 69ft x 28ft 1in)
Machinery: Twin screws, diesel engines
Top speed: 15 knots
Launched: June 1928

In the 1920s, the development of the motor ship reached a new peak with the laying down of the *Highland Chieftain* and her four sister ships.

Although not fast, they were quite economical to run and only required 10,000hp to drive them at a steady 15 knots. Accommodation was for 135 first-class

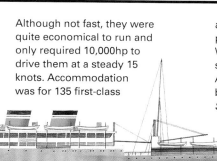

and 66 intermediate-class passengers, plus 600 steerage. After World War II, *Highland Chieftain* served on the London to South America route until she was sold to become the whaling ship *Calpean Star* in 1958. While under tow off Montevideo in 1960, an engine-room explosion caused her to become grounded and she became a total loss.

Himalaya

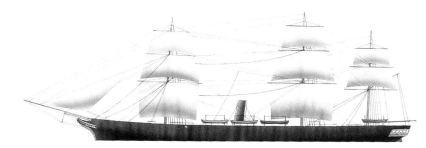

Type: British liner
Displacement: 4,765 tonnes (4,690 tons)
Dimensions: 103.7m x 14m x 6.5m (340ft 5in x 46ft 2in x 21ft 5in)
Machinery: Single screw, horizontal direct-acting trunk engines
Top speed: 14 knots
Launched: May 1853

In 1851 the Peninsular and Oriental Steam Navigation Company

decided to build a large iron-hulled paddle steamer, but while still under construction, *Himalaya* was converted to screw propulsion. She entered service in 1854, but proved to be too expensive to run and was sold to the British government as a troop ship. She served during the Crimean War, and became a depot ship during World War I. In 1920 she was sold as a coal hulk. She was sunk at Portland in 1940.

Hoche

Type: French battleship
Displacement: 10,993 tonnes (10,820 tons)
Dimensions: 102.6m x 20.2m x 8.3m (336ft 8in x 66ft 4in x 27ft 3in)
Machinery: Twin screws, vertical compound engines
Main armament: Eighteen 140mm

(5.5in), two 274mm (10.8in), two 340mm (13.4in) guns
Armour: 254-450mm (10-

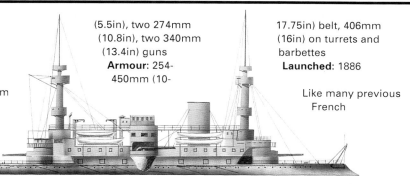

17.75in) belt, 406mm (16in) on turrets and barbettes
Launched: 1886

Like many previous French

battleships, *Hoche* carried her main guns in the lozenge-shaped layout, but the two fore and aft guns were carried in turrets instead of being mounted in open barbettes, and had wide arcs of fire. Laid down in 1881, *Hoche* was completed in 1890. She was re-engined in 1898-99, and her high superstructure was reduced to improve stability. She was sunk as a target in 1913.

Holland No 1

Type: US submarine
Displacement: 2.2 tonnes (2.2 tons)
Dimensions: 4.4m x 0.9m (14ft 6in x 3ft)
Machinery: Single screw, petrol engine
Launched: May 1878
Date of profile: 1878

Holland No 1 was John P. Holland's first successful submarine design. The diminutive craft was originally to have been hand-cranked like previous submarines, but with the introduction of the newly developed Brayton four-horsepower petrol engine, Holland was able to produce a more reliable vessel. *Holland No 1* was built at the Albany Iron Works

and was completed in 1878. After successful trials the engine was removed and she was scuttled in 4.2m (14ft) of

water on the Upper Passaic River. Years later she was raised, and she is now housed in the Paterson Museum, USA.

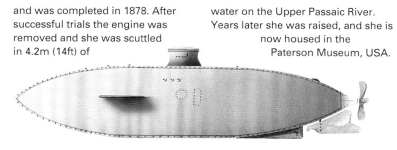

Holland VI

Type: US submarine
Displacement: 64 tonnes (63tons)
(surface), 76 tonnes (74 tons)
(submerged)
Dimensions: 16.3m x 3.1m x 3.5m
(53ft 3in x 10ft 3in x 11ft 6in)
Machinery: Single screw, petrol
engine (surface), electric motor
(submerged)

Top speed: 8 knots (surface), 5 knots
(submerged)
Main armament: One pneumatic
gun, one 457mm (18in) torpedo tube
Launched: May 1897

Holland VI was the first modern US
submarine, and later became the
prototype for British and Japanese
submarines which combined petrol
engine and battery power with

hydroplanes. *Holland VI* entered
service with the US Navy as *Holland*
in 1900. Her petrol engines
developed 45hp and her electric

motors 75hp when submerged.
Diving depth was 22.8m (75ft). She
served as a training ship until 1905,
was re-numbered *SS1*, and scrapped
in 1913.

Hood

Type: British battlecruiser
Displacement: 45,923 tonnes
(45,200 tons)
Dimensions: 262m x 31.7m x 8.7m
(860 ft x 104ft x 28ft 6in)
Machinery: Quadruple screws,
turbines
Top speed: 32
knots

Main armament: Twelve
140mm (5.5 in), eight
381mm (15in) guns
Launched: August 1918

After the Battle of
Jutland in 1916, in
which

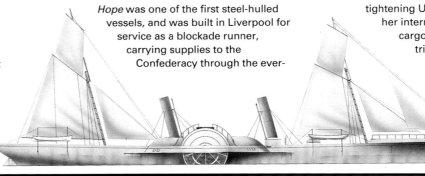

three of Britain's battlecruisers blew
up, designs were put in hand for a
more well-
protected
vessel. *Hood*
was to have

been the first of four such ships, but
was the only one completed. Her
engines developed 144,000hp, and
range was 7,600km (4,000 miles) at
10 knots. She was sunk on 21 May
1941 during an encounter with the
German battleship *Bismarck* and
the cruiser *Prinz Eugen*.

Hope

Type: Confederate blockade runner
Displacement: 1,727 tonnes (1,700 tons)
Dimensions: 85.6m x 10.6m x 2.4m (281ft x
35ft x 8ft)
Machinery: Paddle wheels, two-cylinder
oscillating engine
Top speed: 16 knots
Launched: 1864

Hope was one of the first steel-hulled
vessels, and was built in Liverpool for
service as a blockade runner,
carrying supplies to the
Confederacy through the ever-

tightening Union stranglehold. Over half
her internal space was given over to
cargo. After several successful
trips, *Hope* was captured by
USS *Eolus* in 1864. She
was sold and re-named
Savannah in 1865,
and in 1866 she
was sold to
Spain and
was broken
up in 1885.

Hosho

Type: Japanese aircraft carrier
Displacement: 10,160 tonnes (10,000
tons)
Dimensions: 168m x 21.3m x 6m

(551ft 6in x 70ft x 20ft 3in)
Machinery: Twin screws, turbines
Top speed: 25 knots
Main armament: Four 140mm (5.5in)
guns
Aircraft: 26

Launched: 1921

Hosho was the
world's first
commissioned

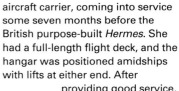

aircraft carrier, coming into service
some seven months before the
British purpose-built *Hermes*. She
had a full-length flight deck, and the
hangar was positioned amidships
with lifts at either end. After
providing good service,
Hosho was relegated to
secondary duties by
the 1930s. She was
scrapped in 1947.

Housatonic

Type: US cruiser
Displacement: 1,964 tonnes (1,934
tons)
Dimensions: 62m x 11.5m x 5m
(205ft x 38ft x 16ft 6in)
Machinery: Single screw, horizontal
direct-acting engines
Top speed: 10 knots
Main armament: One 280mm (11in),

one 100-pounder, three 30-pounder guns
Launch date: 1861

Housatonic was laid down in 1861 as part of the
Union Navy's expansion programme, and in 1862
she briefly engaged the Confederate ironclad
Chicora off Charleston. In 1864 *Housatonic* was
attacked by the Confederate submarine *H. L.
Hunley*, which succeeded in exploding a spar
torpedo under her hull. *H. L. Hunley* was dragged
down by the sinking ship and all her crew were lost.

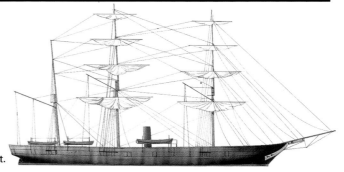

Huascar

Type: Peruvian battleship
Displacement: 2,062 tonnes (2,030 tons)
Dimensions: 60.9m x 10.6m x 5.5m (200ft x 35ft x 18ft)
Machinery: Single screw, single expansion engine
Top speed: 12.3 knots
Main armament: Two 254mm (10in), two 40-pounder guns
Armour: 102-127mm (4-5in) belt, 203mm (8in) on turret face, 152mm (6in) on turret sides
Launched: October 1865
Date of profile: 1865

Huascar was built at Birkenhead, England, for the Peruvian Navy. She was remarkably small and light, with an iron hull and low freeboard. She had an armoured belt some 127mm (5in) thick amidships, which tapered to 63mm (2.5in) at the ends. There were two transverse armoured bulkheads which protected vital spaces and equipment from raking fire. She also had a 51mm (2in) thick armoured deck. Her 254mm (10in) main armament was mounted in a single, heavily protected Coles turret, mounted low on the main deck aft of the foremast but in front of the light bridge. The freeboard at this point was only 1.52m (5ft), and when the ship was not in action, hinged metal bulwarks were raised to give the deck some protection. She had a raised forecastle and ram bow, while her mainmast was a light tripod design. She fought her first action in May 1877, against two British warships, after her crew had mutinied. She was one of only two effective Peruvian warships in the 1879 war with Chile. In October 1879, she was caught by two Chilean ironclads, and surrendered after a hard fight. She was then rebuilt and used by Chile. She is now preserved as a museum ship.

Hudson Rex

Type: Panamanian cargo carrier
Displacement: 12,192 tonnes (12,000 tons)

Dimensions: 148.5m x 20.6m x 9.4m (487ft 3in x 67ft 7in x 31ft)
Machinery: Single screw, diesel engines
Top speed: 19.2 knots
Launched: October 1991

The design of *Hudson Rex* saw a move away from modern, fully automated cargo-handling methods to the conventional derrick booms used previously in large cargo vessels. She carries eight derrick booms, one for each cargo hold, and these are operated by electro-hydraulic winches. Fans supply cold air to the refrigerated area, and there is also a comprehensive insulation system. The refrigeration system is installed in the engine room, which also houses the single main engine. Steam is supplied by a composite boiler, and power for all electrical requirements is supplied by three alternators. Temperature control is monitored from the main control centre in the engine room.

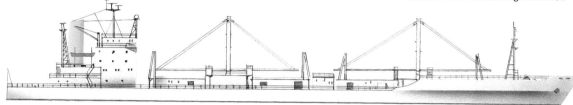

Humber

Type: British monitor
Displacement: 1,544 tonnes (1,520 tons)
Dimensions: 81m x 14.9m x 1.7m (266ft 9in x 49ft x 5ft 8in)
Machinery: Twin screws, triple expansion engines
Top speed: 9.6 knots
Main armament: Two 152 (6in) mm guns, two 120mm (4.7in) mortars
Armour: 76mm (3in) on hull, 51mm (2in) thick deck over magazines

Launched: June 1913

Humber was originally named *Javary*. She was one of a trio of light-draught monitors built for Brazil and taken over by the Royal Navy at the start of World War I. As first completed, the ship almost achieved her designed speed of 12 knots, but alterations increased the draught, so reducing *Humber*'s speed to 9.6 knots. In 1915 she served off the beaches of the Dardanelles and in 1916 was laid up in Alexandria, where she was re-fitted and given new guns. In 1918 she was sent to Mudros. After the Armistice, she spent three months in Istanbul before returning to Britain in 1919. In 1920 she was sold to a Dutch salvage company and converted to a crane barge, and was still serving in this capacity at the outbreak of World War II. She was broken up some time after 1945.

Humboldt

Type: US liner
Displacement: 2,387 tonnes (2,350 tons)
Dimensions: 85.9m x 12m (282ft x 40ft)
Machinery: Paddle wheels, side-lever engines
Top speed: 10 knots
Launched: 1850
Date of profile: 1853

Humboldt was one of the pioneer steamships of the New York and Le Havre Steam Navigation Company, which had been set up to take over the US mail contract formerly handled by the Ocean Steam Navigation Company. *Humboldt* entered service in 1851, and successfully plied the route between New York, Southampton and Le Havre until she was wrecked on the Sister's Rock off Halifax, Nova Scotia, in 1853. The loss was due to a local fisherman who had falsely claimed to be an experienced pilot.

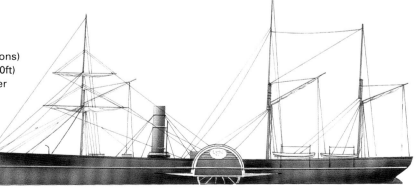

Hunley

Type: US submarine tender
Displacement: 19.304 tonnes (19,000 tons)
Dimensions: 182.6m x 25.3m x 8.2m (599ft x 83ft x 27ft)
Machinery: Single screw, diesel/electric engines
Main armament: Four 20mm (0.8in) guns

Launched: September 1961

Hunley and her sister *Holland* were specifically designed to provide repair and supply services to fleet ballistic missile submarines, and were commissioned in June 1962. *Hunley* has 52 separate workshops and can handle several submarines at once. She also has a helicopter platform. Her crew numbers about 2,500 men.

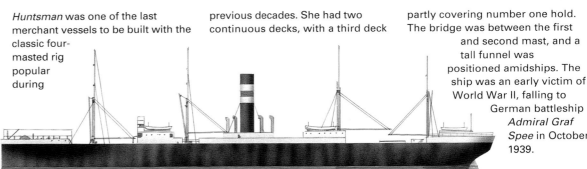

Huntsman

Type: British cargo vessel
Displacement: 12,151 tonnes (11,960ft)
Dimensions: 153m x 17.6m x 8.4m (502ft x 58ft x 27ft 6in)
Machinery: Single screw, turbines
Top speed: 13 knots
Launched: July 1921
Date of profile: 1921

Huntsman was one of the last merchant vessels to be built with the classic four-masted rig popular during previous decades. She had two continuous decks, with a third deck partly covering number one hold. The bridge was between the first and second mast, and a tall funnel was positioned amidships. The ship was an early victim of World War II, falling to German battleship *Admiral Graf Spee* in October 1939.

Huntsville

Type: Confederate ironclad
Displacement: not recorded
Dimensions: 45m x 10.3m x 3.2m (150ft x 34ft x 10ft 6in)
Machinery: not recorded (single screw)
Top speed: 3 knots
Main armament: One 162.5mm (6.4in), three 32-pounder guns

Launched: February 1863

Huntsville was one of a quartet of ironclads ordered by the Confederate Navy and built at Selma, Alabama. One of the ships was never completed, but *Huntsville* formed a pair with her sister *Tuscaloosa*. The fourth vessel was *Tennessee*. *Huntsville* had a low freeboard hull surmounted by a long armoured casemate which housed the guns. The 162.5mm (6.4in) gun was positioned forward, while the 32-pounders were on the broadside, with one able to fire aft. In company with *Tennessee*, *Huntsville* was towed to Mobile to receive her machinery. When Mobile fell to Union forces, *Huntsville* and *Tuscaloosa* were ordered up the Tombigbee River where they were scuttled on 12 April 1864.

Hvalen

Type: Swedish submarine
Displacement: 189 tonnes (186 tons) (surface), 233 tonnes (230 tons) (submerged)
Dimensions: 42.4m x 4.3m x 2.1m (139ft x 14ft x 6ft 11in)
Machinery: Single screw, petrol engines (surface), electric motors (submerged)
Top speed: 14.8 knots (surface), 6.3 knots (submerged)
Main armament: Two 457mm (18in) torpedo tubes
Launched: 1909

Hvalen was the only large submarine to be constructed for Sweden by a foreign power. She was bought from the Italian firm of Fiat-San Giorgio so that the Swedes could examine a leading European design, and she made headline news with her epic 7,600km (4,000 miles) voyage from Italy to Sweden without escort. *Hvalen* was removed from the effective list in 1919 and sunk as a target in 1924. Later the wreck was raised and scrapped.

Hydra

Type: Greek battleship
Displacement: 4,885 tonnes (4,808 tons)
Dimensions: 102m x 15.8m x 5.4m (334ft 8in x 51ft 10in x 18ft)
Machinery: Twin screws, vertical triple expansion engines

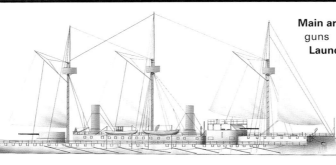

Main armament: Five 150mm (5.9in), three 274mm (10.8in) guns
Launched: 1889

Hydra was of an unusual design, with two of the 274mm (10.8in) guns mounted in the top storey of a two-tier battery situated forward. The lower tier housed four of the 150mm (5.9in) guns, and the fifth was positioned under the bridge. *Hydra* was re-fitted in 1900 and given two military masts.

Hyundai Admiral

Type: South Korean container ship
Displacement: 62,131 tonnes (61,153 tons)
Dimensions: 275m x 37m x 13.6m (902ft 3in x 121ft 9in x 44ft 7in)
Machinery: Single screw, diesel engines
Launch date: 1992

Fitted with the world's most powerful diesel engine (developing over 67,000bhp), *Hyundai Admiral* is the first of five new large container ships built at the massive Hyundai shipyard at Ulsan, South Korea, and designed for service on the Far East/West coast shipping routes of the Hyundai Corporation. The ship is largely automated, with surveillance monitors in each control centre enabling a single watchkeeping system to be employed. There are seven holds, which can carry over 4,400 containers. There is an area for dangerous cargo situated in the fore holds. *Hyundai Admiral* has a double hull, and the rigidity of it is maintained by box passages. Her single propeller weighs 82.5 tonnes (81 tons).

I 7

Type: Japanese submarine
Displacement: 2,565 tonnes (2,525 tons) (surface), 3,640 tonnes (3,583 tons) (submerged)
Dimensions: 109.3m x 9m x 5.2m (358ft 7in x 29ft 6in x 17ft)
Machinery: Twin screws, diesel engines (surface), electric motors (submerged)
Main armament: One 140mm (5.5in) gun, six 533mm (21in) torpedo tubes, one light floatplane
Launched: July 1935

I7 and her sister *I8* were the largest submarines built for the Japanese Navy prior to World War II. Both operated as long-range scouts with a surfaced range of 26,600km (14,000 miles) at 16 knots. *I7* was badly damaged by USS *Monaghan* in July 1943, and was scuttled by her crew to prevent her capture.

I 21

Type: Japanese submarine
Displacement: 728 tonnes (717 tons) (surface), 1,063 tonnes (1,047 tons) (submerged)
Dimensions: 65.6m x 6m x 4.2m (215ft 3in x 19ft 8in x 13ft 9in)
Machinery: Twin screws, diesel engines (surface), electric motors (submerged)
Top speed: 13 knots (surface), 8 knots (submerged)
Main armament: Five 457mm (18in) torpedo tubes
Launched: November 1919

One of two vessels that were Japan's first ocean-going submarines, *I21* was built from Italian plans of the Fiat-Laurenti F1 type. She was built at Kawasaki Kobe and completed in 1920. Her number changed to *RO-2* in 1924. She was stricken in 1930.

I 201

Type: Japanese submarine
Displacement: 1,311 tonnes (1,291 tons) (surface), 1,473 tonnes (1,450 tons) (submerged)
Dimensions: 79m x 5.8m x 5.4m (259ft 2in x 19ft x 17ft 9in)
Machinery: Twin screws, diesel engines (surface), electric motors (submerged)
Top speed: 15.7 knots (surface), 19 knots (submerged)
Main armament: Four 533mm (21in) torpedo tubes
Launched: 1944

I201 was a high-speed submarine, and twice as fast underwater as her US contemporaries. She had an all-welded hull. Surfaced range was 15,200km (8,000 miles) at 11 knots, but submerged it was only 256km (135 miles) at 3 knots. In August 1945 she surrendered to US forces.

I 351

Type: Japanese submarine
Displacement: 3,568 tonnes (3,512 tons) (surface), 4,358 tonnes (4,290 tons) (submerged)
Dimensions: 110m x 10.2m x 6m (361ft x 33ft 6in x 20ft)
Machinery: Twin screws, diesel engines (surface), electric motors (submerged)
Top speed: 15.7 knots (surface), 6.3 knots (submerged)
Main armament: Four 533mm (21in) torpedo tubes
Launched: 1944

I351 was intended to support seaplanes in forward areas where shore facilities and surface ships were not available. She was sunk by the US submarine *Bluefish* on 14 July 1945, after only six months in service.

I-400

Type: Japanese submarine
Displacement: 5,316 tonnes (5,233 tons) (surface), 6,665 tonnes (6,560 tons) (submerged)
Dimensions: 122m x 12m x 7m (400ft 3in x 39ft 4in x 23ft)
Machinery: Twin screws diesel engines (surface), electric motors (submerged)
Top speed: 18.7 knots (surface), 6.5 knots (submerged)
Main armament: One 140mm (5.5in) gun, eight 533mm (21in) torpedo tubes
Launched: 1944
Date of profile: 1945

Prior to World War II, many navies tried to build an effective aircraft-carrying submarine. Only the Japanese managed to produce a series of workable vessels, the most notable being the STo class. Of the nineteen planned vessels only two (I-400 and I-401) were completed. A third, I-402, was completed as a submersible tanker transport. I-400 was a huge vessel, with a large,

aircraft hanger offset to starboard. The bridge and conning tower was attached to this, offset to port. Inside the hangar was space for three M6A1 *Seiran* floatplanes, plus components for a fourth. To launch the aircraft, I-400 would surface, then the machines would be warmed up in the hangar. They would be rolled forward, their wings unfolded, then

launched down a 26m (85ft) long catapult rail. All three aircraft could be airborne in 45 minutes. The Japanese planned to use these vessels to raid US bases, but the mission was changed to attacking the locks on the Panama Canal. In the event the raid was never flown. I-400 and her sisters surrendered to US warships at the end of the war. These were the largest diesel electric submarines ever made, and were not overtaken in size until the US Ethan Allen class of SSBN.

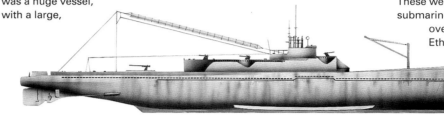

Ibuki

Type: Japanese battlecruiser
Displacement: 15,844 tonnes (15,595 tons)
Dimensions: 148m x 23m x 8m (465ft x 75ft 4in x 26ft 1in)
Machinery: Twin Fourteen 120mm, eight 203mm, four 304mm guns

screws, turbines
Top speed: 21 knots
Main armament: Armour: 102-178mm (4-7in) belt, 127-178mm (5-7in) on turrets
Launched: November 1907

Ibuki was the first Japanese warship to be fitted with turbine engines. Laid down in May 1907,

she was quickly built, but the launch was delayed due to other construction work already in hand. The delay enabled her design to be modified, prior to completion, to include the installation of turbine machinery, which developed 24,000hp. Coal supply was 2,032 tonnes (2,000 tons), plus 221 tonnes (218 tons) of oil fuel. *Ibuki* served as an escort for Australian troops on their way to the Dardanelles during the early part of World War I. She was scrapped in 1924.

Idaho

Type: US cruiser
Displacement: 3,295 tonnes (3,241 tons)
Dimensions: 90m x 13.5m x 5m (298ft x 44ft6in x 17ft)
Machinery: Twin screws, single compound engine
Top speed: 8.3 knots
Main armament: Six 32-pounder guns
Launched: October 1864
Date of profile: 1868

Idaho was laid down in 1863 as one of a group of seven light cruisers. She was originally

intended to have a designed speed of 15 knots, but this could not be reached because the fire grate area needed to develop such power was inadequate. She was rejected by the Trial Board in May 1866 but her designer managed to get Congress to accept the vessel. With her engines removed, she served as a store ship and proved exceptionally fast under sail, often making over 18 knots. She was badly damaged in a typhoon in 1869 and was never repaired. She was scrapped in 1874.

Idaho

Type: US battleship
Displacement: 33,528 tonnes (33,000 tons)
Dimensions: 190.2m x 29.7m x 9.1m (624ft x 97ft 6in x 29ft 10in)
Machinery: Quadruple screws, turbines

Top speed: 21 knots
Main armament: Twelve 356mm (14in), fourteen 127mm (5in) guns
Launched: June 1917
Date of profile: 1919

Idaho was one of a trio of battleships that introduced a new 356mm (14in) gun that could be elevated

independently; with previous guns, all weapons in a turret had been locked into the same elevation. The main guns were housed in triple turrets. Originally 22 127mm (5in) guns were planned. The number was reduced to 14, allowing extra armour in some areas. *Idaho* was extensively rebuilt in 1930-31, and by 1943 she had had all her 127mm (5in) guns removed. *Idaho* was stricken in 1947; her sister ships were *New Mexico* and *Mississippi*.

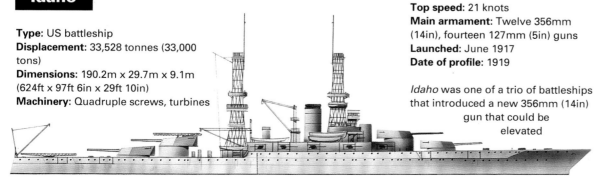

Impavido

Type: Italian destroyer
Displacement: 4,054 tonnes (3,990 tons)
Dimensions: 131.3m x 13.7m x 4.4m (430ft 9in x 45ft x 14ft 5in)
Machinery: Twin screws, turbines
Main armament: Two

127mm (5in) guns, one Tartar missile launcher
Launched: May 1962

Impavido and her sister are the first missile-armed destroyers in the Italian Navy. Derived from the conventional gun-armed Impetuoso-class

destroyers, they retained the forward 127mm (5in) twin gun turret, but the after turret was replaced with a US Mk 13 launcher for Tartar surface-to-air missiles. The after funnel was made taller to keep exhaust away from the fire control tracker on top of the aft structure. *Impavido* has four 76mm (3in) AA guns, and submarine defence is provided by two triple torpedo tubes. In 1976-77 *Impavido* underwent modernisation.

Imperator

Type: German liner
Displacement: 52,951 tonnes (52,117 tons)
Dimensions: 277.1m x 29.9m (909ft 2in x 98ft)
Machinery: Quadruple screws, turbines
Top speed: 24 knots
Launched: May 1912
Date of profile: 1913

When completed in April 1913, *Imperator* was the world's largest

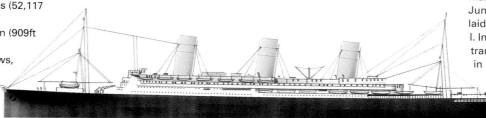

ship. She was built for the Hamburg-Amerika Line as an answer to the

giant White Star liner *Olympic* (sister to the *Titanic*). *Imperator* made her maiden voyage to New York in June 1914, and on her return was laid up in Hamburg for World War I. In 1919 she became a US Army transport and was sold to Cunard in 1921, becoming *Berengaria*. She was damaged by fire at New York in 1938, and was finally scrapped in 1946.

Imperator Pavel I

Type: Russian battleship
Displacement: 17,678 tonnes (17,400 tons)
Dimensions: 140.2m x 24.4m x 8.2m (460ft x 80ft x 27ft)
Machinery: Twin screws, vertical triple expansion engines
Main armament: Four 305mm (12in), fourteen 203mm (8in) and twelve 119mm (4.7in) guns

Armour: 127-216mm (5-8.5in) thick belt, 102-203mm (4-8in) on main turrets and 127-165mm (5-6.5in) on battery
Launched: September 1907

Imperator Pavel I was laid down in April 1904, but construction was delayed to incorporate lessons learned in the Russo-Japanese War of 1904-05. The hull was completely armoured and was flush decked. The superstructure housed six of the 203mm (8in) guns and all the 119mm (4.7in) guns, with twin 203mm (8in) turrets

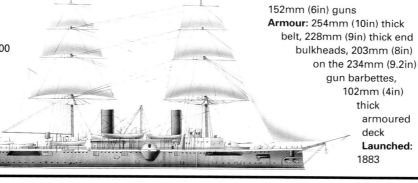

mounted on the upper deck at each corner of the superstructure. The 305mm (12in) guns were in turrets. She was renamed *Respublika* in 1917 and was scrapped in 1923.

Imperieuse

Type: British cruiser
Displacement: 8,636 tonnes (8,500 tons)
Dimensions: 96m x 18.9 x 8.3m (315ft x 62ft x 27ft 3in)
Machinery: Twin screws, inverted compound engines
Top speed: 16.7 knots
Main armament: Four 234mm (9.2in), ten

152mm (6in) guns
Armour: 254mm (10in) thick belt, 228mm (9in) thick end bulkheads, 203mm (8in) on the 234mm (9.2in) gun barbettes, 102mm (4in) thick armoured deck
Launched: 1883

Imperieuse and her sister *Warspite* were the only British warships to carry their main armament in four separate positions. They were also the last British vessels to be fitted with a square rig. This rig increased displacement by 1,016 tonnes (1,000 tons). To reduce weight, four 152mm (6in) guns were removed and the two masts replaced by a single military mast. *Imperieuse* was scrapped in 1913.

Inconstant

Type: British cruiser
Displacement: 5,872 tonnes (5,780 tons)
Dimensions: 102.8m x 15.3 x 7.8m (337ft 3in x 50ft 2in x 25ft 6in)
Machinery: Single screw, horizontal single expansion

engines
Top speed: 16.2 knots
Main armament: Ten 228mm (9in), six 178mm (7in) guns
Launched: December 1868

Inconstant was an iron-hulled broadside unarmoured cruiser

built as an answer to the fast American cruisers of the Wampanoag class. When completed in 1869, she was the fastest ship in the world and for many years was one of the fastest ships in the Royal Navy. On trials the vessel maintained over 15 knots for 24 hours. *Inconstant* was an excellent sea boat and was broken up in 1956.

Independence

Type: US sailing battleship
Displacement: 2,293 tonnes (2,257 tons)
Dimensions: 57.9m x 15.2m (190ft x 50ft)
Main armament: Thirty long 32-pounder, 33 medium 32-pounder guns, 24 32-pounder carronades
Launched: July 1814

Independence was one of three 74-gun sailing line-of-battle ships that were modelled upon an earlier class of 1799, although the plans for *Independence* were never submitted to the Navy Department. When she was ready for sea, it was found that the sills of the lower gunports were only 1.2m (3ft 10in) above the waterline when the full war complement and stores for six months were on board. In 1836 it was decided to cut her three-decks down to two to improve performance. After this, *Independence* became a very successful vessel and a smart sailer, thanks to the retention of the earlier rig of a 74-gun ship; she also became the largest frigate in the US Navy. *Independence* was finally broken up in 1914.

Independence

Type: US aircraft carrier
Displacement: 13,208 tonnes (13,000 tons)
Dimensions: 190m x 33m x 7.6m (623ft x 109ft 3in x 25ft 11in)
Machinery: Quadruple screws, turbines
Main armament: Two 127mm (5in) guns
Aircraft: 45
Launched: August 1942

During 1942 the US Navy lost four aircraft carriers, and for a time had only *Enterprise* in the Pacific. The first of the large Essex-class carriers were not expected to enter service until the following year, so plans were put in hand to convert some of the 39 light cruisers of the Cleveland class then under construction.

Emergency work was carried out on nine of the vessels and they all entered service in 1943. *Independence* had 45 aircraft, but she had room to 'ferry' up to 100. . She was used as a target in the Bikini atomic bomb tests, and was sunk as a target in 1951.

Independencia

Type: Peruvian battleship
Displacement: 3,556 tonnes (3,500 tons)
Dimensions: 65.5m x 13.6m x 6.7m (215ft x 44ft 9in x 22ft)
Machinery: Single screw, horizontal compound engines
Top speed: 12 knots
Main armament: Two 178mm (7in), twelve 70-pounder guns
Armour: 114mm belt (4.5in), 114mm (4.5in) over battery
Launched: August 1865

Independencia and *Huascar* were the only major armoured vessels built for Peru, and their loss in the war with Chile in 1879 was disastrous. Early in the war both ships went to Iquique to raise the blockade by two small Chilean gunboats. During the action *Independencia* ran aground while trying to ram one of the enemy vessels. She caught fire and was lost.

India

Type: Russian submarine
Displacement: 3,251 tonnes (3,200 tons) (surface), 4,064 tonnes (4,000 tons) (submerged)
Dimensions: 106m x 10m (347ft 9in x 32ft 10in)
Machinery: Twin screws, diesel engines (surface), electric motors (submerged)
Top speed: 15 knots (surface), 10 knots (submerged)
Main armament: Four 533mm (21in) torpedo tubes
Launched: 1979

India was designed for salvage and rescue operations. Her hull was built

for high surface speeds so she can be rapidly deployed in operational areas. Two rescue submarines are carried in semi-recessed deck wells aft, and can enter the parent boat when it is submerged. *India* can also operate under ice.

Indiana

Type: US battleship
Displacement: 45,231 tonnes (44,519 tons) (680ft x 108ft x 35ft)
Dimensions: 207.2m x 32.9m x 10.6m
Machinery: Quadruple screws, turbines
Main armament: Twenty 127mm (5in), nine 406mm (16in) guns
Armour: 309mm (12.2in) belt, 457mm (18in) facings on turrets
Launched: November 1941

Indiana was one of a class of four units that were the last US battleships designed within the limits of the London Treaty. All *Indiana*'s 127mm (5in) guns were concentrated on two levels in twin turrets amidships, and her single funnel was faired into the rear of the bridge. She saw extensive service in the Pacific during World War II. She was sold in 1963.

Indianapolis

Type: US cruiser
Displacement: 12,960 tonnes
(12,755 tons)
Dimensions: 185.9m x 20m x 6.4m
(610ft x 66ft x 21ft)
Machinery: Quadruple screws,
turbines
Top speed: 32.8 knots
Main armament: Eight 127mm (5in),
nine 203mm (8in) guns
Launched: November 1931
Date of profile: 1932

Indianapolis and her sister *Portland*
were originally intended to be part
of a class of five fast, heavy cruisers.
In the event design trends were

moving towards better-protected
vessels, as well as to cruisers able
to carry a larger number of lighter
guns, and so these two were the
only ships in the class to be
completed. *Indianapolis* mounted
her 127mm (5in) main guns in triple
armoured turrets, with two forward
and one aft. She was driven by four
powerful steam turbines, which
developed a total of 107,000hp.
Her fuel supply was a maximum

of 2,146 tonnes (2,125 tons), which
gave her an operational range of
19,000km (10,000 miles) at 15 knots.
Both vessels underwent extensive
rebuilds during their careers,
including modifications to reduce
the bridge structure and also to
increase their anti-aircraft
armament. *Portland* survived the
war, and was broken up in 1959.

Indianapolis herself became the last
major US surface ship to be lost in
World War II. She had been used on
a secret mission to deliver an atom
bomb (one of the two to be dropped
on Japan) to the forward air base at
Trinian. On 29 July 1945 she was
returning from this task, when she
was torpedoed and sunk by a
Japanese submarine. A large part
of her crew survived the initial
sinking, but owing to the secrecy of
her mission, rescue attempts were
slow to be launched. Many of the
men left in the water were attacked
and killed by large
groups of sharks
which were drawn to
the scene.

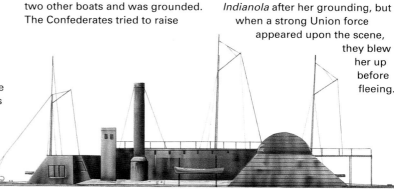

Indianola

Type: US ironclad
Displacement: 520 tonnes (511
tons)
Dimensions: 53m x 15m x 1.5m
(175ft x 52ft x 5ft)
Machinery: Twin screws,
paddlewheels
Top speed: 6 knots
Main armament: Two 228mm (9in),
two 280mm (11in) guns
Launched: 1862

Indianola had one of the shortest
careers of any Union ironclad
serving in the American Civil War.
She was ordered by the US Army
for service on the Mississippi, and
was taken over by the US Navy in
early 1863. Despite the fact that she
was not yet finished, *Indianola* was
rushed into service to help defend
Cincinnati against a strong
Confederate force. However, on
24 February 1863 she was
attacked by the Confederate
ram *Queen of the West* and

two other boats and was grounded.
The Confederates tried to raise

Indianola after her grounding, but
when a strong Union force
appeared upon the scene,
they blew
her up
before
fleeing.

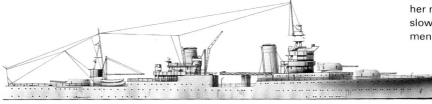

Infanta Maria Teresa

Type: Spanish cruiser
Displacement: 7,000 tonnes (6,890
tons)
Dimensions: 110.9m x 19.8m x
6.5m (364ft x 65ft 2in x 21ft 7in)
Machinery: Twin screws,
vertical triple expansion
engines
Main armament:
Ten 140mm
(5.5in), two

280mm (11in) guns
Armour: 254-305mm (10-12in) thick belt
Launched: August 1890

Infanta Maria Teresa was designed along the lines of the
5,080-tonne (5,000-ton) British Orlando class, but had
increased displacement. She was designed to be a fast,
powerful vessel for service in Spain's empire. During the
Spanish-American War of 1898, *Infanta Maria Teresa* and
her two sister ships were blockaded in
Santiago harbour by a US fleet. On 3
July 1898 the Spanish fleet tried to
break through the blockade, and *Infanta
Maria Teresa* was lost in action.

Inflexible

Type: British battleship
Displacement: 12,070 tonnes (11,880
tons)
Dimensions: 104.8m x 22.8m x 7.7m
(344ft x 75ft x 25ft 6in)
Machinery: Twin screws, compound
engines
Top speed: 14.7 knots
Main armament: Four 406mm (16in)
guns
Launched: April 1876

Designed by Nathaniel Barnaby,
Inflexible was one of the most
powerful vessels of her time. She
was built in direct response to
the giant Italian battleships
Duilio and *Dandolo*, and to
French moves towards
arming their new ships with
large guns. As
completed,
Inflexible had the
heaviest muzzle-
loading rifled guns

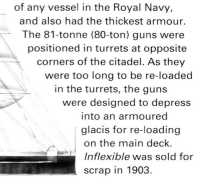

of any vessel in the Royal Navy,
and also had the thickest armour.
The 81-tonne (80-ton) guns were
positioned in turrets at opposite
corners of the citadel. As they
were too long to be re-loaded
in the turrets, the guns
were designed to depress
into an armoured
glacis for re-loading
on the main deck.
Inflexible was sold for
scrap in 1903.

Inflexible

Type: British battlecruiser
Displacement: 20,320 tonnes (20,000 tons)
Dimensions: 172.8m x 23.9m x 8m (567ft x 78ft 6in x 26ft 10in)
Machinery: Quadruple screws, turbines
Main armament: Sixteen 102mm (4in), eight 305mm (12in) guns
Armour: 102-152mm (4-6in) belt,

178mm (7in) on turrets
Launched: June 1907

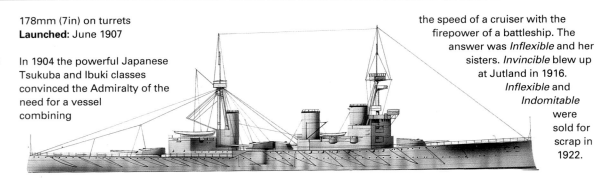

In 1904 the powerful Japanese Tsukuba and Ibuki classes convinced the Admiralty of the need for a vessel combining the speed of a cruiser with the firepower of a battleship. The answer was *Inflexible* and her sisters. *Invincible* blew up at Jutland in 1916. *Inflexible* and *Indomitable* were sold for scrap in 1922.

Intelligent Whale

Type: US submarine
Displacement: Unknown
Dimensions: 9.4m x 2.6m x 2.6m (31ft x 8ft 6in x 8ft 6in)
Machinery: Single screw, hand-cranked
Top speed: 4 knots
Launched: 1862
Date of profile: 1862

Intelligent Whale was the first submarine constructed for the Union Navy, and was built in answer to the increasing threat from Confederate vessels of the same type. Thirteen men were carried, six of them propelling the cylindrical cigar-shaped hull by hand, and the remainder intended to leave the vessel by a trap

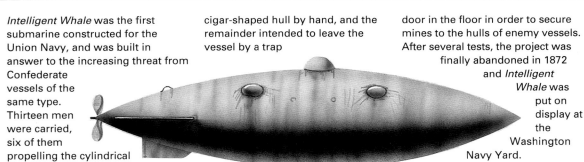

door in the floor in order to secure mines to the hulls of enemy vessels. After several tests, the project was finally abandoned in 1872 and *Intelligent Whale* was put on display at the Washington Navy Yard.

Intrepid

Type: British assault ship
Displacement: 12,313 tonnes (12,120 tons)
Dimensions: 158m x 24m x 6.2m (520ft x 80ft x 20ft 6in)
Machinery: Twin screws, turbines
Main armament: Two 40mm (1.6in) guns, four Seacat anti-aircraft missile launchers
Launched: June 1964

Intrepid was one of a pair of advanced assault ships combining the role of commando carrier and assault vessel. She was able to operate her own fleet of landing craft, as well as carrying up to 700 troops plus a crew of 556. The rear half of the vessel comprises a landing dock from which the landing craft load up. With landing craft in

operation, *Intrepid*'s displacement increases to 17,221 tonnes (16,950 tons), and her aft draught rises to 9.7m (32ft). Above the landing dock is a flight deck for the vessel's six helicopters, and the hangars are in the aft section of the super-structure.

Iosco

Type: US gunboat
Displacement: 1,191 tonnes (1,173 tons)
Dimensions: 62m x 10.6m x 2.9m (205ft x 35ft x 9ft 6in)
Machinery: Paddle wheels, direct acting inclined engines
Top speed: 13 knots
Main armament: Four 228mm (9in), two 24-

pounder, two 100-pounder guns
Launched: 1863

Iosco was one of a class of 28 wooden-hulled vessels designed to combat the Confederate forces stationed along the inland waterways. The hazards of turning vessels under such conditions called for speedy craft with a shallow draught that could travel well in both directions, and for this reason *Iosco* and her class were given a rudder at each end and became known as the 'double enders'. Machinery and boilers were positioned amidships, and both bow and stern were pointed.

Iowa

Type: US battleship
Displacement: 56,601 tonnes (55,710 tons)
Dimensions: 270.4m x 33.5m x 11.6m (887ft 2in x 108ft 3in x 38ft)
Machinery: Quadruple screws, turbines
Top speed: 32.5 knots

Main armament: Twenty 127mm (5in), nine 406mm (16in) guns
Launched: August 1942
Date of profile: 1948

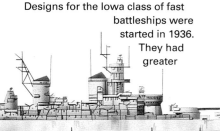

Designs for the Iowa class of fast battleships were started in 1936. They had greater displacement than the previous South Dakota class, and had more power and protection. *Iowa* was an escort for carriers in World War II, and was used to bombard shore positions during the Korean War.

Iris

Type: British cruiser
Displacement: 3,790 tonnes (3,730 tons)
Dimensions: 101m x 14m x 6.7m (333ft x 46ft x 22ft)
Machinery: Twin screws, horizontal direct acting compound engines
Main armament: Ten 64-pounder guns
Launched: April 1877

For a time *Iris* and her sister *Mercury* were the fastest large vessels in the Royal Navy, having been designed specifically for speed at the expense of protection and armament. *Iris* was the first British warship to be built from steel, and her hull was divided into numerous small compartments to limit damage should she suffer a direct hit. Large coal bunkers were positioned alongside the engine spaces to give side protection. Her armament underwent several changes during

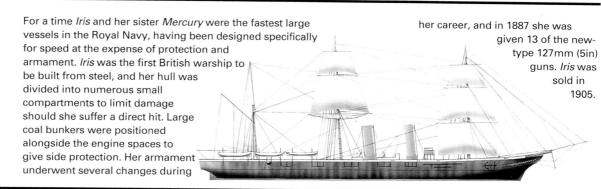

her career, and in 1887 she was given 13 of the new-type 127mm (5in) guns. *Iris* was sold in 1905.

Iron Duke

Type: British battleship
Displacement: 30,866 tonnes (30,380 tons)
Dimensions: 189.8m x 27.4m x 9m (622ft 9in x 90ft x 29ft 6in)
Machinery: Quadruple screws, turbines
Top speed: 21.6 knots
Main armament: Twelve 152mm (6in), ten 342mm

(13.5in) guns
Armour: 102-305mm belt (4-12in), 228mm (9in) middle belt, 51-152mm (2-6in) on battery
Launched: October 1912

Iron Duke was the British flagship at the Battle of Jutland in 1916, and was one of the longest

serving pre-World War I dreadnought battleships. She was one of a class of four vessels that formed the third group of super-dreadnoughts. They were all armed with 342mm (13.5in) guns, and the Iron Duke class were the first major capital ships to revert to 152mm (6in) guns for anti-torpedo boat defence. Minor changes were later made to the secondary armament. *Iron Duke* became a training ship in 1931 and was a depot ship at Scapa Flow in 1939. She was scrapped in 1946.

Isaac Peral

Type: Spanish submarine
Displacement: 499 tonnes (491 tons) (surface), 762 tonnes (750 tons) (submerged)
Dimensions: 60m x

5.8m x 3.4m (196ft 10in x 19ft x 11ft 2in)
Machinery: Twin screws, diesel engines (surface), electric motors

(submerged)
Main armament: Four 457mm (18in) torpedo tubes, one 76mm (3in) gun on disappearing mount
Launched: July 1916
Date of profile: 1918

Isaac Peral was Spain's first major submarine. She was built by the Fore River Company in America and modelled on the Holland design. She attained 15.36 knots on the surface during trials. Surface range was 5,386km (2,835 miles) at 11 knots; range submerged was 130km (80 miles) at full power from the 480hp electric motors. She was renamed *O1* in 1930, later being hulked and renumbered *A0*.

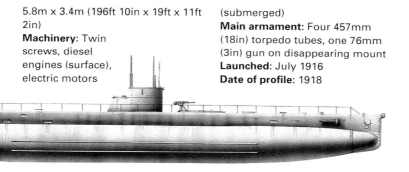

Ise

Type: Japanese battleship
Displacement: 32,576 tonnes (32,063 tons)
Dimensions: 208.2m x 28.6m x 8.8m (683ft x 94ft x 29ft)
Machinery: Quadruple screws, turbines
Top speed: 23 knots
Main armament: Twenty 140mm

(5.5in), twelve 355mm (14in) guns
Launched: November 1916
Date of profile: 1918

Ise was an improved version of the previous Fuso class, and carried two twin superfiring guns amidships. She was extensively modernised between World Wars I and II, and by 1937 had

been lengthened aft by 7.6m (25ft). Following the large loss of Japanese aircraft carriers at Midway in June 1942, *Ise* was converted to a hybrid battleship-carrier. She was sunk at Kure in early 1945 and was raised and scrapped in 1946.

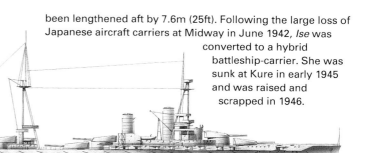

Ishikari

Type: Japanese ferry
Displacement: 7,050 tonnes (6,938 tons)
Dimensions: 192.5m x 27m x 6.9m (631ft 6in x 88ft 7in x 22ft 8in)
Machinery: Twin screws, diesel engines
Top speed: 21.5 knots
Launched: November 1990

Ishikari was one of the first of a new series of luxury, high-speed ferries to enter Japanese service and is able to carry 850 passengers, 151 cars and 165 lorries. Her hull is designed for high speed and economy, and she burns 76 tonnes (75 tons) of oil a day in

regular service. The box-shaped upper part of the hull houses nine separate decks, the top three being devoted to passengers. The large

internal decks are allocated to vehicles. Passenger areas are fully air-conditioned, with cabins arranged in classes in a choice of Japanese or western style. *Ishikari* also has shops, restaurants and an observation lounge, and features a central staircase surrounding a tall living tree.

Italia

Type: Italian battleship
Displacement: 15,904 tonnes (15,654 tons)
Dimensions: 124.7m x 22.5m x 8.7m (409ft 2in x 73ft 10in x 28ft 6in)
Machinery: Twin screws, vertical compound engines
Top speed: 17.8 knots
Main armament: Four 431mm (17in) guns
Armour: 102mm (4in) thick deck, 482mm (19in) on citadel
Launched: September 1880
Date of profile: 1882

In the late 1870s, the impoverished Italian Navy realised that they could not outbuild the French, so instead decided to build a few high-quality ships, so powerful that they could outfight anything else afloat. *Italia* and her sister *Lepanto* were the result. At the time of her completion, *Italia* was one of the fastest vessels afloat, beaten only by her sister. This was partially due to the lack of side armour, these ships having no armoured belt. Instead they had a thick armoured deck which curved down to the waterline, and which was supplemented by an extensive honeycomb of watertight compartments. Their 104-tonne (102-ton) main guns were mounted in pairs on turntables, which were placed on a huge single oval-shaped armoured barbette. Ammunition had to be trundled up from below the armoured deck, and each gun could only fire one shell every five minutes. In the event technology overtook these vessels, and by the time they entered service, the quick-firing gun and improved high-explosive shell had rendered them obsolete. *Italia* was transferred to harbour duties in 1914, and was scrapped in 1921.

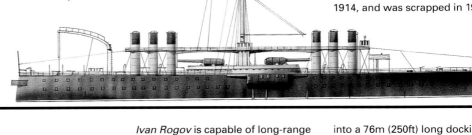

Ivan Rogov

Type: Russian amphibious assault ship
Displacement: 13,208 tonnes (13,000 tons)
Dimensions: 158m x 24m x 8.2m (521ft 8in x 80ft 5in x 21ft 4in)
Machinery: Twin screws, gas turbines
Top speed: 23 knots
Main armament: Two 76mm (3in) guns, plus missiles
Launched: 1977

Ivan Rogov is capable of long-range operation, having a range of some 22,800km (14,170 miles) at 14 knots and 15,200km (9,445 miles) at 20 knots. Her complement numbers 200, and she can also carry 550 troops, plus 40 tanks and other supporting vehicles. She has a bow ramp for beaching capability, and her rear doors open into a 76m (250ft) long docking area housing landing craft and two 86-tonne (84.6-ton) Lebed-class hovercraft. The rear of the superstructure houses a hangar for four helicopters, with a flight deck behind it. The twin 76mm (3in) gun turret is situated forward. On top of the superstructure are two staggered funnels that are combined to form a single structure connected by the mainmast support. During the first half of 1979, *Ivan Rogov* was transferred from the Black Sea to the Pacific Fleet.

Iwo Jima

Type: US assault ship
Displacement: 18,330 tonnes (18,042 tons)
Dimensions: 183.6m x 25.7m x 8m (602ft 8in x 84ft x 26ft)
Machinery: Single screw, turbines
Main armament: Four 76mm (3in) guns
Launched: September 1960

Iwo Jima was the world's first ship designed specifically to carry and operate helicopters. She is can also carry a Marine battalion of 2,000 troops, plus their artillery and support vehicles. The flight deck allows for the simultaneous take-off of up to seven helicopters, and *Iwo Jima* has hangar facilities for up to 20 helicopters. The two lifts are situated at the very edges of the deck, so as not to reduce the flight-deck area. Storage capacity is provided for 1,430 litres (6,500 gallons) of petrol for the vehicles, plus over 88,000 litres (400,000 gallons) for the helicopter force. In 1970 a Sea Sparrow missile launcher was installed, and a second was installed three years later. *Iwo Jima* and her six sisters have extensive medical facilities, including operating theatres and a large hospital.

Izumrud

Type: Russian cruiser
Displacement: 3,098 tonnes (3,050 tons)
Dimensions: 110.9m x 12.2m x 5m (345ft x 49ft x 16ft)
Machinery: Twin screws, triple expansion engine
Top speed: 25 knots
Main armament: Six 120mm (4.7in) guns
Launched: 1903

Izumrud had a 51mm (2in) thick armoured deck running the full length of the vessel. A light three-masted rig was carried, which was extended to carry the newly installed Russian-made wireless. Engines developed over 24,000hp, and consumed over 25 tonnes (25 tons) of coal per hour. *Izumrud* was one of the few Russian warships to survive the Battle of Tsushima in May 1905, but shortly afterwards she ran aground in thick fog near Vladivostok due to compass failure.

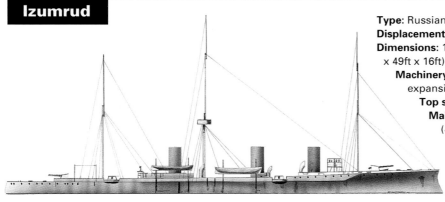

Izumrud

Type: Russian frigate
Displacement: 1,219 tonnes (1,200 tons)
Dimensions: 72m x 10m x 3.7m (236ft 3in x 32ft 10in x 12ft 2in)
Machinery: Triple screws, one gas turbine, two diesel engines
Main armament: Two 57mm (2.25in) guns, SAM missiles
Launched: 1970

Izamrud was one of a large group of small anti-submarine frigates built at the rate of three per year, and divided into three groups according to the equipment carried. *Izumrud* belongs to the first group. Her twin 57mm (2.25in) gun turret is carried aft, and the SAM SA-N-4 missiles are mounted forward of the bridge and are fired up through a circular hatchway in the deck. Two twin, multi-barrel rocket launchers are also fitted in front of the bridge. Twin, 533mm (21in) torpedo tubes are mounted amidships. Turbines develop 24,000hp, and the diesels produce 16,000hp. Range is 1,805km (950 miles) at 27 knots and 8,550km (4,500 miles) at 10 knots. *Izumrud* is intended primarily for inshore anti-submarine patrols.

J1

Type: British submarine
Displacement: 1,223 tonnes (1,204 tons) (surface), 1,849 tonnes (1,820 tons) (submerged)
Dimensions: 84m x 7m x 4.3m (275ft 7in x 23ft x 14ft)
Machinery: Triple screws, diesel engines (surface), electric motors (submerged)
Main armament: One 76mm (3in) gun, six 457mm (18in) torpedo tubes
Launched: November 1915

J1 was built in response to a possible threat from German submarines then entering service and reputed to be capable of 22 knots. As first completed, *J1*'s large forward free-flooding tank brought the bows down in the water, causing loss of speed when surfaced. Later the bows were raised, and the submarine was then able to maintain 17 knots surfaced in heavy seas. Range at 12.5 knots surfaced was 9,500km (5,000 miles). Later a 102mm (4in) gun was positioned high up at the front of the conning tower in place of the 76mm (3in) weapon. *J1* was handed over to Australia in 1919. She was broken up in 1924.

Jacob van Heemskerck

Type: Dutch cruiser
Displacement: 4,282 tonnes (4,215 tons)
Dimensions: 131m x 12m x 4.5m (433ft x 40ft 9in x 15ft)
Machinery: Twin screws, turbines
Top speed: 34.5 knots
Main armament: Eight 102mm (4in) guns
Launched: September 1939

Jacob van Heemskerck was originally to have been a 2,540-tonne (2,500-ton) flotilla leader. However, although the ship was authorised in 1931, she was not laid down until 1938, by which time her displacement had been greatly increased. She was intended to carry six 150mm (5.9in) guns, but with the invasion of Holland at the start of World War II, the ship was taken to Britain for completion and eight 102mm (4in) guns were mounted instead, as the heavier armament was not available there. *Jacob van Heemskerck* was scrapped in 1958.

Jakob Maersk

Type: Danish tanker
Displacement: 42,523 tonnes (42,523 tons)
Dimensions: 185m x 27.4m x 12.5m (607ft x 90ft x 41ft)
Machinery: Single screw, diesel engines
Top speed: 17.3 knots
Launched: March 1991

Jakob Maersk was an updated version of an already successful design, and incorporated greater cargo capacity. She has four large holds, each with wing tanks. Each hold contains free-standing, self-supporting cargo tanks covered with 120mm (4.7in) thick polyurethane to protect them from damage. The cargo is handled by eight multi-stage centrifugal pumps that can load or discharge two tanks at a time. The system also includes an inert-gas generator and drying plant with its own heater and compressor. Thrusters are provided to assist bow and stern pitch, a design feature unique in tanker design. The 23 crew members are all accommodated in single cabins.

James Clark Ross

Type: British research vessel
Displacement: 7,439 tonnes (7,322 tons)
Dimensions: 99m x 10.8m x 6.5m (325ft x 35ft 5in x 21ft 4in)
Machinery: Single screw, diesel engines
Launched: December 1990

James Clark Ross was specifically designed to carry out oceanic research in the Antarctic, and is well equipped to transport supplies through seas covered by thick ice. Her hull is strengthened to allow her to break up newly formed ice, and she can navigate through broken ice up to 1.5m (5ft) thick, or fragmented ice over 3m (10ft) thick. *James Clark Ross* can remain at sea for up to ten months at a time, and has fully equipped laboratory facilities. Should they be required, extra laboratories are stowed in containers.

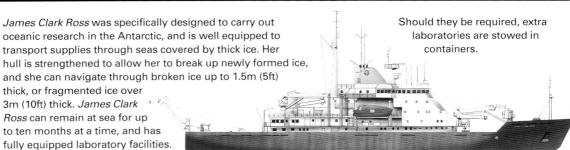

James Watt

Type: British steamship
Displacement: Not known
Dimensions: 43m x 14.3m (141ft 8in x 47ft) over the paddle boxes
Machinery: Paddle wheels, twin cylinder engine
Top speed: 9 knots
Launched: 1820

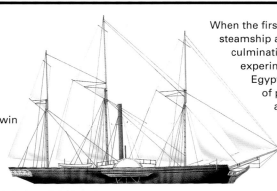

When the first working paddle-wheel steamship appeared, it was the culmination of centuries of experimentation. The Ancient Egyptians had already had the idea of paddle-wheel propulsion, and as early as 1685 the Frenchman Denis Papin had designed a single steam cylinder which drove a piston. By the early 1800s, several successful small steamships were in operation, and James Watt was the largest of them all at the time of her completion. She entered service as a passenger and cargo vessel, and spent her career operating along Britain's east coast, with London as her main port of call. Each of her paddle wheels was 5.4m (18ft) in diameter, and they were driven by two cylinders each measuring 508mm (20in) in diameter and developing 100hp.

Jason

Type: US repair ship
Displacement: 16,418 tonnes (16,160 tons)
Dimensions: 161.3m x 22.3m x 7m (529ft 2in x 73ft 2in x 23ft 4in)
Machinery: Twin screws, turbines
Top speed: 19.2 knots
Main armament: Four 127mm (5in) guns
Launched: December 1940

By the end of the 1930s, the US Navy felt the need to increase its fleet repair force, as it had been relying on converted merchant vessels. In 1938 the US Navy authorised Jason, a purpose-built repair vessel, with three more ships to follow. These ships were able to handle a multitude of tasks, and could serve several major surface vessels at once. On completion in 1941, Jason was classified as a heavy hull repair ship. By the 1980s her 127mm (5in) guns had been replaced with lighter armament of four 20mm (0.8in) guns. Accommodation for 1,336 crew is situated on the upper levels, with the extensive repair shops below.

Jauréguiberry

Type: French battleship
Displacement: 11,823 tonnes (11,637 tons)
Dimensions: 108.5m x 22m x 8.4m (356ft x 72ft 8in x 27ft 8in)
Machinery: Twin screws, vertical triple expansion engines
Top speed: 17.7 knots
Main armament: Eight 140mm (5.5in), two 274mm (10.8in), two 305mm (12in) guns
Launched: October 1893
Date of profile: 1897

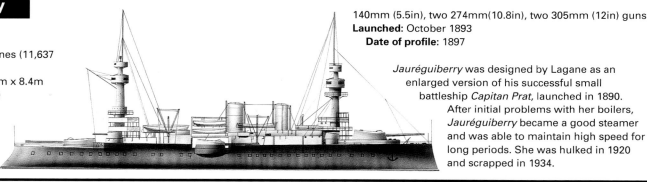

Jauréguiberry was designed by Lagane as an enlarged version of his successful small battleship Capitan Prat, launched in 1890. After initial problems with her boilers, Jauréguiberry became a good steamer and was able to maintain high speed for long periods. She was hulked in 1920 and scrapped in 1934.

Java

Type: Dutch cruiser
Displacement: 6,776 tonnes (6,670 tons)
Dimensions: 155m x 16m x 5.4m (509ft 6in x 52ft 6in x 18ft)
Machinery: Triple screws, turbines
Top speed: 31.5 knots
Main armament: Ten 150mm (5.9in) guns
Launched: August 1921

Designed and constructed in Germany, Java was the largest warship to be built in a German yard in the years following World War I. She was laid down in 1916 with the intention of completing in 1917, but this was delayed until 1925. In 1935 she underwent a major refit and was given a new tubular foremast and a short pole mainmast near the second funnel. Java was sunk in action on 27 February 1942 by superior Japanese forces.

Javary

Type: Brazilian battleship
Displacement: 3,699 tonnes (3,641 tons)
Dimensions: 73m x 17m x 3.4m (240ft x 57ft x 11ft 5in)
Machinery: Twin screws, compound double cylinder engines
Top speed: 11 knots
Main armament: Four 254mm (10in) guns
Launched: January 1875

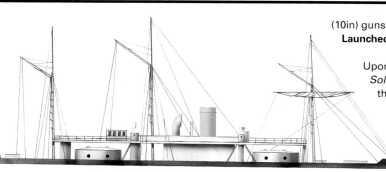

Upon completion, Javary and her sister Solimoes were the most powerful vessels in the Brazilian Navy. During the Brazilian revolution of 1893, Javary sank as a result of leaks in the hull which were caused by the constant firing of her guns during her bombardment of government shore fortifications.

Jeanne D'Arc

Type: French cruiser
Displacement: 11,270 tonnes (11,092 tons)
Dimensions: 145.3m x 19.4m x 8m (477ft x 63ft 8in x 26ft 7in)
Machinery: Triple screws, vertical triple expansion engines
Top speed: 21.8 knots
Main armament: Fourteen 140mm (5.5in), two 193mm (7.6in) guns

Armour: 40-152mm (1.6-6in) belt, 120-160mm (4.7-6.3in) on turrets, 38mm (1.5in) and 51mm (2in) decks
Launched: June 1899
Date of profile: 1902

Jeanne D'Arc was the first in a series of large French armoured cruisers, and her configuration set the pattern for many future designs. Her profile was distinctive, with a high freeboard and six tall funnels, installed in two groups of three. She was well protected for a cruiser, with a thick armoured belt along her complete length, which met with an armoured deck at its top and bottom edges to form a closed armoured box. Behind this was a cellular network of watertight compartments, passageways, cofferdams and coal bunkers. Her 193mm (7.6in) main guns were mounted singly in turrets placed at the extreme ends of the ship, the bow one being some 11m (36ft) above the waterline. The 140mm (5.5in) secondary armament was on two levels on the broadside, either being mounted in armoured sponsons or behind shields. She had two groups of boilers, each of which were served by three funnels. In between these was the engines. During her trials, excessive heat built up in the stokehold, which caused delays while improved ventilation was fitted. Jeanne D'Arc was relegated to training ship status prior to World War I. She was struck off and scrapped in 1934.

Jeanne D'Arc

Type: French helicopter carrier
Displacement: 13,208 tonnes (13,000 tons)
Dimensions: 180m x 25.9m x 6.2m (590ft 6in x 85ft x 20ft 4in)
Machinery: Twin screws, turbines
Top speed: 26.5 knots
Main armament: Four 100mm (3.9in) guns
Aircraft: Eight
Launched: September 1961
Date of profile: 1964

Originally to be named La Résolue, this ship was authorised in 1957 as a training cruiser to replace the pre-World War I Jeanne D'Arc. As a result of the cancellation of a large carrier, La Résolue underwent major design changes, finally emerging as Jeanne D'Arc, a combination of cruiser, helicopter carrier and assault ship. Her superstructure is situated forward, with the aft end of the vessel being given over to a helicopter deck below which is housed the narrow hangar. Two of the 100mm (3.9in) guns are carried in single turrets, one each side of the bridge, and the remaining two guns are positioned aft. In her role as a troop carrier, Jeanne D'Arc can transport 700 men and eight large helicopters. In 1975 Exocet missiles were fitted, giving her a full anti-ship role. In peacetime shel also retains her role as a training ship, providing facilities for up to 198 cadets at a time.

Jervis Bay

Type: British passenger/cargo vessel
Displacement: 23,601 tonnes (23,230 tons)
Dimensions: 167m x 20m x 10m (549ft x 68ft x 33ft)
Machinery: Twin screws, turbines
Top speed: 15 knots
Launched: 1922

Jervis Bay was built for the Australian emigrant trade. Cargo was handled by two electric cranes and 23 derricks. Engines developed 9,000hp, and fuel supply was 3,454 tonnes (3,400 tons) of oil. As originally completed, Jervis Bay carried 732 third-class passengers in two-, four- and six-berth cabins. Only 12 first-class passengers were carried, usually government officials. By the early 1930s the ship had been taken over by the P & O Line, and tourist-class replaced third-class. In 1939 Jervis Bay was fitted out as an armed merchant cruiser and given eight 152mm (6in) guns. In November 1939 her 38-ship convoy was attacked by the German battleship Admiral Scheer. Jervis Bay attacked in order to give the convoy time to scatter. Thirty-two vessels managed to escape, but Jervis Bay was sunk with heavy loss of life.

Jo Alder

Type: Italian tanker
Displacement: 12,801 tonnes (12,600 tons)
Dimensions: 139m x 21.2m x 8m (456ft x 69ft 9in x 26ft 5in)
Machinery: Single screw, diesel engines
Top speed: 14.5 knots
Launched: 1991
Date of profile: 1993

Jo Alder is a specialised chemical tanker able to carry food products, non-contaminable chemicals and general petroleum products in stainless steel cargo tanks. The tanks are completely separate, with 25 cargoes being handled by individual loading/discharge pumps. Cargoes are computer-controlled, and in Jo Alder the usually bulky computer console has been replaced by a simple screen, keyboard and light pen. The hull of the vessel is double-skinned and has a double bottom with toughened longitudinal and transverse bulkheads, which also form the outer casings of the cargo tanks. The engine room is designed for unmanned operation.

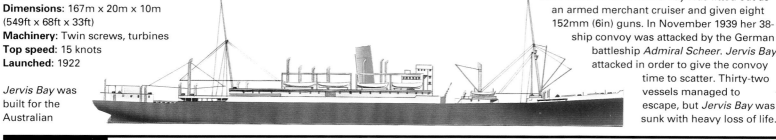

John Bell

Type: British liner
Displacement: 1,118 tonnes (1,101 tons)
Dimensions: 70m x 10m (231ft x 33ft)
Machinery: Single screw, compound engines
Launched: 1854

John Bell started life as a sailing ship, but in 1856 she was chartered by the Anchor Line and given engines. The following year she was put into service on the Glasgow-Canada route. During the Indian Mutiny *John Bell* saw brief service as a troop transport, but was back in service on the Glasgow-Quebec-Montreal run by July 1859. She was purchased by the Anchor Line in 1862 and her name changed to *Saint Patrick*. She continued to serve until 1875, when her engines were removed. She later became *Diamant*. The layout of the vessel was typical of the period, with a large saloon cabin, first-class passenger cabins forward, plus steerage. The engine room was aft with the boiler room just in front of the mizzen mast.

Jorge Juan

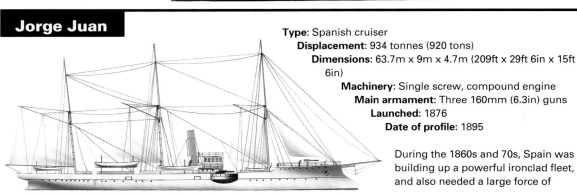

Type: Spanish cruiser
Displacement: 934 tonnes (920 tons)
Dimensions: 63.7m x 9m x 4.7m (209ft x 29ft 6in x 15ft 6in)
Machinery: Single screw, compound engine
Main armament: Three 160mm (6.3in) guns
Launched: 1876
Date of profile: 1895

During the 1860s and 70s, Spain was building up a powerful ironclad fleet, and also needed a large force of small cruisers and gunboats to police her many overseas colonies. Spain built many of these vessels herself, but limited facilities forced her to go abroad for the rest. *Jorge Juan* and her sister *Sanchez Barcáiztegui* were composite-built barque-rigged cruisers built in France. *Jorge Juan*'s engines developed 1,100hp, and her coal supply was just 130 tonnes (128 tons) as she was expected to cruiser under sail for most of her patrols.

Jurien de la Gravière

Type: French cruiser
Displacement: 5,588 tonnes (5,500 tons)
Dimensions: 134m x 14.8m x 6.7m (440ft x 48ft 8in x 22ft)

Machinery: Triple screws
Top speed: 22.9 knots
Main armament: Eight 160mm (6.4in) guns
Launched: June 1899

Jurien de la Gravière was the last cruiser built without side armour for the French Navy until 1922, when the Duguay-Trouin class were put into construction. Laid down in late 1897, *Jurien de la Gravière* was completed in 1903. Her hull was constructed from copper-sheathed wood and had a 76mm (3in) thick armoured deck which extended the full length of the ship and had 'crowns' over the funnel bases, plus a cellulose belt and a cofferdam. Machinery developed 17,400hp, and with only 14,000hp she could still make 21.7 knots. *Jurien de la Gravière* was stricken in 1922.

K 26

Type: British submarine
Displacement: 2,174 tonnes (2,140 tons) (surface), 2,814 tonnes (2,770 tons) (submerged)
Dimensions: 107m x 8.5m (351ft 6in x 28ft)
Machinery: Twin screws, turbines (surface), electric motors (submerged)
Main armament: Three 102mm (4in)

guns, ten 533mm (21in) torpedo tubes
Launched: August 1919

In 1915 the British decided to design a class of exceptionally fast ocean-going submarines that could keep up with

the battlefleet. As diesel engines of the period could not develop adequate power to sustain a surface speed of 24 knots, steam turbines were used instead, with electric motors for

underwater operation. The turbine machinery took up nearly 40 per cent of *K 26*'s length, and had to be shut down when she was submerged, with giant lids covering the funnel uptakes. *K 26* was completed in 1923. She was scrapped in 1931.

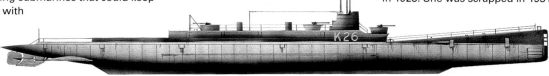

Kaiser

Type: Austrian battleship
Displacement: 5,811 tonnes (5,720 tons)
Dimensions: 77.7m x 17.7m x 7.3m (255ft x 58ft 3in x 24ft 2in)
Machinery: Single screw, horizontal

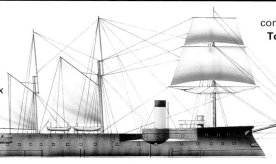

compound engines
Top speed: 11.5 knots
Main armament: Ten 228mm (9in) guns
Launched: 1862

Kaiser was originally a wooden-hulled two-decker battleship. She took part in the Battle of Lissa in

1866, when she suffered severe damage. Due to lack of funds for new construction, the damaged vessel was converted into an ironclad central battery ship in 1869. She was rebuilt in iron from the waterline up, and in 1874 re-joined the fleet. She was re-armed in 1882, and again in 1885. *Kaiser* served as a barrack hulk from 1902 to 1918. Scrapped in 1920.

Kaiser

Type: German battleship
Displacement: 26,998 tonnes (26,573 tons)
Dimensions: 172.4m x 29m x 8.3m (565ft 8in x 95ft 2in x 27ft 3in)
Machinery: Triple screws, turbines
Top speed: 23.5 knots
Main armament:

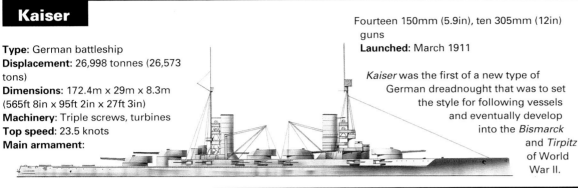

Fourteen 150mm (5.9in), ten 305mm (12in) guns
Launched: March 1911

Kaiser was the first of a new type of German dreadnought that was to set the style for following vessels and eventually develop into the *Bismarck* and *Tirpitz* of World War II.

There were five units in the Kaiser class. All had superfiring turrets aft and diagonally offset wing turrets. Machinery developed 31,000hp, coal supply was 3,000 tonnes (2,953 tons), and range at 12 knots was nearly 15,200km (8,000 miles). *Kaiser* was in action at Jutland, and all vessels in the class were interned at Scapa Flow and scuttled in 1919. From 1929 to 1937 they were salvaged and broken up.

Kaiser Franz Josef I

Type: Austrian liner
Displacement: 17,170 tonnes (16,900 tons)
Dimensions: 152.4m x 18.8m x 8.8m (500ft x 62ft x 29ft)
Machinery: Twin screws, quadruple expansion engines
Top speed: 19 knots
Launched: September 1911

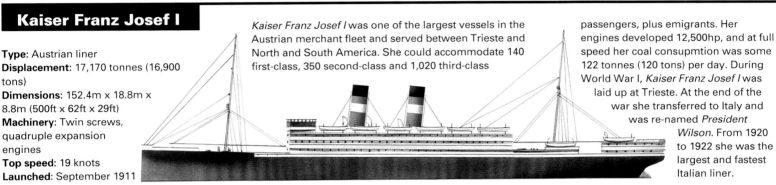

Kaiser Franz Josef I was one of the largest vessels in the Austrian merchant fleet and served between Trieste and North and South America. She could accommodate 140 first-class, 350 second-class and 1,020 third-class passengers, plus emigrants. Her engines developed 12,500hp, and at full speed her coal consumption was some 122 tonnes (120 tons) per day. During World War I, *Kaiser Franz Josef I* was laid up at Trieste. At the end of the war she transferred to Italy and was re-named *President Wilson*. From 1920 to 1922 she was the largest and fastest Italian liner.

Kaiser Friedrich

Type: German liner
Displacement: 12,680 tonnes (12,480 tons)
Dimensions: 177m x 18.8m (582ft x 62ft)
Machinery: Twin screws, quadruple expansion engines
Top speed: 20 knots
Launched: 1898

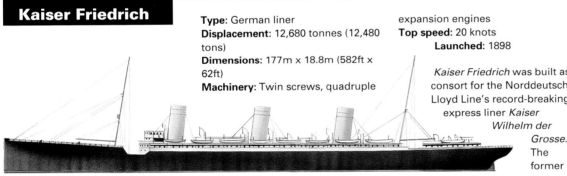

Kaiser Friedrich was built as a consort for the Norddeutscher Lloyd Line's record-breaking express liner *Kaiser Wilhelm der Grosse*. The former ship differed considerably from her running mate, having twin masts with three large funnels. However, her performance was disappointing, and after a year her owners returned her to her builders. She was then chartered to the Hamburg American Line. In 1912 she became the Cie Sud-Atlantique's *Burdigala* and served on the South American route. In 1916 she was torpedoed and sunk in the Mediterranean.

Kaiser Friedrich III

Type: German battleship
Displacement: 11,784 tonnes (11,599 tons)
Dimensions: 125.3m x 20.4m x 8.2m (411ft x 67ft x 27ft)
Machinery: Triple screws, triple expansion engines
Top speed: 18 knots
Main armament: Twelve

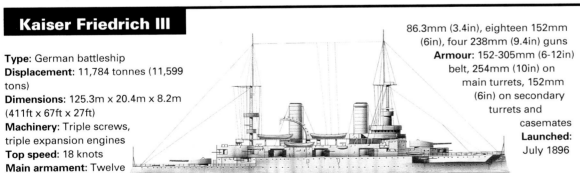

86.3mm (3.4in), eighteen 152mm (6in), four 238mm (9.4in) guns
Armour: 152-305mm (6-12in) belt, 254mm (10in) on main turrets, 152mm (6in) on secondary turrets and casemates
Launched: July 1896

Kaiser Friedrich III was laid down in 1895 and completed in 1898. Six of her 152mm (6in) guns were in single turrets high on the superstructure, with the remainder in casemates. The 86.3mm (3.4in) guns were carried singly behind shields on the upper deck. *Kaiser Friedrich III's* total armour weight was 3,860 tonnes (3,800 tons). She was eventually scrapped in 1920.

Kaiser Max

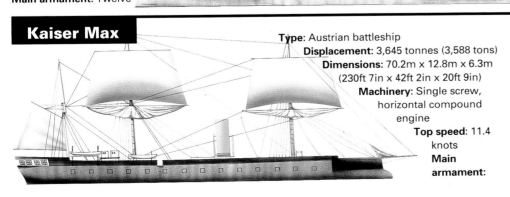

Type: Austrian battleship
Displacement: 3,645 tonnes (3,588 tons)
Dimensions: 70.2m x 12.8m x 6.3m (230ft 7in x 42ft 2in x 20ft 9in)
Machinery: Single screw, horizontal compound engine
Top speed: 11.4 knots
Main armament:

Fourteen 14-pounder, sixteen 48-pounder guns
Armour: 110mm (4.3in) belt
Launched: March 1862

Kaiser Max was one in a three-unit class of ironclads built for the Austrian Navy. They were modified versions of the preceding class, with uprated engines, more guns and sternchasers. Within a few years *Kaiser Max's* hull was found to be rotten. Her machinery was removed and put into another vessel of the same name. The hull was scrapped in 1878.

Kaiser Wilhelm der Grosse

Type: German liner
Displacement: 14,578 tonnes (14,349 tons)
Dimensions: 191m x 20m (627ft x 66ft)
Machinery: Twin screws, triple expansion engines
Top speed: 23 knots
Launched: May 1897

In the forty years up to the late 1890s, the British had dominated the North Atlantic crossing routes. In an attempt to break this stranglehold, Germany sent a number of engineers and designers to work in British yards to gain vital experience. One of these was Robert Zimmermann, who after 11 years in Britain returned home to design the *Kaiser Wilhelm der Grosse*, the first German liner built specifically to win the Blue Riband of the Atlantic. She was completed in 1897, and provided accommodation for 332 first-class, 343 second-class and 1,074 third-class passengers. Then the largest passenger ship in the world, she quickly showed her ability to run at high speeds, taking the eastbound Blue Riband title in 1897, and the westbound in 1898. She worked the North Atlantic route until 1914, when she was converted to an auxiliary cruiser and armed with six 105mm (4.1in) guns. She sunk three ships on her first raid, before being sunk by the British cruiser *Highflyer* on 27 August 1914.

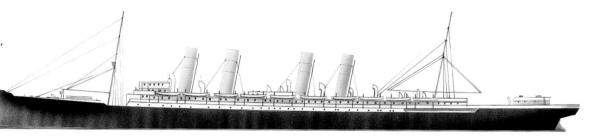

Kaiserin Augusta

Type: German cruiser
Displacement: 6,317 tonnes (6,218 tons)
Dimensions: 123.2m x 15.6m x 7.4m (405ft 6in x 51ft 2in x 24ft 3in)
Machinery: Triple screws, triple expansion engines
Main armament: Eight 102mm (4in), four 152mm (6in) guns
Launched: January 1892

Kaiserin Augusta was Germany's first triple-screw warship. Plans were drawn up in 1887, and the designs were a foretaste of the successful German cruisers to be built much later, during World War I. *Kaiserin Augusta* was laid down at Krupps Germania yard in 1890, and was completed in 1892. In 1898 her armament was increased to 12 x 152mm (6in) guns, so greatly improving her offensive powers. Her engines developed 12,000hp. Range was 7,600km (4,000 miles) at 10 knots. In 1914 *Kaiserin Augusta* became a gunnery school ship. She was broken up in 1920.

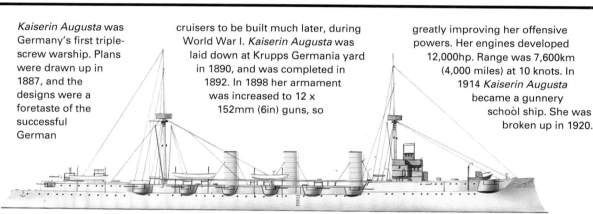

Kaiserin Elisabeth

Type: Austrian cruiser
Displacement: 4,565 tonnes (4,494 tons)
Dimensions: 103.7m x 14.7m x 5.7m (340ft 3in x 48ft 5in x 18ft 8in)
Machinery: Twin screws, horizontal triple expansion engines
Top speed: 20 knots
Main armament: Six 152mm (6in), two 238mm (9.4in) guns
Launched: 1890

Kaiserin Elisabeth was the only major Austrian warship to be sunk outside home waters during wartime. Her 238mm (9.4in) guns were in single, open mounts. Four of the 152mm (6in) guns were in casemates on the main deck level with the fore and aft bridge, and the other two were in the waist of the ship. Her engines developed 9,000hp. In 1905-1906, the 238mm (9.4in) weapons were replaced by two more 152mm (6in) guns. She was stationed at the German port of Tsingtao in China upon the outbreak of World War I. She was scuttled in November 1914 to prevent her falling into Japanese hands.

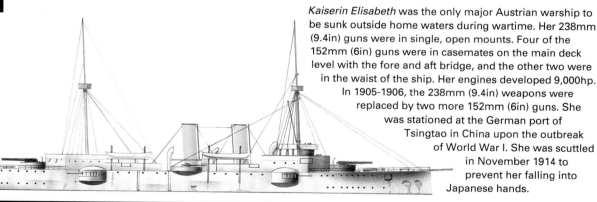

Kalamazoo

Type: US battleship
Displacement: 5,690 tonnes (5,600 tons)
Dimensions: 105m x 17m x 5.3m (345ft 5in x 56ft 8in x 17ft 6in)
Machinery: Twin screws, horizontal direct acting engines
Top speed: 11 knots
Main armament: Four 380mm (15in) guns

Kalamazoo was one of a class of four units that, with the exception *Dunderberg*, were the largest warships in the US Navy at the time. *Kalamazoo* was a double-turreted monitor with two massive funnels and a single, large, armoured ventilating trunk. Her hull was plated with 152mm (6in) armour with a 762mm (30in) thick wooden backing. The deck armour was 76mm (3in) thick, laid on top of a 152mm (6in) thick wooden deck, with another 76mm (3in) of wood laid on top of the armour plating. As a result, the hulls and decks of *Kalamazoo* and her sisters were very strong, but as they were made from unseasoned wood they rapidly deteriorated. *Kalamazoo* was laid down in 1863, but after the end of the American Civil War, construction work on all ships in the class was slow. All four units had been broken up by 1884. The US Navy were not to possess such powerful vessels again until the early 1890s.

Kapitan Saken

Type: Russian torpedo gunboat
Displacement: 610 tonnes (600 tons)
Dimensions: 64m x 7.3m x 3.3m
(210ft x 24ft x 11ft)

Machinery: Twin screws, vertical triple expansion engines

Top speed: 18.5 knots
Main armament: Four three-pounder guns, four 431mm (17in) torpedo tubes
Launched: May 1889
Date of profile: 1890

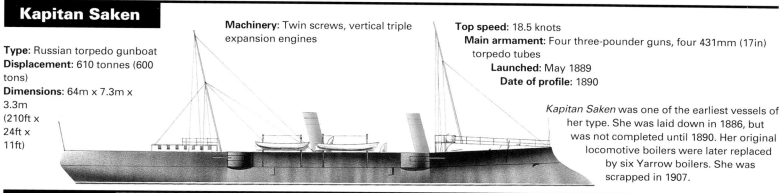

Kapitan Saken was one of the earliest vessels of her type. She was laid down in 1886, but was not completed until 1890. Her original locomotive boilers were later replaced by six Yarrow boilers. She was scrapped in 1907.

Karlsruhe

Type: German cruiser
Displacement: 6,290 tonnes (6,191 tons)
Dimensions: 142.2m x 13.7m x 5.5m
(466ft 6in x 45ft x 18ft)
Machinery: Twin screws, turbines
Top speed: 28.5 knots
Main armament: Twelve 105mm (4.1in) guns

Armour: 18-60mm (0.7-2.4in) waterline belt, 40-60mm (1.6-2.4in) armoured deck
Launched: November 1912

Although *Karlsruhe*'s career was one of the shortest of any German cruiser, she inflicted a great deal of damage on the British merchant marine. Upon the outbreak of World War I she was stationed in the Caribbean, and sank 17 merchant vessels amounting to over 77,834 tonnes (76,609 tons). In November 1914 *Karlsruhe* was in company with two supply tenders when she was destroyed by a magazine explosion.

Kasuga

Type: Japanese cruiser
Displacement: 7,750 tonnes (7,628 tons)
Dimensions: 111.7m x 18.9m x 7.3m
(366ft 7in x 62ft x 24ft)
Machinery: Twin screws, vertical triple expansion engines
Top speed: 20 knots
Main armament: Fourteen 152mm (6in), two 203mm (8in), one 254mm

(10in) guns
Launched: October 1902
Date of profile: 1904

Kasuga was originally built for Argentina at Ansaldo, Genoa, but was purchased by Japan in 1903 just prior to her

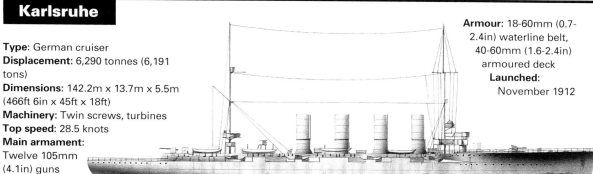

completion. She was almost a duplicate of the successful Italian Garibaldi type, with good protection, powerful armament and fair speed. She was partially disarmed in the 1920s, and became a training ship. *Kasuga* was scrapped in 1948.

Katahdin

Type: US ram
Displacement: 2,421 tonnes (2,383 tons)
Dimensions: 76.4m x 13.2m x 4.6m

(250ft 9in x 43ft 5in x 15ft)
Machinery: Twin screws, horizontal triple expansion engines
Main armament: Four six-pounder

guns
Launched: 1893

Katahdin was an armoured ram intended for harbour defence work, but was also expected to act with a battle fleet, ramming enemy vessels in the thick smoke of battle. Her 'turtle-back' hull was fully armoured, 51mm (2in) thick on top, increasing to 152mm (6in) at the waterline. Taken out of service in 1897, she was re-commissioned during the war with Spain in 1898. She was stricken from the Navy List in 1909, and became a target ship.

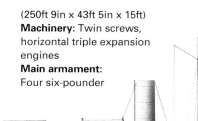

KDD Ocean Link

Type: Japanese cable layer
Displacement: 9,662 tonnes (9,510 tons)
Dimensions: 133m x 19.6m x 7.4m
(437ft x 64ft 4in x 24ft 3in))
Machinery: Twin screws, diesel

engines
Launched: August 1991

KDD Ocean Link, one of the most advanced cable layers in the world, is able to operate in the severest conditions of the North Pacific. She has two full-length decks, beneath which are three large holds for the cables. High-speed Optical Fibre Cable is laid over the stern, while cable burying is executed with a burial plough towed aft. The plough has a TV camera, plus forward scanning sonar, and is monitored from the main control room.

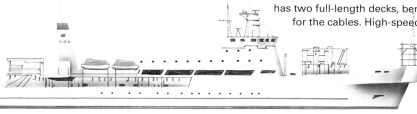

Kearsarge

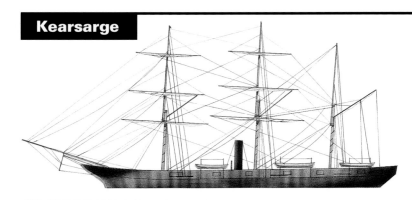

Type: US cruiser
Displacement: 1,511 tonnes (1,488 tons)
Dimensions: 60.5m x 10m x 4.8m (198ft 6in x 33ft 10in x 15ft 9in)
Machinery: Single screw, horizontal back-acting engine
Top speed: 11 knots
Main armament: Two 280mm (11in), four 32-pounder guns
Launched: September 1861
Date of profile: 1864

Kearsarge was built for the Union under the war programme of 1861. She was commissioned in 1862, and was immediately sent off to Europe to locate Sumter, a Confederate raider that had already destroyed a number of Union vessels. In 1864 Kearsarge engaged CSS Alabama off Cherbourg and sank her. In 1894 Kearsarge ran aground off Nicaragua, was looted by the populace, and became a total loss.

Keokuk

Type: US battleship
Displacement: 687 tonnes (677 tons)
Dimensions: 48.6m x 10.9m x 2.6m (159ft 6in x 36ft x 8ft 6in)
Machinery: Twin screws, condensing engines
Main armament: Two 280mm (11in) guns
Armour: 102mm (4in) thick strips 25.4mm (1in) apart, with the

intervening spaces filled with wood
Launched: December 1862

Keokuk was one of the designs submitted to the ironclad design board of 1861 in an attempt to produce

a vessel able to combat the powerful Confederate ironclads then building. One of the other designs was the famous Monitor.

During action off Charleston in 1863, Keokuk was hit 90 times and sank in shallow water. The Confederates salvaged her 280mm (11in) guns and left her hull as a wreck.

Kerch

Type: Russian cruiser
Displacement: 9,855 tonnes (9,700 tons)
Dimensions: 173m x 18.6m x 6.7m (567ft 7in x 61ft x 22ft)
Machinery: Twin screws, gas turbines
Main armament: Four 76.2mm (3in) guns, two twin SA-N-

3 missile launchers
Launched: 1973

Kerch and her six sisters are the largest vessels to have been fitted

with all gas-turbine propulsion. The turbines develop 120,000hp, giving a range of 5,700km (3,000 miles) at full speed, or 16,720km (8,800 miles) at 15 knots. The vessels were developed from the

successful Kresta II design, and have major air and anti-submarine capabilities. Kerch has a heavy gun armament, and extensive command and control facilities. The sizeable superstructure is dominated by the large, low exhaust funnel. The hangar is just forward of the aft flight deck, and slightly lower, with a lift connecting the two for handling the single helicopter.

Kiautschou

Type: German liner
Displacement: 11,085 tonnes (10,911 tons)
Dimensions: 164.5m x 18m x 8.8m (540ft x 60ft x 29ft 11in)
Machinery: Twin screws, quadruple expansion engines
Launched: 1899

In the late 1890s the Germans began a colosssal building programme to bolster their regular mail and passenger service to the Far East. Kiautschou was built for the Hamburg

American Line, and had accommodation for 240 first-class, 162 second-class and 1,950 steerage-class passengers. In 1904 she changed ownership and was re-named Prinzess Alice. After World War I she was taken over by the US merchant marine and re-named City of Honolulu. She caught fire in 1922 and was abandoned.

Kiev

Type: Russian aircraft carrier
Displacement: 38,608 tonnes (38,000 tons)
Dimensions: 273m x 47.2m x 8.2m (895ft 8in x 154ft 10in x 27ft)
Machinery: Quadruple screws, turbines
Main armament: Four

76.2mm (3in) guns, plus missiles
Aircraft: 36
Launched: December 1972

Kiev was the first Russian aircraft carrier to be built with a full flight deck and a purpose-

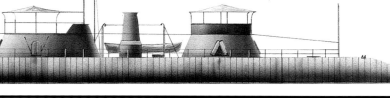

built hull. She was laid down in September 1970 in the Black Sea Nikolayev Dockyard. She was completed in May 1975. The flight deck is angled, with

most of the armament carried forward, and comprising a full range of anti-ship, anti-air and anti-submarine missiles. Twenty-four of the lethal SS-N-12 Shaddock type missiles are carried. The large bridge structure is set on Kiev's starboard side, and houses an array of radar equipment.

Kilo

Type: Russian submarine
Displacement: 2,336 tonnes (2,300 tons) (surface), 2,946 tonnes (2,900 tons) (submerged)
Dimensions: 73m x 10m x 6.5m (239ft 6in x 32ft 10in x 21ft 4in)
Machinery: Single screw, diesel engines (surface), electric motors (submerged)
Top speed: 12 knots (surface), 18 knots (submerged)
Main armament: Six 533mm (21in) torpedo tubes
Launched: 1981

Unlike the United States Navy, the Soviet Navy in the 1970s remained

convinced that there was a place for the conventionally-powered submarine. Cheaper and simpler than nuclear attack boats, diesel electric vessels are smaller, quieter and more manoeuvrable than their larger brethren. The Kilo class were the first such boats of Russian design to use a modern teardrop hull form, which gives a high underwater speed for comparatively low power. They have a double hull, which increases the chances of surviving a hit. They have a distinctive, typically

Russian, long fin, and a prominent raised deck casing. The diesel engines develop 4,000hp, while the electric motors develop 5,000hp. These are small, popular boats, although they have relatively simple navigation and sensor systems, and are not armed with the latest

submarine launched anti-ship missiles. They are fast, highly manoeuvrable and well suited to operations in restricted waters. A number have been successfully sold to other navies, often to replace their 1950s-vintage diesel boats. Construction was at the rate of 2-4 per year, although with the break up of the Soviet Union, it is not known whether manufacture will continue.

Kirov

Type: Russian cruiser
Displacement: 11,684 tonnes (11,500 tons)
Dimensions: 191m x 18m x 6m (626ft 8in x 59ft x 20ft)
Machinery: Twin screws, turbines

Top speed: 35.9 knots
Main armament: Six 100mm (3.9in), nine 180mm (7.1in) guns
Armour: 76mm (3in) belt
Launched: November 1936

Built with Italian technical help, *Kirov* was a great advance in Russian cruiser design. Initial plans had been for a 7,112-tonne (7,000-

ton) vessel, but extra tonnage was added to strengthen the hull. Final designs were approved in 1934, and *Kirov* was laid down in October 1935 and completed in September 1938. Her 180mm (7.1) guns were mounted in triple turrets, with the battery of 100mm (3.9in) guns concentrated in single mounts alongside the second funnel. A catapult was situated between the two large sloping funnels. *Kirov* was deleted from the effective list in the late 1970s.

Kirov

Type: Russian guided-missile cruiser
Displacement: 28,000 tonnes (28,000 tons)
Dimensions: 248m x 28m x 8.8m (813ft 8in x 91ft 10in x 28ft 10in)
Machinery: Twin screws, turbines, two

pressurised water-type reactors
Main armament: Two 100mm (3.9in) guns, two twin SA-N-4

launchers, twelve SA-N-6 launchers plus twenty anti-ship missiles
Launch date: December 1977

Apart from aircraft carriers, *Kirov* is the largest ship to have been built since the end of World War II. She has a huge superstructure with numerous

radars and early warning antennae. The majority of the missile-launching systems are forward, and housed below deck, leaving the aft section of the vessel for machinery and the helicopter hangar. *Kirov* and her sister are the only vessels to use both steam turbines and nuclear power. Two nuclear reactors are coupled with oil-fired superheaters that intensify the heat of the steam to increase power for more speed.

Kniaz Pojarski

Type: Russian battleship
Displacement: 5,220 tonnes (5,138 tons)
Dimensions: 83m x 15m x 7.4m (272ft 4in x 49ft 3in x 24ft 6in)
Machinery: Single screw, horizontal direct-acting engines
Top speed: 11.7 knots
Main armament: Eight 228mm (9in) guns
Launched: September 1867

Kniaz Pojarski was the first Russian ironclad to serve in the Pacific. She was laid down in 1864 as part of Russia's rapidly growing fleet, but unlike her sister vessels, she was the only one of her type to be designed as a

cruising ironclad. She had a good spread of sail for extended patrolling and a steady gun platform. She was modernised in 1884-86. Two 152mm (6in) guns were mounted fore-and-aft on the upper deck, and 203mm (8in) guns replaced the 228mm (9in) weapons on the battery deck. She was broken up in 1907.

Kniaz Suvarov

Type: Russian battleship
Displacement: 13,730 tonnes
(13,513 tons)
Dimensions: 121m x 23m x 7.9m
(397ft x 76ft 2in x 26ft 2in)
Machinery: Twin screws, vertical
triple expansion engines
Top speed: 17.5 knots
Main armament: Twelve 152mm
(6in), four 305mm (12in) guns

Launched: September 1902
Date of profile: 1904

Kniaz Suvarov was the Russian
flagship at Tsushima in May
1905, and was sunk by enemy
torpedoes. She was one of a
class of five vessels, and
Borodino and
Alexander were
also sunk at
Tsushima,

while *Orel* surrendered to
Japanese forces. The
remaining ship in the
class, *Slavia*, was not
completed in time
to join her ill-
fated sisters.

Köln

Type: German cruiser
Displacement: 7,605
tonnes (7,486
tons)
Dimensions:
155.5m x 14.3m x 6m
(510ft 2in x 47ft

19ft 8in)
Machinery: Twin screws, turbines
Main armament: Eight 150mm
(5.9in) guns
Launched: October 1916

The evolution of the light
to medium cruiser in
the German Navy
was very
systematic,
progressing from

the Bremen class, capable of 23
knots, through several classes, each
an improvement over the preceding
group, to the *Köln* class of ten units.
Laid down in 1915-16, *Köln* and her
sister *Dresden* were the only ships
to be completed, the remainder
being broken up before completion.
Köln had a range of 10,260km (5,400
miles) at 12 knots, or 2,280km (1,200
miles) at full speed. She was
scuttled at Scapa Flow in 1919.

Köln

Type: German cruiser
Displacement: 8,260 tonnes (8,130
tons)
Dimensions: 174m x 15.3m x 6.3m
(570ft 10in x 50ft 2in x 20ft 8in)
Machinery: Twin screws, turbines,
diesel engines
Top speed: 32 knots
with turbines, 10
knots with diesels

Main armament: Nine 150mm (5.9in) guns
Launched: May 1928

Köln and her two sisters were a completely new
design, and incorporated electric welding, which
saved weight. They also carried the new triple
turret, with the two after turrets offset
from the centreline, giving a

good all-round field of fire. As completed, *Köln* had a catapult
and 12 x 500mm (19.7in) torpedo tubes in triple mounts, but
the catapult and two of the mounts
were removed early in World War
II. *Köln* was sunk during a
bombing raid while undergoing a
refit. She was later raised, and
was scrapped in 1946.

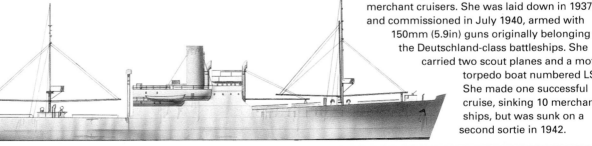

Komet

Type: German commerce raider
Displacement: 7,620 tonnes (7,500
tons)
Dimensions: 115m x 15.3m x 6.5m
(377ft 4in x 50ft 2in x 21ft 4in)
Machinery: Single screw,
diesel engines
Main armament: Six
150mm (5.9in) guns
Launched: 1939

Komet, originally named *Ems*, was the smallest
and best equipped of the German armed
merchant cruisers. She was laid down in 1937
and commissioned in July 1940, armed with
150mm (5.9in) guns originally belonging to
the Deutschland-class battleships. She
carried two scout planes and a motor
torpedo boat numbered LS2.
She made one successful
cruise, sinking 10 merchant
ships, but was sunk on a
second sortie in 1942.

König Wilhelm

Type: German battleship
Displacement: 10,933 tonnes (10,761
tons)
Dimensions: 112m x 18.3m x 8.5m
(368ft x 60ft x 28ft)
Machinery: Single screw, horizontal
single expansion engine
Top speed: 14.7 knots

Main armament: Five 210mm (8.3in),
eighteen 238mm (9.4in) guns
Launched: April 1868
Date of profile: 1869

König Wilhelm was laid down in
Britain for the Turkish Navy, but was
bought by Germany prior to
completion. In 1878 she collided with
Grosser Kurfürst and sank her. She

then underwent extensive
repairs and was re-
boiled, given a stronger
ram and extra smaller
guns. She emerged
re-rated as a heavy
cruiser. She became
a school ship in
1907 and was
scrapped in 1921.

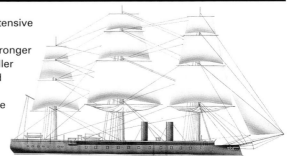

Koning Willem II

Type: Dutch liner
Displacement: 4,361 tonnes (4,293 tons)
Dimensions: 124m x 13.7m x 7m (408ft x 45ft x 23ft 3in)
Machinery: Single screw, quadruple expansion engines
Launched: 1899
Date of profile: 1904

Koning Willem II was one of a group of mail steamers built for the Nederland Steamship Company for service between Europe and the East Indies. She carried 70 first-class passengers, about 30 second-class passengers and up to 40 troops making the journey to and from the Dutch possessions in the East. Her engines developed 4,000hp. She was fitted out with a good spread of awnings for tropical climates, and was a fine seaboat. In 1913 she was sold to Italy and re-named *Atene*. She was wrecked in 1926.

Korietz

Type: Russian gunboat
Displacement: 1,290 tonnes (1,270 tons)
Dimensions: 66.7m x 10.6m x 3.7m (219ft x 35ft x 12ft 4in)
Machinery: Twin screws, horizontal compound engines
Main armament: One 152mm (6in), two 203mm (8in) guns
Launched: August 1886

Korietz was laid down in 1885 at Stockholm. She was a barquentine-rigged vessel, with the two 203mm (8in) guns firing forward from sponsons protected by armour shields. The 152mm (6in) gun was mounted aft, and four 107mm (4.2in) weapons were mounted on the broadside. She and her sister *Mandjur* were heavily armed for their size, and ideal for patrol work. *Korietz* was one of the first warships lost in the Russo-Japanese War. She was scuttled in Korea on 9 February 1904 to prevent her falling into enemy hands.

Kormoran

Type: German commerce raider
Displacement: 20,218 tonnes (19,900 tons)
Dimensions: 164m x 20m x 8.5m (538ft x 66ft 3in x 27ft 10in)
Machinery: Twin screws, diesel engines, electric motors
Main armament: Six 150mm (5.9in) guns
Launched: 1939

Kormoran, formerly the *Steiermark*, was laid down in 1938 and commissioned in 1940. She immediately set out on a 350-day sortie, sinking or capturing 11 merchant ships totalling 69,366 tonnes

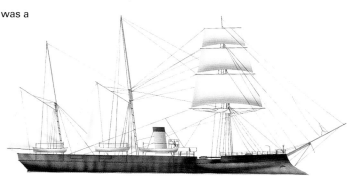

(68,274 tons). She was tracked down by the Australian cruiser *Sydney* off Western Australia on 11 November 1941. At first *Sydney*'s crew thought *Kormoran* was a Dutch merchant

vessel, but then *Kormoran* opened fire on her. Soon both ships were out of action. *Sydney* later blew up with the loss of all hands. *Kormoran* later sank.

Kota Wijaya

Type: Malayan container ship
Displacement: 22,695 tonnes (22,695 tons)
Dimensions: 184.5m x 27.6m x 9.5m (605ft 4in x 90ft 6in x 31ft 3in)

Machinery: Single screw, diesel engines
Top speed: 19 knots
Launched: February 1991
Date of profile: 1992

Kota Wijaya is one of a new generation of container ships able to

carry a mixed cargo of 6m (20ft) and 12m (40ft) containers in six holds, with a total capacity of 1,186 TEU, plus a further 200 refrigerated containers on the upper deck. The hull is double-skinned over the midships section, and the side tanks are used for fuel while the starboard

water ballast heeling tanks are used during loading and unloading operations. *Kota Wijaya*'s engines develop 14,000hp at 100 revolutions per minute, and fuel consumption is 40.8 tonnes (40.2 tons) per day, a further two tonnes also being consumed by auxiliary engines.

Krasnograd

Type: Russian cargo ship
Displacement: 26,630 tonnes (26,630 tons)
Dimensions: 173.5m x 23m x 10m (569ft 3in x 75ft 6in x 32ft 10in)
Machinery: Single screw, diesel engines
Launched: 1992

Krasnograd is among the first foreign-built cargo carriers to enter Russian service for many years. The hold features two through-decks with four cargo holds. Containers of (6m (20ft) and (12m (40ft) are carried, having a total capacity of 728 TEU. Thirty are refrigerated.

Krasnyi Kavkaz

Type: Russian cruiser
Displacement: 9,174 tonnes (9,030 tons)
Dimensions: 169.5m x 15.7m x 6.2m (556ft x 51ft 6in x 20ft 4in)
Machinery: Twin screws, turbines
Top speed: 29 knots
Main armament: Four 100mm (3.9in), four 180mm (7.1in) guns
Launched: June 1916
Date of profile: 1935

This ship was laid down for the Imperial Russian Navy in 1913 and launched in 1916 as the light cruiser *Admiral Lazarev*. The chaos of the revolution and the ensuing civil war prevented her from being worked on until 1927, and she was not finally completed until 1932. Once work was restarted, her builders tried to take advantage of the advances in ship design that had taken place in the previous nine years and she was extensively modified from her earlier design. Her hull was lengthened by some 9m (30ft), while her armour protection was carried further aft than was originally planned. She was also fitted with an experimental gun design of 180mm (7.1in) calibre, which was mounted singly in turrets along the centreline. This gun was later used in follow-on Soviet cruiser designs. She had a distinctive outline, with two large upright funnels, a crowded bridge and a large crane forming an integral part of the mainmast. In January 1932 she joined the Soviet Navy as the light cruiser *Krasnyi Kavkaz*. She served throughout World War II, and suffered severe combat damage on more than one occasion. She went into dock and had a major overhaul in 1944. She was not long on the active list after the war, and became a training ship in 1947. She was later used as a target ship, and was eventually sunk sometime in 1956, during the development of the SSN-1 anti-shipping missile.

Kreml

Type: Russian battleship
Displacement: 4,064 tonnes (4,000 tons)
Dimensions: 67.6m x 16m x 5.9m (221ft 9in x 53ft x 19ft 6in)
Machinery: Single screw, horizontal direct acting engine
Top speed: 9 knots
Main armament: Eight 86mm (3.4in), six 152mm (6in), eight 203mm (8in) guns
Launched: 1865

Kreml was one of five vessels that formed the basis of the Russian ironclad fleet. She had two near-sisters, one of which, *Pervenetz*, was designed by George Mackrow and built in Britain. *Kreml* was laid down in 1864 and completed in 1866. She was an iron-hulled broadside ironclad. Her engines, taken from a Russian wooden screw ship, developed 1,630hp. She eventually became a gunnery training ship before being scrapped in 1905.

Kronprinz Wilhelm

Type: German liner
Displacement: 15,147 tonnes (14,908 tons)
Dimensions: 202m x 20.2m x 8.8m (663ft x 66ft 3in x 29ft)
Machinery: Twin screws, quadruple expansion engines
Top speed: 23.3 knots
Launched: March 1901

Kronprinz Wilhelm was one of a group of large express liners built for Norddeutscher Lloyd at the turn of the century. Upon completion, *Kronprinz Wilhelm* had the largest quadruple expansion engines of the period, with the largest cylinder having a diameter of some 2,590mm (102in) and a stroke of 1,955mm (77in). The ship was an immediate success, maintaining high speeds across the North Atlantic. When World War I broke out she became a commerce raider until forced to intern herself in a US port. When the USA entered the war in 1917, she became the troop transport *Von Steuben*. She was scrapped in 1940.

Kurfürst Friedrich Wilhelm

Type: German battleship
Displacement: 10,210 tonnes (10,050 tons)
Dimensions: 115.7m x 19.5m x 7.9m (379ft 7in x 64ft x 26ft)
Machinery: Twin screws, triple expansion engines
Main armament: Six 105mm (4.1in), six 280mm (11in) guns
Armour: 305-406mm (12-16in) belt, 305mm (12in) on barbettes, 127mm (5in) on gun houses
Launched: June 1891

Kurfürst Friedrich Wilhelm was one of four powerful vessels that formed the basis of the German Navy in the early 1900s. She was sold to Turkey in 1910, becoming *Heireddin Barbarossa*. She was sunk by a British submarine in 1915.

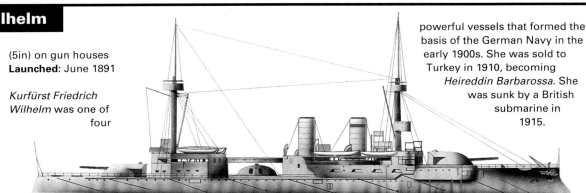

L 2

Type: Russian submarine
Displacement: 1,219 tonnes (1,200 tons) (surface), 1,574 tonnes (1,550 tons) (submerged)
Dimensions: 81m x 7.5m x 4.8m (265ft 9in x 24ft 7in x 15ft 9in)
Machinery: Twin screws, diesel engines

(surface), electric motors (submerged)
Main armament: One 100mm (3.9in) gun, six 533mm (21in) torpedo tubes
Launched: July 1931

L 2 was one of a large class of Russian submarines. She was noted for being the most successful of the entire class, having sunk the 5,313-

tonne (5,230-ton) German steamship *Goya* in the Baltic in April 1945, at a time when such relatively large merchant ships were very precious to Germany. L 2 was broken up in 1959.

L 3

Type: US submarine
Displacement: 457 tonnes (450 tons) (surface), 556 tonnes (548 tons) (submerged)
Dimensions: 51m x 5.3m x 4m (167ft 4in x 17ft 4in x 13ft5in)
Machinery: Twin screws, diesel engines (surface), electric motors (submerged)
Main armament: One 76mm (3in)

gun, four 457mm (18in) torpedo tubes
Launched: February 1915

L 3 was the first US submarine to carry a deck gun. This was a 23-calibre weapon that retracted vertically into a deckhouse until only a small portion of the barrel was left exposed, so cutting down on underwater drag.

Range at 11 knots surfaced was 6,270km (3,300 miles) and at five knots submerged was 285km (150 miles). L 3 was broken up in 1932.

L 23

Type: British submarine
Displacement: 904 tonnes (890 tons) (surface), 1,097 tonnes (1,080 tons) (submerged)
Dimensions: 72.7m x 7.2m x 3.4m (238ft 6in x 23ft 8in x 11ft2in)
Machinery: Twin screws,

diesel engines (surface), electric motors (submerged)
Top speed: 17.5 knots (surface), 10.5 knots (submerged)
Main

armament: One 102mm (4in) gun, four 533mm (21in) torpedo tubes
Launched: July 1919
Date of profile: 1920

L 23 was one of the last surviving units of a large, successful class of single-hull submarines built during World War I. By World War II, only L 23 and two others remained in service. L 23 foundered on her way to the breakers in 1946.

La Champagne

Type: French liner
Displacement: 6,858 tonnes (6,750 tons)
Dimensions: 154.8m x 15.7m x 7.3m (508ft x 51ft 8in x 24ft)
Machinery: Single screw, three-cylinder compound engines
Top speed: 18.6 knots
Launched: April 1885

La Champagne served on the North Atlantic. She and her sister *Bretagne* were France's first luxury liners, and carried 390 first-class, 65 second-class and 620 third-class passengers. While at anchor on 28 May 1915, *La Champagne* grounded, broke her back and was a total loss.

Lafayette

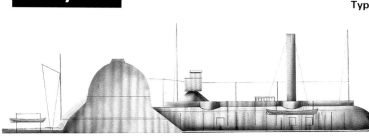

Type: US gunboat
Displacement: 1,016 tonnes (1,000 tons)
Dimensions: 85.3m x 13.7m x 2.4m (280ft x 45ft x 8ft)
Machinery: Paddlewheels, single-stroke engines
Main armament: Four 228mm (9in), two 280mm (11in), two 100-pounder guns
Launched: 1858
Date of profile: 1863

Lafayette was one of the most powerful river gunboats on the Mississippi. Formerly the *Alick Scott*, she was taken over by the US Army as a transport under the name of *Fort Henry* before being re-named *Lafayette*. She was converted at St Louis in 1862, and was in service by 1863. She was laid up in 1865 and was sold the following year.

Lafayette

Type: French liner
Displacement: 15,138 tonnes (14,900 tons)
Dimensions: 171.6 m x 19.5m x 7.4m (563ft x 64ft x 24ft 3in)
Machinery: Quadruple screws, four-cylinder compound engines
Top speed: 18.9 knots
Launched: May 1914

Ordered as the *Ile de Cuba* for the French Line, the ship was completed as *Lafayette* in October 1915. She was taken over as a hospital ship in 1916. In 1919 she resumed her original service, carrying 336 first-class, 110 second-class and 90 third-class passengers, plus 714 emigrants. *Lafayette* had a two-tier public section above the boat deck, giving her a unique appearance. The drawing room, garden lounge and luxury appartments were situated on the boat deck. In 1928 the ship was re-named *Mexique*. She hit a mine and sank in June 1940.

Lake Champlain

Type: British liner
Displacement: 7,510 tonnes (7,392 tons)
Dimensions: 140m x 15.8m (460ft x 52ft)
Machinery: Twin screws, triple expansion engines
Top speed: 13 knots
Launched: 1900

Lake Champlain had a long and varied career. In May 1901 she commenced service on the North Atlantic, carrying the first wireless to be fitted to a North Atlantic liner. In 1913 she transferred to the Austrians and was re-named *Tyrolia*. She returned to Britain in 1914, and during World War I was disguised as a dreadnought battleship in an attempt to conceal the true position of the main British fleet. In 1915 she became the oiler *Ruthenia*. She was sent to Singapore as an oil hulk in 1929, captured by the Japanese in 1942 and re-named *Choran*. She was re-taken in 1945 and eventually scrapped in 1949.

Lancashire

Type: British liner
Displacement: 9,704 tonnes (9,552 tons)
Dimensions: 152m x 17.4m x 8.5m (500ft x 57ft 3in x 28ft 1in)
Machinery: Twin screws, quadruple expansion engines
Top speed: 15 knots
Launched: 1917
Date of profile: 1918

Lancashire was one of the last vessels to carry four masts. She entered service for the Bibby Line in July 1917, and in 1930 became a troop transport for the Indian Service. She continued as a troop transport during World War II, and was broken up in 1956.

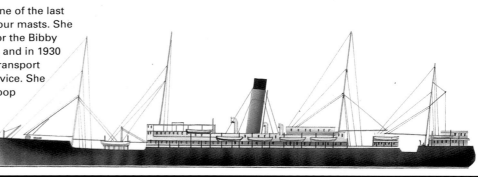

Landsort

Type: Swedish tanker
Displacement: 165,646 tonnes (163,038 tons)

Dimensions: 274m x 48m x 17m (899ft x 157ft 6in x 55ft 9in)
Machinery: Single screw, diesel engines
Launched: June 1991

Landsort was the first double-hulled oil tanker to be completed in line with the new, stricter regulations for this type of vessel. She was specifically designed to carry crude oil and oil products of heavier specific gravity. She has nine full-width cargo tanks. Cargo capacity is 172,850 cubic metres (6,105,150 cubic ft). The 2.5m (8ft) space within the double hull is divided into five pairs of tanks for carrying water ballast. The main engine develops nearly 21,000hp. Her rudder is the largest in the world, covering an overall area of 58 sq m (624 sq ft).

Leonardo Da Vinci

Type: Italian battleship
Displacement: 25,250 tonnes (25,086 tons)
Dimensions: 176m x 28m x 9.3m (577ft 9in x 91ft 10in x 30ft 10in)
Machinery: Quadruple screws, turbines
Top speed: 21.6 knots
Main armament: Eighteen 120mm (4.7in), thirteen 305mm (12in) guns
Armour: 127-248mm (5-9.8in) belt, 280mm (11in) on turrets, 110-127mm (4.3-5in) on secondary battery
Launched: October 1911
Date of profile: 1916

Leonardo da Vinci and her two sisters were an improvement on the previous Dante Alighieri class, having 13 big guns mounted in five centreline turrets, with superfiring twin turrets fore and aft. Instead of carrying the secondary armament in twin turrets, the battery was concentrated amidships in casemates. Machinery developed 31,000hp, and range at 10 knots was 9,120km (4,800 miles). *Leonardo da Vinci* was completed in 1914, but sank as a result of a magazine explosion at Taranto harbour in 1916. She was raised in 1919 and scrapped in 1923.

Lepanto

Type: Italian battleship
Displacement: 16,154 tonnes (15,900 tons)
Dimensions: 124.7m x 22.3m x 9.6m (409ft 1in x 73ft 2in x 31ft 6in)
Machinery: Twin screws, vertical compound engines
Top speed: 18.4 knots
Main armament: Eight 152mm (6in), four 431mm (17in) guns
Armour: 483mm (19in) on central citadel
Launched: March 1883

Upon completion in 1887, Benedetto Brin's *Lepanto* was the fastest capital ship in the world and, together with her sister *Italia*, was also one of the largest and most powerful. She had no side armour, but her armoured deck curved almost down to the waterline, and she was extensively compartmentalised. What armour she had was concentrated amidships on a large oval barbette that lay at an oblique angle across the hull. On this were mounted two turntables, each one of which carried two 431mm (17in) guns. Her four funnels were linked by a narrow flying bridge, the front of which was connected to a tiny conning bridge. A mast protruded from the centre. Her engines developed 15,797hp, and range at 10 knots was 16,530km (8,700 miles). She could carry large numbers of troops in times of emergency, an important consideration when the vessel was laid down in 1876, with Italy threatened from France on one side and by the Austrian Navy on the other. By the time she and her sister entered service, however, great strides had been made in the development of quick-firing guns and high-explosive shells. These fine ships, with their inadequate armour and slow rate of fire (one shot every five minutes from each gun), were soon incapable of meeting a modern battleship face to face. In later years, *Lepanto* had more quick-firing light guns fitted to her maindeck. She was finally stricken from the effective list in 1914.

Lexington

Type: American gunboat
Displacement: 455 tonnes (448 tons)
Dimensions: 54m x 11m x 1.8m (177ft 7in x 36ft 10in x 6ft)
Machinery: Paddlewheels
Top speed: 7 knots
Main armament: Four 203mm (8in), two 32-pounder guns
Launched: 1860

Lexington was built at Pittsburgh for service as a passenger and freight steamer on the Mississippi. In 1861 she was sold to the government and high, 127mm (5in) thick bulwarks were built up around her decks to protect her crew from rifle fire. The decks were strengthened and guns were positioned forward, firing through ports cut in the bulwarks. *Lexington* was initially converted for the Union Army, who were trying to build up their own gunboat fleet. Later she was taken over by the navy. She was sold in 1865.

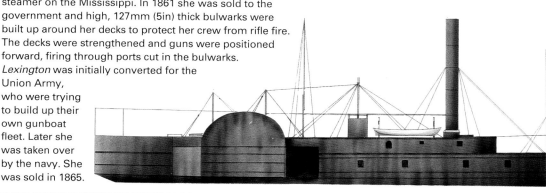

Lexington

Type: US aircraft carrier
Displacement: 48,463 tonnes (47,700 tons)
Dimensions: 270.6m x 32.2m x 9.9m (88ft x 105ft 8in x 32ft 6in)
Machinery: Quadruple screws, turbo electric drive
Top speed: 33.2 knots
Main armament: Twelve 127mm (5in), eight 203mm (8in) guns
Aircraft: 80
Launched: October 1925
Date of profile: 1939

Lexington was the first effective carrier completed for the US Navy. She was laid down in 1921 as a battlecruiser, but work was stopped as a result of the 1922 Washington Naval Treaty. Her design was then changed to that of an aircraft carrier, though her cruiser-type hull form was retained. A 137m x 21m (450ft x 70ft) hangar was installed and for many years, she remained the largest aircraft carrier afloat. In 1942 she was set on fire during action with Japanese forces, and was scuttled by the US destroyer *Phelps*.

Libia

Type: Italian cruiser
Displacement: 4,537 tonnes (4,466 tons)
Dimensions: 111.8m x 14.5m x 5.5m (366ft 10in x 47ft 7in x 18ft)
Machinery: Twin screws, vertical triple expansion engines
Top speed: 22.9 knots
Main armament: Eight 120mm (4.7in), two 152mm (6in) guns
Launched: November 1912

This vessel was originally ordered by Turkey as the *Drama* in 1907, and the design followed that of Elswick's *Hamidieh* of 1902-04. When Italy declared war on Turkey she was taken over by the Italians, and was completed in 1913 as *Libia*. Her 152mm (6in) guns were positioned fore and aft, but in 1925 were removed. The 120mm (4.7in) guns were positioned on the broadside and in the waist. *Libia*'s engines developed 11,530hp, and range was 5,985km (3,150 miles) at 10 knots, 2,394km (1,260 miles) at 18 knots. She was removed from the effective list in 1937.

Lion

Type: British battlecruiser
Displacement: 30,154 tonnes (29,680 tons)
Dimensions: 213.3m x 27m x 8.7m (700ft x 88ft 6in x 28ft 10in)
Machinery: Quadruple screws, turbines
Main armament: Sixteen 102mm (4.2in), eight 343mm (13.5in) guns

Armour: 127-228mm (5-9in) main belt, 102-152mm (4-6in) upper belt, 102-228mm (4-9in) on turrets
Launched: August 1910

Lion had eight 343mm (13.5in) guns, and

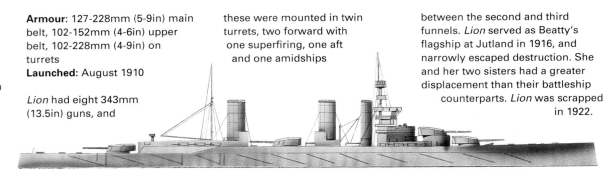

these were mounted in twin turrets, two forward with one superfiring, one aft and one amidships

between the second and third funnels. *Lion* served as Beatty's flagship at Jutland in 1916, and narrowly escaped destruction. She and her two sisters had a greater displacement than their battleship counterparts. *Lion* was scrapped in 1922.

Littorio

Type: Italian battleship
Displacement: 46,698 tonnes (45,963 tons)
Dimensions: 237.8m x 32.9m x 9.6m (780ft 2in x 108ft x 31ft 6in)

Machinery: Quadruple screws, turbines
Top speed: 28 knots
Main armament: Twelve 89mm

(3.5in), four 120mm (4.7in), twelve 152mm (6in), nine 380mm (15in) guns
Launched: August 1937
Date of profile: 1940

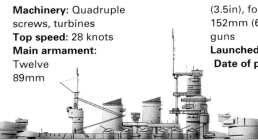

Littorio was one of the last battleships to be built for the Italian Navy. Her impressive outline was all the more striking due to the raised height of the aft turret, which was designed to avoid blast damage to the two fighter planes carried on the poop deck. *Littorio* was broken up between 1948 and 1950.

Lord Nelson

Type: British battleship
Displacement: 17,945 tonnes (17,663 tons)
Dimensions: 135m x 24m x 7.9m (443ft 6in x 79ft 6in x 26ft)
Machinery: Twin screws, triple expansion engines
Top speed: 18.7 knots
Main armament: Ten 233mm (9.2in), four 305mm (12in) guns

Armour: 203-305mm (8-12in) belt, 178-203mm (7-8in) on turrets
Launched: September 1906

Lord Nelson and her sister *Agamemnon* were the last pre-dreadnoughts built for the Royal Navy. *Lord Nelson* was

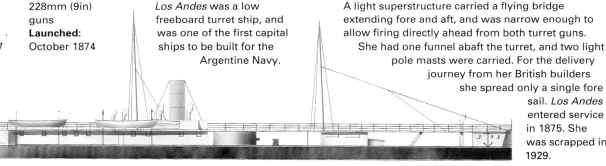

completed in October 1908. The 305mm (12in) guns were in twin turrets, with the 233mm (9.2in) guns in a mix of twin and single turrets on the broadside. The main belt ran her full length, supplemented by an upper belt which ran to the base of the 'Y' turret. Further protection was provided by a number of solid bulkheads, the first to be fitted to a British battleship. She saw extensive service during World War I, and was scrapped in 1920.

Los Andes

Type: Argentinian battleship
Displacement: 1,703 tonnes (1,677 tons)
Dimensions: 56.4m x 15.7m x 3.2m (185ft 4in x 51ft 7in x 10ft 6in)
Machinery: Twin screws, compound engines
Top speed: 9.5 knots
Main armament: Two

228mm (9in) guns
Launched: October 1874

Los Andes was a low freeboard turret ship, and was one of the first capital ships to be built for the Argentine Navy.

A light superstructure carried a flying bridge extending fore and aft, and was narrow enough to allow firing directly ahead from both turret guns. She had one funnel abaft the turret, and two light pole masts were carried. For the delivery journey from her British builders she spread only a single fore sail. *Los Andes* entered service in 1875. She was scrapped in 1929.

Louisiana

Type: Confederate ironclad
Displacement: 1,422 tonnes (1,400 tons)
Dimensions: 80m x 18.8m (260ft x 62ft)
Machinery: Twin

screws, paddlewheels
Main armament: Two 178mm (7in), four 203mm (8in), three 228mm (9in), seven 32-

pounder guns
Armour: 102mm (4in) on casemate, plus wooden backing
Launched: April 1862

Louisiana was one of three powerful ironclads intended for the defence of the lower Mississippi. Lack of suitable materials

meant that much 'green' wood was used in her construction, and she leaked so badly that water was knee deep on the gun deck during action. In April 1862 she put up a fierce defence against overwhelming odds, but when the Union fleet pushed past her to New Orleans, *Louisiana* was set on fire by her commander and left to explode down river.

Luigi Cadorna

Type: Italian cruiser
Displacement: 7,113 tonnes (7,001 tons)
Dimensions: 169.3m x 15.5m x 5.5m (555ft 6in x 50ft 10in x 18ft)
Machinery: Twin screws, turbines
Main armament: Six 100mm (3.9in), 8 152mm (6in) guns

Launched: 1931

By the end of the 1920s, Italy was building some outstanding cruisers. They were well armed and faster than most of their contemporaries, speed being

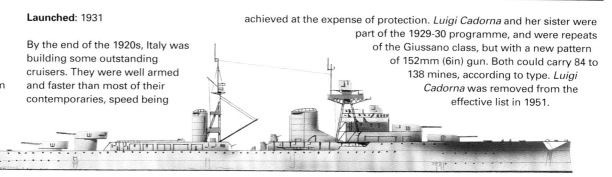

achieved at the expense of protection. *Luigi Cadorna* and her sister were part of the 1929-30 programme, and were repeats of the Giussano class, but with a new pattern of 152mm (6in) gun. Both could carry 84 to 138 mines, according to type. *Luigi Cadorna* was removed from the effective list in 1951.

Luigi Settembrini

Type: Italian submarine
Displacement: 968 tonnes (953 tons) (surface), 1,171 tonnes (1,153 tons) (submerged)
Dimensions: 69m x 6.6m x 4.4m (226ft 8in x 21ft 8in x 14ft 5in)
Machinery: Twin screws, diesel engines (surface), electric motors (submerged)
Top speed: 17 knots (surface), 7.5 knots (submerged)
Main armament: One 102mm (4in) gun, eight 533mm (21in) torpedo tubes
Launched: 1930

Luigi Settembrini was a fast, short-range, partial-double-hulled boat with great manoeuvrability. Until 1940 she

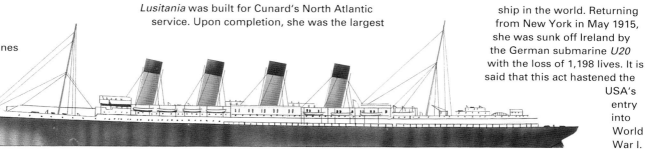

served in the Red Sea. From 1940 to 1943 she alternated combat patrols and supply runs to North Africa with periods of service at the Submarine School. After Italy joined the Allies, the boat was used for training until she was accidentally rammed and sunk by the US destroyer *Framet* in 1944.

Lusitania

Type: British liner
Displacement: 32,054 tonnes (31,550 tons)
Dimensions: 232m x 27m (761ft x 88ft)
Machinery: Quadruple screws, turbines
Launched: 1906

Lusitania was built for Cunard's North Atlantic service. Upon completion, she was the largest

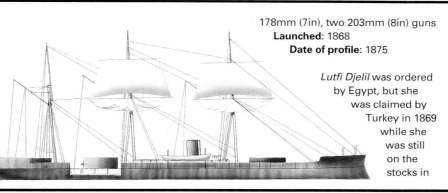

ship in the world. Returning from New York in May 1915, she was sunk off Ireland by the German submarine *U20* with the loss of 1,198 lives. It is said that this act hastened the USA's entry into World War I.

Lutfi Djelil

Type: Turkish battleship
Displacement: 2,580 tonnes (2,550 tons)
Dimensions: 62m x 14m x 4.2m (203ft 4in x 46ft x 13ft 9in)
Machinery: Twin screws, compound engines
Top speed: 12 knots
Main armament: Two 178mm (7in), two 203mm (8in) guns
Launched: 1868
Date of profile: 1875

Lutfi Djelil was ordered by Egypt, but she was claimed by Turkey in 1869 while she was still on the stocks in

France. She had twin turrets, the larger fore turret housing the two 203mm (8in) guns and the aft turret housing the 178mm (7in) guns. Both turrets were manually operated, needing 24 crew to rotate them. Hinged bulwarks amidships were lowered to protect the crew during action. In May 1877 *Lutfi Djelil* was off Braila when rounds from the Russian shore batteries pierced her magazine and she blew up.

M1

Type: British submarine
Displacement: 1,619 tonnes (1,594 tons) (surface), 1,977 tonnes(1,946 tons) (submerged)
Dimensions: 90m x 7.5m x 4.9m (295ft 7in x 24ft 7in x 16ft)
Machinery: Twin screws, diesel engines (surface), electric motors (submerged)
Top speed: 15 knots (surface), 9 knots (submerged)
Main armament: One 305mm (12in) gun, four 533mm (21in) torpedo tubes
Launched: July 1917

M1 was armed with a single 305mm (12in)

gun carried in the front part of the extended conning tower and, if already loaded, it could be fired from periscope depth in 30 seconds, or 20 seconds if breaking the surface. *M1* served briefly in the war and was sunk in November 1925 after she was rammed by the merchant vessel *Vidar*.

Magdalena

Type: British liner
Displacement: 5,459 tonnes (5,373 tons)
Dimensions: 128m x 15m x 6.4m (421ft x 50ft x 21ft)
Machinery: Twin screws, triple expansion engines
Top speed: 15 knots

Launched: 1889
Date of profile: 1889

Magdalena was one of a series of liners built for the Royal Mail Line, who were adding a number of vessels to their fleet at that time. Her design was an interesting mix of old and new. She was one of the last liners to sport the distinctive clipper bow, but one of the first to carry pole masts without any provision for sails. Her propulsion was of the new triple expansion type, a style that had just been introduced and was proving to be economical and reliable to run. She entered service on the Royal Mail Line's South American route, and quickly proved to be a popular ship. She had accommodation for 170 first-class, 40 second-class, and 330 third-class passengers. The first-class passengers were carried in the sumptuous two-tier deck house, which was another design innovation. After a long career, she was due to be scrapped in 1914. World War I intervened, however, and she was impressed into government service, for use as a transport. She managed to survive the war, and was scrapped in 1921.

Magenta

Type: French battleship
Displacement: 6,832 tonnes (6,715 tons)
Dimensions: 86m x 57.7m x 8.4m (282ft x 56ft 8in x 27ft 8in)
Machinery: Single screw, horizontal return connecting rod engine
Top speed: 13 knots
Main armament: Thirty-four 162mm (6.4in), sixteen 55-pounder guns,

plus two 223mm (8.8in) howitzers
Armour: 120mm (4.7in) belt
Launched: June 1861

Magenta and her sister *Solferno* were the only two-decker, broadside ironclads to be built. The armour was concentrated amidships where the guns were housed on main and upper decks, with shotproof transverse bulkheads. The two-tier placing gave the upper-deck guns increased elevation and range, as well as lightening the ends of the vessel. *Magenta* was an imposing-looking ship, with a pronounced tumble-home to the hull and a prominent ram. On 31 October 1875 she blew up as a result of a fire that started in the wardroom galley.

Maine

Type: US battleship
Displacement: 6,789 tonnes (7,180 tons)
Dimensions: 98.9m x 17.4m x 6.9m (318ft x 57ft x 21ft 6in)
Machinery: Twin screws, triple expansion engines
Top speed: 16.4 knots
Main armament: Six 152mm (6in), four 254mm (10in) guns

Launched: November 1889
Date of profile: 1898

Initial designs for *Maine* showed a three-masted sail rig, but this was abandoned and she entered service with two military masts instead. In January 1898 she was sent to Havana, Cuba, to protect US interests there, but in February she was sunk by an explosion. This was thought to be the result of Spanish sabotage, and war began between the USA and Spain. Later evidence suggested that a coal bunker fire was the cause.

Majestic

Type: British battleship
Displacement: 16,317 tonnes (16,060 tons)
Dimensions: 128.3m x 22.8m x 8.2m (421ft x 75ft x 27ft)
Machinery: Twin screws, triple expansion engines
Top speed: 17.5 knots
Main armament: Twelve 152mm (6in), four 305mm (12in) guns
Armour: 228mm belt (9in), 305-355mm (12-14in) bulkheads, 355mm (14in) on barbettes, 254mm (10in) on turrets, 152mm (6in) on casemates
Launched: January 1895

With *Majestic* and her eight sisters, designer Sir William White produced the best battleships of the 1890s, and set the pattern for all battleship design until the coming of the *Dreadnought* in 1905. The use of improved armour allowed for adequate protection at less cost in weight. The armoured hull curved down to meet the lower edge of the belt, so increasing internal protection. *Majestic* was sunk in the Dardanelles on 27 May 1915, after being struck by two torpedoes from the German submarine *U21*

Marathon

Type: British liner
Displacement: 6,903 tonnes (6,795 tons)
Dimensions: 150m x 16m x 9m (490ft x 55ft x 30ft)
Machinery: Twin screws, triple expansion engine

Launched: 1904

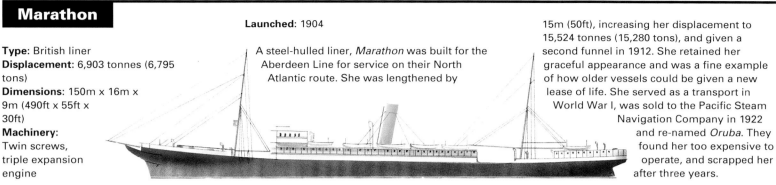

A steel-hulled liner, *Marathon* was built for the Aberdeen Line for service on their North Atlantic route. She was lengthened by 15m (50ft), increasing her displacement to 15,524 tonnes (15,280 tons), and given a second funnel in 1912. She retained her graceful appearance and was a fine example of how older vessels could be given a new lease of life. She served as a transport in World War I, was sold to the Pacific Steam Navigation Company in 1922 and re-named *Oruba*. They found her too expensive to operate, and scrapped her after three years.

Marco Polo

Type: Italian cruiser
Displacement: 5,000 tonnes (4,930 tons)
Dimensions: 106m x 14.7m x 6.2m (347ft 9in x 48ft x 20ft 4in)

Machinery: Twin screws, vertical triple expansion engines
Top speed: 17.8 knots
Main armament: Ten 120mm (4.7in), six 152mm (6in) guns
Armour: 100mm belt
Launched: 1892
Date of profile: 1896

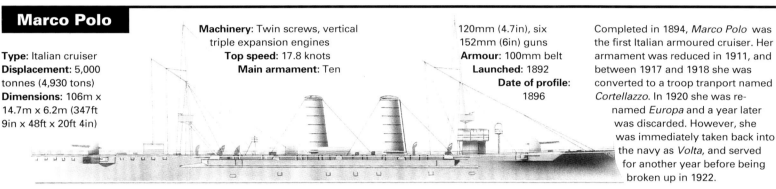

Completed in 1894, *Marco Polo* was the first Italian armoured cruiser. Her armament was reduced in 1911, and between 1917 and 1918 she was converted to a troop tranport named *Cortellazzo*. In 1920 she was re-named *Europa* and a year later was discarded. However, she was immediately taken back into the navy as *Volta*, and served for another year before being broken up in 1922.

Marinor

Type: Dutch tanker
Displacement: 10,842 tonnes (10,672 tons)
Dimensions: 112.2m x 18m x 7.6m (368ft x 59ft x 25ft)
Machinery: Single screw, diesel engine
Top speed: 14.4 knots
Launched: 1992

Marinor is an unusual tanker in that she can transport a cargo mix of china clay and chemicals. She was designed for a specific charter centred on the east coast of North America and the Caribbean, which involved carrying china clay liquid for the paper industry alongside chemicals such as sulphuric acid. Twelve tanks are formed along the centreline bulkhead, and these are all lined with stainless steel to resist strong chemicals. The steel also strengthens the

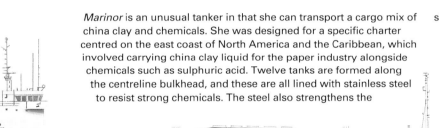

ship's structure and saves weight. The tanks are connected in pairs, six being for clay and six, plus a small bow tank, for chemicals. All the tanks have deck-mounted heaters connected to the main boilers.

Marsala

Type: Italian cruiser
Displacement: 4,207 tonnes (4,141 tons)
Dimensions: 140.3m x 13m x 4.1m (460ft 4in x 42ft 8in x 13ft 5in)
Machinery: Triple screws, turbines
Top speed: 27.6 knots
Main armament: Six 76mm (3in), six 120mm (4.7in) guns

Launched: March 1912

Completed in 1914, *Marsala* was one of two ships in a class of light cruisers designed by Engineer Captain Rota. Two of her 120mm (4.7in) guns were carried side-by-side on the forecastle, two were placed aft on the centreline, and two were placed in echelon amidshipsl. An armoured deck protected the machinery spaces, extending along the vessel's midships section before reducing at the bow and stern, where it curved down to below the waterline. Four small funnels rose up through a light superstructure. *Marsala* was discarded in 1927.

Marshal Soult

Type: British monitor
Displacement: 7,010 tonnes (6,900 tons)
Dimensions: 108.4m x 27m x 3m (355ft 8in x 90ft 3in x 10ft 6in)
Machinery: Twin screws, diesel engines
Top speed: 6 knots

Main armament: Two 380mm (15in) guns
Launched: August 1915

Marshal Soult was

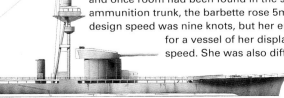

designed to operate in shallow waters. Fitting the 380mm (15in) gun mountings on a draught of only 3m (10ft) was a serious challenge, and once room had been found in the shallow hull for the ammunition trunk, the barbette rose 5m (17ft) above the deck. Her design speed was nine knots, but her engines were underpowered for a vessel of her displacement to reach such speed. She was also difficult to steer. She became a training ship in 1921 and was discarded in 1946.

MAS 9

Type: Italian motor torpedo boat
Displacement: 16 tonnes (16 tons)
Dimensions: 16m x 2.6m x 1.2m
(52ft 6in x 8ft 8in x 4ft)
Machinery: Twin screws, petrol
engines
Top speed: 25.2
knots
Main armament:
One 47mm (1.85in)

gun, two 450mm (17.7in) torpedoes
Launched: 1916
Date of profile: 1916

MAS 9 was one of a group of

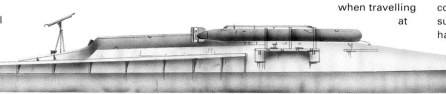

unusual vessels designed for rapid
attack by Engineer Bisio. Total crew
for each vessel numbered eight.
Their small size offered a poor
target to the enemy, especially
when travelling
at

full speed. Engines developed
450hp. Torpedoes were carried one
each side amidships, on the
whaleback foredeck. One night in
December 1917 *MAS 9*,
commanded by Luigi Rizzo,
successfully penetrated Trieste
harbour and sank the Austrian
battleship *Wein*.
MAS 9 was
discarded in
1922.

Masséna

Type: French battleship
Displacement: 11,922 tonnes (11,735
tons)
Dimensions: 112.6m x 20.2m x 8.8m
(369ft 7in x 66ft 6in x 29ft)
Machinery: Triple screws, triple expansion
engines
Top speed: 18 knots
Main armament: Eight
100mm (3.9in), eight

140mm (5.5in), two 274mm (10.8in), two
305mm (12in) guns
Launched: July 1885
Date of profile: 1898

Masséna was the first French warship to have triple screws.
She had a long, sleek hull, pronounced tumble-home and
prominent bow ram. Her 305mm (12in) guns were
housed in single turrets, one high up on the bows and
the other right aft, at main deck level. The 274mm
(10.8in) guns were mounted singly on each side, and
were on deep barbettes which protruded
outwards from the hull to allow the
guns to fire in line with the keel.
Masséna was hulked in 1915 and used
as a breakwater during the 1916
Gallipoli evacuations.

Maya

Type: Japanese cruiser
Displacement: 12,985 tonnes
(12,781 tons)
Dimensions: 202m x 18m x 6m
(661ft 8in x 59ft x 20ft)
Machinery: Quadruple screws,
turbines
Top speed:

35.5 knots
Main armament: Four 120mm
(4.7in), ten 203mm (8in) guns
Launched:
November
1930

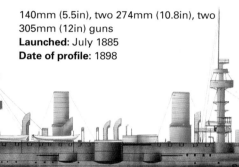

Maya was one of four heavy
cruisers that formed part of Japan's
programme of naval construction
between 1927 and 1931. *Maya* and
her sisters were improved
versions of *Nachis*, with an
enlarged bridge
that carried
light

armour. The 203mm (8in) guns had
an elevation of 70 degrees, making
them effective weapons against
some forms of air attack. However,
in 1943 *Maya* was badly damaged at
Rabaul by gunfire from US aircraft,
and had to be completely rebuilt. In
October 1944 she was sunk by four
torpedoes fired from a US
submarine during the
actions which lead to the
Battle of Leyte Gulf.

Mayon Spirit

Type: Liberian tanker
Displacement:
100,000 tonnes
(98,507 tons)
Dimensions:
244.8m x 41.2m x
14.4m
(830ft 2in x
135ft 2in x

47ft 3in)
Machinery: Single screw, diesel
engine
Launched: December 1981

Mayon Spirit is of an
improved tanker design,
with better anti-pollution

provision given by the introduction
of a double hull with a 2m (6ft 6in)
space between the hulls in the
double bottom and a greater space
in the wing tanks. Within this double
skin arrangement, there is only one
central cargo tank in a midship

position, plus small side tanks.
Carrying capacity is 120,043 cubic
metres (4,239,285 cubic ft). Cargo is
handled by three pumps monitored
from the control room. Total
complement for
this large ship
is only 38.

McRae

Type: Confederate gunboat
Displacement: 843 tonnes (830 tons)
Dimensions: Unknown
Machinery: Single screw, compound
engine
Top speed: 8 knots
Main armament: One 228mm (9in),
six 32-pounder guns
Launched: Unknown

Date of profile: 1861

McRae was originally the
barque-rigged pirate ship
Marques de la Habana,
which was captured
by *Saratoga* in
1860. In 1861
*Marques de la
Habana* was
bought by the

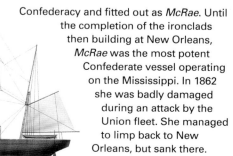

Confederacy and fitted out as *McRae*. Until
the completion of the ironclads
then building at New Orleans,
McRae was the most potent
Confederate vessel operating
on the Mississippi. In 1862
she was badly damaged
during an attack by the
Union fleet. She managed
to limp back to New
Orleans, but sank there.

Memphis

Type: US cruiser
Displacement: 9,660 tonnes (9,508 tons)
Dimensions: 169.5m x 16.9m x 4m (555ft 9in x 55ft 6in x 13ft 6in)
Machinery: Quadruple screws, turbines
Top speed: 34.4 knots
Main armament: Twelve 152mm (6in) guns
Launched: April 1924
Date of profile: 1926

After the last of the Chester class cruisers were delivered to the US Navy in 1908, there was a hiatus in construction until this class of 10 was authorised in 1916. *Memphis* and her sisters were laid down

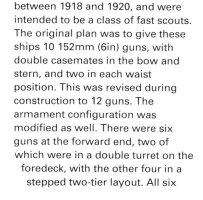

between 1918 and 1920, and were intended to be a class of fast scouts. The original plan was to give these ships 10 152mm (6in) guns, with double casemates in the bow and stern, and two in each waist position. This was revised during construction to 12 guns. The armament configuration was modified as well. There were six guns at the forward end, two of which were in a double turret on the foredeck, with the other four in a stepped two-tier layout. All six

guns were thus able to fire directly ahead, while four could fire on each broadside. The six aft guns were housed in a similar way, giving a full broadside of eight barrels. *Memphis* had little protection, although a strip of 76mm (3in) armour covered the waterline near her machinery spaces. Her steam turbines developed over 90,000hp, while 2,020 tonnes (2,000 tons) of fuel oil gave her a range of 19,000km (10,000 miles) at 15 knots. She had a distinctive outline, with four funnels, and a steeply sloping deckline dropping down from the high forecastle. *Memphis* was discarded in 1946.

Mendez Nuñez

Type: Spanish cruiser
Displacement: 6,140 tonnes (6,043 tons)
Dimensions: 140.8m x 14m x 4.7m (462ft x 46ft x 15ft 5in)
Machinery: Quadruple screws, turbines
Top speed: 29.2 knots

Main armament: Six 152mm (6in) guns
Launched: March 1923

Mendez Nuñez was one of two fast, light cruisers that were authorised in 1915, laid down in 1917, but not completed until 1924 due to

difficulties in obtaining materials both during and after World War I. The ships were based on the British C-class cruisers, with three guns grouped at either end of the vessel. Engines developed

43,776hp, and coal supply was 800 tonnes (787 tons), plus 500 tonnes (492 tons) of oil. Seventy-six millimetre (3in) thick armour was concentrated amidships, reducing to 31mm (1.25in) at either end of the ship. Twelve 533mm (21in) torpedo tubes were carried in triple mounts, two each side just aft of amidships. *Mendez Nuñez* was discarded in 1963. Her sister, *Blas de Lezo*, was wrecked in July 1932.

Messaggero

Type: Italian despatch vessel
Displacement: 1,000 tonnes (1,005 tons)
Dimensions: 72m x 9m x 3m (236ft 3in x 30ft x 10ft 4in)
Machinery: Paddle wheels, reciprocating engines
Top speed: 14 knots
Main armament: Four 75mm (3in) guns
Launched: July 1885

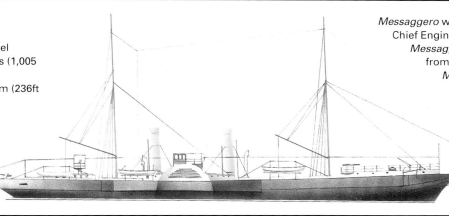

Messaggero was a steel-hulled vessel designed by Chief Engineer Masdea, who based the plans on *Messaggiere*, launched in 1863. The machinery from *Messaggiere* was re-used in *Messaggero*, and the new vessel also had a two-masted gaff rig. Her 75mm (3in) guns were later replaced by four 57mm (2.25in) guns, and in 1889 four 37mm (1.5in) machine guns were added. *Messaggero* was discarded in 1907, but served for a while as a depot ship at Panigaglia.

Messaggiere

Type: Italian despatch vessel
Displacement: 1,240 tonnes (1,220 tons)
Dimensions: 72m x 9m x 3.6m (235ft 6in x 30ft x 11ft 10in)
Machinery: Paddle wheels, reciprocating engines
Main armament: Two 120mm (4.7in) guns
Launched: May 1863

Designed and built by Wigram of London, this wooden-hulled, three-masted, schooner-rigged vessel was laid down in July 1862 and completed in August 1863. She and her sister ship proved exceptionally useful in the war against Austria in 1866, during which they acted as fast

scouts as well as despatch vessels. *Messaggiere* was discarded in 1885, but her engines were installed in a new vessel named *Messaggero*, which was launched in 1885.

Messina

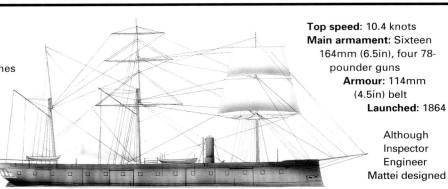

Type: Italian battleship
Displacement: 4,382 tonnes (4,313 tons)
Dimensions: 75.8m x 15m x 7.3m (248ft 8in x 49ft 6in x 24ft)
Machinery: Single screw, single expansion six-cylinder engine

Top speed: 10.4 knots
Main armament: Sixteen 164mm (6.5in), four 78-pounder guns
Armour: 114mm (4.5in) belt
Launched: 1864

Although Inspector Engineer Mattei designed

Messina as a wooden-hulled frigate, she was converted into a broadside ironclad before her completion in 1867. Built at the Castellammare Naval Dockyard, she formed part of the second group of ironclads built for the Italians, and the first built in Italy. In about 1870 her armament was changed to eight 164mm (6.5in), four 203mm (8in) and two 254mm (10in) guns. She was removed from the effective list in 1880.

Messudieh

Type: Turkish battleship
Displacement: 9,865 tonnes (9,710 tons)
Dimensions: 101m x 17.9m x 7.9m (331ft 4in x 59ft x 26ft)
Machinery: Single screw, horizontal compound engines
Main armament: Three 178mm (7in), twelve 254mm (10in) guns
Armour: 152-305mm belt (6-12in), 178-254mm (7-10in) on battery
Launched: October 1874

Messudieh was a fully rigged, central battery ship with a ram bow. She combined considerable firepower with good protection, speed and endurance, plus good seakeeping qualities. She was sunk in 1914.

Michigan

Type: US battleship
Displacement: 18,186 tonnes (17,900 tons)
Dimensions: 138.2m x 24.5m x 7.5m (453ft 5in x 80ft 4in x 24ft 7in)
Machinery: Twin screws, vertical triple expansion engines

Main armament: Twenty-two 76mm (3in), eight 305mm (12in)guns
Armour: 228-305mm (9-12in) belt, 203-305mm (8-12in) on turrets
Launched: December 1906

Michigan was designed before, but built after, the epoch-

making *Dreadnought*. Her design introduced the concept of all-big-guns on the centreline. Most of the 76mm (3in) guns were concentrated in a box battery amidships, with the rest on the upper deck. Cage masts greatly reduced the target area offered to enemy gunners. As the turbine was still in the development stage, triple expansion engines were installed instead. *Michigan* was stricken in 1923.

Mikasa

Type: Japanese battleship
Displacement: 15,422 tonnes (15,179 tons)
Dimensions: 131.7m x 23.2m x 8.2m (432ft x76ft 3in x 27ft 2in)
Machinery: Twin screw, vertical triple expansion engines
Top speed: 18 knots

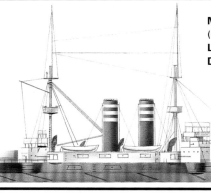

Main armament: Fourteen 152mm (6in), four 305mm (12in) guns
Launched: November 1900
Date of profile: 1902

Mikasa was the last battleship built under the Japanese naval expansion programme of

1896, and was the flagship of Vice-Admiral Togo during the Russo-Japanese War of 1904-05. She sank in Sasebo harbour after suffering a mazagine explosion in 1905, but was raised and repaired in 1907. In 1921 she was re-classified as a coast defence ship. She retired in 1923 after running aground, and is now on permanent public display as the last surviving battleship of her period.

Minas Gerais

Type: Brazilian battleship
Displacement: 21,540 tonnes (21,200 tons)
Dimensions: 165.8m x 25.3m x 8.5m (544ft x 83ft x 27ft 10in)
Machinery: Twin screws, vertical triple expansion engines
Top speed: 21 knots

Main armament: Twenty-two 120mm (4.7in), twelve 305mm (12in) guns
Launched: September 1908

Minas Gerais was originally designed as a pre-dreadnought battleship in answer to the powerful

vessels then building for Chile. Her design was later modified and she became the first powerful

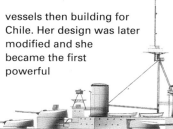

dreadnought to be built for a minor navy. She was built in Britain and completed in 1910. She was extensively modernised in the USA in 1923, and again in Brazil from 1934 to 1937. She was scrapped in 1954.

Minerva

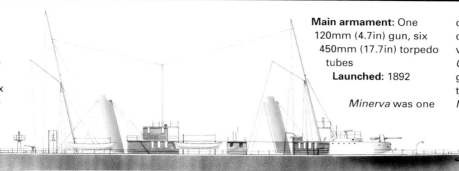

Type: Italian cruiser
Displacement: 1,027 tonnes (1,011 tons)
Dimensions: 73.9m x 8.2m x 3.7m (242ft 6in x 27ft x 12ft)
Machinery: Twin screws, triple expansion engines
Top speed: 20.5 knots

Main armament: One 120mm (4.7in) gun, six 450mm (17.7in) torpedo tubes
Launched: 1892

Minerva was one of eight steel-hulled cruisers designed by Engineer Vigna. All vessels in the class differed slightly: *Caprera* had two 120mm (4.7in) guns, and *Montebello* had three tall, closely-spaced funnels. *Minerva*'s engines developed 4,500hp. Laid down in 1889, she was completed in 1892. The class was one of the largest built for the Italian Navy. She was discarded in 1921.

Minin

Type: Russian cruiser
Displacement: 6,234 tonnes (6,136 tons)
Dimensions: 89.9m x 15m x 7.7m (295ft x 49ft 6in x 25ft 5in)
Machinery: Single screw, vertical compound twelve-cylinder engine
Main armament: Twelve 152mm (6in), four 203mm (8in) guns
Launched: 1869

Minin was laid down in 1866 as a low freeboard ironclad carrying twin turrets armed with four 280mm (11in) guns and a full sail rig. Work was halted after her launch following the loss of the British turret ship *Captain*, and *Minin* was completed as an armoured cruiser in 1878. She now had a long box battery that housed the powerful armament. She served in the Pacific during the 1880s, and in 1909 was converted to a minelayer named *Ladoga*. On 15 August 1915 she was sunk by a mine laid by the German U-boat *UC4*.

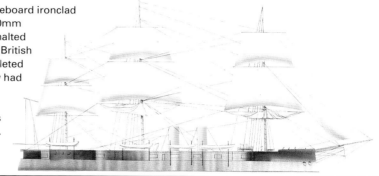

Minnehaha

Type: US liner
Displacement: 13,615 tonnes (13,401 tons)
Dimensions: 187.8m x 19.8m (616ft 2in x 65ft)
Machinery: Twin screws, quadruple expansion engines
Top speed: 16 knots
Launched: 1900

Minnehaha was built for service on the North Atlantic and was ordered in the late 1890s when trade between Europe and North America was on the increase. On her maiden voyage she collided with and sank the tug *American* in New York harbour. In 1910 she ran aground on the Scilly Isles. In September 1917 she was torpedoed by the German U-boat *U48* and sank within four minutes.

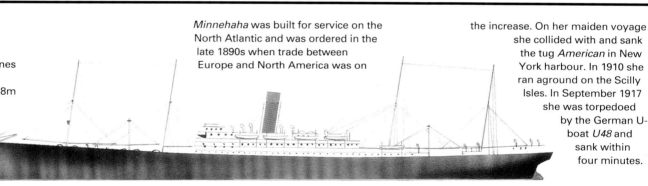

Minnekahda

Type: US liner
Displacement: 17,500 tonnes (17,221 tons)
Dimensions: 196.9m x 20.3m (646ft x 66ft 3in)
Machinery: Triple screws, turbines and triple expansion engines

Launched: March 1917

Minnekahda was originally ordered in 1913 as a luxury liner for the Atlantic Transport Line. Laid down in 1914, she was completed in time to serve as a cargo carrier during World War I. She made her first civilian voyage as a cargo vessel in early 1918. In 1920 she entered the emigrant trade after the Bethlehem Steel Company had built in extra accommodation for 2,150 third-class passengers. In 1926 she was modified to carry 750 tourist-class passengers. She was laid up in New York in 1935, and was sold for scrap the following year.

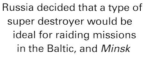

Minsk

Type: Russian destroyer
Displacement: 2,623 tonnes (2,582 tons)
Dimensions: 127.5m x 11.7m x 4m (418ft 4in x 38ft 4in x 13ft 4in)
Machinery: Triple screws, turbines
Main armament: Two 76mm (3in), five 130mm (5.1in) guns
Launched: November 1935

During World War I, the Imperial Russian Navy had conducted some outstandingly successful operations with the large, fast destroyer *Novik*. The type was later repeated, but with a reduced displacement. By the early 1930s Russia decided that a type of super destroyer would be ideal for raiding missions in the Baltic, and *Minsk* was laid down between 1932 and 1934 with technical aid from France and Italy. She was sunk in 1941, but re-floated in 1942. In 1959 she became a training vessel.

Mississippi

Type: US cruiser
Displacement: 3,271 tonnes (3,220 tons)
Dimensions: 67m x 20m (over paddle boxes) x 6.6m (220ft x 66ft 6in x 21ft 9in)
Machinery: Paddle wheels, side-lever engines
Top speed: 11 knots
Main armament: Eight 203mm (8in), two 254mm (10in) guns
Launched: May 1841

In 1839 the US Navy finally decided to build two or more steam vessels. After much deliberation, two large cruisers were ordered. *Mississippi* was laid down in Philadelphia in 1839, and completed in 1842. The *Missouri* was also delivered in that year, but was destroyed in 1845 by fire at Gibraltar. *Mississippi* was designed by Copeland. She had a wooden hull, and was barque-rigged, with 1,765 square metres (19,000 sq ft) of canvas. Her steam engine provided its motive force via two side-mounted paddle wheels. She turned out to be a good sailor, performing equally well under sail or steam. At the time there were only 23 engineers serving in the Navy; their conditions were poor, as there was little official enthusiasm for steam. *Mississippi* helped amend this, as she proved to be an effective fighting ship. She served in the Mexican War of 1847, and the American Civil War. She was part of Admiral Farragut's Mississippi river squadron. In March 1863 she was set on fire, after having run aground at Port Hudson.

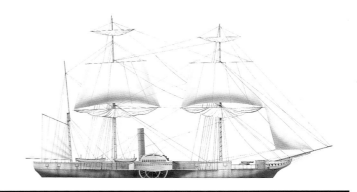

Mississippi

Type: US cruiser
Displacement: 11,176 tonnes (11,000 tons)
Dimensions: 178.5m x 19.2m x 9m (585ft 4in x 63ft x 29ft 6in)
Machinery: Twin screws, nuclear-powered turbines
Main armament: Two 127mm (5in) guns, two twin launchers for Tartar and Harpoon missiles, Asroc launcher
Launched: July 1976

Mississippi was one of a class of four units that were improved versions of the preceding California class, with Mk 26 missile launchers and provision for a helicopter hangar and elevator in the stern. The group were the first US ships to be built since World War II that incorporated the hangar and elevator feature, but unfortunately it was found to be impossible to keep the hangar area completely watertight, and so the hangars were removed during the early 1980s. Three Tomahawk launchers with 12 missiles were put in their place. The 127mm (5in) Mk 45 guns fire 20 rounds per minute, and have a range of over 14,630 metres at an elevation of 85 degrees.

Missouri

Type: Confederate gunboat
Displacement: Unknown
Dimensions: 55.7m x 17m x 2.6m (183ft x 55ft 8in x 8ft 6in)
Machinery: Single paddle wheel, poppet valve engines
Top speed: 6 knots
Main armament: One 228mm (9in), one 280mm (11in), one 32-pounder guns
Launched: April 1863
Date of profile: 1865

Missouri was the last Confederate ironclad to see active service during the American Civil War. She was laid down in December 1862 and was completed by the following September for service on the rivers still under Confederate control. The vessel had a 40m (130ft) long casemate housing her mixed armament. The single 6.7m (22ft) diameter paddle wheel was situated aft in the casemate, which was plated with 114mm (4.5in) thick railroad iron laid at an angle to avoid having to cut it. The armour was laid in two interlocking layers, and extended 1.8m (6ft) below the waterline. *Missouri* served as a troop transport and minelayer until she was surrendered to Union forces in June 1865, some two months after the official Confederate surrender.

Mogami

Type: Japanese cruiser
Displacement: 11,169 tonnes (10,993 tons)
Dimensions: 201.5m x 18m x 5.5m (661ft x 59ft x 18ft)
Machinery: Quadruple screws, turbines
Main armament: Eight 127mm (5in) dual-purpose, fifteen 155mm (6.1in) guns
Launched: March 1934

Mogami was one of four vessels that were designed as light cruisers, but which were actually larger than conventional heavy cruisers. The 155mm (6.1in) guns were positioned in triple mounts along the centreline, and the dual-purpose 127mm (5in) guns were placed in twin mounts amidships. Initial sea experience revealed weaknesses in the vessels' hull structure, caused by problems with the welding. During trials the turrets jammed due to distortion of the hulls. The problem was cured by strengthening the hulls, which increased displacement by several hundred tonnes. *Mogami* was sunk in 1944 by US torpedo bombers.

Monadnock

Type: US Monitor
Displacement: 3,454 tonnes (3,400 tons)
Dimensions: 78.8m x 16m x 3.9m (258ft 6in x 52ft 9in x 12ft 8in)
Machinery: Twin screws, vibrating lever engines
Top speed: 9 knots
**Main

armament: Four 380mm (15in) guns
Armour: 254mm (10in) on turrets, 127mm (5in) on hull, 51mm (2in) thick deck
Launched: 1864
Date of profile: 1866

In 1862 four powerful, double-turreted monitors were ordered by the US Navy. Like their predecessors, they had wooden hulls which quickly deteriorated. Early plans specified a Coles turret, but this was dropped in favour of the Ericsson type, which was not so effective. *Monadnock* was completed too late to serve in the American Civil War, and she was sent to serve on the Pacific coast. All vessels in her class were good seaboats, and were very steady gun platforms even when the sea was washing across the deck. *Monadnock* was scrapped in 1875.

Monarch

Type: British battleship
Displacement: 8,455 tonnes (8,322 tons)
Dimensions: 100.5m x 17.5m x 7.3m (330ft x 57ft 6in x 24ft 2in)
Machinery: Single screw, return connecting rod engines
Main armament: Four 305mm (12in) guns
Armour: 114-178mm (4.5-7in) belt, 203-254mm (8-10in) on turrets
Launched: May 1868

Monarch was the first large, ocean-going turret ship of the monitor type. She had a forecastle and poop, and still carried a full sailing rig. Her engines developed 7,842hp, and upon completion *Monarch* was the fastest battleship in the world. Her twin turrets were surmounted by a flying bridge. She was sold in 1906.

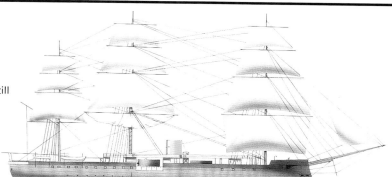

Monarch

Type: British battleship
Displacement: 26,284 tonnes (25,870 tons)
Dimensions: 177m x 26.9m x 8.7m (580ft x 88ft 6in x 28ft 9in)
Machinery: Quadruple screws, turbines
Top speed: 20.8 knots
Main armament: Sixteen 102mm (4in), ten 343mm (13.5in) guns
Armour: 203-305mm (8-12in) belt, 280mm (11in) on turrets
Launched: March 1911

Monarch was one of four units that were the first vessels to carry 343mm (13.5in) guns since the days of the Royal Sovereign class of 1889. With a massive increase of 2,540 tonnes (2,500 tons) displacement over contemporary dreadnoughts, *Monarch* and her sisters were called 'super-dreadnoughts'. They were the first capital ships of the dreadnought era to carry all the main guns on the centreline. Armour protection was thorough, the side armour rising to upper deck level 5m (17ft) above the waterline. All ships in the class served at Jutland in 1916. *Monarch* was sunk as a target in 1925.

Monitor

Type: US monitor
Displacement: 1,000 tonnes (987 tons)
Dimensions: 52m x 12.6m x 2.5m (172ft x 41ft 6in x 8ft 4in)
Machinery: Single screw, double trunk engines
Top speed: 6 knots
Main armament: Two 280mm (11in) guns
Armour: 203mm (8in) on turrets, 127mm (5in) on hull
Launched: January 1862

Before the Civil War, the US Navy had shown little interest in the ironclad warship. But by the end of 1861 news of the Confederate's rapid progress in converting the *Merrimack* into a powerful ironclad had reached Union forces. In response to this threat, Congress immediately authorised the building of several similar vessels. Of 16 designs submitted, three were chosen, including John Ericsson's design for *Monitor*. She was a well-armoured vessel, and had a low freeboard which presented a poor target. She fought *Merrimack* at Hampton Roads in 1862, then served on the James River until she sank in a storm on 31 December 1862.

Montebello

Type: Italian cruiser
Displacement: 827 tonnes (814 tons)
Dimensions: 73.4m x 7.9m x 4.6m (241ft x 26ft x 15ft)
Machinery: Triple screws, triple expansion engines
Top speed: 18 knots
Main armament: Six 57mm (2.25in) guns
Launched: March 1888

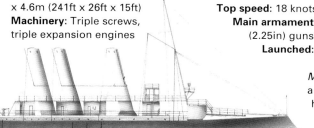

Montebello was a light, steel-hulled cruiser. She and her three sisters were designated as torpedo cruisers. All had slight differences in hull shape, machinery, boilers and armament. A flying bridge ran from the top of the conning tower beneath a light bridge aft, to just behind the last of the three funnels. *Montebello* was laid down in 1885 and completed in 1889. She was discarded in 1920.

Monterey

Type: US monitor
Displacement: 4,000 tonnes (4,084 tons)
Dimensions: 78m x 18m x 4.2m (256ft x 59ft x 14ft 10in)

Machinery: Twin screws, vertical triple expansion engines
Main armament: Two 254mm (10in), two 305mm (12in) guns
Armour: 127-330mm (5-13in) thick belt, 190-203mm (7.5-8in) on turrets
Launched: April 1891

Monterey was the last twin turret monitor built for the US Navy, and was one of the most powerful vessels on a 4,064-tonne (4,000-ton) displacement. The 305mm (12in) guns were mounted in the fore turret, and the 254mm (10in) guns were positioned in a turret aft. The raised central superstructure carried six six-pounder guns for anti-torpedo-boat defence. When going into action, *Monterey*'s low freeboard could be further reduced by flooding the water ballast tanks, thereby reducing the hull target area. The vessel was laid down in 1889 and completed in 1893 for service as a coast defence ship on the US Pacific coastline. She served in the Philippines from 1898 to 1917, and was then stationed at Pearl Harbor until her sale in 1921.

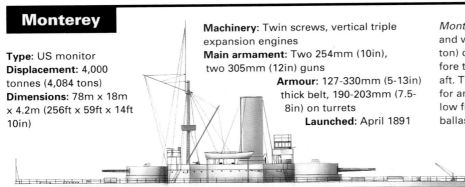

Moon

Type: British destroyer
Displacement: 910 tonnes (895 tons)
Dimensions: 114m x 8m x 2.9m (375ft x 26ft 8in x 9ft 6in)
Machinery: Twin screws, turbines
Main armament: Three 102mm (4in) guns
Launched: April 1915

Moon was one of four special boats built at Yarrow. They formed part of the massive World War I emergency programme which was put in hand in September 1914, in which repeats of the 'M' class were ordered in large numbers. *Moon* and her three sisters had increased length over the rest of the 'M' class, and had raked stems and sloping sterns to improve seakeeping qualities. The central gun was on a raised platform to improve local fire control. There were also two twin mounts for 533mm (21in) torpedo tubes. There were problems in completing the vessels due to the shortage of zinc. *Moon* was sold for breaking up in 1921.

Moravian

Type: British liner
Displacement: 4,646 tonnes (4,573 tons)
Dimensions: 119m x 14m x 8m (390ft 4in x 47ft x 27ft 4in)
Machinery: Single screw, triple expansion engines
Top speed: 15 knots
Launched: 1899

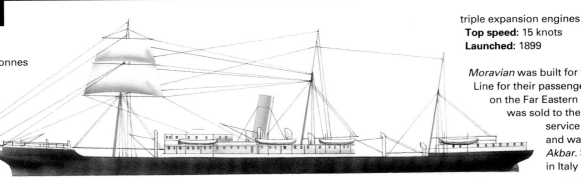

Moravian was built for the Aberdeen Line for their passenger/cargo service on the Far Eastern route. In 1914 she was sold to the Mogul Line for service as a pilgrim ship and was re-named *Akbar*. She was scrapped in Italy in 1923.

Moreno

Type: Argentinian battleship
Displacement: 30,500 tonnes (30,000 tons)
Dimensions: 173.8m x 29.4m x 8.5m (270ft 3in x 96ft 9in x 27ft 10in)
Machinery: Triple screws, turbines
Top speed: 22.5 knots
Main armament: Twelve 152mm (6in), twelve 305mm (12in) guns
Launched: September 1911
Date of profile: 1915

Rivalry between South American republics reached a new height around 1910, when Brazil ordered two powerful dreadnoughts from British yards. Argentina answered with a programme of three dreadnoughts, but owing to financial limitations only two were ordered, from US yards. *Moreno* and her sister *Rivadavia* were modernised in 1924-25. They were converted to oil, the lattice mast forward was shortened and the pole mast aft was replaced by a tripod. Displacement increased by 1,016 tonnes (1,000 tons). *Moreno* was sold in 1956.

Moskva

Type: Russian helicopter carrier
Displacement: 14,800 tonnes (14,567 tons)
Dimensions: 191m x 34m x 7.6m (626ft 8in x 111ft 6in x 25ft)

Machinery: Twin screws, turbines
Main armament: One twin SUW-N-1 launcher, two twin SA-N-3 missile launchers
Aircraft: 18 helicopters
Launched: 1964

Moskva was the first helicopter carrier built for the Russian Navy. She was laid down in 1962 and completed in 1967. She was designed to counteract the growing threat from the US nuclear-powered missile submarines that first entered service in 1960. *Moskva* has a massive central block which dominates the vessel and houses the major weapons systems.

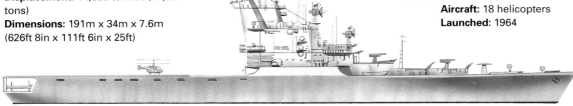

Mount Whitney

Type: US command ship
Displacement: 19,598 tonnes (19,290 tons)
Dimensions: 189m x 25m x 8.2m (620ft 5in x 82ft x 27ft)
Machinery: Single screw, turbines
Top speed: 23 knots
Main armament: Four 76mm (3in) guns, two eight-tube Sea Sparrow missile launchers
Launched: January 1970

America's Pacific battles during World War II convinced the US Navy and Marine Corps of the value of specialised amphibious assault forces. There was a core of experience in mounting amphibious operations, which was used to construct the Guam class assault ships. Amphibious operations are complex and multi-faceted, and require comprehensive command, control and communications facilities. The Navy's earlier command ships were not up the demands of modern warfare, so a new class of two vessels were built, the first ships to be designed from the outset for this role. *Mount Whitney*, and her sister ship *Blue Ridge*, use the same hull form and machinery as the Guam class, and have flat open decks to allow maximum antenna placement. There is a helicopter flight deck aft. These ships are crammed with communications equipment, while there are extensive briefing areas, planning facilities and command spaces. They have space for 200 staff officers and 500 men. Their engines develop 22,000hp, and range at 16 knots is 25,650km (13,500 miles). They have limited self defence weapons, and normally rely on an escorting task force for protection.

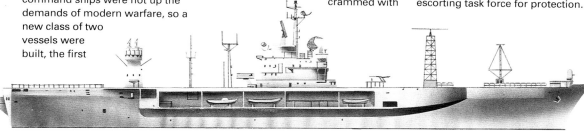

Muzio Attendolo

Type: Italian cruiser
Displacement: 9,133 tonnes (8,990 tons)
Dimensions: 182.2m x 16.6m x 6m (597ft 9in x 54ft 6in x 19ft 8in)
Machinery: Twin screws, turbines
Main armament: Six 100mm (3.9in), eight 152mm (6in) guns
Launched: 1934

Muzio Attendolo was one of a class that were slightly larger versions of the previous Cadorna class, with an additional 203 tonnes (200 tons) given over to armour protection. She had a 60mm (2.4in) thick belt, a 20-30mm (0.8-1.1in) thick armoured deck plus armoured bulkheads around the magazines and engine-room spaces. The main command centre was protected by 100mm (3.9in) thick plating. Total armour protection amounted to some 1,371 tonnes (1,350 tons). The 152mm (6in) guns were mounted in twin turrets, two forward, two aft. The ship also carried four 533mm (21in) torpedo tubes in twin mounts amidships. An aircraft catapult was carried on the shelter deck amidships, and the two aircraft could be launched to either side. *Muzio Attendolo* was sunk during an air attack on Naples in December 1942. Her sister, *Raimondo Montecuccoli*, became a training vessel after World War II and was scrapped in June 1964.

N1

Type: US submarine
Displacement: 353 tonnes (348 tons) (surface), 420 tonnes (414 tons) (submerged)
Dimensions: 45m x 4.8m x 3.8m (147ft 4in x 15ft 9in x 12ft 6in)
Machinery: Twin screws, diesel engines (surface), electric motors (submerged)
Top speed: 13 knots (surface), 11 knots (submerged)
Main armament: Four 457mm (18in) torpedo tubes
Launched: December 1916

When the USA entered World War I in 1917 there were around 50 submarines in service with the US Navy. These ranged from the small A and B boats in the Philippines, to the more advanced boats of the L class. The N class of seven units were slightly smaller than the previous L class, and had reduced engine power in order to achieve greater engine reliability. This led to the adoption of more moderate power in the subsequent O, R and S classes, the last of which were launched in 1922. *N1* and her class were the first US submarines to have metal bridges, and the last until 1946 to be designed without deck guns. *N1*, re-numbered *SS 53* in 1920, was broken up in 1931.

Nagara

Type: Japanese cruiser
Displacement: 5,560 tonnes (5,570 tons)
Dimensions: 163m x 14.2m x 4.6m (535ft x 46ft 9in x 15ft 10in)
Machinery: Quadruple screws, turbines
Main armament: Seven 140mm (5.5in) guns
Launched: April 1921

Nagara was the first Japanese Navy ship to carry 610mm (24in) torpedo tubes. They were placed in twin mounts, with two in the break between the bridge and first funnel, and two placed aft of the third funnel. Above the foredeck was a flying-off platform for a light floatplane. The hangar was positioned in the front part of the bridge. It was removed in 1931-1932, and during the refit *Nagara* was given a tripod mainmast. She was sunk in August 1944.

Nagato

Type: Japanese battleship
Displacement: 39,116 tonnes (38,500 tons)
Dimensions: 215.8m x 29m x 9m (708ft x 95ft 1in x 29ft 10in)
Machinery: Quadruple screws, turbines
Top speed: 23 knots
Main armament: Twenty 140mm (5.5in), eight 406mm (16in) guns

Launched: November 1919
Date of profile: 1920

Nagato and her sister *Mutsu* heralded a new era in battleship design with the adoption of the 406mm (16in) gun. It had a range of some 40,233 m (44,000yd), and this with great accuracy coupled with greater destructive power. A massive tripod foremast rose above a large bridge structure, and in the mid-1920s the first funnel was angled back to clear the bridge and mast of smoke fumes. New machinery requiring only one funnel was installed between 1934 and 1936, and the first funnel was then removed. *Nagato* was destroyed as a target in the Bikini atomic bomb tests of July 1946.

Naldera

Type: British liner
Displacement: 23,368 tonnes (23,000 tons)
Dimensions: 182.8m x 20.6m x 8.9m (600ft x 67ft 6in x 29ft 3in)
Machinery: Twin screws, quadruple expansion engines

Launched: 1917

Naldera was ordered in 1914 for the P & O Line's Far Eastern service. Construction was slowed down during World War I because of demands for other types of ship, but in 1917 the Admiralty decided that the vessel should be an armed merchant cruiser. However, they then decided that she should be completed as a fast cargo boat, then a troopship, a hospital ship and an aircraft carrier, but none of the conversions were ever completed. At the end of 1918 the cut-about hull was returned to P & O, who finally completed her for service as a liner in 1920. *Naldera* was scrapped in 1938.

Naniwa

Type: Japanese cruiser
Displacement: 3,708 tonnes (3,650 tons)
Dimensions: 91.4m x 14m x 6m (300ft x 46ft x 20ft)
Machinery: Triple screws, horizontal compound engines
Main armament: Six 152mm (6in), two 262mm (10.3in) guns
Launched: March 1885

Naniwa was the first modern cruiser built for the Japanese Navy. She and her sister ship *Takachiho* were designed by William White and developed from the Chilean vessel *Esmeralda*. They had a double cellular bottom with a complete 51-76mm-thick (2-3in) armoured deck. The 25-tonne (25-ton), 262mm (10.3in) guns were placed one forward and one aft, with the 152mm (6in) guns mounted on sponsons, three on each broadside. *Naniwa* was wrecked in July 1912.

Napoli

Type: Italian battleship
Displacement: 14,338 tonnes (14,112 tons)
Dimensions: 144.6m x 22.4m x 8.5m (474ft 5in x 73ft 6in x 27ft 10in)
Machinery: Twin screws, vertical triple expansion engines
Top speed: 22 knots
Main armament: Twelve 203mm (8in), two 305mm (12in) guns
Launched: September 1905

Napoli was designed by Vittorio Cuniberti, and evolved from a project to build an 8,128-tonne (8,000-ton) ship, protected with 152mm (6in) armour and armed with twelve 203mm (8in) guns that could achieve 22 knots. From this idea Cuniberti developed *Napoli*, a battleship that was faster than any afloat, as well as being far more powerful than any cruiser. She was a forerunner of the battlecruiser. Her 305mm (12in) guns were in turrets fore and aft, and the 203mm (8in) guns were in twin turrets, three on each beam. *Napoli* was removed from service in 1926.

Nashville

Type: Confederate ironclad
Displacement: Unknown
Dimensions: 82m x 18.8m (30m over paddle boxes) x 3.2m (271ft x 62ft (95ft 6in) x 10ft 6in)
Machinery: Paddlewheels, side-lever engines
Top speed: 6 knots
Main armament: Three 178mm (7in) guns, one 24-pounder howitzer
Launched: 1864

Nashville was built at Montgomery, Alabama, and was completed at Mobile. She entered service in early 1865, forming part of the main Confederate defence force against Union forces in and around Mobile. When Mobile fell in 1865, *Nashville* headed up river to make a final stand, but she ran aground on 10 May 1865.

Nassau

Type: German battleship
Displacement: 20,533 tonnes (20,210 tons)
Dimensions: 146m x 27m x 8.5m (479ft 4in x 88ft 3in x 27ft 10in)
Machinery: Triple screws, vertical

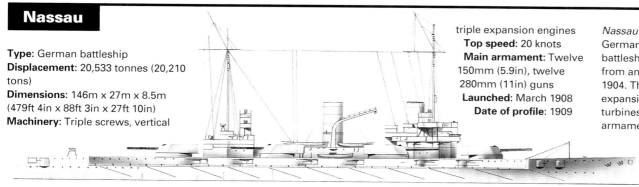

triple expansion engines
Top speed: 20 knots
Main armament: Twelve 150mm (5.9in), twelve 280mm (11in) guns
Launched: March 1908
Date of profile: 1909

Nassau and her three sisters were Germany's first dreadnought battleships, and were developed from an earlier all-big-gun design of 1904. The adoption of triple expansion engines instead of turbines meant that the main armament had to be arranged in six twin turrets, one forward, one aft and two on each beam. Nassau was scrapped in 1921.

Nautilus

Type: US submarine
Displacement: 19 tonnes (19 tons) (surface)
Dimensions: 6.4m x 1.1m (21ft x 3ft 7in)
Machinery: Single screw, hand-cranked
Main armament: Single detachable explosive charge
Launched: 1800

Nautilus was designed by Robert Fulton. Having no success with his designs in America, Fulton went to France in 1797, where his plans for Nautilus were accepted. She was to become the first submarine to be built to a government contract. The hull was composed of an iron framework covered with copper sheets, and buoyancy was controlled by hand pumps. Nautilus was propelled by sail when on the surface, and by hand-cranked propeller when submerged. During trials in Le Havre harbour, Nautilus remained underwater at a depth of 7.6m (25ft) for one hour. A detachable explosive charge was secured just above the conning tower, ready to be fastened to the hull of an enemy vessel. Crew numbered three. Later Fulton took Nautilus to Britain, where she was consistently successful during trials, but she never went into service. Finally her hull began to leak, and she was left to rot.

Nautilus

Type: British submarine
Displacement: 1,464 tonnes (1,441 tons)
Dimensions: 78.8m x 7.9m x 5.4m (258ft 6in x 26ft x 17ft 9in)
Machinery: Twin screws, diesel engines (surface), electric motors (submerged)
Main armament: Eight 457mm (18in) torpedo tubes

Launched: December 1914

Nautilus was built in response to a request from the Admiralty for a 1,016-tonne (1,000-ton) submarine with a surface speed of 20 knots. However, calculations showed that the best speed possible was 17 knots, and that on a displacement of 1,290 tonnes (1,270 tons). Vickers, the designers, approached Fiat, but they could not guarantee the required 1,850hp from their new 12-cylinder diesel engines.

However, Nautilus was laid down in 1913 and the big diesel engines were installed. She never entered operational service, but was stationed at Portsmouth as a depot ship. She was scrapped in 1922.

Nautilus

Type: US submarine
Displacement: 2,773 tonnes (2,730 tons) (surface), 3,962 tonnes (3,900 tons) submerged

Dimensions: 113m x 10m (370ft x 33ft 3in)
Machinery: Twin screws, diesel engines (surface),

electric motors (submerged)
Main armament: Two 152mm guns, six 533mm torpedo tubes
Launched: March 1930
Date of profile: 1931

Nautilus was one of three V-class submarines designed as powerfully armed ocean-going boats. They were slow to dive due to their huge size and flat deck, which had a raised centre section to improve the guns' field of fire. She was re-numbered SS168 in 1931, and re-fitted in 1940 to carry 5,104 litres (19,320 gallons) of aviation fuel for long-range seaplanes. She was scrapped in 1945.

Nautilus

Type: US submarine
Displacement: 4,157 tonnes (4,091 tons) (surface), 4,104 tonnes (4,040) (submerged)
Dimensions: 97m x 8.2m (323ft 7in x 27ft 6in)
Machinery: Twin screws, nuclear reactor, turbines
Main armament: Six 533mm (21in)

torpedo tubes
Launched: January 1954
Date of profile: 1954

Nautilus was the world's first nuclear-powered submarine. Apart from her revolutionary propulsion plant, she was of a conventional design. Early trials established new records, including nearly 2,250km (1,400 miles) submerged in 90 hours at 20 knots, at that time the longest period spent submerged by a US submarine, as well as being the fastest speed achieved underwater.

Navarin

Type: Russian battleship
Displacement: 10,370 tonnes
(10,206 tons)
Dimensions: 109m x 20.4m x 8.3m
(357ft 7in x 67ft x 27ft 6in)
Machinery: Twin screws,
vertical triple expansion
engines
Top speed: 15.5 knots
Main armament: Eight 152mm (6in),
four 305mm (12in) guns
Armour: 203-406mm (8-16in) belt,
305mm (12in) on turrets, 127mm
(5in) on battery
Launched:
October 1891

Date of profile: 1896

Navarin was based upon the successful British Nile class of battleship. She was laid down in 1889 in St Petersburg. She had a rectangular central superstructure which held the 152mm (6in) guns in broadside, protected by 127mm (5in) armour. Her main 305mm (12in) guns were mounted in two twin armoured turrets, fore and aft of the superstructure. She had

four funnels in a rectangular configuration, which earned her the nickname, the 'upturned table'. She was well protected, with her main belt covering the centre section in two strakes. There was also a 76mm (3in) thick armoured deck which rested on top of the main belt. Her engines developed 9,140hp and coal supply was 707 tonnes (700 tons). *Navarin* took part in the Battle of Tsushima in May 1905, where the Russian fleet was demolished by superior Japanese gunnery and ship handling. She took numerous hits from heavy shells, but her armour stood up well and she remained relatively unscathed. The next day, on 28 May 1905, she made a run for Vladivostock, but was torpedoed by Japanese destroyers. They didn't stop to pick up survivors, and she sank with heavy loss of life.

Nedlloyd Europa

Type: Dutch container ship
Displacement: 48,768 tonnes (48,000 tons)
Dimensions: 266m x 32.2m x 13m
(872ft 9in x 105ft 9in x 42ft 8in)
Machinery: Single screw, diesel
engine
Top speed: 23 knots
Launched: September 1991

Nedlloyd Europa is of an unusual design which does away with standard hatch covers

to the cargo holds. Instead, she features container guides which extend from the holds up above the deck to secure deck-carried containers. This system ensures greater security for the cargo in transit, minimising the risk of

damage or loss in heavy weather. Tests proved the safety of the design, confirming that hatch covers do not add strength to the structure of the hull. However, removal of any water that finds its way into a hatchless vessel is a priority, and duplicate pumping and drainage systems are incorporated. She has seven cargo holds, two of them positioned aft in the bridge structure.

Nelson

Type: British cruiser
Displacement: 7,592 tonnes (7,473 tons)
Dimensions: 85.3m x 18.2m x 7.5m
(280ft x 60ft x 24ft 10in)
Machinery: Twin screws, inverted compound engines
Top speed: 14 knots
Main armament: Eight 228mm (9in), four 254mm (10in) guns
Launched: November 1876
Date of profile: 1878

Nelson was built in answer to the growing number of Russian armoured cruisers then in service or under construction. She and her sister *Northampton* were intended for overseas service, mainly in the Pacific where lack of coaling stations meant long periods at sea under sail alone. *Nelson* carried 1,168 tonnes (1,150 tons) of coal herself, giving her a range of 9,500km (5,000 miles) at 10 knots, and 14,250km (7,500 miles) at seven knots. She also carried a barque rig of 2,201 square metres (23,690 sq ft). She. became a stokers' training ship in 1901 and was sold in 1910.

Nelson

Type: British
battleship
Displacement:
38,608 tonnes
(38,000 tons)
Dimensions:
216.8m x 32.4m

x 9.6m (711ft x 106ft 4in x 31ft 6in)
Machinery: Twin screws, turbines
Top speed: 23.5 knots
Main armament: Twelve 152mm (6in), nine 406mm (16in) guns
Launched: September 1925
Date of profile: 1945

Nelson and her sister ship *Rodney* were the first battleships to be completed within the limits of the Washington Treaty of 1922, which fixed the maximum displacement for each class of vessel. *Nelson's* main armament was concentrated forward of the tower bridge in three triple turrets, so saving on the weight of armour that would

have been required had they been placed at each end of the vessel as originally planned. More weight was saved by adopting less powerful machinery. The secondary battery was carried in twin turrets level with the main mast. The engine rooms were placed forward of the boiler rooms in order to keep the bridge structure clear of funnel smoke. *Nelson* and *Rodney* were both scrapped in 1948/49.

Neptune

Type: British battleship
Displacement: 9,276 tonnes
(9,130 tons)
Dimensions: 91.4m x
19.2m x 7.6m (300ft x 63ft
x 25ft)
Machinery: Single
screw, horizontal trunk
engines
Top speed: 14.2 knots

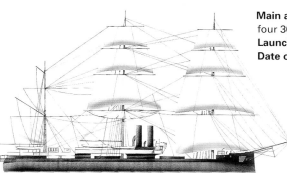

Main armament: Two 228mm (9in),
four 305mm (12in) guns
Launched: September 1874
Date of profile: 1881

Neptune was originally
Independencia, designed by
Reed for the Brazilian Navy in
1872. She was taken over
during a period when war
between Britain and
Russia seemed likely, and

she was converted at Portsmouth for
service in the Royal Navy. The
305mm (12in) guns were in twin
turrets amidships, separated by a
short superstructure that supported a
flying bridge. The two 228mm (9in)
guns were under the forecastle.
Because the sails on the mainmast
were so close to the funnels, the sails
had to be replaced several times due
to smoke rot. *Neptune* was broken up
in 1903.

Nereide

Type: Italian submarine
Displacement: 228 tonnes (225
tons) (surface), 325 tonnes (320
tons) (submerged)
Dimensions: 40m x 4.3m x 2.8m
(134ft 2in x 14ft 1in x 9ft 2in)
Machinery: Twin screws, diesel
engines (surface), electric motors
(submerged)
Top speed: 13.2 knots (surface), 8

knots (submerged)
Main armament: Two 450mm
(1.7in) torpedo tubes
Launched: July 1913

Nereide and her sister *Nautilus*
were the first submarines designed
by Engineer Bernardis, later to
become renowned as a submarine
designer. Both were laid down on 1
August 1911 and completed in 1913.
Nereide's smooth, sleek hull shape

was similar to that of a torpedo
boat, and she had two torpedo
tubes mounted in the bow. A third
deck-
mounted
torpedo tube
was
planned,

but never fitted. *Nereide* was sunk
on 5 August 1915 by torpedoes from
the Austrian submarine *U5*.

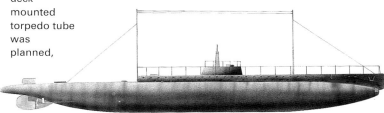

Nerissa

Type: British liner
Displacement: 5,672 tonnes (5,583
tons)
Dimensions: 106m x 16.4m x
6.3m (349ft 6in x 54ft x 29ft
8in)
Machinery: Single screw,
triple expansion engines
Top speed: 16 knots
Launched: March 1926

Nerissa was built very quickly, as her owners, the Red
Cross Line, required her for the 1926 season on the
New York run. Contracts were signed in November
1925, she was running trials at the end of May 1926,

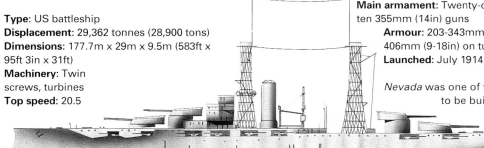

and she set out on her maiden voyage on 5
June. Her hull was strengthened, and the
icebreaker-type stem sloped sharply back
to the keel from the waterline. There was
accommodation for 163 first-class and 66
second-class passengers. During the
depression of 1927, *Nerissa* was sold to
the Furness Withy Group and served
on the West Indies-New
York route. She was sunk
by a German U-boat in
1941.

Nevada

Type: US battleship
Displacement: 29,362 tonnes (28,900 tons)
Dimensions: 177.7m x 29m x 9.5m (583ft x
95ft 3in x 31ft)
Machinery: Twin
screws, turbines
Top speed: 20.5

knots
Main armament: Twenty-one 127mm (5in),
ten 355mm (14in) guns
Armour: 203-343mm (8-13.5in) belt, 228-
406mm (9-18in) on turrets
Launched: July 1914

Nevada was one of the first battleships
to be built on the 'all-or-

nothing' principle, adopted by other
navies after World War I, in which
the thickest possible armour was
applied to vital areas, leaving the
rest virtually unprotected. *Nevada*
was badly damaged at Pearl Harbor
in December 1941. After repairs,
she served reliably during World
War II, and survived the Bikini
bomb tests in July 1946. She was
sunk off Hawaii during target
practice in 1948.

New Ironsides

Type: US battleship
Displacement: 4,277 tonnes
(4,210 tons)
Dimensions: 70m x 17.5m
x 4.8m (232ft x 57ft
6in x 15ft 8in)
Machinery: Single
screw, horizontal

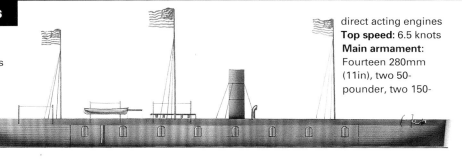

direct acting engines
Top speed: 6.5 knots
Main armament:
Fourteen 280mm
(11in), two 50-
pounder, two 150-

pounder guns
Launched: May 1862

New Ironsides was one of three
ironclads ordered in 1861. She
served as the Union flagship, and
although she saw almost constant
action during the Civil War, her
armour was never pierced. She was
destroyed by a fire in 1865.

New York

Type: US cruiser
Displacement: 9,165 tonnes (9,021 tons)
Dimensions: 117m x 19.7m x 7.2m (384ft x 64ft 10in x 23ft 10in)

Machinery: Twin screws, vertical triple expansion engines
Top speed: 21 knots
Main armament: Twelve 102mm

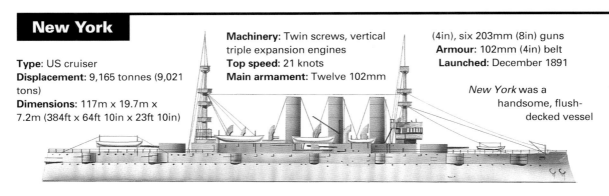

(4in), six 203mm (8in) guns
Armour: 102mm (4in) belt
Launched: December 1891

New York was a handsome, flush-decked vessel

and the USA's first armoured cruiser. She was laid down in September 1890 and completed in August 1893. She served as Admiral Sampson's flagship during the Spanish-American War of 1898. In 1905-09 her armament was revised. She became the *Saratoga* in 1911 and *Rochester* in 1917. She served until 1933, then remained in the Philippines until she was scuttled to prevent capture by Japanese forces during World War II.

New York

Type: US battleship
Displacement: 28,854 tonnes (28,400 tons)
Dimensions: 174.6m x 29m x 9m (573ft x 95ft 2in x 29ft 6in)
Machinery: Twin screws, triple expansion engines

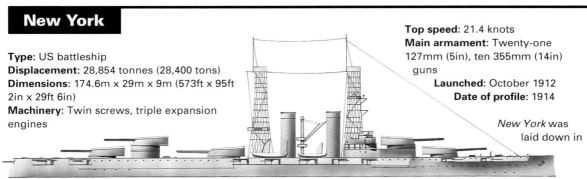

Top speed: 21.4 knots
Main armament: Twenty-one 127mm (5in), ten 355mm (14in) guns
Launched: October 1912
Date of profile: 1914

New York was laid down in

September 1911 and completed in April 1914. Her engines developed 29,687hp and coal supply was 2,964 tonnes (2,917 tons), plus 406 tonnes (400 tons) oil fuel. During World War I she served with the British fleet. She underwent major recon-struction from 1925 to 1927. Having survived World War II, *New York* went on to survive the Bikini atomic bomb tests in 1946. She was sunk as a target off Pearl Harbor in 1948.

Newark

Type: US cruiser
Displacement: 4,665 tonnes (4,592 tons)
Dimensions: 100m x 15m x 5.7m (328ft x 49ft 2in x 18ft 10in)
Machinery: Twin screws, horizontal triple expansion engines
Main armament: Twelve 152mm (6in) guns
Launched: March 1890

Newark was the last US warship to carry a full sailing rig. Originally she carried a barque rig, but this was later removed, as was the main mast. Engines developed 8,500hp and coal supply was 812 tonnes (800 tons). She was laid down in Philadelphia in 1888, and completed in 1891. In 1913 she was removed from the navy list, but served as a quarantine hulk and hospital annex until she was sold in 1926.

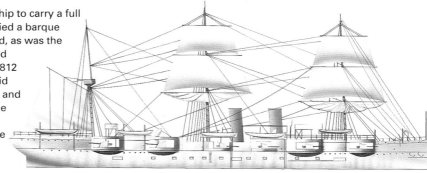

Nibbio

Type: Italian torpedo boat
Displacement: 26 tonnes (25.5 tons)
Dimensions: 24.3m x 3m x 1m (80ft x 10ft x 3ft 6in)
Machinery: Single screw, triple expansion reciprocating engine

Top speed: 18 knots
Main armament: Two 355mm (14in) torpedo tubes
Launched: 1878

Nibbio was Italy's first torpedo boat. She was built by Thornycroft, who had already built such small, high-speed vessels for Norway, France, Denmark, Sweden and Austria. Her engines developed

250hp, and steam was supplied by a single locomotive boiler. Two torpedoes were carried amidships, and she also had a one-pounder gun. Crew numbered 10. *Nibbio* was first commissioned in 1881, and in 1886 she was re-designated *IT*. She was discarded in 1904, but was later used as a steam boat and was re-numbered *PE44*.

Niels Juel

Type: Danish coast defence ship
Displacement: 4,165 tonnes (4,100 tons)
Dimensions: 90m x 16.3m x 5m (295ft 3in x 53ft 6in x 16ft 5in)
Machinery: Twin screws, vertical triple expansion engines

Top speed: 16 knots
Main armament: Ten 150mm (5.9in) guns
Launched: 1918
Date of profile: 1939

Niels Juel was laid down in 1914 at Copenhagen, but her construction was delayed due to the demands of the Danish fleet, then busily engaged in neutrality patrols. As built, the vessel had a tripod foremast and a light main-

mast, but this was changed to a built-up foremast equipped with range finders, and a light pole mast. During World War II, *Niels Juel* tried to escape to Sweden but she was captured by the Germans. They converted her to a cadet ship named *Nordland*. She then served as a refugee ship for officers and their families until she was bombed and sunk near Kiel in 1945.

Nile

Type: British battleship
Displacement: 12,791 tonnes (12,590 tons)
Dimensions: 105m x 22m x 8.6m (345ft x 73ft x 28ft 6in)
Machinery: Twin screws, triple expansion engines
Top speed: 17 knots
Main armament: Six 120mm (4.7in), four 343mm (13.5in) guns
Launched: March 1888

Nile and her sister *Trafalgar* were the heaviest battleships in the Royal Navy at the time of their construction. They were extremely well armoured, carrying over 4390 tonnes (4,320 tons) of protective steel plate. In order to enable them to carry this heavier armour, the belt was only 70m (230ft) long amidships, and extended from 1.6m (5ft 6in) below the waterline to 0.9m (3ft) above it. The 76mm (3in) thick armoured deck extended the full length of the vessel. In *Nile*, the weaponry also reflected the principle of combining the heaviest armament with maximum protection. The 343mm (13.5in) guns were mounted in twin, hydraulically operated, turrets on the centreline some 4.2m (14ft) above the waterline. These were positioned fore and aft of the octagonal citadel. This held the 120mm (4.7in) guns, which were protected by bulkheads some 127mm (5in) thick. Later the 120mm (4.7in) guns were replaced by more modern 152mm (6in) weapons. When she was completed in 1891, many naval officers felt that she would be one of the last capital ships to be built, because of the perceived threat of the rapidly developing torpedo boats then entering service. *Nile* spent most of her service in the Mediterranean before ending up as a training ship. She was scrapped in 1912.

Nisshin

Type: Japanese cruiser
Displacement: 1,514 tonnes (1,490 tons)
Dimensions: 61.8m x 8.7m x 4.2m (202ft 9in x 28ft 9in x 13ft 9in)
Machinery: Single screw, reciprocating engine
Main armament: One 178mm (7in), six 30-pounder guns

Launched: 1869

Nisshin was laid down in 1867, for the Shogun, but was not completed until after the civil war, when the Shogun' forces were defeated at Hakodate. This led to the abolition of the feudal fleets, and all warships were enrolled in the Imperial Navy. *Nisshin* was commissioned into the Japanese Navy in 1870. She was a wooden-hulled, barque-rigged corvette, and her 178mm (7in) gun was mounted on the centreline between the foremast and the bridge, with the 30-pounder guns on the broadside. She was scrapped in 1893.

Nordenfelt 1

Type: Greek submarine
Displacement: 61 tonnes (60 tons)
Dimensions: 19.5m x 2.7m (64ft x 9ft)
Machinery: Single screw, compound engine
Top speed: 9 knots (surface), 4 knots (submerged)
Main armament: One 355mm (14in) torpedo tube, one 25.4mm (1in) gun fitted later
Launched: 1885
Date of profile: 1885

Laid down in 1882, *Nordenfelt 1* was one of the world's first steam-propelled submarines. Her hull was almost circular in section, with frames spaced 0.6m (2ft) apart along its length. Diving depth was 15m (50ft). Most of her interior was taken up with the machinery, boilers and a steam accumulator, which had a heat exchanger at the bottom. Steam from the boiler was conveyed through the coils of the heater, giving up its latent heat to the water in the accumulator, which was then returned to the boiler via a feed pump. By this means, a large store of superheated water could be stored in the pear-shaped tank. When this was released into the main boiler at a lower pressure, it turned into steam. The engine was fired in harbour, and took three days to heat up the reservoir fully.

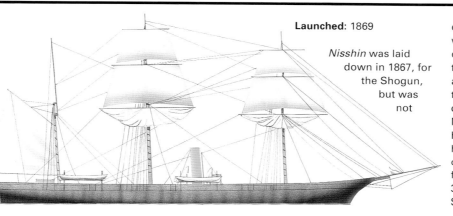

Norman

Type: British liner
Displacement: 13,614 tonnes (13,400 tons)
Dimensions: 154.5m x 16.2m x 8.5m (507ft x 53ft 2in x 27ft 9in)
Machinery: Twin screws, triple expansion engines
Top speed: 17 knots
Launched: 1894

Norman served on the South African route and was the largest vessel on the mail service at the time. She had luxurious accommodation for 250 first-class passengers, and also carried 100 third-class passengers. In 1899 she served as a troop transport in the Boer War. She underwent a major refit in 1904, and was placed on reserve in 1910. She resumed her South African service in 1914. *Norman* was laid up in 1925 and was sold for scrap in 1926.

North Carolina

Type: US battleship
Displacement: 47,518 tonnes (46,770 tons)
Dimensions: 222m x 33m x 10m (728ft 9in x 108ft 3in x 32ft 10in)
Machinery: Quadruple screws, turbines
Top speed: 28 knots

Main armament: Twenty 127mm (5in), nine 406mm (16in) guns
Launched: June 1940
Date of profile: 1942

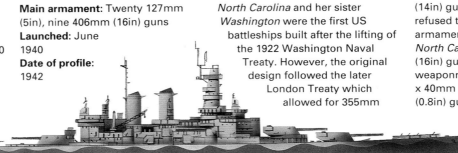

North Carolina and her sister *Washington* were the first US battleships built after the lifting of the 1922 Washington Naval Treaty. However, the original design followed the later London Treaty which allowed for 355mm (14in) guns, but as the Japanese refused to restrict their main armament, the US decided to fit *North Carolina* with triple 406mm (16in) gun turrets. By 1945 her weaponry had been replaced by 96 x 40mm (1.6in), and 36 x 20mm (0.8in) guns. She was stricken in 1960, and is now preserved at Wilmington, North Carolina.

November

Type: Russian submarine
Displacement: 4,572 tonnes (4,500 tons) (surface), 5,384 tonnes (5,300 tons) (submerged)
Dimensions: 110m x 9m x 7.7m (360ft 10in x 29ft 6in x 25ft 3in)
Machinery: Twin screws, pressurised-water nuclear reactors, turbines
Main armament: Four 400mm (15.7in), eight 533mm (21in) torpedo tubes
Launched: 1958

Even by Soviet standards, the November-class submarines were large when they first appeared, dwarfing contemporary vessels of other nations. The US Navy were the first to recognise the advantages of nuclear propulsion: the single hull construction, large saving in weight and increase in underwater speed. The Russians were not slow to follow suit. The Novembers' eight bow tubes are for 533mm (21in) anti-ship torpedoes,

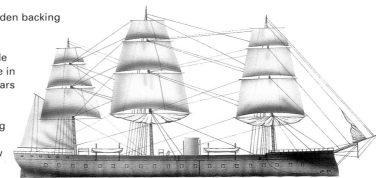

while the 400mm (15.7in) tubes are for anti-submarine torpedoes and are positioned aft. The fully rounded bow sections made it possible to house eight tubes, with a large area aft of the torpedo room housing two re-loads per tube.

Novgorod

Type: Russian coast defence vessel
Displacement: 2,500 tonnes (2,491 tons)

Dimensions: 36.9m x 36.9m x 4.1m (121ft x 121ft x 13ft 6in)
Machinery: Six screws, horizontal compound engines
Top speed: 6 knots

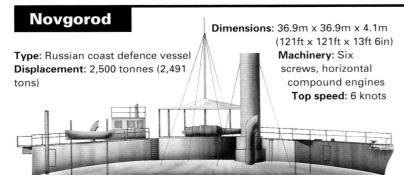

Main armament: Two 86mm (3.4in), two 280mm (11in)guns
Launched: 1873
Date of profile: 1876

During the 1860s, there was a tendency towards an increase in beam with a corresponding decrease in the length of ironclads, so making it possible to increase the weight of armour protection carried. This principle reached a peak with *Novgorod*, one of two completely circular battleships. She was ordered by Admiral Popoff, and laid down in 1872. She was built in sections and was assembled and completed in 1874. Her sloping deck rose to over 1.5m (5ft) above the waterline in the centre, where the two 280mm (11in) guns were housed in a tall, open barbette. Two propellers were later removed. She was scrapped around 1900.

Numancia

Type: Spanish battleship
Displacement: 7,304 tonnes (7,189 tons)
Dimensions: 96m x 17.3m x 8.2m (315ft x 57ft x 27ft)
Machinery: Single screw, non-compound engines
Top speed: 13 knots
Main armament: Forty 68-pounder guns

Armour: 102-140mm belt, 444mm wooden backing
Launched: November 1863

Numancia was an iron-hulled, broadside ironclad and was laid down at La Seyne in 1861. She served during the Spanish wars with Peru and Chile, and was badly damaged during the Carlist conflict of 1873. She was completely rebuilt during 1897-98. By 1914 she was a gunnery training ship. She sank while under tow to the breakers in 1916.

Oberon

Type: British submarine
Displacement: 1,513 tonnes (1,490 tons) (surface), 1,922 tonnes (1,892 tons) (submerged)
Dimensions: 83.4m x 8.3m x 4.6m (273ft 8in x 27ft 3in x 15ft)
Machinery: Twin screws, diesel engines (surface), electric motors (submerged)
Main armament: Eight 533mm (21in) torpedo tubes
Launched: September 1926
Date of profile: 1939

Oberon was an ocean-going paddle-tank type submarine developed from the L type of World War I. Originally *O 1*, the boat was of an advanced design for long-range operation, and was ideal for service in the Far East. Surfaced range at nine knots was 9,500km (5,000 miles), and submerged at four knots was 114km (60 miles). She was scrapped in 1945.

Oceanic

Type: British liner
Displacement: 17,550 tonnes (17,274 tons)

Dimensions: 209m x 20.7m (686ft x 68ft)
Machinery: Twin screws, triple expansion engines
Top speed: 19.5 knots

Launched: January 1899
Date of profile: 1899

In *Oceanic*, the White Star Line

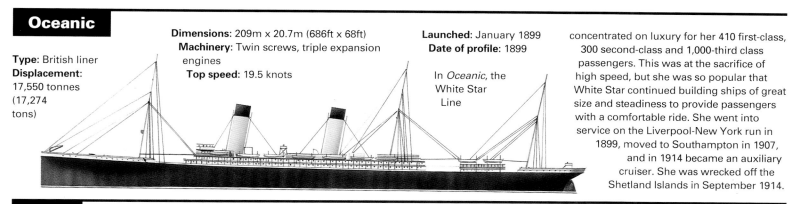

concentrated on luxury for her 410 first-class, 300 second-class and 1,000-third class passengers. This was at the sacrifice of high speed, but she was so popular that White Star continued building ships of great size and steadiness to provide passengers with a comfortable ride. She went into service on the Liverpool-New York run in 1899, moved to Southampton in 1907, and in 1914 became an auxiliary cruiser. She was wrecked off the Shetland Islands in September 1914.

Ohio

Type: US submarine
Displacement: 16,360 tonnes (16,764 tons) (surface), 19,050 tonnes (18,750 tons) (submerged)
Dimensions: 170.7m x 12.8m x 11m (560ft x 42ft x 36ft 5in)
Machinery: Single screw, pressurised -water nuclear reactor, turbines
Top speed: 28 knots (surface), 30+ knots (submerged)

Main armament: 24 Trident missiles, four 533mm (21in) torpedo tubes
Launched: April 1976

This submarine is the lead ship in a large class of boats intended to form the third arm of the USA's nuclear defence force. She is the

largest submarine to be built in the West, only surpassed by the Russian Typhoon class. Her size was determined by the size of her nuclear reactor plant. *Ohio* first entered service in October 1981, and can remain submerged at sea for periods

of up to 70 days. Originally the Ohio class were armed with the Trident C-4 missile, but from the ninth boat they were built to carry the improved D-5 missile, with the preceding eight boats being re-fitted accordingly.

Olympia

Type: US cruiser
Displacement: 6,663 tonnes (6,558 tons)
Dimensions: 104.8m x 16m x 6.5m (344ft x 53ft x 21ft 6in)

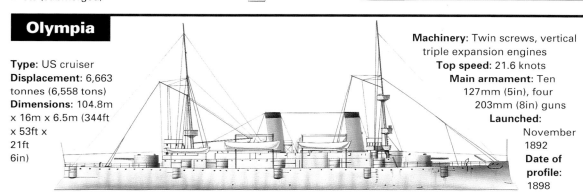

Machinery: Twin screws, vertical triple expansion engines
Top speed: 21.6 knots
Main armament: Ten 127mm (5in), four 203mm (8in) guns
Launched: November 1892
Date of profile: 1898

In 1898 *Olympia* was the flagship of the US fleet at the Battle of Manila during the war with Spain. She was powerfully armed, with excellent protection on a moderate displacement. The 203mm (8in) guns were mounted in twin turrets fore and aft. The 127mm (5in) guns were fitted in the superstructure, protected by 102mm (4in) thick shields. *Olympia* served during World War I and was decommissioned in 1922.

Oregon

Type: US battleship
Displacement: 10,452 tonnes (10,288 tons)
Dimensions: 106.9m x 21m x 7.3m (351ft x 69ft 3in x 24ft)
Machinery: Twin screws, vertical triple expansion engines
Top speed: 15 knots

Main armament: Four 152mm (6in), eight 203mm (8in), four 330mm (13in) guns
Launched: October 1893
Date of profile: 1896

In 1889 Congress denied a request for 192 warships to be built over a 15-year period, and the US Navy had to make do with three 'sea-going coastline battleships'. This designation was the only way the Navy could get the approval of Congress. The ships were the three Oregons, and they carried heavy armament and protection on a small displacement which resulted in a low freeboard, limited endurance and low speed. In 1898 *Oregon* took part in the war with Spain. She was sold in 1956.

Orzel

Type: Polish submarine
Displacement: 1,117 tonnes (1,100 tons) (surface), 1,496 tonnes (1,473 tons) (submerged)
Dimensions: 84m x 6.7m x 4m (275ft 7in x 22ft x 13ft 8in)
Machinery: Twin screws, diesel engines (surface), electric motors (submerged)

Main armament: One 105mm (4.1in) gun, twelve 550mm (21.7in) torpedo tubes
Launched: January 1938

Orzel was ordered in January 1935 and was funded by public subscription. She was a large, ocean-going submarine with excellent all-round qualities. She

and her sister ship were built in Holland. Diving depth was 80m (200ft), surfaced range at ten knots was 13,300km (7,000 miles), and submerged range at five knots was 190km

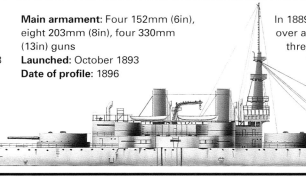

(100 miles). *Orzel* went into service in February 1939, and escaped to Britain in September after having carried out the last patrol of any Polish warship. She sank after striking a mine in June 1940.

Palestro

Type: Italian battleship
Displacement: 2,642 tonnes (2,600 tons)
Dimensions: 64.8m x 13m x 5.6m (212ft 7in x 42ft 8in x 18ft 4in)
Machinery: Single screw, reciprocating engines
Top speed: 8 knots
Main armament: One 165mm (6.5in), four 203mm (8in) guns
Armour: 120mm (4.7in) belt, 120mm (4.7in) on battery
Launched: September 1865

Palestro was laid down at La Seyne in August 1864 and completed in January 1866. She and her sister ship

Varese had iron hulls, and carried a full barque rig. Her steam engines were capable of generating 930hp, and she carried 180 tonnes (177 tons) of coal, which gave her a range of 1520km (945 miles) at eight knots. It was intended that she should rely on sail for most of her motive force. On 20 July 1866, she and two other Italian ironclads, *Re d'Italia* and *San Martino*, met up with seven Austrian ironclads near Lissa. A confused swirling battle took place, shrouded in thick smoke. *Re d'Italia* was taking heavy damage, and *Palestro* tried to come to her aid. She was then raked from her stern and suffered numerous hits. Fires were started, and she had to limp out of the battle.

Two other Italian ships took her in tow, and boats were launched to take off the crew. Captain Capellini refused to abandon ship, and his crew volunteered to stay and fight

the fire. It was to no avail, as shortly afterwards she exploded and sank. Only 19 men from 250 survived. *Varese* served until 1891, although in her later years as a hospital ship.

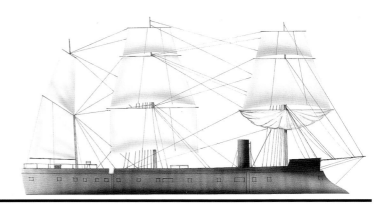

Palestro

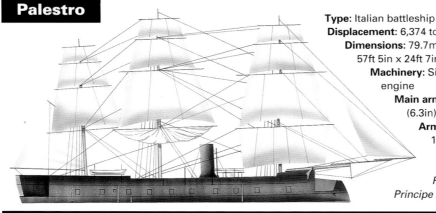

Type: Italian battleship
Displacement: 6,374 tonnes (6,274 tons)
Dimensions: 79.7m x 17.5m x 7.5m (261ft 6in x 57ft 5in x 24ft 7in)
Machinery: Single screw, single expansion engine
Main armament: Twelve 160mm (6.3in) guns
Armour: 220mm (8.7in) belt, 140mm (5.5in) on battery
Launched: October 1871

Palestro and her sister *Principe Amedeo* were the first

ironclads to be built in Italian yards. They were also the last to have composite hulls with iron framing and wooden planking, and to carry sails. Due to the aftermath of the war with Austria in 1866, *Palestro* and her sister were six years on the stocks and took another four years completing, *Palestro* entering service in July 1875. She had a full-length belt, a pronounced ram bow, and carried 3,413 square metres (36,740 sq ft) of canvas. She was removed from the effective list in 1900.

Panther

Type: Austrian cruiser
Displacement: 1,582 tonnes (1,557 tons)
Dimensions: 73m x 10m x 4.2m (240ft x 34ft x 14ft)
Machinery: Twin

screws, vertical compound engines
Top speed: 18.4 knots
Main armament: Four 47mm (1.85in),

two 120mm (4.7in) guns
Launched: June 1885

Panther was Austria's first modern cruiser. She was laid down at Armstrong's yard in 1884. She and her sister *Leopard* were to provide Austria

with invaluable experience in the construction of modern cruisers such as the *Tiger*, which was laid down nearly one year later. *Panther's* engines developed 5,940hp, and were of the twin cylinder type then about to be superseded by the new triple expansion engine. Her main armament was removed in 1909/10, and she was attached to a submarine training squadron. In 1917 *Panther* served at Cattaro as a sea-going training ship. She was scrapped in 1920.

Parisian

Type: British liner
Displacement: 5,444 tonnes (5,359 tons)
Dimensions: 134.4m x 14m (441ft x 46ft)
Machinery: Single screw, compound engines
Top speed: 14 knots
Launched: 1881

Parisian was the first North Atlantic liner to have bilge keels. She was built from steel, and was much larger and faster than any previous liner belonging to her owners, the Allan Line. She could

accommodate 150 first-class, 100 second-class and 1,000 third-class

passengers. In 1899 she was rebuilt and given triple expansion engines. In 1914 she was broken up.

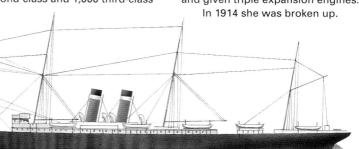

Passaic

Type: US monitor
Displacement: 1,905 tonnes (1,875 tons)
Dimensions: 61m x 14m x 3.2m (200ft x 46ft x 10ft 6in)
Machinery: Single screw, trunk engines
Top speed: 7 knots

Main armament: One 280mm (11in), one 381mm (15in) gun
Armour: 127mm (5in) on hull, 280mm (11in) on turret
Launched: August 1862

Passaic was the lead ship in a

class of ten single turreted monitors that formed the backbone of the Union Navy during the American Civil War. The class was a direct development of the original *Monitor*, with increased displacement and many of *Monitor*'s shortcomings ironed

out. During the attack on Charleston in April 1863, all ships in *Passaic*'s class that were present were badly damaged by the well-directed fire from the Confederate forts. Two were lost in the war, and several served as coast defence vessels in the Spanish American War of 1898. *Passaic* survived both wars, and was sold in 1899.

Pawnee

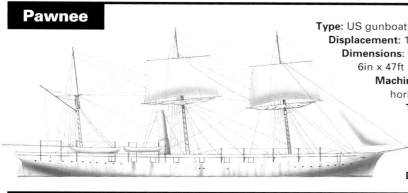

Type: US gunboat
Displacement: 1,557 tonnes (1,533 tons)
Dimensions: 67.5m x 14.3m x 3m (221ft 6in x 47ft 10in x 10ft)
Machinery: Twin screws, horizontal direct acting engines
Top speed: 10 knots
Main armament: Eight 228mm (9in), two 32-pounder guns
Launched: 1859
Date of profile: 1862

Pawnee had an unusual concave hull form that enabled a heavy armament to be carried on a shallow draught. Later this proved invaluable in the shallow rivers of the Confederacy. Laid down in 1858, she was completed in 1860. When the Gosport Navy Yard fell to the Confederates, *Pawnee* towed the sailing frigate *Cumberland* to safety. In 1869 *Pawnee*'s machinery was removed and she was fitted out as a sailing ship. She served as a hospital and store ship until her sale in 1884.

Pegaso

Type: Italian torpedo boat
Displacement: 210 tonnes (207 tons)
Dimensions: 50.3m x 5.3m x 1.7m (165ft 2in x 17ft 5in x 5ft 8in)
Machinery: Twin screws, vertical triple expansion engines

Main armament: Two 57mm (2.25in) guns, three 450mm (17.7in) torpedo tubes

Launched: August 1905

Pegaso was the lead ship of five vessels in a class that eventually increased to 27 units. Their design was very successful, proving strong and seaworthy. *Pegaso* was laid down at Pattison's yard in August 1904, and was completed in September 1905. Her engines developed 3,200hp, and range at full speed was nearly 646km (340 miles). She was converted to oil fuel in 1908, and later served in World War I. *Pegaso* was discarded in March 1923.

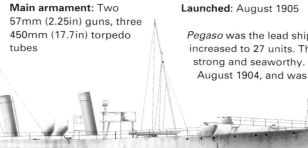

Pelayo

Type: Spanish battleship
Displacement: 9,900 tonnes (9,745 tons)
Dimensions: 102m x 20m x 7.5m (334ft 8in x 66ft 3in x 24ft 9in)
Machinery: Twin screws, vertical compound engines
Top speed: 16.7 knots
Main armament: Twelve 120mm (4.7in), one 162mm (6.4in), two

280mm (11in), two 317mm (12.5in) guns
Launched: February 1887
Date of profile: 1890

Pelayo was Spain's most powerful warship for over 20 years. She was built in France to designs by Lagane, one of the world's leading naval architects. She was based upon the French *Marceau*, with slightly increased length and beam, and with

reduced draught to allow her passage through the Suez Canal. *Pelayo* was rebuilt in 1897, and was given new boilers and armour over the midship battery. She

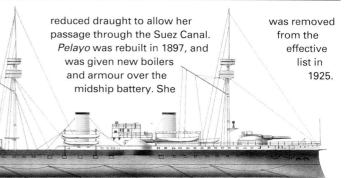

was removed from the effective list in 1925.

Pellicano

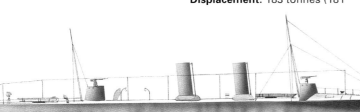

Type: Italian torpedo boat
Displacement: 183 tonnes (181 tons)
Dimensions: 48.7m x 5.7m x 1.5m (159ft 10in x 18ft 10in x 5ft)
Machinery: Twin screws, vertical triple expansion engines
Top speed: 21 knots
Main armament: Two 37mm (1.5in) guns, two 355mm (14in) torpedo tubes
Launched: April 1899

Pellicano was commissioned in 1900 as a first-class torpedo boat with a design speed of 25.7 knots, but because of unreliable machinery this speed was never achieved. She was an excellent seaboat, however, and served as a prototype for a later group of ocean-going vessels launched in 1905-06. She was discarded in 1920.

Petr Veliki

Type: Russian battleship
Displacement: 10,572 tonnes (10,406 tons)
Dimensions: 103.5m x 18.9m x 8.2m (339ft 8in x 62ft 3in x 27ft)
Machinery: Twin screws, horizontal return connecting rod engines
Top speed: 10 knots
Main armament: Six 86mm

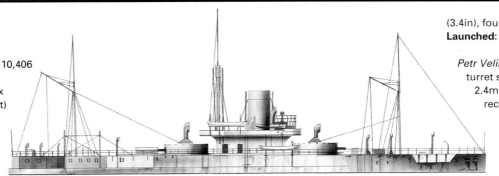

(3.4in), four 305mm (12in) guns
Launched: August 1872

Petr Veliki was a large, breastwork turret ship with an iron hull and 2.4m (8ft) freeboard. She was reconstructed in 1905/06. Renamed *Respublikanets*, she served as a gunnery training ship with the Baltic fleet. She was scrapped in 1922.

Piemonte

Type: Italian cruiser
Displacement: 2,824 tonnes (2,780 tons)
Dimensions: 97.8m x 11.6m x 5.1m (320ft 10in x 38ft x 16ft 9in)
Machinery: Twin screws, triple expansion engines
Top speed: 22.3 knots
Main armament: Six 120mm (4.7in), six 152mm (6in) guns

Launched: August 1888

Piemonte was the first warship in the world to be armed exclusively with the quick-firing gun. The vessel was laid down in 1887 and completed in 1889. Her 152mm (6in) guns could fire at a rate of seven rounds per minute, and the 120mm (4.7in) guns at 12 rounds per minute. Unfortunately the armament proved too heavy, so the 152mm guns were reduced in number, and were then finally removed in 1912. She had good armour protection, with a complete 76mm (3in) thick deck. *Piemonte* was discarded in May 1920.

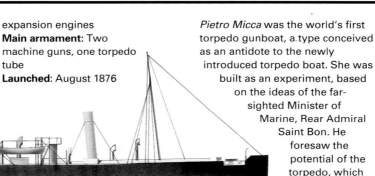

Pietro Micca

Type: Italian cruiser
Displacement: 607 tonnes (598 tons)
Dimensions: 61.8m x 5.9m x 3.6m (203ft x 19ft 7in x 11ft 10in)
Machinery: Single screw, vertical single expansion engines
Main armament: Two machine guns, one torpedo tube
Launched: August 1876

Pietro Micca was the world's first torpedo gunboat, a type conceived as an antidote to the newly introduced torpedo boat. She was built as an experiment, based on the ideas of the far-sighted Minister of Marine, Rear Admiral Saint Bon. He foresaw the potential of the torpedo, which was already establishing a reputation. *Pietro Micca* was designed by Engineer Mattei Pietro Micca, and had an iron hull with machinery that developed 571hp. Steam was supplied by four locomotive boilers. She was laid down in 1875, and was completed in 1877, some nine years before any similar boat in the French and British navies. She was used for test work and was discarded in 1893.

Pietro Micca

Type: Italian submarine
Displacement: 1,595 tonnes (1,570 tons) (surface), 2,000 tonnes (1,970 tons) (submerged)
Dimensions: 90.3m x 7.7m x 5.3m (296ft 3in x 25ft 3in x 17ft 4in)
Machinery: Twin screws, diesel engines (surface), electric motors (submerged)
Main armament: Two 120mm (4.7in) guns, six 533mm (21in) torpedo tubes
Launched: 1935

Pietro Micca was a long-range, torpedo and minelaying boat with a partial double hull and an operational depth of 90m (295ft). Although she was an experimental vessel, and not repeated, she was a good, manoeuvrable seaboat. Surfaced range at full speed was 4,185km (2,600 miles), and at nine knots was 10,300km (6,400 miles). She was sunk in July 1943 by torpedoes from the British submarine *Trooper*.

Pillau

Type: German cruiser
Displacement: 5,336 tonnes (5,252 tons)
Dimensions: 135.3m x 13.6m x 6m (443ft 10in x 44ft 7in x 19ft 8in)
Machinery: Twin screws, turbines
Main armament: Two 88mm (3.5in), eight 150mm (5.9in) guns
Launched: April 1914

Pillau was originally ordered from Schichau of Danzig for the Russian Navy. Laid down in 1913, *Pillau* was to have been named *Muraviev Amurski*, and was nearly ready by the time World War I broke out. Germany took her over and re-named her. *Pillau* was handed over to Italy at the end of the war, and was officially taken over in July 1920 and re-named *Bari*. She underwent a major rebuild in 1934/35, when her funnels were reduced to two. US bombers sank her in 1943.

Pioneer

Type: Confederate submarine
Displacement: 4 tonnes (4 tons)
Dimensions: 10.3m x 1.2m x 1.2m
(34ft x 4ft x 4ft)
Machinery: Single screw, hand-
cranked
Top speed: Unknown
Main armament: One spar torpedo
Launched: February 1862

Both sides in the American Civil War experimented with submarines, and the Confederacy was especially interested in any development which promised to break the Union maritime blockade. This early submersible was typical of these fledgling efforts, and was the only privateer submarine ever to be built. She was laid down in late 1861 at the government yard at New Basin in New Orleans, although materials were supplied by the Leeds Foundry. She had an oval shaped hull, which resembled the shape of others that came after her. She was to be operated by a three-man crew, two of whom would work the hand cranking system which in turn was to drive the single external propeller. Her only armament was a spar torpedo, a long shaft with explosive at the end which had to be rammed into the side of the target vessel. This was a dangerous process, as was later evidenced by the submarine *H.L Hanley*, when she sunk both herself and the *USS Housatonic* in the same explosion. In March 1862 *Pioneer* was issued with a Letter of Marque, which licensed her to sink Union warships. Should she do so, the captain and crew would collect a bounty of 20 per cent of the estimated value of their victim. In the event, she never went into action. Before the vessel could be used, New Orleans fell to the Union and *Pioneer* was sunk in a bayou to prevent her capture. She was raised 16 years later and was left abandoned on the riverbank. In 1952 she was moved to the Louisiana State Museum.

Pisa

Type: Italian cruiser
Displacement: 10,770 tonnes
(10,600 tons)
Dimensions: 140.5m x 21m x 7.1m
(461ft x 68ft 10in x 23ft 4in)
Machinery: Twin screws, vertical
triple expansion engines
Top speed: 23.4 knots
Main armament:
Sixteen 76mm (3in),
eight 190mm (7.5in),
four 254mm (10in) guns
Launched: September 1907
Date of profile: 1909

Pisa, designed by Engineer Orlando, was laid down at Leghorn in February 1905, and was completed in September 1909. Her 254mm (10in) guns were mounted in twin turrets, one fore and one aft. She had three tall funnels and a single mast aft, with searchlight platforms and two spotting tops. Later a foremast was added. In July 1921 *Pisa* was re-classified as a coast defence vessel and was employed on training duties. From 1925 to 1930 she served as a cadet training ship. She was stricken in 1937.

Planter

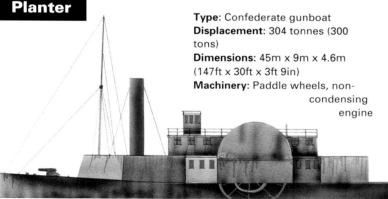

Type: Confederate gunboat
Displacement: 304 tonnes (300
tons)
Dimensions: 45m x 9m x 4.6m
(147ft x 30ft x 3ft 9in)
Machinery: Paddle wheels, non-
condensing
engine
Top speed: 6 knots
Main armament: One 24-pounder,
one 32-pounder guns
Launched: 1860

Planter was a wooden-hulled, shallow draught gunboat built at Charleston, South Carolina. She served as an armed transport and despatch boat, carrying supplies and armaments to the local forts and batteries. She had white officers and a black slave crew of eight. In early May 1862, the crew plotted to seize the steamer and escape. At 03.00, when the crew and their families were safely aboard and the officers were asleep ashore, *Planter* headed down towards the harbour mouth, giving the correct signals to the forts as she passed. The fugitives succeeded in reaching the blockading Union fleet, where they surrendered to the nearest gunboat. *Planter* was not retained by the Union Navy because she was a wood burner.

Pobieda

Type: Russian battleship
Displacement: 12,872 tonnes (12,670
tons)
Dimensions: 133m x 21.7m x 8.3m
(436ft 4in x 71ft 5in x 27ft 3in)
Machinery: Triple screws, vertical
triple expansion engines
Top speed: 18.5 knots
Main armament: Twenty 76mm
(3in), eleven 152mm (6in), four
254mm (10in) guns
Launched: May 1900

Pobieda's engines developed 15,000hp, and coal supply was 2,032 tonnes (2,000 tons). During the war with Japan, she struck a mine off Port Arthur, but survived due to the protection given by her coal bunker and her internal armour. She was captured by the Japanese in 1905 and was re-named *Suwo*. She was scrapped in 1922.

Pola

Type: Italian cruiser
Displacement: 13,747 tonnes
(13,531 tons)
Dimensions: 182.8m x 20.6m x 7.2m
(599ft 9in x 67ft 7in x 23ft 8in)
Machinery: Twin screws, turbines
Top speed: 34.2 knots
Main armament: Sixteen
100mm (3.9in), eight
203mm (8in) guns

Launched: December 1931
Date of profile: 1932

Pola and her three sisters were
completed between 1931 and
1932. To keep the displacement
within reasonable limits, the
superstructure was reduced and
the continuous

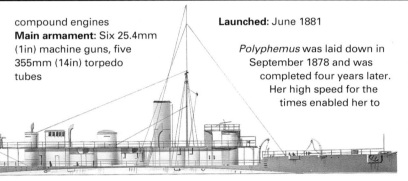

flush deck of the Trento class, upon which the four vessels were based,
was done away with. Pola could be distinguished from her sisters by the
merging of the bridge structure and fore funnel. Her
engines developed over 100,000hp, and range at 16
knots was 9,937km (5,230 miles), at 25 knots it was
6,289km (3,310 miles) and at full speed it was just
under 3,800km (2,000 miles). Additional anti-
aircraft guns were added in the late 1930s.
Pola was sunk in March 1941.

Polyphemus

Type: British torpedo ram
Displacement: 2,682 tonnes 2,640
tons)
Dimensions: 73m x 12m x 6.2m
(240ft x 40ft x 20ft 6in)
Machinery: Twin screws,

compound engines
Main armament: Six 25.4mm
(1in) machine guns, five
355mm (14in) torpedo
tubes

Launched: June 1881

Polyphemus was laid down in
September 1878 and was
completed four years later.
Her high speed for the
times enabled her to

use her large torpedo armament to
best advantage when in action. She
had a 76mm (3in) thick sloping deck
on a cigar-shaped hull, over which
was built a conventional hull to
improve sea-keeping qualities and to
provide crew accommodation. The
machine guns were placed in towers
with a good field of fire. One torpedo
tube was carried in the bows, with
two on each broadside. She was
broken up in 1903.

Powerful

Type: British cruiser
Displacement: 14,427 tonnes (14,200
tons)
Dimensions: 152.3m x 21.6m x
9.4m (499ft 8in x 70ft 10in x 31ft)
Machinery:
Twin
screws,
triple
expansion

engines
Main armament:
Twelve 152mm (6in),
two 233mm (9.2in)
guns

Launched: 1895

Powerful and her sister *Terrible*
were built in answer to the
powerful Russian cruisers *Rurik*
and *Rossia*. The British vessels
were the first warships to use the
large tube Belleville boiler, 48 of
which were carried in eight boiler
rooms. Engines developed over
25,000hp. *Powerful* was completed
in June 1897 and was sold in 1929.

Powhatan

Type: US cruiser
Displacement: 3,825 tonnes
(3,765 tons)
Dimensions: 76.2m
x 21.2m (over
paddle boxes) x 6.3m
(250ft x 69ft 6in x 20ft
9in)
Machinery: Paddle
wheels, inclined

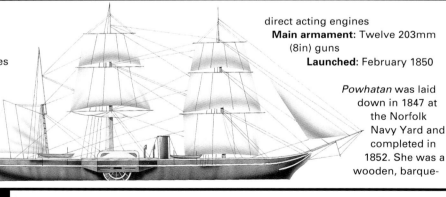

direct acting engines
Main armament: Twelve 203mm
(8in) guns
Launched: February 1850

Powhatan was laid
down in 1847 at
the Norfolk
Navy Yard and
completed in
1852. She was a
wooden, barque-

rigged vessel, and proved a popular
ship as she was very reliable as
well as being comfortable. Her
armament was concentrated on the
upper deck, and was modified to
one 280mm (11in) and ten 228mm
(9in) guns in 1861. During the
American Civil War she also carried
several 100-pounder rifled guns.
She continued in active service until
the early 1880s. She was sold in
1886 and was scrapped in 1887.

Prince Albert

Type: British battleship
Displacement: 3,942 tonnes (3,880
tons)
Dimensions: 73.1m x 14.6m x 6.2m
(240ft x 48ft x 20ft 6in)
Machinery: Single screw, horizontal
direct acting engines
Top speed: 11.2 knots

Main armament: Four 228mm (9in) guns
Launched: May 1864
Date of profile: 1886

Prince Albert was Britain's first turret
ship. The turrets were all carried on the
centreline, two forward of the midship
superstructure and two aft. She was
laid down in 1862, but not completed
until 1866. She was sold in 1899.

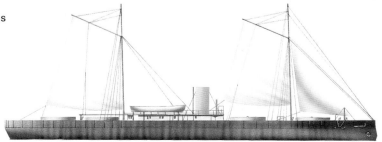

Principe di Carignano

Type: Italian battleship
Displacement: 4,152 tonnes (4,086 tons)
Dimensions: 75.8m x 15.2m x 7.2m (248ft 8in x 50ft x 23ft 8in)
Machinery: Single screw, single expansion engine
Top speed: 10.2 knots
Main armament: Twelve 164mm (6.5in), ten 203mm (8in) guns
Launched: September 1863

Principe di Carignano was designed as a screw frigate by Engineer Mattei, but was converted to an ironclad while still on the stocks. She was a broadside vessel with most of her armament carried on the main deck behind the iron armour. Her engine developed 1,960hp, and range at 10 knots was around 2,280km (1,200 miles). In July 1866, *Principe di Carignano* took part in the Lissa campaign. She was re-armed in 1870, her 203mm (8in) guns reduced to four in number, and her 164mm (6.5in) guns increased to 16. She was discarded in 1875 and broken up between 1877 and 1879.

Principe Umberto

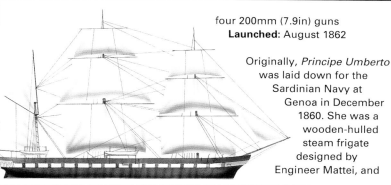

Type: Italian cruiser
Displacement: 4,165 tonnes (4,100 tons)
Dimensions: 75.8m x 15.2m x 7.2m (248ft 8in x 50ft x 23ft 8in)
Machinery: Single screw, single compound engine
Top speed: 11 knots
Main armament: Five 80mm (3.1in), sixteen 160mm (6.3in), four 200mm (7.9in) guns
Launched: August 1862

Originally, *Principe Umberto* was laid down for the Sardinian Navy at Genoa in December 1860. She was a wooden-hulled steam frigate designed by Engineer Mattei, and was originally to have been armed with 54 x 80mm (3.1in) guns. Her engine, supplied by Penn of London, developed 600hp, and she had four locomotive boilers. *Principe Umberto* was completed in November 1863, and was a classic example of the wooden, single-deck cruiser. In 1866 she took part in the Lissa campaign during the war with Austria. She was deleted from the effective list in 1875.

Quaker City

Type: US privateer
Displacement: 1,625 tonnes (1,600 tons)
Dimensions: 74.6m x 10.9m x 3.9m (244ft 8in x 36ft x 13ft)
Machinery: Paddle wheels, side-lever engine
Main armament: Two 6-pounder, two 32-pounder guns
Launched: 1854

Quaker City was the only Union privateer to operate during the American Civil War. She was built at Philadelphia, and was a two-masted, schooner-rigged vessel. She was fitted out and armed by means of a subscription organised by the Union Defense Committee of New York, and was chartered in April 1863 for a fee of $1,000 per day for 30 days. She cruised in the Chesapeake Bay area, capturing four Confederate vessels. Later, the Navy Department took *Quaker City* over and re-armed her. She served in the North Atlantic, and in Mexican waters. She was decommissioned in 1865, and was sold in 1869.

Quarto

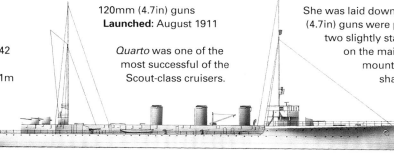

Type: Italian cruiser
Displacement: 3,497 tonnes (93,442 tons)
Dimensions: 131.6m x 12.8m x 4.1m (431ft 9in x 42ft x 13ft 5in)
Machinery: Quadruple screws, turbines
Main armament: Six 76mm (3in), six 120mm (4.7in) guns
Launched: August 1911

Quarto was one of the most successful of the Scout-class cruisers. She was laid down in 1909 and completed in 1913. Her 120mm (4.7in) guns were positioned in pairs, two on the forecastle, two slightly staggered aft of the superstructure and two aft on the main deck. The 76mm (3in) guns were on single mounts amidships. During World War I, *Quarto*'s shallow draught saved her from destruction by torpedoes fired from submarines which had misjudged her depth below the waterline. She was very fast, and maintained 28 knots throughout her career. She was stricken in 1939.

Queen Elizabeth

Type: British battleship
Displacement: 33,548 tonnes (33,020 tons)
Dimensions: 196.8m x 27.6m x 10m (646ft x 90ft 6in x 30ft)
Machinery: Quadruple screws, turbines
Top speed: 23 knots
Main armament: Sixteen 152mm (6in), eight 380mm (15in) guns
Launched: October 1913
Date of profile: 1916

Queen Elizabeth was a major advance in battleship development, and was the first capital ship to be built with oil burning boilers. She was fast, but her reliance upon oil fuel concerned critics, who foresaw disaster if oil supplies were ever interrupted. The following Revenge class carried coal and oil fuel. *Queen Elizabeth* was scrapped in 1948/49.

R1

Type: British submarine
Displacement: 416 tonnes (410 tons)
(surface), 511 tonnes (503 tons)
(submerged)
Dimensions: 49.9m x 4.6m x 3.5m
(163ft 9in x 15ft x 11ft 6in)
Machinery: Single screw, diesel
engine (surface), electric motor
(submerged)
Top speed: 9.5 knots (surface), 15
knots (submerged)
Main armament: Six
457mm (18in)

torpedo tubes
Launched: April 1918
Date of profile: 1918

In early 1917, the Royal Navy were
desperately trying to counter the
German submarine force, which was
exacting a fearful toll of British
merchant shipping. The most

significant development was the
instigation of the convoy system, but
they also looked at designs for
submarines able to hunt other
submarines. R1 was the first of this
new class of vessel, and is the
forerunner of the modern ASW
hunter-killer fleet submarine. Ten
vessels were completed. They were
intended to be fast enough to chase
U-Boats on the surface, and to be
sink them with torpedoes. R1 had a
hull form similar to that of the earlier
H class, and a pronounced raised
bulge above the bow. She
was highly streamlined, with
internal ballast tanks and no
gun. There were six 457mm
(18in) torpedo tubes around

her bow, and five powerful
hydrophones with bearing
instruments were carried in the large
bow compartment. She had a single
240hp diesel engine, and an electric
motor which could produce 1,200hp.
A small 25hp auxiliary motor was
also mounted on the drive shaft. On
the surface, she had a range of
3,800km (2,000 miles) at eight knots.
These vessels were a daring solution
to a problem which nearly brought
Britain to disaster, but they arrived
too late to have any effect. Only one
vessel, R8, actually saw any action,
making an inconclusive attack which
was spoiled by a faulty torpedo. It
would be nearly 30 years before the
ASW submarine came of age.

Rapido

Type: Italian despatch boat
Displacement: 1,456 tonnes (1,433
tons)
Dimensions: 78m x 9.2m x
3.8m (256ft 5in x 30ft 5in
x 12ft 6in)
Machinery:
Single screw,
vertical
double
expansion
engine

Top speed : 13.1 knots
Main armament: Five 76mm (3in) guns
Launched: November 1876

Rapido was an iron-hulled, four-masted
topsail schooner laid down in 1873.
She had evenly spaced masts and two
raked funnels. Her engines developed
1,920hp, and steam was supplied by
four cylindrical boilers. Armament was
modified in 1890. Her crew numbered
144 in 1891, 137 in 1897 and 124 in
1905. After 1907 she served as a hulk
at Genoa. She was scrapped in 1912.

Rattlesnake

Type: British torpedo gunboat
Displacement: 558 tonnes (550
tons)
Dimensions: 60.9m x 7m x 3m
(200ft x 23ft x 10ft 4in)
Machinery: Twin screws, triple
expansion engines
Top speed: 19.2 knots
Main armament: One 102mm (4in)
gun, four 355mm (14in) torpedo
tubes
Launched: September 1886

Rattlesnake was one of the
world's first torpedo gunboats,
and was the first in the Royal
Navy. She was built to
counteract the expanding
fleets of torpedo boats then
being built by many
countries. Earlier vessels
built for the
same
purpose,
such as the
British 1,605-
tonne (1,580-

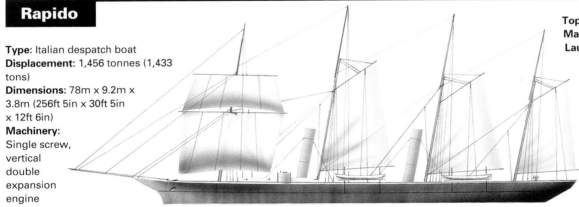

ton) *Scout* and the French
1,300-tonne (1,280-ton)
Condor, had proved
too large and
unwieldy, and so
it was decided
to build a

smaller vessel able to maintain
high speed. *Rattlesnake*'s
engines developed
2,700hp and she had a
19mm (0.75in) thick
protective deck.
She was sold
in 1910.

Re d'Italia

Type: Italian battleship
Displacement: 5,791 tonnes (5,700
tons)
Dimensions: 84.3m x
16.6m x 6.7m (276ft
7in x 54ft 6in x 22ft)
Machinery: Single
screw, single
compound engine
Top speed: 12 knots
Main armament: Thirty

160mm (6.3in), two
200mm (7.9in), two
72-pounder guns
Launched:
1863

Upon completion *Re d'Italia* and her
sister *Re di Portogallo* were Italy's
heaviest warships. Being wooden
hulled, they had no internal
subdivisions, and although the
armour stretched end-to-end, the
steering compartment was
unprotected. *Re d'Italia* was rammed
and sunk by the Austrian flagship at
the Battle of Lissa in July 1866 after
her steering had been disabled.

Re Galantuomo

Type: Italian battleship
Displacement: 3,860 tonnes (3,800 tons)
Dimensions: 58.4m x 15.5m x 7m
(191ft 7in x 50ft 10in x 23ft 3in)
Machinery: Single screw, single direct acting engine
Top speed: 9 knots
Main armament: 64 cannon
Launched: June 1858
Date of profile: 1861

Re Galantuomo was Italy's only wooden steam line-of-battle ship. A two-decker, she was laid down at Cantiere di Castellammare di Stabia, and was completed in 1861. Her engines developed 1,351hp. Crew numbered 976. *Re Galantuomo* carried her guns on two decks. She was re-armed in the early 1870s, when she was given eighteen 160mm (6.3in) guns plus smaller weapons. In 1863, the ship transported the crews needed for *Re d'Italia* and *Re di Portogallo*, then building at Webbs yard in New York, from Italy to America. *Re Galantuomo* then served as a coast defence ship and was at Taranto during the war with Austria in 1866. She was scrapped in 1875.

Re Umberto

Type: Italian battleship
Displacement: 15,701 tonnes (15,454 tons)
Dimensions: 127.6m x 23.4m x 9.3m (418ft 8in x 76ft 10in x

30ft 6in)
Machinery: Twin screws, two-cylinder vertical compound engines
Top speed: 20 knots
Main armament: Sixteen 120mm (4.7in), eight 152mm (6in), four 343mm (13.5in) guns
Launched: October 1888
Date of profile: 1894

Designed by Benedetto Brin, *Re Umberto* was one of three capital ships which, upon completion, were the fastest of their type in the world. The two barbettes housing the 343mm (13.5in) guns were mounted on a central pivot, so allowing for all-round loading and a faster rate of fire. This system was adopted by the Royal Navy in 1898. *Re Umberto* was laid down in 1884, completed in 1893, and scrapped in 1920. Her sister *Sardegna* was the first warship to have triple expansion engines.

Regina Margherita

Type: Italian battleship
Displacement: 13,426 tonnes (13,215 tons)
Dimensions: 138.6m x 23.8m x 8.8m (454ft 10in x 78ft 3in x 28ft 10in)
Machinery: Twin screws, triple expansion engines
Top speed: 20.3 knots
Main armament: Twenty 76mm (3in), twelve 152mm (6in), four 203mm

(8in), four 305mm (12in) guns
Launched: May 1901
Date of profile: 1903

Regina Margherita was designed by Benedetto Brin, and the emphasis was placed on speed. As originally designed, the vessel was to have had four 305mm (12in) guns, together with twelve 203mm (8in) weapons. However, after Brin's death the plans were revised to feature the mixed armament listed. *Regina Margherita* sank in 1916 after striking two German mines.

Regina Maria Pia

Type: Italian battleship
Displacement: 4,599 tonnes (4,527 tons)
Dimensions: 81.2m x 15.2m x 6.3m (266ft 5in x 50ft x 20ft 10in)
Machinery: Single screw, single expansion reciprocating engine
Top speed: 13 knots
Main armament: Twenty two 164mm (6.5in), four 72-pounder

guns
Launched: April 1863

Anxious to build a powerful fleet, Italy ordered four broadside ironclads from France, including *Regina Maria Pia*. She was laid down in 1862 and completed in 1864. Her engine developed 2,924hp, and range at ten knots was 4,940kms (2,600 miles). In 1866 she saw action at Porto San Giorgio. She was re-armed to carry two 220mm (8.7in) and nine 203mm (8in) guns, and was later given eight 152mm (6in) and five 120mm (4.7in) guns. In 1895 she was rebuilt as a coast defence ship and stricken in 1904.

Reginaldo Giuliani

Type: Italian submarine
Displacement: 1,184 tonnes (1,166 tons)

(surface), 1,507 tonnes (1,484 tons) (submerged)
Dimensions: 76m x 6.9m x 4.5m (249ft 8in x 23ft x 15ft)

Machinery: Twin screws, diesel engines (surface), electric motors (submerged)
Top speed: 17.5 knots (surface), 8.4 knots (submerged)
Main armament: One 100mm (3.9in) gun, eight 533mm (21in) torpedo tubes
Launched: December 1939

Reginaldo Giuliani and her three sisters were developments of the Brin class, but were slightly larger. Maximum diving depth was 90m (295ft). In 1943 she was converted to transport cargo to the Far East. She was seized by the Japanese at Singapore, and handed over to Germany. In 1944 she was sunk by the British submarine *Tally-Ho*.

Remo

Type: Italian submarine
Displacement: 2,245 tonnes (2,210 tons) (surface), 2,648 tonnes (2,606 tons) (submerged)
Dimensions: 70.7m x

7.8m x 5.3m (232ft x 25ft 9in x 17ft 6in)
Machinery: Twin screws, diesel engines (surface), electric motors (submerged)

Main armament: Three 20mm (0.8in) guns
Launched: March 1943

Remo was a partial-double-hulled transport submarine laid down in September 1942 and completed in June 1943. She had four watertight holds with a total capacity of 600 cubic metres

(21,190 cubic ft). Maximum diving depth was 100m (328ft). She and her one operational sister, *Romolo*, were developed to transport cargo to and from the Far East. Ten more vessels in the class were laid down: two were launched in 1946 and then scrapped; two were scrapped on the slip; and six were seized by German forces. *Remo* was sunk during her maiden voyage in July 1943 by the British submarine *United*.

Resurgam II

Type: British submarine
Displacement: 30 tonnes (30 tons) (surface)
Dimensions: 13.7m x 2.1m (45ft x 7ft)
Machinery: Single screw, Lamm steam locomotive
Top speed: 3 knots
Launched: December 1879
Date of profile: 1879

Resurgam II was designed by George Garrett. She had a cigar-shaped hull with spindle ends, and was able to withstand a pressure of 71 pounds per square inch (32 kg per sq mm), enabling her to dive to a depth of about 45.5m (150ft). Propulsion was by steam on the Lamm fireless principle then in use on London's underground railways. A coal furnace heated water in a large steam boiler. The fire door and

smoke-escape valve leading to a short funnel inside the superstructure were then closed. Latent head turned the water into steam when the throttle valve was opened, thereby supplying the engine. Initial trials were promising, and Garrett decided to set up base on

the Welsh coast. However, as *Resurgam II* was being towed to her new berth in February 1880, she sank during a storm. She still lies where she sank off the British coast, although there are plans to raise her.

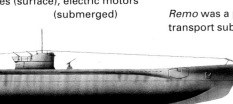

Retvisan

Type: Russian battleship
Displacement: 13,106 tonnes (12,900 tons)
Dimensions: 117.8m x 22m x 7.9m (386ft 8in x 72ft 2in x 26ft)
Machinery: Twin screws, vertical triple expansion engines
Top speed: 18.8 knots
Main armament: Twelve 152mm (6in), four 305mm (12in), twenty 11-

pounder guns
Launched: October 1900
Date of profile: 1901

Retvisan was the only capital ship to be built for the

Russians by a US yard, and her design was standard US type, with a flush-deck and central superstructure. In 1904 she was torpedoed off Port Arthur. When Port Arthur fell in 1905 she was surrendered to the Japanese. Re-named *Hizen*, she was sunk as a target in 1924.

Riachuelo

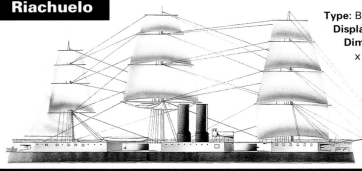

Type: Brazilian battleship
Displacement: 6,100 tonnes (6,100 tons)
Dimensions: 92.9m x 15.8m x 6m (305ft x 52ft x 19ft 8in)
Machinery: Twin screws, vertical compound engines
Main armament: Six 140mm (5.5in), four 234mm (9.2in) guns
Armour: 178-280mm (7-11in) belt, 254mm (10in) on turrets and conning tower

Launched: June 1883

Riachuelo was a twin-turreted, fully-rigged ship and was built to replace *Independencia*, which had been sold to Britain. *Riachuelo* was an excellent example of armour and offensive power on a 6,100-tonne (6,000-ton) displacement, and for many years she was a major unit. She was scrapped in 1910.

Roanoke

Type: US battleship
Displacement: 6,400 tonnes (6,300 tons)
Dimensions: 80.7m x 16m x 7.4m (265ft x 52ft 6in x 24ft 3in)
Machinery: Single screw, horizontal direct acting engines
Main armament: Two 280mm (11in), two 380mm (15in), two

150-pounder guns
Armour: 114mm (4.5in) on hull sides, 280mm (11in) on turrets
Launched: 1855

Roanoke was the only multi-turreted ironclad to see service in the American Civil War. Originally she

was a wooden-hulled, 40-gun steam frigate laid down in 1853. In March 1862 she was nearly lost when the Confederates attacked her at

Hampton Roads. In May 1862 she was cut down to just above the waterline and the low freeboard was plated with iron armour. Three turrets were installed and she was re-armed. She was taken out of service in 1865 and sold in 1883.

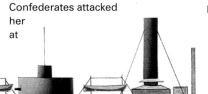

Rolf Krake

Type: Danish battleship
Displacement: 1,341 tonnes (1,320 tons)
Dimensions: 56m x 11.6m x 3.2m (183ft 9in x 38ft 2in x 10ft 6in)
Machinery: Single screw, single expansion compound engine
Top speed: 9.5 knots
Main armament: Four 68-pounder guns
Armour: 76-114mm (3-4.5in) hull, 114mm (4.5in) on turrets plus 228mm (9in) wood backing
Launched: July 1863

Denmark was the first Scandinavian country to possess an ironclad fleet of any size, beginning in the 1860s with large deep-draught broadside vessels. In 1862, with increasing tension between Denmark and Prussia over Schleswig-Holstein, the Danes boosted their defences. They ordered a coastal defence monitor-type vessel from Napier in Glasgow, which was laid down in December 1862. *Rolf Krake* had a shallow draught, and low freeboard, and while ideal for coastal defence would have been ill-suited to deep sea operations. Her main armament was mounted in pairs, in two of the new Coles turrets. She had a low silhouette, with her turrets mounted directly on the maindeck and only a small armoured bridge towards the rear of the ship. Hinged metal bulwarks gave the deck some protection from high seas, and these were dropped down when in action. During the Prusso-Danish war of 1864, she fought an inconclusive duel with enemy artillery while trying to prevent the Prussians crossing between Schleswig and Alsen. In 1867 the forward guns were replaced by a single 203mm (8in) weapon. She became a training ship in 1893 and was sold in 1907.

Roma

Type: Italian battleship
Displacement: 6,250 tonnes (6,250 tons)
Dimensions: 79.6m x 17.5m x 7.6m (261ft 2in x 57ft 5in x 25ft)
Machinery: Single screw, single expansion engine
Top speed: 13 knots
Main armament: Twelve 203mm (8in), five 254mm (10in) guns
Armour: 150mm belt (5.9in)
Launched: December 1865
Date of profile: 1873

Roma, a wooden-hulled broadside ironclad with 2,960 square metres (31,933 sq ft) of sail, was laid down in 1863 and completed in 1869. She was re-armed in 1874/75. In 1886 she served as the flagship of the defending force guarding La Spezia. She was removed from the effective list in 1895, and used as a floating ammunition depot ship until she was scuttled to prevent an explosion after being set ablaze by lightning in July 1896. She was re-floated in August, and was then broken up.

Royal Sovereign

Type: British battleship
Displacement: 5,161 tonnes (5,080 tons)
Dimensions: 73.3m x 18.9m x 7.6m (240ft 6in x 62ft x 25ft)
Machinery: Single screw, return connecting rod engine
Top speed: 11 knots
Main armament: Five 266mm (10.5in) guns
Armour: 114-140mm (4.5-5.5in) belt, 140-254mm (5.5-10in) on turrets
Launched: 1857

With the introduction of the ironclad, Britain was left with a large fleet of obsolete wooden battleships. In 1862, work began to convert one such vessel, *Royal Sovereign*, into Britain's first ironclad turret ship. The five 266mm (10.5in) guns were mounted in four turrets, the fore turret housing two guns and the single turrets being placed on the centreline. A light steadying rig was fitted. As originally built, she had achieved 12.2 knots but with the increased weight of her new armour, her speed fell to 11 knots. She was sold for breaking up in 1885.

Royal Sovereign

Type: British battleship
Displacement: 15,830 tonnes (15,580 tons)
Dimensions: 125m x 22.8m x 8.3m (410ft 6in x 75ft x 27ft 6in)
Machinery: Twin screws, triple expansion engines
Top speed: 16.5 knots
Main armament: Ten 152mm (6in), four 343mm (13.5in) guns
Launched: February 1891
Date of profile: 1892

Designed by Sir William White, *Royal Sovereign* was laid down at Portsmouth Dockyard in September 1889 and was completed in 1892. She was one of 70 vessels ordered under the Naval Defence Act of 1889, and set the standard for most of the pre-dreadnought capital ships that followed. The idea of the new design was increased fighting efficiency, plus the maintenance of speed in a seaway. These requirements were only possible in a barbette ship carrying its guns high above the waterline, with a high freeboard for better seakeeping. *Royal Sovereign* was scrapped in 1919.

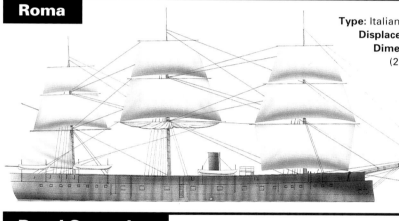

Rurik

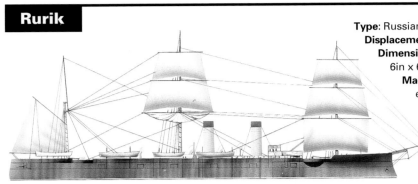

Type: Russian cruiser
Displacement: 11,108 tonnes (10,933 tons)
Dimensions: 130m x 20.4m x 9m (426ft 6in x 67ft x 30ft)
Machinery: Twin screws, triple expansion engines
Main armament: Six 120mm (4.7in), sixteen 152mm (6in), four 203mm (8in) guns
Armour: 127-254mm (5-10in) belt, 305mm (12in) bulkhead fore, 254mm (10in) bulkhead aft
Launched: November 1892

Rurik was the last major Russian warship to carry sails. Her main battery of 152mm (6in) guns amidships had no side protection, but she had bulkheads fore and aft. *Rurik* was a powerful vessel, able to defeat any standard cruiser then patrolling the oceans. She was sunk by the Japanese on 14 August 1904.

Rurik

Type: Russian cruiser
Displacement: 15,433 tonnes (15,190 tons)
Dimensions: 161.2m x 22.8m x 7.9m (529ft x 75ft x 26ft)
Machinery: Twin screws, vertical triple expansion engines
Main armament: Twenty 120mm (4.7in), eight 203mm (8in), four 254mm (10in) guns
Armour: 102-152mm (4-6in) belt, 178-203mm (7-8in) on main turrets, 152-178mm (6-7in) on secondary turrets, 76mm (3in) on battery
Launched: 1906

Rurik was the last major Russian

warship to be constructed abroad. She was built by Vickers, and her design was similar to that of the Italian Pisa class. One of several units ordered after the losses incurred during the war with Japan, she was laid down in 1905, and was completed in 1908. The magazines were fitted with rapid flooding equipment and drenching sprays, which were unique to the Russian Navy. *Rurik* was broken up in 1923.

Russia

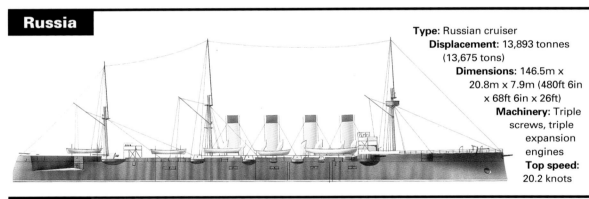

Type: Russian cruiser
Displacement: 13,893 tonnes (13,675 tons)
Dimensions: 146.5m x 20.8m x 7.9m (480ft 6in x 68ft 6in x 26ft)
Machinery: Triple screws, triple expansion engines
Top speed: 20.2 knots
Main armament: Twelve 76mm (3in), sixteen 152mm (6in), four 203mm (8in) guns
Armour: 127-254mm (5-10in) belt
Launched: May 1896

Russia carried four small torpedo boats and was a complete weapons system, able to destroy any standard cruiser of the period. She survived the Russo-Japanese War and World War I, and was scrapped in 1922.

Ryujo

Type: Japanese aircraft carrier
Displacement: 10,150 tonnes (9,990 tons)
Dimensions: 175.3m x 23m x 5.5m (575ft 5in x 75ft 6in x 18ft 3in)
Machinery: Twin screws, turbines
Top speed: 29 knots
Main armament: Twelve 127mm (5in) guns
Aircraft: 48
Launched: April 1931

Ryujo was Japan's first major purpose-built aircraft carrier. She was designed with a cruiser hull, which restricted her width, and so a second hangar was built above the first. This resulted in increased top weight, and almost immediately after her completion in May 1933 she was back in the dockyards for modification. Between 1934 and 1936 her hull was strengthened and her bulges widened. She was sunk by aircraft from USS *Saratoga* in 1942.

S1

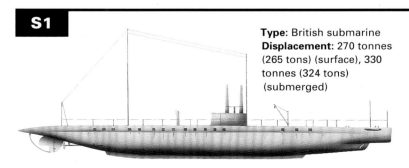

Type: British submarine
Displacement: 270 tonnes (265 tons) (surface), 330 tonnes (324 tons) (submerged)
Dimensions: 45m x 4.4m x 3.2m (148ft x 14ft 5in x 10ft 6in)
Machinery: Twin screws, diesel engines (surface), electric motors (submerged)
Top speed: 13 knots (surface), 8.5 knots (submerged)
Main armament: Two 457mm (18in) torpedo tubes, one 12-pounder gun,
Launched: February 1914

S1 was based on the Italian Laurenti type, having a partial double hull with ten watertight compartments. Her diesel engines developed 650hp, electric motors developed 400hp, and surfaced range at 8.5 knots was 3,040km (1,600 miles). In 1915, *S1* and two sisters, *S2* and *S3*, were transferred to the Italian Navy. They were all discarded in 1919.

Sachsen

Type: German battleship
Displacement: 5,767 tonnes (5,677 tons)
Dimensions: 98.2m x 18.3m x 6.5m (322ft

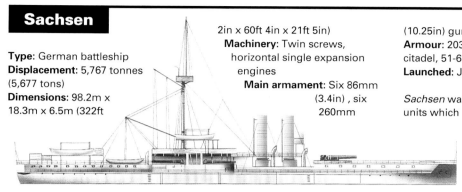

2in x 60ft 4in x 21ft 5in)
Machinery: Twin screws, horizontal single expansion engines
Main armament: Six 86mm (3.4in) , six 260mm

(10.25in) guns
Armour: 203-254mm (8-10in) on citadel, 51-63.5mm (2-2.5in) deck
Launched: July 1877

Sachsen was one of a class of four units which were a break away from previous designs for German central battery and broadside ironclads. Two of the 260mm (10.25in)

guns were carried in a pear-shaped redoubt on the forecastle, the rest being positioned in a rectangular barbette abaft the funnels. Armour covered the central citadel, and the armoured deck protected her ends. *Sachsen* did not have sails, but she carried a single military mast aft. In 1886 she was given three torpedo tubes, and in the late 1890s she was given new armour and engines. She was discarded in 1910.

Saetta

Type: Italian torpedo cruiser
Displacement: 400 tonnes (394 tons)
Dimensions: 56.7m x 6.3m x 2.2m (186ft x

20ft 8in x 7ft 5in)
Machinery: Twin screws, double expansion engines
Top speed: 17 knots
Main armament: Two

57mm (2.25in) guns, three 356mm (14in) torpedo tubes
Launched: May 1887

Saetta was designed by

Benedetto Brin. Her engines developed 2,130hp, and steam was supplied from four locomotive boilers. A low freeboard was linked to a whaleback foredeck to improve performance when running at speed in heavy seas. *Saetta* was used for experiments with oil fuel in 1892. Between 1897 and 1900 she served as a torpedo training ship, and in 1901 she became a training ship for gunners. She was discarded in 1908.

Salamander

Type: Austrian battleship
Displacement: 3,075 tonnes (3,027 tons)
Dimensions: 62.8m x 13.9m x 6.3m (206ft x 45ft 7in x 20ft 8in)
Machinery: Single screw, horizontal low pressure engines
Top speed: 11.3 knots
Main armament: Fourteen 150mm (5.9in), fourteen 68-pounder guns

Launched: August 1861

Salamander was Austria's first ironclad. She was laid down in 1861 and completed in 1862, one of the fastest building times for a new type of vessel. She was a wooden-hulled broadside, with a full-length waterline belt which rose at the foremast to protect the battery. She was re-fitted in 1867/68 and given an increased sail area. Stricken in

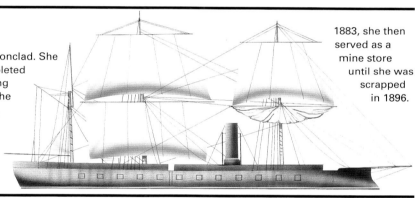

1883, she then served as a mine store until she was scrapped in 1896.

San Francisco

Type: US submarine
Displacement: 6,300 tonnes (6,200 tons) (surface), 7,010 tonnes (6,900 tons) (submerged)
Dimensions: 110m x 10m x 9.8m (360ft x 33ft x 32ft 4in)
Machinery: Single screw,

nuclear powered pressurised-water reactor, turbines
Top speed: 30+ knots (submerged)
Main armament: Four 533mm (21in) torpedo tubes, Harpoon and Tomahawk missiles
Launched: October 1979

San Francisco is a large attack submarine belonging to the world's largest class of nuclear-

powered boats. The class was developed to counter the Russian Victor-class fast attack submarines. *San Francisco* is larger than the preceding Sturgeon-class vessels in order to accommodate a more capable reactor plant. The reactor has an estimated fuel core life of 10 to 13 years, and *San Francisco* need only enter port to change crews and refit. A patrol can last up to three months, with the boat keeping in touch with base via satellite.

San Giorgio

Type: Italian cruiser
Displacement: 11,480 tonnes (11,300 tons)
Dimensions: 140.8m x 21m x 7.3m (462ft x 68ft 10in x 24ft)
Machinery: Twin screws, vertical triple expansion engines

Top speed: 23.7 knots
Main armament: Eighteen 76mm (3in), eight 190mm (7.5in), four 254mm (10in) guns
Launched: July 1908
Date of profile: 1910

San Giorgio was laid down in 1905, and was an improved version of *Pisa*, then building. *San Giorgio* was rebuilt as a training ship in 1937/38,

and was used as a floating battery in World War II. She was scuttled in 1941 to prevent her capture, was refloated in 1952, but sank in heavy seas while under tow off Tobruk.

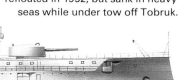

San Jacinto

Type: US cruiser
Displacement: 2,184 tonnes (2,150 tons)
Dimensions: 64m x 11.5m x 5.2m (210ft x 37ft 9in x 17ft 3in)
Machinery: Single screw, horizontal engine
Top speed: 11 knots
Main armament: Sixteen 203mm (8in) guns
Launched: April 1850
Date of profile: 1852

San Jacinto was a wooden-hulled vessel laid down in August 1847 at the New York Navy Yard and completed in early 1852. Her hull design was similar to that of the side-wheel steamer *Saranac*, although she had screw propulsion rather than side paddles. This was done in order to compare the merits of both forms of drive on two similar hulls. However, *San Jacinto* was not as successful as *Saranac* because the small space allocated to her engines caused overheating and difficulties with maintenance. Her large seven-tonne screw was set off the centreline and projected 1.5m (5ft) beyond the rudder. The ship served in the Far East, and was involved in the capture of the Chinese forts at Canton. She was recalled during the American Civil War, when under Captain Wilkes she seized the British steamer *Trent*, which was carrying the Confederate commissioners to Europe. This episode very nearly led the Union into war with Britain. She spent most of the rest of her war service on the blockade of southern ports. During this time she suffered two outbreaks of yellow fever, another one of the hazards faced by sailors of that era. On 1 January 1865 she struck a reef at Great Abasco Island and became a total loss.

Savannah

Type: US steamship
Displacement: 325 tonnes (320 tons)
Dimensions: 33.5m x 7.8m x 3.9m (110ft x 25ft 8in x 13ft)
Machinery: Paddle wheels, single cylinder engine
Top speed: 6 knots
Launched: August 1818
Date of profile: 1819

Savannah was the first steam-propelled vessel to cross the Atlantic. She was a wooden-hulled vessel built in New York by Francis Fickett, and was originally intended as a sailing packet for service to France. However, before her completion she was purchased by the Savannah Steam Ship Company who had her adapted for auxiliary steam propulsion with collapsible paddle wheels that could be stored on deck. The engine and boilers occupied most of the hold between the fore and main mast, leaving little room for cargo. Accommodation was two well-furnished state rooms, plus 32 berths. *Savannah* sailed from New York for Liverpool in May 1819, making the journey in 27 days and 11 hours. Upon her return to America her engines were removed. She served as a sailing ship until she ran aground during a storm off Long Island in 1821 and became a total wreck.

Savannah

Type: US cargo ship
Displacement: 14,112 tonnes (13,890 tons)
Dimensions: 195m (639ft 9in)long (other dimensions unknown)
Machinery: Twin screws, nuclear reactor, turbines
Top speed: 20.5 knots
Launched: July 1959

Savannah was an experimental merchant ship, being the first to be powered by atomic propulsion. She was designed to demonstrate the possibilities of the peaceful application of atomic energy. She made her maiden voyage in August 1962, and then undertook a number of demonstration cruises around the world. Range was 638,400km (336,000 miles) at top speed. Crew numbered 110, and she could accommodate 60 passengers. *Savannah* was withdrawn from service in 1972 when her high operational costs made her commercially unattractive.

Savoia

Type: Italian royal yacht
Displacement: 3,318 tonnes (3,266 tons)
Dimensions: 93.8m x 12.8m x 5.8m (307ft 9in x 42ft x 19ft)
Machinery: Single screw, three-cylinder horizontal engine
Main armament: Six 57mm (2.25in), two 75mm (3in) guns
Launched: June 1883

Savoia was laid down in 1880 at Cantiere di Castellammare di Stabia. She was completed for service as the Royal Yacht in 1885, but classified as a light cruiser. A three-masted vessel with a light rig. Her engines developed 3,340hp, and range at 10 knots was 28,500km (15,000 miles). From 1902-05 she was converted to a repair ship and re-named *Vulcano*. She was discarded in 1923.

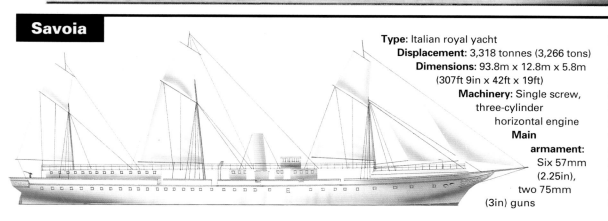

Sciota

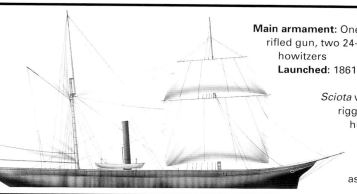

Type: US gunboat
Displacement: 515 tonnes (507 tons)
Dimensions: 48m x 8.5m x 3.3m (158ft x 28ft x 11ft)
Machinery: Single screw, horizontal back-acting engines
Top speed: 11 knots

Main armament: One 20-pounder rifled gun, two 24-pounder howitzers
Launched: 1861

Sciota was a schooner-rigged, wooden-hulled gunboat in a class of 33 units which became known as the '90-day gunboats' due to the speed with which they were built. They had been ordered to form part of the blockading force around the Confederate ports during the American Civil War. *Sciota* was laid down in July 1861 and was in service by November 1861. During a mine-clearing operation off the Texas coast in April 1865 she struck a mine and sank. Three months later she was raised and sold.

Seeadler

Type: German commerce raider
Displacement: 4,572 tonnes (4,500 tons)
Dimensions: 74.8m x 11.8m x 6.7m (245ft 6in x 38ft 9in x 22ft)
Machinery: Twin screws, diesel engines
Main armament: Two 104mm (4.1in) guns, two 508mm (20in) torpedo tubes

Launched: 1888

Seeadler was the only raiding sailing ship to serve in World War I. She was formerly the US vessel *Pass of Balmaha*, built in Glasgow. Crossing the North Sea in 1915, she was taken by the British, but re-taken by the German submarine *U36*. Converted as a commerce raider and re-named *Seeadler*, she captured over 30,000 tonnes (30,099 tons) of enemy shipping for the Germans until she was wrecked in 1917.

Selandia

Type: Danish passenger/cargo ship

Displacement: 9,956 tonnes (9,800 tons)

Dimensions: 117.6m x 16.2m (386ft x 53ft 2in)
Machinery: Twin screws, diesel engines
Top speed: 12 knots
Launched: 1911

Selandia was the world's first ocean-going

motorship. She carried 7,518 tonnes (7,400 tons) of cargo and had accommodation for 26 passengers. Her first voyage in 1912 covered 35,405km (22,000 miles) and during the next 12 years she travelled over 1,140,000km (600,000 miles) with only ten days lost in port due to engine trouble. In 1936 she was sold to Norway and re-named *Norseman*. She was wrecked off Japan in January 1942.

Selma

Type: Confederate gunboat
Displacement: 600 tonnes (590 tons)
Dimensions: 76.8m x 9m x 1.8m (252ft x 30ft x 6ft)
Machinery: Paddle wheels
Top speed: 9 knots
Main armament: One 152mm (6in), one

203mm (8in), two 228mm (9in) guns
Launched: 1856

Formerly named *Florida* and owned by the Mobile Mail Line, the vessel

was taken into Confederate service in 1861 and was rebuilt with extra framing to strengthen the hull. Her superstructure was reduced in length, and she was given iron plating on her upper deck and sides to protect the

boilers and machinery. She then joined the small squadron in Mobile Bay. She saw extensive action against Union gunboats, but had to deal with a severe desertion problem among the crew. *Selma* was forced to surrender to Farragut's superior Union force in 1863, and she became part of the Union fleet. She was sold in 1865.

Seraph

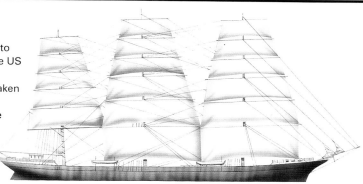

Type: British submarine
Displacement: 886 tonnes (872 tons) (surface), 1,005 tonnes (990 tons) (submerged)
Dimensions: 66.1m x 7.2m x 3.4m (216ft 10in x 23ft 8in x 11ft 2in)
Machinery: Twin screws,

diesel engines (surface), electric motors (submerged)
Main armament: One 76mm (3in) gun, six

533mm (21in) torpedo tubes
Launched: October 1941
Date of profile: 1942

Seraph, one of 63 successful units, was a medium-range boat with a diving depth of 95m (310ft). Her diesel engines developed 1,900hp, and surfaced range at 10 knots was 11,400km (6,000 miles). The electric motors developed 1,300hp. She was broken up in 1965.

Sevastopol

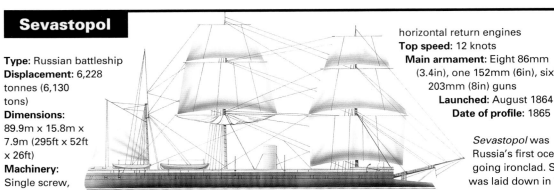

Type: Russian battleship
Displacement: 6,228 tonnes (6,130 tons)
Dimensions: 89.9m x 15.8m x 7.9m (295ft x 52ft x 26ft)
Machinery: Single screw, horizontal return engines
Top speed: 12 knots
Main armament: Eight 86mm (3.4in), one 152mm (6in), sixteen 203mm (8in) guns
Launched: August 1864
Date of profile: 1865

Sevastopol was Russia's first ocean-going ironclad. She was laid down in 1860 as a wooden-hulled, unarmoured frigate mounting 28 60-pounders. Conversion began in 1862, and she was completed as a battleship in 1865. Her armoured battery was 60m (195ft) long, and was positioned amidships. Two of the 203mm (8in) guns were placed outside the battery. Armoured bulkheads ran the length of the battery. *Sevastopol* was removed from the effective list during the 1880s.

Sfax

Type: French cruiser
Displacement: 4,634 tonnes (4,561 tons)
Dimensions: 91.5m x 15m x 7.6m (300ft 5in x 49ft 4in x 25ft 2in)
Machinery: Twin screws, horizontal compound engines
Main armament: Ten 140mm (5.5in), six 163mm (6.4in) guns
Launched: May 1884

Sfax was laid down in 1882 and completed in 1887. She was a two-funnelled vessel with a pronounced ram bow and tumble-home, and a 60mm (2.4in) thick armoured deck. Originally she carried 1,988 square metres (21,400 sq ft) of sail, but this was removed during the early 1890s. In 1900 *Sfax* was re-fitted, and her main mast was removed. She was stricken in 1906.

Shah

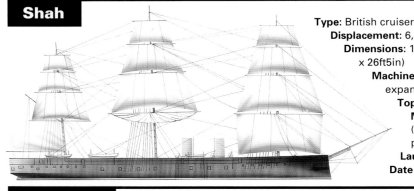

Type: British cruiser
Displacement: 6,350 tonnes (6,250 tons)
Dimensions: 101.8m x 15.8m x 8m (334ft x 52ft x 26ft5in)
Machinery: Single screw, horizontal single expansion engine
Top speed: 16.2 knots
Main armament: Sixteen 178mm (7in), two 228mm (9in), eight 64-pounder guns
Launched: September 1873
Date of profile: 1877

Shah was a fast, iron-hulled cruiser with copper sheathing. She carried 2,476 square metres (26,655 sq ft) of canvas, and made 13.5 knots under sail alone. In May 1877 *Shah* fought an inconclusive action against the powerful Peruvian turret ship *Huascar*. This action brought about a change in British policy, and thereafter they employed second-class battleships on all their foreign stations. *Shah* was sold in 1919.

Shanghai

Type: Chinese fast attack/patrol boat
Displacement: 137 tonnes (135 tons)
Dimensions: 38.8m x 5.4m x 1.7m (127ft 4in x 17ft 8in x 5ft 7in)
Machinery: Quadruple screws, diesel engines
Top speed: 28.5 knots
Main armament: Four 37mm (1.45in) guns, four 25.4mm (1in) cannon
Launched: 1962

Shanghai is one vessel in a class of around 500 fast attack/patrol craft, 350 of which are in service with the Chinese Navy. The Shanghai craft are mainly intended for coastal work, and carry a relatively powerful armament of light weapons, plus depth charges and mines. Within the class there are variations in bridge structure, armament and radar equipment. Many vessels have been exported to Asia, the Middle East and Africa, and more are being built under licence by European navies.

Shannon

Type: British cruiser
Displacement: 5,670 tonnes (5,670 tons)
Dimensions: 79.2m x 16.4m x 6.7m (260ft x 54ft x 22f 3in)
Machinery: Single screw, compound horizontal return connecting rod engines
Main armament: Seven 228mm (9in), two 254mm (10in), six 20-pounder guns
Launched: November 1875

Shannon was Britain's first armoured cruiser. She was laid down in 1873 and completed in 1877. A 203-228mm (8-9in) thick armoured screen ran across the vessel at the end of the forecastle, behind which were positioned two 254mm (10in) muzzle-loading rifled guns. This gave *Shannon* both straight ahead and broadside firepower. *Shannon* was sold at the end of 1899.

Shenandoah

Type: Confederate raider
Displacement: 1,179 tonnes (1,160 tons)
Dimensions: 70m x 9.7m x 6.2m (230ft x 32ft x 20ft 6in)
Machinery: Single screw, single compound engine
Top speed: 9 knots
Main armament: Four 203mm (8in), two 12-pounder, two 32-pounder guns
Launched: 1863

The Confederacy had achieved great success with their commerce raiders, which by 1864 had almost swept the

Union merchant marine from the seas. By this time, they could no longer build ships abroad due to Union political pressure, so they had to look for suitable vessels to buy. They purchased the *Sea King*, a wooden hulled

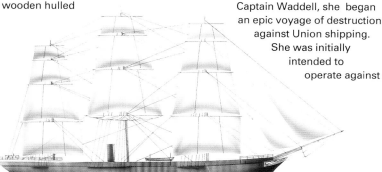

vessel recently built in Glasgow. She was bought by the Confederate agent Bullock in 1864 and was fitted with her guns at sea. She was also renamed *Shenandoah*. Bearing her new flag, and under the command of Captain Waddell, she began an epic voyage of destruction against Union shipping. She was initially intended to operate against

Union whalers in the Pacific, but ended up sailing right around the globe, the only Confederate vessel to carry the Southern flag this far. During her career she captured or sunk more than 30 Union vessels, and at one point the US Navy had more than 100 ships trying to track her down. She was looking for more victims when the Civil War ended, and ignorant of this fact, went on hunting. She only stopped when a British ship told Captain Waddell the news about the surrender. She was sold and later sank during a storm in the Indian Ocean. Surprisingly, at no time in her brief military career did she ever land in her adopted country.

Shinano

Type: Japanese aircraft carrier
Displacement: 74,208 tonnes 973,040 tons)
Dimensions: 266m x 40m x 10.3m (872ft 9in x 131ft 3in x 33ft 9in)
Machinery: Quadruple screws, turbines
Main armament: One hundred and forty-five 25mm

(1in), sixteen 127mm (5in) guns, three hundred and thirty-six rocket launchers
Aircraft: 120
Launched: October 1944

At the time of her completion, *Shinano* was the world's largest

aircraft carrier, but she was to have the shortest career of any major warship of her type when, on 29 November 1944, she was sunk by the US submarine *Archerfish*. *Shinano* was a Yamato-class battleship, and was converted into an auxiliary carrier with masive internal

capacity for transporting supplies of fuel and spares, plus aircraft, to the Japanese task forces. Her single storey hangar was 168m (550ft) long, and her own air group of 40-50 planes were housed forward, with the replacement aircraft for the task forces stowed aft. She was torpedoed and sunk while on her way to Kure for final fitting out.

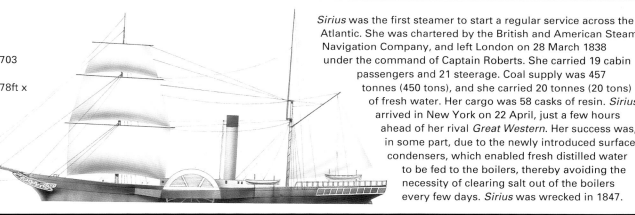

Sirius

Type: British liner
Displacement: 714 tonnes (703 tons)
Dimensions: 54m x 7.6m (178ft x 25ft)
Machinery: Paddle wheels, twin side-lever engines
Top speed: 8 knots
Launched: 1837
Date of profile: 1838

Sirius was the first steamer to start a regular service across the Atlantic. She was chartered by the British and American Steam Navigation Company, and left London on 28 March 1838 under the command of Captain Roberts. She carried 19 cabin passengers and 21 steerage. Coal supply was 457 tonnes (450 tons), and she carried 20 tonnes (20 tons) of fresh water. Her cargo was 58 casks of resin. *Sirius* arrived in New York on 22 April, just a few hours ahead of her rival *Great Western*. Her success was, in some part, due to the newly introduced surface condensers, which enabled fresh distilled water to be fed to the boilers, thereby avoiding the necessity of clearing salt out of the boilers every few days. *Sirius* was wrecked in 1847.

Skipjack

Type: US submarine
Displacement: 3,124 tonnes (3,075 tons) (surface), 3,570 tonnes (3,513 tons) (submerged)
Dimensions: 76.7m x 9.6m x 8.9m (251ft 8in x 31ft 6in x 29ft 2in)
Machinery: Single screw, nuclear reactor, turbines
Main armament: Six 533mm (21in) torpedo tubes
Launched: May 1958

Date of profile: 1960

Skipjack was the lead ship in a class of six boats that were the first to incorporate the teardrop hull, which allowed for high speed underwater, with the endurance of nuclear

propulsion. The diving planes were mounted on the fin to improve underwater manoeuvrability. All the torpedo tubes were in the bow; no stern tubes were fitted because the aft hull shape tapered sharply. *Skipjack*'s engine

developed 15,000hp; her crew numbered 93. She introduced the S5W fast-attack submarine propulsion plant used in all subsequent US attack and ballistic submarines until the Los Angeles class.

Slava

Type: Russian cruiser
Displacement: 11,700 tonnes (11,200 tons)
Dimensions: 186m x 20.8m x 7.6m (610ft

3in x 68ft 3in x 25ft
Machinery: Twin screws, gas

turbines
Main armament: Two 127mm (5in) guns, eight twin SS-N-12 launchers, eight launchers for SA-N-6 missiles plus two twin launchers for SAM missiles
Launched: 1979

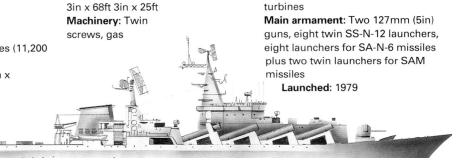

Slava is a smaller version of the Kirov class, for which she and her three sisters are intended to act as a conventional back-up. The SS-N-12 missiles are carried in twin launchers along each side of the bridge. Complex radars are fitted on the massive foremast at the end of the bridge. Another radar fit is mounted on top of the mainmast. *Slava* entered service in 1982. The last unit will be completed in the late 1990s.

Society Adventurer

Type: Bahamian expedition ship
Displacement: 8,512 tonnes (8,378 tons)
Dimensions: 122.7m x 18m x 4.7m (402ft 8in x 59ft x 15ft 5in)
Machinery: Twin screws, diesel engines
Launched: January 1991

Society Adventurer is a new-style luxury cruise expedition ship able to operate for up to eight weeks at a time without taking on fuel or provisions. Range is 16,150km (8,500 miles). She was

designed for cruises to special-interest areas such as Antarctica, the Arctic, the South Pacific and the Amazon River. She can accommodate 188 passengers in

well-appointed twin cabins fitted with closed-circuit televisions so that passengers can watch transmissions from diving teams. There is an observation lounge on top of the bridge.

Sokol

Type: Russian destroyer
Displacement: 224 tonnes (220 tons)
Dimensions: 57.9m x 5.6m x 2.2m (190ft x 18ft 6in x 7ft 6in)
Machinery: Twin screws, vertical triple expansion

engines
Top speed: 30.2 knots
Main armament: Three 3-pounder, one 12-pounder guns, two 380mm (15in) torpedo tubes
Launched: 1895
Date of profile: 1896

Sokol was Russia's first destroyer, laid down in 1894 and completed in 1895. Her 12-pounder gun was mounted on top of the conning tower, at the end of the turtle-back foredeck. Two of the 3-pounder guns were placed just aft of the first funnel, with the third gun mounted aft between the two aft funnels. Her armament was modified during her career, another 12-pounder being added, plus six torpedo tubes. To save weight, light nickel steel and aluminium were used in her construction wherever possible. Re-named *Pruitki*, she served as a minesweeper in World War I and was scrapped in 1922.

Sparviero

Type: Italian aircraft carrier
Displacement: 30,480 tonnes (30,000 tons)
Dimensions: 202.4m x 25.2m x 9.2m

(664ft 2in x 82ft 10in x 30ft 2in)
Machinery: Quadruple screws, diesel engines
Main armament: Four 102mm (4in), six 152mm (6in) guns
Launched: 1927

In 1936 it was suggested that the large liner *Augustus* could provide the possible basis for an aircraft carrier. Although the idea was initially rejected, it was revised in 1942, when it was decided to

convert *Augustus* into an auxiliary carrier. She was re-named *Falco*, then *Sparviero*, but just as her upper works had been removed, she was seized by the Germans for use as a blockship.

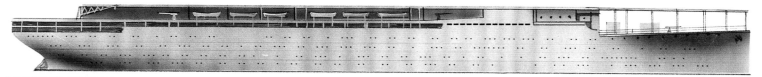

Sparviero

Type: Italian guided missile hydrofoil
Displacement: 62.5 tonnes (62.5 tons)
Dimensions: 23m x 12.1m x 1.5m (75ft 6in x 23ft x 4ft 3in) (foil-borne), 24.6m x 7m x 1.9m (80ft 8in x 39ft 8in x 4ft 3in) (hull-borne)

Machinery: Single gas turbine driving water jet, one diesel engine
Main armament: One 76mm (3in) gun, two OTOMAT SSM launchers
Launched: 1974

During the 1960s, the USA carried out tests with a series of hydrofoils suitable

for patrol work. *Sparviero* is a development of these vessels, but has a larger hull and improved armament. She was authorised as a basis for a NATO hydrofoil. She has successfully fired OTOMAT Mk 1 SSMs, which have a range of 180km (95 miles). No berths are fitted for the crew as she is intended for short-range missions.

Spica

Type: Swedish fast attack torpedo craft
Displacement: 218 tonnes

(215 tons)
Dimensions: 42.7m x 7m x 2.6m (140ft x 23ft 4in x 8ft 6in)
Machinery: Triple screws,

gas turbines
Main armament: One 57mm (2.25in) gun, six 533mm (21in) torpedo tubes
Launched: 1966

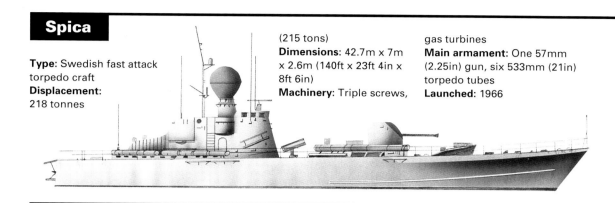

Spica was the first of a group of fast attack craft that were ideally suited to Baltic waters. Bases for these craft are built into the rocky coastline of Sweden, and can withstand most weapons except nuclear. The gas turbines develop 12,720hp and provide rapid acceleration. The Spica group represent a formidable fighting force, and this successful design has been adopted by several world navies.

Spruance

Type: US destroyer
Displacement: 8,168 tonnes (8,040 tons)
Dimensions: 171.7m x 16.8m x 5.8m (563ft 4in x 55ft 2in x 19ft)

Machinery: Twin

screws, gas turbines
Main armament: Two 127mm (5in) guns, Tomahawk and Harpoon missiles
Launched: 1973

The successful hull design of the

Spruance-class destroyers was used, with modifications, on two other classes of US warship, and has reduced rolling and pitching tendencies, so providing a better weapons platform. All vessels in the Spruance class have undergone major weapons changes over the years.

Staffetta

Type: Italian despatch vessel
Displacement: 1,805 tonnes (1,777 tons)
Dimensions: 77m x 9.4m x 3.9m (252ft 10in x 31ft x 13ft)
Machinery: Single screw, double expansion engine
Top speed: 12.5 knots
Main armament: Four 120mm (4.7in) guns

Launched: June 1876

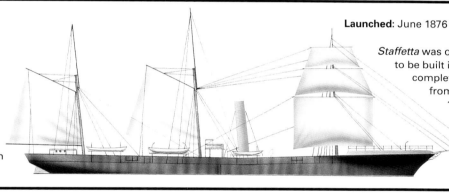

Staffetta was one of the first iron-hulled warships to be built in Italy, laid down in 1873 and completed in 1877. Her machinery, taken from *Cristoforo Colombo*, developed 1,700hp, and range at full speed was 3,420km (1,800 miles). In 1897 *Staffetta* was given four 57mm (2.25in) guns. In 1903 she became a survey ship. She was discarded in 1914.

Stiletto

Type: US torpedo boat
Displacement: 31 tonnes (31 tons)
Dimensions: 29m x 3.5m x 0.9m (94ft x 11ft 6in x 3ft)
Machinery: Single screw, vertical compound engine
Top speed: 18.2 knots

Main armament: None when first completed
Launched: 1886

In 1881 the US Advisory Board recommended the construction of a number of

torpedo boats of the Herreshoff type for harbour and inshore defence work. However, nothing was done until 1888 when the fast, wooden-hulled yacht *Stiletto* was

purchased from the Herreshoff company for experimental trials. Originally she had been laid down as a private speculation at Herreshoff's yard, Bristol, Rhode Island, and had been commissioned in 1887. In 1898 *Stiletto* was given two Howell torpedo tubes. She was removed from the Navy List in early 1911, and was sold in July of the same year.

Stonewall

Type: Confederate battleship
Displacement: 1,585 tonnes (1,560 tons)
Dimensions: 60m x 32m x 16m (194ft x 31ft 6in x 15ft 8in)
Machinery: Twin screws, horizontal direct-acting engines
Main armament: One 228mm (9in), two 70-pounder guns

Armour: 89-115mm (3.5-4.5in) belt, 140mm (5.5in) over bow gun, 850mm (24in) wooden backing behind side armour
Launched: June 1864

Stonewall was the last ironclad to serve in the Confederate Navy. The 228mm (9in) gun was housed in the bows above the ram, and could fire direct ahead or through a port on either side. In May 1865 *Stonewall* was handed over to Union forces. She was sold to Japan and re-named *Adzuma*. In 1888 she was removed from the effective list and was then used as an accommodation ship.

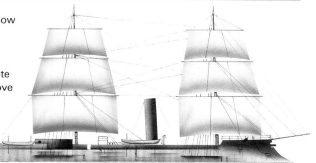

Stromboli

Type: Italian cruiser
Displacement: 3,505 tonnes (3,450 tons)
Dimensions: 91.4m x 13.2m x 6.2m (300ft x 43ft 4in x 20ft 8in)
Machinery: Twin screws, double expansion engines
Top speed: 17 knots
Main armament: Two 254mm (10in), six 152mm (6in) guns
Launched: February 1886
Date of profile: 1895

Italy was one of the first nations to fully appreciate the value of the medium-sized protected cruiser.

Between 1882 and 1890, the Italian Navy ordered 12 of this type of fast, heavily armed vessel, three from Britain and the rest from Italian yards. *Stromboli* was one in a class of four vessels that followed the design of *Giovanni Bausan*, which had been launched in 1883. She was laid down at the Venice Naval

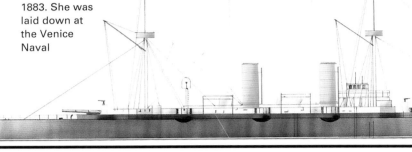

Dockyard in 1883, and completed in March 1888. She had an armoured deck 38mm (1.5in) thick, with 13mm 0.5in) of plate protecting her conning tower. Her engines were capable of some 6,250hp, and her range at 10 knots was over 6,650km (3,500 miles). Her 254mm (10in) main guns were positioned fore and aft, while the 152mm (6in) weapons were on waist-mounted sponsons, three on each side. All her guns were behind protective shields. She was discarded and scrapped in 1907. One of her sister ships, *Etna*, lasted until 1921, having briefly served as a headquarters ship at Taranto.

Sultan

Type: British battleship
Displacement: 9,693 tonnes (9,540 tons)
Dimensions: 99m x 18m x 8m (324ft 10in x 59ft x 26ft 3in)
Machinery: Single screw, horizontal trunk engine
Main armament: Eight 254mm (10in),

four 228mm (9in) guns
Armour: 152-228mm (6-12in) belt with 254-305mm (10-12in) wood backing, 228mm (9in) on main battery, 203mm (8in) on upper battery
Launched: 1870

Sultan was laid down in 1868. All ther 254mm (10in) rifled muzzle-loaders were in a 25.3m (83ft) long armoured battery, with the forward gun firing through an embrasured port to give ahead fire. She was ship rigged, spreading 4,589 square metres (49,395 sq ft) of canvas when carrying studding sails, but was a slow sailer. *Sultan* was a very powerful vessel and one of the most heavily armed central battery ships ever built. Her final days were spent as a mine-sweeping depot ship and she was scrapped in 1945.

Sumter

Type: Confederate raider
Displacement: 456 tonnes (449 tons)
Dimensions: 56.1m x 9.1m x 3.8m (184ft x 30ft x 12ft 6in)
Machinery: Single screw (engine type not recorded)
Top speed: 10 knots
Main armament: One 203mm (8in), four 32-pounder guns
Launched: 1859

Sumter was formerly the passenger steamer

Havana belonging to the McConnell New Orleans Havana Line, and was bought in April 1861 at New Orleans for conversion to a raider. *Sumter* – under the command of Raphael Semmes, who later commanded *Alabama* – left New Orleans on 30 June, penetrating the Union blockade. She captured 18 Union vessels before being forced into Cadiz for repairs in early 1863. She then became the blockade runner *Gibraltar*.

Surcouf

Type: French submarine
Displacement: 3,302 tonnes (3,250 tons) (surface), 4,373 tonnes (4,304 tons) (submerged)
Dimensions: 110m x 9.1m (360ft 10in x 29ft 9in)
Machinery: Twin screws, diesel engines (surface), electric motors (submerged)
Main armament: Two 203mm (8in) guns, eight 551mm (21.7in), four 400mm (15.75in) torpedo tubes

Launched: 1929

Surcouf was the largest submarine in the world until the Japanese 400 series entered service in World War II. She was a double-hulled cruiser-type boat with the enormous range of 19,000km (10,000 miles) at ten knots. She was

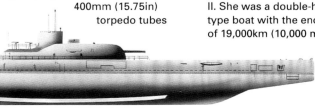

intended for service well away from a French base, and could carry 90-days' worth of stores for her crew of 118. *Surcouf*'s diving depth was 80m (262ft 6in) and she carried 284 tonnes (280 tons) of fuel. The 203mm (8in) guns were carried in a watertight turret forward of the conning tower; these had a range of 27,400m (30,000 yd) and could be fired 2.5 minutes after surfacing, at a rate of three rounds per minute. *Surcouf* was lost in 1942.

Swift

Type: British flotilla leader
Displacement: 2,428 tonnes (2,390 tons)
Dimensions: 107.8m x 10.4m x 3.2m (353ft 8in x 34ft 2in x 10ft 6in)
Machinery: Quadruple screws, turbines
Main armament: Four 102mm (4in) guns, two 457mm (18in) torpedo tubes
Launched: December 1907

Swift was the world's first purpose-built flotilla leader. The design, however, was very ambitious, and the vessel failed to make the contract speed of 36 knots. After many changes to the propeller and with the funnels heightened she finally made just over 35 knots, and was eventually accepted into the navy in 1910, after two years of trials. She was a good sea boat but her light construction made her vulnerable in North Sea storms. The foredeck 102mm (4in) weapons were later replaced with 152mm (6in) guns. *Swift* was broken up in 1921.

Swordfish

Type: British submarine
Displacement: 947 tonnes (932 tons) (surface), 1,123 tonnes (1,105 tons) (submerged)
Dimensions: 70.5m x 7m x 4.5m (231ft 4in x 23ft x 14ft 9in)
Machinery: Twin screws, impulse reaction turbines
Main armament: Two 533mm (21in), four 457mm (18in) torpedo tubes
Launched: March 1916

In spite of the disappointing performance of *Nautilus*, launched in 1914, the British Admiralty pressed ahead with plans for a 20-knot submarine. Laurenti's proposal of 1912 was re-examined, and worked up by Scott. *Swordfish's* small funnel was lowered electrically and the well covered by a plate. Closing down the funnel took 1.5 minutes, with the heat inside the vessel proving bearable. She was the first submarine to fit an emergency telephone buoy. In 1917 *Swordfish* was converted to a surface patrol boat, and was broken up in 1922.

Tage

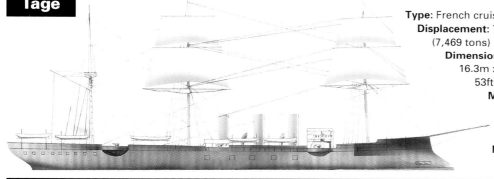

Type: French cruiser
Displacement: 7,589 tonnes (7,469 tons)
Dimensions: 118.9m x 16.3m x 7.7m (390ft x 53ft 6in x 25ft 2in)
Machinery: Twin screws, triple expansion engines
Main armament: Eight 163mm (6.4in), ten 140mm (5.5in) guns
Launched: October 1886

A large, powerful, steel-hulled cruiser, *Tage* was laid down in July 1885 and completed at the end of 1890. Two 140mm (5.5in) guns were later removed, as were three of the original 381mm 15in) torpedo tubes. *Tage* was discarded in 1910.

Taiho

Type: Japanese aircraft carrier
Displacement: 37,866 tonnes (37,270 tons)
Dimensions: 260.6m x 30m x 9.6m (855ft x 98ft 6in x 31ft 6in)
Machinery: Quadruple screws, turbines
Main armament: Twelve 100mm (3.9in), seventy-one 25mm (1in) guns
Launched: April 1943

Taiho was Japan's largest purpose-built aircraft carrier and the first to feature an armoured deck. She was laid down in July 1941 and went into service in March 1944. The two-tier hangars were 150m (500ft) long and unarmoured at the sides. The lower hangar was 124mm (4.9in) thick over the boiler and machinery spaces, which also had 150mm (5.9in) thick side armour; the flight deck had 76mm (3in) thick armour to withstand a 455kg (1,000lb) bomb. Total armour protection came to 8,940 tonnes (8,800 tons). *Taiho* was sunk within a few weeks of entering service, by the US submarine *Albacore* on 19 June 1944.

Takao

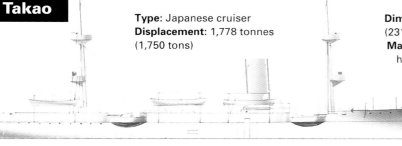

Type: Japanese cruiser
Displacement: 1,778 tonnes (1,750 tons)
Dimensions: 70.4m x 10.5m x 4m (231ft x 34ft 6in x 13ft 2in)
Machinery: Twin screws, horizontal compound engines
Top speed: 15 knots
Main armament: Four 150mm (5.9in), one 119mm (4.7in) guns
Launched: October 1888

Takao was the first steel-hulled warship to be built in Japan. Designed by Emile Bertin, she was laid down in 1886 and completed in 1889. In 1907, *Takao* was rearmed with two 152mm (6in) and two 119mm (4.7in) quick-firers. She served as a survey ship from 1911 until sold in 1918.

Tango

Type: Russian submarine
Displacement: 3,251 tonnes (3,200 tons) (surface), 3,962 tonnes (3,900 tons) (submerged)
Dimensions: 92m x 9m x 7m (301ft 10in x 29ft 6in x 23ft)
Machinery: Twin screws, diesel engines (surface), electric motors (submerged)
Top speed: 15 knots (surface), 16 knots (submerged)
Main armament: Six 533mm (21in) torpedo tubes
Launched: 1972

The nuclear-powered Victor-class attack submarines were the immediate Soviet response to the growing force of US nuclear missile submarines, but they took a long time to build. A vessel that could be more quickly constructed was called for, and the answer was the Tango class of 19 boats. The Tangos are among the largest of the conventionally powered submarines, and weapons include the SS-N-15.

Taranto

Type: Italian cruiser
Displacement: 6,027 5,933 tons) tonnes
Dimensions: 138.7m x 13.4m x 5.7m (455ft x 44ft x 18ft 8in)
Machinery: Twin screws, turbines
Main armament: Seven 150mm (5.9in), two 76mm (3in) guns
Launched: August 1911

Taranto was formerly the German light cruiser Strassburg, and was originally armed with twelve 105mm (4.1in) guns. In 1915 her armament was changed to seven 150mm (5.9in) guns. The vessel was ceded to Italy in July 1920 and received into the Italian Navy in June 1925, after alterations that included re-arming with Italian weapons. In September 1943 she was scuttled in La Spezia but was refloated twice by German forces, each time being sunk by Allied bombs. In 1946/47, she was raised and broken up.

Tegetthoff

Type: Austrian battleship
Displacement: 7,550 tonnes (7,431 tons)
Dimensions: 92.5m x 21.8m x 7.6m (303ft 4in x 71ft 6in x 24ft 10in)
Machinery: Single screw, horizontal low-pressure engine
Top speed: 14 knots
Main armament: Six 280mm (11in), six 90mm (3.5in) guns
Launched: 1878

Tegetthoff was Austria's last central battery ironclad and was the largest capital ship to be added to the navy for over 20 years. In 1897 she became a floating battery at Pola, and was renamed Mars in 1912. She was ceded to Italy in 1918 and scrapped in 1920.

Temeraire

Type: British battleship
Displacement: 8,677 tonnes (8,540 tons)
Dimensions: 86.9m x 18.9m x 8.2m (285ft x 62ft x 27ft)
Machinery: Twin screws, vertical inverted compound engines
Top speed: 14.7 knots
Main armament: Four 280mm (11in), four 254mm (10in) guns
Launched: May 1876
Date of profile: 1878

Temeraire was Britain's first barbette ship, with one 280mm (11in) gun mounted at each end of the upper deck in a pear-shaped barbette. The 254mm (10in) guns were in a central battery. She originally carried 2,322 square metres (25,000 sq ft) of canvas, but her rig was later reduced. In 1902, she became a depot ship and workshop. She was renamed Indus II in 1904 and later Akbar, and was sold in 1921.

Tennessee

Type: Confederate ironclad
Displacement: 1,293 tonnes (1,273 tons)
Dimensions: 64m x 14.6m x 4.3m (209ft x 48ft x 14ft)
Machinery: Single screw, non-condensing engines
Top speed: 7 knots
Main armament: Two 181mm (7.1in), four 152mm (6in) guns
Armour: 127-152mm (5-6in) on sides, 51mm (2in) on deck
Launched: February 1863

Tennessee was the largest ironclad built in the Confederacy and was the main force in the defence of Mobile Bay. Laid down in 1862, after launching she was towed down to Mobile by the ironclad Baltic for completion. The falling waters of the river made it almost impossible to get Tennessee over the bars and giant wooden pontoons were constructed and lashed to the vessel to lift her over. Tennessee was captured by Union forces on 5 August 1864 after a three-hour battle .

Terrible

Type: British cruiser
Displacement: 1,876 tonnes (1,847 tons)
Dimensions: 76m x 16.7m x 7.3m (250ft x 55ft x 24ft)
Machinery: Paddle wheels, single condensing engine
Top speed: 11 knots
Main armament: Twenty-one heavy guns (including 203mm (8in))
Launched: 1845
Date of profile: 1845

From 1822, Britain had attempted to build a

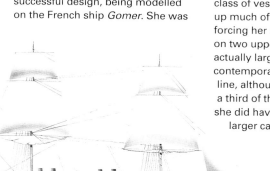

suitable steam-powered paddle-wheel frigate but all attempts had failed. *Terrible* was the first such successful design, being modelled on the French ship *Gomer*. She was the most powerful paddle-cruiser of her time, although she displayed many of the faults endemic to this class of vessel. Her machinery took up much of her internal space, forcing her 21 guns to be mounted on two upper decks. She was actually larger than most contemporary 90-gun ships of the line, although she carried less than a third of their armament. The guns she did have, though, were of a larger calibre. The main problem

with paddle-steamers, however, was the position of their propelling wheels. These were extremely vulnerable to hostile fire, and fragile enough to be easily put out of action. The paddles were also a cumbersome source of drag when not operating, and gave the ship dismal performance under sail. A mixed force of screw and paddle ships usually found it impossible to manoeuvre effectively as a squadron. This short-lived method of propulsion was soon eclipsed by the stern-mounted screw.

Teutonic

Type: British liner
Displacement: 10,143 tonnes (9,984 tons)
Dimensions: 172.5m x 17.6m
(565ft 8in x 57ft 8in)
Machinery: Twin screws, triple expansion engines
Top speed: 20.4 knots
Launched: January 1889

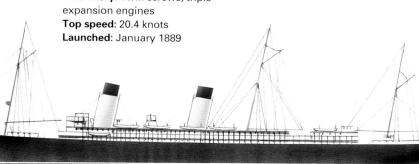

Teutonic and her sister *Majestic* were the first White Star liners to have twin screws, and were the first for that line to be built according to British Admiralty specifications, which required them to have the capability to be converted into armed merchant cruisers in times of war. *Teutonic* provided lavish accommodation for 300 first-class passengers, including a gilt-lined dining hall and a leather-lined smoking room. She also carried 175 second-class passengers, plus 850 steerage. In 1891 she took the Blue Riband for the westbound crossing of the Atlantic. In 1915 she became a troopship. She was broken up in 1921.

Texas

Type: Confederate ironclad
Displacement: Unknown
Dimensions: 66m x 15.3m x 3.9m (217ft x 50ft 4in x 13ft)
Machinery: Twin screws, horizontal direct-acting engines
Top speed: Unknown
Main armament: Six 163mm (6.4in) guns
Armour: 102mm (4in) on battery

Launched: January 1865
Date of profile: 1865

Texas was the last major warship to be launched in the Confederacy. She was one of the most powerful ironclads to be build in the Southern states of America, and was also the

only twin-screw ironclad to be built in a Southern yard. She was laid down at Rocketts, a suburb just outside Richmond, and was moved to Richmond after launching to be fitted out. Four of her guns were mounted on pivots, giving direct ahead and

astern fire, as well as broadside firing through ports. The two remaining guns were positioned on each broadside. All the guns were Brooke rifles – powerful and advanced weapons. When Richmond fell to the Union forces on 3 April 1865, the Confederates failed to blow up *Texas*, and she was seized by the Union and moved to the Norfolk Navy Yard.

Texas

Type: US battleship
Displacement: 6,772 tonnes (6,665 tons)
Dimensions: 91m x 19.5m x 6.8m (299ft x 64ft x 22ft 6in)
Machinery: Twin screws, vertical triple expansion engines
Main armament: Two 152mm (6in), two 305mm (12in) guns
Armour: 152-305mm (6-12in) belt, 305mm (12in) on turrets and

redoubt
Launched: June 1892

Texas was authorised in 1886, laid down in June 1889 and completed in 1895. She was designed in Britain

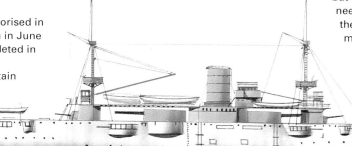

and proved to be a good seaboat, but after initial trials the hull needed strengthening. By 1904 the funnel had been raised and more armour added to the turret hoists. In 1911 she was re-named *San Marcos*, and was expended as a target in 1912.

Theodora

Type: Dutch tanker
Displacement: 9,372 tonnes (9,224 tons)
Dimensions: 110.6m x 17m x 7m (362ft 10in x 55ft 9in x 23ft)
Machinery: Single screw,

diesel engines
Top speed: 14.5 knots
Launched: March 1991

Theodora was specially designed to carry high-temperature cargoes, including boiler oil, naphtha,

bituminous coal, creosote and antracene oil. Cargoes are carried in three separate steel tanks which rest on flexible foundations welded to the ship's hull, thereby allowing for expansion or contraction of the cargo. The

temperature of the tanks is controlled by pumps and heat exchangers. *Theodora* has a double hull with 13 ballast tanks, which are completely separate from the cargo system. All ship's systems are controlled from the bridge. A full set of fire-fighting equipment is carried, and provision for crew safety includes a free-fall lifeboat aft, plus inflatable life rafts.

Thistle

Type: British submarine
Displacement: 1,347 tonnes (1,326 tons) (surface), 1,547 tonnes (1,523 tons) (submerged)
Dimensions: 83.6m x 8m

x 3.6m (274ft 3in x 26ft 6in x 12ft)
Machinery: Twin screws, diesel engines (surface), electric motors (submerged)

Main armament: One 102mm (4in) gun, ten 533mm (21in) torpedo tubes
Launched: 1939

Thistle was one of the first British T-class submarines to be completed. The T-class were built to replace the previous O, P and R classes of ocean-going submarines, and were designed to remain at sea for patrols of up to 42 days. Construction of the 21-unit class began in 1936. *Thistle* was lost in the North Sea on 14 April 1940. Some of the surviving submarines continued to serve until 1963.

Thomas W. Lawson

Type: US sailing ship
Displacement: 5,301 tonnes (5,218 tons)
Dimensions: 120.5m x 15m x 9.8m (395ft 4in x 49ft 3in x 32ft 2in)
Launched: 1902

Thomas W. Lawson was probably the largest schooner ever built. She had seven masts, and carried 4,064 tonnes (4,000

tons) of coal. Although the vessel had a massive 4,000 square metre (43,055 sq ft) spread of canvas, she needed a crew of only 35 to operate the sails because she was fitted with a range of mechanical winches. Built by the Fore River Shipbuilding Co. at Quincy, Massachussetts, she was operated by the Coastwise Transportation Company of Boston. She was wrecked in 1907 after only five years in service.

Tiger

Type: British battlecruiser
Displacement: 35,723 tonnes (35,160 tons)
Dimensions: 214.6m x 27.6m x 8.6m (704ft x 90ft 6in x 28ft 5in)
Machinery: Quadruple screws,

turbines
Top speed: 30 knots
Main

armament: Twelve 152mm (6in), eight 343mm (13.5in) guns
Launched: December 1913

It had been intended to fit *Tiger* with small tube boilers and geared turbines, and had this

suggestion been adopted her top speed may have been 32 knots. However, as it was *Tiger* was still the fastest, as well as the largest, capital ship of her day. She was also the last coal-burning capital ship in the Royal Navy, and was the only British battlecruiser to carry 152mm (6in) guns. *Tiger* was scrapped as a result of the Washington Naval Treaty of 1922.

Tiger

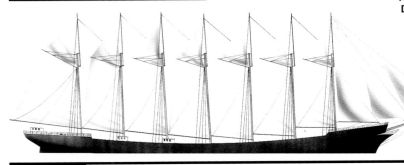

Type: British cruiser
Displacement: 12,273 tonnes (12,080 tons)
Dimensions: 170m x 20m x 6.4m (555ft 6in x 64ft x 21ft 3in)
Machinery: Quadruple screws, turbines
Top speed: 31.5 knots

Main armament: Six 76mm (3in), four 152mm (6in) guns
Launched: October 1945

Tiger was originally laid down in 1941 as one of the Minotaur class. However, work stopped

in 1946 for eight years. Originally named *Bellerophon*, she was finally completed to new designs in 1959, and was one of the last cruisers to enter British service. She was scrapped in the 1960s.

Torbay

Type: British submarine
Displacement: 4,877 tonnes (4,800 tons) (surface), 5,384 tonnes (5,300 tons) (submerged)
Dimensions: 85.4m x 10m x 8.2m (280ft 2in x 33ft 2in x 27ft)
Machinery: Pump jet, pressurised water-cooled reactor, turbines
Main armament: Five 533mm (21in) torpedo tubes

Launched: March 1985

Torbay was one of the first of an improved type of fleet submarine ordered in 1977. She and her sisters have longer-life nuclear reactors, and their main propulsion and auxiliary machinery raft are mounted and suspended from transverse bulkheads in order to provide better sound insulation, making them even harder for an enemy to detect. Anechoic tiles provide further reduction in the acoustic signature. *Torbay* and her sisters carry Tigerfish torpedoes.

Trento

Type: Italian cruiser
Displacement: 13,547 tonnes (13,334 tons)
Dimensions: 196.9m x 20.6m x 6.8m (646ft 2in x 67ft 7in x 22ft 4in)
Machinery: Quadruple screws, turbines
Top speed: 36 knots
Main armament: Sixteen 100mm (3.9in), eight 203mm (8in) guns
Launched: October 1927

Trento was one of two cruisers built under the 1924/25 programme, but difficulties were experienced in keeping within the specified 10,160-tonne (10,000-ton) weight limit. Every effort was made to save weight, but after initial trials the hull had to be strengthened to reduce vibration at high speed. A box citadel with 70mm (2.75in) thick sides and 50mm (1.95in) on top provided protection. Engines developed 146,975hp, and she was one of the fastest cruisers of her time. She was sunk off Malta by the British submarine *Umbra* on 15 June 1942

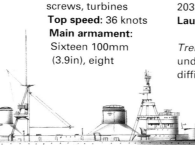

Trenton

Type: US cruiser
Displacement: 3,962 tonnes (3,900 tons)
Dimensions: 257m x 14.6m x 20m (253ft x 48ft x 19ft 6in)
Machinery: Single screw, horizontal compound back acting engine
Main armament: Ten 203mm (8in) guns
Launched: January 1876

Trenton was the last large, wooden-hulled warship built for the US Navy. Her hull was laid down at the New York Navy Yard in December 1873. The vessel was completed in 1877. She was a full-rigged ship and carried a ram with a heavy composition casting, the point being 2.7m (9ft) below the waterline and extending 2.4m (8ft) beyond the stem. She was wrecked in Apia harbour, Samoa in March 1889, after fierce winds had driven her into the USS *Vandalia*, which was already aground, and water flooded in through her anchor ports.

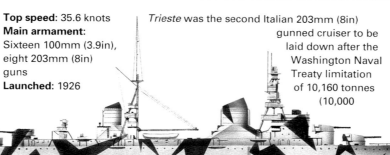

Trieste

Type: Italian cruiser
Displacement: 13,540 tonnes (13,326 tons)
Dimensions: 196.9m x 20.6m x 6.8m (646ft 2in x 67ft 7in x 22ft 4in)
Machinery: Quadruple screws, turbines
Top speed: 35.6 knots
Main armament: Sixteen 100mm (3.9in), eight 203mm (8in) guns
Launched: 1926

Trieste was the second Italian 203mm (8in) gunned cruiser to be laid down after the Washington Naval Treaty limitation of 10,160 tonnes (10,000 tons). Lightly constructed to save weight, her full-load displacement was still some 3,048 tonnes (3,000 tons) over the limit. She was torpedoed by the British submarine *Utmost* in 1942, and though badly damaged managed to escape to Messina. She was sunk during an air raid on Sardinia in 1943.

Tripoli

Type: Italian cruiser
Displacement: 967 tonnes 952 tons)
Dimensions: 73.4m x 7.9m x 4.9m (240ft 9in x 26ft x 16ft)
Machinery: Triple screws, double expansion engines
Top speed: 19 knots
Main armament: Six 57mm (2.25in), one 120mm (4.7in) gun
Launched: August 1886

Tripoli was an experimental cruiser and originally carried a light fore and aft rig. Designed by Benedetto Brin, she was laid down in June 1885 and was completed in December 1886. She was steel-hulled and was classified as a torpedo cruiser armed with five 355mm (14in) torpedo tubes. She was the first Italian warship with triple screws. *Tripoli* served as a minelayer during World War I, and was officially classified as such in 1921. She was discarded in 1923.

Tromp

Type: Dutch destroyer
Displacement: 5,486 tonnes (5,400 tons)
Dimensions: 138.2m x 14.8m x 6.6m (453ft 5in x 48ft 6in x 21ft 8in)
Machinery: Twin screws, gas turbines
Top speed: 28 knots
Main armament: Two 120mm (4.7in) guns, one 8-cell launcher for Sea Sparrow, one Mk 13 SM-1 launcher
Launched: June 1973
Date of profile: 1980

Tromp and her sister ship, *De Ruyter*, were the two most powerful units in the Dutch Navy. They fulfilled the role of flagship to two long-range deep-water task groups, which were assigned to NATO and intended to operate in the Eastern Atlantic. *Tromp* is a powerful, well armed ship, with a good balance of weapons. Her 120mm (4.7in) dual-purpose guns are in a single automated turret, and are able to fire 42 rounds per minute at targets over 20km (32 miles) distant. For area air defence she carries 40 Standard missiles which are fired by the single Mk13 launcher aft. An octuple Sea Sparrow launcher with 60 reloads provides short-range anti-aircraft and anti-missile defence, while a later refit added a Goalkeeper point defence gun system. A single Lynx helicopter is her main ASW weapon, although she carries light torpedo tubes for close-in work. She

has a 44,000hp gas turbine for high speed, and an 8,200hp cruising turbine which gives her a range of 9,500km (5,000 miles). Using gas turbines instead of steam helps to keep manning levels down. She has a distinctive appearance, with a huge bulbous dome covering her 3-D air surveillance radar. She is due to be decommissioned in the late 1990s.

Ts'ao Chiang

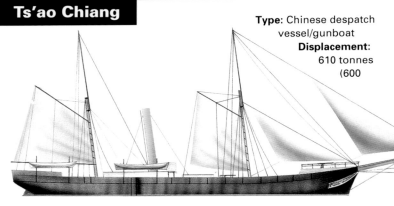

Type: Chinese despatch vessel/gunboat
Displacement: 610 tonnes (600 tons)
Dimensions: 47.7m x 8.6m x 3.2m (156ft 8in x 28ft 3in x 10ft 8in)
Machinery: Single screw, horizontal reciprocating engines
Top speed: 9 knots
Main armament: Four 160mm (6.3in) guns
Launched: 1876

Ts'ao Chiang was the first Chinese warship to be lost in the 1895 war with Japan. She was a composite-built vessel with iron framing and a wooden hull, and was built for the Nanyang Fleet at the Kiangyan Dockyard and completed in 1879. Tension built up between China and Japan during 1895, and on 25 July a small force of Chinese warships, including *Ts'ao Chiang*, were attacked without warning by a force of Japanese cruisers. After a brief chase, *Ts'ao Chiang* was captured. She was taken over by the Japanese Navy and was re-named *Soko*. She was scrapped in 1904.

Tsessarevitch

Type: Russian battleship
Displacement: 13,122 tonnes (12,915 tons)
Dimensions: 118.5m x 23.2m x 7.9m (388ft 9in x 76ft x 26ft)
Machinery: Twin screws, vertical triple expansion engines
Top speed: 18.5 knots
Main armament: Twelve 152mm (6in), four 305mm (12in), twenty 3-pounder guns
Armour: 178-254mm (7-10in) belt, 254mm (10in) on main turrets, 152mm (6in) on secondary turrets
Launched: 1901

Tsessarevitch was part of the Russian naval expansion programme of 1898. She was laid down at La Seyne in June 1899, and was completed in 1903. Her design followed the French practice of the period, having a pronounced tumble-home and high forecastle. She served as flagship to the First Pacific Squadron based at Port Arthur, and was damaged during the Yellow Sea battle in 1904. While serving in the Baltic in World War I, she was re-named *Grashdanin*. She was scrapped in 1922.

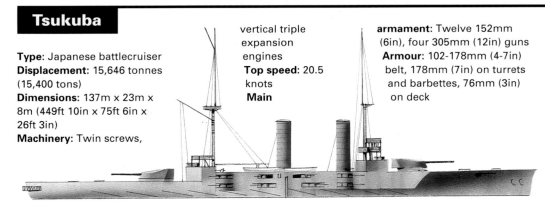

Tsukuba

Type: Japanese battlecruiser
Displacement: 15,646 tonnes (15,400 tons)
Dimensions: 137m x 23m x 8m (449ft 10in x 75ft 6in x 26ft 3in)
Machinery: Twin screws, vertical triple expansion engines
Top speed: 20.5 knots
Main armament: Twelve 152mm (6in), four 305mm (12in) guns
Armour: 102-178mm (4-7in) belt, 178mm (7in) on turrets and barbettes, 76mm (3in) on deck
Launched: December 1905

Tsukuba was ordered in 1904 as a replacement for one of two powerful battleships lost during the war with Russia. She was laid down at Kure Naval Dockyard in 1905, and originally classified as an armoured cruiser. By the time she was completed in 1907, much more powerful battle-cruisers were being built for the Japanese Navy, and in 1921 her sister *Ikoma* was re-rated as a first-class cruiser. In January 1917 her magazine caught fire and she blew up in Yokosuka Bay. She was later raised and broken up.

Tsukushi

Type: Japanese cruiser
Displacement: 1,372 tonnes
(1,350 tons)
Dimensions: 64m x 9.7m x
4.4m (210ft x 31ft
10in x 14ft 5in)

Machinery: Twin screws, reciprocating
horizontal compound engines
Top speed: 16.5 knots
Main armament: Four 120mm
(4.7in), two 254mm (10in)
guns
Launched: August 1880

Tsukushi was
ordered by
Chile during
the war with

Peru. She was completed in 1883,
put up for sale and was purchased
by Japan in 1885. Her engines
developed 2,887hp and steam was
supplied by five cylindrical boilers.
She was one of the fastest warships
of her day. Coal supply was 305
tonnes (300 tons), and range at eight
knots was 10,222km (5,380 miles).
Tsukushi served until 1907, when she
became a training ship. She was
broken up in 1910.

Tsushima

Type: Japanese cruiser
Displacement: 3,420 tonnes (3,366
tons)
Dimensions: 102m x 13.4m x 4.9m
(334ft 8in x 44ft x 16ft 2in)
Machinery: Twin screws,
reciprocating compound
engines
Top speed: 20 knots
Main armament: Six

152mm (6in) guns
Launched: December 1902

Tsushima was the third vessel
to be built entirely to a
Japanese design. She was an

improvement over the previous pair, *Suma* and *Akashi*, because
of her increased displacement. Their 152mm (6in) guns made
Tsushima and her sister *Niitaka* more powerful than many
contemporary cruisers; they were positioned one on the
forecastle, one on the poop and two each side. Ten 12-
pounder guns were spread along the waist. Engines
developed 9,500hp, and steam was supplied by 16
Nillausse boilers. *Tsushima* served in the
Russo-Japanese War of 1904/05. She was
partially disarmed in 1930, and became a
training ship in 1936. She sank during an
air raid in 1944.

Turbinia

Type: British steamer
Displacement: 45 tonnes (44.5 tons)
Dimensions: 30.4m x 2.7m x 0.9m
(100ft x 9ft x 3ft)
Machinery: Triple shafts, turbine
Top speed: 34.5 knots
Launched: 1894
Date of profile: 1894

At one time *Turbinia* was the fastest

vessel in the world; she was the first
vessel to carry the Parsons turbine
engine. Previously the turbine was
being developed for shore
installations. The turbine was a
completely radical approach to

steam engineering. Built by
the inventor C. A. Parsons, the
engine was placed aboard the
specially built *Turbinia* at the
small shipyard in Wallsend-
on-Tyne. Engines developed

2,000hp. *Turbinia* made a
spectacular impact at the British
Naval Review at Spithead in June
1897 as she dashed between the
lines of anchored warships with a
standard naval steam launch
trying, unsuccessfully, to catch her.

Turtle

Type: US submarine
Displacement: 2 tonnes (2 tons)
Dimensions: 1.8m x 1.3m (6ft x 4.5ft)
Machinery: Single screw, hand-
cranked
Top speed: Unknown
Main armament: One 68kg (150lb)
detachable explosive charge
Launched: 1776
Date of profile: 1776

Turtle was the first submarine to
be used in action. She
was built by David
Bushnell who, during the
American War of
Independence in 1775,
had carried out
experiments with floating
tide-borne mines. He
subsequently decided to
build a manned submarine that
could transport the explosive

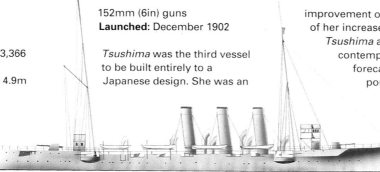

charge to the hull of the enemy ship. *Turtle* comprised two
turtle-like shells made of wood and caulked and bolted all
round. She had a tiny conning tower with glass
ports to enable the sole occupant to find his way
to the target. The interior of the craft was filled
with numerous controls, some being worked with
the feet. A hand-cranked screw drove the vessel through
the water, and she had a vertical screw for downward
thrust. The charge was carried outside the hull, and was
attached to the target by an auger that was screwed into
the hull of the enemy vessel. A clockwork timing device
gave *Turtle* time to escape.

Tycho Brahe

Type: Danish train ferry
Displacement: 10,871
tonnes (10,700 tons)
Dimensions:
111m x
28.2m
x 5.7m
(364ft

2in x 92ft 6in x 18ft 8in)
Machinery: Quadruple thrusters,

diesel engines
Top speed: 13.5 knots
Launched: 1991

Tycho Brahe is the world's
largest
double-
ended train
ferry. She
operates

on the 4.3km (2.7 mile) seaway
between Helsingør, Denmark, and
Helsingborg, Sweden. She runs to a
tight schedule, and so is designed to
reach her maximum speed after
1,500m (1,640yd), and to decelerate
rapidly when 800m (875yd) from the
shore. She can carry 260 lorries, 240
cars and nine railway coaches, plus
up to 1,250 passengers.

261

Typhoon

Type: Russian submarine
Displacement: 25,400 tonnes (21,500 tons) (surface), 26,924 tonnes (26,500 tons) (submerged)
Dimensions: 170m x 24m x 12.5m (562ft 8in x 78ft 9in x 41ft)
Machinery: Twin screws, pressurised water-cooled nuclear reactors, turbines
Top speed: 27 knots (submerged)

Main armament: Twenty SS-N-20 nuclear ballistic missiles, two 533mm (21in) and four 650mm (25.6in) torpedo tubes
Launched: 1979
Date of profile: 1980

Typhoon is the largest submarine in the world, and is nearly half as big again as the powerful US Ohio class of nuclear ballistic missile submarines. Her 20 missile tubes are situated in two rows in front of the large fin, which is aft of midships and houses the main control centre. Her rounded hull and squat fin enable her to force her way up through 3m- (9ft 10in-) thick ice.

U1

Type: German submarine
Displacement: 241 tonnes (238 tons) (surface), 287 tonnes (283 tons)

(submerged)
Dimensions: 42.4m x 3.8m x 3.2m (139ft x 12ft 6in x 10ft 6in)
Machinery: Twin screws,

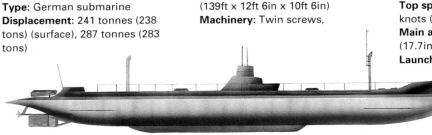

kerosene engines (surface), electric motors (submerged)
Top speed: 10.8 knots (surface), 8.7 knots (submerged)
Main armament: One 450mm (17.7in) torpedo tube
Launched: August 1906

U1 was Germany's first practical submarine, and one of the most successful

and reliable of the period. Two kerosene engines developed 400hp, as did her electric motors, and surfaced range at 10 knots was 2,850km (1,500 miles). Submerged range at 5 knots was 80km (50 miles). *U1* was initially used for trials, and then became a training vessel. She was discarded in 1919 but was purchased by her builder, Germania of Kiel, and donated to the Deutsches Museum, München.

U2

Type: German submarine
Displacement: 254 tonnes (250 tons) (surface), 302 tonnes (298 tons) (submerged)
Dimensions: 40.9m x 4.1m x 3.8m (133ft 2in x 13ft 5in x 12ft 6in)
Machinery: Twin screws, diesel engines (surface), electric motors (submerged)
Main armament: One 20mm (0.8in)

gun, three 533mm (21in) torpedo tubes
Launched: July 1935

Germany was forbidden to build or possess submarines by the 1919 Treaty of Versailles. However, during the 1920s she set up clandestine design teams in Spain, Holland and Russia. The

first boat was built for Finland in 1927, and this was the basis for *U2*, one of the first Type II submarines intended

for coastal service. Diesel engines developed 350hp, and the electric motors developed 180hp. The early Type II boats were all used for training. *U2* was sunk in April 1944.

U12

Type: German submarine
Displacement: 425 tonnes (419 tons) (surface), 457 tonnes (450 tons) (submerged)

Dimensions: 43.9m x 4.6m x 4.3m (144ft x 15ft x 14ft)

Machinery: Single screw, diesel engine (surface), electric motors (submerged)
Top speed: 10 knots (surface), 17 knots (submerged)

Main armament: Eight 533mm (21in) torpedo tubes
Launched: 1968
Date of profile: 1969

U12 was one of the first class of German submarines to be built after World War II. They have since developed into a very successful type, with over 40 boats serving in foreign navies. The hull is of a non-magnetic steel alloy. Diesel engines develop 2,300hp, and the single electric motor develops 1,500hp. It is possible to re-charge the electric fuel cells in 50 minutes.

U32

Type: German submarine
Displacement: 626 tonnes (616 tons) (surface), 745 tonnes (733 tons) (submerged)
Dimensions: 64.5m x 5.8m x 4.4m (211ft 8in x 19ft x 14ft 5in)
Machinery: Twin screws, diesel engines

(surface), electric motors (submerged)
Top speed: 16 knots (surface), 8 knots (submerged)
Main armament: One

88mm (3.5in) gun, five 533mm (21in) torpedo tubes
Launched: April 1937

U32 was one of the first of the Type VII ocean-going submarines and was used as the basis for all later construction. The class were compact, cheap and simple to build, easy to operate and reliable. Between 1941 and 1943 they came close to defeating Britain. *U32* was sunk in October 1940.

U140

Type: German submarine
Displacement: 1,960 tonnes (1,930 tons) (surface), 2,522 tonnes (2,483 tons) (submerged)
Dimensions: 92m x 9m x 5.3m (301ft 10in x 29ft 10in x 17ft 4in)
Machinery: Twin screws, diesel engines (surface), electric motors (submerged)
Top speed: 15.5 knots (surface), 7.5 knots (submerged)
Main armament: Two 150mm (5.9in) guns, six 500mm (19.7in) torpedo tubes
Launched: November 1917

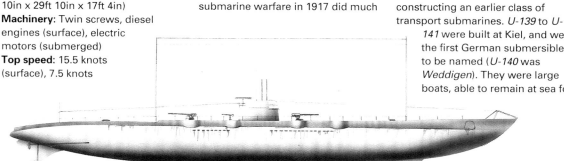

The resumption of unrestricted submarine warfare in 1917 did much to bring the United States into the war. At that time, the Germans were faced with a lack of suitable boats with the range to operate off the US coast. In 1918 they built a class of four long-range boats, which used the experience gained in constructing an earlier class of transport submarines. *U-139* to *U-141* were built at Kiel, and were the first German submersibles to be named (*U-140* was *Weddigen*). They were large boats, able to remain at sea for long periods. Fitted with six torpedo tubes (four in the bow, two in the stern), they only had a limited supply of torpedoes. They were also equipped with two 150mm guns, situated fore and aft of the conning tower. The intention was for the submarine to surface if possible, and sink her merchant ship target with gunfire. *U-140* had a surfaced range of just over 26,600 km (14,000 miles) at 8 knots. Two diesels with electric drive gave 3,950hp, and the two electric motors developed 1,700hp. After the 1918 armistice, *U-139* was commissioned by the French Navy and retained until 1935. *U140* was sunk as a target in July 1921.

U2501

Type: German submarine
Displacement: 1,647 tonnes (1,621 tons) (surface), 2,100 tonnes (2,067 tons) (submerged)
Dimensions: 77m x 8m x 6.2m (251ft 8in x 26ft 3in x 20ft 4in)
Machinery: Twin screws, diesel engines (surface), electric motors (submerged)
Main armament: Four 30mm (1.2in) guns, six 533mm (21in) torpedo tubes
Launched: 1944

U2501, the first of the type XXIs, was a milestone in the development of the submarine, and a transitional step towards today's nuclear-powered vessels. She was a double-hulled, ocean-going vessel, with high submerged speed plus the capability to run silent at 3.5 knots. The outer hull was built of light plating to aid streamlining. The inner hull was formed from 28-37mm (1.1-1.5in) thick carbon steel plating. She had new, super-light batteries, and could maintain an underwater speed of 16 knots for one hour. At four knots the submarine could run submerged for three days on a single charge. By the end of World War II, 55 type XXI vessels had entered service. *U2501* was scuttled in 1945.

Uebi Scebeli

Type: Italian submarine
Displacement: 710 tonnes (698 tons) (surface), 880 tonnes (866 tons) (submerged)
Dimensions: 60m x 6.5m x 4.7m (197ft 6in x 21ft 2in x 15ft 4in)
Machinery: Twin screws, diesel engines (surface), electric motors (submerged)
Top speed: 14 knots (surface), 7.5 knots (submerged)
Main armament: One 100mm (3.9in) gun, six 533mm (21in) torpedo tubes
Launched: October 1937

Uebi Scebeli was a short-range, single-hull boat with ballast tanks amidships. She was one of the large '600' class that gave good service throughout World War II. There were minor differences between the submarines in the class as they were built in various yards. In the early 1940s, two were modified to carry small assault craft fitted inside watertight containers aft of the conning tower. Standard maximum diving depth was 80m (262ft), and surfaced range at 14 knots was 4,180km (2,200 miles). She was scuttled off Crete in 1940 after being hit by a depth charge.

Ugolini Vivaldi

Type: Italian destroyer
Displacement: 2,621 tonnes (2,580 tons)
Dimensions: 107.3m x 10.2m x 3.4m (352ft x 33ft 6in x 11ft 2in)
Machinery: Twin screws, turbines
Top speed: 38 knots
Main armament: Six 120mm (4.7in) guns
Launched: January 1929
Date of profile: 1932

Ugolini Vivaldi was one of a group of powerful destroyers authorised in 1926 and laid down in 1927/28. Slightly smaller than their French counterparts, the Chacal class, the Italian vessels carried the same armament and were several knots faster. Some vessels in the class achieved considerable speeds. *Alvise da Mosto* developed 70,000hp and reached 45 knots. *Ugolini Vivaldi* was damaged by German shore batteries off Sardinia in September 1943, and was finally sunk by German aircraft attack.

Ulpio Traiano

Type: Italian cruiser
Displacement: 5,420 tonnes (5,334 tons)
Dimensions: 143m x 14.4m x 4.9m (468ft 10in x 47ft 3in x 16ft)
Machinery: Twin screws, turbines
Main armament: Eight 135mm (5.3in) guns
Launched: 1942

Ulpio Traiano was one of a large class of super-fast cruisers built to counter the French destroyers of the Mogador and Le Fantasque classes, with their design speeds of up to 40 knots. The vessels in *Ulpio Traiano*'s class were initially limited to only 3,454 tonnes (3,400 tons) to keep costs down. Final designs produced a larger vessel, but with only 15mm (0.6in) thick protective plating on the bridge, and 20mm (0.8in) on the four twin turrets. Many vessels in the class were scrapped on the stocks, and only a few were completed. *Ulpio Traiano* was sunk by British human torpedoes while completing at Palermo harbour in 1943.

Unebi

Type: Japanese cruiser
Displacement: 3,672 tonnes (3,615 tons)
Dimensions: 98m x 13m x 5.7m (321ft 6in x 43ft x 18ft 9in)
Machinery: Twin screws, horizontal compound triple expansion engines
Main armament: Seven 150mm (5.9in), four 238mm (9.4in) guns
Launched: April 1886

Unebi was one of the most heavily armed cruisers to be built on a displacement of under 4,064 tonnes (4,000 tons). The 238mm (9.4in) guns were positioned on large sponsons and the 150mm (5.9in) guns were placed on the upper deck. After trials, *Unebi* was despatched to Japan, but before she could reach her destination she was caught in a typhoon and sank in October 1887.

Unicorn

Launched: November 1941

Type: British aircraft carrier
Displacement: 20,624 tonnes (20,300 tons)
Dimensions: 186m x 27.4m x 7.3m (610ft x 90ft x 24ft)
Machinery: Twin screws, turbines
Main armament: Eight 102mm (4in) guns
Aircraft: 36

Unicorn was built as part of the 1938 Naval Expansion Programme, and was intended to be a depot/maintenance support ship. She was modified during construction so that she could operate her own aircraft, as well as maintain aircraft from other carriers. Her engines developed 40,000hp, and range at 13 knots was 20,900km (11,000 miles). During World War II she served in the Mediterranean, then on Atlantic patrols, before moving to the Pacific. She later became a depot ship in Hong Kong, and was scrapped in 1959/60.

Union

Type: Peruvian cruiser
Displacement: 1,727 tonnes (1,700 tons)
Dimensions: 67m x 9m x 4.8m (220ft x 30ft x 16ft)
Machinery: Single screw, single expansion engine
Top speed: 14 knots
Main armament: Fourteen 30-pounder rifled guns
Launched: 1865

Union was one of a quartet of fast cruisers ordered from France by the Confederate Navy for use as commerce raiders. While nearing completion, the French authorities refused to allow the vessels to leave for America, and two were sold to Germany and two to Peru. *Union* took part in many actions during Peru's war with Chile (1879-83), and after the loss of *Huascar*, was Peru's only surviving seagoing warship. She was scuttled at Callao in 1881 to prevent her capture by the Chileans.

Upholder

Type: British submarine
Displacement: 2,220 tonnes (2,185 tons) (surface), 2,494 tonnes (2,455 tons) (submerged)
Dimensions: 70.3m x 7.6m x 5.5m (230ft 8in x 25ft x 18ft)
Machinery: Single screw, diesel engine (surface), electric motors (submerged)
Top speed: 12 knots (surface), 20 knots (submerged)
Main armament: Six 533mm (21in) torpedo tubes
Launched: December 1986

By the end of the 1970s, the Royal Navy was in need of a non-nuclear-powered patrol submarine – the previous diesel powered class having proved successful and quieter than their nuclear counterparts. Her teardrop-shaped hull is single-skinned. The high tensile steel of the hull gives her the strength to reach depths of 200m (656ft). She carries Tigerfish and Spearfish torpedoes.

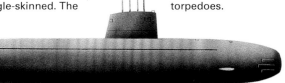

Uragan

Type: Russian torpedo boat
Displacement: 629 tonnes (619 tons)
Dimensions: 71.5m x 7.4m x 2.6m (234ft 7in x 24ft 9in c 8ft 6in)

Machinery: Twin screws, turbines
Top speed: 24 knots
Main armament: Three 102mm (4in) guns

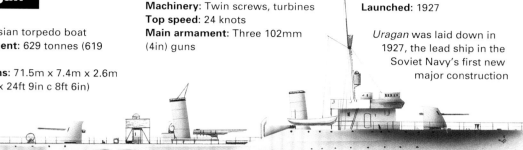

Launched: 1927

Uragan was laid down in 1927, the lead ship in the Soviet Navy's first new major construction

programme. Eighteen ships were ordered but only 12 were laid down, with the remaining six being held over for five years. Their engines developed 6,300hp and designed speed (unattained) was 29 knots. Additional anti-aircraft armament was added before World War II, and complement was increased from 70 to 108. All served in the war. Many survived, including *Uragan*. She was discarded in 1959.

Urania

Type: Italian cruiser
Displacement: 946 tonnes (931 tons)
Dimensions: 73.1m x 8.2m x 3.6m (239ft 9in x 27ft x 11ft 9in)

Machinery: Twin screws, triple expansion engines
Main armament: One 119mm (4.7in)

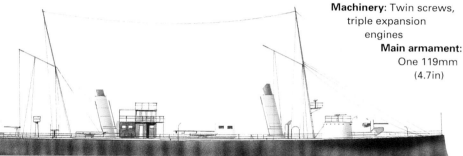

gun, six 450mm (17.7in) torpedo tubes
Launched: June 1891

Urania was one in a large group of small torpedo cruisers designed as improved versions of *Tripoli*. All differed in minor detail, with *Caprera* having two 119mm (4.7in) guns. *Urania* was laid down at Genoa in 1889 and was completed in July 1893. She was discarded in 1912.

Vanderbilt

Type: US liner
Displacement: 3,413 tonnes (3,360 tons)
Dimensions: 100m x 14.5m (331ft x 47ft 6in)
Machinery: Paddle wheels, single beam engine
Top speed: 14 knots

Launched: 1857

When first completed for the North Atlantic Mail

Steamship Line, *Vanderbilt* was one of the largest and fastest and most luxurious liners on the route. In March 1862 she was taken over by the US Navy and sent on a year-long patrol in search of the elusive Confederate vessel *Alabama*. After an overhaul, she was sent out again, sometimes missing *Alabama* by only a few hours. She was retained in the US Navy until 1873, then sold to a shipping company. They removed her machinery and gave her a full rig. Re-named *Three Brothers*, she then spent most of the rest of her career in the grain trade. She was scrapped in 1899.

Vanguard

Type: British battleship
Displacement: 6,106 tonnes (6,010 tons)
Dimensions: 85.3m x 16.4m x 6.8m (280ft x 54ft x 22ft 7in)
Machinery: Twin screws, horizontal return connecting rod engines
Main armament: Four 152mm (6in), ten 228mm (9in) guns

Armour: 152-203mm (6-8in) belt, 203-254mm (8-10in) teak backing, 152mm (6in) on battery
Launched: 1870

Vanguard was a successful central battery ship built for overseas service, where

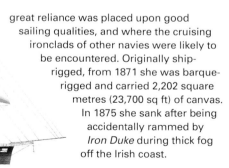

great reliance was placed upon good sailing qualities, and where the cruising ironclads of other navies were likely to be encountered. Originally ship-rigged, from 1871 she was barque-rigged and carried 2,202 square metres (23,700 sq ft) of canvas. In 1875 she sank after being accidentally rammed by *Iron Duke* during thick fog off the Irish coast.

Vanguard

Type: British battleship
Displacement: 52,243 tonnes (51,420 tons)
Dimensions: 248m x 32.9m x 10.9m (813ft 8in x 108ft x 36ft)
Machinery: Quadruple screws, turbines

Top speed: 30 knots
Main armament: Sixteen 140mm (5.5in), eight 381mm (15in) guns
Armour: 114-355mm

(4.5-14in) belt, 152-330mm (6-13in) on main turrets, 280-330mm (11-13in) on barbettes
Launched: 1944

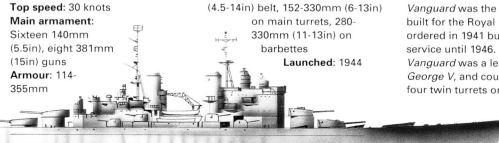

Vanguard was the last battleship built for the Royal Navy. She was ordered in 1941 but didn't enter service until 1946. Basically, *Vanguard* was a lengthened *King George V*, and could accommodate four twin turrets on the centreline. She was sold for scrap in 1960.

Vanguard

Type: British submarine
Displacement: 15,240 tonnes (15,000 tons) (submerged)
Dimensions: 148m x 12.8m x 12m (486ft 6in x 42ft x 39ft 4in)
Machinery: Single screw, pressurised water-cooled nuclear reactor
Top speed: 25+ knots (submerged)
Main armament: Sixteen Trident D5 missiles, four 533mm (21in) torpedo tubes
Launched: 1990

In 1980 the British government were faced with the need to replace their ageing Resolution class submarines and their Polaris nuclear ballistic

missile system. They decided to build a class of much larger boats, carrying the more powerful Trident missile. HMS Vanguard is the lead ship of this class, and carries 16 missiles in vertical launch tubes aft of the sail. The original plan was to operate the Trident C-4 missile, but this was later changed to the larger D-5 when the US Navy decided to upgrade. Each missile can carry up to 14 warheads to targets more than 12,350km (6,500 miles) distant,

giving each submarine a fearsome destructive capability. Vanguard is larger than any previous British submarine, although smaller then the US Ohio and Russian Typhoon ballistic missile boats. Vanguard was laid down in September 1986. Her machinery develops 27,500hp, and she is scheduled to need a refit and re-coring of the nuclear reactor every eight years. Like all submarines of this type, she is expected to operate independently for long periods,

remaining undetected and submerged for many months at a time. The increased range of Trident over Polaris gives her a much greater choice of patrol area, thus reducing the chances of detection. The original plan was to buy four of these boats to provide one on station at all times, but budget problems and the end of the Cold War may change this.

Varese

Type: Italian cruiser
Displacement: 8,230 tonnes (8,100 tons)
Dimensions: 111.8m x 18.2m x 7.3m (366ft 9in x 59ft 9in x 24ft)
Machinery: Twin screws, vertical triple expansion engines

Main armament: Fourteen 152mm (6in), two 203mm (8in), one 254mm guns(10in)
Armour: 102-152mm (4-6in) belt, 152mm (6in) on turrets and battery
Launched: 1899

Varese was part of a group of successful Italian cruisers, and individual units were eagerly snapped up by foreign navies whenever one became available for sale. Varese and her sisters combined high speed with excellent protection and a powerful armament. Designed by Engineer Masdea, the vessels were often classified as second-class battleships in navy lists of the period. Two of

the class served with the Japanese Battle Fleet during the Russo-Japanese War of 1904/05, after the Japanese had lost two of their own battleships to Russian mines. The 254mm (10in) gun was housed in a single turret forward, with the 203mm (8in) guns being positioned in a twin turret aft. Ten of the 152mm (6in) weapons were in a battery on the main deck, with four more behind shields on the upper deck, level with each of the funnels. Varese was discarded in 1923.

Variag

Type: Russian cruiser
Displacement: 6,604 tonnes (6,500 tons)
Dimensions: 129.5m x 15.8m x 6.3m (425ft x 52ft x 20ft 8in)
Machinery: Twin screws, vertical triple expansion engines
Top speed: 23 knots
Main armament: Twelve 152mm (6in) guns
Launched: October 1899
Date of profile: 1903

Variag was one of three cruisers ordered as part of the Russian naval programme of 1898 to evaluate which type of 152mm (6in) gunned cruiser to introduce into the Russian Navy. Variag was built in the USA

and was completed in 1900. Although she was not accepted as a general type for the navy, she was a fast, powerful vessel, and was ideal as a short-range scout with the battle fleet.

The Japanese sunk her in 1904, raising her and re-naming her Soya. She was scrapped in 1921.

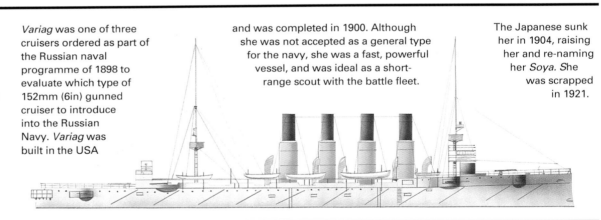

VAS 205

Type: Italian anti-submarine launch
Displacement: 70 tonnes (69.4 tons)
Dimensions: 28m x 4.3m x 1.5m (91ft 10in x 14ft x 4ft 5in)
Machinery:

Twin screws, petrol engines
Top speed: 19 knots

Main armament: Two 20mm (0.8in) guns, two 450mm (17.7in) torpedo tubes

Launched: 1942

A large number of anti-submarine launches were laid down in 1941, and eventually classified in three basic groups. VAS 205 was one of the first group, and was designed as a submarine chaser, armed with

torpedoes to enable her to attack surfaced vessels near the coast. The Fiat petrol engine developed 1,620hp, and her Carraro engine developed 300hp. Fuel capacity was 11.7 tonnes (11.5 tons). Thirty depth charges were carried. Range on main engines at 19 knots was 665km (350 miles), and on auxiliary engines at 12 knots was 2,470km (1,300 miles). She was completed in 1942, and scuttled by the Germans at Naples in 1943.

VAS 301

Type: Italian anti-submarine launch
Displacement: 91 tonnes (90 tons)
Dimensions: 30m x 4.5m x 4m (98ft 5in x 14ft 9in x 13ft 2in)
Machinery: Triple screws, diesel engines
Main armament: Two 20mm (0.8in) guns, two 450mm torpedo tubes (17.7in)
Launched: 1942

VAS 301 was the first of the final batch of Vedette Antisommergibili. She was laid down in January 1942 and delivered in September the same year. She had a round, steel bilge hull and was fitted with three 350hp Fiat diesel engines. Range at 14 knots was 1,450km (900 miles). The torpedo tubes were on fixed mounts just before the bridge. The secondary armament of each vessel in the class varied. The entire class was captured in 1943. *VAS 301* was taken into the German Navy as *RA 254*, and was scuttled at Genoa on 25 April 1945.

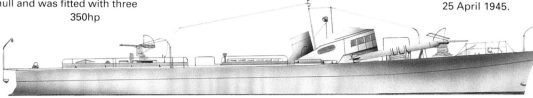

Vasco da Gama

Type: Portuguese battleship
Displacement: 2,518 tonnes (2,479 tons)
Dimensions: 65.8m x 12m x 5.4m (216ft x 40ft x 18ft)
Machinery: Twin screws, compound engines
Main armament: One 152mm (6in), two 260mm (10.2in), two 40-pounder guns
Armour: 228mm (9in) belt and (10in) battery, 254mm wood backing
Launched: 1875

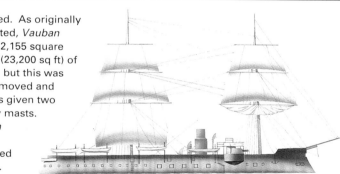

Vasco da Gama was Portugal's only capital ship, and was originally intended primarily for the defence of Lisbon. She was built by the Thames Ironworks, London, and was a compact and powerful vessel. Her octagonal battery rose up above the main deck, housing the two 260mm (10.2in) guns. It had a 0.9-metre (3ft) overhang on each side, so providing axial fire. In the 1890s the rig was reduced to two masts. Between 1901 and 1903 she underwent a major refit, which included new armament and structural modifications.

Vauban

Type: French battleship
Displacement: 6,210 tonnes (6,112 tons)
Dimensions: 81m x 17.5m x 7.7m (265ft 9in x 57ft 3in x 25ft 3in)
Machinery: Twin screws, vertical compound engines
Top speed: 14.5 knots
Main armament: Six 150mm (5.9in), one 190mm (7.5in), four 238mm (9.4in) guns
Armour: 150-254mm (5.9-10in) belt, 198mm (7.8in) on barbette
Launched: July 1882
Date of profile: 1885

The French battleship *Vauban* was the epitome of the French ironclad cruising ship. She was based on the preceding Bayard class, but instead of having a wooden hull, she had a steel hull, sheathed with wood and coppered. As originally completed, *Vauban* carried 2,155 square metres (23,200 sq ft) of canvas, but this was later removed and she was given two military masts. *Vauban* was discarded in 1905.

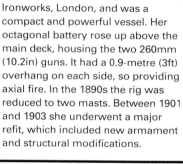

Vedetta

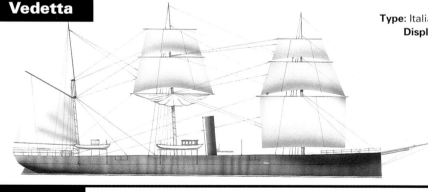

Type: Italian sloop
Displacement: 827 tonnes (814 tons)
Dimensions: 56m x 8.2m x 3.5m (184ft 6in x 27ft x 11ft 8in)
Machinery: Single screw, reciprocating engine
Main armament: Four 120mm (4.7in) guns
Launched: 1866

Vedetta was the first iron-hulled warship to be built for Italy, laid down in 1862 and completed in 1869. She was barque rigged, with all guns mounted on the upper deck. Engines developed 670hp, coal supply was 139 tonnes (137 tons), and range at nine knots was 1,900km (1,000 miles). She became a depot ship in 1901, and was discarded in 1903 and finally transferred for preservation at the Garaventa Institute, Genoa.

Velella

Type: Italian submarine
Displacement: 806 tonnes (794 tons) (surface), 1,034 tonnes (1,018 tons) (submerged)
Dimensions: 63m x 6.9m x 4.5m (207ft x 22ft 9in x 14ft 8in)
Machinery: Twin screws, diesel engines (surface), electric motors (submerged)
Top speed: 14 knots (surface), 8 knots (submerged)
Main armament: One 100mm (3.9in) gun, six 533mm (21in) torpedo tubes
Launched: 1936

Velella was originally laid down for Portugal in 1931. However, when the contract was cancelled *Velella* and a sister ship were acquired by the Italian Navy. *Velella* was completed in 1937. She served in World War II, but was sunk by the British submarine *Shakespeare* in 1943 in the Gulf of Salerno.

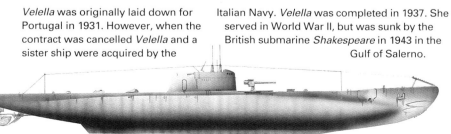

Venezia

Type: Italian cruiser
Displacement: 4,487 tonnes (4,417 tons)
Dimensions: 130.6m x 12.8m x 5.3m (428ft 6in x 42ft x 17ft 4in)
Machinery: Twin screws, turbines
Top speed: 27 knots
Main armament: Nine 100mm (3.9in) guns
Launched: October 1912

Venezia was formerly the fast scout *Saida*, completed for Austria in May 1914 and acquired by Italy in September 1920. One 100mm (3.9in) gun was positioned on the forecastle with two more aft and the rest in the waist of the ship on each broadside. She had a strip of 60mm (2.4in) thick armour at the waterline, and 20mm (0.8in) on the armoured deck. Range at 24 knots was 3,040km (1,600 miles), and at full speed was 1,634km (860 miles). After an extensive refit, *Venezia* entered the Italian Navy in 1921. She became an accommodation ship in 1930, and was stricken in 1937.

Vesuvio

Type: Italian cruiser
Displacement: 3,481 tonnes (3,427 tons)

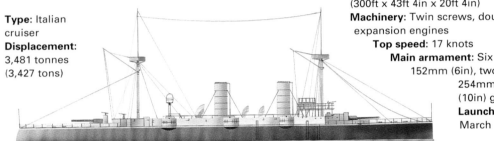

Dimensions: 91m x 13.2m x 6.2m (300ft x 43ft 4in x 20ft 4in)
Machinery: Twin screws, double expansion engines
Top speed: 17 knots
Main armament: Six 152mm (6in), two 254mm (10in) guns
Launched: March 1886

Vesuvio was one of four units in a class that was a follow-on from the highly successful British-built *Giovanni Bausan*, the first modern cruiser constructed for the Italian Navy. *Vesuvio* was a fine example of the protected cruiser as built in the 1880s, combining a powerful armament with speed. She was designed by Engineer Vigna. Her engines developed 6,820hp, and her endurance at 10 knots was approximately 9,500km (5,000 miles). The heavy 254mm (10in) guns were later abandoned in favour of 152mm (6in) quick-firers. *Vesuvio* was discarded in 1911.

Vesuvius

Type: US cruiser
Displacement: 944 tonnes (929 tons)
Dimensions: 76.9m x 8m x 2.7m (252ft 4in x 26ft 5in x 9ft)
Machinery: Twin screws, vertical triple expansion engines
Top speed: 21.6 knots
Main armament: Three 381mm (15in) dynamite guns
Launched: April 1888

Vesuvius was the only warship in the world to be fitted with the dynamite gun. The three guns were carried side-by-side in the bows. Each shell weighed 444kg (980lb), and carried a 226kg (500lb) charge of dynamite. Each gun was 16.7m (55ft) long, and ten shells were carried for each gun. Basic range was 1,554m (1,700yd). She was later used for experimental work with torpedoes. She was sold in 1921.

Vettor Pisani

Type: Italian cruiser
Displacement: 7,357 tonnes 7,242 tons)
Dimensions: 105.7m x 18m x 7.5m (346ft 9in x 59ft x 24ft 7in)
Machinery: Twin screws,

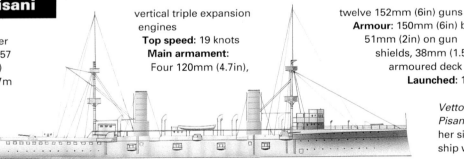

vertical triple expansion engines
Top speed: 19 knots
Main armament: Four 120mm (4.7in), twelve 152mm (6in) guns
Armour: 150mm (6in) belt, 51mm (2in) on gun shields, 38mm (1.5in) armoured deck
Launched: 1895

Vettor Pisani and her sister ship were a follow-on pair to Italy's first armoured cruiser, *Marco Polo*, completed in 1894. Like *Marco Polo*, the main armament of the new vessels consisted of 152mm (6in) guns. *Vettor Pisani* was laid down in 1892 at La Spezia Naval Dockyard. She was completed in April 1899 and discarded in 1920. Her sister, *Carlo Alberto*, was used in 1902 during experiments for Marconi's radio.

Viborg

Type: Russian torpedo boat
Displacement: 169 tonnes (166 tons)
Dimensions: 43.4m x 5m x 2m (142ft 6in x 17ft x 7ft)
Machinery: Twin screws, vertical compound engines
Top speed: 20 knots
Main armament: Three 381mm (15in) torpedo tubes

Launched: 1886

Viborg was the largest torpedo boat of her period. She was built at Thompson's Yard, Clydebank, Scotland, specialists at constructing this type of vessel. Two 37mm (1.5in) revolving Hotchkiss cannon were placed forward, abreast of the funnels. The forward part of her turtle deck was thickly plated in front of the conning tower. *Viborg* was discarded in 1910.

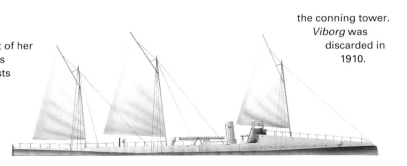

Victor III

Type: Russian submarine
Displacement: 6,400 tonnes (6,300 tons) (submerged)
Dimensions: 104m x 10m x 7m (347ft 9in x 32ft 10in x 23ft)
Machinery: Single screw, pressurised water-cooled nuclear reactor, turbines
Top speed: 30 knots
Main armament: Six 533mm (21in) torpedo tubes
Launched: 1978

The 1960 introduction of the first American ballistic missile submarine, the *George Washington*, posed major

problems for the Soviet Navy, and caused a significant upgrade of anti-submarine warfare capability. One result of this was the introduction of a new class of nuclear-powered hunter-killer submarine, given the NATO codename Victor. This was an ambitious programme, with a completely new reactor design and a broad streamlined teardrop hull. They have a long sail which is blended into the hull, and strenuous

attempts were made to quieten the machinery. The Victor II was an improved version introduced in 1972. This class had the hull and sail covered by a coating of sound-absorbing rubber tiles to reduce the chance of detection. They were also capable of operating the nuclear-tipped SS-N 15 anti-submarine missile. In 1978, this variant was in turn

superseded by the Victor III, which had an improved sonar fit and could fire the SS-N-16 missile. This delivers a conventional homing torpedo to a greater range than is otherwise possible. There have been more than 43 Victors of all types produced, at least 20 of them the more capable Victor III. Recent production had shifted to the Akula class, but financial troubles in post-Soviet Russia are hindering construction.

Victoria

Type: Australian gunboat
Displacement: 538 tonnes (530 tons)
Dimensions: 42m x 8.2m x 3.3m (140ft x 27ft x 11ft)
Machinery: Twin screws, compound engines
Top speed: 12 knots
Main armament: One 254mm (10in) gun
Launched: 1883

During the 1880s, Britain's Australian colony began to build up a sizeable navy for local defence. As Australia had no suitable construction facilities, the new additions were built in

Britain. *Victoria* was a steel-hulled vessel armed with a single 254mm (10in) gun mounted forward behind a raised bulwark. The entire vessel had to be turned in order to train the gun on its target. Engines developed 800hp and coal supply was 91 tonnes (90 tons). Although relatively small, vessels such as *Victoria* proved a useful deterrent against raiding cruisers, which could not afford to run the risk of being badly damaged so far from home. She was sold in 1896.

Victorian

Type: British liner
Displacement: 10,805 tonnes (10,635 tons)
Dimensions: 158.5m x 18m (520ft x 60ft)
Machinery: Triple screws, turbines
Top speed: 19 knots
Launched: 1905

Victorian was the first triple screw, turbine-driven liner in service on the North Atlantic.

She was ordered in 1903 for the Allan Line and was among the fastest liners on the route, well able to

maintain 18 knots. *Victorian* had accommodation for 346 first-class, 344 second-class, and 1,000 third-class passengers, and served between Liverpool, England, and various Canadian ports. In 1914 she became an auxiliary cruiser and was armed with eight 120mm (4.7in) guns. Later she was given six 152mm (6in)

weapons. In 1920 she was returned to her owners, and two years later she was given new machinery. She was scrapped in 1929.

Vincenzo Gioberti

Type: Italian destroyer
Displacement: 2,326 tonnes (2,290 tons)
Dimensions: 106.7m x 10m x 3.4m (350ft x 33ft 4in x 11ft 3in)
Machinery: Twin screws, turbines
Top speed: 39 knots
Main armament: Four 120mm (4.7in) guns
Launched: September 1936

Vincenzo Gioberti was one unit in a class of four vessels that were repeats of the Maestrale class, but which had increased power. The 120mm (4.7in) guns were in twin

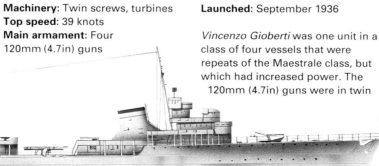

mounts, one forward and one aft on the raised superstructure. Six 533mm (21in) torpedo tubes were mounted on triple carriages down the centreline. She also had eight 13.2mm (5.2in) weapons, later replaced by 20mm (0.8in) anti-aircraft guns. She was laid down by Odero-Terni-Orlando of Leghorn in January 1936, and was completed in October 1937. On 9 August 1943 she was sunk by a torpedo fired from the British submarine *Simoon*.

Vincenzo Giordano Orsini

Type: Italian destroyer
Displacement: 864 tonnes (850 tons)
Dimensions: 73.5m x 7.3m x 2.8m (241ft x 24ft x 9ft)
Machinery: Twin screws, turbines
Top speed: 33.6 knots
Main armament: Six 102mm (4in), four 500mm (17.7in) torpedo tubes
Launched: April 1917
Date of profile: 1918

Vincenzo Giordano Orsini was one of a quartet of fast destroyers that were improved versions of the Pilo class. A higher-calibre gun armament was now carried, plus twin torpedo mountings. Engines developed 15,000hp, and range at 14 knots was 3,800km (2,000 miles) or 760km (400 miles)

at 29 knots. All vessels in the class were re-classified as torpedo boats in 1929. *Vincenzo Giordano Orsini* was scuttled on 8 April 1941.

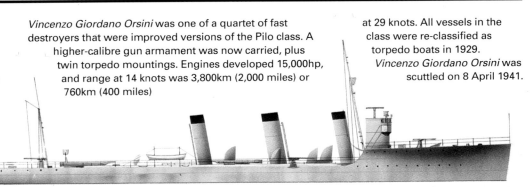

Viper

Type: British destroyer
Displacement: 350 tonnes (344 tons)
Dimensions: 64m x 6.4m x 3.8m (210ft 3in x 21ft x 12ft 6in)

Machinery: Eight screws, turbines
Top speed: 37 knots
Main armament: One 12-pounder gun, two 457mm (18in) torpedo tubes
Launched: September 1899
Date of profile: 1899

Viper was the world's first turbine-driven warship. The principle of the turbine had been known for centuries, but it was not until the 1880s that Charles Parsons succeeded in making practical use of a steam turbine. *Viper* had eight screws on four shafts, and on a three-hour trial she developed 1,041hp for 33.9 knots. She had not been in service long when she ran aground in a thick mist off the Channel Islands in August 1901.

Vitoria

Type: Spanish battleship
Displacement: 7,250 tonnes (7,135 tons)
Dimensions: 96.3m x 17.3m x 8m (316ft 2in x 57ft x 26ft 3in)
Machinery: Single screw, single compound engine
Top speed: 12.5 knots
Main armament: Thirty 68-pounder guns

Launched: November 1865
Date of profile: 1688

Upon her completion in 1867, *Vitoria* helped to push Spain into fifth place among the world's naval powers behind Britain, France, Italy and Austria. She was an iron-hulled, broadside frigate with a ram bow and all her guns mounted on the main deck. She was re-built in France in 1897/98 and was given quick-firing guns. She was stricken in 1912.

Vittorio Emanuele

Type: Italian battleship
Displacement: 12,800 (12,600 tons) (approx) tonnes
Dimensions: 144.6m x 22.4m x 8m (474ft 4in x 73ft 6in x 26ft 3in) (approx)
Machinery: Twin screws, vertical triple expansion

engines
Top speed: 21.3 knots
Main armament: Sixteen 76mm (3in), twelve 203mm (8in), two 305mm (12in) guns
Launched: October 1904
Date of profile: 1908

Vittorio Emanuele was one of a quartet of battleships built to a revolutionary design which combined a powerful

armament with good protection and high speed on a relatively light displacement. The 305mm (12in) guns were mounted in single turrets, one forward and one aft, and the 203mm (8in) guns were in twin turrets at main deck level. *Vittorio Emanuele* was laid down in 1901 and completed in 1908. She was removed from service in 1923.

Vittorio Veneto

Type: Italian battleship
Displacement: 46,484 tonnes (45,752 tons)
Dimensions: 237.8m x 32.9m x 9.6m (780ft 2in x 108ft x 31ft 6in)
Machinery: Quadruple screws, turbines

Top speed: 31.4 knots
Main armament: Twelve 89mm (3.5in), four 120mm (4.7in), twelve 152mm (6in), nine 381mm (15in) guns

Launched: July 1937
Date of profile: 1941

Vittorio Veneto was badly damaged several times during World War II. When Italy joined the Allies, she was laid up in the Suez Canal. She was broken up between 1948 and 1950.

Vittorio Veneto

Type: Italian helicopter cruiser
Displacement: 8,991 tonnes (8,850 tons)
Dimensions: 179.5m x 19.4m x 6m (589ft x 63ft 8in x 19ft 8in)
Machinery: Twin screws, turbines
Top speed: 32 knots
Main armament: Twelve 40mm (1.6in), eight 76mm

(3in) guns, four Teseo SAM launchers, one ASROC launcher
Aircraft: Nine helicopters
Launched: February 1967

Vittorio Veneto was a purpose-built helicopter cruiser that followed on from the smaller

Andrea Doria class of the 1950s. The addition of a second deck aft gave her greater hangar capacity. A large central lift is set immediately aft of the superstructure, and two sets of fin stabilisers make her a steady helicopter platform. Laid down in 1965 and completed in 1969, the ship underwent a major refit between 1981 and 1984.

Volage

Type: British cruiser
Displacement: 3,129 tonnes (3,080 tons)
Dimensions: 82.2m x 12.8m x 6.7m (270ft x 42ft x 22ft)
Machinery: Single screw, horizontal single expansion engine
Main armament: Six 178mm (7in), four 64-pounder guns

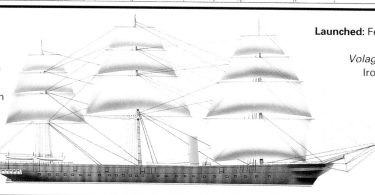

Launched: February 1869

Volage was laid down in 1867 at the Thames Ironworks, London. The slide-mounted 178mm (7in) guns were carried in the waist on the broadside; two 64-pounders were also in the waist, with the other two forward as chase guns. *Volage* carried 1,475 square metres (16,593 sq ft) of canvas and made 13 knots under sail. Her engines developed 4,530hp. She was sold in 1904.

Volframio

Type: Italian submarine
Displacement: 726 tonnes (715 tons) (surface), 883 tonnes (870 tons) (submerged)
Dimensions: 60m x 6.4m x 4.7m (197ft 6in x 21ft 2in x 15ft 8in)
Machinery: Twin screws, diesel engines (surface), electric motors (submerged)
Top speed: 14 knots (surface), 7.3

knots (submerged)
Main armament: One 100mm (3.9in) gun, six 533mm (21in) torpedo tubes
Launched: November 1941

Volframio was one of a class of 13 boats developed from the '600' class. Diving depth was 80m (262ft), and fuel supply was 41

tonnes (41 tons). Her diesel engines developed 1,400hp and her electric motors produced 800hp. Range surfaced at full speed was 4,370km (2,300 miles), and at 8.5 knots was

9,500km (5,000 miles). Submerged range at seven knots was 13km (7 miles), and at three knots was 152km (80 miles). She was scuttled at La Spezia in 1943, refloated by the Germans and finally sunk in 1944.

Von der Tann

Type: German battlecruiser
Displacement: 22,150 tonnes (21,802 tons)
Dimensions: 172m x 26.6m x 8m (563ft 4in x 87ft 3in x 26ft 7in)

Machinery: Quadruple screws, turbines
Top speed: 27.7 knots
Main armament: Ten 150mm (5.9in), eight 280mm (11in) guns

Armour: 100-248mm belt, 228mm on barbettes and turrets
Launched: March 1909

Von der Tann was Germany's first battlecruiser, and the first major German warship to

have turbines. Her protection was good, and though she was hit by four shells at the Battle of Jutland in 1916, which caused severe fire and put all her main guns out of action, she reached home without difficulty. She was surrendered at the end of World War I, and scuttled at Scapa Flow in June 1919. She was raised in December 1930, and was broken up at Rosyth between 1931 and 1934.

Voragine

Type: Italian armoured battery
Displacement: 2,389 tonnes (2,352 tons)
Dimensions: 56m x 14.4m x 4.2m (183ft 9in x 47ft 4in x 14ft)
Machinery: Single screw, single expansion engine
Top speed: 6.9 knots
Main armament: Twelve guns

Armour: 140mm (5.5in) on battery and waterline
Launched: June 1866

Voragine was built at La Foca, Genoa, for coastal defence purposes. The guns were positioned in a large raised battery amidships. Engines developed 588hp, and a light rig was carried for steadying sails. She was discarded in March 1875. A sister vessel, *Guerriera*, was launched in May 1866.

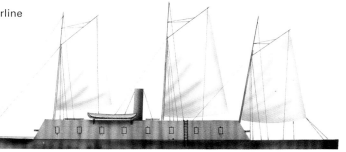

Vulcan

Type: British torpedo depot ship
Displacement: 6,705 tonnes (6,000 tons)
Dimensions: 113.6m x 17.6m x 6.7m (373ft x 58ft x 22ft)
Machinery: Twin screws, triple expansion engines
Top speed: 20 knots
Main armament: Eight 120mm (4.7in) guns
Launched: June 1889
Date of profile: 1898

Vulcan was the world's first purpose-built torpedo depot ship. She was designed to

accompany the main fleet and launch her squadron of six second-class torpedo boats at the first suitable opportunity. Her boats were normally stowed on cross-trees on the upper deck, aft of the two funnels. They were launched and retrieved by the two large goose-necked cranes in the centre of the hull. She could also act as a depot and resupply ship to other torpedo boats as the situation required. She had a full length armoured deck, 64mm (2.5in) thick on the flat, and 128mm (5in) thick on the slopes and engine hatches. She had a reasonable armament of eight 120mm (4.7in) guns, two positioned forward of the bridge, two down each side and two more aft. Her engines developed 12,000hp from four double-ended boilers. A further boiler provided steam to power the machinery in the vessel's repair shop. *Vulcan* became a training hulk in 1931 and was finally broken up in 1955.

W2

Type: Italian submarine
Displacement: 336 tonnes (331 tons) (surface), 507 tonnes (499 tons) (submerged)
Dimensions: 52.4m x 4.7m x 2.7m (172ft x 15ft 5in x 8ft 10in)
Machinery: Twin screws, diesel engines (surface), electric motors (submerged)
Main armament: Two 457mm (18in) torpedo tubes plus external drop collars for four

457mm (18in) torpedoes
Launched: February 1915

Following a visit to Fiat-San Giorgio in 1911, a British Admiralty team then went to the Schneider yard at Toulon to study

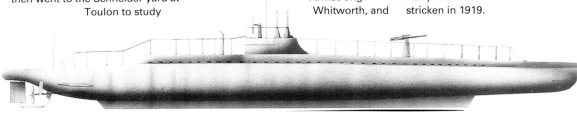

designs using the advanced double-hull system of construction, plus drop collars for torpedoes. As a result, *W1* and *W2* were ordered from Armstrong Whitworth, and

W2 was laid down in 1913. By 1916 the Royal Navy had a surplus of non-standard medium-sized submarines, and so in August *W1* and *W2* were both handed over to the Italian Navy. *W2* was stricken in 1919.

Wacht

Type: German cruiser
Displacement: 1,498 tonnes (1,475 tons)
Dimensions: 85.5m x 9.6m x 4.6m (280ft 6in x 31ft 6in x 15ft 4in)
Machinery: Twin screws,

double expansion engines
Top speed: 19.6 knots
Main armament: Three 105mm (4.1in) guns
Launched: August 1887
Date of profile: 1892

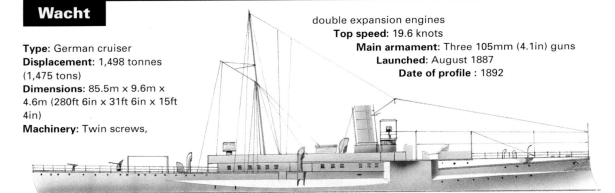

Wacht was designed for service in the North Sea and the Baltic. She carried a relatively heavy armament for her displacement, plus three 350mm (13.8in) torpedo tubes. Two of the 105mm (4.1in) guns were mounted side by side next to the bridge, with the remaining gun mounted aft. She was later re-armed with 88mm (3.5) weapons. *Wacht* was lost in the Baltic on 4 September 1901 after colliding with the German battleship *Sachsen*.

Wallaroo

Type: Australian cruiser
Displacement: 2,616 tonnes (2,575 tons)
Dimensions: 85m x 12.5m x 4.7m (278ft x 41ft x 15ft 6in)
Machinery: Twin screws, triple expansion engines
Main armament: Eight 120mm (4.7in) guns

Launched: February 1890

Wallaroo was a P class vessel laid down in the late 1880s. Under the terms of the Imperial

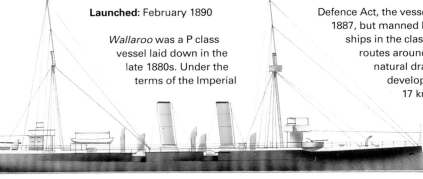

Defence Act, the vessels were paid for by Australia in 1887, but manned by Royal Navy personnel. All five ships in the class were sent to patrol the trade routes around Australia's coastline. Under natural draught, *Wallaroo*'s engines developed 4,000hp and gave a speed of 17 knots. Under forced draught, engines developed 7,500hp and gave 19 knots. She was sold for breaking up in 1920, but she was retained and became the hulk *Wallington* in 1949.

Walrus

Type: US submarine
Displacement: 398 tonnes (392 tons) (surface), 530 tonnes (521 tons) (submerged)

Dimensions: 47m x 5m x 4m (153ft 10in x 16ft 9in x 13ft 2in)
Machinery: Twin screws, diesel engines (surface), electric motors (submerged)

Top speed: 14 knots (surface), 10.5 knots (submerged)
Main armament: Four 457mm (18in) torpedo tubes
Launched: March 1914

Walrus was one of an eight-unit class developed from earlier classes. There was trouble at first with the

NLSE diesel engines, and in spite of complete overhauls, this persisted in three of the group. Diesel engines developed 950hp, electric motors developed 680hp. Surfaced range at 10 knots was 5,396km (2,406 miles), and diving depth was 61m (200ft). *Walrus*, the last US submarine to have a name for many years to come, was later numbered *K4*. She served in the Azores during World War I, and was broken up in 1931.

Walrus

Type: Dutch submarine
Displacement: 2,490 tonnes (2,450 tons) (surface), 2,800 tonnes (2,800 tons) (submerged)
Dimensions: 67.5m x 8.4m x 6.6m (222ft x 27ft7in x 21ft 8in)
Machinery: Single screw, diesel engines (surface), electric motors (submerged)
Top speed: 13 knots (surface), 20

knots (submerged)
Main armament: Four 533mm (21in) torpedo tubes
Launched: October 1985

Walrus was the first of a new type of advanced submarine. She was laid down in October 1979, but not completed until 1991 because in August 1986 a

fire gutted her internally. This also delayed the completion of three follow-on boats, and *Zeeleeuw*, commissioned in 1989, became the class leader. The use of high-tensile steel gave a diving depth of 300m (985ft), an

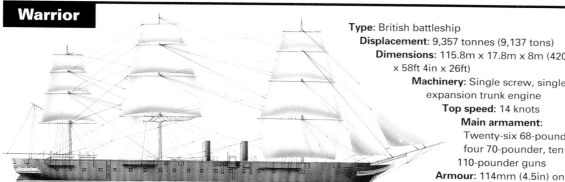

increase of 50 per cent over the previous Zwaardvis class. The new Gipsy fire control and automated electronic command systems reduced crew numbers from 65 to 49.

Warrior

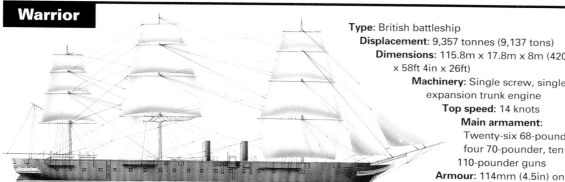

Type: British battleship
Displacement: 9,357 tonnes (9,137 tons)
Dimensions: 115.8m x 17.8m x 8m (420ft x 58ft 4in x 26ft)
Machinery: Single screw, single expansion trunk engine
Top speed: 14 knots
Main armament: Twenty-six 68-pounder, four 70-pounder, ten 110-pounder guns
Armour: 114mm (4.5in) on

belt and battery, 457mm wood (18in) backing
Launched: December 1860

Warrior was the world's first iron-hulled capital ship. Designed by Isaac Watts, she was laid down in May 1859. High speed was achieved by the 'V' formation of the forward part of the hull. *Warrior* was restored during the 1980s, and she is now stationed at Portsmouth, England.

Warspite

Type: British battleship
Displacement: 33,548 tonnes (33,020 tons)
Dimensions: 197m x 28m x 9m (646ft x 90ft 6in x 29ft 10in)
Machinery: Quadruple screws, turbines
Main armament: Sixteen 152mm (6in), eight

381mm (15in) guns
Armour: 102-330mm (4-13in) belt, 127-330mm (5-13in) on turrets, 102-254mm (4-10in) on barbettes
Launched: November 1913

Warspite belonged to the Queen Elizabeth class, developed from the Iron Duke class, but displacement was increased by 2,540 tonnes (2,500 tons), and 6m (20ft) were added to the length. The 381mm (15in) guns fired an 871kg (1,916lb) shell to a range of 32,000m (35,000yd) with extreme accuracy. *Warspite* was extensively modernised after World War I. She was scrapped in 1948.

Warspite

Type: British submarine
Displacement: 4,368 tonnes (4,300 tons) (surface), 4,876 tonnes (4,800 tons) (submerged)
Dimensions: 87m x 10m x 8.4m (285ft x 33ft 2in x 27ft 7in)
Machinery: Single screw, pressurised water-cooled nuclear reactor,

turbines
Top speed: 28 knots (submerged)
Main armament: Six 533mm (21in) torpedo tubes
Launched: September 1965
Date of profile: 1968

Warspite was one of a group of five boats that formed the first complete

class of British nuclear-powered submarines. The class followed Britain's first nuclear-powered submarine *Dreadnought*. Turbines develop 15,000hp and there is an

emergency battery with diesel generator and electric motor.

Washington

Type: US liner
Displacement: 1,666 tonnes (1,640 tons)
Dimensions: 70m x 11.8m (230ft x 39ft)
Machinery: Paddle wheels, side-lever engines
Top speed: 9 knots
Launched: 1847

The Oceanic Steam Navigation Company was set up in 1847. Initially four liners were planned to provide a service between New York and Europe, but funds were limited and only *Washington* and a sister ship were ordered. *Washington* could carry 40 first-class and 44 second-class passengers. She gave good service until 1858, when she was sold and based in the Pacific. She was scrapped in 1863.

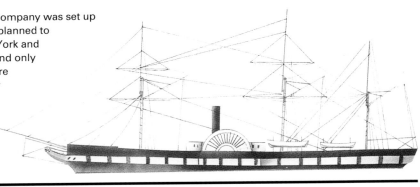

Washington

Type: French liner
Displacement: 3,462 tonnes (3,408 tons)

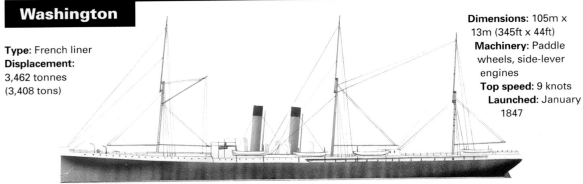

Dimensions: 105m x 13m (345ft x 44ft)
Machinery: Paddle wheels, side-lever engines
Top speed: 9 knots
Launched: January 1847

Washington was the first liner built for the Compagnie Générale Transatlantique, and was the forerunner of such famous liners as *Normandie* of 1936. *Washington* had luxurious accommodation for 128 first-class and 54 second-class passengers, and she also carried 29 third-class passengers in steerage. In 1868 she was converted to a twin screw vessel with single expansion engines. She was scrapped in 1900.

Washington

Type: US battleship
Displacement: 47,518 tonnes (46,770 tons)
Dimensions: 222m x 33m x 10m (728ft 9in x 108ft 4in x 33ft)
Machinery: Quadruple screws, turbines
Top speed: 28 knots
Main armament: Twenty 127mm (5in), nine 406mm

(16in) guns
Armour: 168-305mm belt (6.6-12in), 178-406mm (7-16in) on main turrets
Launched: June 1940

Washington and her sister *North Carolina* were the first US battleships built after the lifting of the

1922 Washington Naval Treaty. Original designs complied with the 356mm (14in) gun limitations of the later London Treaty, but when Japan refused to ratify the agreement the design was re-cast to carry three triple 406mm (16in) gun turrets. The additional weight of the larger weapons caused a two-knot reduction in top speed. *Washington*, along with *South Dakota*, sank the Japanese battlecruiser *Kirishima* at Guadalcanal in November 1942. She was scrapped in 1960/61.

Werra

Type: German liner
Displacement: 5,190 tonnes (5,109 tons)
Dimensions: 132m x 14m (433ft x 46ft)
Machinery: Single screw, compound engines
Top speed: 16 knots
Launched: 1882

Werra was one of a group of express liners built for Norddeutscher Lloyd's North Atlantic service. Lack of construction facilities in Germany as a result of a rapid influx of work, meant that *Werra* was built by Elder in Britain. She was a handsome vessel, with accommodation for 125 first-class, 130 second-class and 1,000 third-class passengers. She was scrapped in 1903.

Westernland

Type: Belgian liner
Displacement: 5,827 tonnes (5,736 tons)
Dimensions: 134m x 14m (440ft x 47ft)
Machinery: Single screw, compound engines
Top speed: 14 knots

Launched: 1883

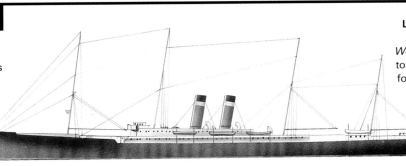

Westernland was one of the first steel-hulled ships to serve on the North Atlantic route. She was built for the Red Star Line which, during the early 1880s, was rapidly expanding its fleet and carrying well over 25,000 passengers a year. *Westernland* entered service between Antwerp and New York in 1883. She transferred to the American Line in 1901, and was scrapped in 1912.

Whidbey Island

Type: US dock landing ship
Displacement: 15,977 tonnes
(15,726 tons)
Dimensions: 186m x 25.6m x 6.3m
(609ft x 84ft x 20ft 8in)
Machinery: Twin screws, diesel
engines
Top speed: 20+ knots
Main armament: Two 20mm (0.8in)
Vulcan guns
Launched: June 1983

Whidbey Island was the first of a
class of eight advanced dock
landing ships (LSD), and was a
development of the Anchorage
class. She was laid down in 1981

and completed in February 1985.
She provides powerful support to
an assault landing task force,
having a large well deck to the stern
which can be flooded to allow boats
and landing craft to sail in and out.
This deck measures 134m x 15m
(440ft x 50ft). It is large enough to
carry four LCAC hovercraft or up to
21 smaller 61-tonne (60-ton)
landing craft. The LCAC is a
gas-turbine powered air
cushion vehicle, which the Navy
uses to deliver heavy equipment
and vehicles directly on to the

beach. She has accommodation
for 450 troops, plus a crew of
340. Cargo capacity is 1,524 cubic
metres (53,820 cubic ft) for
marine cargo, plus 3,810 square
metres (41,010 sq ft) parking
capacity for military vehicles. She
has a small flight deck aft, which
can operate up to two CH-46 Sea
Knight or CH-53 Sea

Stallion/Super Stallion assault and
transport helicopters. She can also
operate AV-8B Harrier vertical take-
off aircraft. Eight of this class were
built in total, and the intention was
to build a follow-on design. Her
engines develop 41,600hp, and a
range at 18 knots is 18,050km
(9,500 miles). She has only light
point defence weapons.

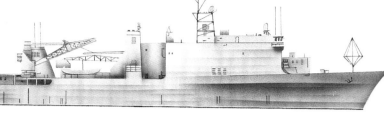

Whiskey

Type: Russian submarine
Displacement: 1,066 tonnes (1,050
tons) (surface), 1,371 tonnes (1,350
tons) (submerged)
Dimensions: 76m x 6.5m x 5m
(249ft 4in x 21ft 4in x 16ft)

Machinery: Twin screws, diesel
engines (surface), electric motors
(submerged)
Top speed: 18 knots (surface), 14
knots (submerged)
**Main
armament:**
Two

406mm (16in), four 533mm (21in)
torpedo tubes
Launched: 1956

'Whiskey' was a large class of post-
World War II attack submarine.
About 240 were built between
1951 and 1957. Originally it

had been planned to built 340, but as
nuclear propulsion became available,
so the number was reduced.
Between 1959 and 1963, four units
were converted to early warning
boats, but the introduction of the
long-range Bear aircraft in 1963
reduced their strategic importance
in some areas, and
by the 1980s, these
submarines had
disappeared from the
effective list.

Wilmington

Type: US gunboat
Displacement: 1,716 tonnes (1,689
tons)
Dimensions: 76.4m x 12.4m x 2.7m
(250ft 9in x 41ft x 9ft)
Machinery: Twin screws, triple
expansion engines
**Main
armament:**
Eight 102mm
(4in) guns

Launched: October 1895

Wilmington was laid down in
1894 and completed in May 1897.
She and her sister *Helena* were
patrol gunboats for use in the
waters around Florida. They
had one tall funnel and the

hull cut down aft to form a long poop. Two of the
102mm (4in) guns were mounted on the foredeck,
with two more mounted aft and two on each
broadside behind 38mm (1.5in) armour.
The ships had a shallower draught
than other US gunboats, making
them ideal for river work.
Engines developed
1,900hp. She saw
service in the 1898
war with Spain,
later served as a
training ship and
was sold in 1946.

Winnebago

Type: US monitor
Displacement: 1,320 tonnes (1,300
tons)
Dimensions: 70m x 17m x 1.8m
(229ft x 56ft x 6ft)
Machinery: Quadruple screws,
horizontal compound engines
Top speed: 9 knots
Main armament: Four
279mm (11in) guns
Armour: 76mm (3in)

on sides, 203mm (8in) on turrets
Launched: 1863

Winnebago was one of
the most successful of
the monitor-type
warships to see
service in the
American Civil War.
By May

1862 it had been decided to
increase the number of shallow-
draught armoured vessels for
service on the
rivers. These
were to be
twin-turreted

vessels driven by screws instead of
paddle wheels. Two different types
of turret were fitted – a standard
Ericsson, and one produced by
James Eades, builder of *Winnebago*
and her three sisters Only the two
turrets, the funnel and a single
ventilator showed above the
turtleback deck. Side armour was
solid plate. *Winnebago* was
sold in 1874.

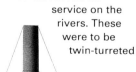

Winnepec

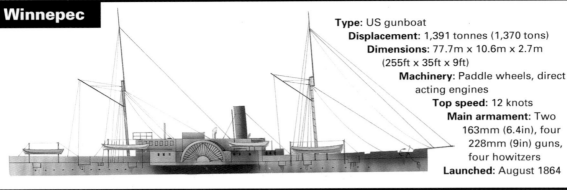

Type: US gunboat
Displacement: 1,391 tonnes (1,370 tons)
Dimensions: 77.7m x 10.6m x 2.7m (255ft x 35ft x 9ft)
Machinery: Paddle wheels, direct acting engines
Top speed: 12 knots
Main armament: Two 163mm (6.4in), four 228mm (9in) guns, four howitzers
Launched: August 1864

Winnepec was one of a large group of wooden-hulled gunboats built by the Union Navy for service on the rivers of the Confederacy. She was laid down in 1863, launched in 1864 and completed in 1865. A long rudder at each end gave her the capacity to steer forwards or backwards with equal ease, and for this reason *Winnepec* and her six sisters were known as 'double-enders'. She was sold in 1869.

Wivern

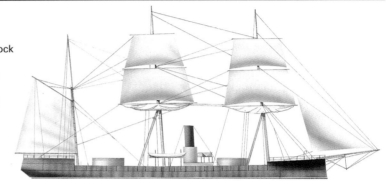

Type: British battleship
Displacement: 2,794 tonnes (2,750 tons)
Dimensions: 68.4m x 12.9m x 4.9m (224ft 6in x 42ft 6in x 16ft 3in)
Machinery: Single screw, horizontal direct acting engine
Top speed: 10.5 knots
Main armament: Four 228mm (9in) guns

Launched: August 1863

The Confederate Navy agent John Bullock commissioned *Wivern* from Laird Brothers in 1861. She was laid down as *Mississippi*, but was seized by the neutral British government in 1864 and became HMS *Wivern*. Completed in 1865, she was the first vessel to have Cowper Coles' new tripod masts. In 1898 she took up duties in Hong Kong harbour. She was sold in 1922.

Wolverine

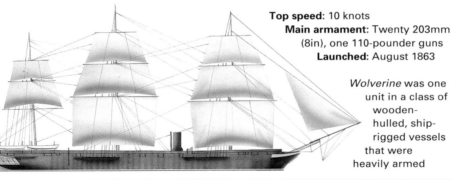

Type: British cruiser
Displacement: 2,462 tonnes (2,424 tons)
Dimensions: 68.5m x 12.3m x 5.7m (225ft x 40ft 8in x 19ft)
Machinery: Single screw, double piston rod engine

Top speed: 10 knots
Main armament: Twenty 203mm (8in), one 110-pounder guns
Launched: August 1863

Wolverine was one unit in a class of wooden-hulled, ship-rigged vessels that were heavily armed

according to the broadside principle. The single 110-pounder pivot gun was an early example of the breechloader. *Wolverine*'s engines developed 1,339hp, giving her the lowest speed of her class, which averaged 12 knots. In 1876 she was re-engined with return connecting rod machinery, which developed 1,493hp. Her top speed then increased to 11.3 knots. She was sold in 1905.

Worden

Type: US cruiser
Displacement: 8,334 tonnes (8,203 tons)
Dimensions: 162.5m x 16.6m x 7.6m (533ft 2in x 54ft 6in x 25ft)
Machinery: Twin screws, turbines
Top speed: 32.7 knots
Main armament: Two 20mm (0.8in) Vulcan guns, two quad Harpoon launchers, two

twin launchers for Standard SM-2 ER missiles
Launched: June 1962

Worden was one of the units in the Leahy class, a group of nine vessels designed to

replace the USA's ageing cruisers from World War II. Their basic design set the pattern for later cruiser-design, with a twin stack layout supporting a complex and effective radar/tracking system. The Harpoon missiles are active homing to 130km (80 miles) at Mach 0.9; the Standard missiles have a range of 175km (92 miles), but at Mach 2.5+, with high explosive warheads. The class was re-fitted in the late 1960s.

X1

Type: British submarine
Displacement: 3,098 tonnes (3,050 tons) (surface), 3,657 tonnes (3,600 tons) (submerged)
Dimensions: 110.8m x 9m x 4.8m

(363ft 6in x 29ft 10in x 15ft 9in)
Machinery: Twin screws, diesel engines (surface), electric motors (submerged)
Top speed: 20 knots

(surface), 9 knots (submerged)
Main armament: Four 132mm (5.2in) guns, six 533mm (21in) torpedo tubes.
Launched: 1925

X1 was designed to see how a very large submarine would perform underwater. She was one of the first submarines to have Asdic, and her battery of 132mm (5.2in) guns was intended to defeat any destroyer or armed merchant cruiser in a surface action. *X1* proved to be an excellent sea boat, and a steady gun platform. She was scrapped in 1936.

X1

Type: US submarine
Displacement: 31 tonnes (31 tons) (surface), 36 tonnes (36 tons) (submerged)

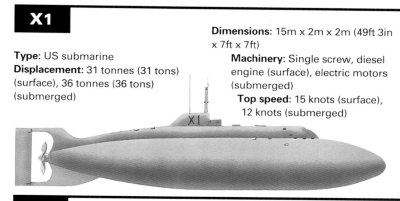

Dimensions: 15m x 2m x 2m (49ft 3in x 7ft x 7ft)
Machinery: Single screw, diesel engine (surface), electric motors (submerged)
Top speed: 15 knots (surface), 12 knots (submerged)

Launched: 1954

X1 was an experimental submarine completed in 1955. She was intended to be a prototype for a series of midget submarines that would penetrate enemy harbours, and her design was based upon the British *X5*. *X1* normally carried a four-man crew, but on short missions she could accommodate six. Originally, she was fitted with a

hydrogen-peroxide propulsion unit, which allowed her diesel engines to be used while submerged. A small electrical motor was fitted to allow her to 'creep' undetected below water. In 1958 an explosion of the hydrogen peroxide blew her into three pieces. After repair, she was laid up in 1960, and was later used for research purposes until 1973. *X1* was the only midget submarine built for the US Navy.

X2

Type: Italian submarine
Displacement: 409 tonnes (403 tons) (surface), 475 tonnes (468 tons) (submerged)
Dimensions: 42.6m x 5.5m x 3m (139ft 9in x 18ft x 10ft 4in)
Machinery: Twin screws, diesel engines (surface), electric motors (submerged)
Top speed: 8.2 knots (surface), 6.2

knots (submerged)
Main armament: One 76mm (3in) gun, two 450mm (17.7in) torpedo tubes
Launched: April 1917

X2 was a single-hulled minelaying submarine with 'saddle' tanks, based upon the

Austrian *U24* (ex-German *UC12*), which sank off Taranto after hitting one of her own mines. *U24* was raised by the Italians, who then commissioned her as *X1*. *X2* was laid down in August

1916 and completed in 1918. Maximum diving depth was 40m (130ft). Surfaced range at 8 knots was 2,280km (1,200 miles), and submerged range at 3 knots was 112km (70 miles). *X2* was laid up in 1940.

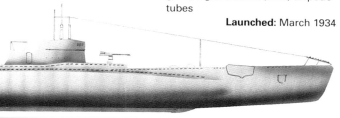

X2

Type: British submarine
Displacement: 1,000 tonnes (985 tons) (surface), 1,280 tonnes (1,259 tons) (submerged)

Dimensions: 70.5m x 6.8m x 4m (231ft 3in x 22ft 4in x 13ft 6in)
Machinery: Twin screws, diesel

engines (surface), electric motors (submerged)
Main armament: Two 100mm (3.9in) guns, eight 533mm (21in) torpedo tubes

Launched: March 1934

X2 was formerly the Italian submarine *Galileo*, captured by the British during her first patrol in 1940. As *X2* she served with the Royal Navy until she was scrapped in 1946. She was a long-range boat with a partial double hull. Operational diving depth was 90 metres, surfaced range at 16 knots was 6,270km (3,300 miles), and submerged range at 3 knots was 200km (105 miles), or 13km (7 miles) at full speed.

X5

Type: British submarine
Displacement: 27 tonnes (27 tons) (surface), 30 tonnes (29.5 tons) (submerged)
Dimensions: 15.7m x 1.8m x 2.6m (51ft 6in x 6ft x 8ft 6in)
Machinery: Single screw, diesel engine (surface), electric motors (submerged)

Top speed: 6.5 knots (surface), 5 knots (submerged)
Main armament: Two side charges
Launched: 1942

In 1942 two prototype midget submarines were built, and from these an operational X-type (including *X5*) was developed. The most notable event involving the class was the unsuccessful attempt

to sink the German battleship *Tirpitz* in 1943. A number of X-craft had been towed to Altenfjord, Norway, where German surface units lay at anchor. *X6* and *X7* managed to lay charges that damaged

Tirpitz, but *X5*, having successfully negotiated the minefields and barrages protecting the German ships, disappeared without trace during the mission.

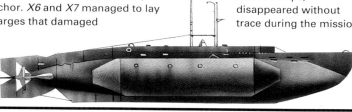

Xia

Type: Chinese submarine
Displacement: 8,128 (8,000 tons) tonnes

(submerged)
Dimensions: 120m x 10m x 8m (393ft 8in x 32ft 10in x 26ft 3in)
Machinery: Single screw, pressurised water-cooled nuclear reactor

Top speed: 22 knots (submerged)
Main armament: Twelve tubes for CSS-N-3 missiles, six 533mm (21in) torpedo tubes
Launched: April 1981
Date of profile: 1990

Xia was laid down at Huludao in 1978. She has a typical SSBN layout

and a large turtleback more prominent than on Western counterparts, which resembles that of the Russian Delta class. Missiles are two-stage solid fuel rockets with inertial guidance ballistic flight to 3,249km (1,710 miles) and a nuclear warhead of two megatons. More of the type are under construction at the time of writing, so giving China a credible nuclear capability.

Yakumo

Type: Japanese cruiser
Displacement: 10,000 tonnes (9,850 tons)
Dimensions: 132.3m x 19.5m x 7.2m (434ft x 64ft 3in x 23ft 9in)
Machinery: Twin screws, vertical triple expansion engines
Top speed: 20.7 knots
Main armament: Twelve 152mm (6in), four 203mm (8in) guns
Launched: July 1899

Yakumo was the only major warship to be built directly for the Japanese Navy by Germany. She was ordered under the Japanese Naval Expansion Programme of 1896-97, and was laid down in March 1898 with completion in June 1900. She was a fine example of the armoured cruiser which was then at its peak of development, but was soon to be eclipsed. Her armament was powerful for a ship of her size, and was balanced by heavy and effective protection. Her main 203mm (8in) guns were mounted in twin armoured turrets fore and aft, while her 152mm (6in) secondary weapons were placed on two levels. Six were installed behind shields, while the rest were in a battery on the main deck, protected by 152mm (6in) of armour plate. She had an armoured belt which ran for almost the full length of her hull, and was from 89mm to 178mm (3.5-7in) thick and was also covered by an armoured deck which reached 127mm (5in) thick in the centre. Her total armour weighed 2,003 tonnes (2,000 tons). This class of vessel was soon to be superseded by advances in naval technology and the advent of the more powerful battlecruiser. She became a training ship in 1920, and was scrapped in 1947.

Yamato

Type: Japanese cruiser
Displacement: 15,000 tonnes (1,476 tons)
Dimensions: 62.7m x 10.7m x 4.6m (206ft x 35ft x 15ft)
Machinery: Single screw, reciprocating horizontal compound engine
Main armament: One 76mm (3in), five 120mm (4.7in), two 170mm (6.7in) guns

Launched: April 1885

Yamato was one of three vessels which, at the time, constituted the largest group of cruisers in the Japanese Navy. *Yamato* was composite-built, with iron framing and a wooden hull with recessed gunports forward to allow for head-on fire. She was originally barque rigged, but this was reduced during a re-fit in 1900. All three vessels in the group were re-classified as survey ships in 1907. *Yamato* became a drill ship in 1935, and in September of the same year she sank in Kobe harbour during a storm. The wreck was not removed until 1950.

Yamato

Type: Japanese battleship
Displacement: 71,110 tonnes (71,659 tons)
Dimensions: 263m x 36.9m x 10.3m (862ft 10in x 121ft x 34ft)
Machinery: Quadruple screws, turbines
Top speed: 27 knots
Main armament: Twelve 127mm (5in), twelve 155mm (6.1in), nine 460mm (18.1in) guns
Armour: 408mm (16.1in) belt, 200-231mm (7.9-9.1in) deck, 546mm (21.5in) on barbettes, 193-650mm (7.6-25.6in) on main turrets
Launched: August 1940

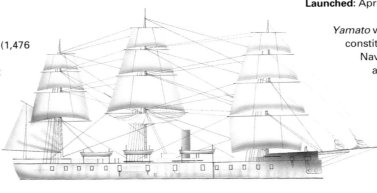

Yamato, together with her sister *Musashi*, were the world's largest and most powerful battleships ever. No fewer than 23 designs were prepared for *Yamato* between 1934 and 1937 when she was laid down. When she was launched, her displacement was only surpassed by that of the British liner *Queen Mary*. Her main turrets each weighed 2,818 tonnes (2,774 tons), and each 460mm (18.1in) gun could fire two 1,473kg (3,240lb) shells per minute over a distance of 41,148m (45,000yd). *Yamato* was sunk on 7 April 1945.

Yang Wei

Type: Chinese cruiser
Displacement: 1,566 tonnes (1,542 tons)
Dimensions: 64m x 9.7m x 4.5m (210ft x 32ft x 15ft)
Machinery: Twin screws, horizontal return reciprocating engines
Main armament: Four 120mm (4.7in), two 254mm (10in) guns
Launched: January 1881

Yang Wei was a small, steel-hulled vessel designed by George Rendel for the Peiyang Fleet. Her engines developed 2,580hp, coal supply was 305 tonnes (300 tons), and range at 8 knots was 10,203km (5,370 miles). The armoured deck covered only the machinery and boiler rooms, the unprotected ends of the ship being divided into compartments to reduce the effect of any damage. She was sunk during the Battle of Yalu in 1894.

Yankee

Type: Russian submarine
Displacement: 9,450 tonnes (9,300 tons) (submerged)
Dimensions: 129.5m x 11.6m x 7.8m (424ft 10in x 38ft x 25ft 7in)
Machinery: Twin screws, nuclear reactors, turbines
Top speed: 30 knots (submerged)
Main armament: Sixteen SS-N-6 missile tubes, six 533mm (21in) torpedo tubes

Launched: 1967

The vessels of the Yankee class, the first of which was completed in 1907, were far larger and more

powerful than any previous Russian submarine, and were slightly larger than the equivalent missile submarines of the West. The first group of the class was

deployed off the eastern seaboard of the USA. A second group was sent to the Pacific coast, where they could direct their missiles as far as the eastern side of the Rocky Mountains.

Yeoman Burn

Type: Norwegian bulk carrier
Displacement: 78,740 tonnes (77,500 tons)
Dimensions: 245m x 32.2m x 14m (830ft 10in x 105ft 8in x 46ft)

Machinery: Single screw, diesel engines
Top speed: 14.6 knots
Launched: October 1990

Yeoman Burn is under a 20-year contract to a British company, and

carries iron ore, coal, limestone, salt, coke or grain in bulk. The hull has nine separate holds and is double-skinned and double-bottomed. She has self-loading and unloading machinery and a crew of 25.

York

Type: British cruiser
Displacement: 8,382 tonnes (8,250 tons)
Dimensions: 175m x 17.3m x 6m (574ft x 56ft 9in x 19ft 8in)
Machinery: Quadruple screws, turbines
Main armament: Four 102mm (4in), six 203mm (8in) guns
Launched: July 1928

The Washington Naval Treaty of 1922 restricted cruiser displacement to a maximum of 10,160 tons (10,000 tons). *York* was the first attempt by a signatory nation at building a heavy cruiser that was not at the limit. In order to give her the same speed and protection as the Kent class, while saving 1,625 tons (1,600 tons), two 203mm (8in) guns were

sacrificed. Engines developed 80,000hp, and range at 12 knots was about 19,000km (10,000 miles). In 1941 *York* was beached at Suda Bay after being hit by an explosive motor boat. Her wreck was scrapped in 1952.

Yoshino

Type: Japanese cruiser
Displacement: 4,216 tonnes (4,150 tons)
Dimensions: 109.7m x 14m x 5m (360ft x 46ft 6in x 17ft
Machinery: Twin screws, reciprocating compound engines
Main armament: Eight 120mm (4.7in), four 152mm (6in) guns
Launched: December 1892

Upon her completion in 1893, *Yoshino* was the world's fastest cruiser. Her armament of quick-firing guns was unmatched, and *Yoshino* was the first warship to employ these weapons in a major sea battle when she formed part of the Japanese fleet at the

Battle of Yalu in September 1894. During the action, in which *Yoshino* fired about 1,200 rounds, spent cartridge cases were ankle deep on the deck, and her crew had to sweep them down the hatches to clear the area around the guns. *Yoshino* sank on 15 May 1905 after being rammed by the armoured cruisr *Kasuga* in thick fog off Port Arthur while on patrol during the Russo-Japanese War.

Zara

Type: Italian cruiser
Displacement: 11,866 tonnes (11,680 tons)
Dimensions: 182.8m x 20m x 7.2m (599ft 9in x 67ft 8in x 23ft 8in)
Machinery: Twin screws, turbines
Main armament: Sixteen 100mm (3.9in), eight 203mm (8in) guns
Launched: April 1930

Zara was the lead ship in a class of four vessels. All were better protected than the preceding Trento class,

although this reduced designed speed. However, all the Zaras made over 33 knots during trials. *Zara*'s engines developed 120,000hp, and range at 25 knots was 5,150km (3,200 miles). She was sunk in 1941 by a British battleship.

Zaragosa

Type: Spanish battleship
Displacement: 5,618 tonnes (5,530 tons)
Dimensions: 85.3m x 16.6m x 8m (280ft x 54ft 7in x 26ft 6in)
Machinery: Single screw, horizontal single expansion engines

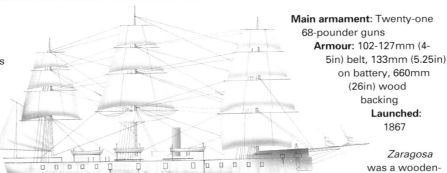

Main armament: Twenty-one 68-pounder guns
Armour: 102-127mm (4-5in) belt, 133mm (5.25in) on battery, 660mm (26in) wood backing
Launched: 1867

Zaragosa was a wooden-hulled broadside battleship. She was originally armed with 68-pounder guns, but in 1885 she was given four 228mm (9in) guns on the main deck, one 180mm (7.1in) gun under the forecastle and two more 180mm (7.1in) weapons on sponsons. She formed part of the Spanish force sent to Cuba in 1873. She was recalled to Spain upon the outbreak of the civil war, became a training ship in 1895 and was stricken in 1899.

Zealous

Type: British battleship
Displacement: 6,197 tonnes (6,100 tons)
Dimensions: 76.8m x 17.8m x 7.7m (252ft x 58ft 6in x 25ft 5in)
Machinery: Single screw, return connecting rod engine
Main armament: Twenty 178mm (7in) guns
Armour: 63.5-114mm (2.5-4.5in) belt, 114mm (4.5in) on battery
Launched: March 1864

In 1861 seven wooden two-deckers were selected for conversion into ironclads in answer to France's ambitious building programme. Only four were completed, of which *Zealous* was one. Her engines could give her a speed of only 11.7 knots. However, with 2,713 square metres (29,200 sq ft) of canvas she could cover greater distances under sail than her contemporaries. She was sold in 1886.

Zieten

Type: German torpedo gunboat
Displacement: 1,170 tonnes (1,152 tons)
Dimensions: 79.4m x 8.5m x 4.6m (260ft 6in x 28ft x 15ft 2in)
Machinery: Twin screws, horizontal compound engines
Top speed: 16 knots
Main armament: Two 380mm (15in) torpedo tubes
Launched: 1876

Designed and built by the Thames Ironworks, London, *Zieten* was Germany's first major torpedo vessel. She was initially armed with one submerged torpedo tube bow and stern. Later six 50mm (1.95in) guns were added, making her an effective torpedo gun boat From 1899 she served as a fishery protection vessel, and in 1914 she became a coastal patrol ship. She was scrapped in 1921.

Zoea

Type: Italian submarine
Displacement: 1,354 tonnes (1,333 tons) (surface), 1,685 tonnes (1,659 tons) (submerged)
Dimensions: 82.8m x 7m x 5.3m (271ft 8in x 23ft 6in x 17ft 5in)
Machinery: Twin screws, diesel engines (surface), electric motors (submerged)
Main armament: One 99mm (3.9in) gun, six 533mm (21in) torpedo tubes, 36 mines
Launched: December 1937

Zoea was a long-range torpedo and minelaying boat. Surfaced range at 14 knots was 4,025km (2,500 miles), and submerged range at 7 knots was 193km (120 miles). Maximum diving depth was 90m (295ft). During World War II, *Zoea* was mainly used as a cargo vessel, and she made 21 trips transporting a total of 1,130 tonnes (1,113 tons) of vital supplies to North Africa. She was later used for anti-submarine training by the Allies and was scrapped in 1947.

Zuikaku

Type: Japanese aircraft carrier
Displacement: 32,618 tonnes32,105 tons)
Dimensions: 257m x 29m x 8.8m (843ft 2in x 95ft x 29ft)
Machinery: Quadruple screws, turbines
Main armament: Sixteen 127mm (5in) guns
Aircraft: 84
Launched: November 1939

Zuikaku and her sister *Shokaku* were the most successful carriers operated by the Japanese Navy. They were considerably larger than previous purpose-built carriers, and were better armed, better protected and carried more aircraft. The wooden flight deck was 240m (787ft) long and 29m (95ft) wide, and was serviced by three lifts. *Zuikaku* was sunk in action with American forces on 25 October 1944.

Index of Ships by Type

Note: The information given in brackets beside the name of each ship indicates its country of service and its launch date. Where the launch date of a vessel is unknown, the date of conversion is given, indicated by a single asterisk (∗). In cases where the vessel was never completed, the date when it was laid down is given, indicated by a double asterisk (∗∗).

Aircraft carriers *(including escort carriers)*
Akagi (Jap, 1925) 12
America (USA, 1964) 14
Aquila (It, 1926) 15
Ark Royal (GB, 1937) 19
Attu (USA, 1944) 25
Audacity (GB, 1941) 26
Béarn (Fr, 1920) 34
Ben-My-Chree (GB, 1908) 35
Clémenceau (Fr, 1957) 65
Courageous (GB, 1916) 74
Dédalo (Sp, 1943) 84
Dixmude (Fr, 1940) 92
Eagle (GB, 1918) 103
Eagle (GB, 1948) 103
Enterprise (USA, 1936) 112
Enterprise (USA, 1960) 112
Essex (USA, 1942) 118
Formidable (GB, 1939) 135
Forrestal (USA, 1954) 135
Furious (GB, 1916) 145
Gambier Bay (USA, 1943) 152
George Washington, (USA, 1989) 158
Giuseppe Garibaldi (It, 1983) 162
Graf Zeppelin (Ger, 1938) 171
Hermes (GB, 1919) 188
Hermes (GB, 1953) 188
Hosho (Jap, 1921) 190
Independence (USA, 1942) 196
Kiev (Rus, 1972) 208
Lexington (USA, 1925) 215
Ryujo (Jap, 1931) 246
Shinano (Jap, 1944) 251
Sparviero (It, 1927) 252
Taiho (Jap, 1943) 255
Unicorn (GB, 1941) 264
Zuikaku (Jap, 1939) 280
(see also: helicopter carriers; seaplane carriers)

Amphibious assault force vessels
Appalachian (USA, 1943) 15
Caorle (It, 1957) 53
Denver (USA, 1965) 87
Grillo (It, 1918) 174
Gustave Zédé (Fr, 1934) 179
Intrepid (USA, 1964) 198
Ivan Rogov (Rus, 1977) 200
Iwo Jima (USA, 1960) 200
Mount Whitney (USA, 1970) 227
Whidbey Island (USA, 1983) 275

Armoured battery vessels
Foudroyante (Fr, 1855) 136
Guerriera (It, 1866) 177
Voragine (It, 1866) 271

Auxiliary naval vessels
Basento (It, 1970) 32
Bengasi (It, 1904) 36
Blenheim (GB, 1919) 38
Bronte (It, 1904) 46
Chazhma (Rus, 1959) 60
Cyclop (Ger, 1916) 78
Dalmazia (It, 1922) 79
Deutschland (Ger, 1960) 89
Engadine (GB, 1966) 110
Filicudi (It, 1954) 129
Fort Grange (GB, 1976) 136
Foudre (Fr, 1895) 136
Frank Cable (USA, 1978) 139
Friendship (GB, 1780) 141
Fulton (USA, 1940) 144
General John Pope (USA, 1943) 156

George Washington Parke Custis (USA, 1855) 158
Hunley (USA, 1961) 192
Vulcan (GB, 1889) 272

Battlecruisers
Australia (Aus, 1911) 27
Derfflinger (Ger, 1913) 87
Dunkerque (Fr, 1935) 100
Glorious (GB, 1916) 166
Gneisenau (Ger, 1936) 166
Goeben (Ger, 1911) 167
Graf Spee (Ger, 1917) 170
Guam (USA, 1943) 177
Haruna (Jap, 1912) 185
Hood, (GB, 1918) 190
Ibuki (Jap, 1907) 194
Inflexible (GB, 1907) 198
Lion (GB, 1910) 216
Tiger (GB, 1913) 258
Tsukuba (Jap, 1905) 260
Von der Tann (Ger, 1909) 271

Battleships
Admiral Graf Spee (Ger, 1933) 11
Affondatore (It, 1865) 11
Agincourt (GB, 1862) 12
Almirante Cochrane (Chile, 1874) 13
Ammiraglio di Saint Bon (It, 1897) 14
Andrea Doria (It, 1913) 14
Arapiles (Sp, 1854) 16
Arciduca Ferdinand Max (Austria, 1865) 16
Armide (Fr, 1867) 20
Arminius (Ger, 1864) 20
Arpad (Austria, 1901) 20
Asahi (Jap, 1898) 21
Assari Tewfik (Turk, 1868) 22
Audacious (GB, 1911) 25
Barham (GB, 1914) 32
Basileus Georgios (Greece, 1867) 33
Bayern (Ger, 1915) 34
Belleisle (GB, 1876) 35
Benbow (GB, 1885) 35
Benedetto Brin (It, 1901) 36
Bismarck (Ger, 1939) 38
Bouvet (Fr, 1896) 42
Bretagne (Fr, 1855) 44
Bretagne (Fr, 1913) 44
Caimen (Fr, 1885) 49
Canada (GB, 1913) 52
Canopus (GB, 1897) 52
Capitan Prat (Chile, 1890) 53
Captain (GB, 1869) 53
Carl XIV Johan (Swed, 1824) 54
Castelfidardo (It, 1863) 56
Centurion (GB, 1892) 57
Charlemagne (Fr, 1895) 58
Charles Martel (Fr, 1893) 59
Chen Yuan (China, 1882) 60
Clémenceau (Fr, 1943) 64
Colbert (Fr, 1875) 66
Collingwood (GB, 1882) 66
Colossus (GB, 1910) 66
Connecticut (USA, 1904) 69
Conqueror (GB, 1881) 70
Conqueror (GB, 1911) 70
Conte di Cavour (It, 1911) 70
Conte Verde (It, 1867) 71
Courbet (Fr, 1882) 74
Couronne (Fr, 1861) 74
Custoza (Austria, 1872) 77
Cyclops (GB, 1871) 78
Danmark (Den, 1864) 80
Dante Alighieri (It, 1910) 81
Danton (Fr, 1909) 81
Demologos (USA, 1814) 86
Deutschland (Ger, 1874) 88
Deutschland (Ger, 1904) 89
Devastation (GB, 1871) 90
Dévastation (Fr, 1879) 90
Dictator (USA, 1863) 91

Dreadnought (GB, 1875) 96
Dreadnought (GB, 1906) 96
Duguesclin (Fr, 1883) 99
Duilio (It, 1876) 99
Duilio (It, 1913) 99
Duke of Wellington (GB, 1852) 99
Dunderberg (USA, 1865) 100
Ekaterina II, (Rus, 1886) 106
Emanuele Filiberto (It, 1897) 107
Enrico Dandolo (It, 1878) 110
Erin (GB, 1913) 114
Erherzog Albrecht (Austria, 1872) 115
Erherzog Karl (Austria, 1903) 115
España (Sp, 1912) 117
Feth-I-Bulend (Turk, 1870) 129
Flandre (Fr, 1864) 131
Flandre (Fr, 1914) 131
Formidabile (It, 1861) 135
Formidable (Fr, 1885) 135
Francesco Caracciolo (It, 1920) 137
Francesco Morosini (It, 1885) 138
Friedrich der Grosse (Ger, 1874) 140
Friedrich Carl (Ger, 1867) 141
Frithjof (Ger, 1891) 141
Fuji (Jap, 1896) 143
Fulminant (Fr, 1877) 143
Furieux (Fr, 1883) 144
Fuso (Jap, 1877) 146
Fuso (Jap, 1914) 146
Gangut (Rus, 1893) 152
Gangut (Rus, 1911) 153
General Admiral Apraksin (Rus, 1896) 155
Georgia (USA, 1904) 159
Giulio Cesare (It, 1911) 162
Glatton (GB, 1871) 164
Gloire (Fr, 1859) 165
Grosser Kurfürst (Ger, 1913) 176
Habsburg (Austria, 1900) 181
Hansa (Ger, 1872) 184
Helgoland (Den, 1878) 186
Helgoland (Ger, 1909) 186
Henri IV (Fr, 1899) 187
Hercules, (GB, 1868) 187
Hoche (Fr, 1886) 189
Huascar (Peru, 1865) 191
Hydra (Greece, 1889) 192
Idaho (USA, 1917) 194
Imperator Pavel I (Rus, 1907) 195
Independencia (Peru, 1865) 196
Indiana (USA, 1941) 196
Inflexible (GB, 1876) 197
Iowa (USA, 1942) 198
Iron Duke (GB, 1912) 199
Ise (Jap, 1916) 199
Italia (It, 1880) 200
Jauréguiberry (Fr, 1893) 202
Javary (Braz, 1875) 202
Kaiser (Austria, 1862) 204
Kaiser (Ger, 1911) 205
Kaiser Friedrich III (Ger, 1896) 205
Kaiser Max (Austria, 1862) 205
Kalamazoo (USA, 1863∗∗) 206
Keokuk (USA, 1862) 208
Kniaz Pojarski (Rus, 1867) 209
Kniaz Suvarov (Rus, 1902) 210
König Wilhelm (Ger, 1868) 210
Kreml (Rus, 1865) 212
Kurfürst Friedrich Wilhelm (Ger, 1891) 212
Leonardo Da Vinci (It, 1911) 214
Lepanto (It, 1883) 215
Littorio (It, 1937) 216
Lord Nelson (GB, 1906) 216
Los Andes (Arg, 1874) 216
Lutfi Djelil (Turk, 1868) 217
Magenta (Fr, 1861) 218
Maine (USA, 1889) 218
Majestic (GB, 1895) 218
Masséna (Fr, 1885) 220
Messina (It, 1864) 222
Messudieh (Turk, 1874) 222
Michigan (USA, 1906) 222

Mikasa (Jap, 1900) 222
Minas Gerais (Braz, 1908) 222
Monadnock (USA, 1864) 225
Monarch (GB, 1868) 225
Monarch (GB, 1911) 225
Moreno (Arg, 1911) 226
Nagato (Jap, 1919) 228
Napoli (It, 1905) 228
Nassau (Ger, 1908) 229
Navarin (Rus, 1891) 230
Nelson (GB, 1925) 230
Neptune (GB, 1874) 231
Nevada (USA, 1914) 231
New Ironsides (USA, 1862) 231
New York (USA, 1912) 232
Nile (GB, 1888) 233
North Carolina (USA, 1940) 234
Numancia (Sp, 1863) 234
Oregon (USA, 1893) 235
Palestro (It, 1865) 236
Palestro (It, 1871) 236
Pelayo (Sp, 1887) 237
Petr Veliki (Rus, 1872) 238
Pobieda (Rus, 1900) 239
Prince Albert (GB, 1864) 240
Principe di Carignano (It, 1863) 241
Queen Elizabeth (GB, 1913) 241
Re d'Italia (It, 1863) 242
Re Galantuomo (It, 1858) 243
Re Umberto (It, 1888) 243
Regina Margherita (It, 1901) 243
Regina Maria Pia (It, 1863) 243
Retvisan (Rus, 1900) 244
Riachuelo (Braz, 1883) 244
Roanoke (USA, 1855) 244
Rolf Krake (Den, 1863) 245
Roma (It, 1865) 245
Royal Sovereign (GB, 1857) 245
Royal Sovereign (GB, 1891) 245
Sachsen (Ger, 1877) 247
Salamander (Austria, 1861) 247
Sevastopol (Rus, 1864) 250
Stonewall, (Confed, 1864) 253
Sultan (GB, 1870) 254
Tegetthoff (Austria, 1878) 256
Temeraire (GB, 1876) 256
Texas (USA, 1892) 257
Tsessarevitch (Rus, 1901) 260
Vanguard (GB, 1870) 265
Vanguard (GB, 1944) 265
Vasco da Gama (Port, 1875) 267
Vauban (Fr, 1882) 267
Vitoria (Sp, 1865) 270
Vittorio Emanuele (It, 1904) 270
Vittorio Veneto (It, 1937) 270
Warrior (GB, 1860) 273
Warspite (GB, 1913) 273
Washington (USA, 1940) 274
Wivern (GB, 1863) 276
Yamato (Jap, 1940) 278
Zaragosa (Sp, 1867) 280
Zealous (GB, 1864) 280

Blockade runners
Banshee (Confed, 1863) 31
Bermuda (Confed, 1861) 37
Flamingo (Confed, 1864) 130
Hope (Confed, 1864) 190

Bulk carriers
Front Driver (Swed, 1991) 141
Futura (Neth, 1992) 147
Halla No 2 (S Kor, 1991) 182
Yeoman Burn (Nor, 1990) 279

Cable layer
KDD Ocean Link (Jap, 1991) 207

Cargo vessels
Barbara (Ger, 1926) 31
Bowes (GB, 1852) 42

Cabotia (GB, 1917)	48	Boyarin (Rus, 1901)	42
Candiope (It, 1918)	52	Bremse (Ger, 1916)	43
Centennial State (USA, 1920)	57	Breslau (Ger, 1911)	43
Clan Macalister (GB, 1930)	64	Brindisi (It, 1912)	44
Cleopatra (GB, 1877)	65	Brooklyn (USA, 1895)	47
Cockerill (Belg, 1910)	66	Brooklyn (USA, 1936)	47
Connector (GB, 1852)	69	Buenos Aires (Arg, 1895)	47
Cunene (Port, 1911)	76	Caio Duilio (It, 1962)	49
Darino (GB, 1917)	82	Caio Mario (It, 1941)	49
Hakuryu Maru (Jap, 1991)	182	Calliope (GB, 1884)	50
Helena (Swed, 1990)	186	Calliope (GB, 1914)	51
Helice (Nor, 1990)	187	Campania (It, 1914)	51
Hudson Rex (Pan, 1991)	191	Cardenal Cisneros (Sp, 1897)	54
Huntsman (GB, 1921)	192	Carlo Alberto (It, 1896)	54
Krasnograd (Rus, 1992)	211	Carola (It, 1880)	55
Savannah (USA, 1969)	248	Caroline (GB, 1914)	55
(see also: passenger/cargo vessels)		Cécille (Fr, 1888)	57
		Chao Yung (China, 1880)	58
Coastal defence vessels		Charleston (USA, 1888)	59
Barrozo (Braz, 1864)	32	Chester (USA, 1907)	60
Dristigheten (Swed, 1900)	97	Chicago (USA, 1885)	60
Drottning Victoria (Swed, 1917)	97	Chin Yuan (China, 1886)	61
Faà Di Bruno (It, 1916)	126	Chishima (Jap, 1890)	62
Glatton (GB, 1914)	165	Chiyoda (Jap, 1890)	62
Gorgon (GB, 1871)	168	Circé (Fr, 1860)	63
Gorm (Den, 1870)	168	Coatit (It, 1899)	66
Göta (Swed, 1891)	168	Columbia (USA, 1892)	67
Haai (Neth, 1871)	181	Comus (GB, 1878)	68
Harald Haarfagre (Nor, 1897)	184	Condé (Fr, 1902)	69
Niels Juel (Den, 1918)	232	Confienza (It, 1889)	69
Novgorod (Rus, 1873)	234	Cornwall (GB, 1926)	72
		Coronel Bolognesi (Peru, 1906)	72
Commerce raiders		Cosmao (Fr, 1889)	73
Alabama (Confed, 1862)	12	Cossack (GB, 1886)	73
Atlantis (Ger, 1937)	24	Cristobal Colon (Sp, 1896)	75
Châteaurenault (Fr, 1898)	60	Cristoforo Colombo (It, 1875)	75
Komet (Ger, 1939)	210	Cristoforo Colombo (It, 1892)	76
Kormoran (Ger, 1939)	211	Curacoa (GB, 1917)	76
Quaker City (USA, 1854)	241	D'Assas (Fr, 1896)	82
Seeadler (Ger, 1888)	249	Davout (Fr, 1889)	83
Shenandoah (Confed, 1863)	251	De Grasse (Fr, 1946)	83
Sumter (Confed, 1859)	254	De Ruyter (Neth, 1944)	84
		Defence (GB, 1907)	85
Container ships		Delhi (India, 1932)	85
Ever Globe (Taiwan, 1984)	123	D'Entrecasteaux (Fr, 1896)	86
Hannover Express (Ger, 1990)	184	Denver (USA, 1902)	87
Hyundai Admiral (S Kor, 1992)	193	Des Moines (USA, 1946)	88
Kota Wijaya (Malaya, 1991)	211	Devonshire (GB, 1904)	90
Nedlloyd Europa (Neth, 1991)	230	Dido (GB, 1896)	91
		Dido (GB, 1939)	91
Corvettes		Dmitri Donskoi (Rus, 1883)	93
Danaide (It, 1942)	80	Dmitri Donskoi (Rus, 1953)	93
Folaga (It, 1942)	133	Dogali (It, 1885)	93
Gladiator (GB, 1944)	163	Drake (GB, 1901)	96
(see also: escort vessels)		Dubourdieu (Fr, 1884)	98
		Duca di Genova (It, 1860)	98
Cruise ship		Duguay-Trouin (Fr, 1923)	98
Society Adventurer (Bah, 1991)	252	Dupetit-Thouars (Fr, 1874)	101
		Dupleix (Fr, 1930)	101
Cruisers		Dupuy de Lôme (Fr, 1890)	101
Aboukir (GB, 1900)	11	Duquesne (Fr, 1876)	102
Aoba (Jap, 1926)	14	Edgar (GB, 1890)	105
Aragon (Sp, 1879)	16	Edgar Quinet (Fr, 1907)	105
Arethusa (GB, 1934)	18	Effingham (GB, 1921)	105
Ariadne (GB, 1943)	18	Elba (It, 1893)	106
Asama (Jap, 1898)	22	Elisabeta (Romania, 1887)	106
Askold (Rus, 1900)	22	Emanuele Filiberto Duca D'Aosta (It, 1935)	107
Astoria (USA, 1933)	23	Emden (Ger, 1908)	108
Atlanta (USA, 1941)	24	Emden (Ger, 1925)	108
Attentive (GB, 1904)	24	Emerald (GB, 1920)	108
Attilio Regolo (It, 1940)	24	Emperador Carlos V (Sp, 1895)	108
Aurora (GB, 1900)	26	Erherzog Friedrich (Austria, 1872)	115
Averroff (Greece, 1910)	27	Esmeralda (Chile, 1883)	116
Bacchante (GB, 1876)	28	Esmeralda (Chile, 1894)	116
Bahia (GB, 1909)	28	Etna (It, 1885)	119
Baleares (Sp, 1932)	28	Etna (It, 1942)	119
Baltimore (USA, 1942)	30	Etruria (It, 1891)	120
Basilicata (It, 1914)	33	Eugenio Di Savoia (It, 1935)	120
Bayan (Rus, 1900)	33	Euridice (It, 1890)	121
Belfast (GB, 1938)	34	Euryalus (It, 1853)	122
Bellona (GB, 1942)	35	Euryalus (GB, 1877)	123
Berlin (Ger, 1903)	36	Exeter (GB, 1929)	124
Birmingham (GB, 1913)	37	Extremadura (Sp, 1900)	125
Bismarck (Ger, 1877)	37	Fabert (Fr, 1874)	126
Black Prince (GB, 1904)	38	Fieramosca (It, 1888)	129
Blake (GB, 1889)	38	Fiume (It, 1930)	130
Blücher (Ger, 1908)	39	Flavio Gioia (It, 1883)	132
Bogatyr (Rus, 1901)	39	Florida (Confed, 1861)	132
Boston (USA, 1884)	41	Florida (USA, 1864)	132

Forbin (Fr, 1888)	134	Nagara (Jap, 1921)	227
Foresight (GB, 1904)	134	Naniwa (Jap, 1885)	228
Forfait (Fr, 1879)	135	Nelson (GB, 1876)	230
Forte (GB, 1893)	136	New York (USA, 1891)	232
Forth (GB, 1886)	136	Newark (USA, 1890)	232
Francesco Ferruccio (It, 1902)	138	Nisshin (Jap, 1869)	233
Freya (Ger, 1874)	140	Olympia (USA, 1892)	235
Friant (Fr, 1893)	140	Panther (Austria, 1885)	236
Frithjof (Nor, 1896)	141	Piemonte (It, 1888)	238
Fu Ch'ing (China, 1893)	142	Pietro Micca (It, 1876)	238
Fürst Bismarck (Ger, 1897)	145	Pillau (Ger, 1914)	238
Furutaka (Jap, 1925)	145	Pisa (It, 1907)	239
Fylgia (Swed, 1905)	147	Pola (It, 1931)	240
Galatea (GB, 1859)	148	Powerful (GB, 1895)	240
Galatea (GB, 1887)	149	Powhatan (USA, 1850)	240
Galatea (GB, 1914)	149	Principe Umberto (It, 1862)	241
Galveston (USA, 1945)	151	Quarto (It, 1911)	241
Gambia (GB, 1940)	152	Rurik (Rus, 1892)	246
Garibaldi (It, 1860)	153	Rurik (Rus, 1906)	246
Garnet (GB, 1877)	153	Russia (Rus, 1896)	246
Gefion (Ger, 1893)	154	San Giorgio (It, 1908)	247
Geiser (Den, 1892)	154	San Jacinto (USA, 1850)	248
Gelderland (Neth, 1898)	154	Sfax (Fr, 1884)	250
General Admiral (Rus, 1873)	155	Shah (GB, 1873)	250
General Garibaldi (Arg, 1895)	156	Shannon (GB, 1875)	250
Georgia (Confed, 1863)	159	Slava (Rus, 1979)	252
Gerona (Sp, 1864)	160	Stromboli (It, 1886)	254
Giovanni Bausan (It, 1883)	161	Tage (Fr, 1886)	255
Giovanni delle Bande Nere (It, 1930)	161	Takao (Jap, 1888)	255
Giuseppe Garibaldi (It, 1899)	162	Taranto (It, 1911)	256
Giuseppe Garibaldi (It, 1934)	162	Terrible (GB, 1845)	257
Gladiator (GB, 1896)	163	Tiger (GB, 1945)	258
Glasgow (GB, 1861)	163	Trento (It, 1927)	259
Glasgow (GB, 1909)	164	Trenton (USA, 1876)	259
Glasgow (GB, 1936)	164	Trieste (It, 1926)	259
Gloire (Fr, 1900)	165	Tripoli (It, 1886)	259
Gloire (Fr, 1935)	166	Tsukushi (Jap, 1880)	261
Gneisenau (Ger, 1906)	166	Tsushima (Jap, 1902)	261
Goito (It, 1887)	167	Ulpio Traiano (It, 1942)	264
Göta Lejon (Swed, 1945)	168	Unebi (Jap, 1886)	264
Gotland (Swed, 1933)	169	Union (Peru, 1865)	264
Graudenz (Ger, 1913)	172	Urania (It, 1891)	265
Gravina (Sp, 1881)	172	Varese (It, 1899)	266
Greif (Ger, 1886)	174	Variag (Rus, 1899)	266
Gromoboi (Rus, 1899)	175	Venezia (It, 1912)	268
Guerriere (USA, 1865)	178	Vesuvio (It, 1886)	268
Guichen (Fr, 1898)	178	Vesuvius (USA, 1888)	268
Hampshire (GB, 1903)	183	Vettor Pisani (It, 1895)	268
Hartford (USA, 1858)	185	Vittorio Veneto (It, 1967)	271
Heroine (GB, 1881)	188	Volage (GB, 1869)	271
Hiei (Jap, 1877)	189	Wacht (Ger, 1887)	272
Housatonic (USA, 1861)	190	Wallaroo (Aus, 1890)	272
Idaho (USA, 1864)	194	Wolverine (GB, 1863)	276
Imperieuse (GB, 1883)	195	Worden (USA, 1962)	276
Inconstant (GB, 1868)	195	Yakumo (Jap, 1899)	278
Indianapolis (USA, 1931)	197	Yamato (Jap, 1885)	278
Infanta Maria Teresa (Sp, 1890)	197	Yang Wei (China, 1881)	278
Iris (GB, 1877)	199	York (GB, 1928)	279
Izumrud (Rus, 1903)	200	Yoshino (Jap, 1892)	279
Jacob van Heemskerck (Neth, 1939)	201	Zara (It, 1930)	279
Java (Neth, 1921)	202		
Jeanne D'Arc (Fr, 1899)	203	**Cruisers, auxiliary**	
Jorge Juan (Sp, 1876)	204	Augusta Victoria (It, 1888)	26
Jurien de la Gravière (Fr, 1899)	204	Città di Catania (It, 1910)	63
Kaiserin Augusta (Ger, 1892)	206	Don (Rus, 1890)	94
Kaiserin Elisabeth (Austria, 1890)	206		
Karlsruhe (Ger, 1912)	207	**Deep sea exploration and recovery vessels**	
Kasuga (Jap, 1902)	207	Aluminaut (USA, 1965)	13
Kearsarge (USA, 1861)	208	Deep Quest (USA, 1967)	84
Kerch (Rus, 1973)	208	Deepstar 4000 (Fr, 1965)	85
Kirov (Rus, 1936)	209		
Kirov (Rus, 1977)	209	**Despatch boats**	
Köln (Ger, 1916)	210	Esploratore (It, 1863)	118
Köln (Ger, 1928)	210	Folgore (It, 1886)	133
Krasnyi Kavkaz (Rus, 1916)	212	Fuad (Turk, 1864)	142
Libia (It, 1912)	215	Galileo Galilei (It, 1887)	151
Luigi Cadorna (It, 1931)	217	Messaggero (It, 1885)	221
Marco Polo (It, 1892)	219	Messaggiere (It, 1863)	221
Marsala (It, 1912)	219	Rapido (It, 1876)	242
Maya (Jap, 1930)	220	Staffetta (It, 1876)	253
Memphis (USA, 1924)	221	Ts'ao Chiang (China, 1876)	260
Mendez Nuñez (Sp, 1923)	221		
Minerva (It, 1892)	223	**Destroyers**	
Minin (Rus, 1869)	223	Alberto da Giussano (It, 1930)	12
Mississippi (USA, 1841)	224	Araguaya (Braz, 1946)	16
Mississippi (USA, 1976)	224	Ardent (GB, 1929)	17
Mogami (Jap, 1934)	224	Arleigh Burke (USA, 1989)	19
Montebello (It, 1888)	225	Armando Diaz (It, 1932)	20
Muzio Attendolo (It, 1934)	227	Artigliere (It, 1937)	21

282

Asagumo (Jap, 1966)	21
Asashio (Jap, 1936)	22
Athabaskan (Can, 1970)	23
Audace (It, 1971)	25
Baleno (It, 1931)	29
Bettino Ricasoli (It, 1926)	37
Bodryi (Rus, 1936)	39
Bombardiere (It, 1942)	40
Borea (It, 1902)	40
Borea (It, 1927)	41
Bourrasque (Fr, 1925)	42
Boyky (Rus, 1960)	43
Bullfinch (GB, 1898)	48
Byedovi (Rus, 1902)	48
Calatafimi (It, 1923)	49
Centauro (It, 1954)	57
Cleveland (GB, 1940)	65
Comet (GB, 1944)	67
Confienza (It, 1920)	69
Coronel Bolognesi (Peru, 1955)	73
Corrientes (Arg, 1896)	73
Crescent (GB, 1931)	74
Cushing (USA, 1978)	77
Daring (GB, 1893)	82
Daring (GB, 1949)	82
Decatur (USA, 1900)	84
Devonshire (GB, 1960)	90
Doyle (USA, 1942)	95
Dragone (It, 1943)	96
Duguay-Trouin (Fr, 1973)	98
Duncan (GB, 1932)	100
Duncan (USA, 1944)	100
Dupleix (Fr, 1975)	101
Duquesne (Fr, 1966)	102
Durandal (Fr, 1899)	102
Edinburgh (GB, 1983)	105
Emanuele Pessagno (It, 1929)	107
Erne (GB, 1903)	114
Espero (It, 1904)	117
Espero (It, 1927)	118
Euro (It, 1900)	121
Euro (It, 1927)	121
Euro (It, 1982)	121
Exmoor (GB, 1941)	124
Farragut (USA, 1898)	127
Fasana (It, 1912)	127
Ferret (GB, 1911)	128
Fervent (GB, 1895)	129
Fionda (It, 1942**)	130
Folgore (It, 1931)	134
Framée (Fr, 1899)	137
Francesco Nullo (It, 1914)	138
Freccia (It, 1899)	139
Freccia (It, 1930)	139
Frunze (Rus, 1915)	142
Fulmine (It, 1898)	143
Fulmine (It, 1931)	143
Furor (Sp, 1896)	145
Fuyutsuki (Jap, 1944)	147
G40 (Ger, 1915)	148
G101 (Ger, 1914)	148
G132 (Ger, 1906)	148
Gadfly (GB, 1906)	148
Garibaldino (It, 1910)	153
Garland (GB, 1913)	153
Gatling (USA, 1913)	154
Georges Leygues (Fr, 1976)	159
Gillis (USA, 1919)	160
Giuseppe la Masa (It, 1917)	163
Glasgow (GB, 1976)	164
Göteborg (Swed, 1935)	169
Grasshopper (GB, 1909)	171
Gravina (Sp, 1931)	172
Grom (Pol, c.1952)	174
Gromki (Rus, 1904)	174
Gromki (Rus, 1913)	175
Gromki (Rus, 1936)	175
Gröningen (Neth, 1954)	176
Guadiana (Port, 1914)	177
Guglielmo Pepe (It, 1914)	178
Gwin (USA, 1917)	180
Hamakaze (Jap, 1940)	183
Hamayuki (Jap, 1983)	183
Haruna (Jap, 1972)	185
Havock (GB, 1893)	186
Impavido (It, 1962)	195
Minsk (Rus, 1935)	223
Moon (GB, 1915)	226
Sokol (Rus, 1895)	252

Spruance (USA, 1973)	253
Tromp (Neth, 1973)	260
Ugolini Vivaldi (It, 1929)	263
Vincenzo Gioberti (It, 1936)	269
Vincenzo Giordano Orsini (It, 1917)	270
Viper (GB, 1899)	270
(see also: flotilla leaders)	

Escort vessels
Bayano (GB, 1917)	34
Bombarda (It, 1942)	40
Daffodil (GB, 1915)	78
Daga (It, 1943)	79
Hachijo (Jap, 1940)	181

Exploration and research vessels
Discovery (GB, 1901)	92
Eendracht (Neth, 1600)	105
Endeavour (GB, 1760)	109
Erebus (GB, 1836*)	112
James Clark Ross (GB, 1990)	201

Fast attack craft
Shanghai (China, 1962)	250
Sparviero (It, 1974)	252
Spica (Swed, 1966)	253

Ferries
Baikal (Rus, 1907)	28
Castalia (GB, 1874)	56
Ferry Lavender (Jap, 1991)	129
Frans Suell (Swed, 1991)	139
Ishikari (Jap, 1990)	199
Tycho Brahe (Den, 1991)	261

Flotilla leaders
Augusto Riboty (It, 1916)	26
Exmouth (GB, 1934)	124
Falco (It, 1919)	126
Faulknor (GB, 1914)	127
Swift (GB, 1907)	255

Frigates
Avon (GB, 1943)	27
Broadsword (GB, 1975)	46
Carabiniere (It, 1967)	54
Carlo Bergamini (It, 1960)	54
Chikugo (Jap, 1970)	61
Cigno (It, 1955)	63
Constitution (USA, 1797)	70
Davidson (USA, 1964)	83
D'Estienne d'Orves (USA, 1946)	88
Dido (GB, 1961)	92
Doudart de la Grée (Fr, 1961)	95
Downes (USA, 1969)	95
Doyle (USA, 1982)	95
Galatea (GB, 1963)	149
Gemlik (Turk, 1959)	155
Godavari (India, 1980)	166
Grafton (GB, 1954)	171
Gurkha (GB, 1960)	178
Izumrud (Rus, 1970)	201

Frigates, sailing
Berlin (Ger, 1674)	36
Bonhomme Richard (USA, 1765)	40
Boudeuse (Fr, 1763)	41
Charles (Fr, 1776)	58
Des Geneys (It, 1827)	88
Essex (USA, 1799)	118
General Pike (USA, 1813)	157
Hancock (USA, 1776)	183

Galley
Bucintoro (Venice, various)	47

Gunboats
Alecto (GB, 1839)	13
Benton (USA, 1861*)	36
Cairo (USA, 1861)	49
Comète (Fr, 1884)	68
Cormorant (GB, 1860)	72
Cricket (GB, 1856)	75
Cricket (GB, 1916)	75
Curlew (GB, 1885)	76
Curtatone (It, 1888)	76
Dardo (It, 1964)	81
Delta (China, 1876)	86
Dolphin (USA, 1884)	93

Donetz (Rus, 1887)	94
Dragonfly (GB, 1938)	96
Dunois (Fr, 1897)	100
Eber (Ger, 1887)	104
Eber (Ger, 1903)	104
Erie (USA, 1936)	113
Ermanno Carlotto (It, 1918)	114
Esk (GB, 1877)	115
Étendard (Fr, 1868)	119
Fulton (Fr, 1887)	144
Fusée (Fr, 1884)	146
General Bragg (Confed, 1851)	156
General Concha (Sp, 1883)	156
General Stirling Price (Confed, 1856)	157
Governolo (It, 1894)	170
Governor Moore (Confed, 1854)	170
Grozyaschi (Rus, 1890)	177
Harriet Lane (USA, 1857)	184
Hatteras (USA, 1861*)	185
Iosco (USA, 1863)	198
Korietz (Rus, 1886)	211
Lafayette (USA, 1858)	213
Lexington (USA, 1860)	215
McRae (Confed, 1861*)	220
Missouri (Confed, 1863)	224
Pawnee (USA, 1859)	237
Planter (Confed, 1860)	239
Sciota (USA, 1861)	249
Selma (Confed, 1856)	249
Victoria (Aus, 1883)	269
Wilmington (USA, 1895)	275
Winnepec (USA, 1864)	276
(see also: torpedo gunboats)	

Helicopter carriers
Jeanne D'Arc (Fr, 1961)	203
Moskva (Rus, 1964)	226

Hospital ship
Ferdinando Palasciano (It, 1899)	127

Hovercraft
Gus (Rus, 1970)	179

Hydrofoil
Sparviero (It, 1974)	252

Ironclads
Albemarle (Confed, 1864)	12
Atlanta (Confed, 1862*)	23
Baltic (Confed, 1860)	30
Casco (USA, 1865)	56
Chicora (Confed, 1862)	61
Choctaw (USA, 1855)	62
Galena (USA, 1862)	150
Huntsville (Confed, 1863)	192
Indianola (USA, 1862)	197
Louisiana (Confed, 1862)	216
Nashville (Confed, 1864)	228
Tennessee (Confed, 1863)	256
Texas (Confed, 1865)	257

Launches
Turbinia (GB, 1894)	261
VAS 205 (It, 1942)	266
VAS 301 (It, 1942)	267

Lightship
Calshot Spit (GB, c.1920)	51

Liners, passenger
Arabia (GB, 1851)	15
Arago (USA, 1855)	15
Arctic (USA, 1849)	17
Arizona (GB, 1879)	19
Balmoral Castle (GB, 1909)	29
Baloeran (Neth, 1929)	30
Batavia (GB, 1870)	33
Belgic (GB, 1914)	34
Blücher (Ger, 1901)	39
Bremen (Ger, 1858)	43
Bremen (Ger, 1928)	43
Britannia (GB, 1840)	45
Britannia (Swed, 1929)	45
Britannic (GB, 1874)	45
Britannic (GB, 1914)	45
Caledonia (GB, 1925)	50
Campania (GB, 1893)	51
Canada (Fr, 1866)	51

Canadian (GB, 1854)	52
Canberra (GB, 1960)	52
Cap Trafalgar (Ger, 1913)	53
Carmania (GB, 1905)	55
Carthage (GB, 1931)	55
China (GB, 1862)	61
City of Berlin (GB, 1875)	63
City of Brussels (GB, 1869)	63
City of Glasgow (GB, 1850)	64
City of New York (USA, 1888)	64
City of Rome (GB, 1881)	64
Columbia (GB, 1902)	67
Columbus (Ger, 1922)	67
Conte Biancamano (It, 1925)	70
Conte di Savoia (It, 1931)	71
Conte Grande (It, 1927)	71
Conte Verde (It, 1922)	71
Corsican (GB, 1907)	73
Czar (Rus, 1912)	78
Derbyshire (GB, 1935)	87
Derfflinger (Ger, 1908)	87
Deutschland (Ger, 1900)	89
Doric (GB, 1922)	94
Duilio (It, 1916)	99
Egypt (GB, 1871)	106
Empire Windrush (GB, 1930)	108
Empress of Britain (GB, 1905)	109
Empress of Britain (GB, 1930)	109
Empress of Canada (GB, 1928)	109
Empress of Russia (GB, 1912)	109
Eridan (Fr, 1928)	113
Erinpura (GB, 1911)	114
Esperia (It, 1918)	117
Etruria (GB, 1885)	120
Europa (Ger, 1928)	122
Europa (Den, 1931)	122
Explorateur Grandidier (Fr, 1924)	124
Flandria (Neth, 1922)	131
France (Fr, 1910)	137
France (Fr, 1961)	137
Franconia (GB, 1910)	138
Furnessia (GB, 1880)	145
Fuso Maru (Jap, 1908)	146
Galician (GB, 1901)	150
Gallia (GB, 1879)	151
Gallia (Fr, 1913)	151
Galway Castle (GB, 1911)	152
Gascon (GB, 1896)	154
General Diaz (It, 1911)	156
General Von Steuben (Ger, 1922)	157
George Washington (Ger, 1908)	157
Georges Philippar (Fr, 1930)	159
Germanic (GB, 1874)	160
Gothland (Belg, 1893)	169
Grampian (GB, 1907)	179
Great Britain (GB, 1843)	173
Great Eastern (GB, 1858)	173
Great Western (GB, 1837)	173
Grosser Kurfürst (Ger, 1899)	176
Hanoverian (GB, 1902)	184
Havel (Ger, 1891)	186
Hibernian (GB, 1861)	188
Highland Chieftain (GB, 1928)	189
Himalaya (GB, 1853)	189
Humboldt (USA, 1850)	191
Imperator (Ger, 1912)	195
John Bell (GB, 1854)	204
Kaiser Franz Josef I (Austria, 1911)	205
Kaiser Friedrich (Ger, 1898)	205
Kaiser Wilhelm der Grosse (Ger, 1897)	206
Kiautschou (Ger, 1899)	208
Koning Willem II (Neth, 1899)	211
Kronprinz Wilhelm (Ger, 1901)	212
La Champagne (Fr, 1885)	213
Lafayette (Fr, 1914)	214
Lake Champlain (GB, 1900)	214
Lancashire (GB, 1917)	214
Lusitania (GB, 1906)	217
Magdalena (GB, 1889)	218
Marathon (GB, 1904)	219
Minnehaha (USA, 1900)	223
Minnekahda (USA, 1917)	223
Moravian (GB, 1899)	226
Naldera (GB, 1917)	228
Nerissa (GB, 1926)	231
Norman (GB, 1894)	233
Oceanic (GB, 1899)	235
Parisian (GB, 1881)	236
Sirius (GB, 1837)	251

283

Teutonic (GB, 1889) — 257
Vanderbilt (USA, 1857) — 265
Victorian (GB, 1905) — 269
Washington (USA, 1847) — 274
Washington (Fr, 1847) — 274
Werra (Ger, 1882) — 274
Westernland (Belg, 1883) — 274
(see also: cruisers, auxiliary; passenger/cargo vessels)

Merchant sailing ships
Ariel (GB, 1865) — 19
Bounty (GB, 1780) — 42
Commandant de Rose (Fr, 1918) — 68
Cutty Sark (GB, 1869) — 77
Dar Pomorza (Pol, 1909) — 81
D'Bataviase Eeuw (Neth, 1620) — 83
Flying Cloud (USA, 1851) — 133
Friendship (GB, 1780) — 141
Great Republic (USA, 1853) — 173
Thomas W. Lawson (USA, 1902) — 258

Minehunters, minesweepers
Aster (Belg, 1981) — 22
Bambù (It, 1955) — 31
Daffodil (GB, 1915) — 78
Dromia (It, 1957) — 97
Edera (It, 1955) — 104
Eridan (Fr, 1979) — 113
Fugas (Rus, 1910) — 142
Guadiaro (Sp, 1950) — 177

Minelayers
Artevelde (Belg, 1940) — 21
Chamäleon (Austria, 1913) — 58
Gouden Leeuw (Neth, 1931) — 170

Monitors
Bosna (Austria, 1915) — 41
Erebus (GB, 1916) — 113
Florida (USA, 1901) — 132
Humber (GB, 1913) — 191
Marshal Soult (GB, 1915) — 219
Monadnock (USA, 1864) — 225
Monitor (USA, 1862) — 225
Monterey (USA, 1891) — 226
Passaic (USA, 1862) — 237
Winnebago (USA, 1863) — 275

Paddle steamers
Chaperon (USA, 1884) — 58
Charlotte Dundas (GB, 1801) — 59
Clermont (USA, 1807) — 65
Comet (GB, 1812) — 67
Ferdinando Primo (It, 1818) — 128
Fulton (Fr, 1803) — 144
Savannah (USA, 1818) — 248

Passenger/cargo vessels
Ballarat (GB, 1920) — 29
Baltic (GB, 1903) — 30
Californian (GB, 1901) — 50
Carpathia (GB, 1902) — 55
Esperance Bay (GB, 1921) — 117
Selandia (Den, 1911) — 249

Patrol vessels
Eagle 17 (USA, 1919) — 104
Endurance (GB, 1956) — 110
Fremantle (Aus, 1979) — 140
Shanghai (China, 1962) — 250

Rams
Katahdin (USA, 1893) — 207
Polyphemus (GB, 1881) — 240

Sail training ships
Arethusa (GB, 1932*) — 17
Eagle (USA, 1936) — 103
Esmeralda (Chile, 1951) — 116

Sailing warships
Ark Royal (GB, 1587) — 19
Audacious (GB, 1785) — 25
Centurion (GB, 1732) — 57
Dauphin Royale (Fr, 1658) — 82
Diligente (Fr, 1803) — 92
Golden Hind (GB, 1560) — 167
Henri Grace à Dieu (GB, 1514) — 187
Independence (USA, 1814) — 196

Salvage vessel
Artiglio II (It, 1906) — 21

Seaplane carriers
Chitose (Jap, 1936) — 62
Commandant Teste (Fr, 1929) — 68
Dédalo (Sp, 1901) — 84
Engadine (GB, 1911) — 110
Europa (It, 1895) — 122
Giuseppe Miraglia (It, 1923) — 163

Sloops
Brooklyn (USA, 1858) — 46
Daffodil (GB, 1915) — 78
Diana (It, 1940) — 91
Egeria (GB, 1873) — 106
Enterprise (USA, 1878) — 112
Eritrea (It, 1936) — 114
Vedetta (It, 1866) — 267

Submarines
A1 (GB, 1902) — 11
Aradam (It, 1936) — 15
Archimede (It, 1939) — 17
Argonaut (USA, 1897) — 18
Argonaut (USA, 1927) — 18
Atropo (It, 1912) — 24
B1 (GB, 1904) — 28
Balilla (It, 1915) — 29
Barbarigo (It, 1917) — 31
Barbarigo (It, 1938) — 32
Beta (It, 1916) — 37
Brin (It, 1938) — 44
Bronzo (It, 1941) — 46
C class (GB, 1906) — 48
C1 (Jap, 1943) — 48
CB12 (It, 1943) — 56
Charlie class (Rus, 1967) — 59
Corallo (It, 1936) — 72
D1 (GB, 1908) — 78
Dagabur (It, 1936) — 79
Dandolo (It, 1937) — 80
Daniel Boone (USA, 1962) — 80
Daphné (Fr, 1959) — 81
Delfino (It, 1892) — 85
Delfino (It, 1930) — 85
Delta (Rus, 1971) — 86
Deutschland (Ger, 1916) — 89
Diablo (USA, 1944) — 90
Diaspro (It, 1936) — 91
Dolfijn (Neth, 1959) — 93
Dolphin (USA, 1932) — 94
Domenico Millelire (It, 1927) — 94
Dreadnought (GB, 1960) — 97
Drum (USA, 1941) — 97
Dupuy de Lôme (Fr, 1915) — 102
Durbo (It, 1938) — 102
Dykkeren (Den, 1909) — 103
E20 (GB, 1915) — 103
Enrico Tazzoli (It, 1935) — 111
Enrico Tazzoli (It, 1942) — 111
Enrico Toti (It, 1928) — 111
Enrico Toti (It, 1967) — 111
Entemedor (USA, 1944) — 111
Ersh (SHCH 303) (Rus, 1931) — 115
Espadon (Fr, 1901) — 116
Espadon (Fr, 1926) — 117
Ettore Fieramosca (It, 1929) — 120
Euler (Fr, 1912) — 121
Eurydice (Fr, 1927) — 123
Evangelista Torricelli (It, 1944) — 123
Explorer (GB, 1954) — 124
F1 (GB, 1915) — 125
F1 (It, 1916) — 125
F4 (USA, 1912) — 125
Faà Di Bruno (It, 1939) — 126
Farfadet (Fr, 1901) — 126
Fenian Ram (USA, 1881) — 127
Ferraris (It, 1934) — 128
Ferro (It, 1943**) — 128
Filippo Corridoni (It, 1930) — 130
Fisalia (It, 1912) — 130
Flutto (It, 1942) — 132
Foca (It, 1908) — 133
Foca (It, 1937) — 133
Francesco Rismondo (It, 1928) — 138
Fratelli Bandiera (It, 1929) — 139
Fulton (Fr, 1919) — 144
G1 (GB, 1915) — 147

Galatea (It, 1933) — 149
Galathée (Fr, 1925) — 150
Galerna (Sp, 1981) — 150
Galilei (It, 1934) — 150
Galvani (It, 1938) — 151
Gemma (It, 1936) — 155
General Mola (Sp, 1934) — 157
George Washington (USA, 1959) — 158
George Washington Carver (USA, 1965) — 158
Georgia (USA, 1982) — 159
Giacinto Pullino (It 1913) — 160
Giacomo Nani (It, 1918) — 160
Giovanni Bausan (It, 1928) — 161
Giovanni da Procida (It, 1928) — 161
Giuseppe Finzi (It, 1935) — 162
Glauco (It, 1905) — 165
Glauco (It, 1935) — 165
Golf I (Rus, 1957) — 167
Goubet I (Fr, 1887) — 169
Goubet II (Fr, 1889) — 169
Grayback (USA, 1957) — 172
Grayling (USA, 1909) — 172
Grongo (It, 1943) — 175
Grouper (USA, 1941) — 176
Guglielmo Marconi (It, 1939) — 178
Gustave Zédé (Fr, 1893) — 179
Gustave Zédé (Fr, 1913) — 179
Gymnôte (Fr, 1888) — 180
H. L. Hunley (Confed, 1863) — 180
H1 (It, 1916) — 181
H4 (USA, 1918) — 181
Hai Lung (Taiwan, 1986) — 182
Hajen (Swed, 1904) — 182
Han (China, 1972) — 183
Henri Poincaré (Fr, 1929) — 187
Holland No 1 (USA, 1878) — 189
Holland VI (USA, 1897) — 190
Hvalen (Swed, 1909) — 192
I7 (Jap, 1935) — 193
I21 (Jap, 1919) — 193
I201 (Jap, 1944) — 193
I351 (Jap, 1944) — 193
I400 (Jap, 1944) — 194
India (Rus, 1979) — 196
Intelligent Whale (USA, 1862) — 198
Isaac Peral (Sp, 1916) — 199
J1 (GB, 1915) — 201
K26 (GB, 1919) — 204
Kilo (Rus, 1981) — 209
L2 (Rus, 1931) — 213
L3 (USA, 1915) — 213
L23 (GB, 1919) — 213
Luigi Settembrini (It, 1930) — 217
M1 (GB, 1917) — 217
N1 (USA, 1916) — 227
Nautilus (USA, 1800) — 229
Nautilus (GB, 1914) — 229
Nautilus (USA, 1930) — 229
Nautilus (USA, 1954) — 229
Nereide (It, 1913) — 231
Nordenfelt 1 (Greece, 1885) — 233
November (Rus, 1958) — 234
Oberon (GB, 1926) — 234
Ohio (USA, 1976) — 235
Orzel (Pol, 1938) — 235
Pietro Micca (It, 1935) — 238
Pioneer (Confed, 1862) — 239
R1 (GB, 1918) — 242
Reginaldo Giuliani (It, 1939) — 243
Remo (It, 1943) — 244
Resurgam II (GB, 1879) — 244
S1 (GB, 1914) — 246
San Francisco (USA, 1979) — 247
Seraph (GB, 1941) — 249
Skipjack (USA, 1958) — 251
Surcouf (Fr, 1929) — 254
Swordfish (GB, 1916) — 255
Tango (Rus, 1972) — 256
Thistle (GB, 1939) — 258
Torbay (GB, 1985) — 259
Turtle (USA, 1776) — 261
Typhoon (Rus, 1979) — 262
U1 (Ger, 1906) — 262
U2 (Ger, 1935) — 262
U12 (Ger, 1968) — 262
U32 (Ger, 1937) — 262
U140 (Ger, 1917) — 263
U2501 (Ger, 1944) — 263
Uebi Scebeli (It, 1937) — 263

Upholder (GB, 1986) — 264
Vanguard (GB, 1990) — 266
Velella (It, 1936) — 267
Victor III (Rus, 1978) — 269
Volframio (It, 1941) — 271
W2 (It, 1915) — 272
Walrus (USA, 1914) — 273
Walrus (Neth, 1985) — 273
Warspite (GB, 1965) — 273
Whiskey (Rus, 1956) — 275
X1 (GB, 1925) — 276
X1 (USA, 1954) — 277
X2 (It, 1917) — 277
X2 (GB, 1934) — 277
X5 (GB, 1942) — 277
Xia (China, 1981) — 277
Yankee (Rus, 1967) — 279
Zoea (It, 1937) — 280
(see also: deep sea exploration and recovery vessels)

Survey vessel
Daino (It, 1945) — 79

Tankers, cargo
British Skill (GB, 1980) — 46
Front Driver (Swed, 1991) — 141
Jakob Maersk (Den, 1991) — 201
Jo Alder (It, 1991) — 203
Landsort, (Swed, 1991) — 214
Marinor (Neth, 1992) — 219
Mayon Spirit (Lib, 1981) — 220
Theodora (Neth, 1991) — 258

Torpedo boats
Astore (It, 1907) — 23
Audace (It, 1915) — 25
Avvoltoio (It, 1879) — 27
Avvoltoio (It, 1888) — 27
Balny (Fr, 1886) — 30
Calliope (It, 1906) — 50
Chidori (Jap, 1933) — 61
Cushing (USA, 1890) — 77
Dahlgren (USA, 1899) — 79
Erato (It, 1883) — 112
Euterpe (It, 1883) — 123
Flamingo (Austria, 1889) — 131
Forban (Fr, 1895) — 134
Fu Lung (China, 1886) — 142
Grondeur (Fr, 1892) — 175
Habana (Sp, 1887) — 181
MAS 9 (It, 1916) — 220
Nibbio (It, 1878) — 232
Pegaso (It, 1905) — 237
Pellicano (It, 1899) — 237
Stiletto (USA, 1886) — 253
Uragan (Rus, 1927) — 265
Viborg (Rus, 1886) — 268

Torpedo cruisers
Aretusa (It, 1891) — 18
Saetta (It, 1887) — 247

Torpedo gunboats
Blitz (Austria, 1888) — 39
Bombe (Fr, 1885) — 40
Destructor (Sp, 1886) — 88
Emanuele Russo (It, 1922) — 107
Espora (Arg, 1890) — 118
G5 (Rus, 1938) — 147
Gossamer (GB, 1890) — 168
Grasshopper (GB, 1887) — 171
Gustavo Sampaio (Braz, 1893) — 180
Kapitan Saken (Rus, 1889) — 207
Rattlesnake (GB, 1886) — 242
Zieten (Ger, 1876) — 280

Tugs
Batcombe (GB, 1970) — 33
Cretecable (GB, 1919) — 75

Yachts, racing
America (USA, 1851) — 13
Britannia (GB, 1890) — 45

Yachts, royal
America (Trinacria) (It, 1884) — 13
Artevelde (Belg, 1940) — 21
Grille (Ger, 1857) — 174
Savoia (It, 1883) — 248

Index of Ships by Country

Note: The information given in brackets beside the name of each ship indicates its launch date. Where the launch date of a vessel is unknown, the date of conversion is given, indicated by a single asterisk (*). In cases where the vessel was never completed, the date when it was laid down is given, indicated by a double asterisk (**).

Argentina
Buenos Aires (1895)	47
Corrientes (1896)	73
Espora (1890)	118
General Garibaldi (1895)	156
Los Andes (1874)	216
Moreno (1911)	226

Australia
Australia (1911)	27
Fremantle (1979)	140
Victoria (1883)	269
Wallaroo (1890)	272

Austria
Arciduca Ferdinand Max (1865)	16
Arpad (1901)	20
Blitz (1888)	39
Bosna (1915)	41
Chamäleon (1913)	58
Custoza (1872)	77
Erherzog Albrecht (1872)	115
Erherzog Friedrich (1857)	115
Erherzog Karl (1903)	115
Flamingo (1889)	131
Habsburg (1900)	181
Kaiser (1862)	204
Kaiser Franz Josef I (1911)	205
Kaiser Max (1862)	205
Kaiserin Elisabeth (1890)	206
Panther (1885)	236
Salamander (1861)	247
Tegetthoff (1878)	256

Bahamas
Society Adventurer (1991)	252

Belgium
Artevelde (1940)	21
Aster (1981)	22
Cockerill (1901)	66
Gothland (1893)	169
Westernland (1883)	274

Brazil
Araguaya (1946)	16
Bahia (1909)	28
Barrozo (1864)	32
Gustavo Sampaio (1893)	180
Javary (1875)	202
Minas Gerais (1908)	222
Riachuelo (1883)	244

Canada
Athabaskan (1970)	23

Chile
Almirante Cochrane (1874)	13
Capitan Prat (1890)	53
Esmeralda (1883)	116
Esmeralda (1894)	116
Esmeralda (1951)	116

China
Chao Yung (1880)	58
Chen Yuan (1882)	60
Chin Yuan (1886)	61
Delta (1876)	86
Fu Ch'ing (1893)	142
Fu Lung (1886)	142
Han (1972)	183
Shanghai (1962)	250
Ts'ao Chiang (1876)	260
Xia (1981)	277
Yang Wei (1881)	278

Confederate States of America
Alabama (1862)	12
Albemarle (1864)	12
Atlanta (1862*)	23
Baltic (1860)	30
Banshee (1863)	31
Bermuda (1861)	37
Chicora (1862)	61
Flamingo (1864)	130
Florida (1861)	132
General Bragg (1851)	156
General Sterling Price (1856)	157
Georgia (1863)	159
Governor Moore (1854)	170
H. L. Hunley (1863)	180
Hope (1864)	190
Huntsville (1863)	192
Louisiana (1862)	216
McRae (1861*)	220
Missouri (1863)	224
Nashville (1864)	228
Pioneer (1862)	239
Planter (1860)	239
Selma (1856)	249
Shenandoah (1863)	251
Stonewall (1864)	253
Sumter (1859)	254
Tennessee (1863)	256
Texas (1865)	257

Denmark
Danmark (1864)	80
Dykkeren (1909)	103
Europa (1931)	122
Geiser (1892)	154
Gorm (1870)	168
Helgoland (1878)	186
Jakob Maersk (1991)	201
Niels Juel (1918)	232
Rolf Krake (1863)	245
Selandia (1911)	249
Tycho Brahe (1991)	261

France
Armide (1867)	20
Balny (1886)	30
Béarn (1920)	34
Bombe (1885)	40
Boudeuse (1763)	41
Bourrasque (1925)	42
Bretagne (1855)	44
Bretagne (1913)	44
Caimen (1885)	49
Canada (1866)	51
Cécille (1888)	57
Charlemagne (1895)	58
Charles (1776)	58
Charles Martel (1883)	59
Châteaurenault (1898)	60
Circé (1860)	63
Clémenceau (1943)	64
Clémenceau (1957)	65
Colbert (1875)	66
Comète (1884)	68
Commandant de Rose (1918)	68
Commandant Teste (1929)	68
Condé (1902)	69
Cosmao (1889)	73
Courbet (1882)	74
Couronne (1861)	74
Danton (1909)	81
Daphné (1959)	81
D'Assas (1896)	82
Dauphin Royale (1658)	82
Davout (1889)	83
De Grasse (1946)	83
Deepstar 4000 (1965)	85
D'Entrecasteaux (1896)	86
D'Estienne d'Orves (1973)	88
Dévastation (1879)	90
Diligente (1803)	92
Dixmude (1940)	92
Doudart de la Grée (1961)	95
Dubourdieu (1884)	98
Duguay-Trouin (1923)	98
Duguay-Trouin (1973)	98
Duguesclin (1883)	99
Dunkerque (1935)	100
Dunois (1897)	100
Dupetit-Thouars (1874)	101
Dupleix (1930)	101
Dupleix (1975)	101
Dupuy de Lôme (1890)	101
Dupuy de Lôme (1915)	102
Duquesne (1876)	102
Duquesne (1966)	102
Durandal (1899)	102
Edgar Quinet (1907)	105
Eridan (1928)	113
Eridan (1979)	113
Espadon (1901)	116
Espadon (1926)	117
Étendard (1868)	119
Euler (1912)	121
Eurydice (1927)	123
Explorateur Grandidier (1924)	124
Fabert (1874)	126
Farfadet (1901)	126
Flandre (1864)	131
Flandre (1914)	131
Forban (1895)	134
Forbin (1888)	134
Forfait (1879)	135
Formidable (1885)	135
Foudre (1895)	136
Foudroyante (1855)	136
Framée (1899)	137
France (1910)	137
France (1961)	137
Friant (1893)	140
Fulminant (1877)	143
Fulton (1803)	144
Fulton (1887)	144
Fulton (1919)	144
Furieux (1883)	144
Fusée (1884)	146
Galathée (1925)	150
Gallia (1913)	151
Georges Leygues (1976)	159
Georges Philippar (1930)	159
Gloire (1859)	165
Gloire (1900)	165
Gloire (1935)	166
Goubet I (1887)	169
Goubet II (1889)	169
Grondeur (1892)	175
Guichen (1898)	178
Gustave Zédé (1893)	179
Gustave Zédé (1913)	179
Gustave Zédé (1934)	179
Gymnôte (1888)	180
Henri IV (1899)	187
Henri Poincaré (1929)	187
Hoche (1886)	189
Jauréguiberry (1893)	202
Jeanne D'Arc (1899)	203
Jeanne D'Arc (1961)	203
Jurien de la Gravière (1899)	204
La Champagne (1885)	213
Lafayette (1914)	214
Magenta (1861)	218
Masséna (1885)	220
Sfax (1884)	250
Surcouf (1929)	254
Tage (1886)	255
Vauban (1882)	267
Washington (1847)	274

Germany
Admiral Graf Spee (1933)	11
Arminius (1864)	20
Atlantis (1937)	24
Augusta Victoria (1888)	26
Barbara (1926)	31
Bayern (1915)	34
Berlin (1674)	36
Berlin (1903)	36
Bismarck (1877)	37
Bismarck (1939)	38
Blücher (1901)	39
Blücher (1908)	39
Bremen (1858)	43
Bremen (1928)	43
Bremse (1916)	43
Breslau (1911)	43
Cap Trafalgar (1913)	53
Carola (1880)	55
Columbus (1922)	67
Cyclop (1916)	78
Derfflinger (1908)	87
Derfflinger (1913)	87
Deutschland (1874)	88
Deutschland (1900)	89
Deutschland (1904)	89
Deutschland (1916)	89
Deutschland (1960)	89
Eber (1887)	104
Eber (1903)	104
Emden (1908)	108
Emden (1925)	108
Europa (1928)	122
Freya (1874)	140
Friedrich der Grosse (1874)	140
Friedrich Carl (1867)	141
Frithjof (1891)	141
Fürst Bismarck145	
G40 (1915)	148
G101 (1914)	148
G132 (1906)	148
Gefion (1893)	154
General Von Steuben (1922)	157
George Washington (1908)	157
Gneisenau (1906)	166
Gneisenau (1936)	166
Goeben (1911)	167
Graf Spee (1917)	170
Graf Zeppelin (1938)	171
Graudenz (1913)	172
Greif (1886)	174
Grille (1857)	174
Grosser Kurfürst (1899)	176
Grosser Kurfürst (1913)	176
Hannover Express (1990)	184
Hansa (1872)	184
Havel (1891)	186
Helgoland (1909)	186
Imperator (1912)	195
Kaiser (1911)	205
Kaiser Friedrich (1898)	205
Kaiser Friedrich III (1896)	205
Kaiser Wilhelm der Grosse (1897)	206
Kaiserin Augusta (1892)	206
Karlsruhe (1912)	207
Kiautschou (1899)	208
Köln (1916)	210
Köln (1928)	210
Komet (1939)	210
König Wilhelm (1868)	210
Kormoran (1939)	211
Kronprinz Wilhelm (1901)	212
Kurfürst Friedrich Wilhelm (1891)	212
Nassau (1908)	229
Pillau (1914)	238
Sachsen (1877)	247
Seeadler (1888)	249
U1 (1906)	262
U2 (1935)	262
U12 (1968)	262
U32 (1937)	262

U140 (1917) 263
U2501 (1944) 263
Von der Tann (1909) 271
Wacht (1887) 272
Werra (1882) 274
Zieten (1876) 280

Great Britain
A1 (1902) 11
Aboukir (1900) 11
Agincourt (1862) 12
Alecto (1839) 13
Arabia (1851) 15
Ardent (1929) 17
Arethusa (1932*) 17
Arethusa (1934) 18
Ariadne (1943) 18
Ariel (1865) 19
Arizona (1879) 19
Ark Royal (1587) 19
Ark Royal (1937) 19
Attentive (1904) 24
Audacious (1785) 25
Audacious (1911) 25
Audacity (1941) 26
Avon (1943) 27
B1 (1904) 28
Bacchante (1876) 28
Ballarat (1920) 29
Balmoral Castle (1909) 29
Baltic (1903) 30
Barham (1914) 32
Batavia (1870) 33
Batcombe (1970) 33
Bayano (1917) 34
Belfast (1938) 34
Belgic (1914) 34
Belleisle (1876) 35
Bellona (1942) 35
Ben-My-Chree (1908) 35
Benbow (1885) 35
Birmingham (1913) 37
Black Prince (1904) 38
Blake (1889) 38
Blenheim (1919) 38
Bounty (1780) 42
Bowes (1852) 42
Britannia (1840) 45
Britannia (1890) 45
Britannic (1874) 45
Britannic (1914) 45
British Skill (1980) 46
Broadsword (1975) 46
Bullfinch (1898) 48
C Class submarine (1906) 48
Cabotia (1917) 48
Caledonia (1925) 50
Californian (1901) 50
Calliope (1884) 50
Calliope (1914) 51
Calshot Spit (c.1920) 51
Campania (1893) 51
Canada (1913) 52
Canadian (1854) 52
Canberra (1960) 52
Canopus (1897) 52
Captain (1869) 53
Carmania (1905) 55
Caroline (1914) 55
Carpathia (1902) 55
Carthage (1931) 55
Castalia (1874) 56
Centurion (1732) 57
Centurion (1892) 57
Charlotte Dundas (1801) 59
China (1862) 61
City of Berlin (1875) 63
City of Brussels (1869) 63
City of Glasgow (1850) 64
City of Rome (1881) 64
Clan Macalister (1930) 64
Cleopatra (1877) 65
Cleveland (1940) 65
Collingwood (1882) 66
Colossus (1910) 66
Columbia (1902) 67
Comet (1812) 67
Comet (1944) 67
Comus (1878) 68

Connector (1852) 69
Conqueror (1881) 70
Conqueror (1911) 70
Cormorant (1860) 72
Cornwall (1926) 72
Corsican (1907) 73
Cossack (1886) 73
Courageous (1916) 74
Crescent (1931) 74
Cretecable (1919) 75
Cricket (1916) 75
Curacoa (1917) 76
Curlew (1885) 76
Cutty Sark (1869) 77
Cyclops (1871) 78
D1 (1908) 78
Daffodil (1915) 78
Daring (1893) 82
Daring (1949) 82
Darino (1917) 82
Defence (1907) 85
Derbyshire (1935) 87
Devastation (1871) 90
Devonshire (1904) 90
Devonshire (1960) 90
Dido (1896) 91
Dido (1939) 91
Dido (1961) 92
Discovery (1901) 92
Doric (1922) 94
Dragonfly (1938) 96
Drake (1901) 96
Dreadnought (1875) 96
Dreadnought (1906) 96
Dreadnought (1960) 97
Duke of Wellington (1852) 99
Duncan (1932) 100
E20 (1915) 103
Eagle (1918) 103
Eagle (1946) 103
Edgar (1890) 105
Edinburgh (1983) 105
Effingham (1921) 105
Egeria (1873) 106
Egypt (1871) 106
Emerald (1920) 108
Empire Windrush (1930) 108
Empress of Britain (1905) 109
Empress of Britain (1930) 109
Empress of Canada (1928) 109
Empress of Russia (1912) 109
Endeavour (1760) 109
Endurance (1956) 110
Engadine (1911) 110
Engadine (1966) 110
Erebus (1836*) 112
Erebus (1916) 113
Erin (1913) 114
Erinpura (1911) 114
Erne (1903) 114
Esk (1877) 115
Esperance Bay (1921) 117
Etruria (1885) 120
Euryalus (1853) 122
Euryalus (1877) 123
Exeter (1929) 124
Exmoor (1941) 124
Exmouth (1934) 124
Explorer (1954) 124
F1 (1915) 125
Faulknor (1914) 127
Ferret (1911) 128
Fervent (1895) 129
Foresight (1904) 134
Formidable (1939) 135
Fort Grange (1976) 136
Forte (1893) 136
Forth (1886) 136
Franconia (1910) 138
Friendship (1780) 141
Furious (1916) 145
Furnessia (1880) 145
G1 (1915) 147
Gadfly (1906) 148
Galatea (1859) 148
Galatea (1887) 149
Galatea (1914) 149
Galatea (1963) 149
Galician (1901) 150

Gallia (1879) 151
Galway Castle (1911) 152
Gambia (1940) 152
Garland (1913) 153
Garnet (1877) 153
Gascon (1896) 154
Germanic (1874) 160
Gladiator (1844) 163
Gladiator (1896) 163
Glasgow (1861) 163
Glasgow (1909) 164
Glasgow (1936) 164
Glasgow (1976) 164
Glatton (1871) 164
Glatton (1914) 165
Glorious (1916) 166
Golden Hind (1560) 167
Gorgon (1871) 168
Gossamer (1890) 168
Grafton (1954) 171
Grampian (1907) 171
Grasshopper (1887) 171
Grasshopper (1909) 171
Great Britain (1843) 173
Great Eastern (1858) 173
Great Western (1937) 173
Gurkha (1960) 178
Hampshire (1903) 183
Hanoverian (1902) 184
Havock (1893) 186
Henri Grâce à Dieu (1514) 187
Hercules (1868) 187
Hermes (1919) 188
Hermes (1953) 188
Heroine (1881) 188
Hibernian (1861) 188
Highland Chieftain (1928) 189
Himalaya (1853) 189
Hood (1918) 190
Humber (1913) 191
Huntsman (1921) 192
Imperieuse (1883) 195
Inconstant (1868) 195
Inflexible (1876) 197
Inflexible (1907) 198
Intrepid (1964) 198
Iris (1877) 199
Iron Duke (1912) 199
J1 (1915) 201
James Clark Ross (1990) 201
James Watt (1820) 202
Jervis Bay (1922) 203
John Bell (1854) 204
K26 (1919) 204
L23 (1919) 213
Lake Champlain (1900) 214
Lancashire (1917) 214
Lion (1910) 216
Lord Nelson (1906) 216
Lusitania (1906) 217
M1 (1917) 217
Magdalena (1889) 218
Majestic (1895) 218
Marathon (1904) 219
Marshal Soult (1915) 219
Monarch (1868) 225
Monarch (1911) 225
Moon (1915) 226
Moravian (1899) 226
Naldera (1885) 228
Nautilus (1914) 229
Nelson (1876) 230
Nelson (1925) 230
Neptune (1874) 231
Nerissa (1926) 231
Nile (1888) 233
Norman (1894) 233
Oberon (1926) 234
Oceanic (1899) 235
Parisian (1881) 236
Polyphemus (1881) 240
Powerful (1895) 240
Prince Albert (1864) 240
Queen Elizabeth (1913) 241
R1 (1918) 242
Rattlesnake (1886) 242
Resurgam II (1879) 244
Royal Sovereign (1857) 245
Royal Sovereign (1891) 245

S1 (1914) 246
Seraph (1941) 249
Shah (1873) 250
Shannon (1875) 250
Sirius (1837) 251
Sultan (1870) 254
Swift (1907) 255
Swordfish (1916) 255
Temeraire (1876) 256
Terrible (1845) 257
Teutonic (1889) 257
Thistle (1939) 258
Tiger (1913) 258
Tiger (1945) 258
Torbay (1985) 259
Turbinia (1894) 261
Unicorn (1941) 264
Upholder (1986) 264
Vanguard (1870) 265
Vanguard (1944) 265
Vanguard (1990) 266
Victorian (1905) 269
Viper (1899) 270
Volage (1869) 271
Vulcan (1889) 272
Warrior (1860) 273
Warspite (1913) 273
Warspite (1965) 273
Wivern (1863) 276
Wolverine (1863) 276
X1 (1925) 276
X2 (1934) 277
X5 (1942) 277
York (1928) 279
Zealous (1864) 280

Greece
Averroff (1910) 27
Basileus Georgios (1867) 33
Hydra (1889) 192
Nordenfelt 1 (1885) 233

India
Delhi (1932) 85
Godavari (1980) 166

Italy
Affondatore (1865) 11
Alberto da Giussano (1930) 12
America (Trinacria) (1884) 13
Ammiraglio di Saint Bon (1897) 14
Andrea Doria (1913) 14
Aquila (1926) 15
Aradam (1936) 15
Archimede (1939) 17
Aretusa (1891) 18
Armando Diaz (1932) 20
Artigliere (1937) 21
Artiglio II (1906) 21
Astore (1907) 23
Atropo (1912) 24
Attilio Regolo (1940) 24
Audace (1915) 25
Audace (1971) 25
Augusto Riboty (1916) 26
Avvoltoio (1879) 27
Avvoltoio (1888) 27
Baleno (1931) 29
Balilla (1915) 29
Bamby (1955) 31
Barbarigo (1917) 31
Barbarigo (1938) 32
Basento (1970) 32
Basilicata (1914) 33
Benedetto Brin (1901) 36
Bengasi (1904) 36
Beta (1916) 37
Bettino Ricasoli (1926) 37
Bombarda (1942) 40
Bombardiere (1942) 40
Borea (1902) 40
Borea (1927) 41
Brin (1938) 44
Brindisi (1912) 44
Bronte (1904) 46
Bronzo (1941) 46
Caio Duilio (1962) 49
Caio Mario (1941) 49
Calatafimi (1923) 49

Calliope (1906)	50
Campania (1914)	51
Candiope (1918)	52
Caorle (1957)	53
Carabiniere (1967)	54
Carlo Alberto (1896)	54
Carlo Bergamini (1960)	54
Castelfidardo (1863)	56
CB12 (1943)	56
Centauro (1954)	57
Cigno (1955)	63
Città di Catania (1910)	63
Coatit (1899)	66
Confienza (1889)	69
Confienza (1920)	69
Conte Biancamano (1925)	70
Conte di Cavour (1911)	70
Conte di Savoia (1931)	71
Conte Grande (1927)	71
Conte Verde (1867)	71
Conte Verde (1922)	71
Corallo (1936)	72
Cristoforo Colombo (1875)	75
Cristoforo Colombo (1892)	76
Curtatone (1888)	76
Daga (1943)	79
Dagabur (1936)	79
Daino (1945)	79
Dalmazia (1922)	79
Danaide (1942)	80
Dandolo (1937)	80
Dante Alighieri (1910)	81
Dardo (1964)	81
Delfino (1892)	85
Delfino (1930)	85
Des Geneys (1827)	88
Diana (1940)	91
Diaspro (1936)	91
Dogali (1885)	93
Domenico Millelire (1927)	94
Dragone (1943)	96
Dromia (1957)	97
Duca di Genova (1860)	98
Duilio (1876)	99
Duilio (1913)	99
Duilio (1916)	99
Durbo (1938)	102
Edera (1955)	104
Elba (1893)	106
Emanuele Filiberto (1897)	107
Emanuele Filiberto Duca D'Aosta (1935)	107
Emanuele Pessagno (1929)	107
Emanuele Russo (1922)	107
Enrico Dandolo (1878)	110
Enrico Tazzoli (1935)	111
Enrico Tazzoli (1942)	111
Enrico Toti (1928)	111
Enrico Toti (1967)	111
Erato (1883)	112
Eritrea (1936)	114
Ermanno Carlotto (1918)	114
Esperia (1918)	117
Espero (1904)	117
Espero (1927)	118
Esploratore (1863)	118
Etna (1885)	119
Etna (1942)	119
Etna (1944)	119
Etruria (1891)	120
Ettore Fieramosca (1929)	120
Eugenio Di Savoia (1935)	120
Euridice (1890)	121
Euro (1900)	121
Euro (1927)	121
Euro (1982)	121
Europa (1895)	122
Euterpe (1883)	123
Evangelista Torricelli (1944)	123
F1 (1916)	125
Faà Di Bruno (1916)	126
Faà Di Bruno (1939)	126
Falco (1919)	126
Fasana (1912)	127
Ferdinando Palasciano (1899)	127
Ferdinando Primo (1818)	128
Ferraris (1934)	128
Ferro (1943**)	128
Fieramosca (1888)	129
Filicudi (1954)	129
Filippo Corridoni (1930)	130
Fionda (1942**)	130
Fisalia (1912)	130
Fiume (1930)	130
Flavio Gioia (1883)	132
Flutto (1942)	132
Foca (1908)	133
Foca (1937)	133
Folaga (1942)	133
Folgore (1886)	133
Folgore (1931)	134
Formidabile (1861)	135
Francesco Caracciolo (1920)	137
Francesco Ferruccio (1902)	138
Francesco Morosini (1885)	138
Francesco Nullo (1914)	138
Francesco Rismondo (1928)	138
Fratelli Bandiera (1929)	139
Freccia (1899)	139
Freccia (1930)	139
Fulmine (1898)	143
Fulmine (1931)	143
Galatea (1933)	149
Galilei (1934)	150
Galileo Galilei (1887)	151
Galvani (1938)	151
Garibaldi (1860)	153
Garibaldino (1910)	153
Gemma (1936)	155
General Diaz (1911)	156
Giacinto Pullino (1913)	160
Giacomo Nani (1918)	160
Giovanni Bausan (1883)	161
Giovanni Bausan (1928)	161
Giovanni da Procida (1928)	161
Giovanni della Bande Nere (1930)	161
Giulio Cesare (1911)	162
Giuseppe Finzi (1935)	162
Giuseppe Garibaldi (1899)	162
Giuseppe Garibaldi (1934)	162
Giuseppe Garibaldi (1983)	162
Giuseppe la Masa (1917)	163
Giuseppe Miraglia (1923)	163
Glauco (1905)	165
Glauco (1935)	165
Goito (1887)	167
Governolo (1894)	170
Grillo (1918)	174
Grongo (1943)	175
Guerriera (1866)	177
Guglielmo Marconi (1939)	178
Guglielmo Pepe (1914)	178
H1 (1916)	180
Impavido (1962)	195
Italia (1880)	200
Jo Alder (1991)	203
Leonardo Da Vinci (1911)	214
Lepanto (1883)	215
Libia (1912)	215
Littorio (1937)	216
Luigi Cadorno (1931)	217
Luigi Settembrini (1930)	217
Marco Polo (1892)	219
Marsala (1912)	219
MAS 9 (1916)	220
Messaggero (1885)	221
Messaggiere (1863)	221
Messina (1864)	222
Minerva (1892)	223
Montebello (1888)	225
Muzio Attendolo (1934)	227
Napoli (1905)	228
Nereide (1913)	231
Nibbio (1878)	232
Palestro (1865)	236
Palestro (1871)	236
Pegaso (1905)	237
Pellicano (1899)	237
Piemonte (1888)	238
Pietro Micca (1876)	238
Pietro Micca (1935)	238
Pisa (1907)	239
Pola (1931)	240
Principe di Carignano (1863)	241
Principe Umberto (1862)	241
Quarto (1911)	241
Rapido (1876)	242
Re d'Italia (1863)	242
Re Galantuomo (1858)	243
Re Umberto (1888)	243
Regina Margherita (1901)	243
Regina Maria Pia (1863)	243
Reginaldo Giuliani (1939)	243
Remo (1943)	244
Roma (1865)	245
Saetta (1887)	247
San Giorgio (1908)	247
Savoia (1883)	248
Sparviero (1927)	252
Sparviero (1974)	252
Staffetta (1876)	253
Stromboli (1886)	254
Taranto (1911)	256
Trento (1927)	259
Trieste (1926)	259
Tripoli (1886)	259
Uebi Scabeli (1937)	263
Ugolini Vivaldi (1929)	263
Ulpio Traiano (1942)	264
Urania (1891)	265
Varese (1899)	266
VAS 205 (1942)	266
VAS 301 (1942)	267
Vedetta (1866)	267
Velella (1936)	267
Venezia (1912)	268
Vesuvio (1886)	268
Vettor Pisani (1895)	268
Vincenzo Gioberti (1936)	269
Vincenzo Giordano Orsini (1917)	270
Vittorio Emanuele (1904)	270
Vittorio Veneto (1937)	270
Vittorio Veneto (1967)	271
Volframio (1941)	271
Voragine (1866)	271
W2 (1915)	272
X2 (1917)	277
Zara (1930)	279
Zoea (1937)	280

Japan

Akagi (1925)	12
Aoba (1926)	14
Asagumo (1966)	21
Asahi (1898)	21
Asama (1898)	22
Asashio (1936)	22
C1 (1943)	48
Chidori (1933)	61
Chikugo (1970)	61
Chishima (1890)	62
Chitose (1936)	62
Chiyoda (1890)	62
Ferry Lavender (1991)	129
Fuji (1896)	143
Furutaka (1925)	145
Fuso (1877)	146
Fuso (1914)	146
Fuso Maru (1908)	146
Fuyutsuki (1944)	147
Hachijo (1940)	181
Hakuryu Maru (1991)	182
Hamakaze (1940)	183
Hamayuki (1983)	183
Haruna (1912)	185
Haruna (1972)	185
Hiei (1877)	189
Hosho (1921)	190
I7 (1935)	193
I21 (1919)	193
I201 (1944)	193
I351 (1944)	193
I400 (1944)	194
Ibuki (1907)	194
Ise (1916)	199
Ishikari (1990)	199
Kasuga (1902)	207
KDD Ocean Link (1991)	207
Maya (1930)	220
Mikasa (1900)	222
Mogami (1934)	224
Nagara (1921)	227
Nagato (1919)	228
Naniwa (1885)	228
Nisshin (1869)	233
Ryujo (1931)	246
Shinano (1944)	251
Taiho (1943)	255
Takao (1888)	255
Tsukuba (1905)	260
Tsukushi (1880)	261
Tsushima (1902)	261
Unebi (1886)	264
Yakumo (1899)	278
Yamato (1885)	278
Yamato (1940)	278
Yoshino (1892)	279
Zuikaku (1939)	280

Korea, South

Halla No 2 (1991)	182
Hyundai Admiral (1992)	193

Liberia

Mayon Spirit (1981)	220

Malaya

Kota Wijaya (1991)	211

Netherlands

Baloeran (1929)	30
D'Bataviase Eeuw (1620)	83
De Ruyter (1944)	84
Dolfijn (1959)	93
Eendracht (1600)	105
Flandria (1922)	131
Futura (1992)	147
Gelderland (1898)	154
Gouden Leeuw (1931)	170
Gröningen (1954)	176
Haai (1871)	181
Jacob van Heemskerck (1939)	201
Java (1921)	202
Koning Willem II (1899)	211
Marinor (1992)	219
Nedlloyd Europa (1991)	230
Theodora (1991)	258
Tromp (1973)	260
Walrus (1985)	273

Norway

Frithjof (1896)	141
Harald Haarfagre (1897)	184
Helice (1990)	187
Yeoman Burn (1990)	279

Panama

Hudson Rex (1991)	191

Peru

Coronel Bolognesi (1906)	72
Coronel Bolognesi (1955)	73
Huascar (1865)	191
Independencia (1865)	196
Union (1865)	264

Poland

Dar Pomorza (1909)	81
Grom (c.1952)	174
Orzel (1938)	235

Portugal

Cunene (1911)	76
Guadiana (1914)	177
Vasco da Gama (1875)	267

Romania

Elisabeta (1887)	106

Russia

Askold (1900)	22
Aurora (1900)	26
Baikal (1907)	28
Bayan (1900)	33
Bodryi (1936)	39
Bogatyr (1901)	39
Boyarin (1901)	42
Boyky (1960)	43
Byedovi (1902)	48
Charlie class (1967)	59
Chazhma (1959)	60
Czar (1912)	78
Delta I (1971)	86
Dmitri Donskoi (1883)	93
Dmitri Donskoi (1953)	93
Don (1890)	94
Donetz (1887)	94

Ekaterina II (1886)	106
Ersh (SHCH 303) (1931)	115
Frunze (1915)	142
Fugas (1910)	142
G5 (1938)	147
Gangut (1893)	152
Gangut (1911)	153
General Admiral (1873)	155
General Admiral Apraksin (1896)	155
Golf I (1957)	167
Gromki (1904)	174
Gromki (1913)	175
Gromki (1936)	175
Gromoboi (1899)	175
Grozyaschi (1890)	177
Gus (1970)	179
Imperator Pavel I (1907)	195
India (1979)	196
Ivan Rogov (1977)	200
Izumrud (1903)	200
Izumrud (1970)	201
Kapitan Saken (1889)	207
Kerch (1973)	208
Kiev (1972)	208
Kilo (1981)	209
Kirov (1936)	209
Kirov (1977)	209
Kniaz Pojarski (1867)	209
Kniaz Suvarov (1902)	210
Korietz (1886)	211
Krasnograd (1992)	211
Krasnyi Kavkaz (1916)	212
Kreml (1865)	212
L2 (1931)	213
Minin (1869)	223
Minsk (1935)	223
Moskva (1964)	226
Navarin (1891)	230
Number (1958)	234
Novgorod (1873)	234
Petr Veliki (1872)	238
Pobieda (1900)	239
Retvisan (1900)	244
Rurik (1892)	246
Rurik (1906)	246
Russia (1896)	246
Sevastopol (1864)	250
Slava (1979)	252
Sokol (1895)	252
Tango (1972)	256
Tsessarevitch (1901)	260
Typhoon (1979)	262
Uragan (1927)	265
Variag (1899)	266
Viborg (1886)	268
Victor III (1978)	269
Whiskey (1956)	275
Yankee (1967)	279

Spain

Aragon (1879)	16
Arapiles (1864)	16
Baleares (1932)	28
Cardenal Cisneros (1897)	54
Cristobal Colon (1896)	75
Dédalo (1901)	84
Dédalo (1943)	84
Destructor (1886)	88
Emperador Carlos V (1895)	108
España (1912)	117
Extremadura (1900)	125
Furor (1896)	145
Galerna (1981)	150
General Concha (1883)	156
General Mola (1934)	157

Gerona (1864)	160
Gravina (1881)	172
Gravina (1931)	172
Guadiaro (1950)	177
Habana (1887)	181
Infanta Maria Teresa (1890)	197
Isaac Peral (1916)	199
Jorge Juan (1876)	204
Mendez Nuñez (1923)	221
Numancia (1863)	234
Pelayo (1887)	237
Vitoria (1865)	270
Zaragosa (1867)	280

Sweden

Britannia (1929)	45
Carl XIV Johan (1824)	54
Dristigheten (1900)	97
Drottning Victoria (1917)	97
Frans Suell (1991)	139
Front Driver (1991)	141
Fylgia (1905)	147
Göta (1891)	168
Göta Lejon (1945)	168
Göteborg (1935)	169
Gotland (1933)	169
Hajen (1904)	182
Helena (1990)	186
Hvalen (1909)	192
Landsort (1991)	214
Spica (1966)	253

Taiwan

Ever Globe (1984)	123
Hai Lung (1986)	182

Turkey

Assari Tewfik (1868)	22
Feth-I-Bulend (1870)	129
Fuad (1864)	142
Gemlik (1959)	155
Lutfi Djelil (1868)	217
Messudieh (1874)	222

United States of America

Aluminaut (1965)	13
America (1851)	13
America (1964)	14
Appalachian (1943)	15
Arago (1855)	15
Arctic (1849)	17
Argonaut (1897)	18
Argonaut (1927)	18
Arleigh Burke (1989)	19
Astoria (1933)	23
Atlanta (1941)	24
Attu (1944)	25
Baltimore (1942)	30
Benton (1861*)	36
Bonhomme Richard (1765)	40
Boston (1884)	41
Brooklyn (1858)	46
Brooklyn (1895)	47
Brooklyn (1936)	47
Cairo (1861)	49
Casco (1865)	56
Centennial State (1920)	57
Chaperon (1884)	58
Charleston (1888)	59
Chester (1907)	60
Chicago (1885)	60
Choctaw (1855)	62
City of New York (1888)	64
Clermont (1807)	65
Columbia (1892)	67

Connecticut (1904)	69
Constitution (1797)	70
Cricket (1856)	75
Cushing (1890)	77
Cushing (1978)	77
Dahlgren (1899)	79
Daniel Boone (1962)	80
Davidson (1964)	83
Decatur (1900)	84
Deep Quest (1967)	84
Demologos (1814)	86
Denver (1902)	87
Denver (1965)	87
Des Moines (1946)	88
Diablo (1944)	90
Dictator (1863)	91
Dolphin (1884)	93
Dolphin (1932)	94
Downes (1969)	95
Doyle (1942)	95
Doyle (1982)	95
Drum (1941)	97
Duncan (1944)	100
Dunderberg (1865)	100
Eagle (1936)	103
Eagle 17 (1919)	104
Entemedor (1944)	111
Enterprise (1874)	112
Enterprise (1936)	112
Enterprise (1960)	112
Erie (1936)	113
Essex (1799)	118
Essex (1942)	118
F4 (1912)	125
Farragut (1898)	127
Fenian Ram (1881)	127
Florida (1864)	132
Florida (1901)	132
Flying Cloud (1851)	133
Forrestal (1954)	135
Frank Cable (1978)	139
Fulton (1940)	144
Galena (1862)	150
Galveston (1945)	151
Gambier Bay (1943)	152
Gatling (1943)	154
General John Pope (1943)	156
General Pike (1813)	157
George Washington (1959)	158
George Washington (1989)	158
George Washington Carver (1965)	158
George Washington Parke Custis (1855)	158
Georgia (1904)	159
Georgia (1982)	159
Gillis (1919)	160
Grayback (1957)	172
Grayling (1909)	172
Great Republic (1853)	173
Grouper (1941)	176
Guam (1943)	177
Guerriere (1865)	178
Gwin (1917)	180
H4 (1918)	181
Hancock (1776)	183
Harriet Lane (1857)	184
Hartford (1858)	185
Hatteras (1861*)	185
Holland No 1 (1878)	189
Holland VI (1897)	190
Housatonic (1861)	190
Humboldt (1850)	191
Hunley (1961)	192
Idaho (1864)	194
Idaho (1917)	194
Independence (1814)	196

Independence (1942)	196
Indiana (1941)	196
Indianapolis (1931)	197
Indianola (1862)	197
Intelligent Whale (1862)	198
Iosco (1863)	198
Iowa (1942)	198
Iwo Jima (1960)	200
Jason (1940)	202
Kalamazoo (1863**)	206
Katahdin (1893)	207
Kearsarge (1861)	208
Keokuk (1862)	208
L3 (1915)	213
Lafayette (1858)	213
Lexington (1860)	215
Lexington (1925)	215
Maine (1889)	218
Memphis (1924)	221
Michigan (1906)	222
Minnehaha (1900)	223
Minnekahda (1917)	223
Mississippi (1841)	224
Mississippi (1976)	224
Monadnock (1864)	225
Monitor (1862)	225
Monterey (1891)	226
Mount Whitney (1970)	227
N1 (1916)	227
Nautilus (1800)	229
Nautilus (1930)	229
Nautilus (1954)	229
Nevada (1914)	231
New Ironsides (1862)	231
New York (1891)	232
New York (1912)	232
Newark (1890)	232
North Carolina (1940)	234
Ohio (1976)	235
Olympia (1892)	235
Oregon (1893)	235
Passaic (1862)	237
Pawnee (1859)	237
Powhatan (1850)	240
Quaker City (1854)	241
Roanoke (1855)	244
San Francisco (1979)	247
San Jacinto (1850)	248
Savannah (1818)	248
Savannah (1959)	248
Sciota (1861)	249
Skipjack (1958)	251
Spruance (1973)	253
Stiletto (1886)	253
Texas (1892)	257
Thomas W. Lawson (1902)	258
Trenton (1876)	259
Turtle (1776)	261
Vanderbilt (1857)	265
Vesuvius (1888)	268
Walrus (1914)	273
Washington (1847)	274
Washington (1940)	274
Whidbey Island (1983)	275
Wilmington (1895)	275
Winnebago (1863)	275
Winnepec (1864)	276
Worden (1962)	276
X1 (1954)	277

Venice

Bucintoro (various)	47